ecret World of
Arrietty

Planning by **Hayao Miyazaki**
Based on *The Borrowers* by **Mary Norton**
Original Screenplay by **Hayao Miyazaki** and **Keiko Niwa**
Directed by **Hiromasa Yonebayashi**

Chapter 3

スタジオジブリ作品
STUDIO GHIBLI

Character Introductions

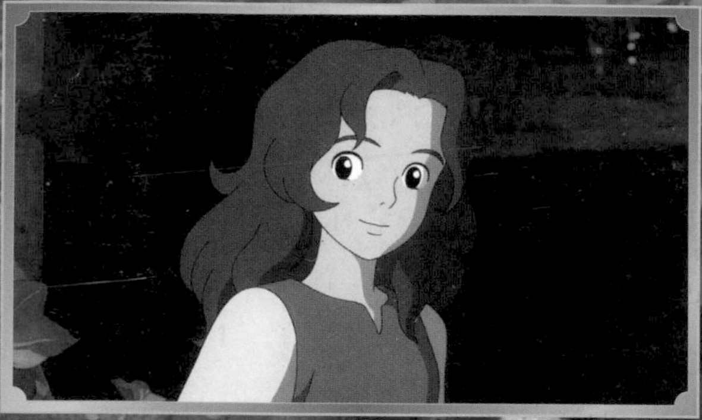

Arrietty

A 14-year-old girl who is one of the little people. She lives with her father and mother under the floorboards of an old house in the country. She is bright and energetic, if not a little heedless. She gets worried when Shawn sees her, so she tries to solve the problem on her own, but…

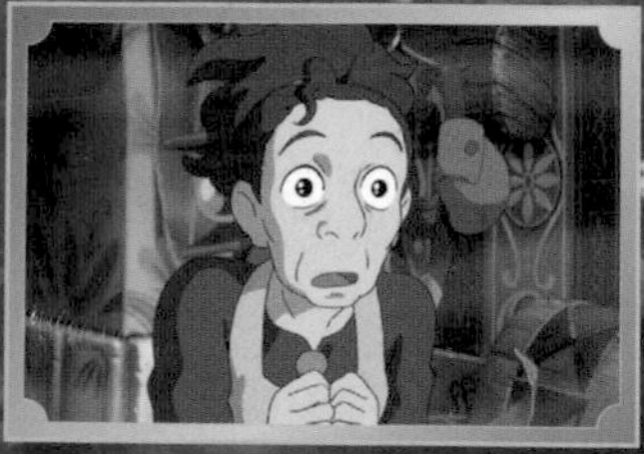

Homily

Arrietty's mother. She handles the housework. She worries a lot.

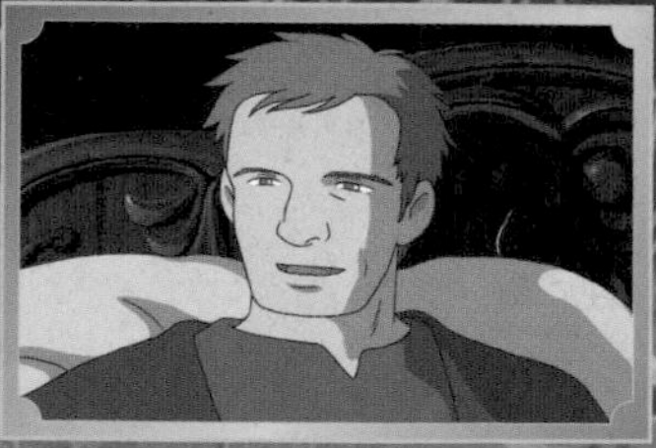

Pod

Arrietty's father. He goes above the floorboards to "borrow" items necessary for living. He is thinking about moving his family because the humans found them.

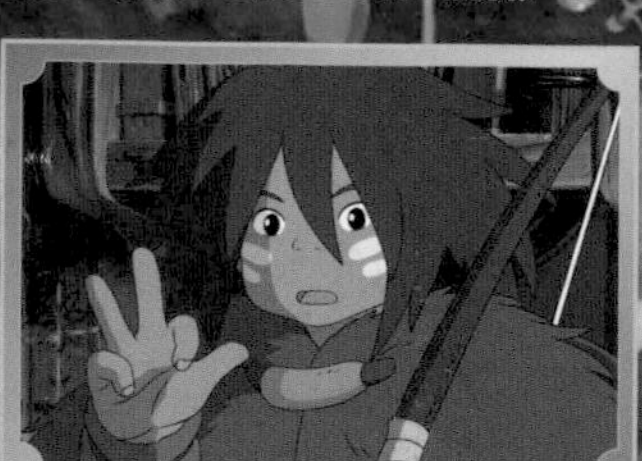

Spiller

A 12-year-old boy who is one of the little people. He carries around a bow and lives alone in the wild.

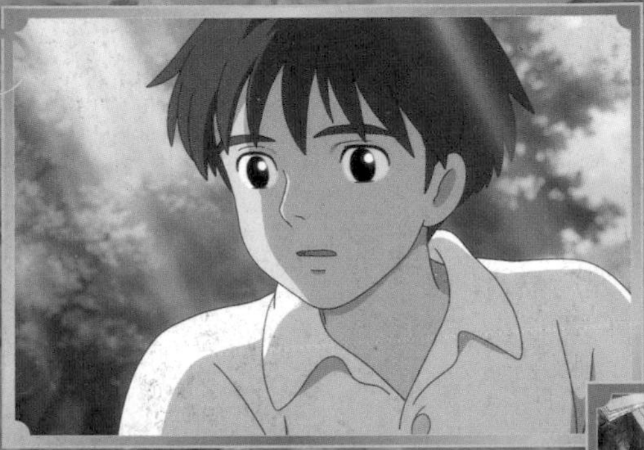

Shawn

A 12-year-old human boy. He has come to stay in the old house where his mother grew up in order to regain his health. He meets Arrietty and is concerned about her.

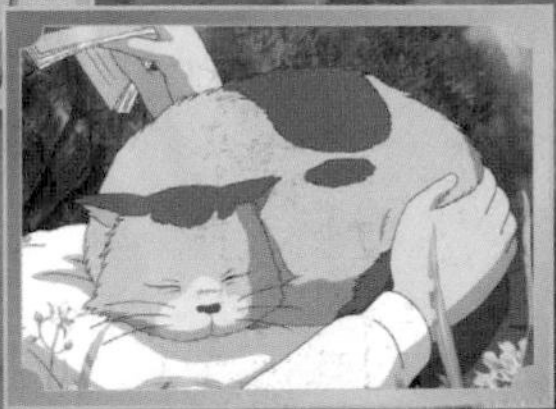

Nina

Jessica's pet cat, who is always dangerously on the prowl.

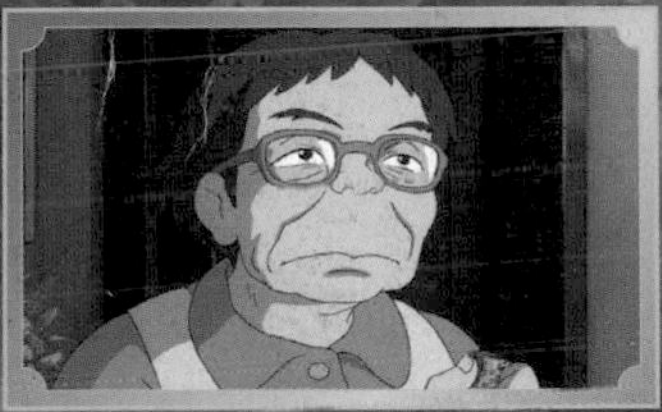

Hara

The maid at Jessica's house. She has lived and worked there for many, many years. She suspects that little people may be living in the house.

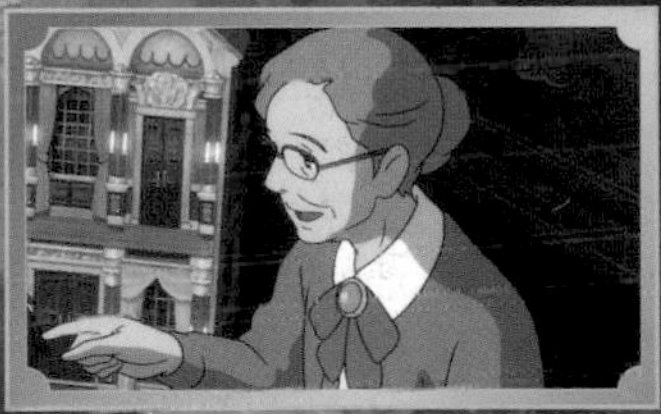

Jessica

Shawn's aunt who owns the old house in the country. She heard about the little people from her now-deceased father.

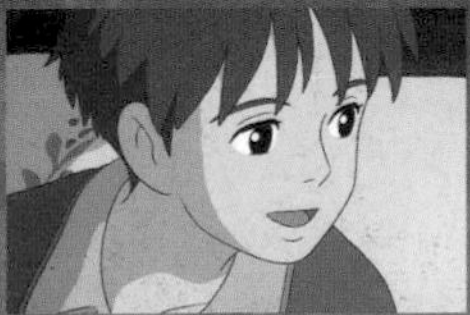

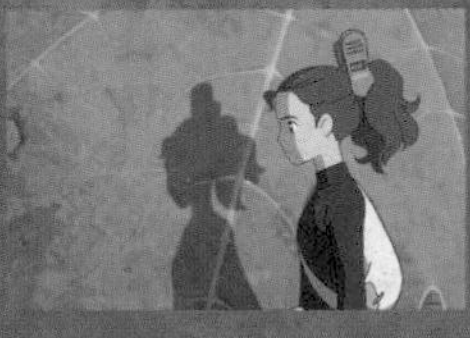

The story so far

While Shawn is staying in the country house of his aunt Jessica he meets Arrietty, who is one of the little people living there. Her family of little people "borrow" items for daily use from the humans while living in secret beneath the floorboards of the house. They have a rule–they mustn't let the humans see them. Shawn starts to be concerned about Arrietty...

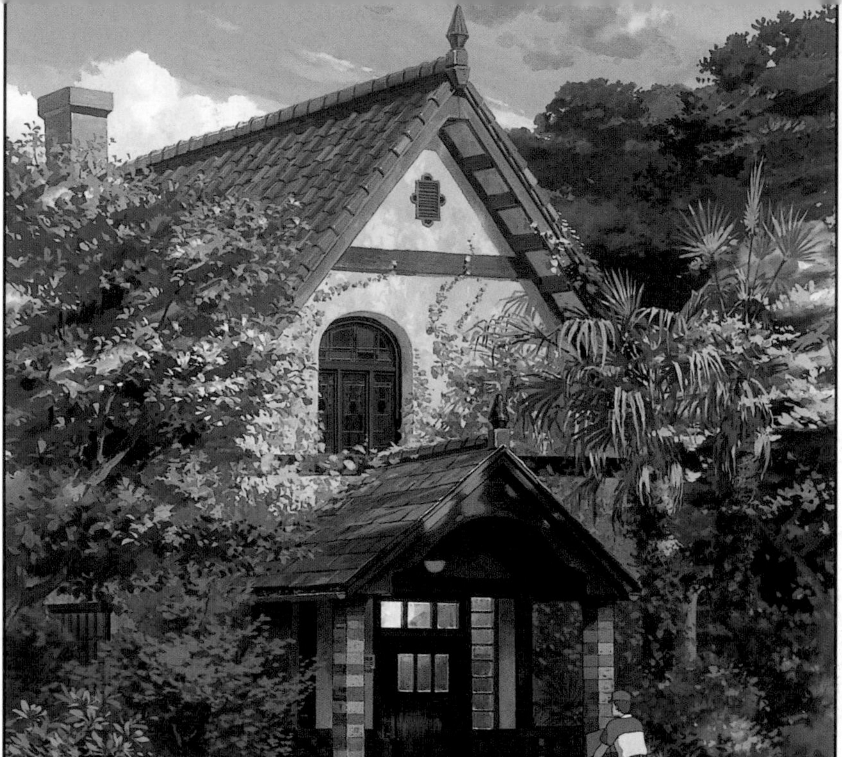

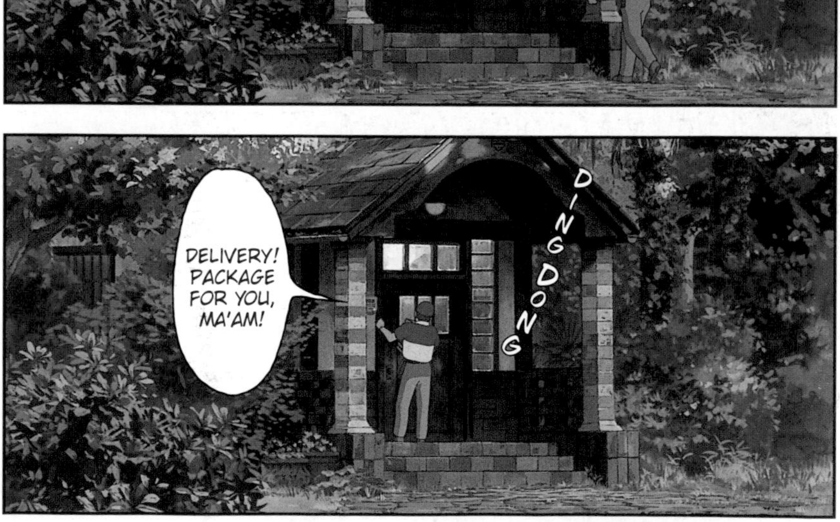
DING DONG
DELIVERY! PACKAGE FOR YOU, MA'AM!

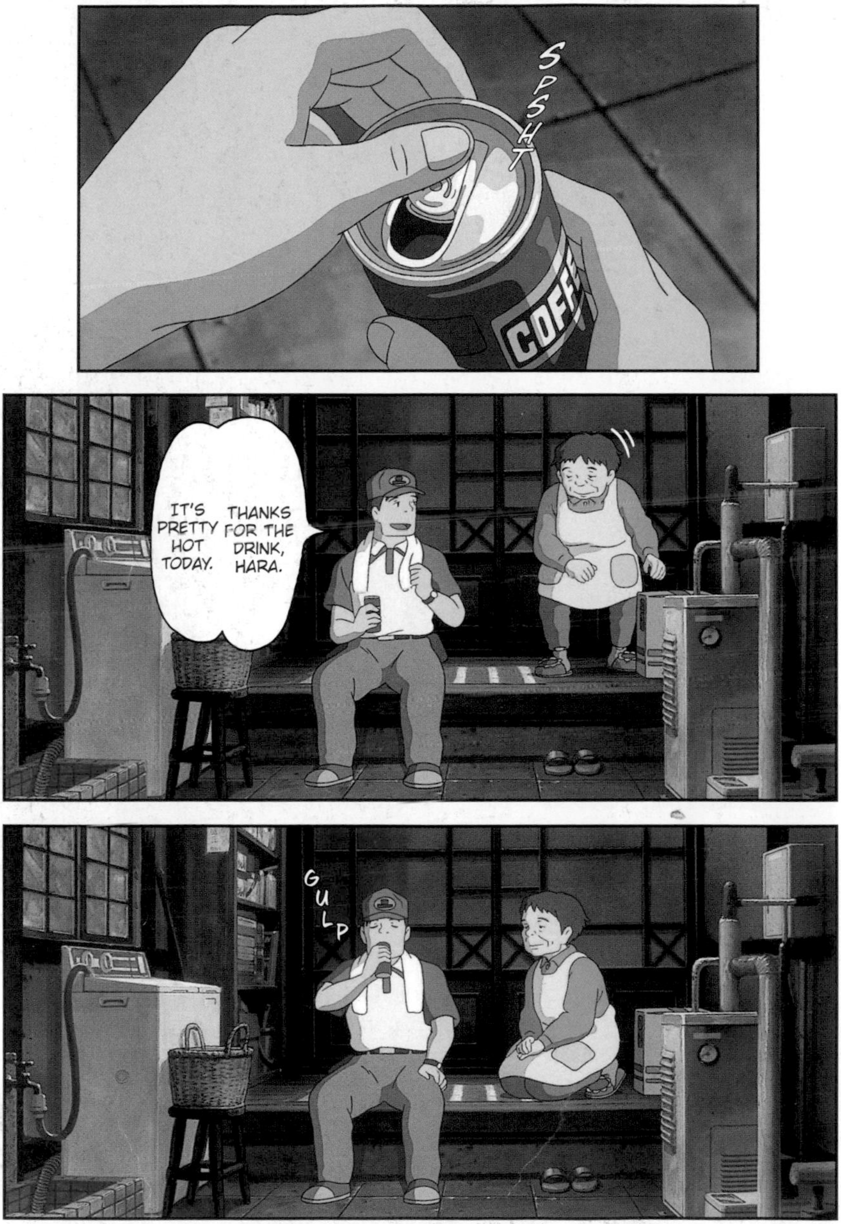
SPSHT
COFFE
IT'S PRETTY HOT TODAY. THANKS FOR THE DRINK, HARA.
GULP

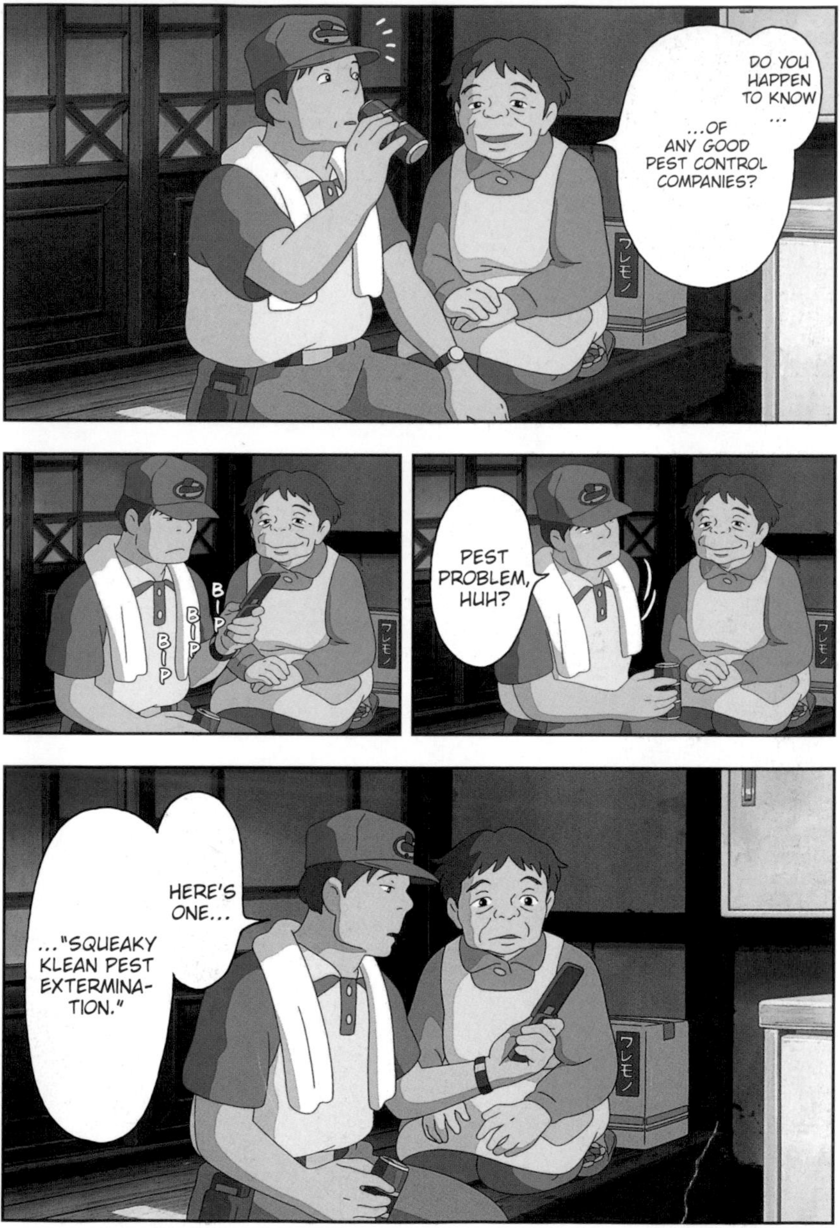
DO YOU HAPPEN TO KNOW ...
...OF ANY GOOD PEST CONTROL COMPANIES?
ワレモノ
PEST PROBLEM, HUH?
BIP BIP BIP
HERE'S ONE...
..."SQUEAKY KLEAN PEST EXTERMINA-TION."

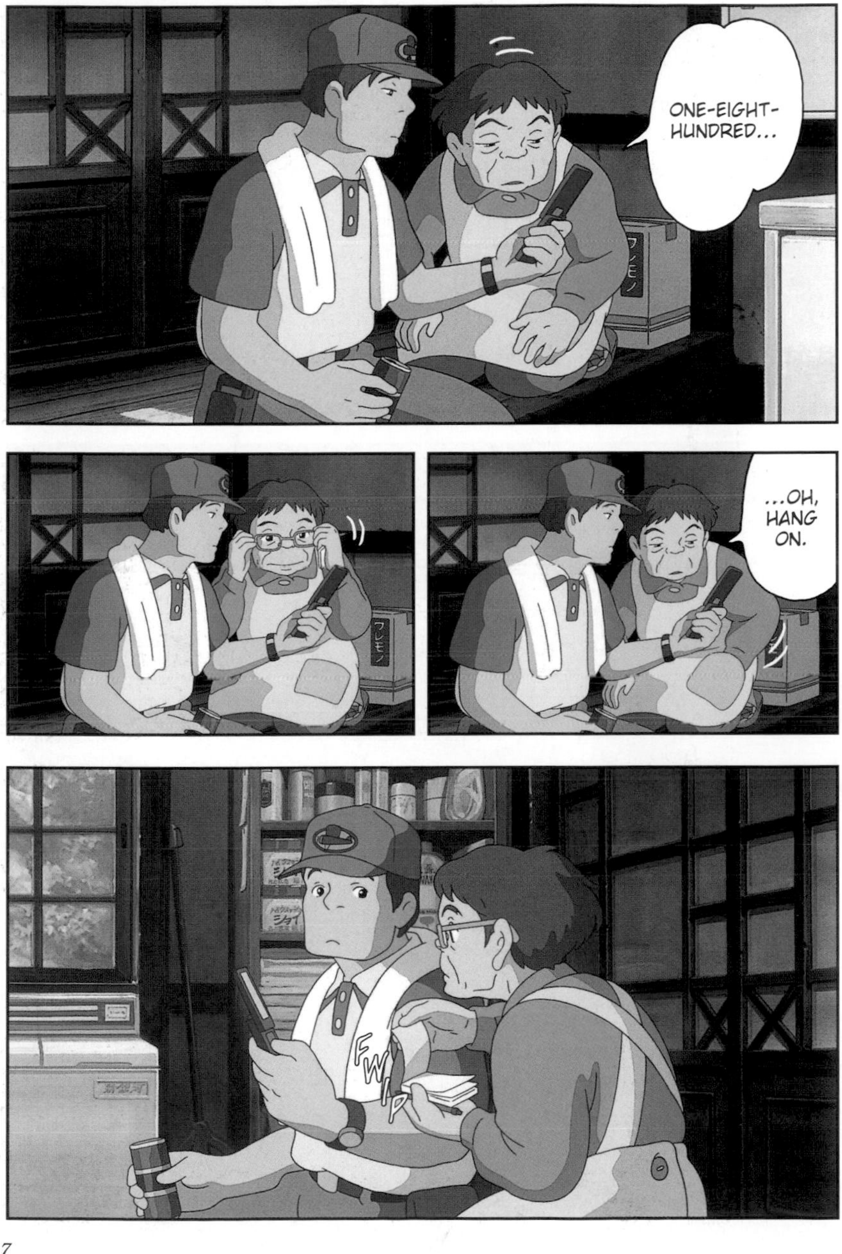
ONE-EIGHT-HUNDRED...
...OH, HANG ON.
FWIP

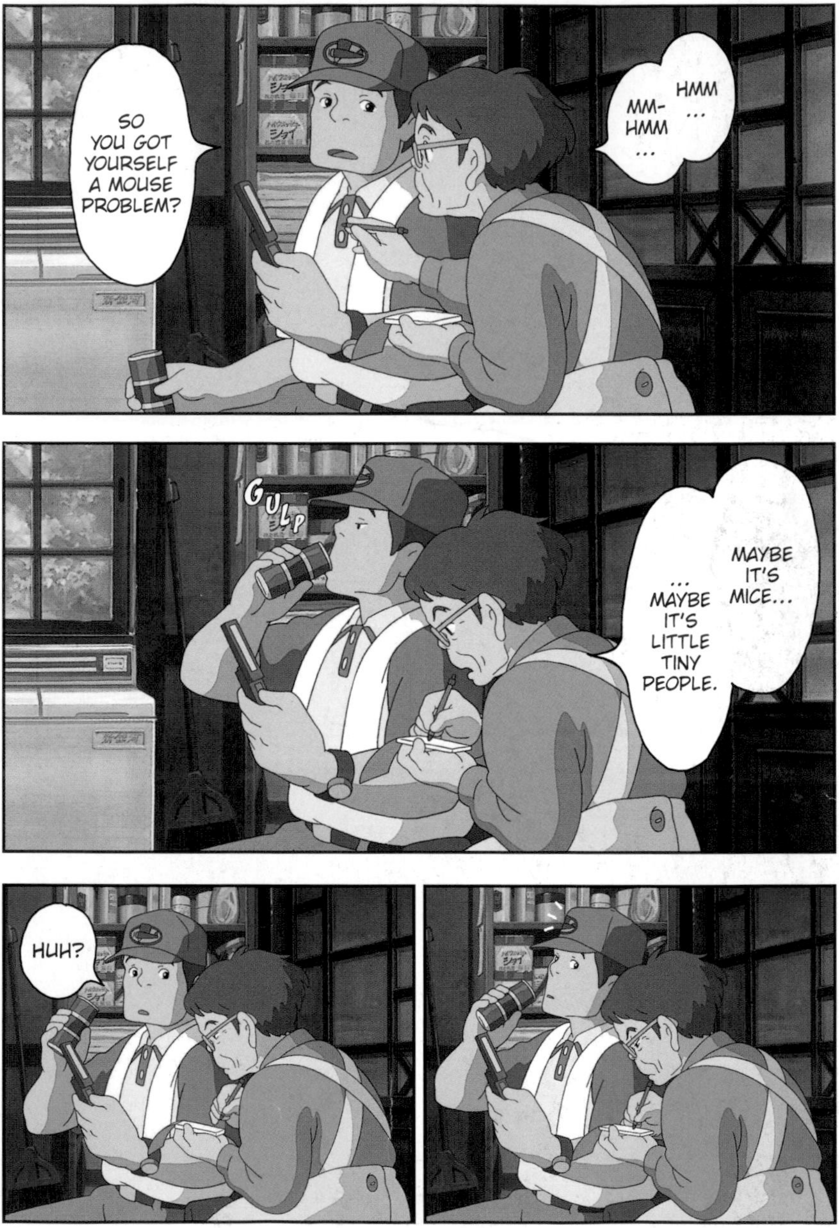
HMM ... MM-HMM ...
SO YOU GOT YOURSELF A MOUSE PROBLEM?
GULP
MAYBE IT'S MICE...
...MAYBE IT'S LITTLE TINY PEOPLE.
HUH?

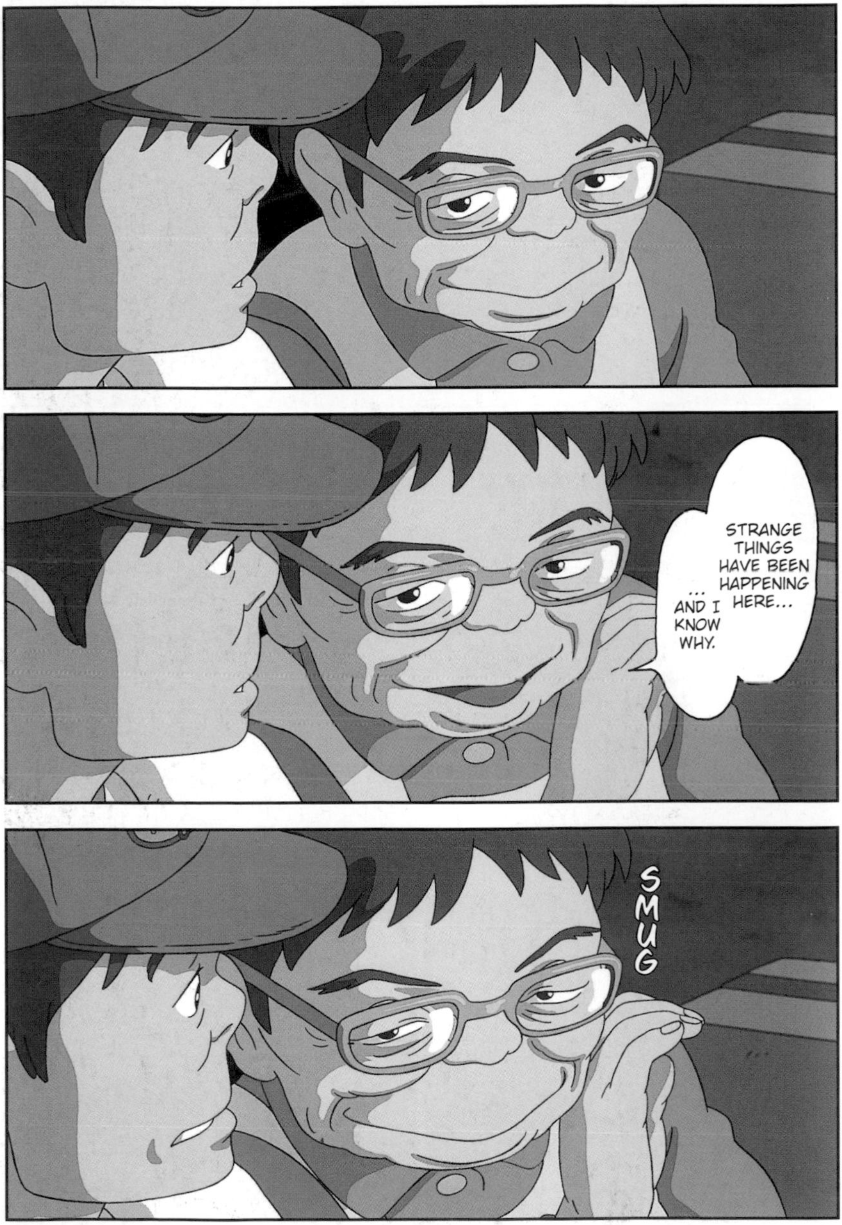
STRANGE THINGS HAVE BEEN HAPPENING HERE...
...AND I KNOW WHY.
SMUG

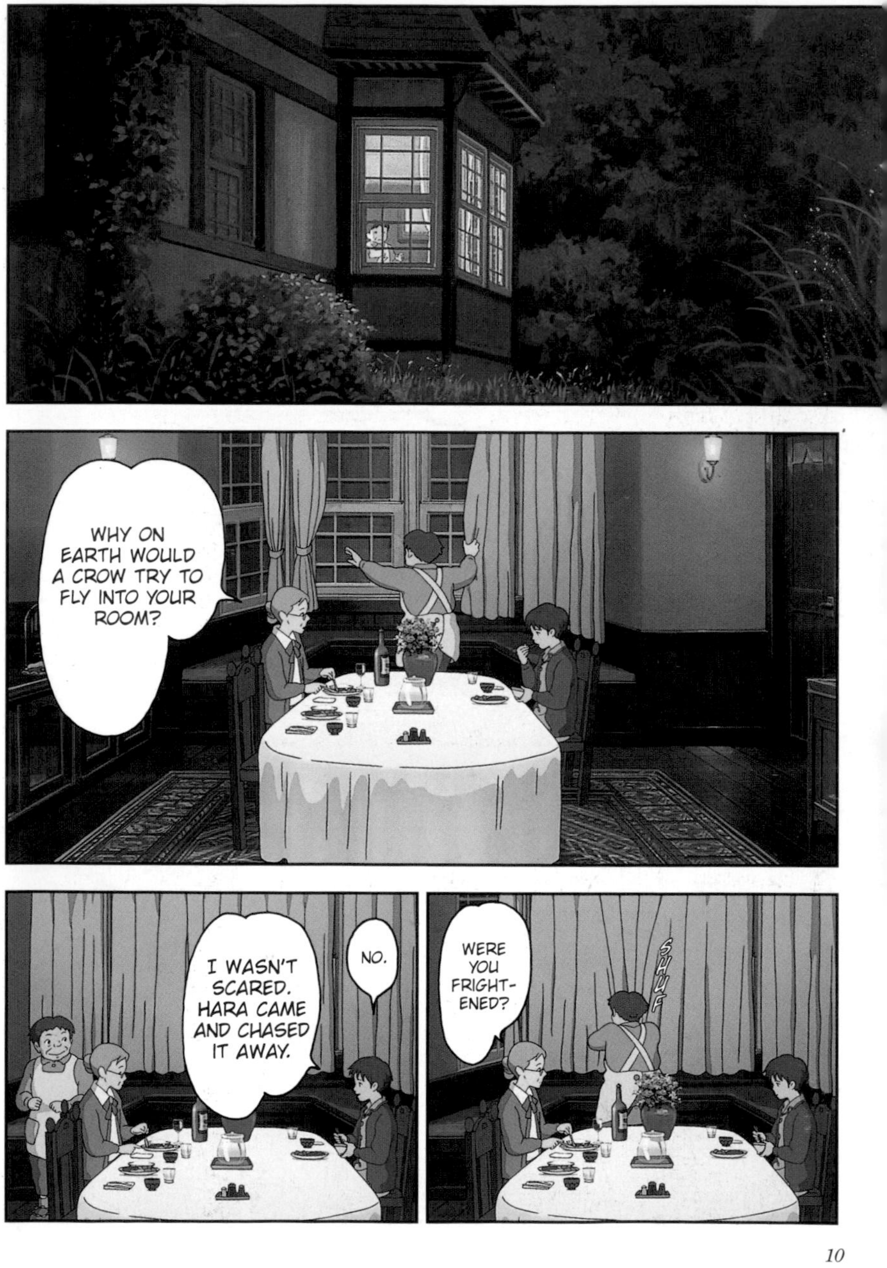
WHY ON EARTH WOULD A CROW TRY TO FLY INTO YOUR ROOM?
WERE YOU FRIGHT-ENED?
SHUF
NO.
I WASN'T SCARED. HARA CAME AND CHASED IT AWAY.

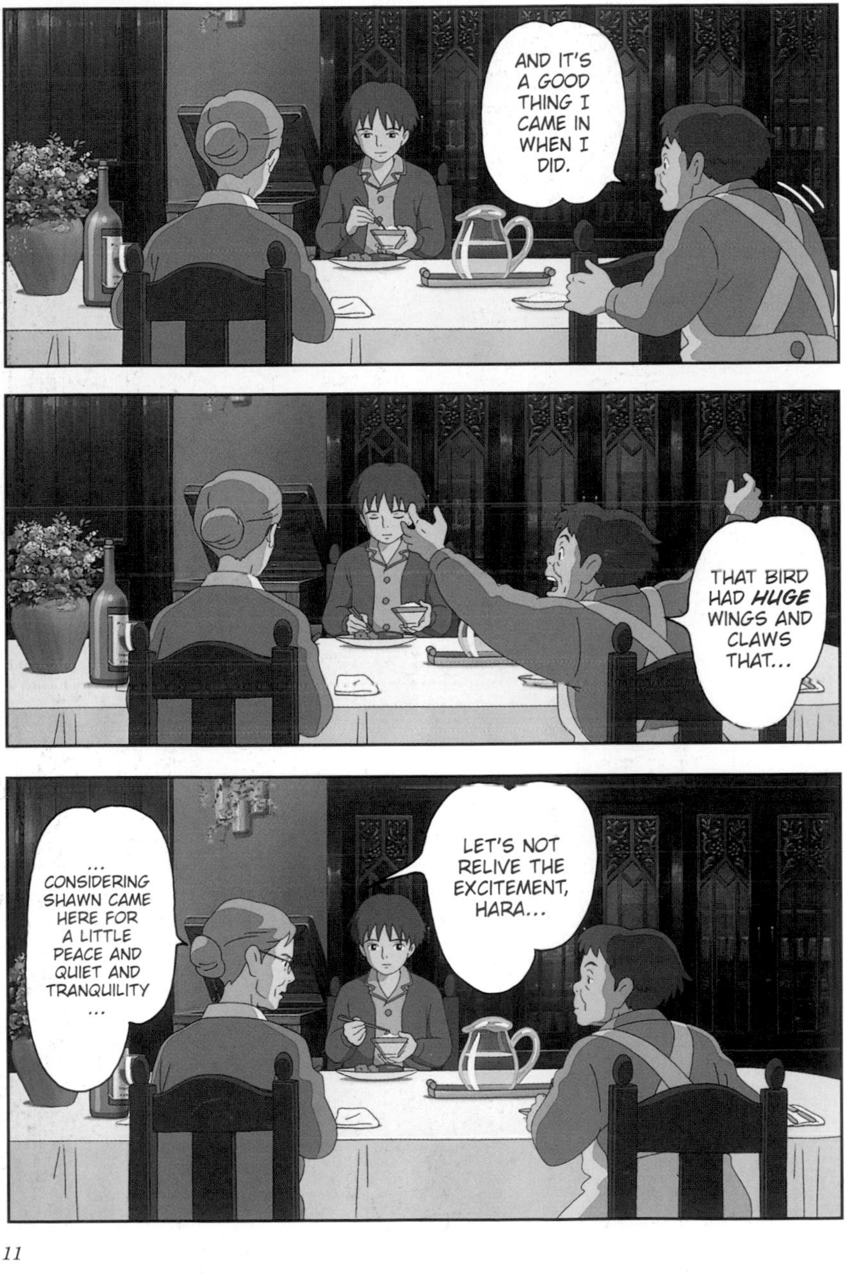
AND IT'S A GOOD THING I CAME IN WHEN I DID.
THAT BIRD HAD ***HUGE*** WINGS AND CLAWS THAT...
LET'S NOT RELIVE THE EXCITEMENT, HARA...
...CONSIDERING SHAWN CAME HERE FOR A LITTLE PEACE AND QUIET AND TRANQUILITY...

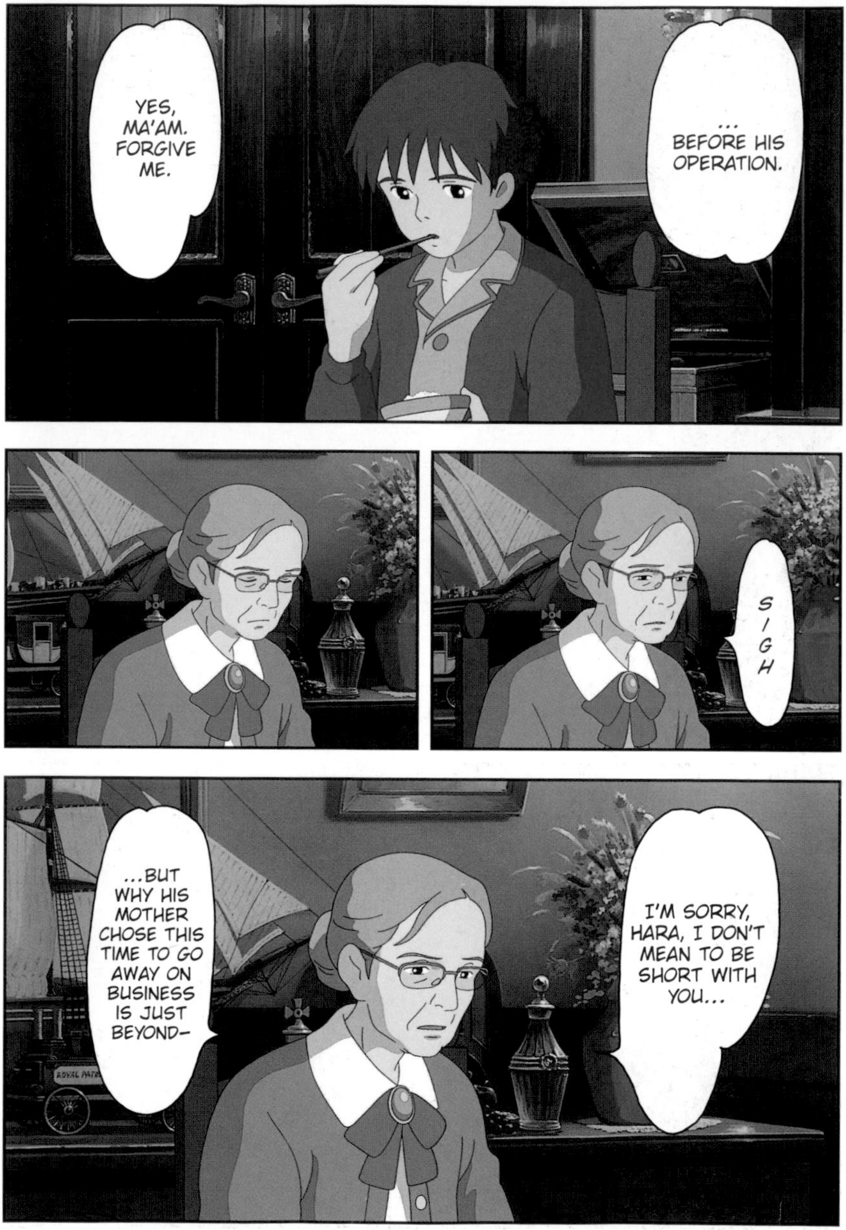
...BEFORE HIS OPERATION.
YES, MA'AM. FORGIVE ME.
SIGH
I'M SORRY, HARA, I DON'T MEAN TO BE SHORT WITH YOU...
...BUT WHY HIS MOTHER CHOSE THIS TIME TO GO AWAY ON BUSINESS IS JUST BEYOND–

IT MUST BE TERRIBLY HARD FOR YOU WITHOUT YOUR MOTHER HERE TO LOOK AFTER YOU.
HMM, YOU KNOW... NOT SO MUCH LATELY.
I SUPPOSE THE DIVORCE COULDN'T BE HELPED, BUT HONESTLY... WHY COULDN'T SHE BE HERE WHEN HER SON NEEDS HER SO?
IT'S THE LAST THING HIS POOR HEART NEEDS.
UH... MMM...

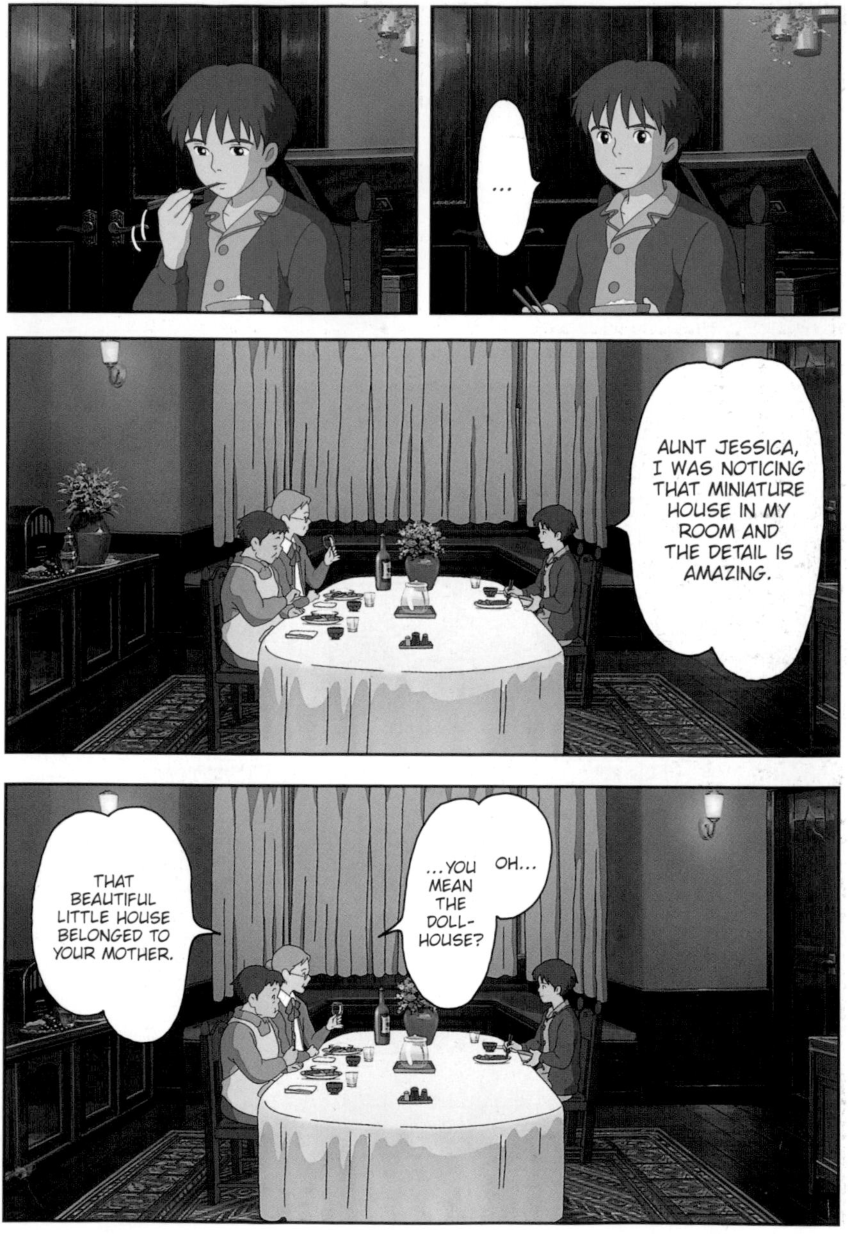
...
AUNT JESSICA, I WAS NOTICING THAT MINIATURE HOUSE IN MY ROOM AND THE DETAIL IS AMAZING.
OH...
...YOU MEAN THE DOLL-HOUSE?
THAT BEAUTIFUL LITTLE HOUSE BELONGED TO YOUR MOTHER.

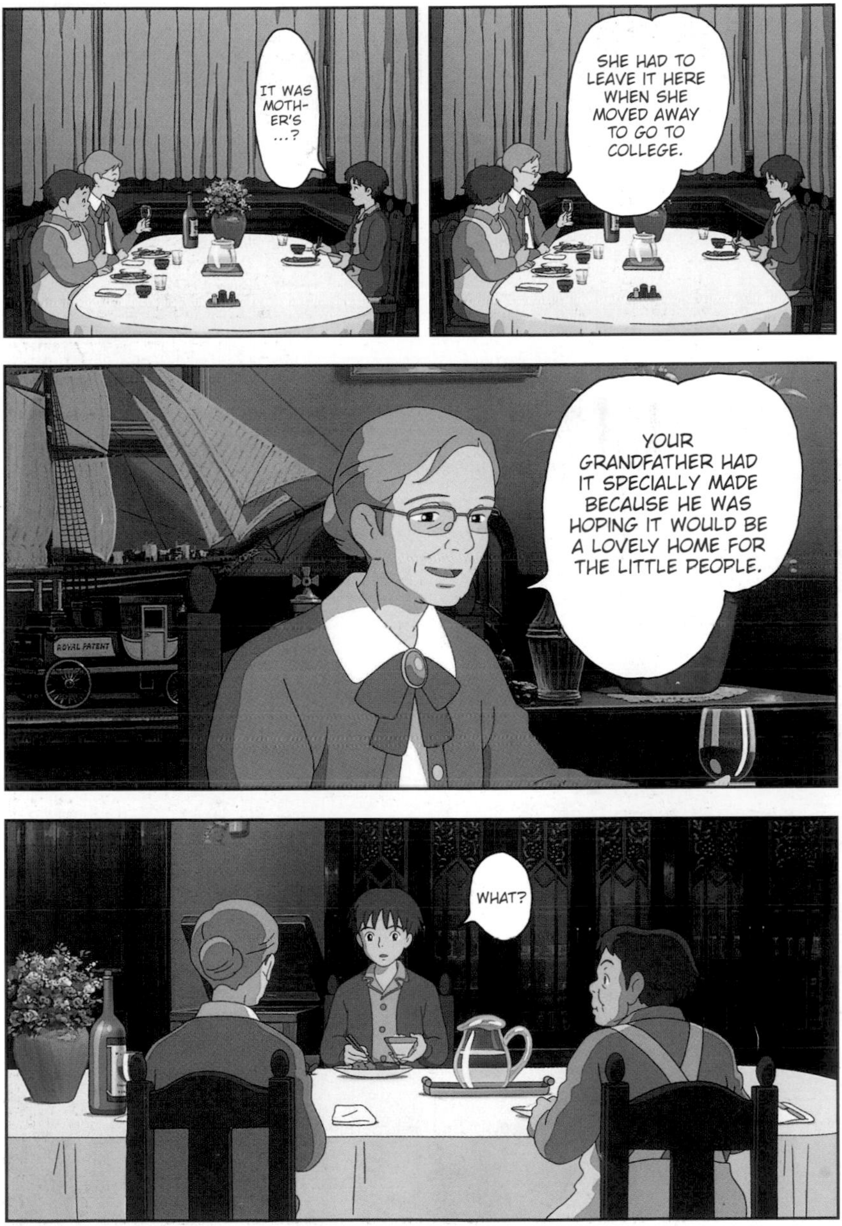
IT WAS MOTHER'S ...?
SHE HAD TO LEAVE IT HERE WHEN SHE MOVED AWAY TO GO TO COLLEGE.
YOUR GRANDFATHER HAD IT SPECIALLY MADE BECAUSE HE WAS HOPING IT WOULD BE A LOVELY HOME FOR THE LITTLE PEOPLE.
ROYAL PATENT
WHAT?

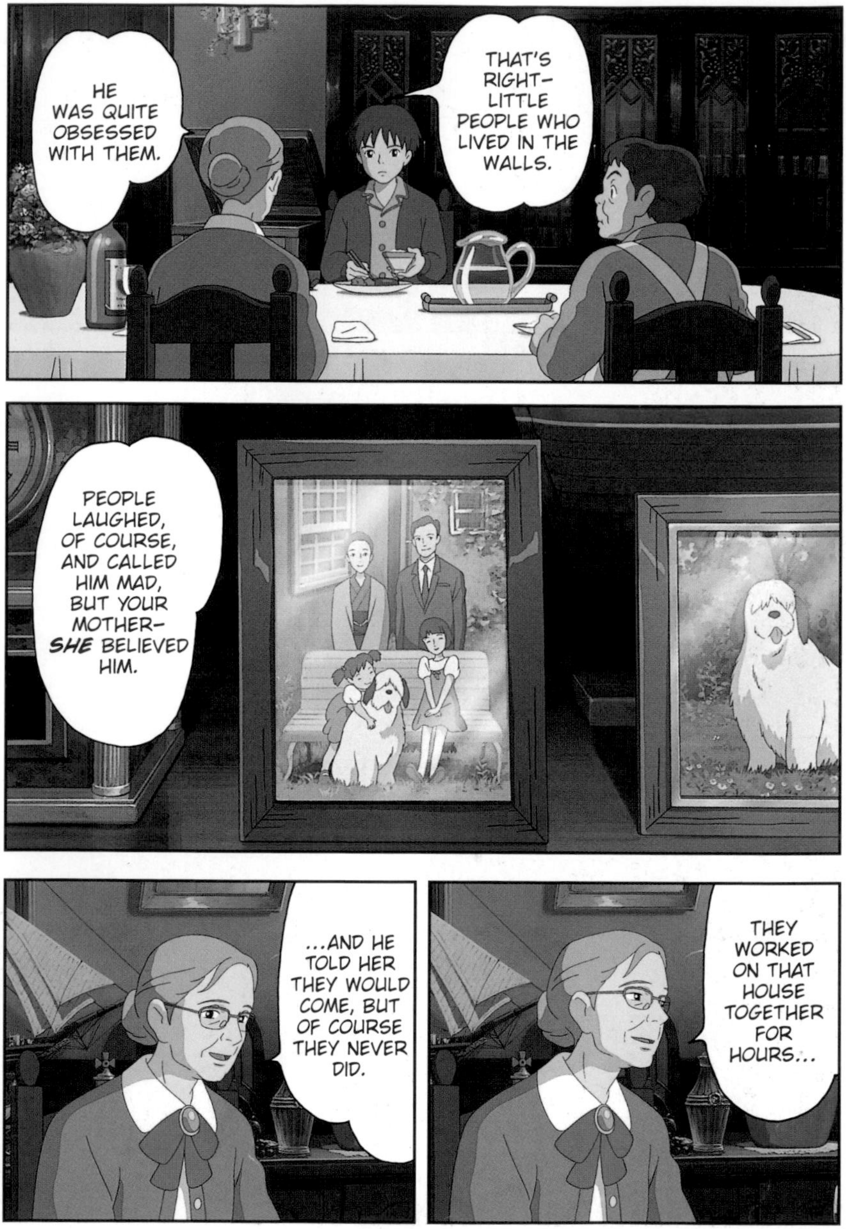
THAT'S RIGHT— LITTLE PEOPLE WHO LIVED IN THE WALLS.
HE WAS QUITE OBSESSED WITH THEM.
PEOPLE LAUGHED, OF COURSE, AND CALLED HIM MAD, BUT YOUR MOTHER— SHE BELIEVED HIM.
THEY WORKED ON THAT HOUSE TOGETHER FOR HOURS...
...AND HE TOLD HER THEY WOULD COME, BUT OF COURSE THEY NEVER DID.

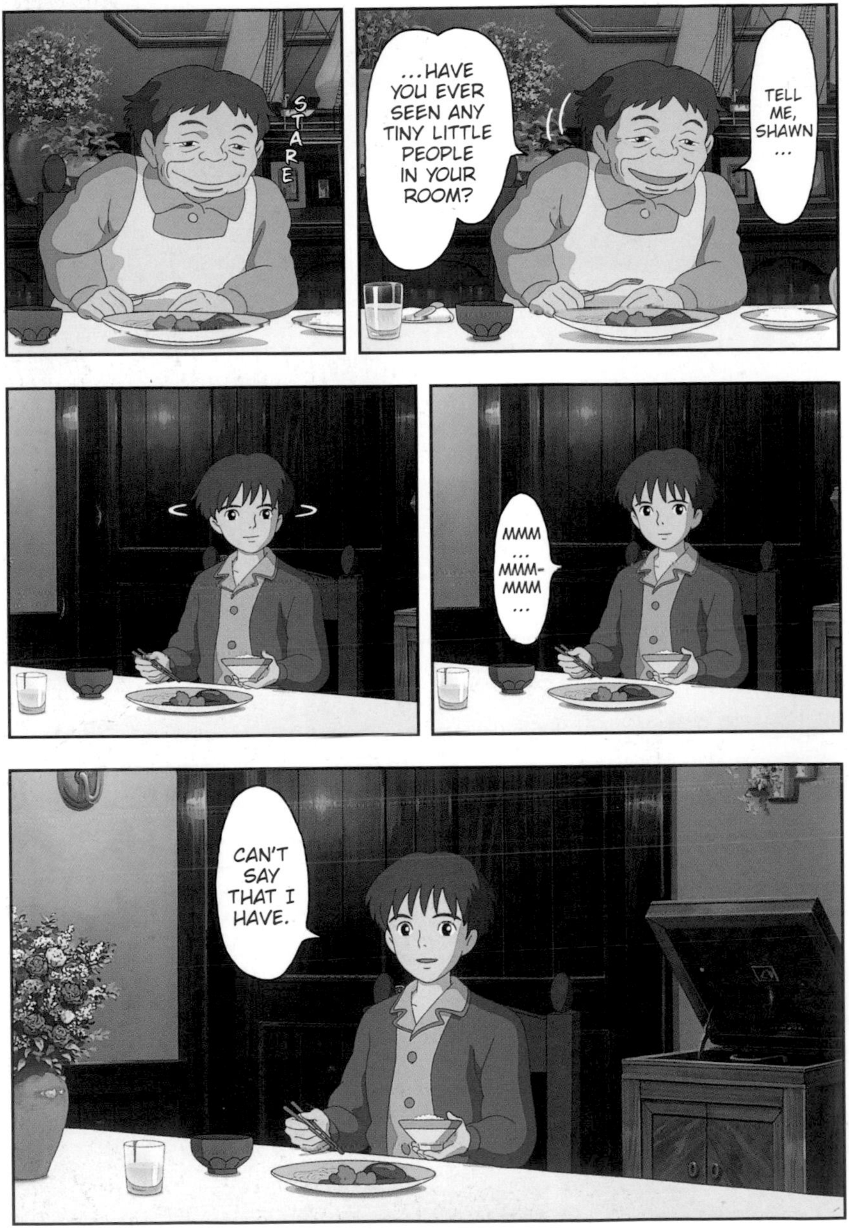
TELL ME, SHAWN...
...HAVE YOU EVER SEEN ANY TINY LITTLE PEOPLE IN YOUR ROOM?
STARE
MMM... MMM-MMM...
CAN'T SAY THAT I HAVE.

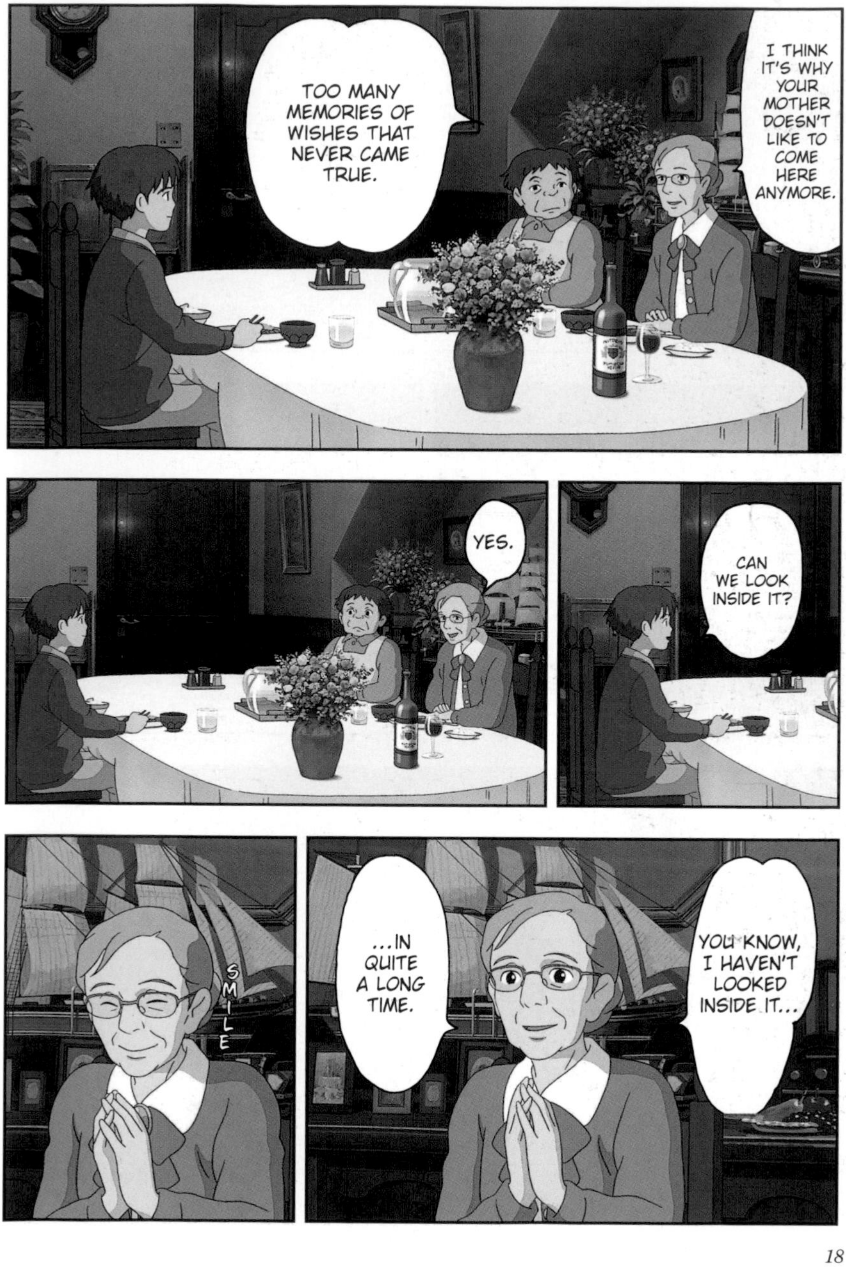
I THINK IT'S WHY YOUR MOTHER DOESN'T LIKE TO COME HERE ANYMORE.
TOO MANY MEMORIES OF WISHES THAT NEVER CAME TRUE.
CAN WE LOOK INSIDE IT?
YES.
YOU KNOW, I HAVEN'T LOOKED INSIDE IT...
...IN QUITE A LONG TIME.
SMILE

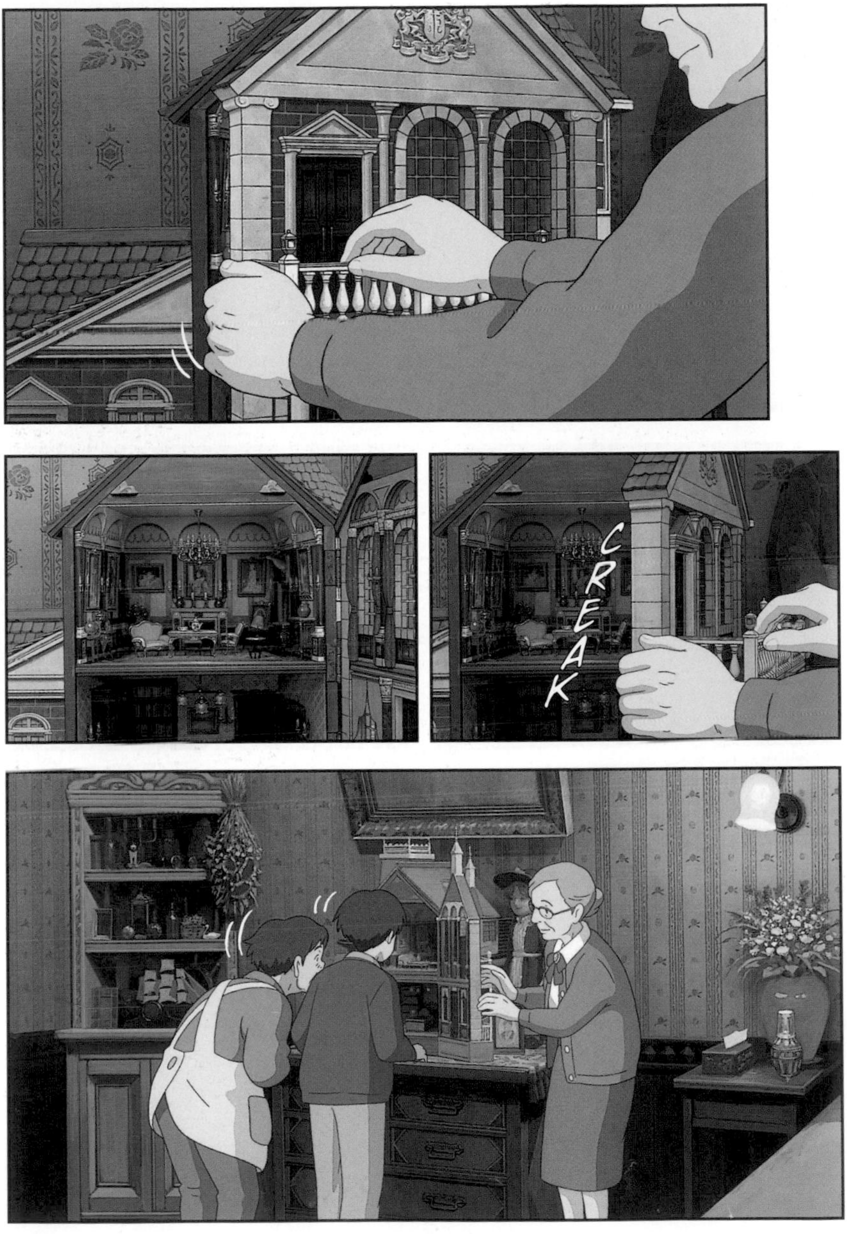
CREAK

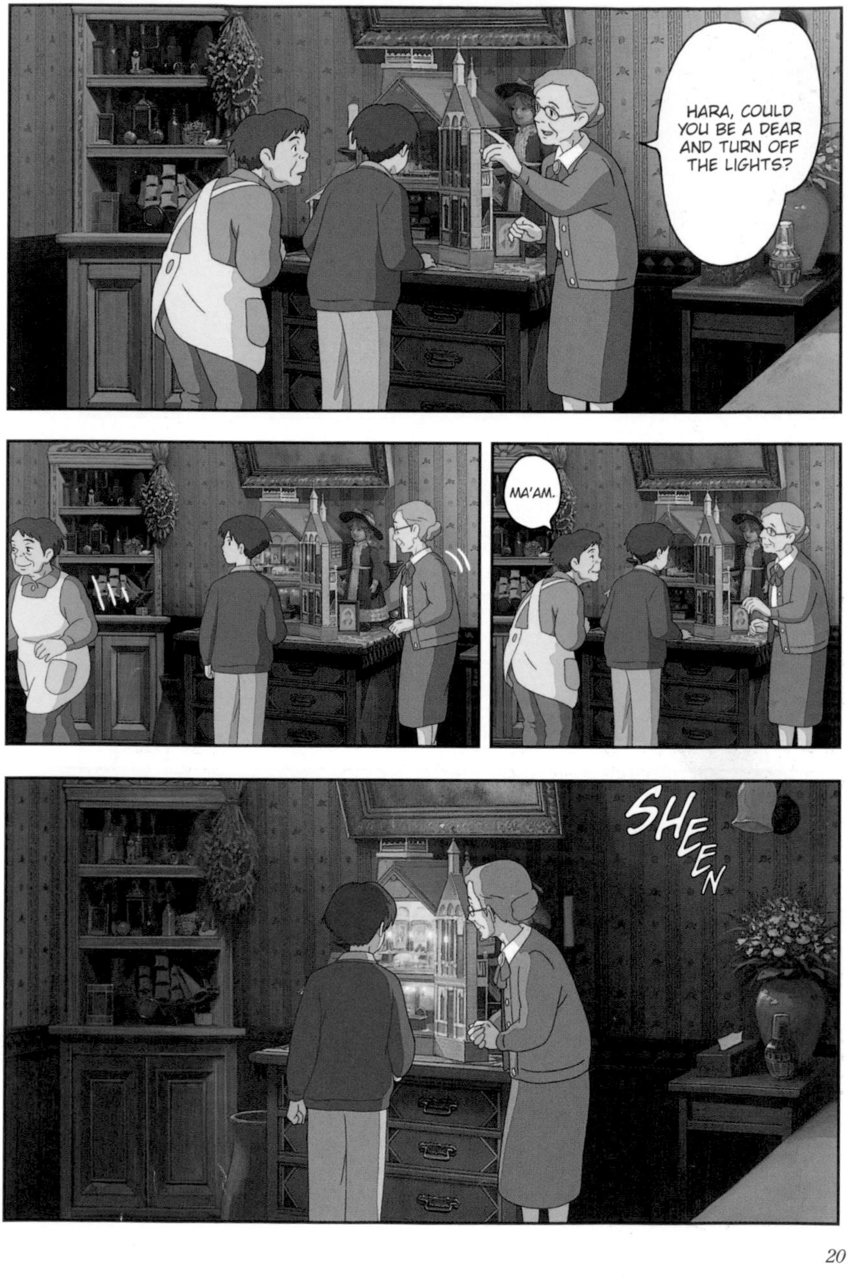
HARA, COULD YOU BE A DEAR AND TURN OFF THE LIGHTS?
MA'AM.
SHEEN

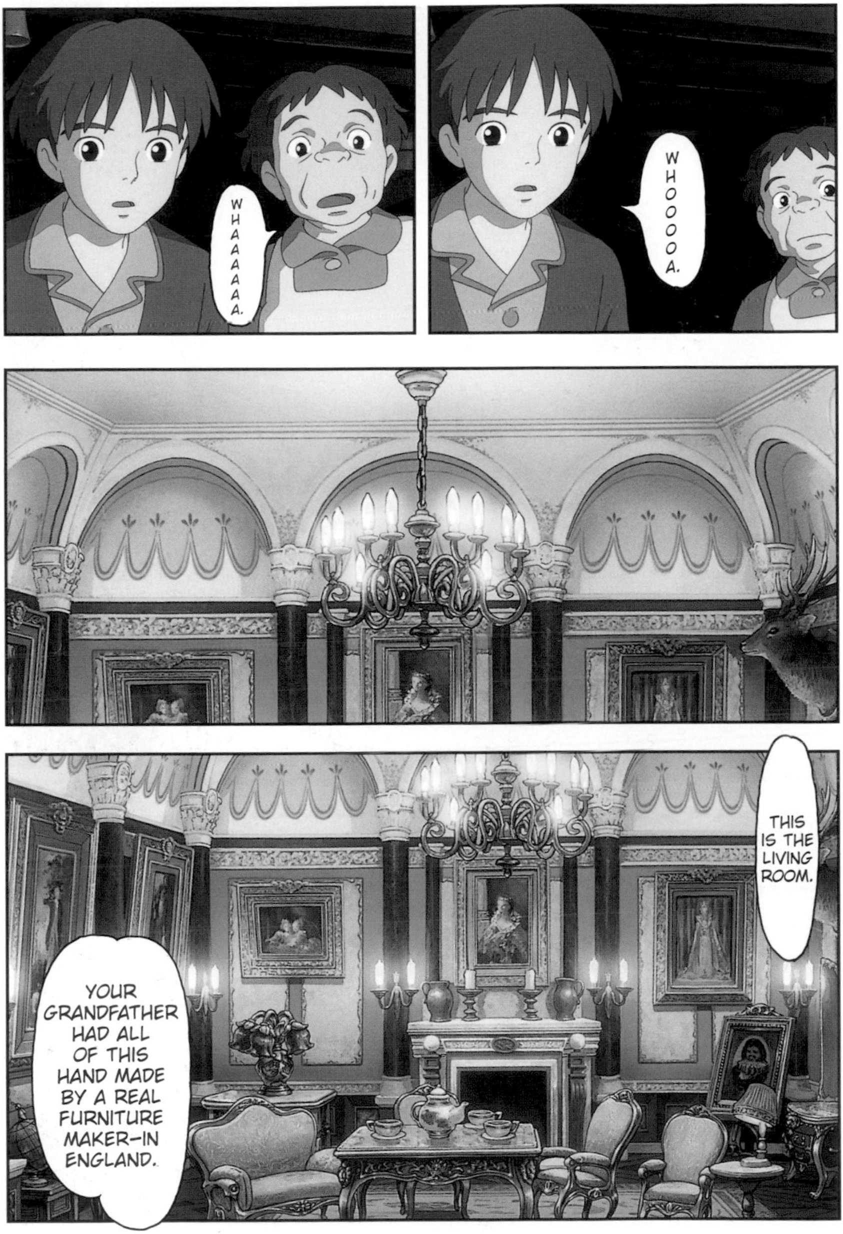
WHOOOOA.
WHAAAAAA.
THIS IS THE LIVING ROOM.
YOUR GRANDFATHER HAD ALL OF THIS HAND MADE BY A REAL FURNITURE MAKER—IN ENGLAND.

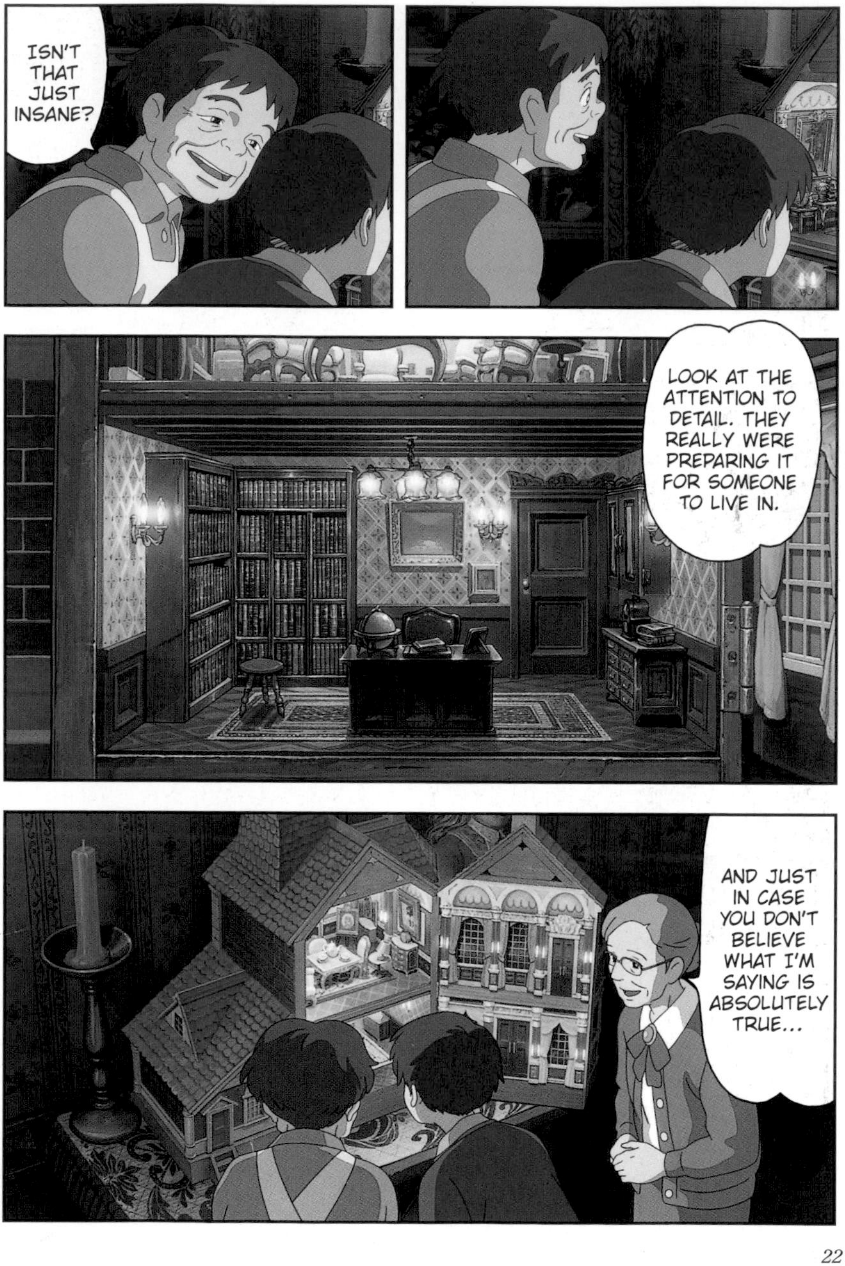
ISN'T THAT JUST INSANE?
LOOK AT THE ATTENTION TO DETAIL. THEY REALLY WERE PREPARING IT FOR SOMEONE TO LIVE IN.
AND JUST IN CASE YOU DON'T BELIEVE WHAT I'M SAYING IS ABSOLUTELY TRUE...

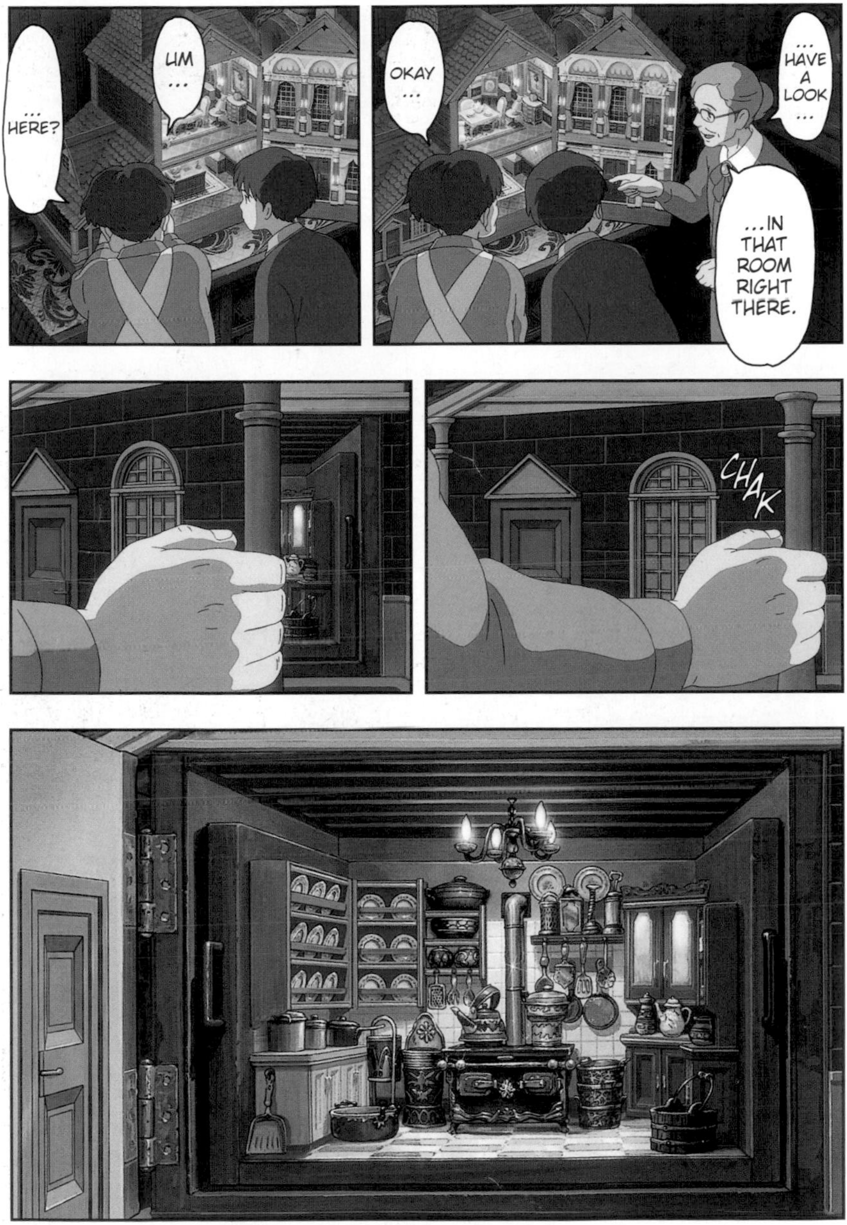
... HAVE A LOOK ...
... IN THAT ROOM RIGHT THERE.
OKAY ...
UM ...
... HERE?
CHAK

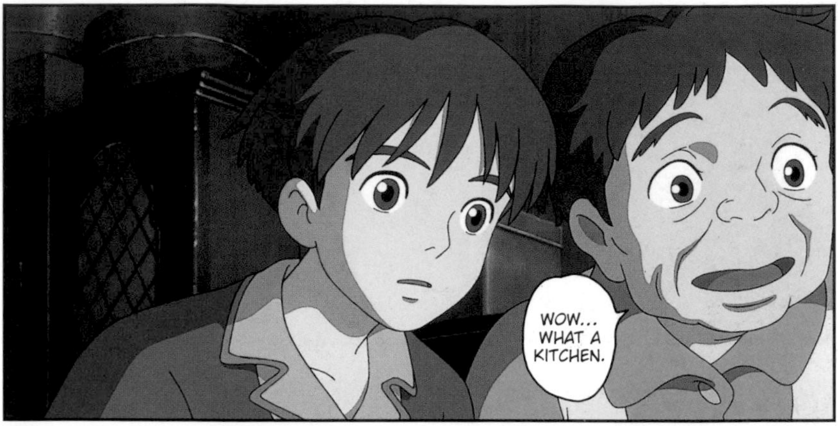
WOW... WHAT A KITCHEN.

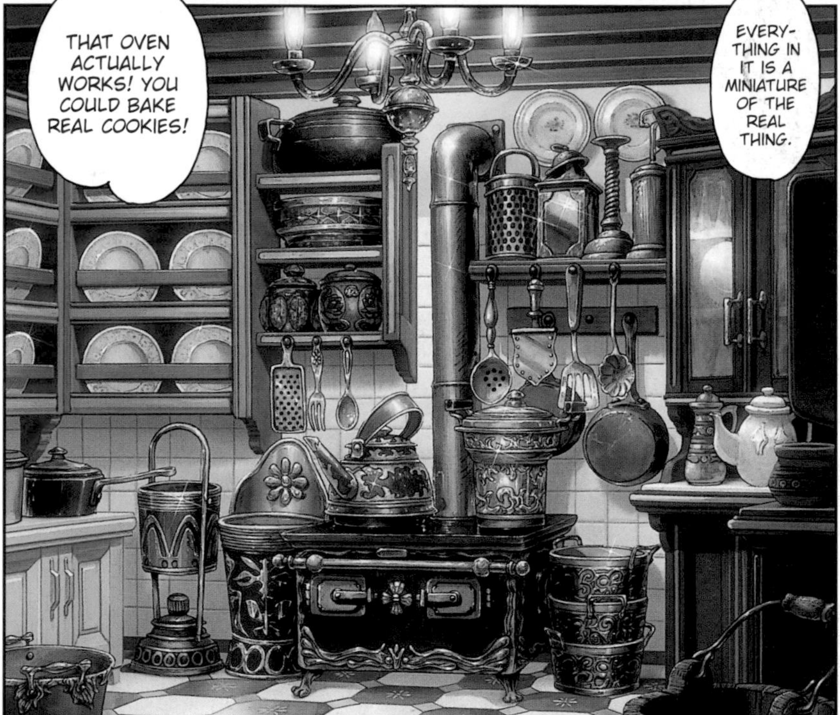
EVERY-THING IN IT IS A MINIATURE OF THE REAL THING.
THAT OVEN ACTUALLY WORKS! YOU COULD BAKE REAL COOKIES!

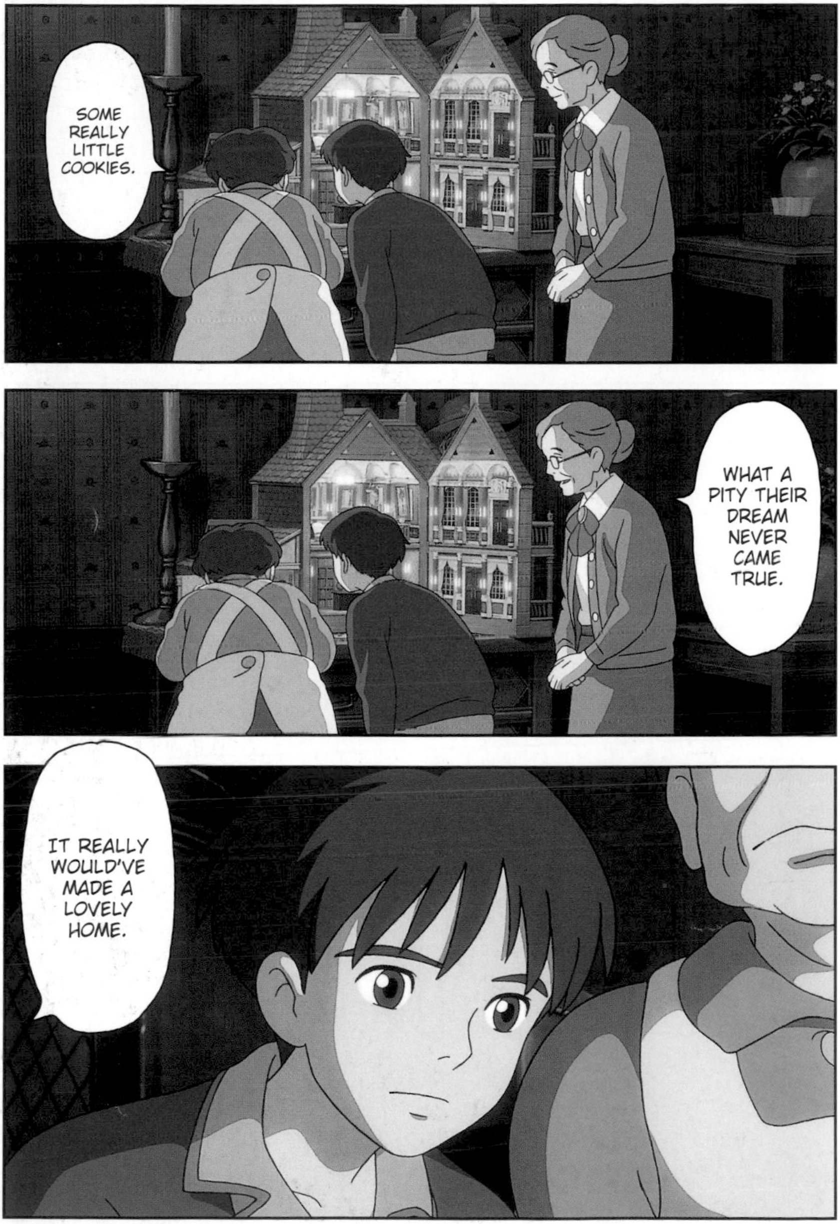
SOME REALLY LITTLE COOKIES.
WHAT A PITY THEIR DREAM NEVER CAME TRUE.
IT REALLY WOULD'VE MADE A LOVELY HOME.

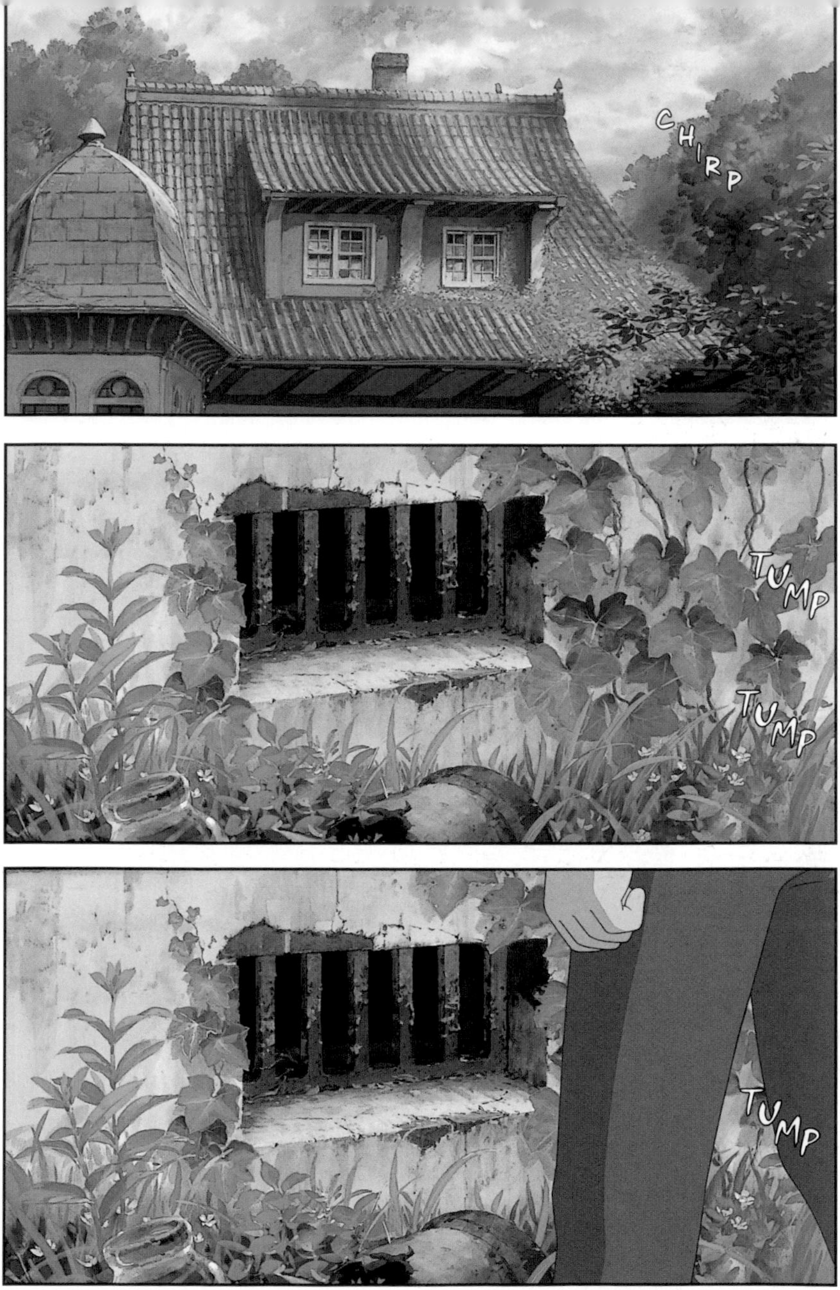
CHIRP
TUMP
TUMP
TUMP

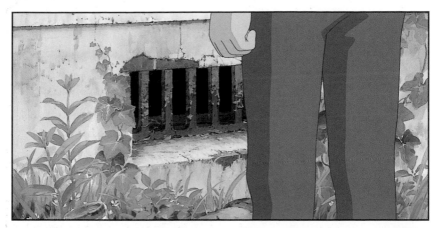

TUMP

TUMP

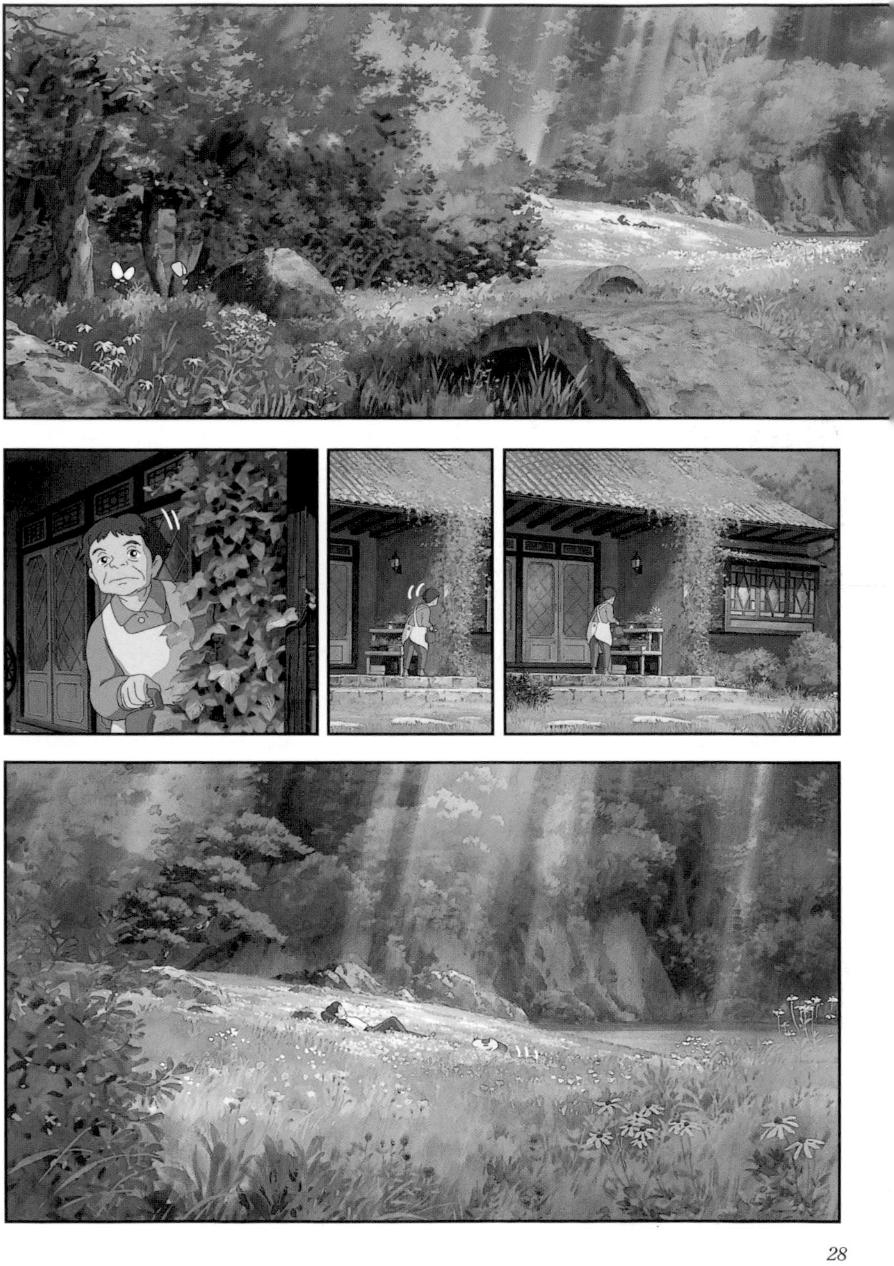

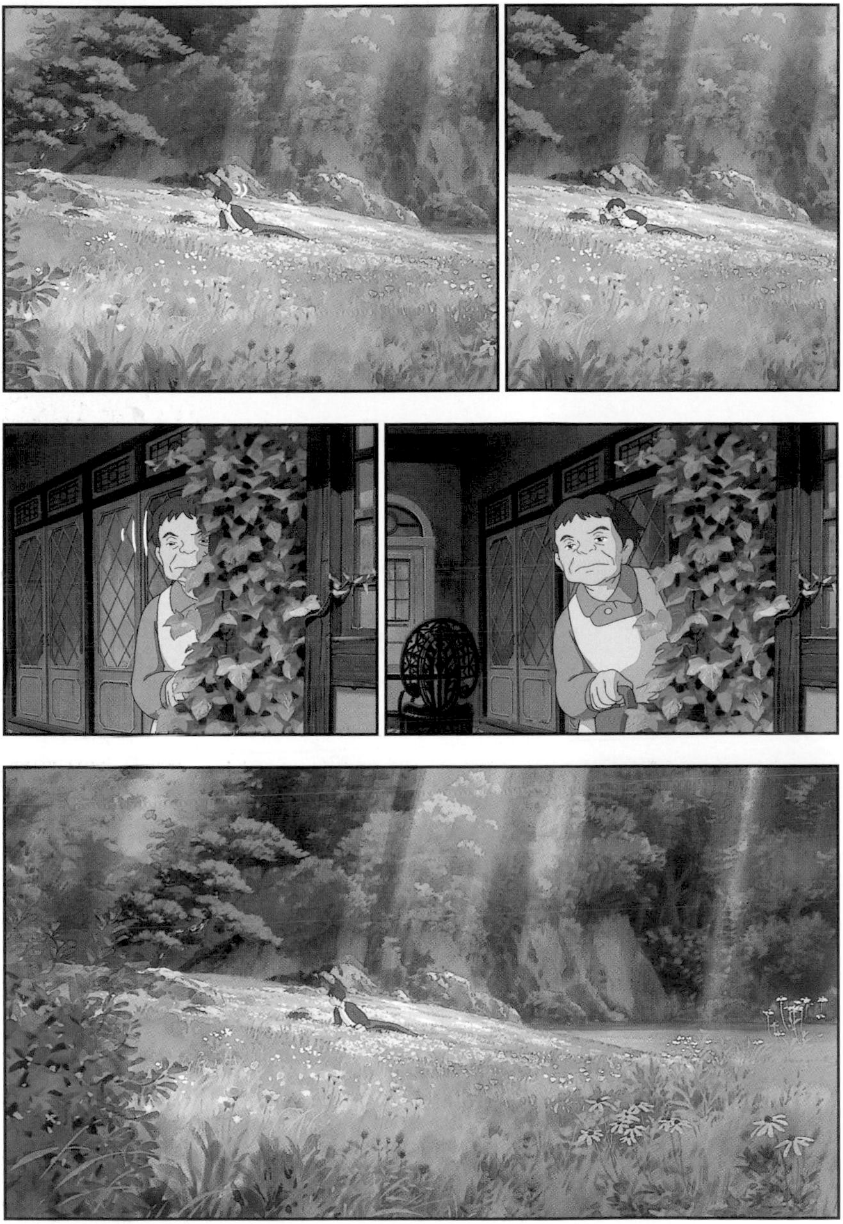

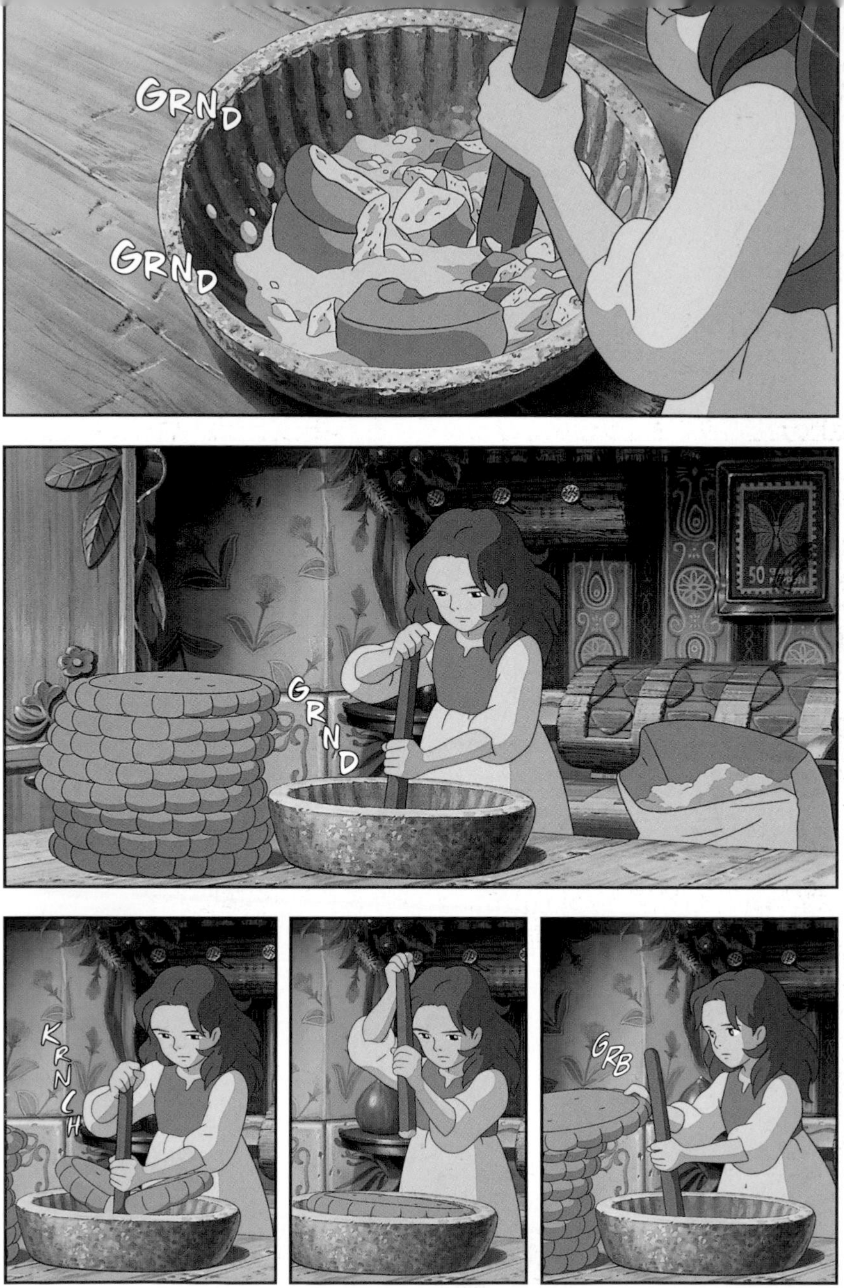
GRND
GRND
GRND
GRB
KRNCH

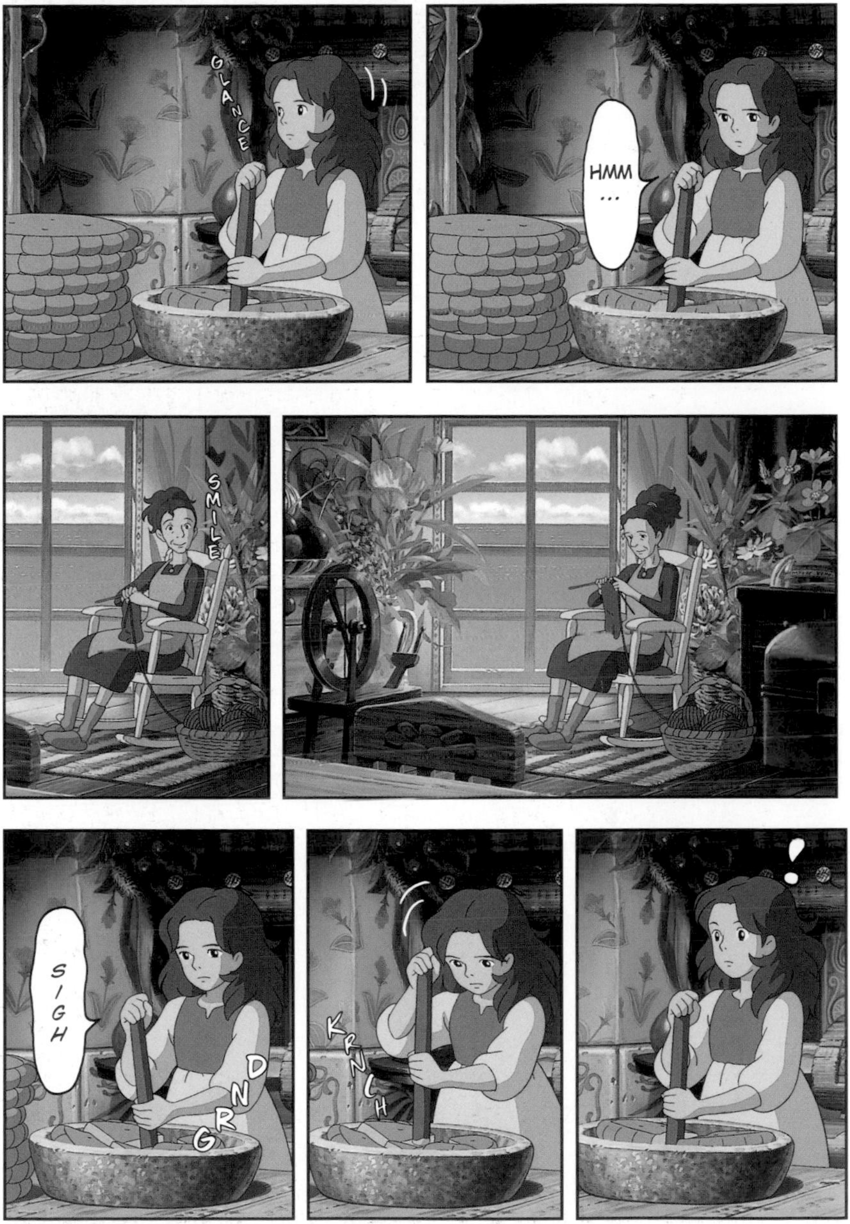
HMM ...
GLANCE
SMILE
!
KRNCH
SIGH
GRND

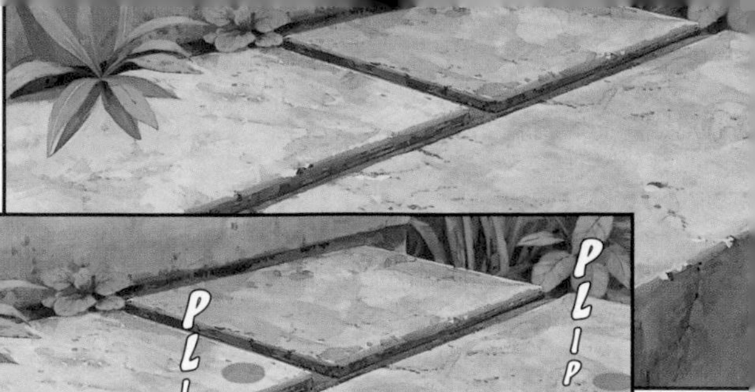

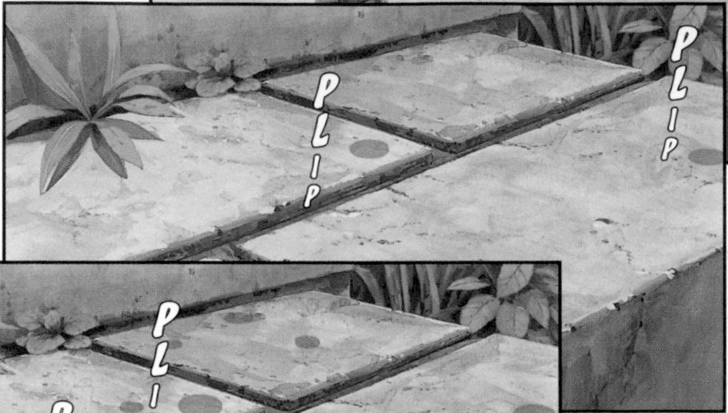
PLIP
PLIP

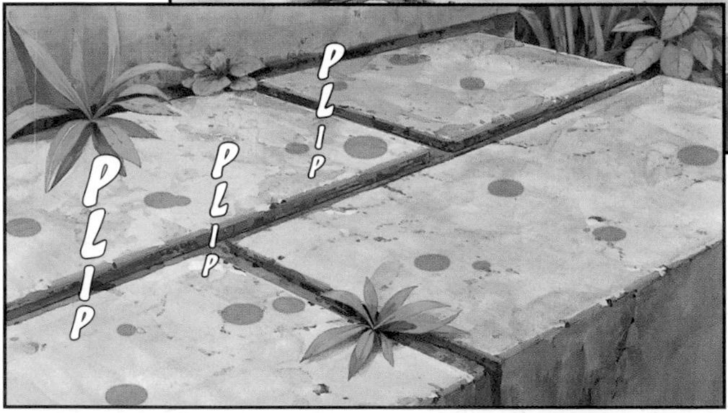
PLIP
PLIP
PLIP

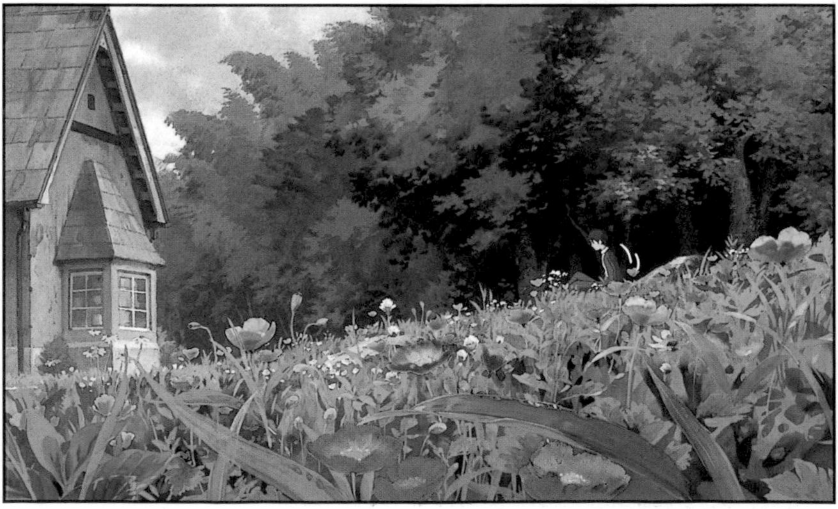

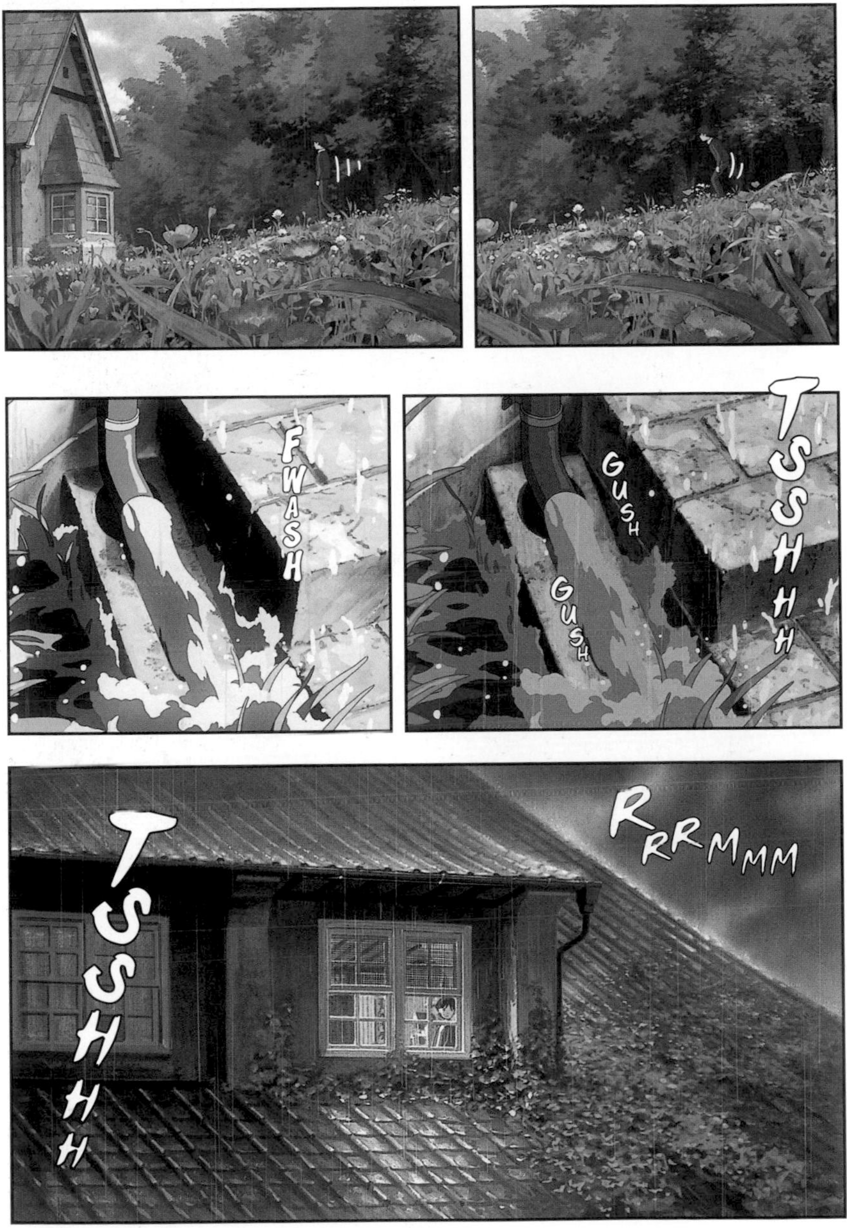
GUSH
GUSH
TSSHHH
FWASH
RRRMMMM
TSSHHH

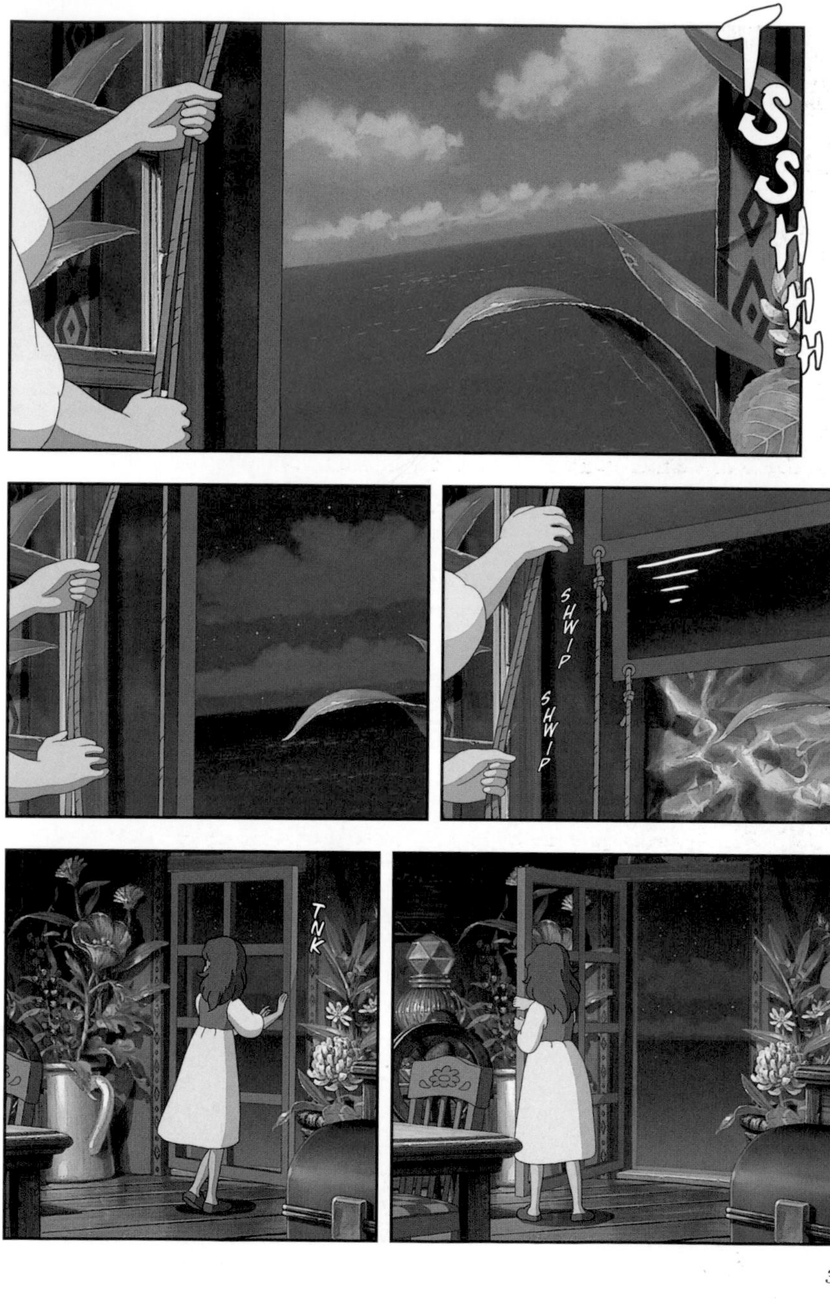
TSSHHH
SHWIP
SHWIP
TNK

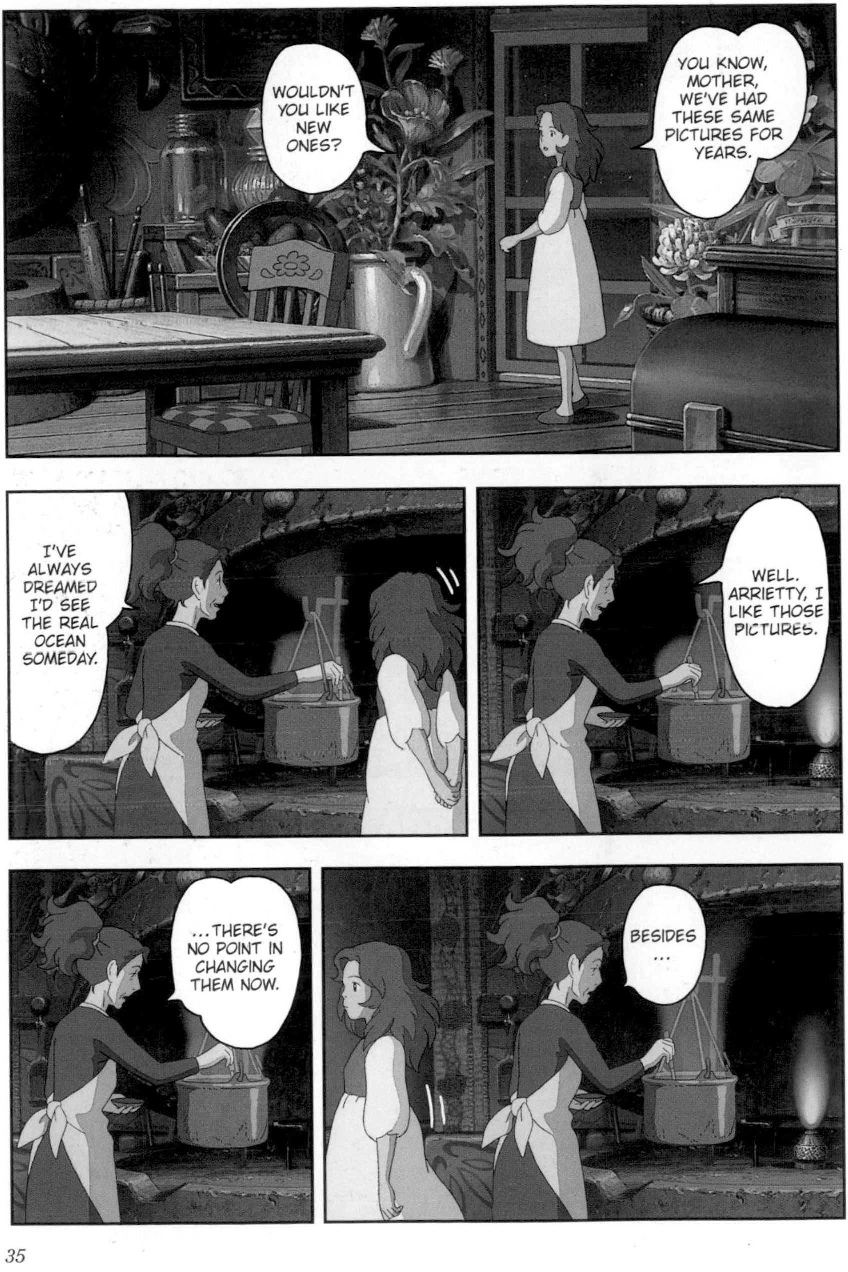
YOU KNOW, MOTHER, WE'VE HAD THESE SAME PICTURES FOR YEARS.
WOULDN'T YOU LIKE NEW ONES?
WELL. ARRIETTY, I LIKE THOSE PICTURES.
I'VE ALWAYS DREAMED I'D SEE THE REAL OCEAN SOMEDAY.
BESIDES ...
...THERE'S NO POINT IN CHANGING THEM NOW.

· · ·

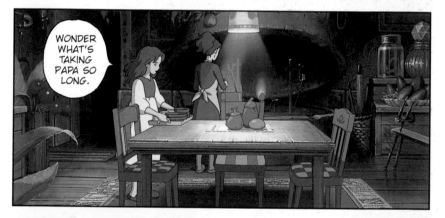

WONDER WHAT'S TAKING PAPA SO LONG.

WHY IS MY FIRST THOUGHT ALWAYS THAT HE GOT EATEN BY THE CAT? WHAT'S WRONG WITH ME?

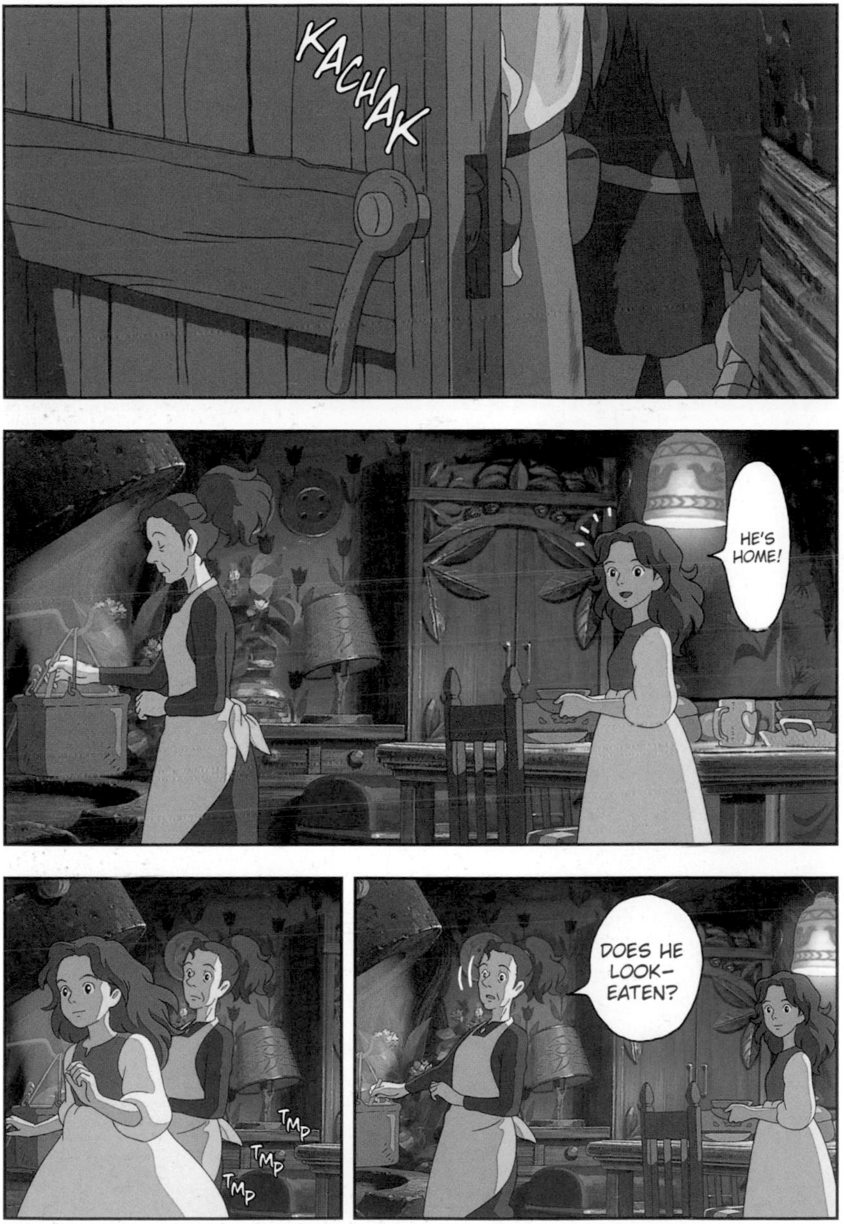
KACHAK
HE'S HOME!
DOES HE LOOK— EATEN?
TMP
TMP
TMP

TMP
TMP
HEY, PAPA! HOW WAS IT OUT THERE? OH...
I SLIPPED AND TWISTED MY LEG.
I'M LUCKY SPILLER HERE FOUND ME.

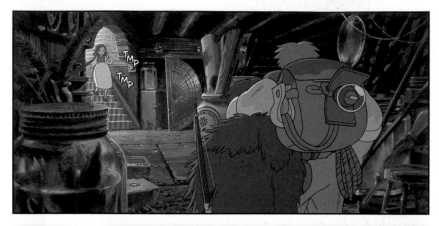

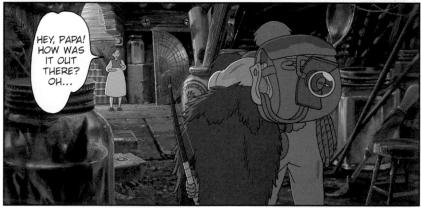

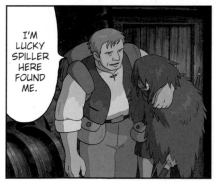

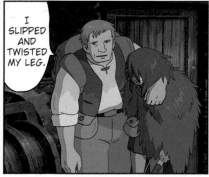

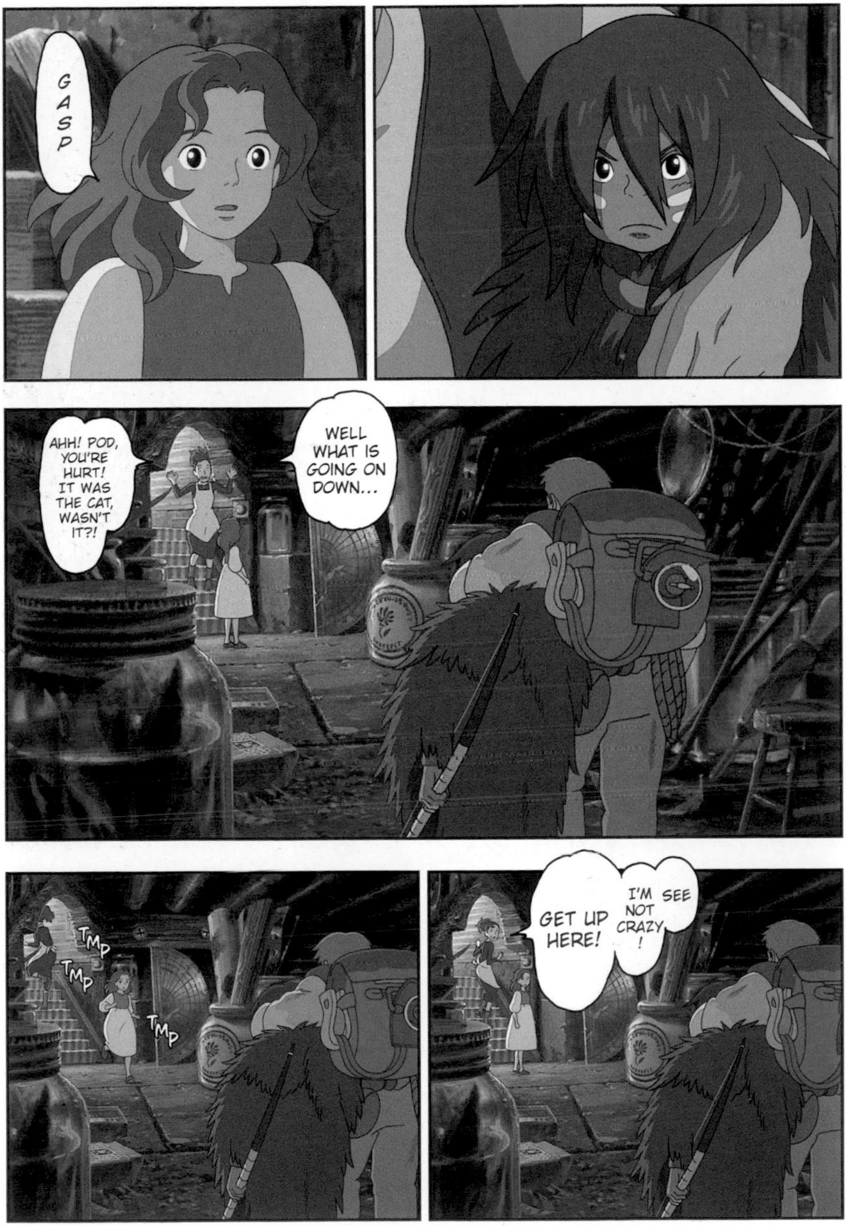
GASP
WELL WHAT IS GOING ON DOWN...
AHH! POD, YOU'RE HURT! IT WAS THE CAT, WASN'T IT?!
SEE I'M NOT CRAZY!
GET UP HERE!
TMP
TMP
TMP

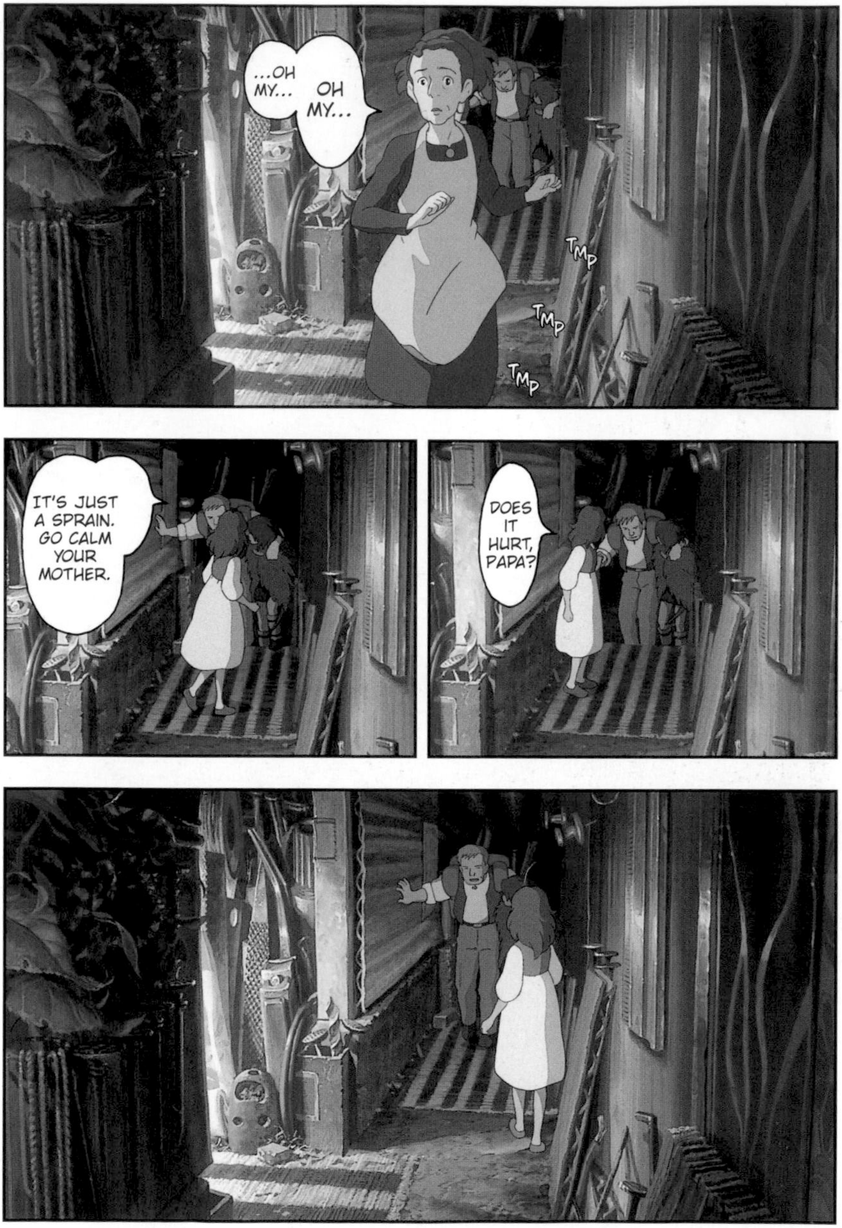
...OH MY... OH MY...
TMP
TMP
TMP
DOES IT HURT, PAPA?
IT'S JUST A SPRAIN. GO CALM YOUR MOTHER.

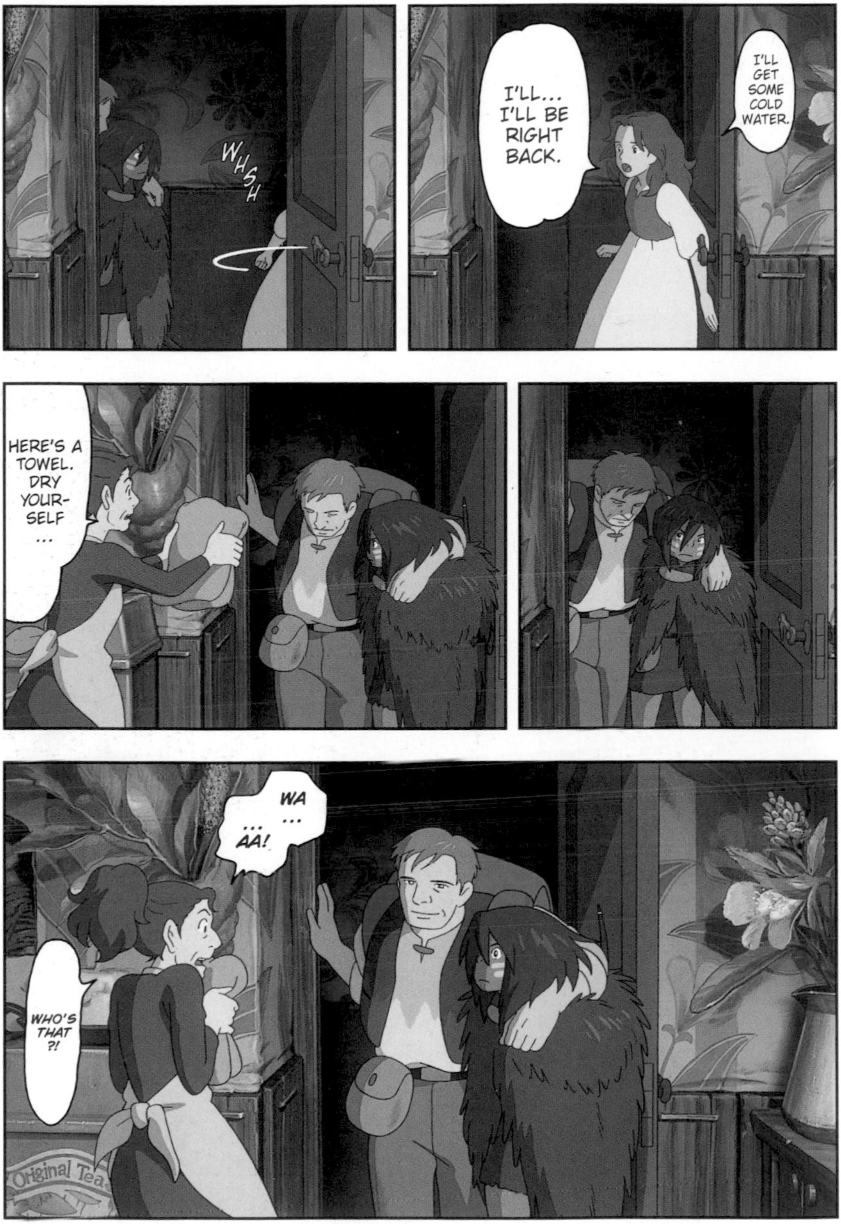
I'LL GET SOME COLD WATER.
I'LL... I'LL BE RIGHT BACK.
WHSH
HERE'S A TOWEL. DRY YOURSELF...
WA... ...ÄA!
WHO'S THAT?!
Original Tea

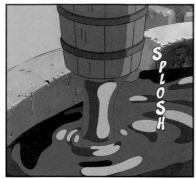

I WONDER IF HE HAS NEWS ABOUT ANY OF THE OTHER BORROWERS!

DRIP

TMP

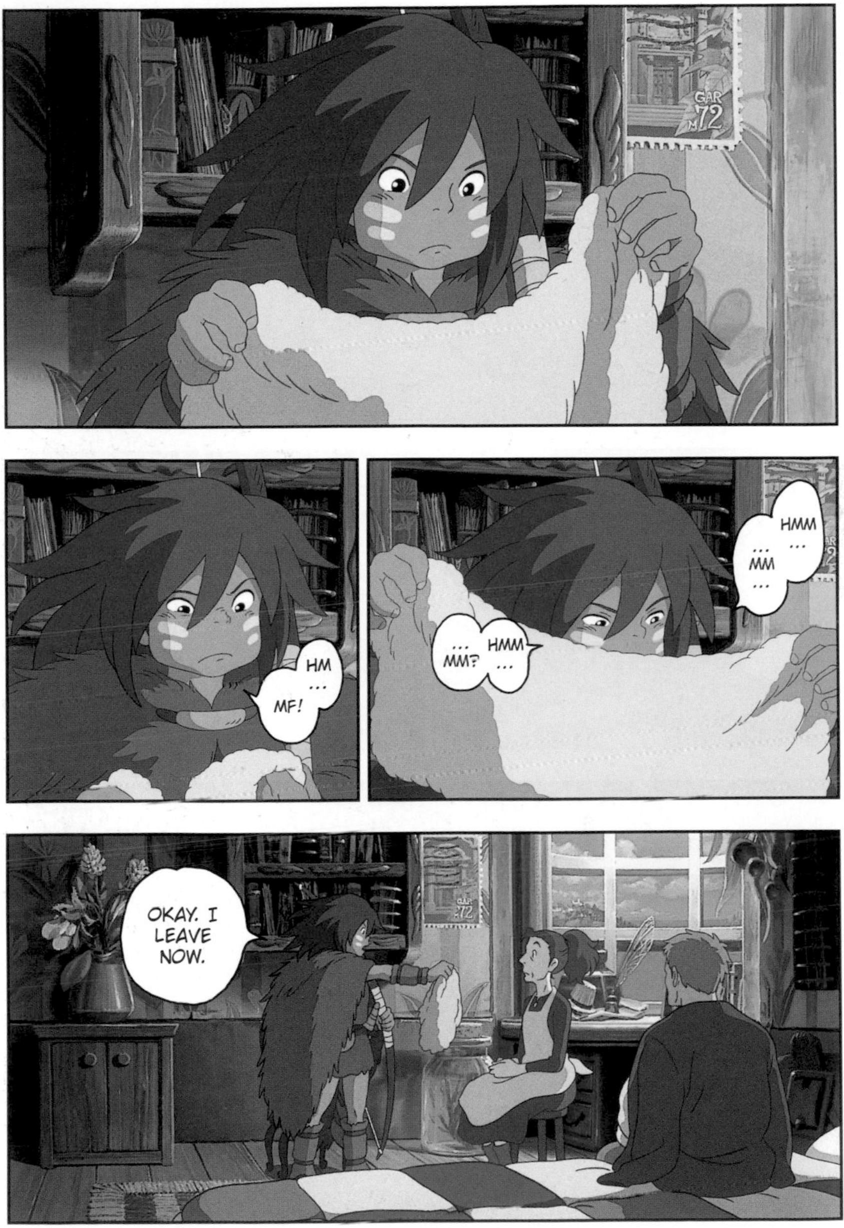
HMM ... ... MM ...
HMM ... ... MM?
HM ... MF!
OKAY. I LEAVE NOW.

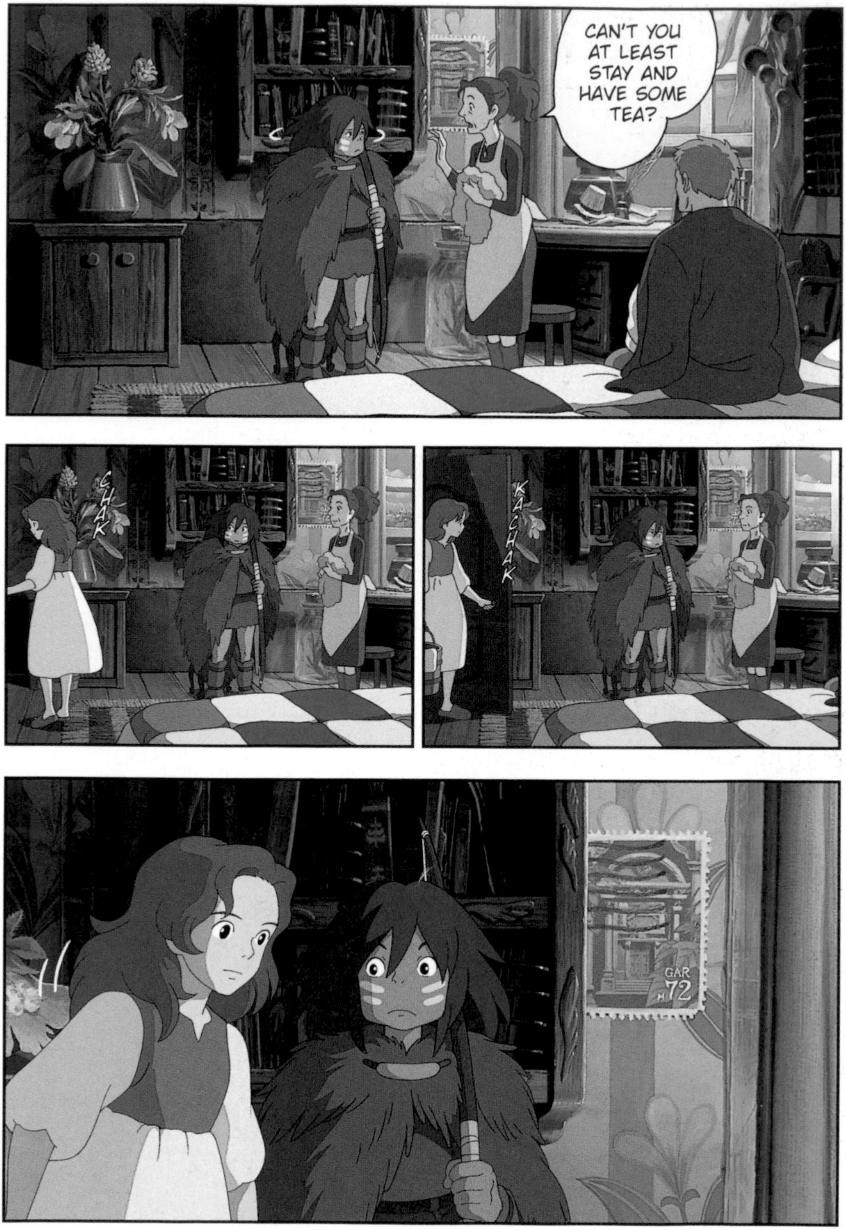
CAN'T YOU AT LEAST STAY AND HAVE SOME TEA?
KACHAK
CHAK
GAR
72

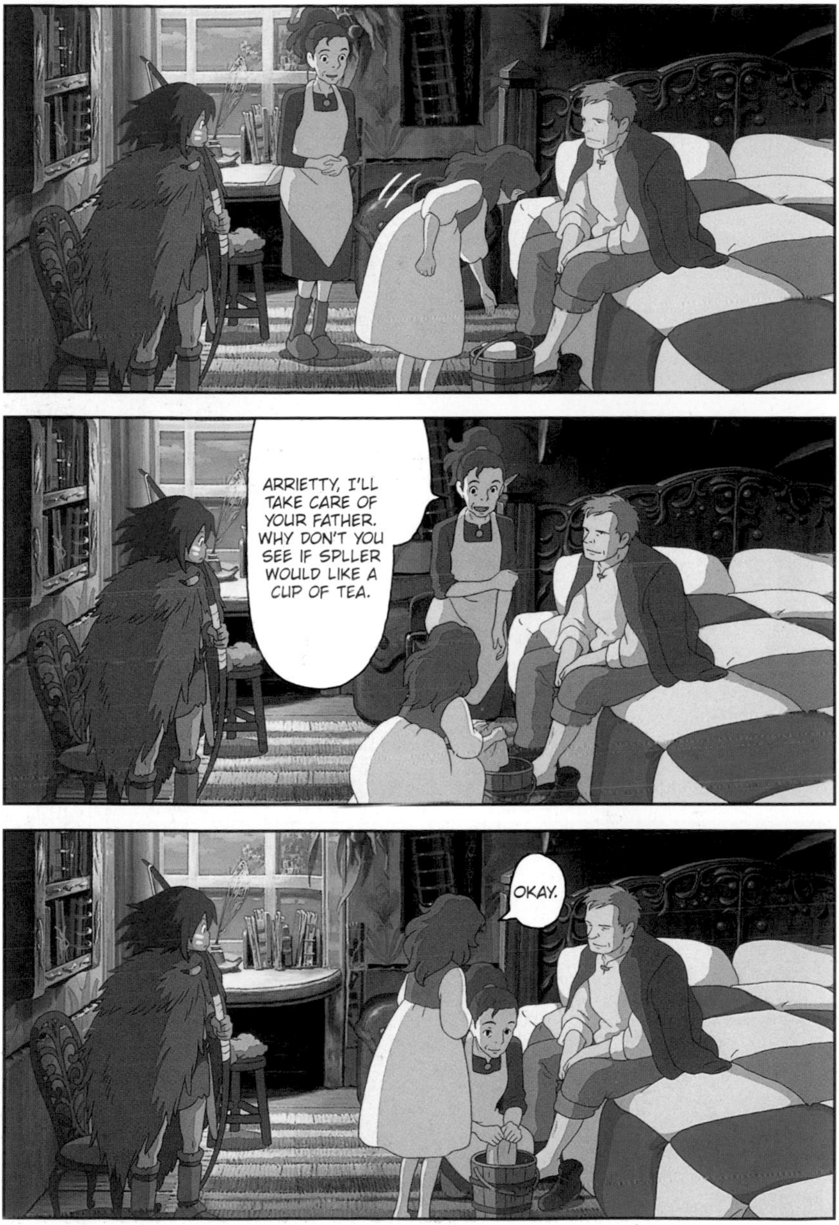
ARRIETTY, I'LL TAKE CARE OF YOUR FATHER. WHY DON'T YOU SEE IF SPLLER WOULD LIKE A CUP OF TEA.
OKAY.

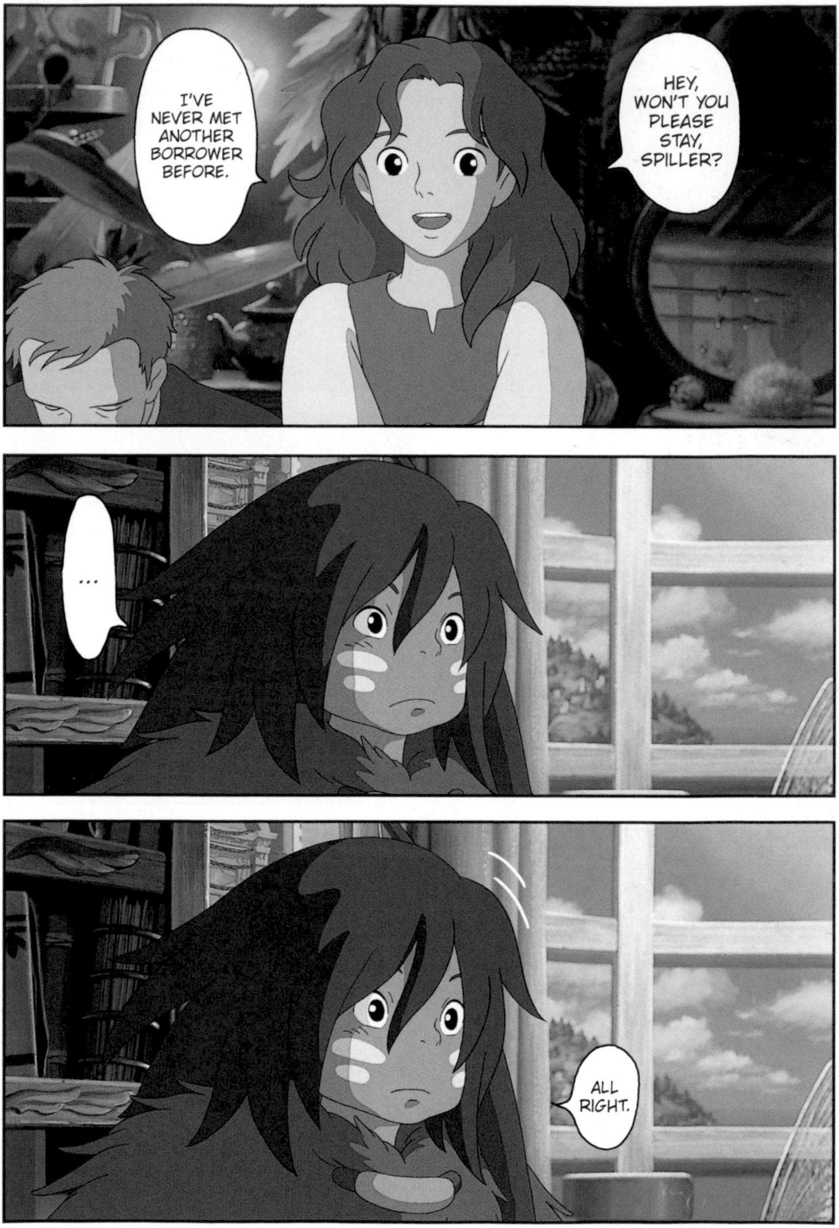
HEY, WON'T YOU PLEASE STAY, SPILLER?
I'VE NEVER MET ANOTHER BORROWER BEFORE.
...
ALL RIGHT.

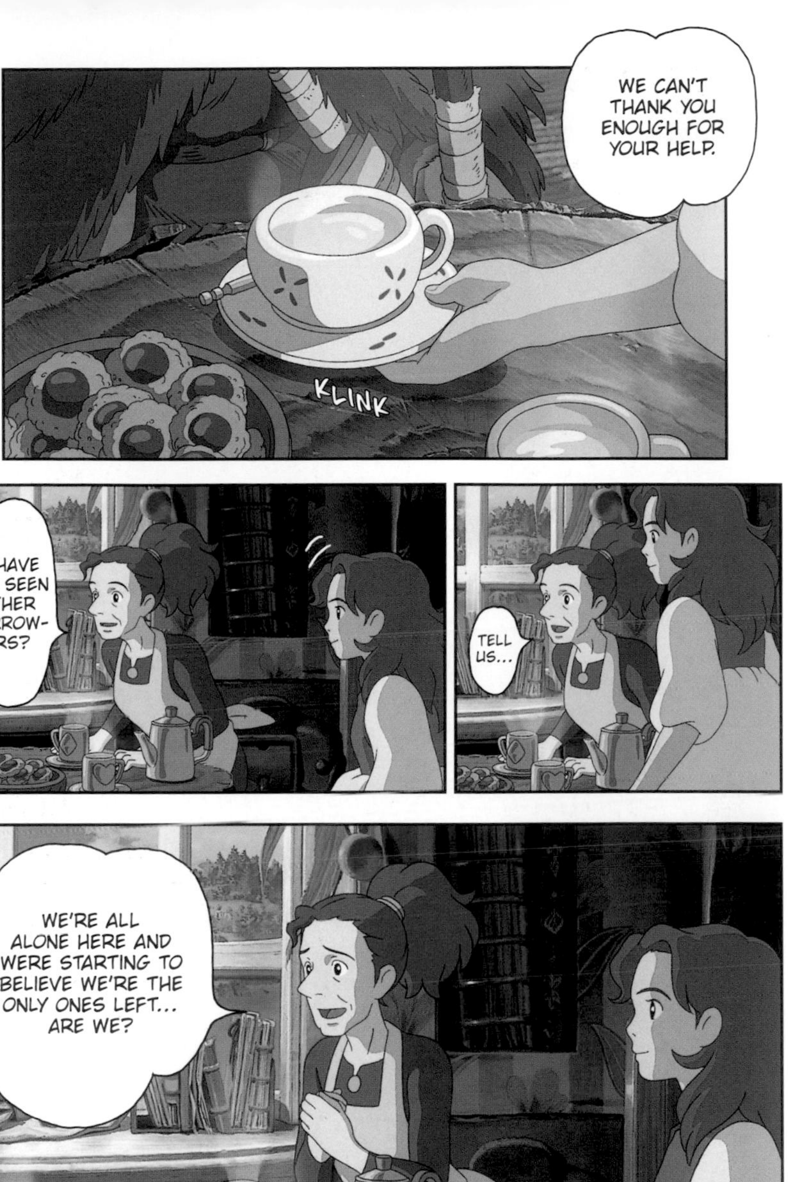
WE CAN'T THANK YOU ENOUGH FOR YOUR HELP.
KLINK
TELL US...
...HAVE YOU SEEN OTHER BORROWERS?
WE'RE ALL ALONE HERE AND WERE STARTING TO BELIEVE WE'RE THE ONLY ONES LEFT... ARE WE?

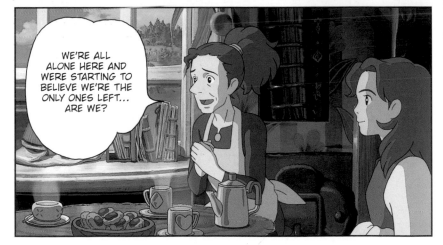

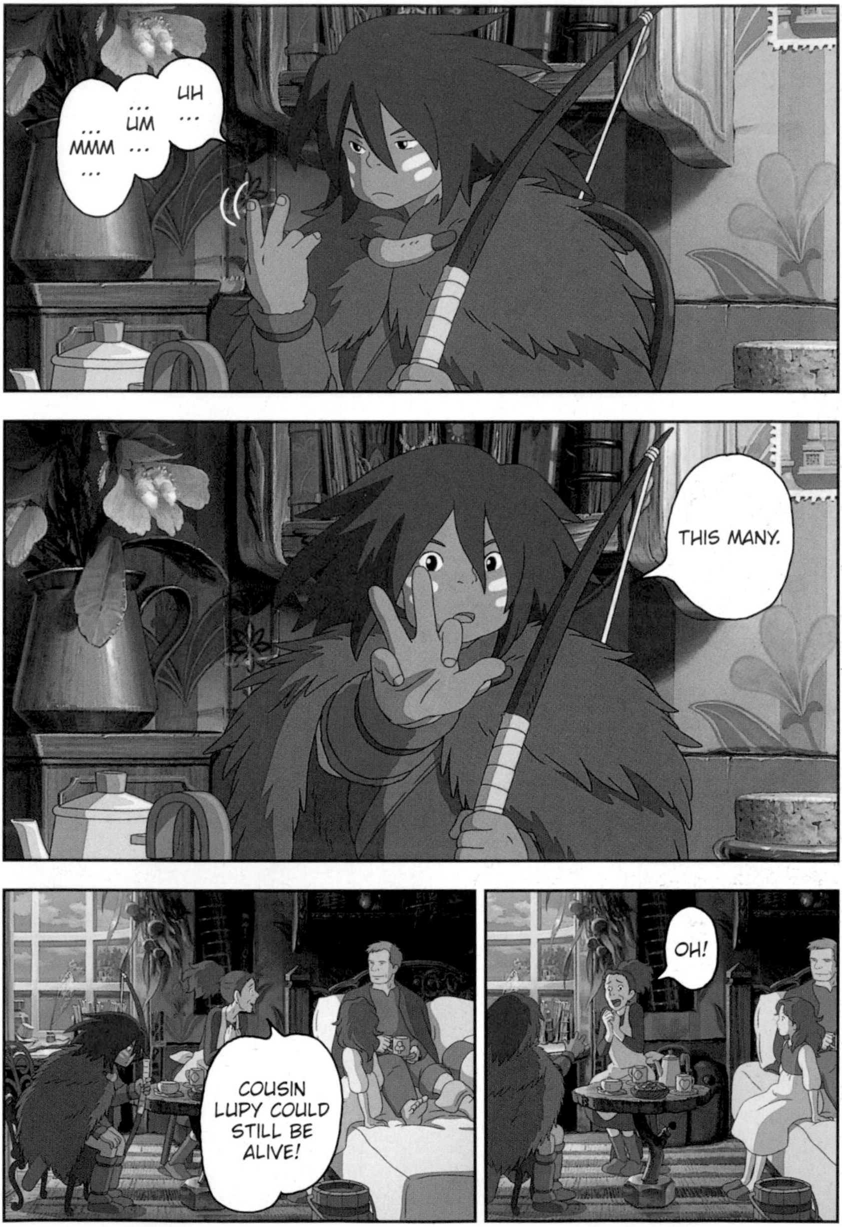
UH ... ... UM ... ... MMM ...
THIS MANY.
OH!
COUSIN LUPY COULD STILL BE ALIVE!

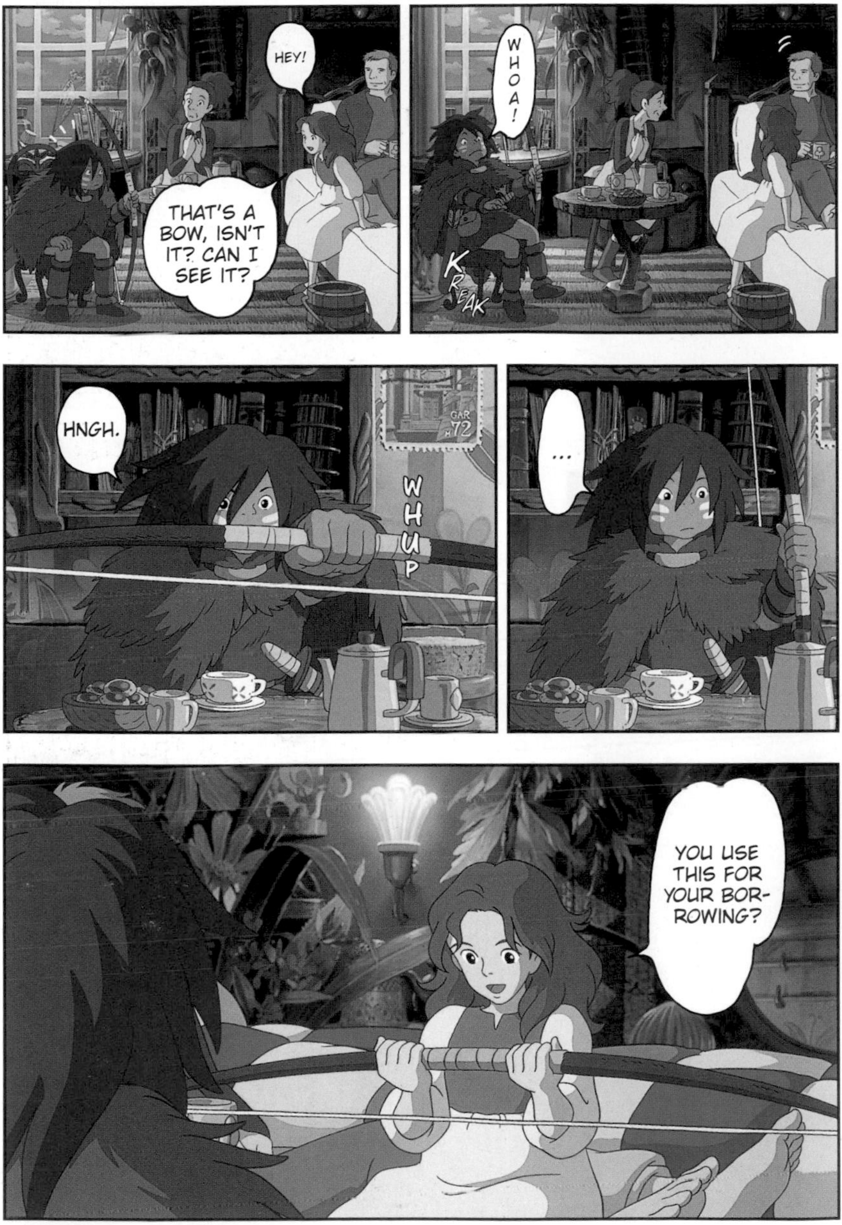
WHOA!
KREAK
HEY!
THAT'S A BOW, ISN'T IT? CAN I SEE IT?
...
HNGH.
WHUP
YOU USE THIS FOR YOUR BOR-ROWING?

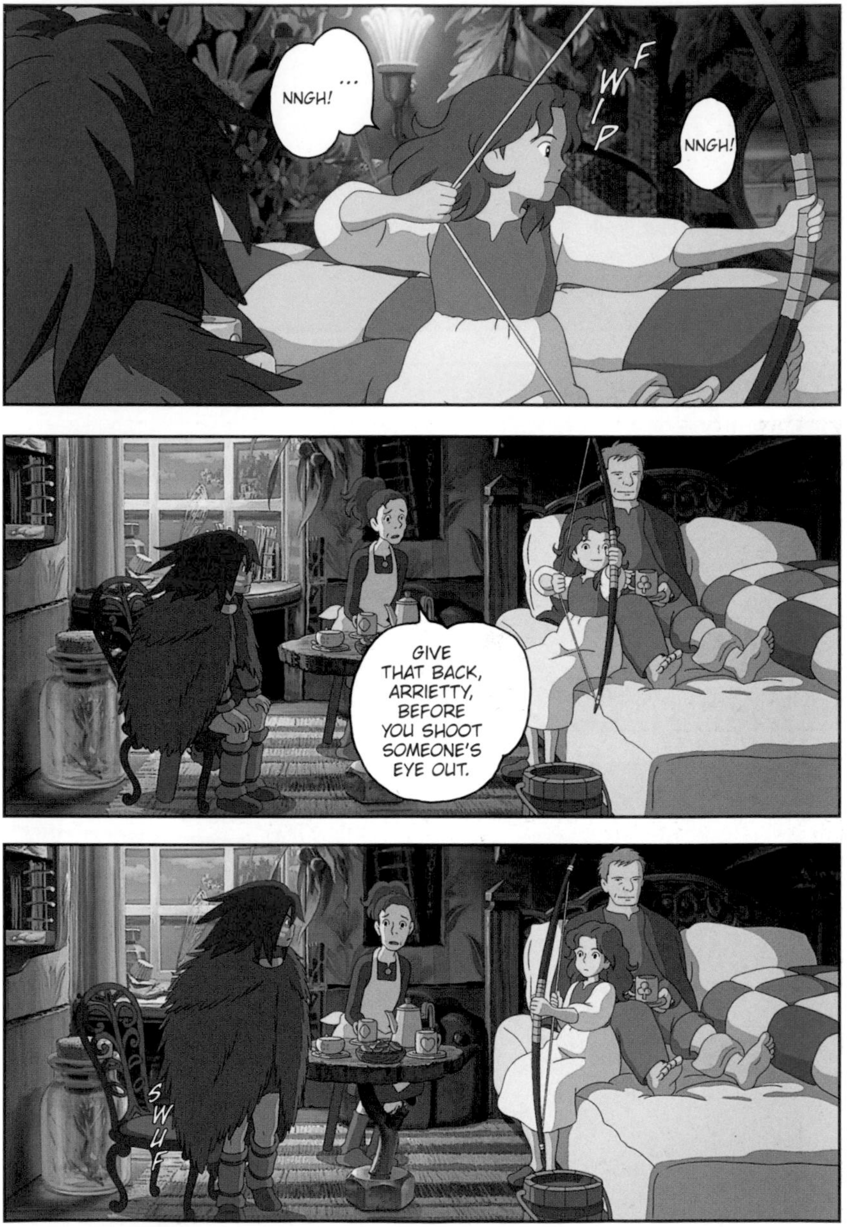
NNGH!
FWIP
... NNGH!
GIVE THAT BACK, ARRIETTY, BEFORE YOU SHOOT SOMEONE'S EYE OUT.
SWUF

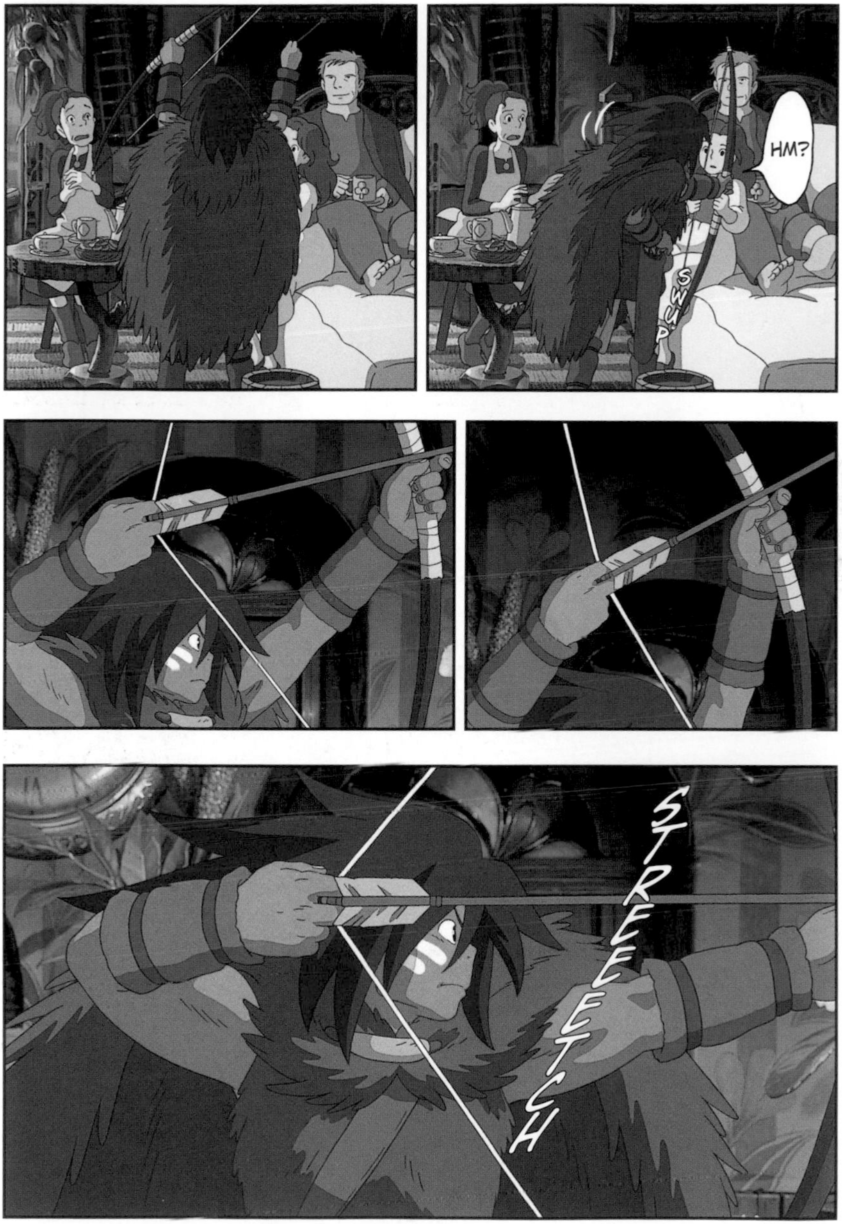
HM?
SWUP
STREEETCH

EEK!
AHHH ...
STRETTTTCH
GRIN
HEH.

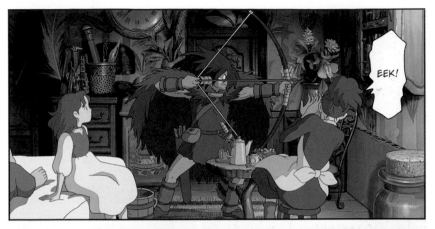

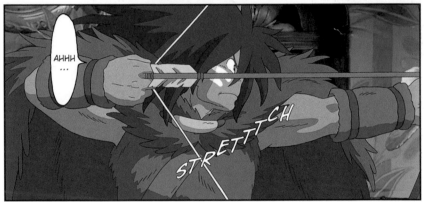

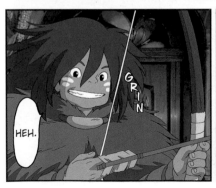

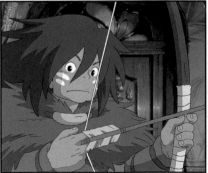

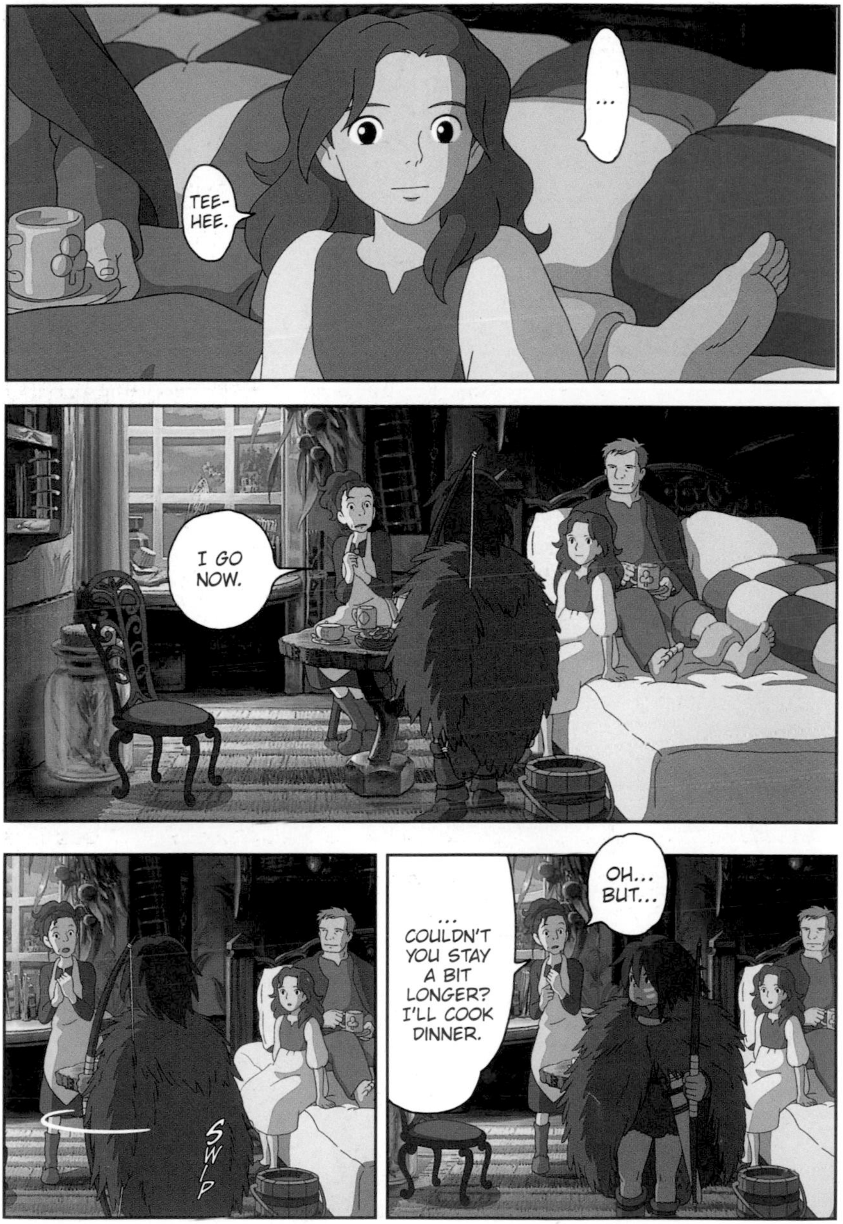
...
TEE-HEE.
I GO NOW.
OH... BUT...
... COULDN'T YOU STAY A BIT LONGER? I'LL COOK DINNER.
SWIP

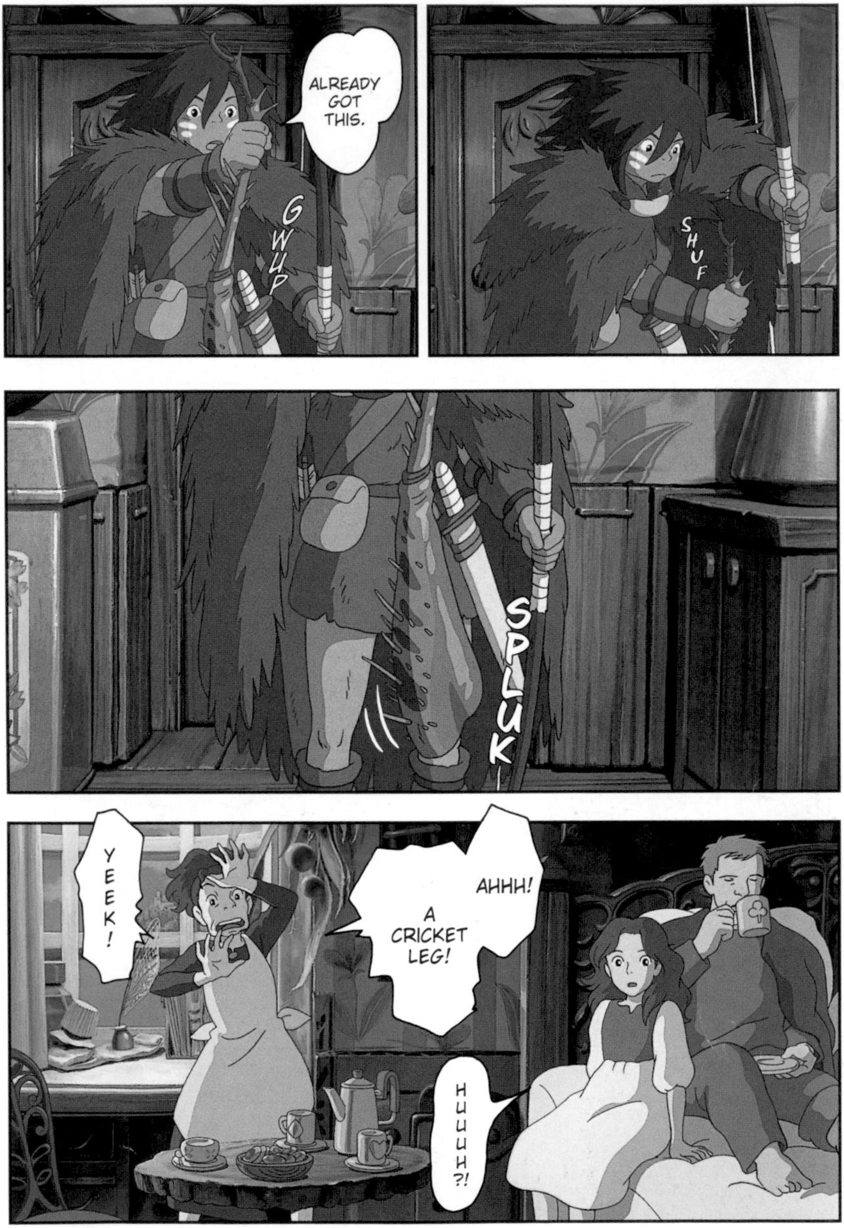
SHUF
ALREADY GOT THIS.
GWUP
SPLUK
AHHH! A CRICKET LEG!
YEEK!
HUUUH?!

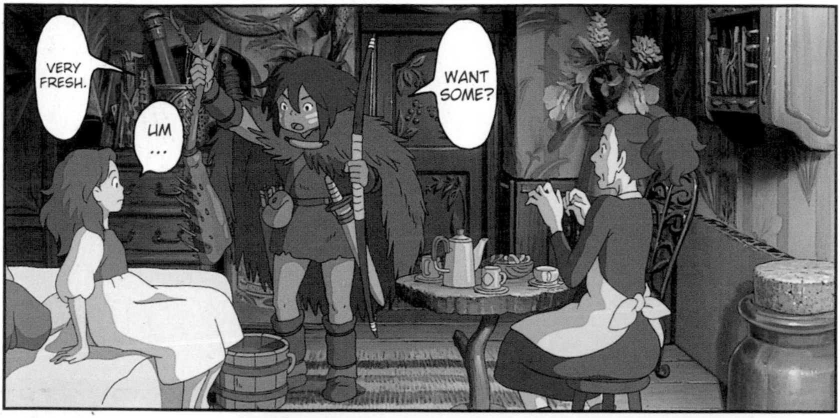
WANT SOME?
VERY FRESH.
UM ...

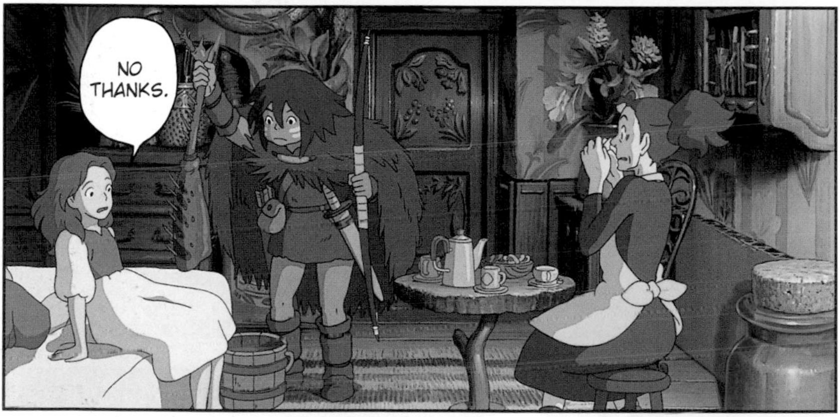
NO THANKS.

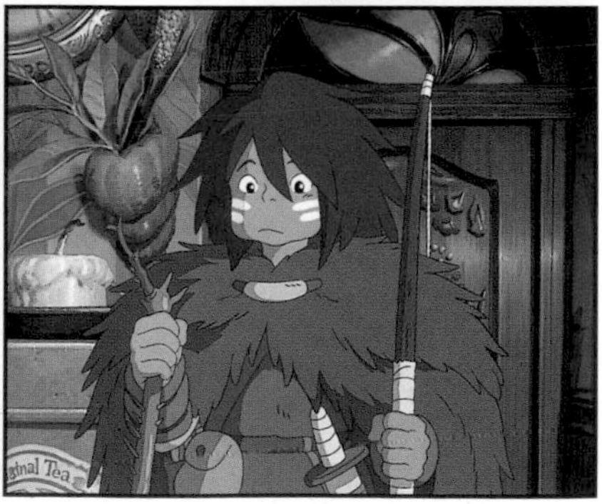

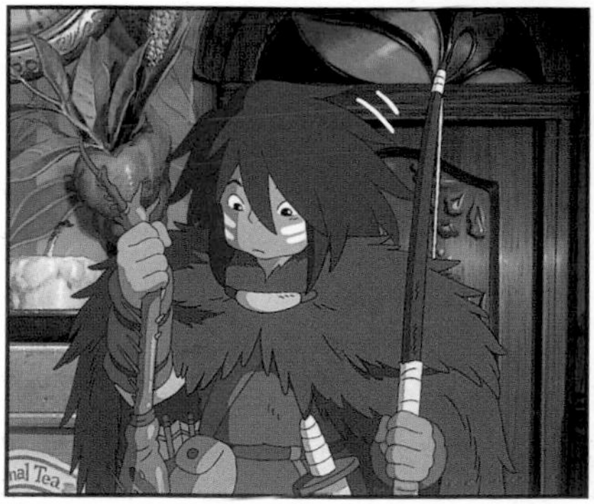

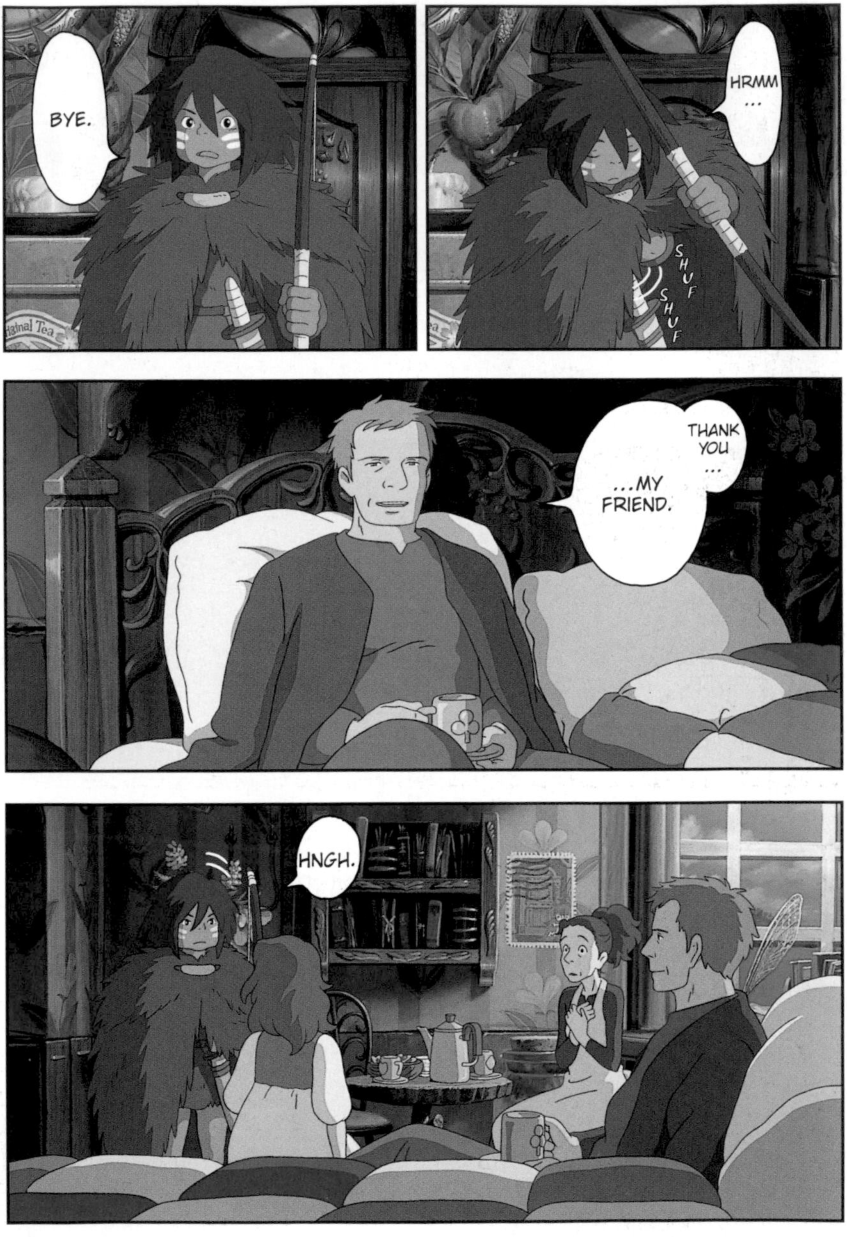
HRMM ...
SHUF SHUF SHUF
BYE.
THANK YOU ...
...MY FRIEND.
HNGH.

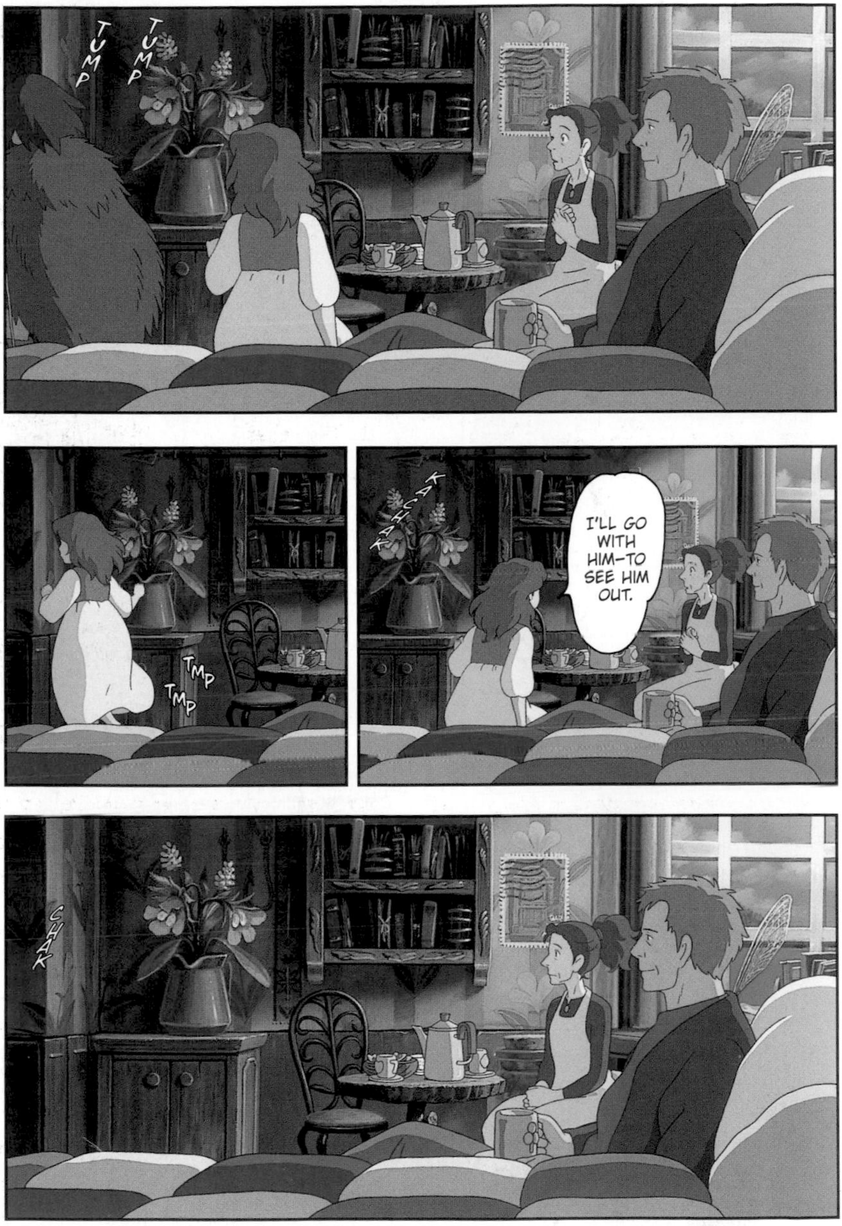
TUMP
TUMP
KACHAK
I'LL GO WITH HIM—TO SEE HIM OUT.
TMP
TMP
CHAK

WHAT WERE YOU DOING OUT THERE IN THAT STORM?

SIGH

OH, POD.

I WAS LOOKING FOR A SAFE ROUTE FOR OUR JOURNEY. AND NOW I KNOW WHICH ROUTE NOT TO TAKE.

SPILLER KNOWS OF MORE BORROWERS A FEW DAYS' JOURNEY AWAY.

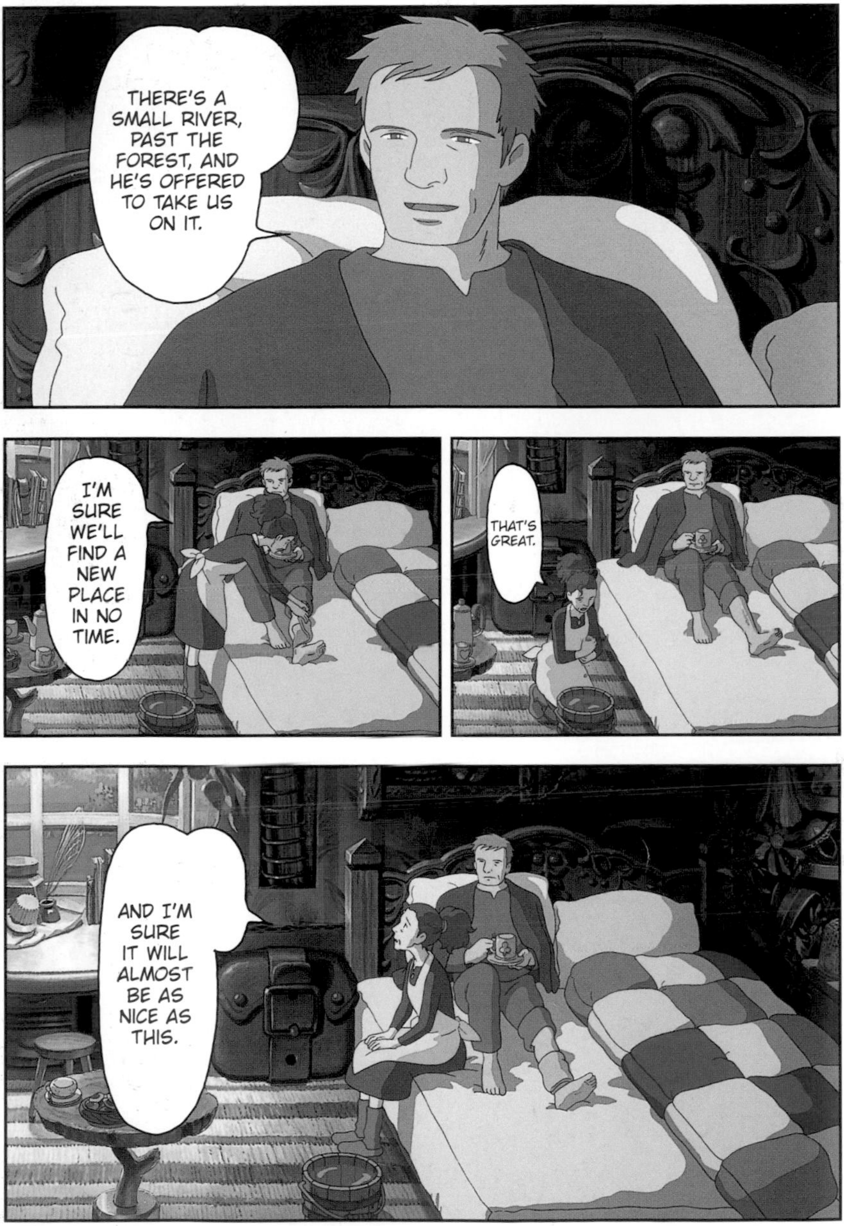
THERE'S A SMALL RIVER, PAST THE FOREST, AND HE'S OFFERED TO TAKE US ON IT.
THAT'S GREAT.
I'M SURE WE'LL FIND A NEW PLACE IN NO TIME.
AND I'M SURE IT WILL ALMOST BE AS NICE AS THIS.

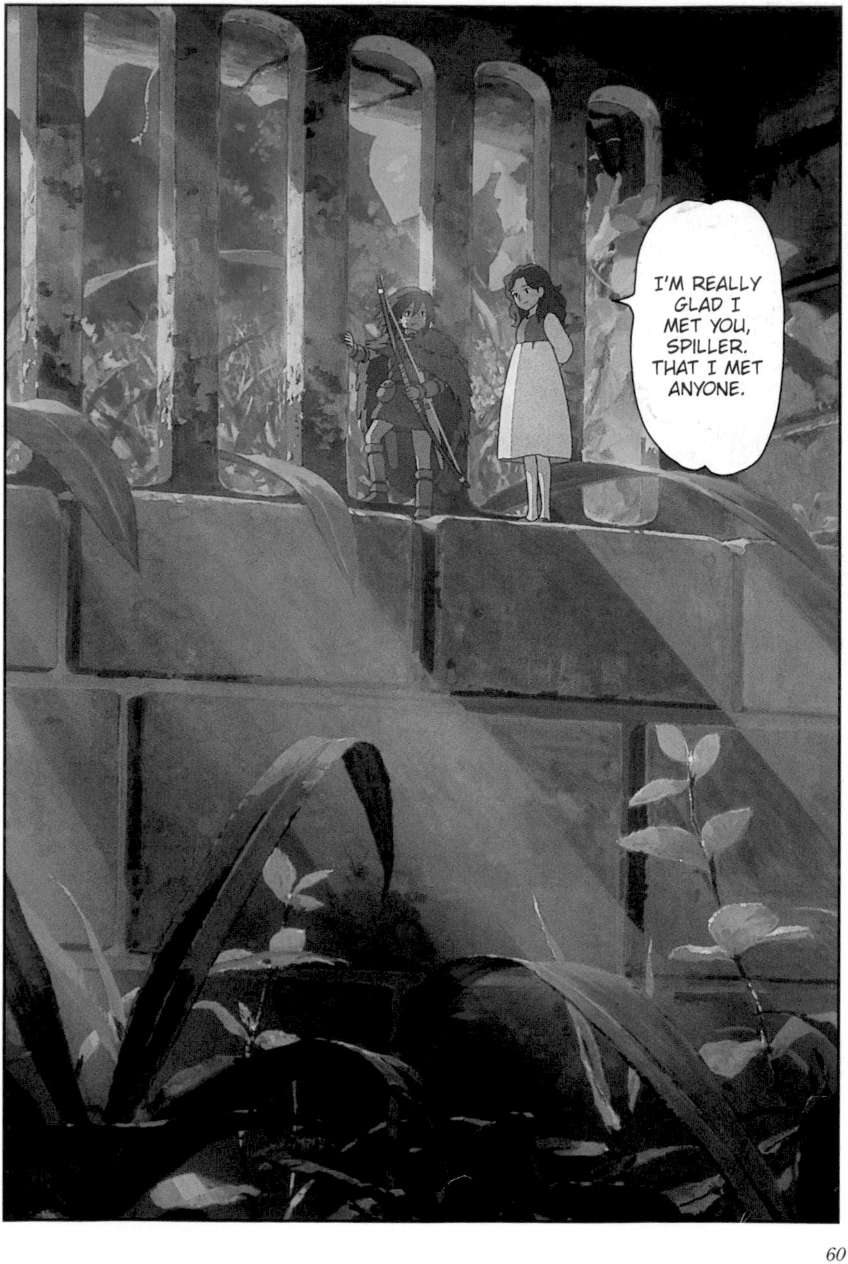
I'M REALLY GLAD I MET YOU, SPILLER. THAT I MET ANYONE.

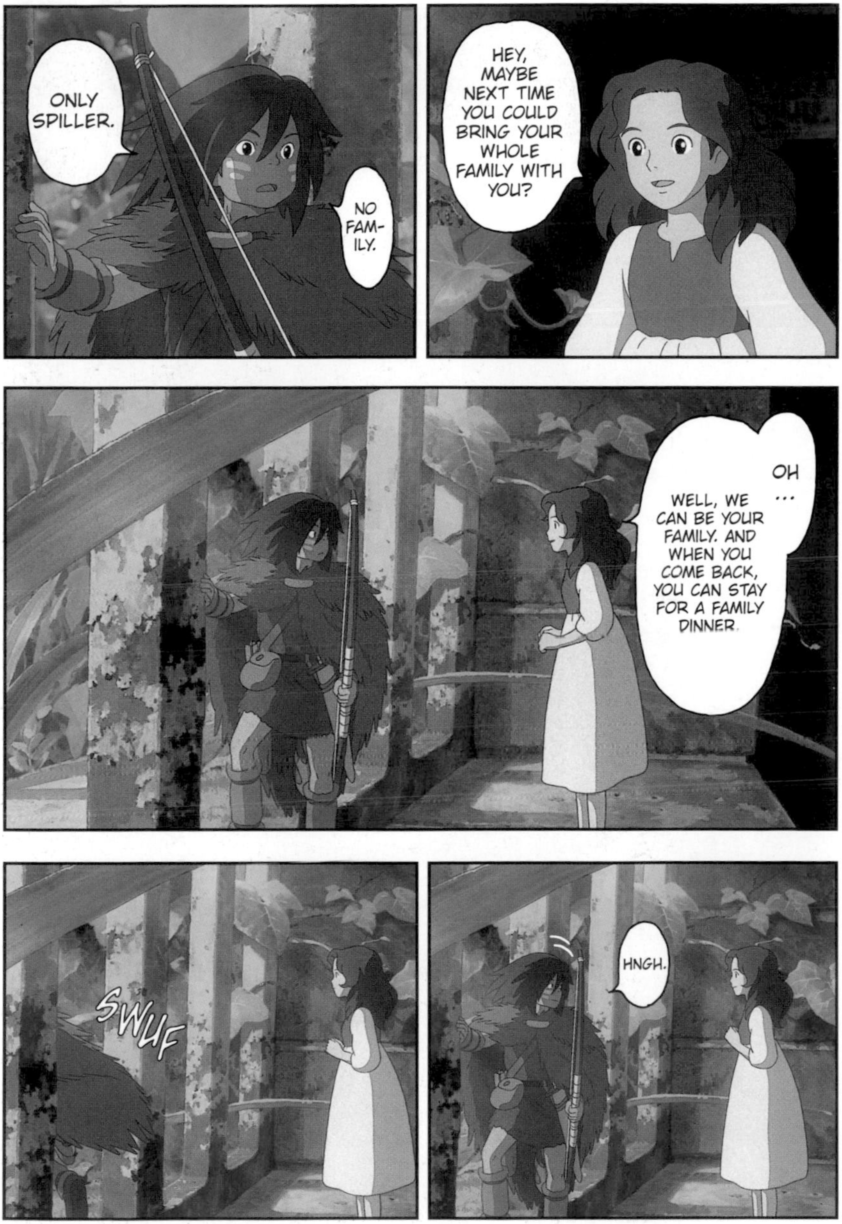
HEY, MAYBE NEXT TIME YOU COULD BRING YOUR WHOLE FAMILY WITH YOU?
ONLY SPILLER.
NO FAM-ILY.
OH ...
WELL, WE CAN BE YOUR FAMILY. AND WHEN YOU COME BACK, YOU CAN STAY FOR A FAMILY DINNER.
HNGH.
SWUF

TMP
UMF!
RUSTLE
RUSTLE
RUSTLE
RUSTLE
OOOH
...

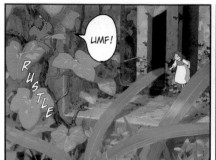

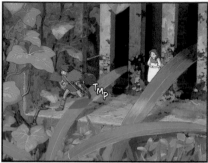

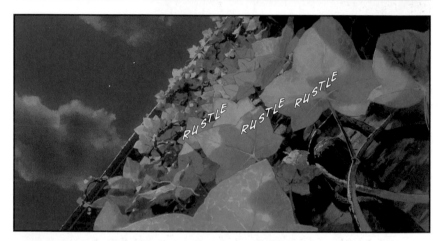

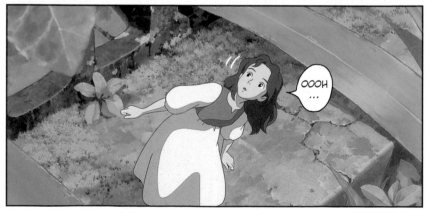

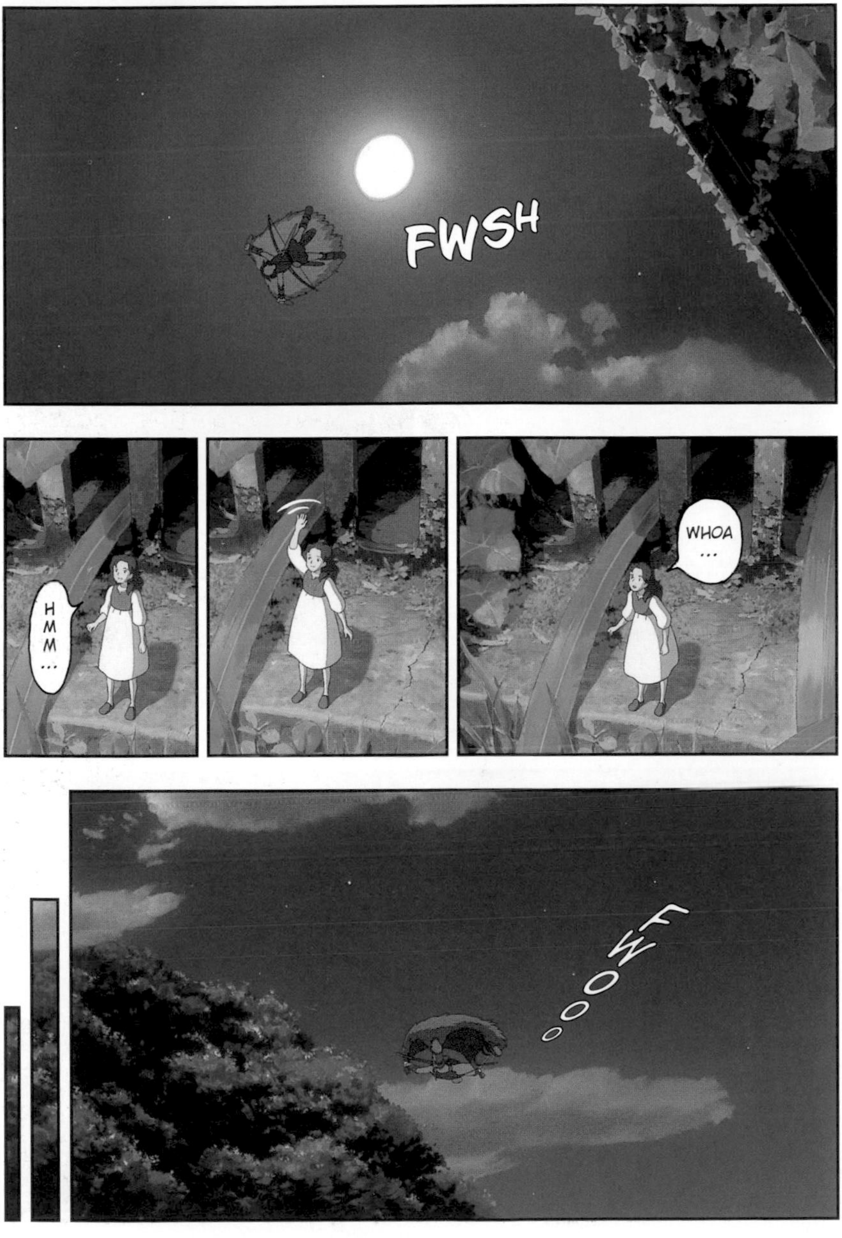
FWSH
WHOA ...
HMM ...
FWOOO

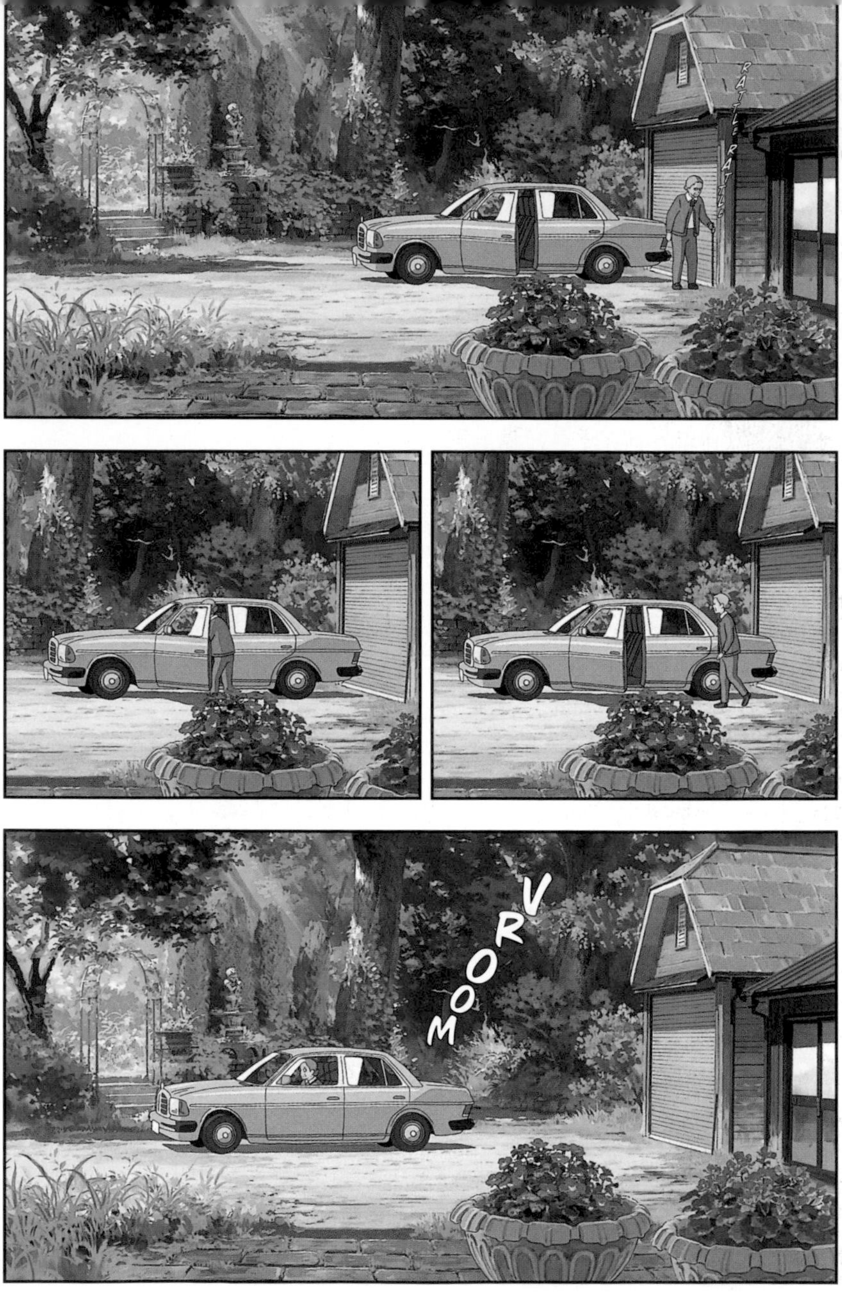
RATTLE RATTLE
VROOOM

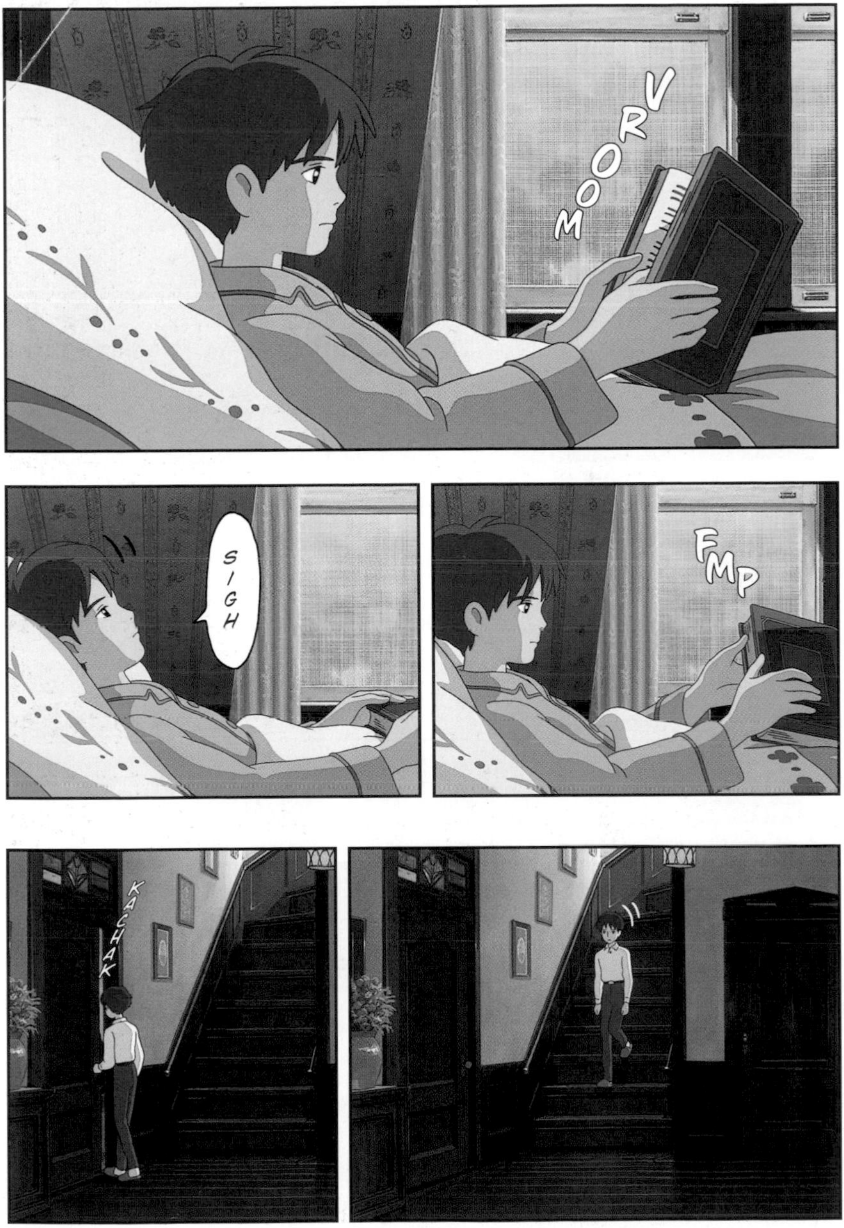
VROOM
FMP
SIGH
KACHAK

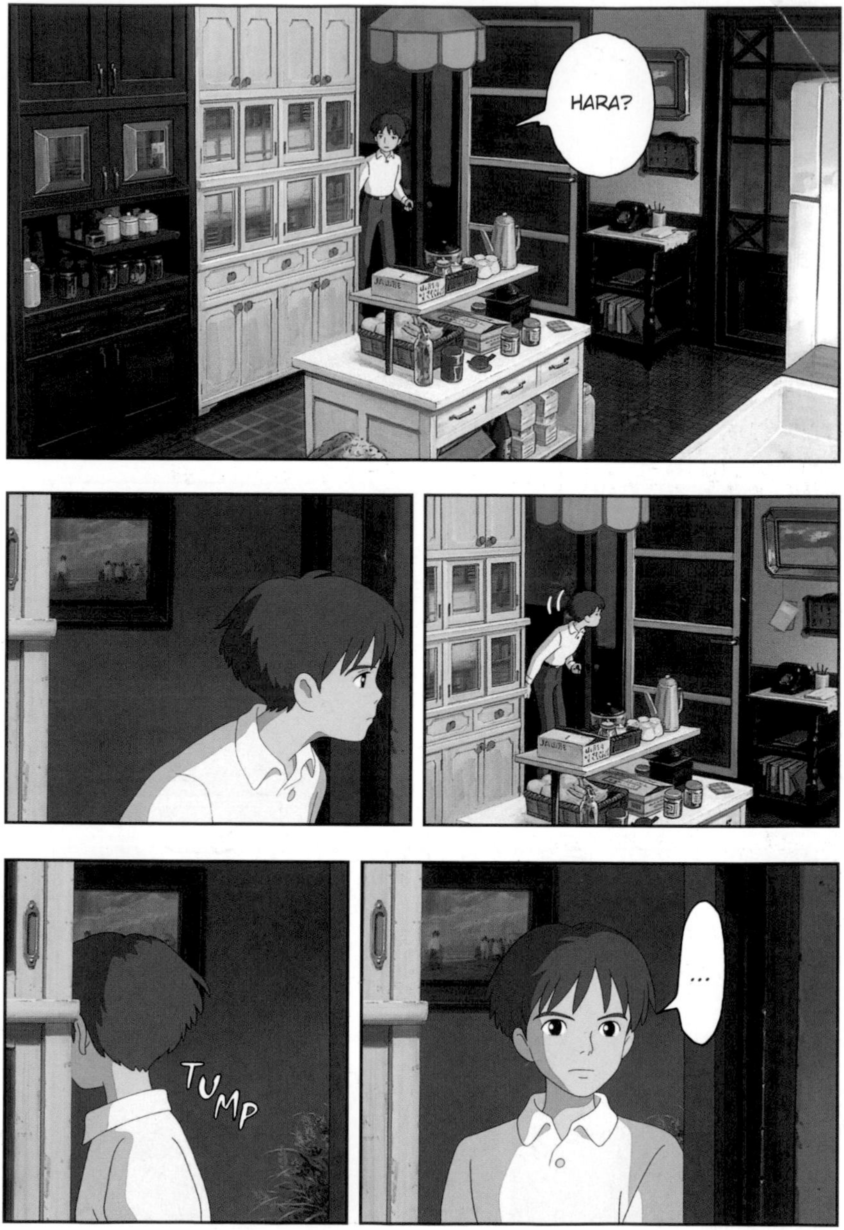
HARA?
...
TUMP

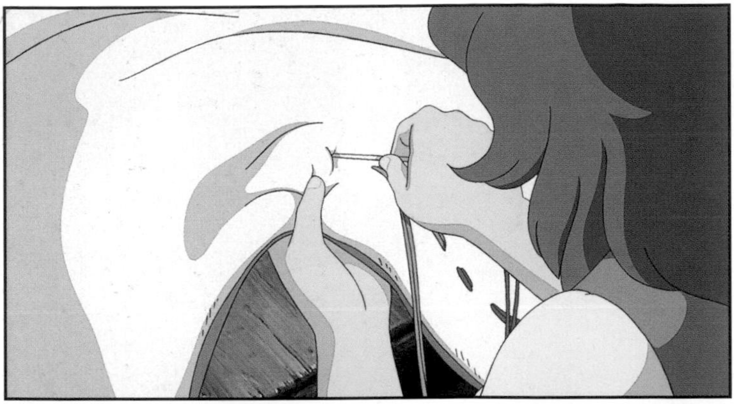

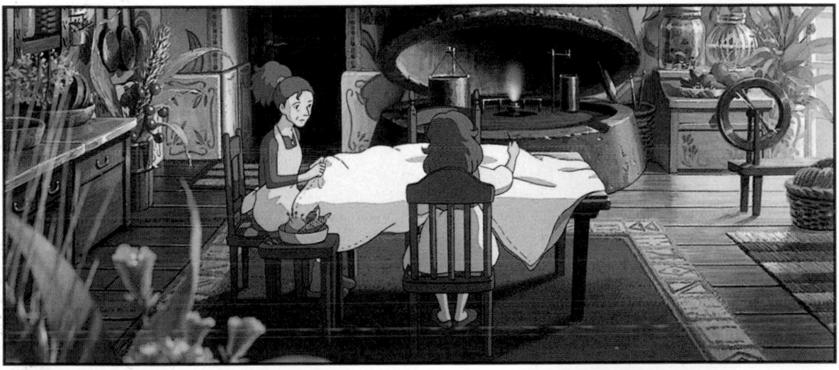

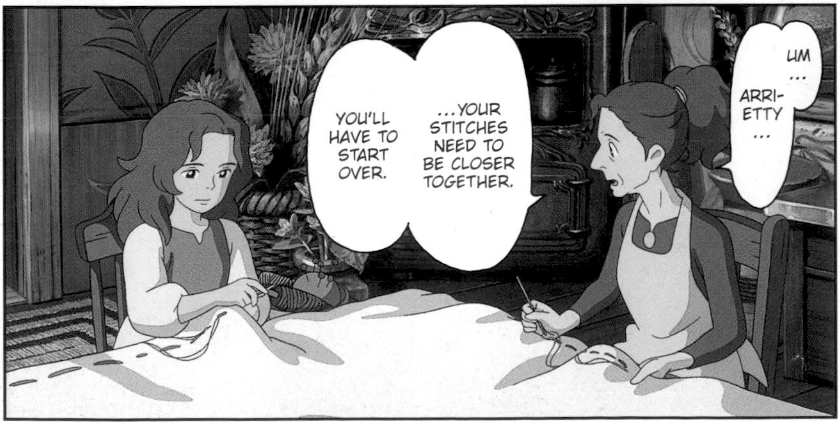
UM ... ARRI-ETTY ...
...YOUR STITCHES NEED TO BE CLOSER TOGETHER.
YOU'LL HAVE TO START OVER.

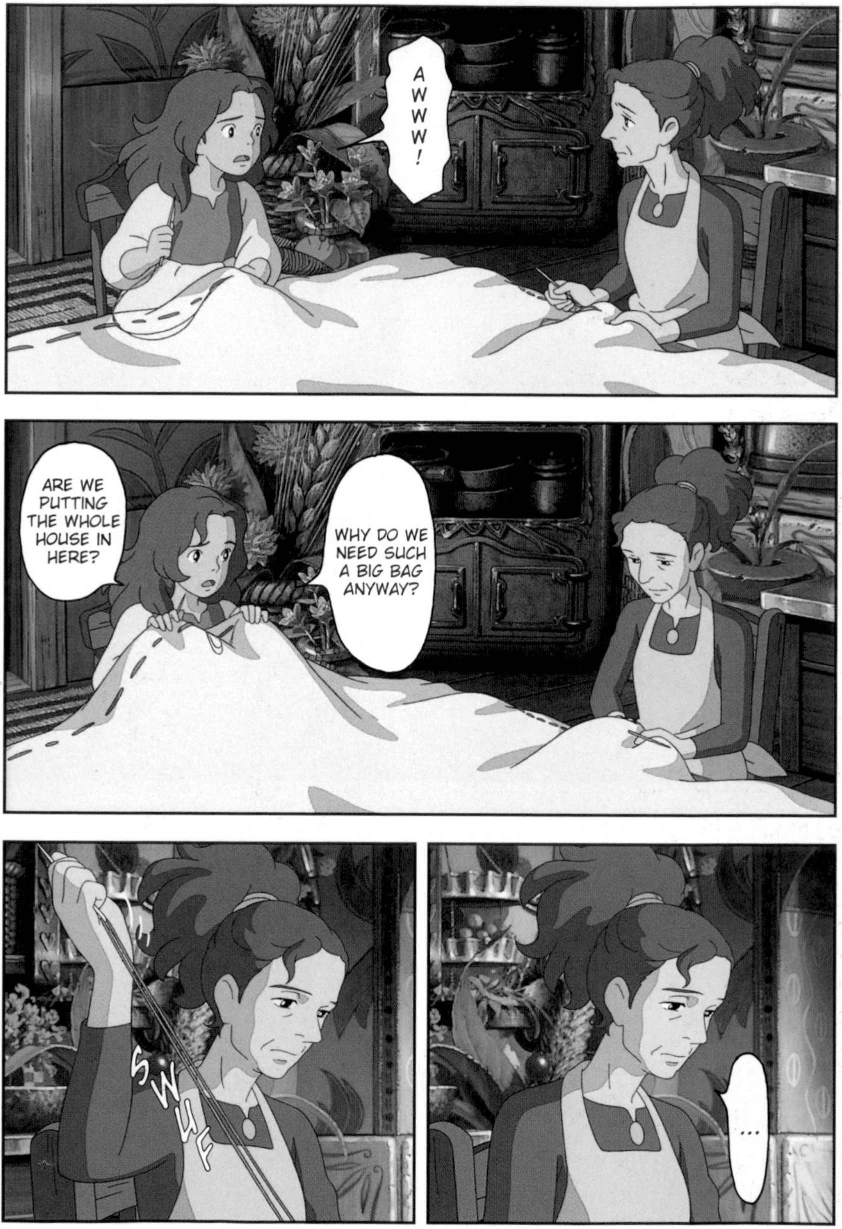
AWWW!
WHY DO WE NEED SUCH A BIG BAG ANYWAY?
ARE WE PUTTING THE WHOLE HOUSE IN HERE?
...
SWUF

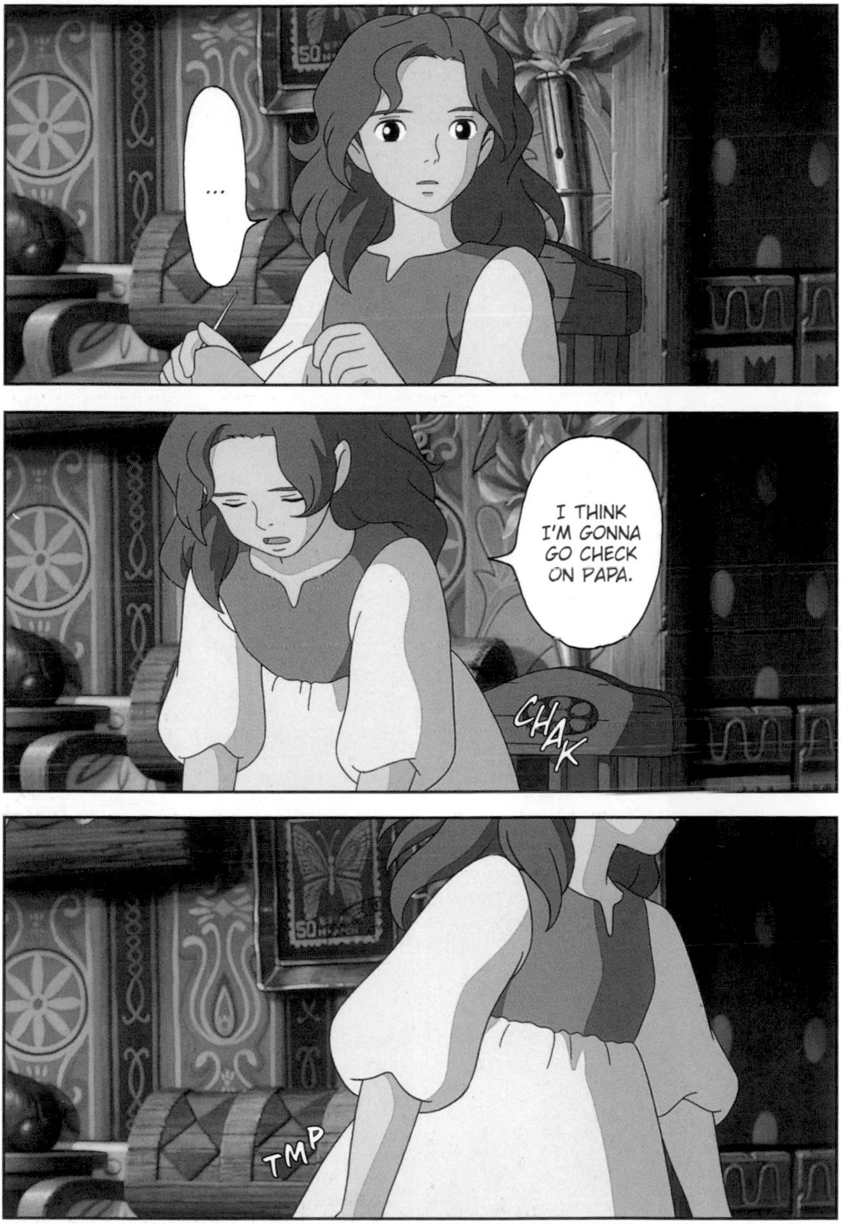
...
I THINK I'M GONNA GO CHECK ON PAPA.
CHAK
TMP

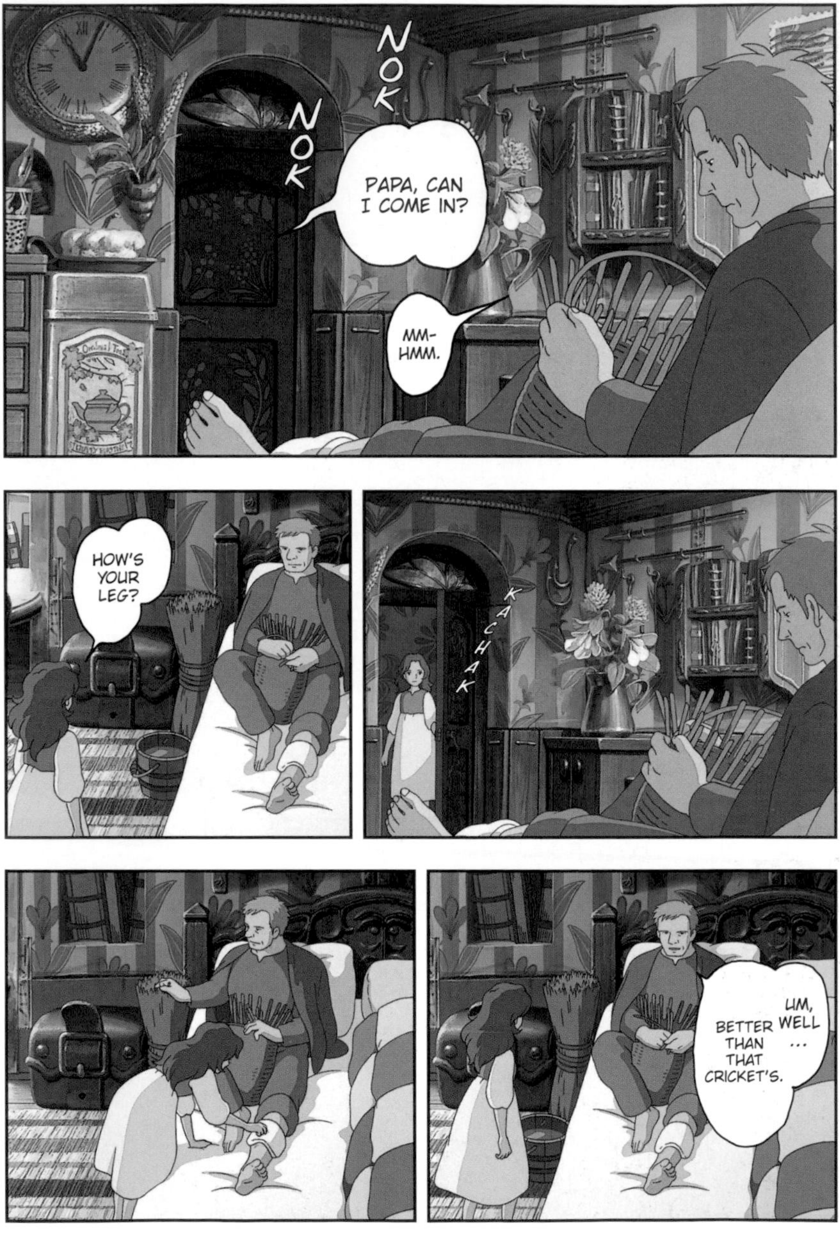
NOK
NOK
PAPA, CAN I COME IN?
MM-HMM.
KACHAK
HOW'S YOUR LEG?
UM, WELL ... BETTER THAN THAT CRICKET'S.

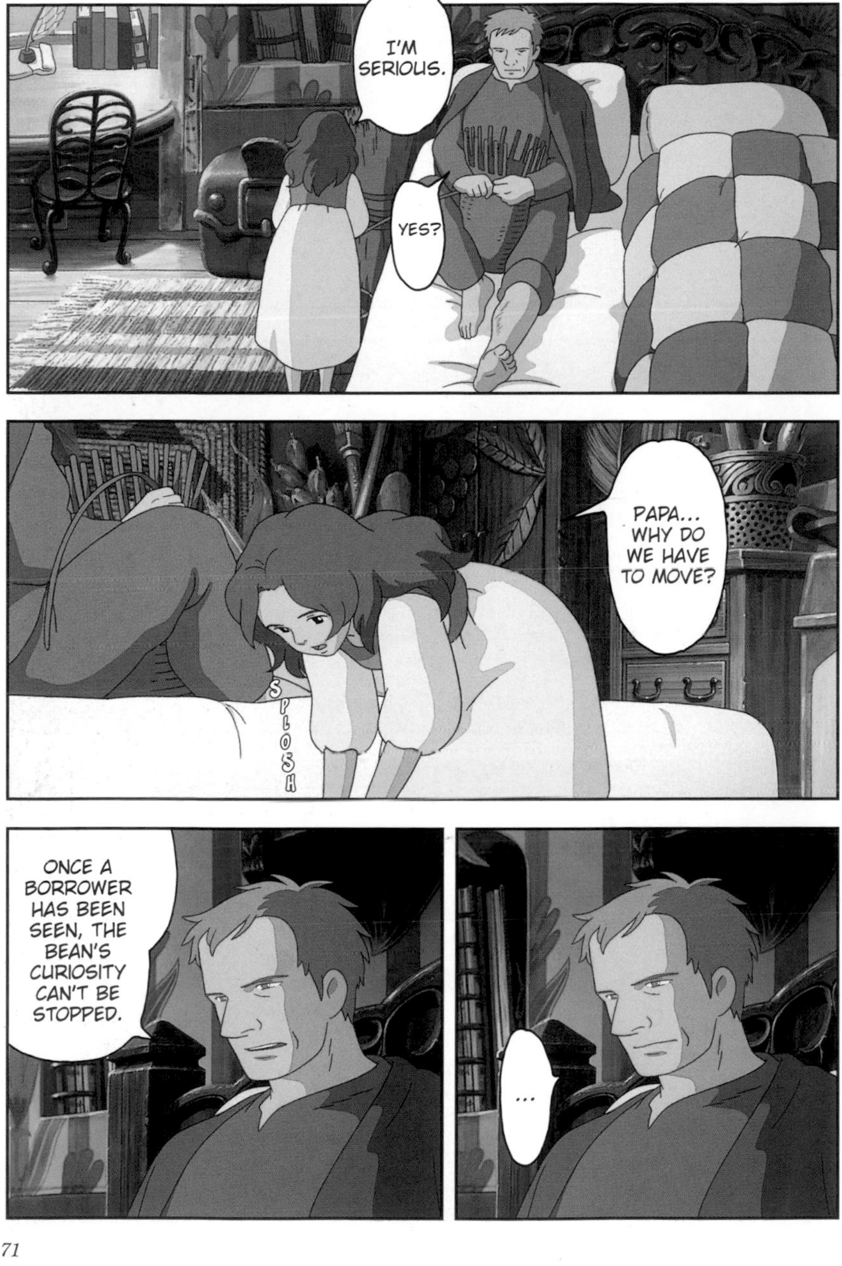
I'M SERIOUS.
YES?
PAPA... WHY DO WE HAVE TO MOVE?
SPLOSH
...
ONCE A BORROWER HAS BEEN SEEN, THE BEAN'S CURIOSITY CAN'T BE STOPPED.

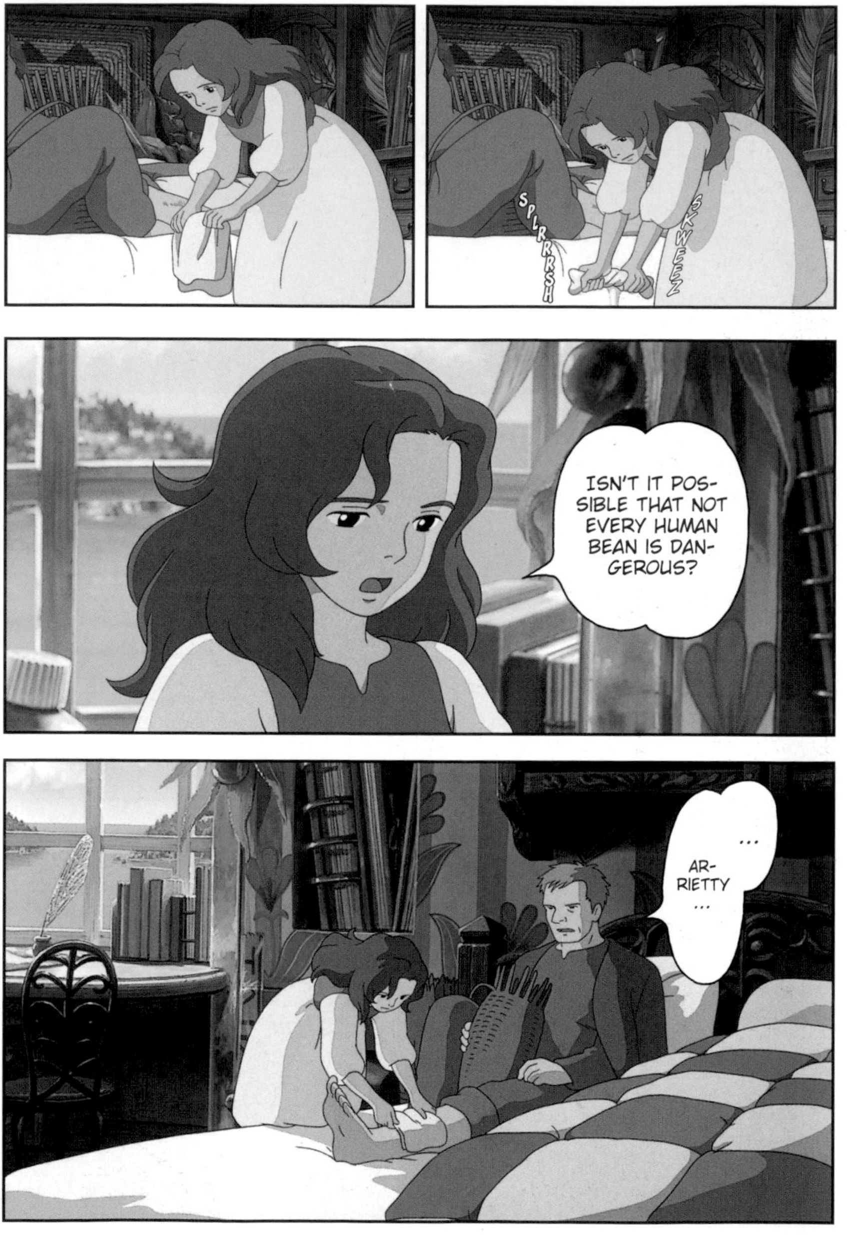
SKWEEZ
SPLRRRSH
ISN'T IT POSSIBLE THAT NOT EVERY HUMAN BEAN IS DANGEROUS?
... ARRIETTY ...

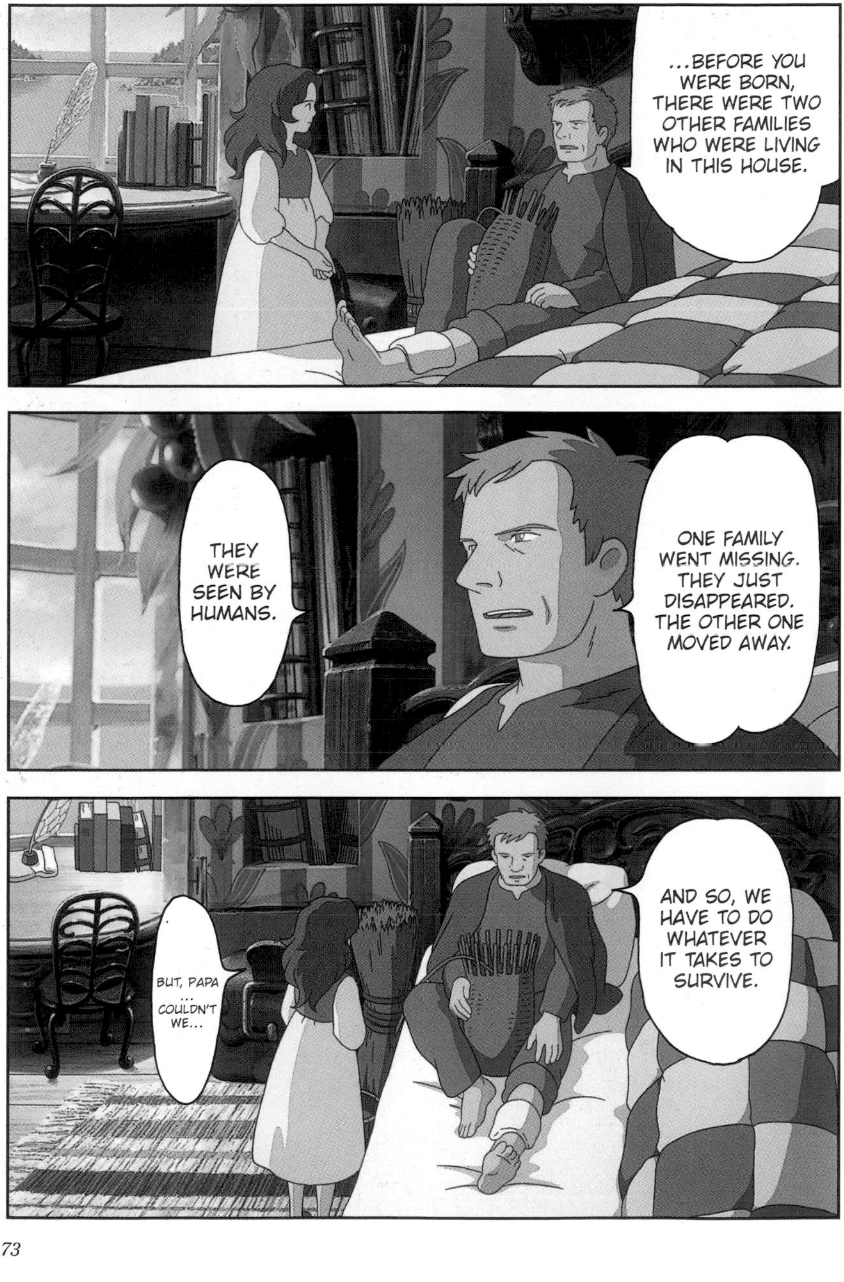
...BEFORE YOU WERE BORN, THERE WERE TWO OTHER FAMILIES WHO WERE LIVING IN THIS HOUSE.
ONE FAMILY WENT MISSING. THEY JUST DISAPPEARED. THE OTHER ONE MOVED AWAY.
THEY WERE SEEN BY HUMANS.
AND SO, WE HAVE TO DO WHATEVER IT TAKES TO SURVIVE.
BUT, PAPA ... COULDN'T WE...

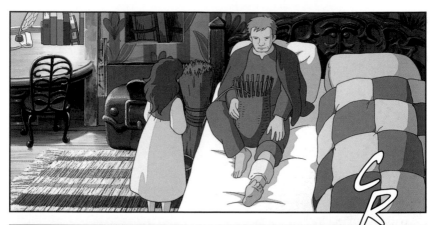

W...

...WHOA!

CRREEEAAAK

K
L
A
T
T
R

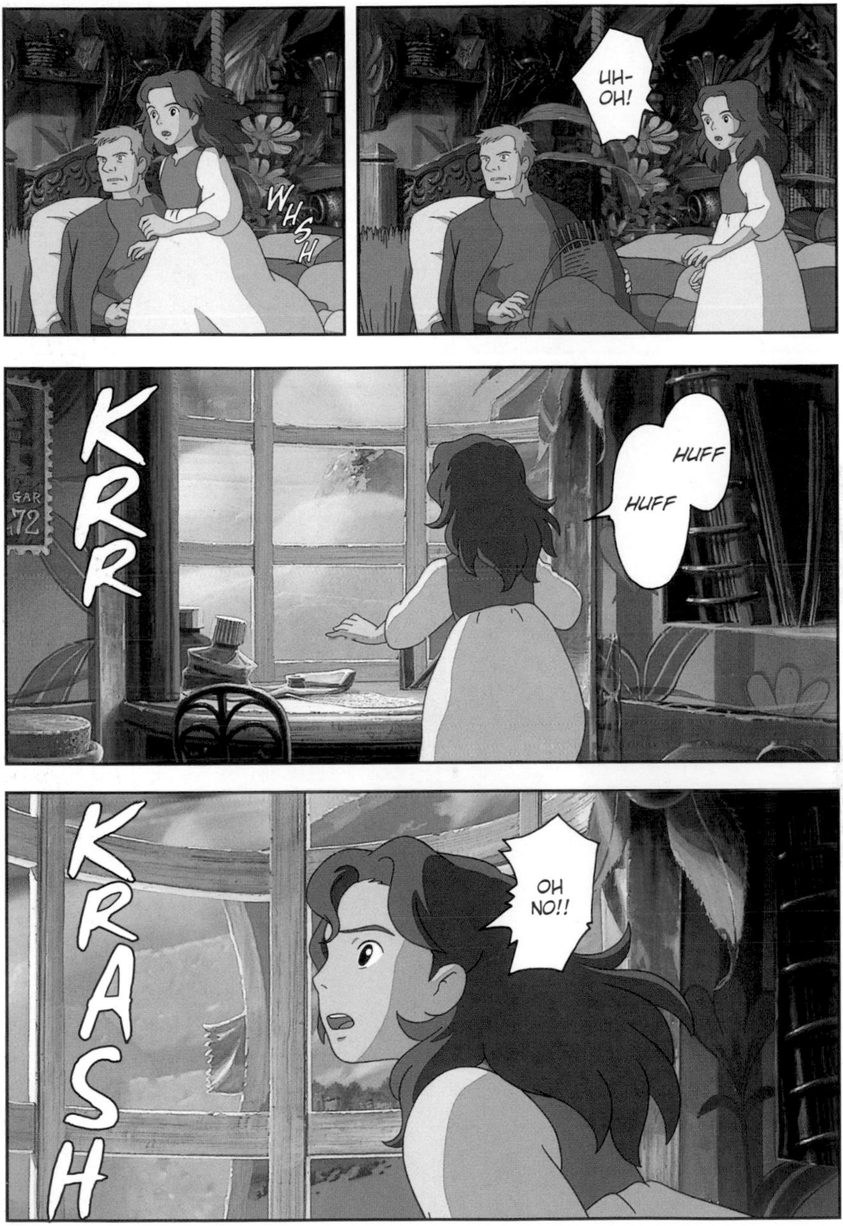
UH-OH!
WHSH
HUFF HUFF
KRRR
OH NO!!
KRASH

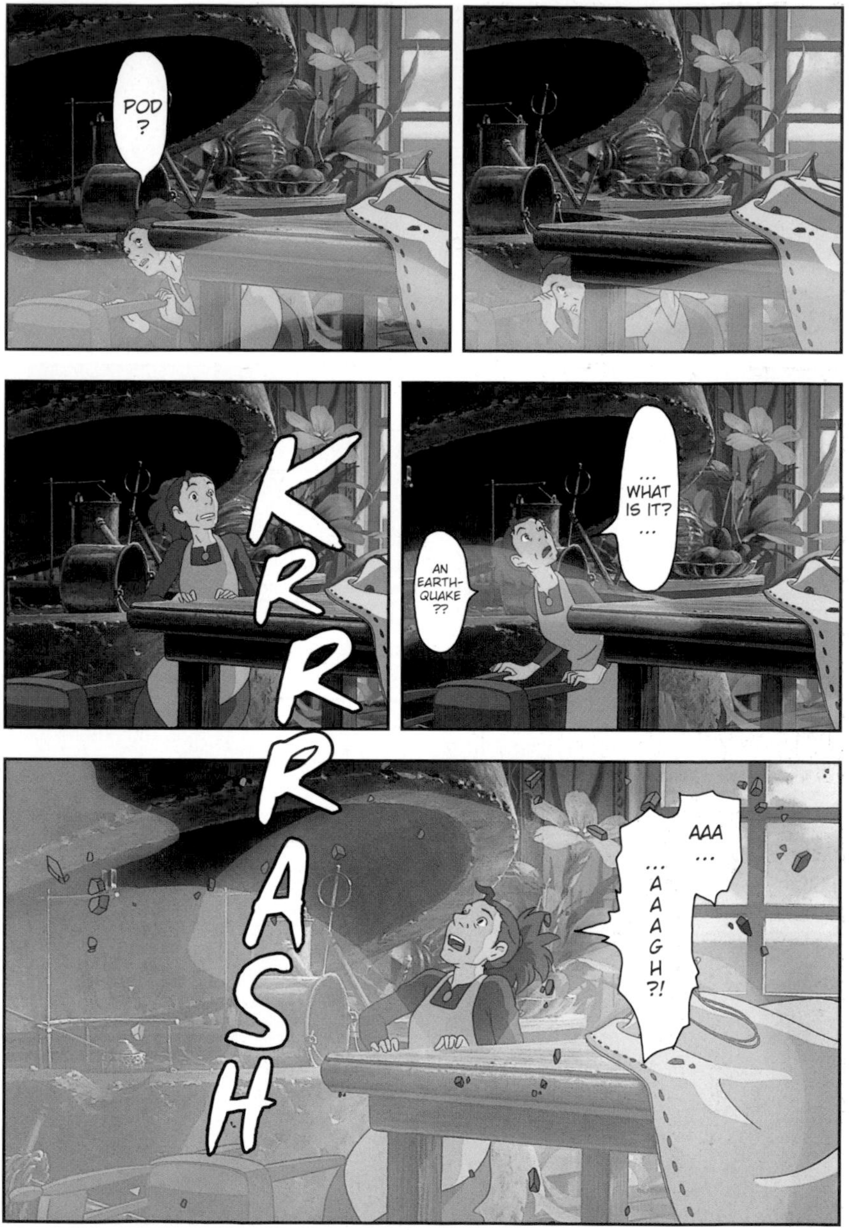
POD ?
... WHAT IS IT? ...
AN EARTH-QUAKE ??
KRRRASH
AAA ... ...AAAAGH?!

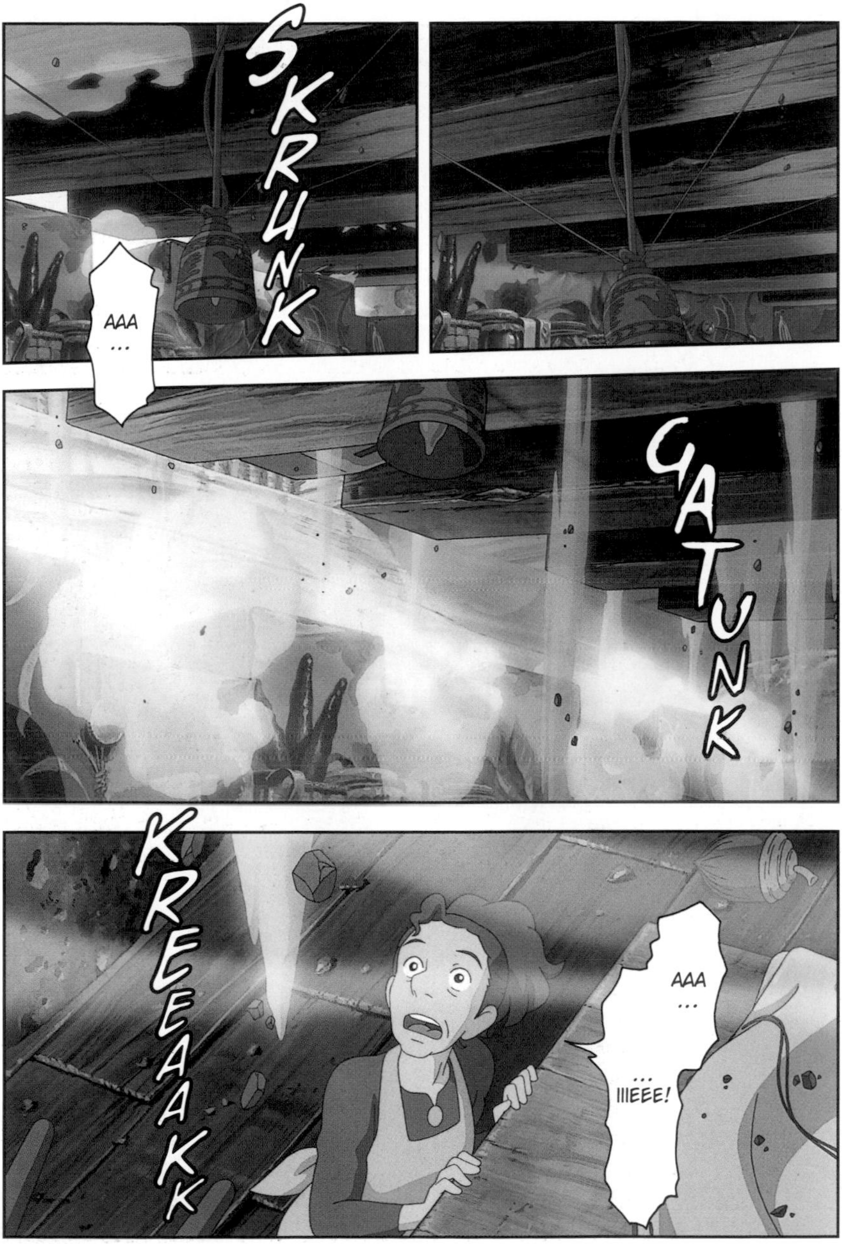
SKRUNK
AAA ...
GATUNK
AAA ...
... IIIEEE!
KREEAAKK

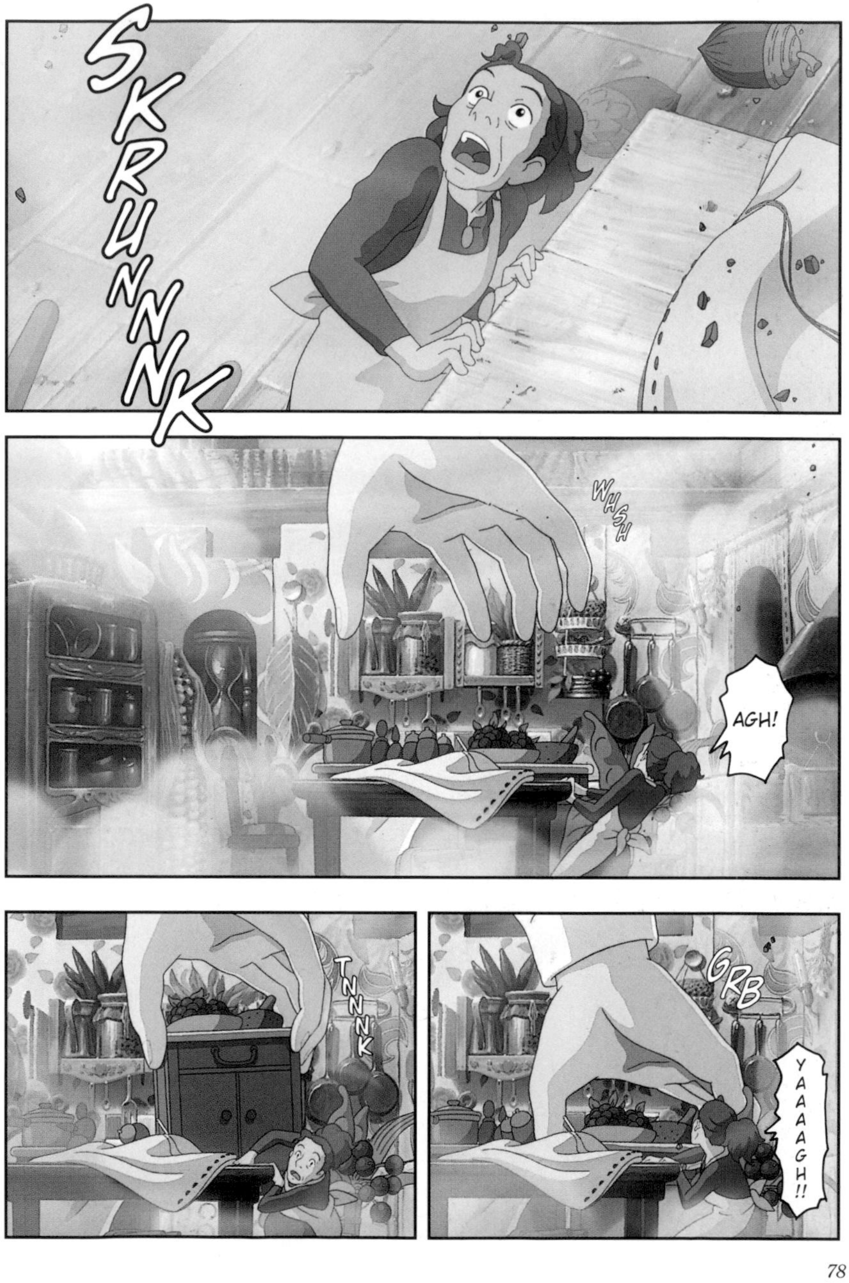
SKRUNNNK
WHSH
AGH!
GRB
YAAAAAGH!!
TNNNK

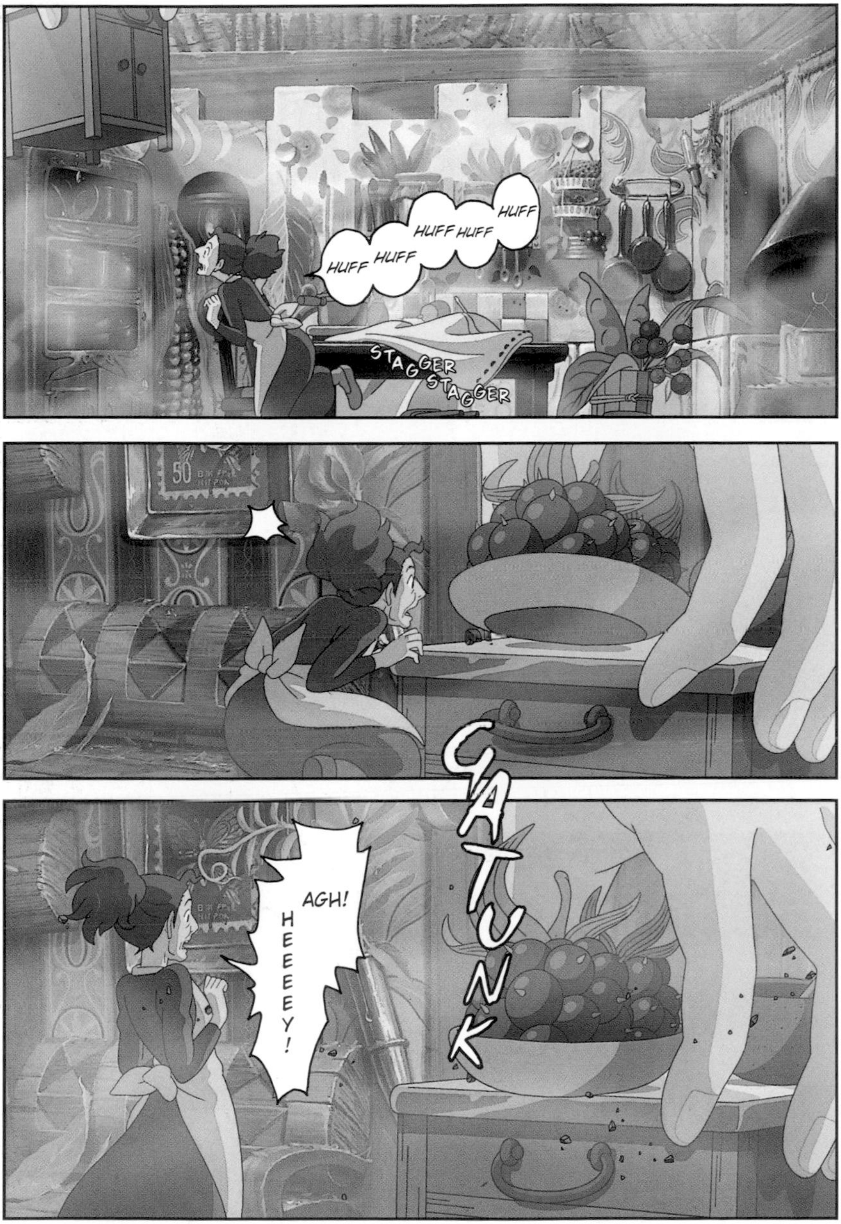
HUFF HUFF HUFF HUFF HUFF
STAGGER STAGGER
GATUNK
AGH! HEEEEEY!

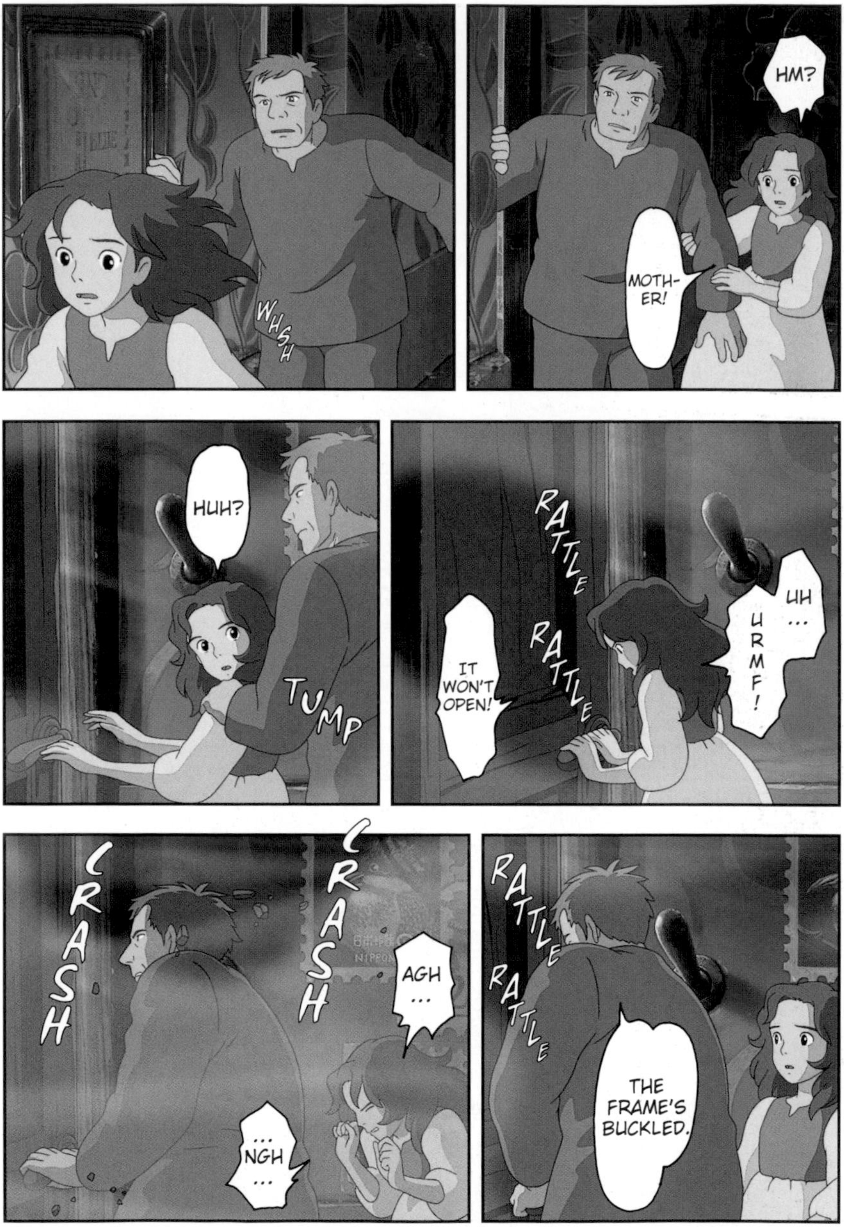
HM?
MOTH-ER!
WHSH
UH ... URMF!
RATTLE RATTLE
IT WON'T OPEN!
HUH?
TUMP
RATTLE RATTLE
THE FRAME'S BUCKLED.
CRASH
AGH ...
CRASH
... NGH ...

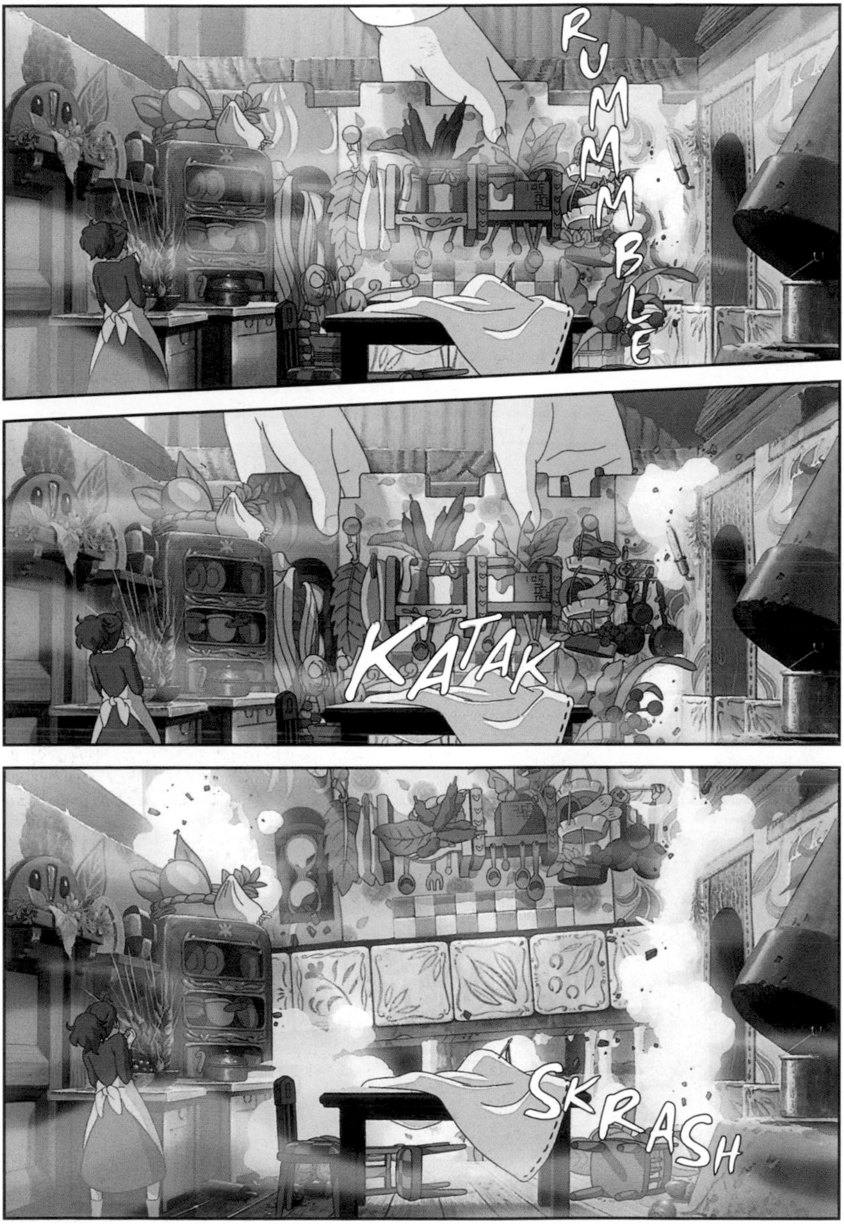
RUMMMBLE
KATAK
SKRASH

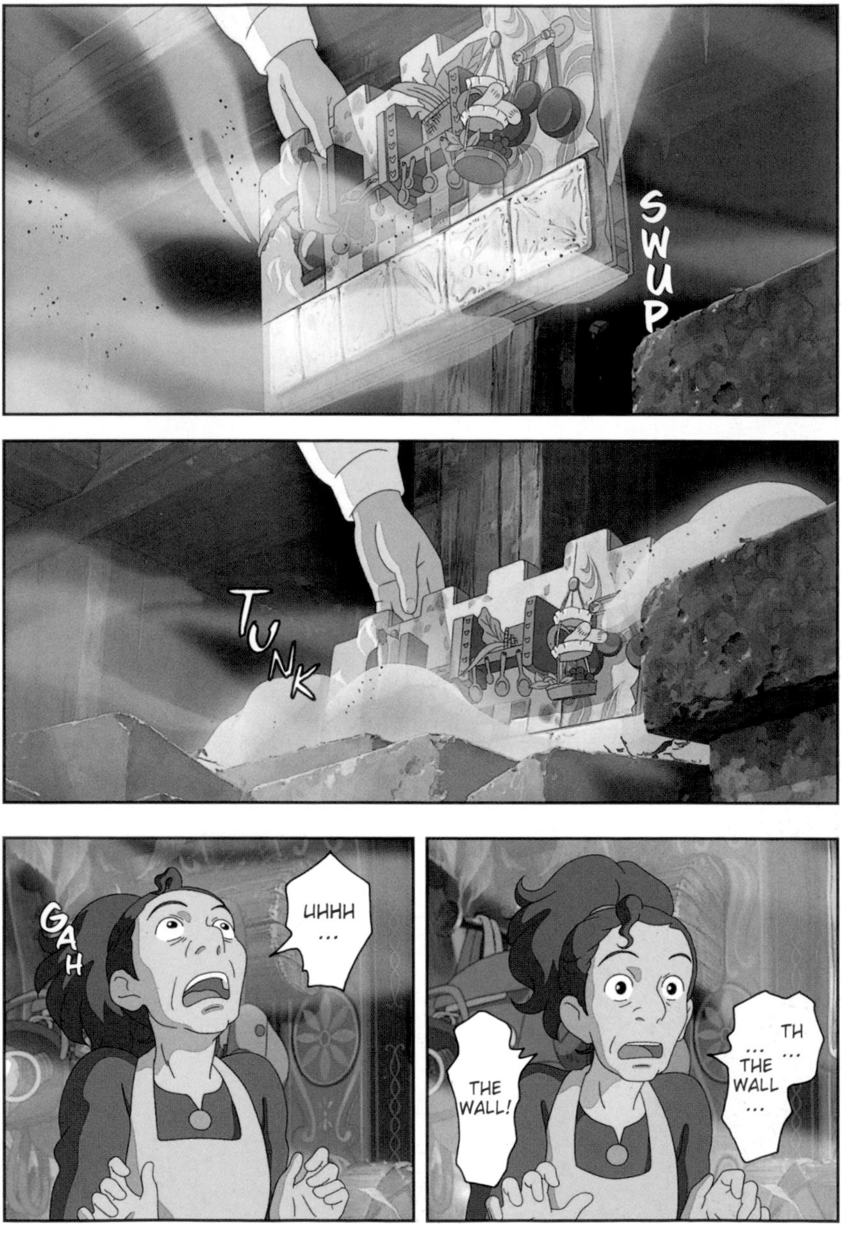
SWUP
TUNK
TH ... THE WALL ...
THE WALL!
GAH
UHHH ...

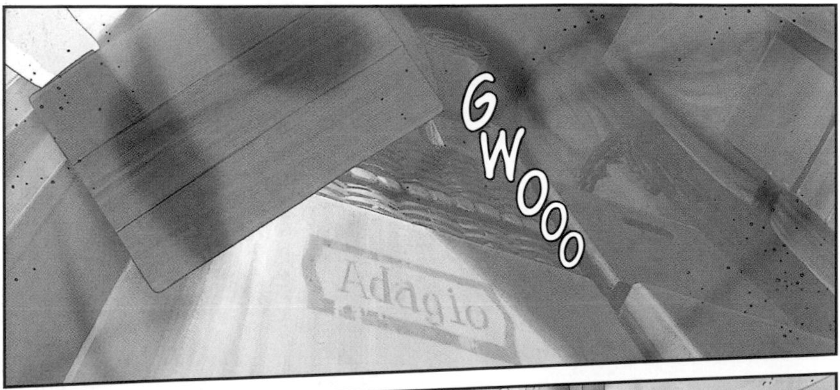
GWOOO
Adagio
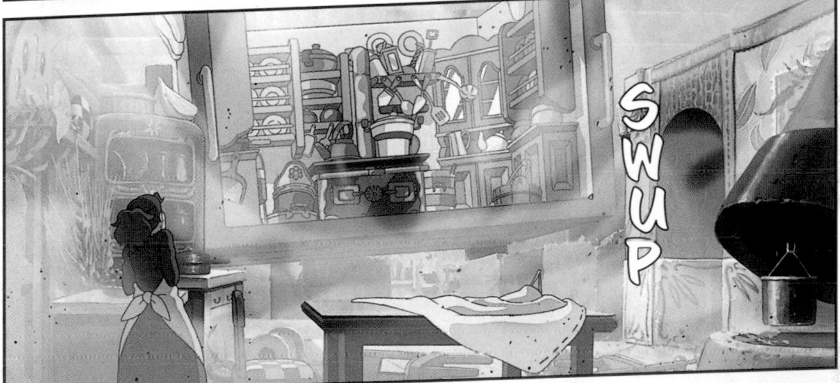
SWUP
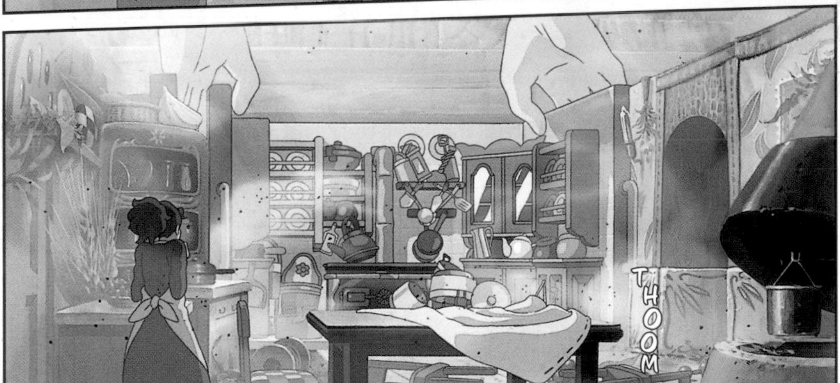
THOOM

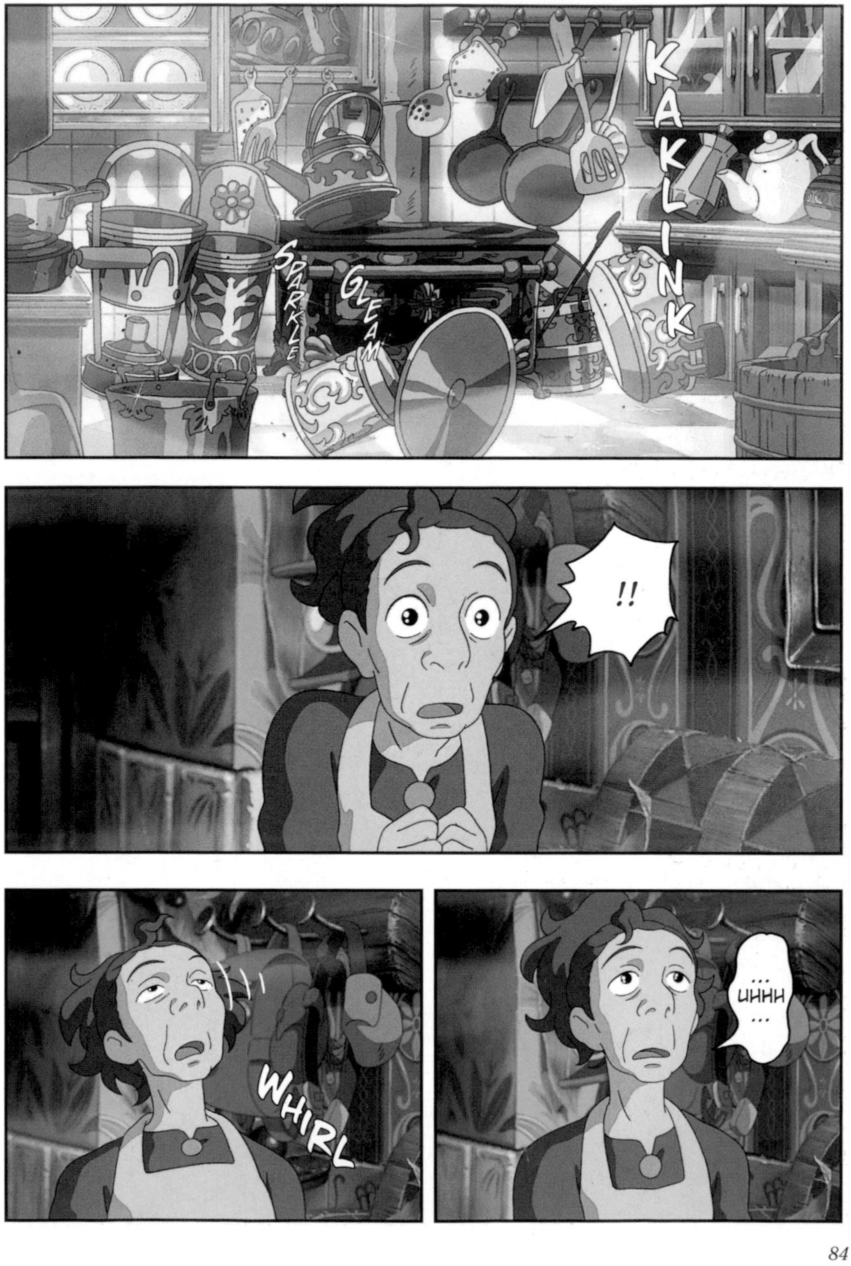
KAKLINK
GLEAM
SPARKLE
!!
...UHHH...
WHIRL

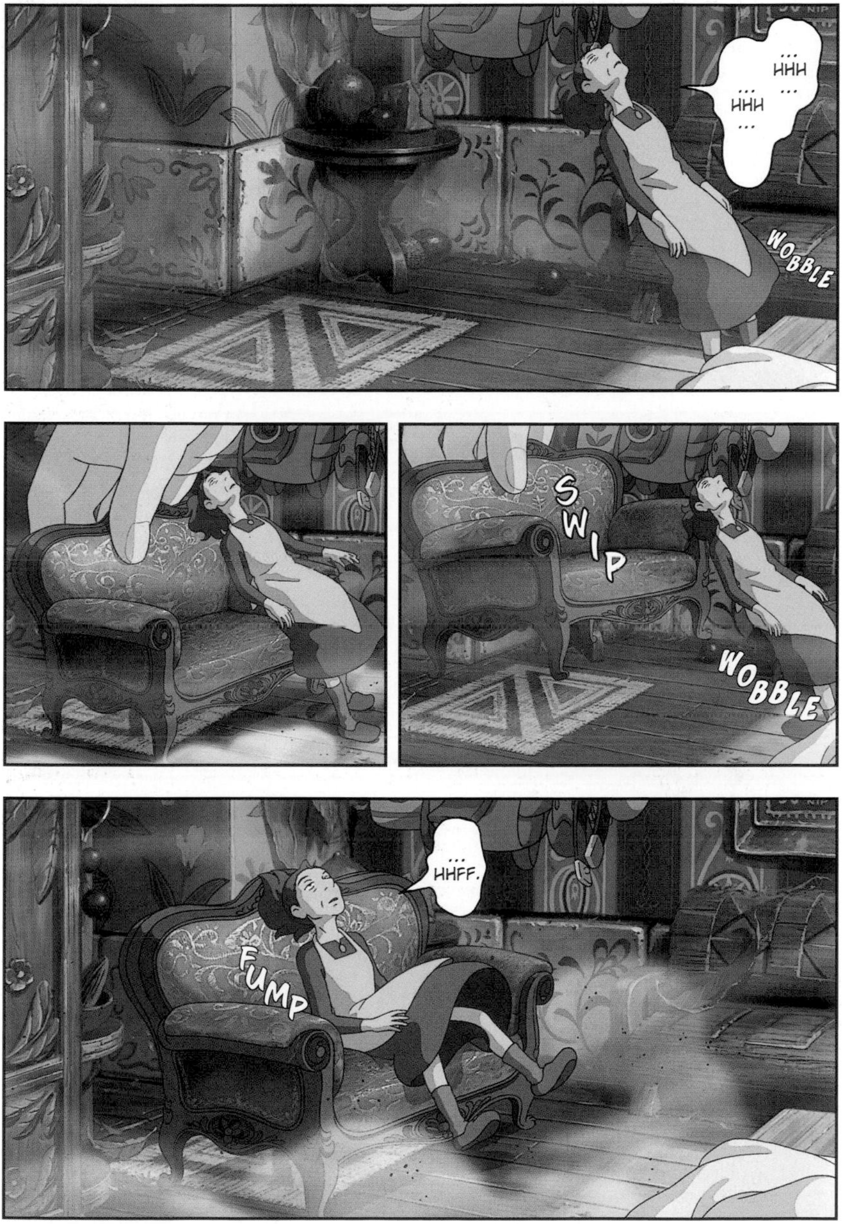
...HHH... HHH...
WOBBLE
SWIP
WOBBLE
...HHFF.
FUMP

BATUNNK
SLAM

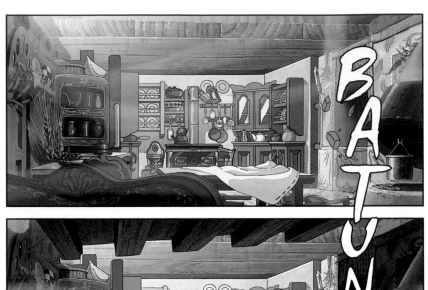

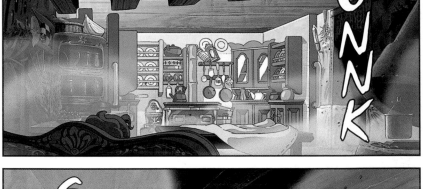

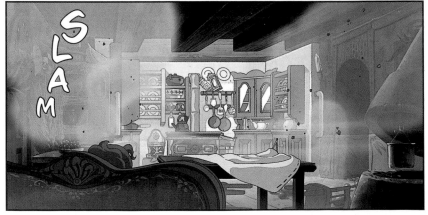

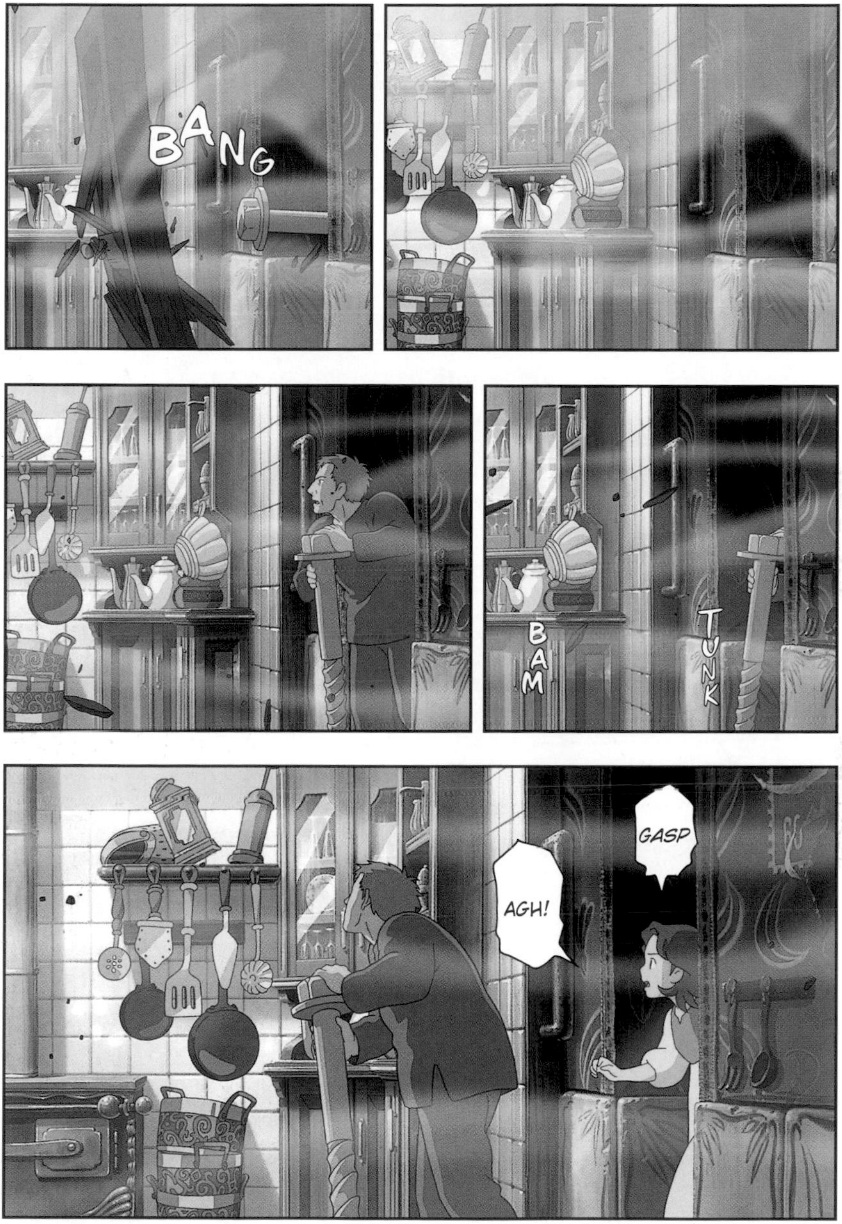
BANG
TUNK
BAM
GASP
AGH!

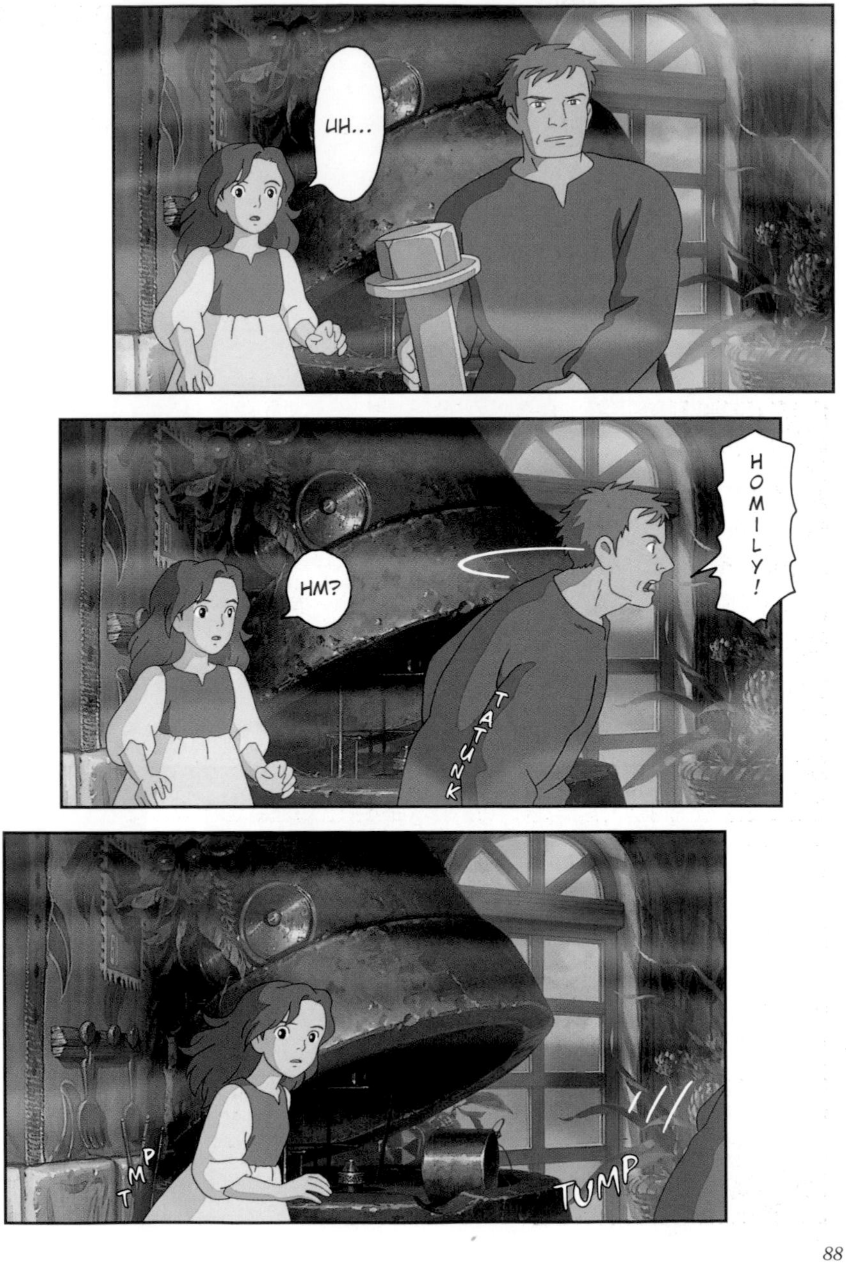
UH...
HOMILY!
TATUNK
HM?
TUMP
TMP

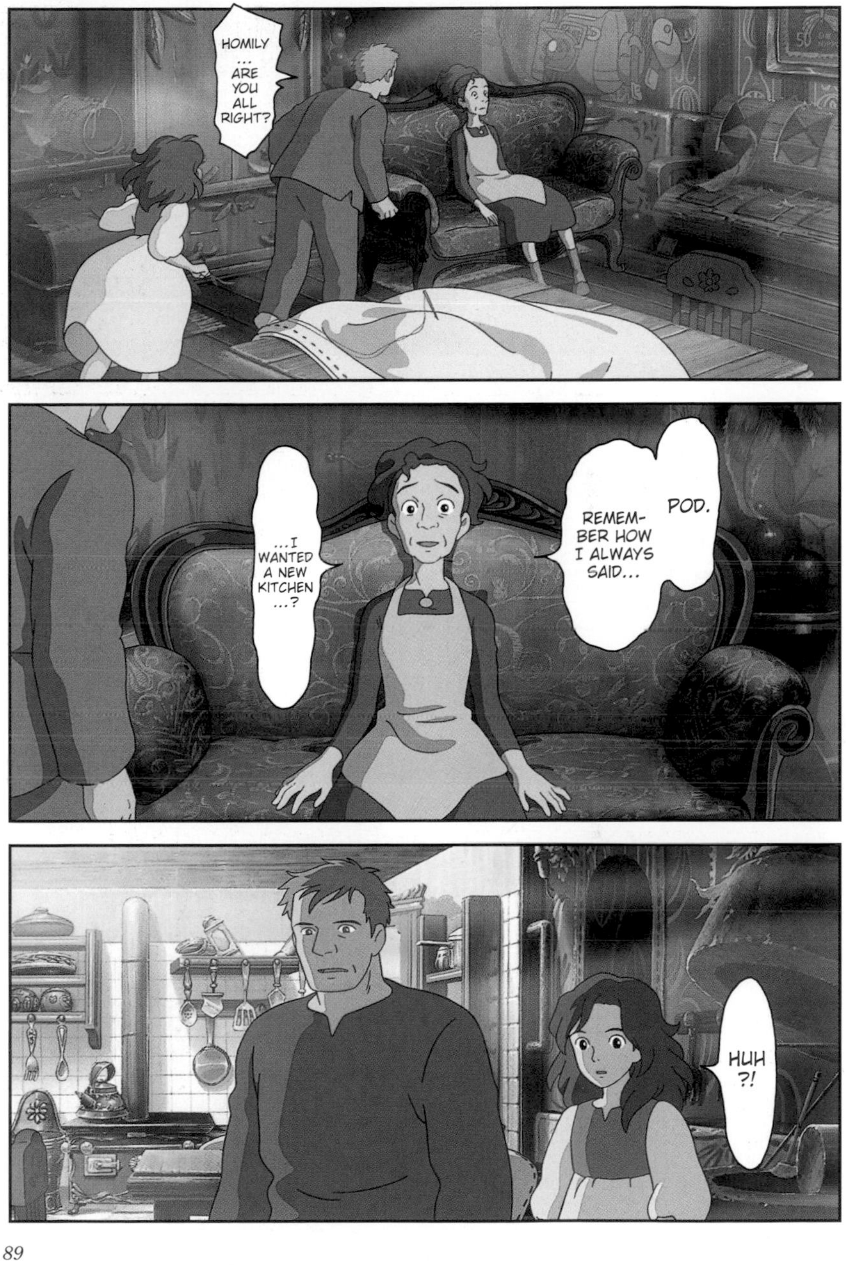
HOMILY ... ARE YOU ALL RIGHT?
POD.
REMEMBER HOW I ALWAYS SAID...
...I WANTED A NEW KITCHEN ...?
HUH ?!

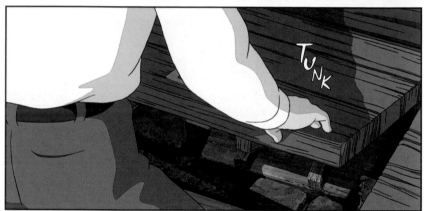

TUNK

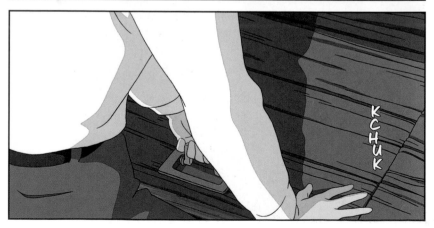

KCHUK

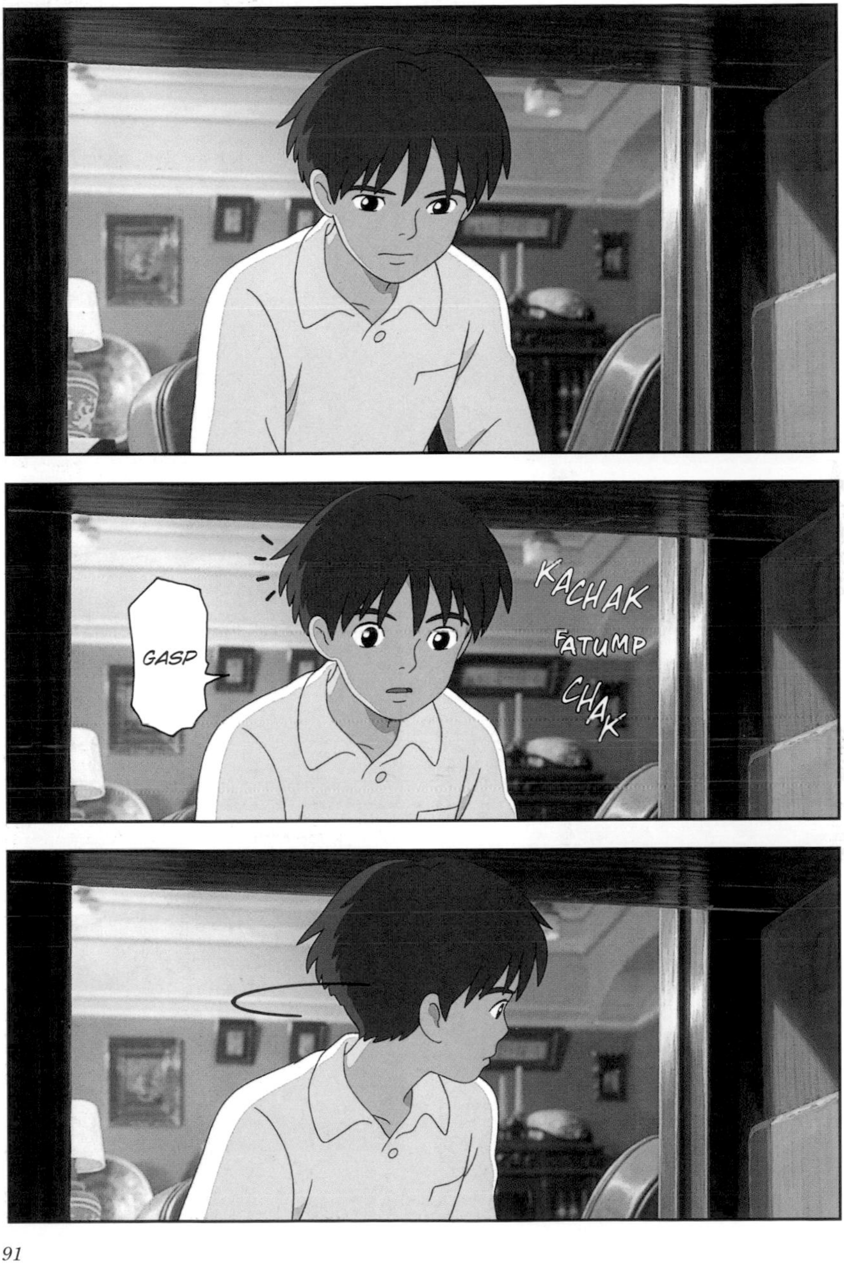
KACHAK
FATUMP
CHAK
GASP

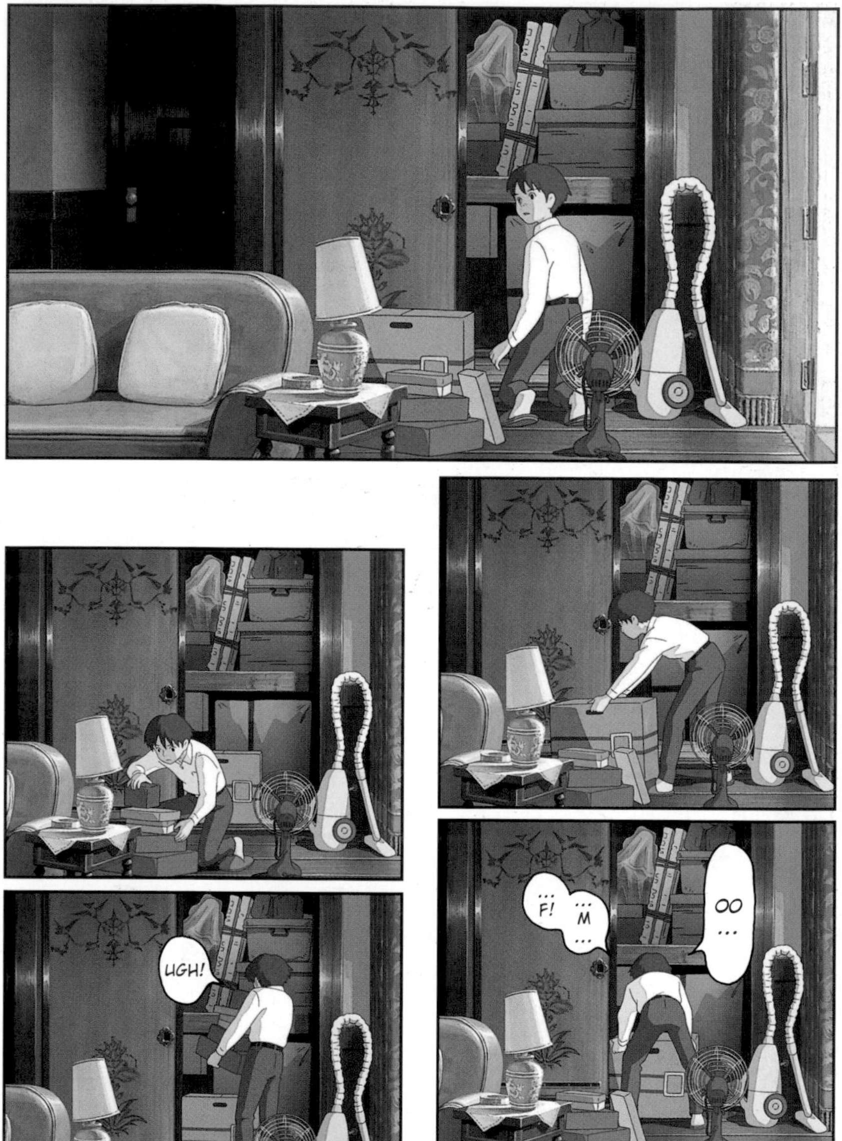
OO
...
...
M
...
...
F!
UGH!

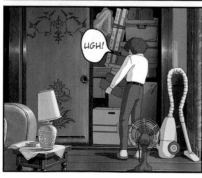

SIGH
HMM ...
THIS ...
... AGAIN ?
HM?

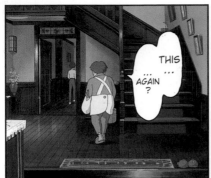

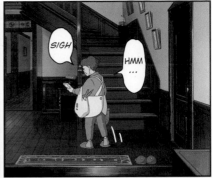

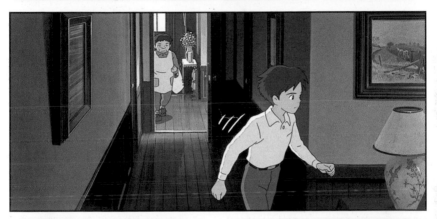

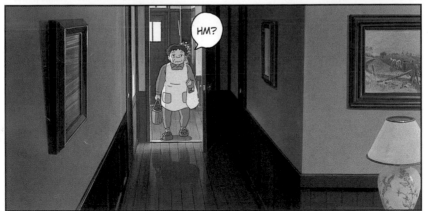

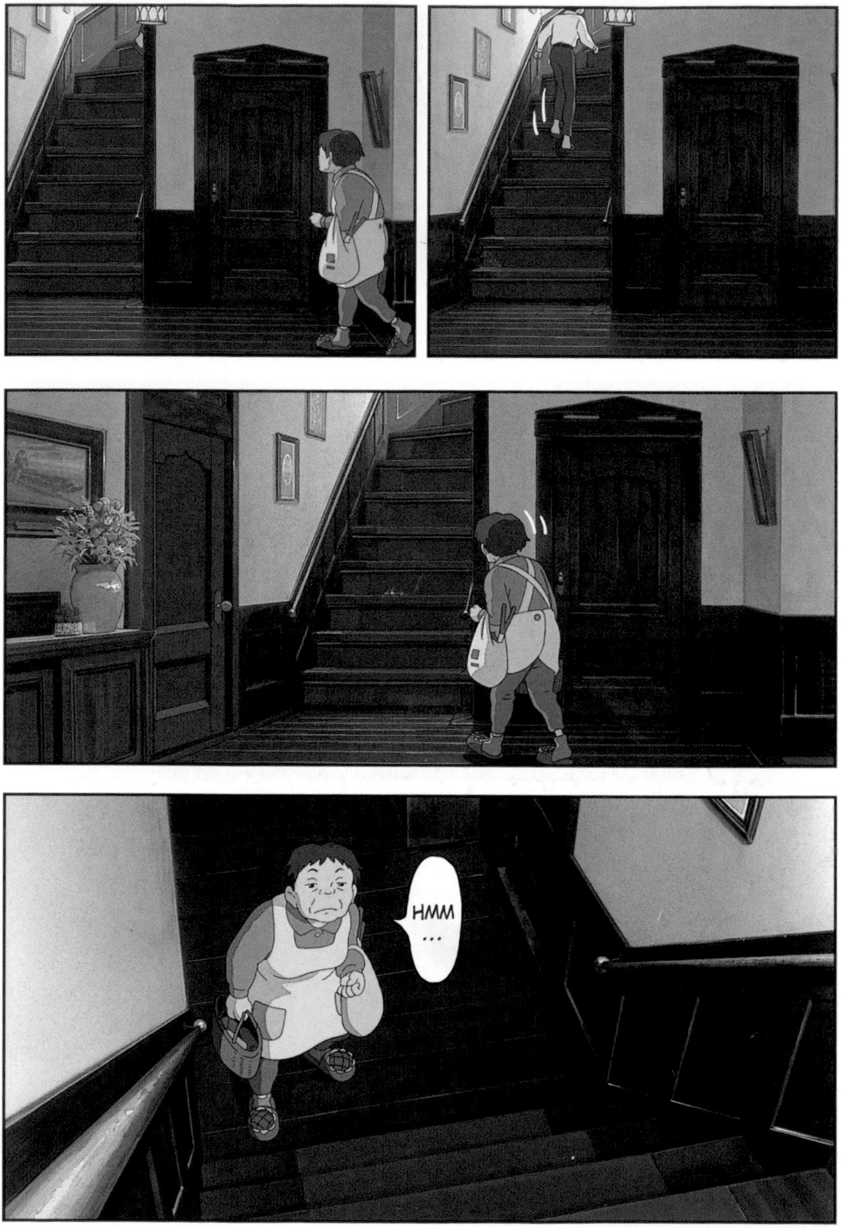
HMM
...

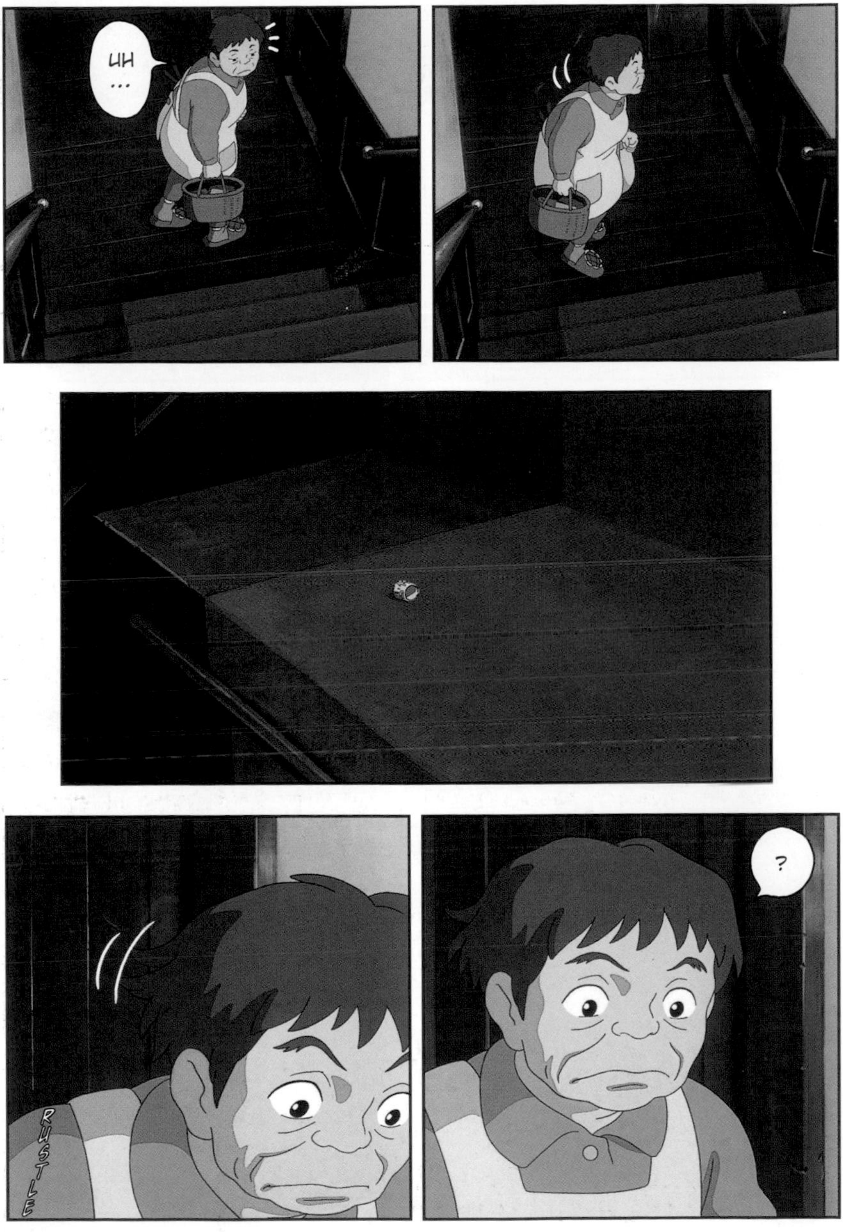
UH ...
?
RUSTLE

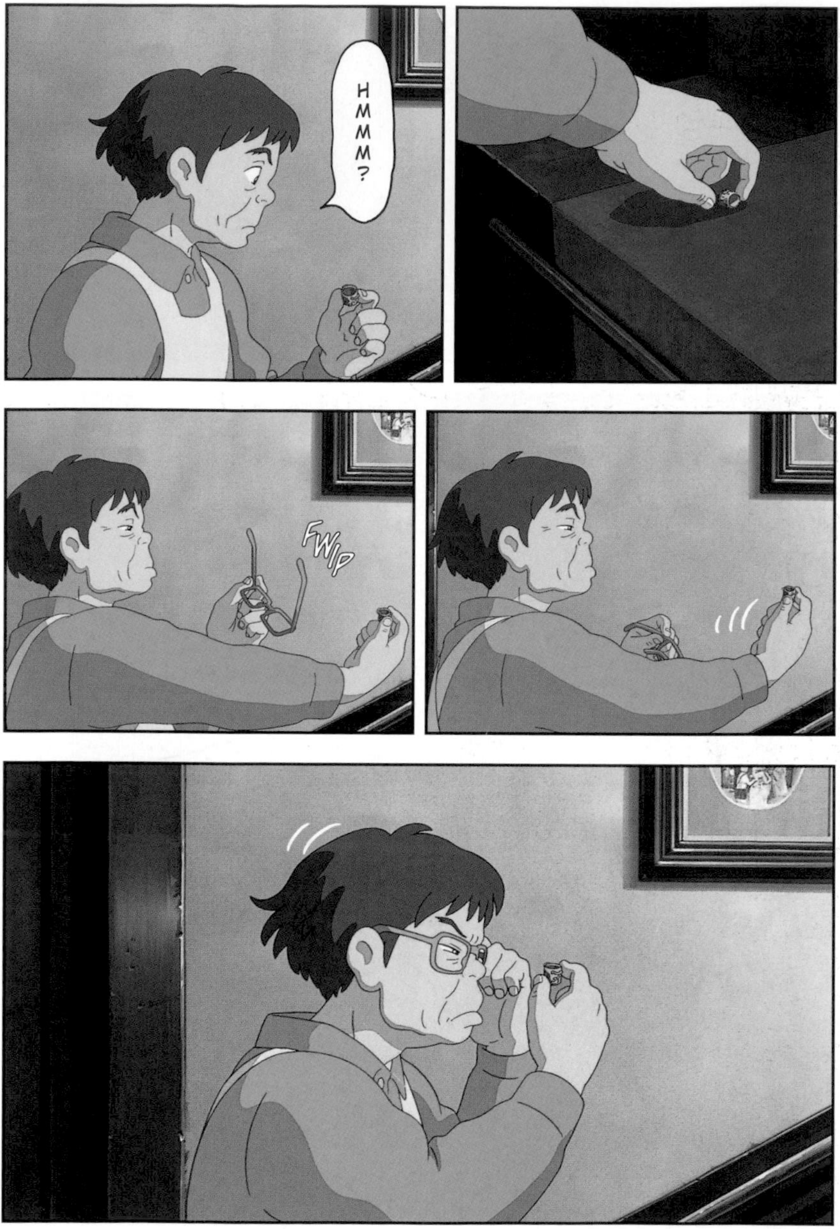
HMMM?
FWIP

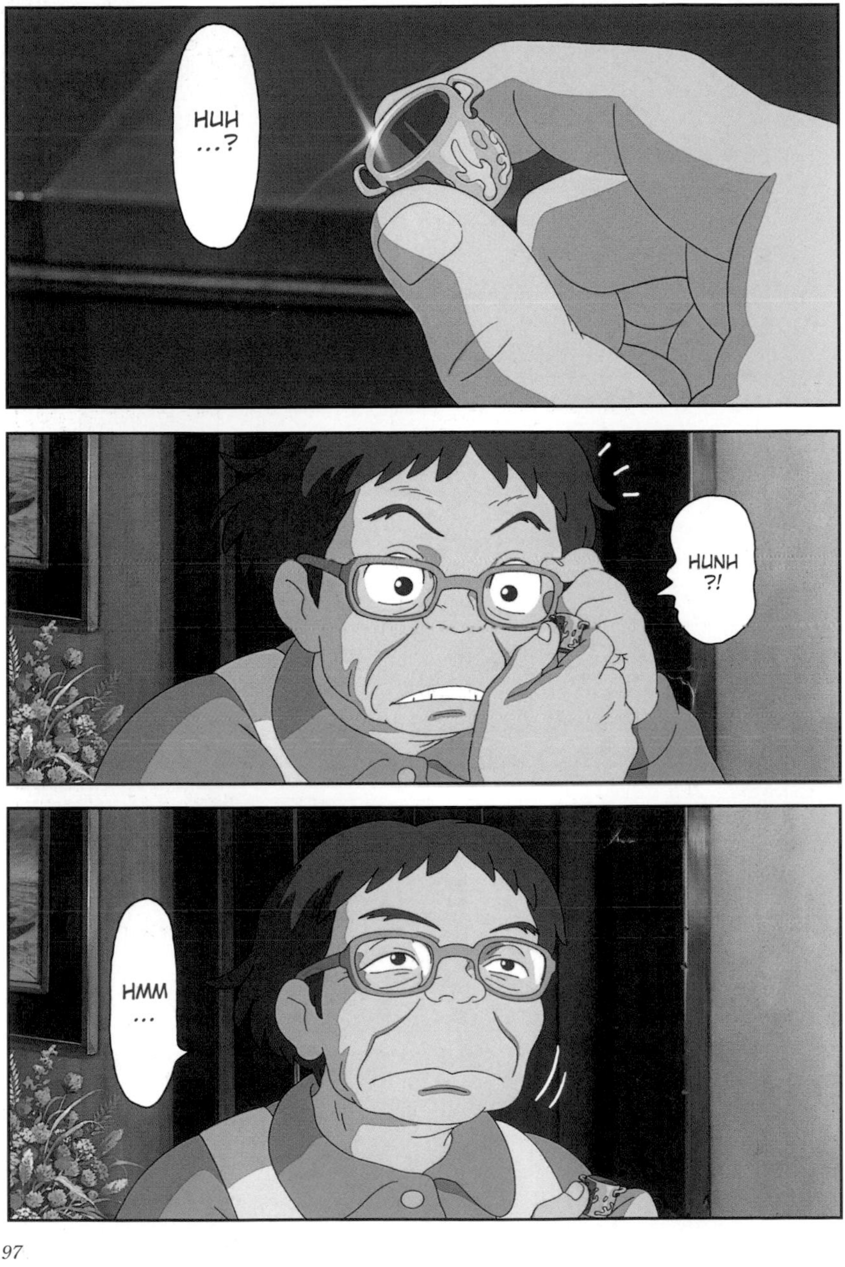
HUH ...?
HUNH ?!
HMM ...

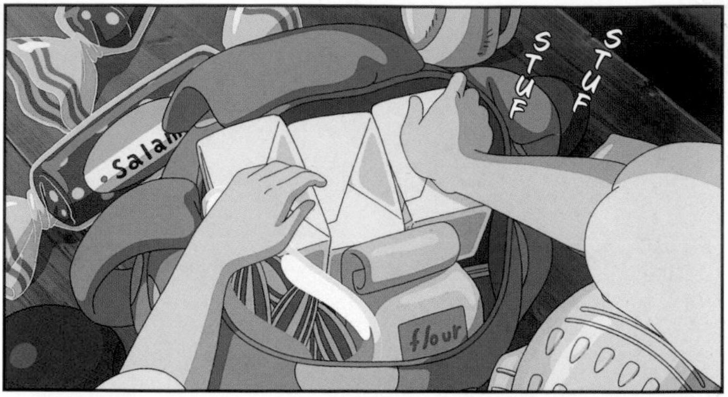
STUF
STUF
Salami
flour

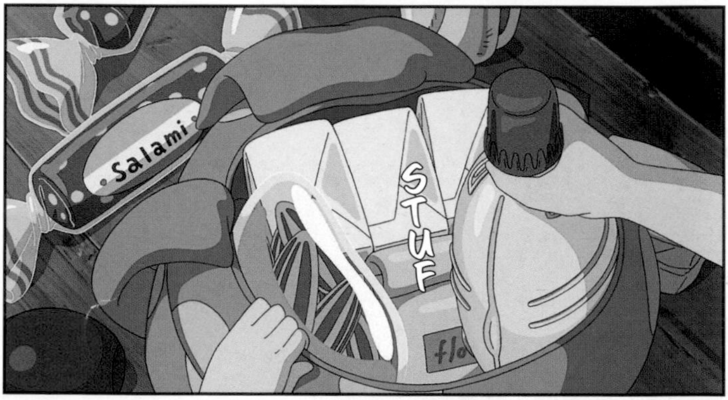
STUF
Salami

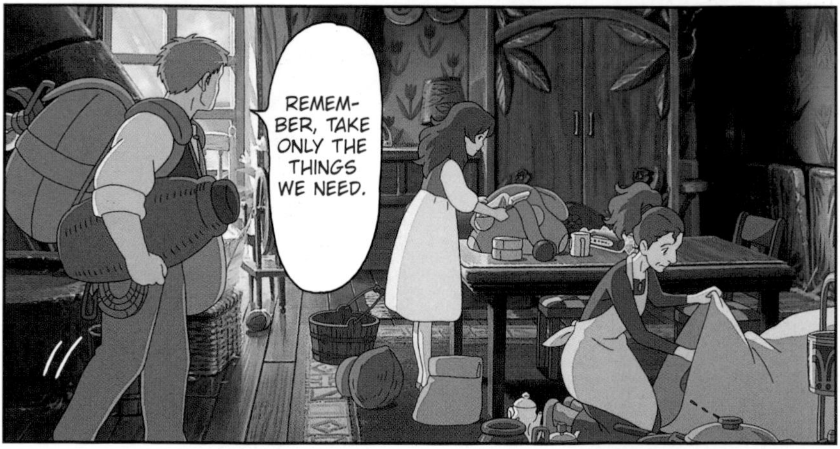
REMEMBER, TAKE ONLY THE THINGS WE NEED.

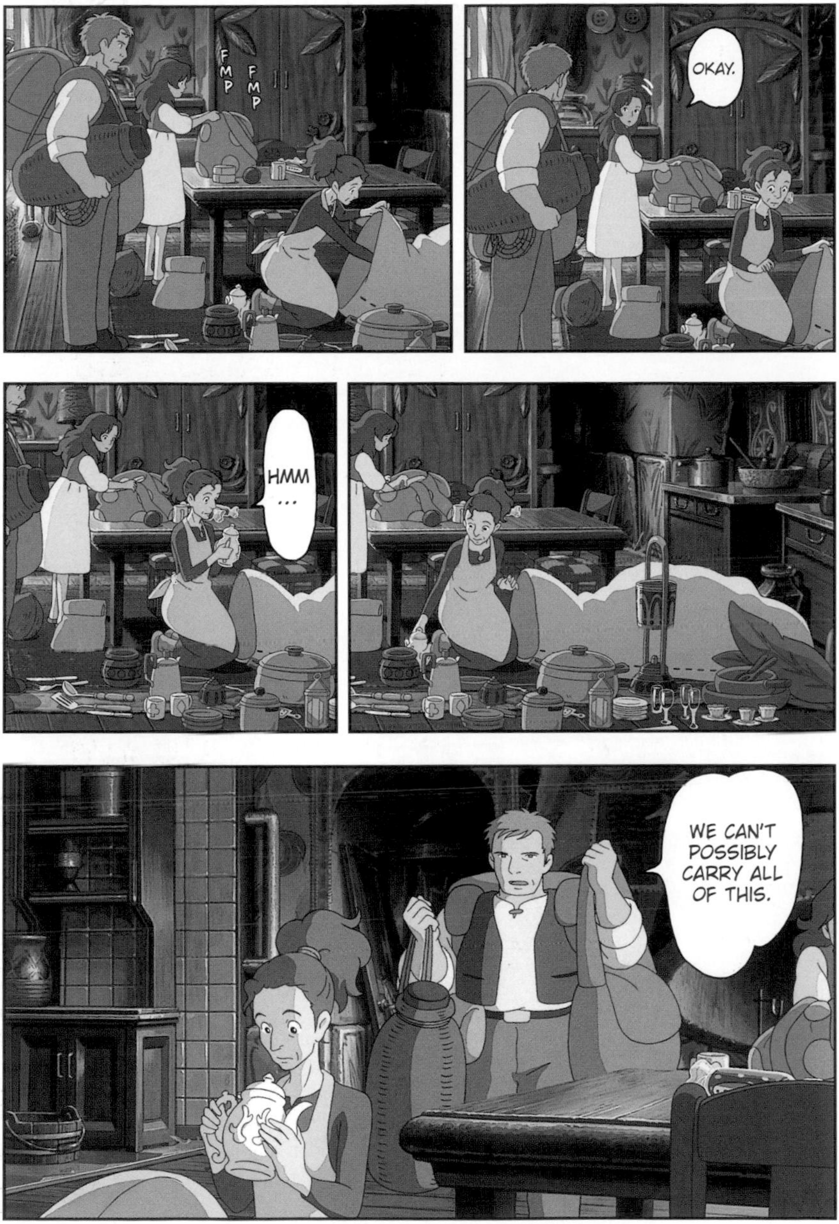
OKAY.
FMP FMP
HMM ...
WE CAN'T POSSIBLY CARRY ALL OF THIS.

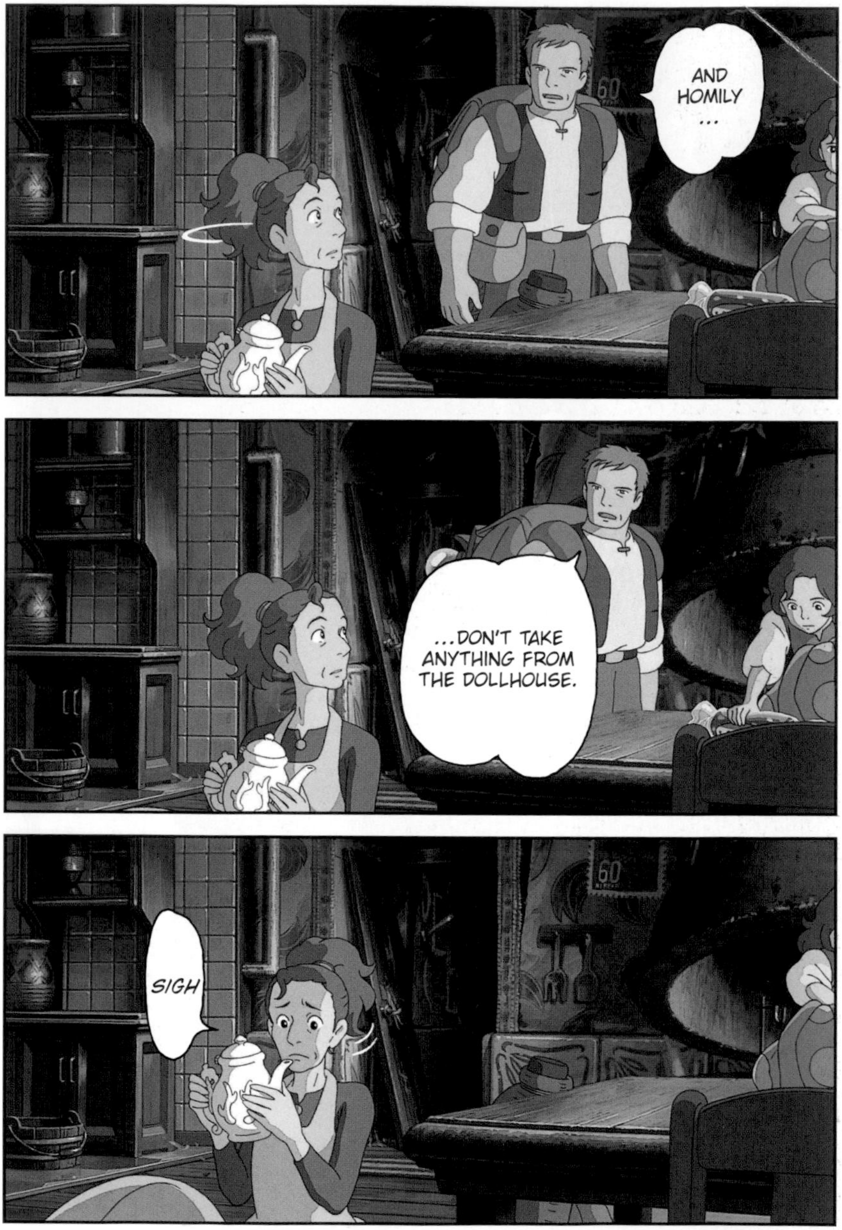
AND HOMILY ...
...DON'T TAKE ANYTHING FROM THE DOLLHOUSE.
SIGH

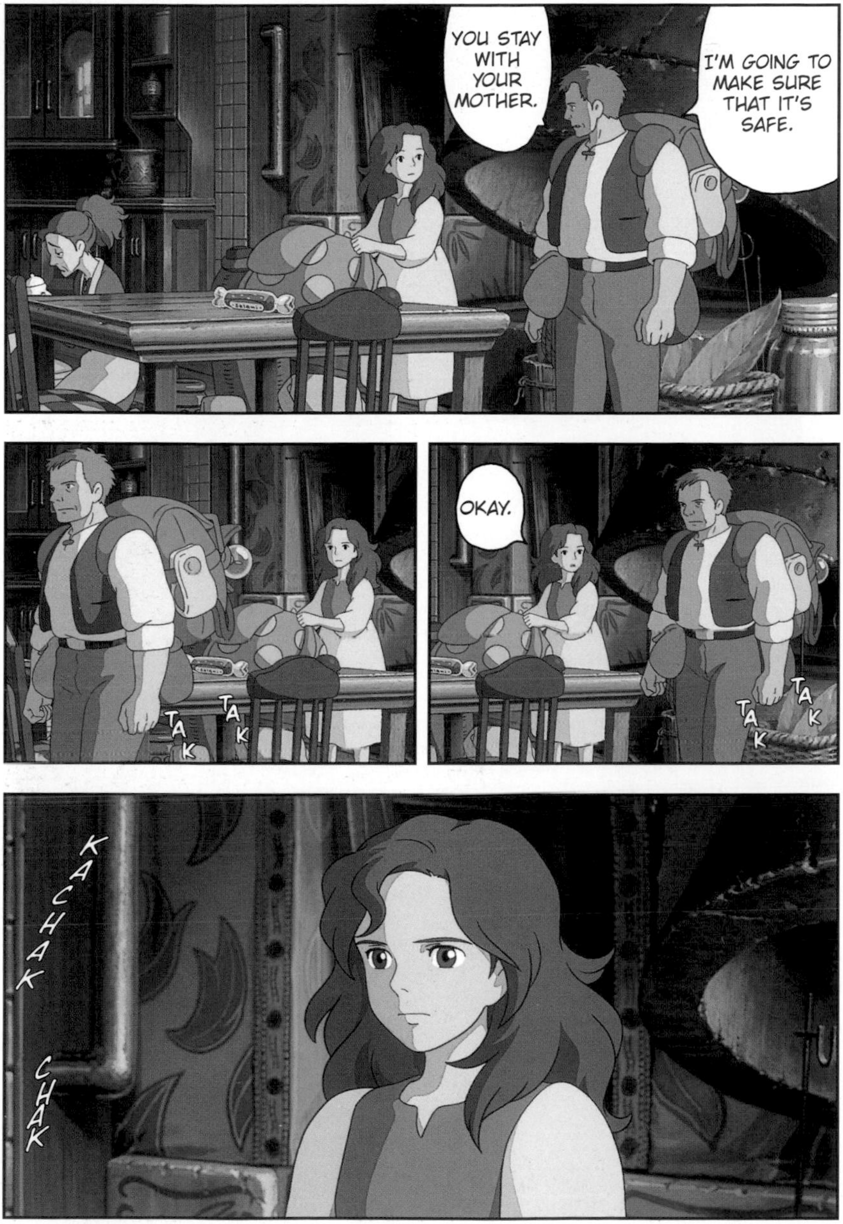
I'M GOING TO MAKE SURE THAT IT'S SAFE.
YOU STAY WITH YOUR MOTHER.
OKAY.
TAK
TAK
TAK
TAK
KACHAK
CHAK

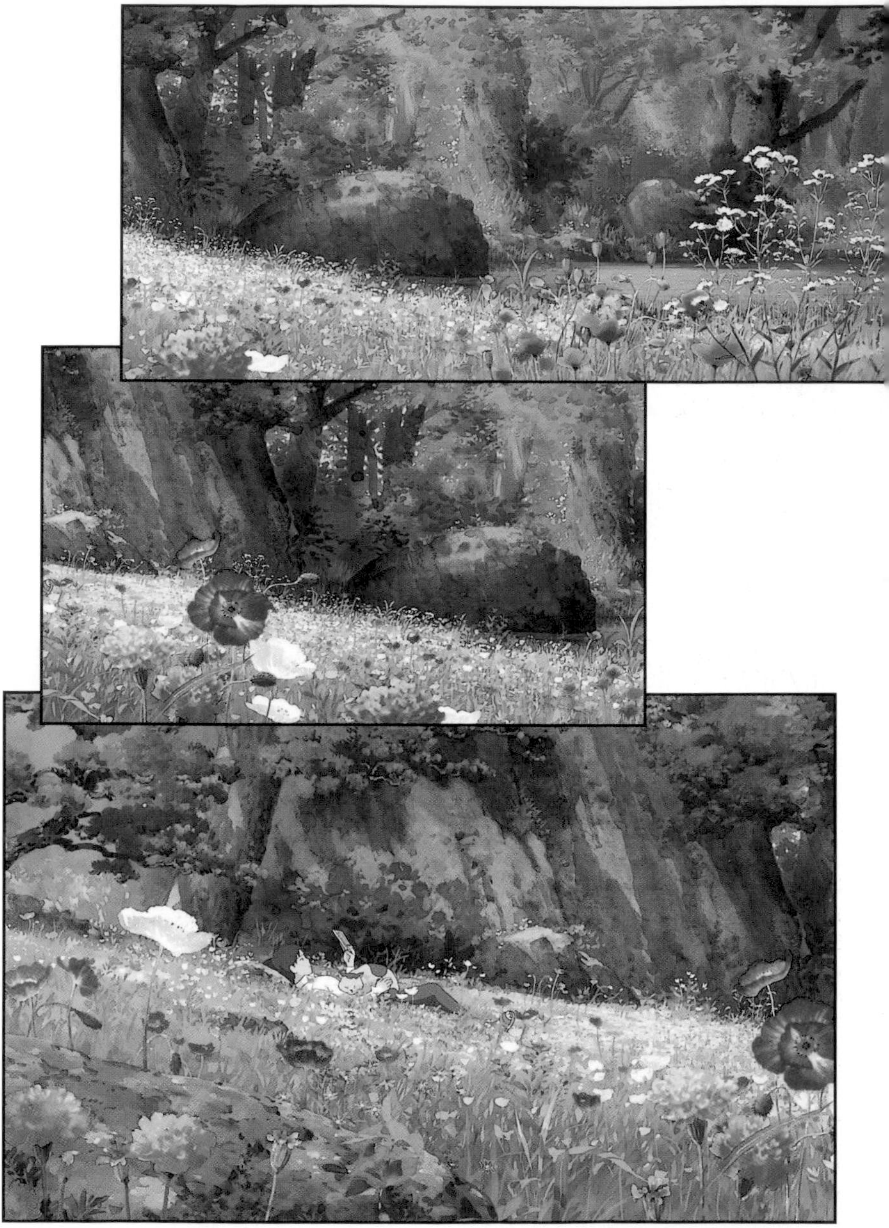

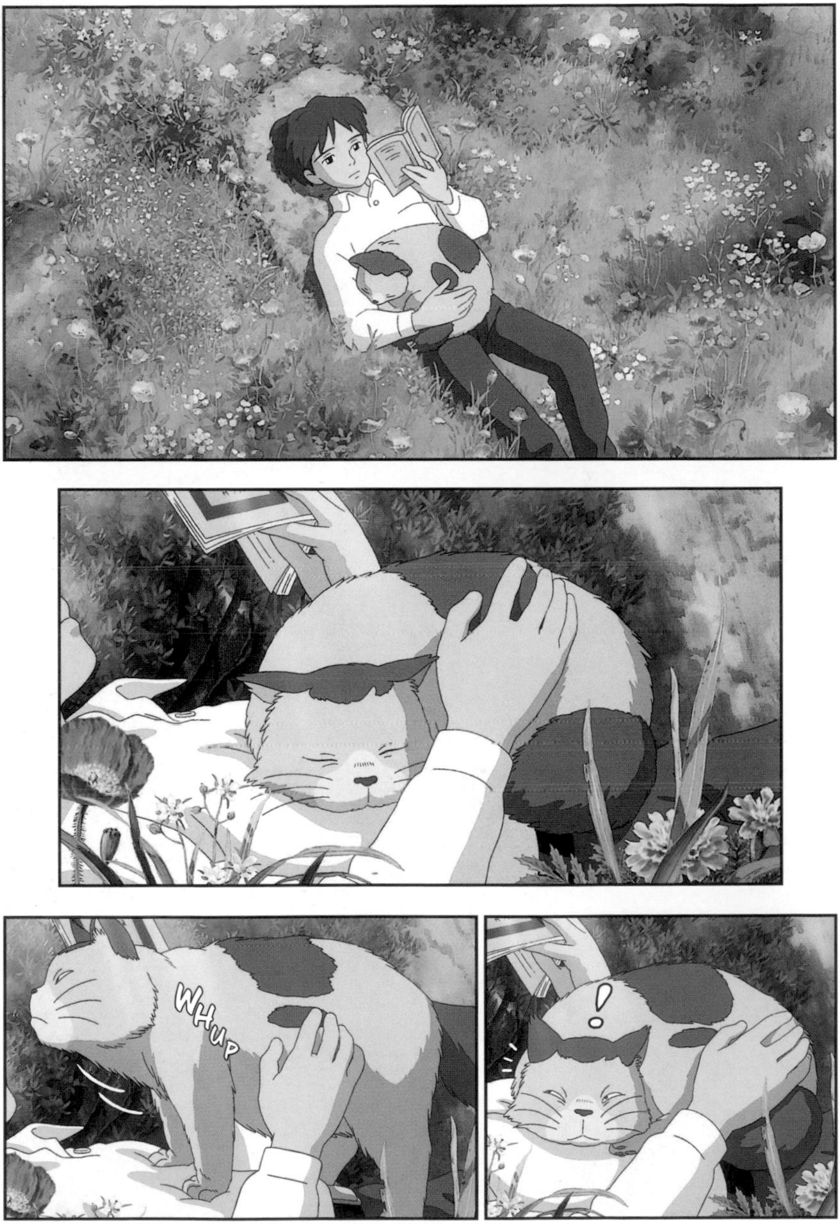
!
WHUP

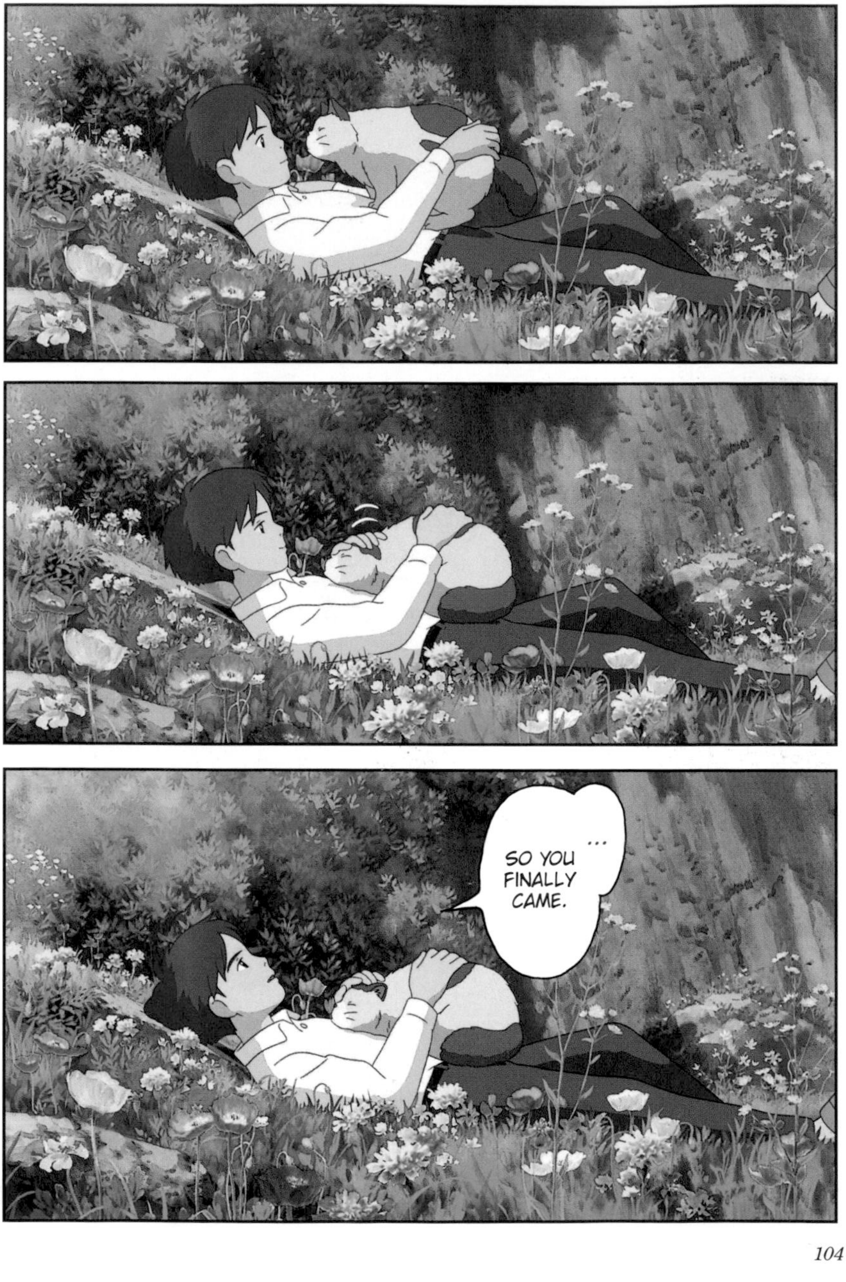
... SO YOU FINALLY CAME.

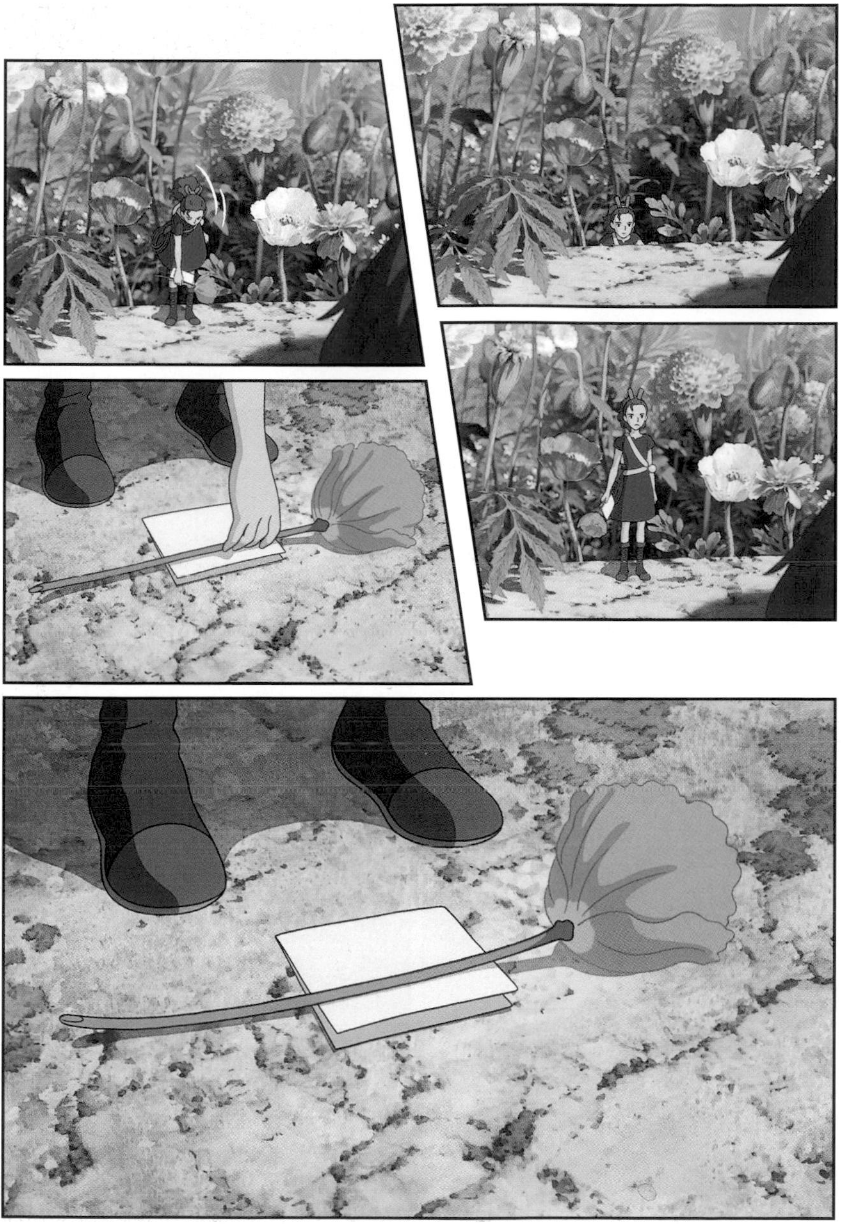

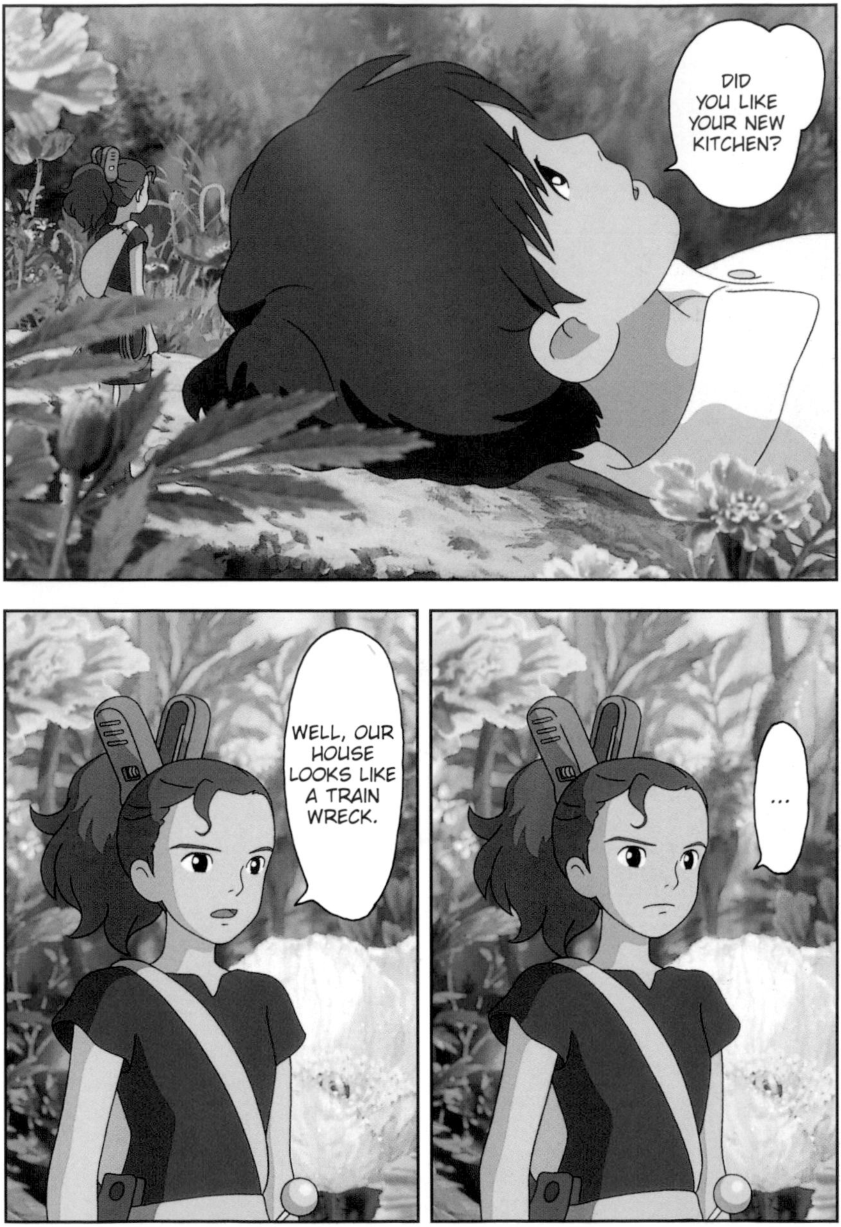
DID YOU LIKE YOUR NEW KITCHEN?
...
WELL, OUR HOUSE LOOKS LIKE A TRAIN WRECK.

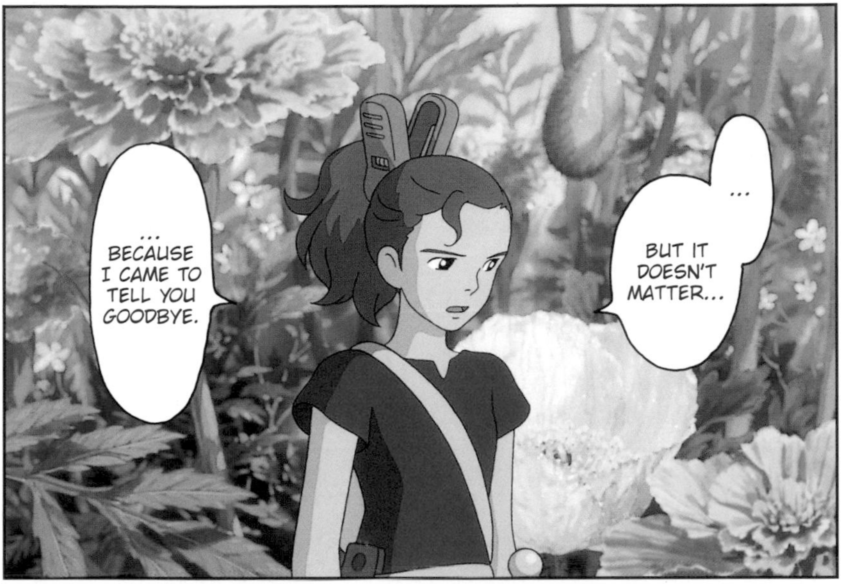
... BUT IT DOESN'T MATTER...
... BECAUSE I CAME TO TELL YOU GOODBYE.

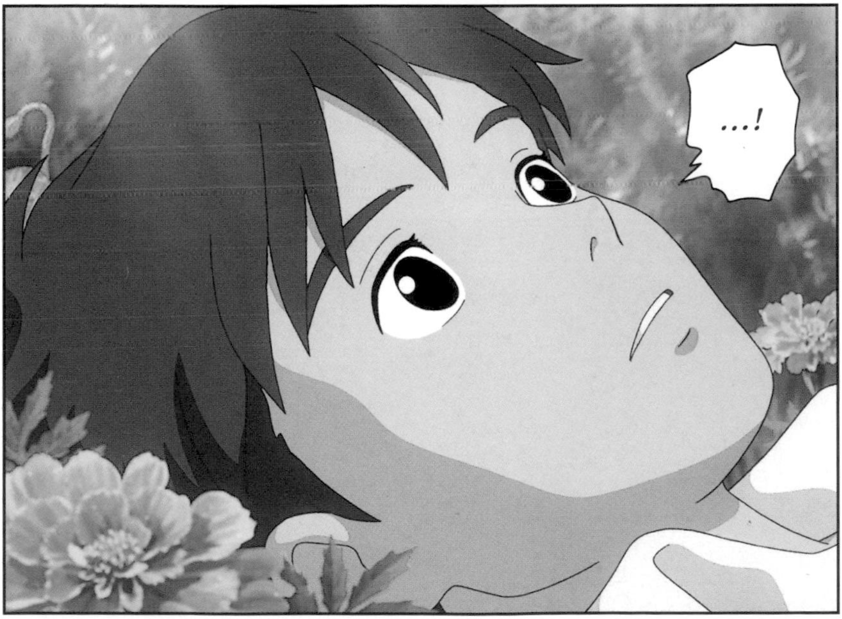
...!

...

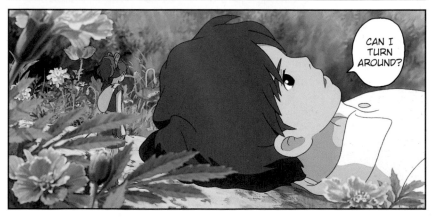

CAN I TURN AROUND?

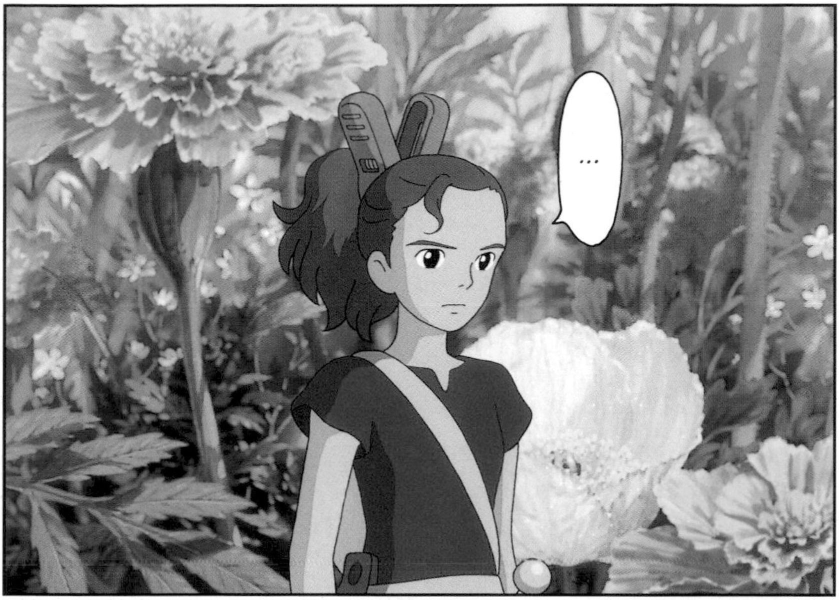
...
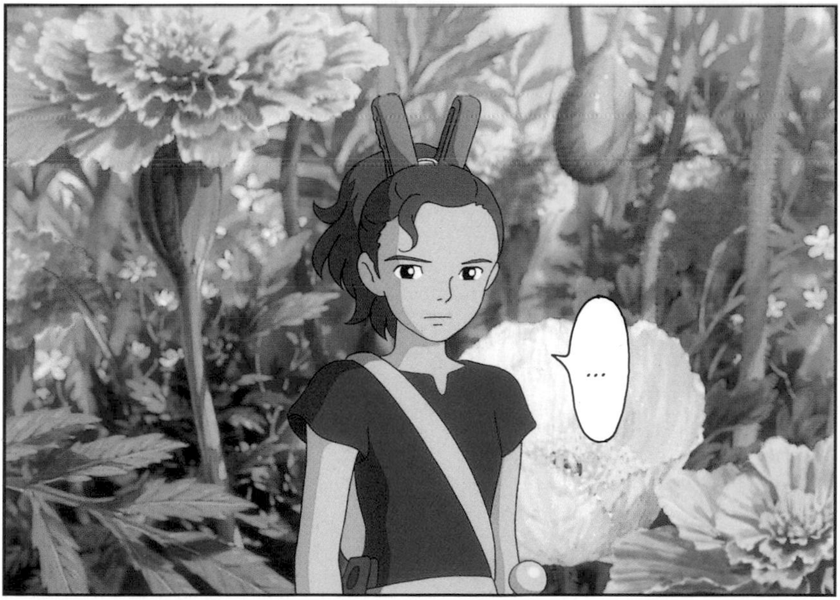
...

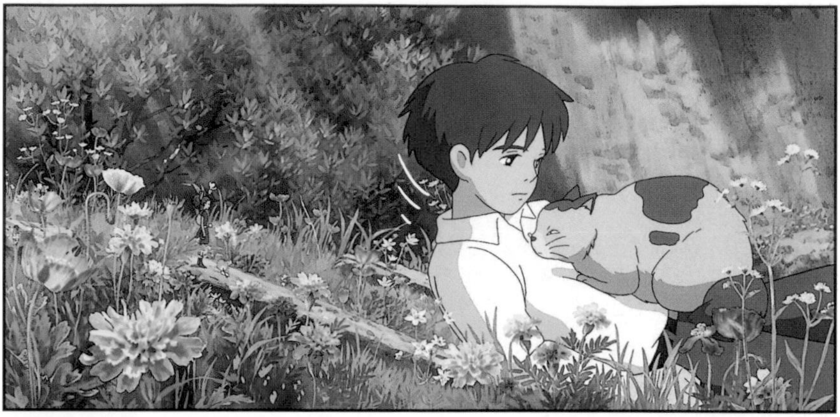

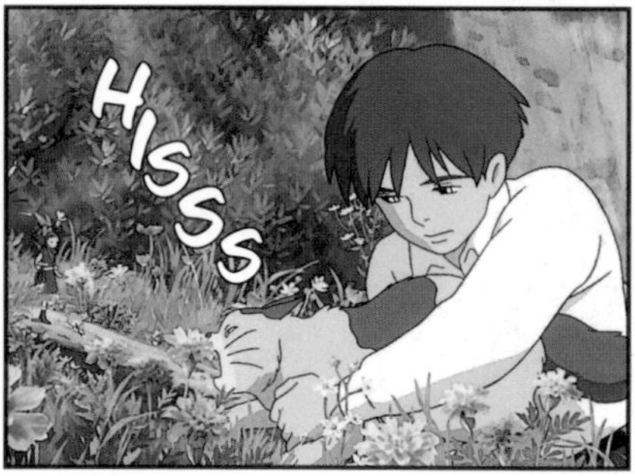
HISSS

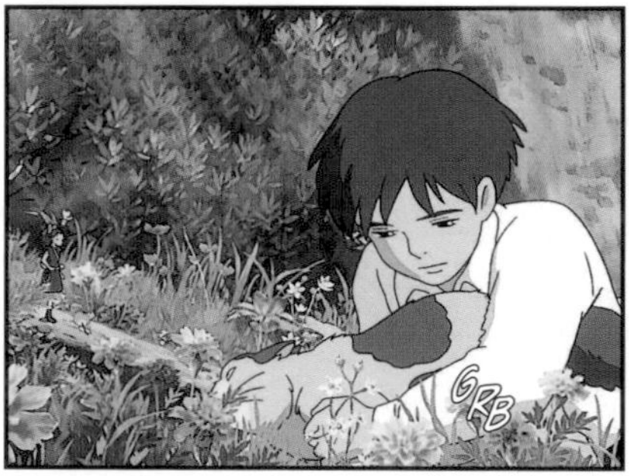
GRB

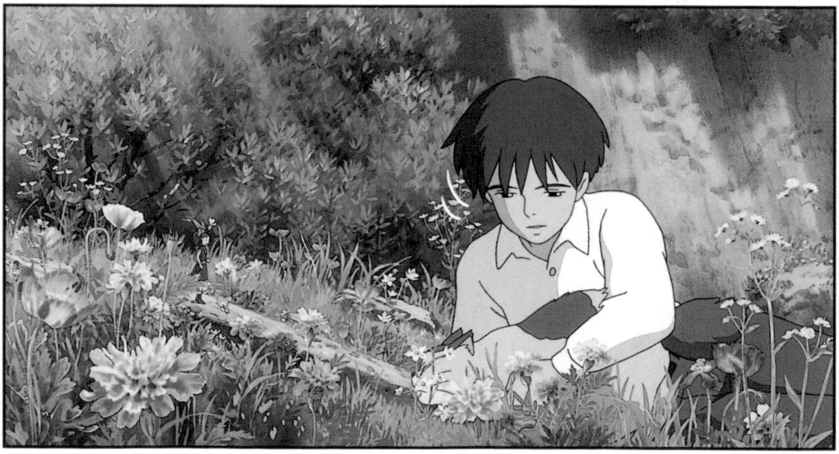

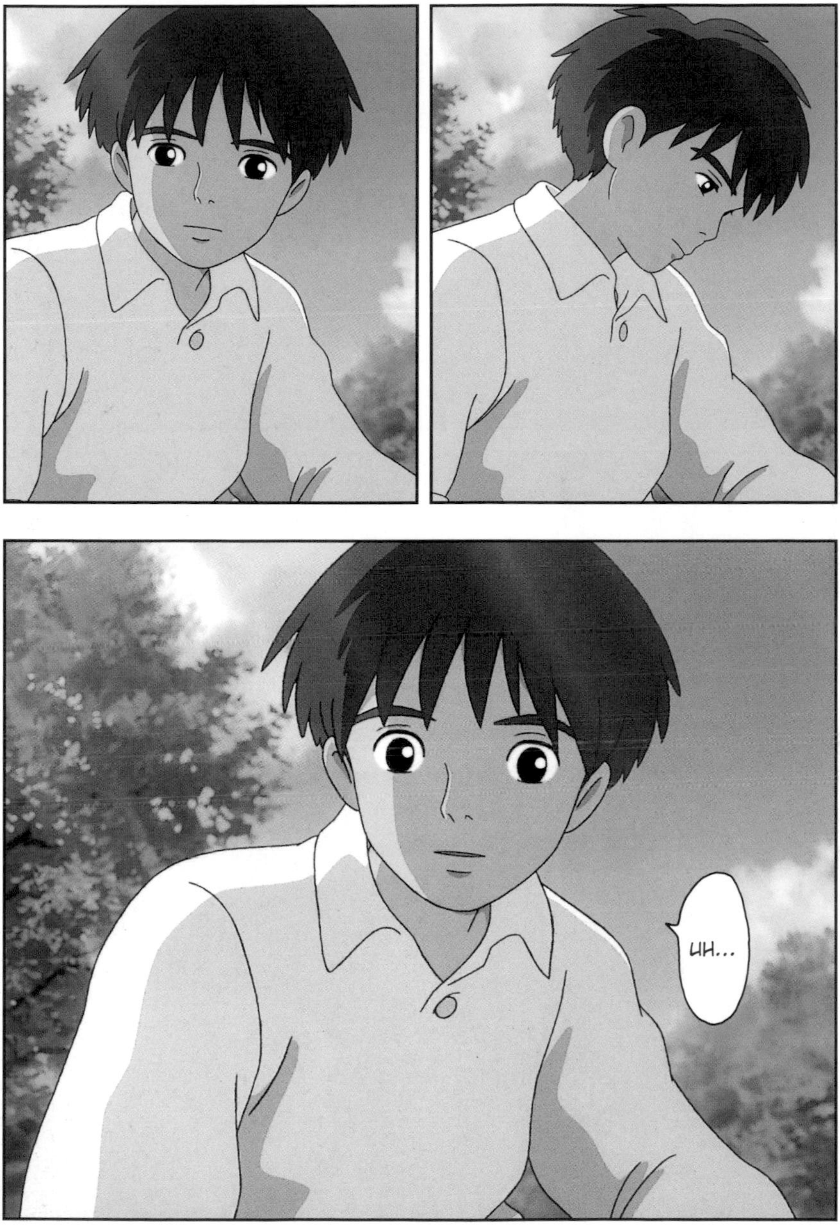
UH...

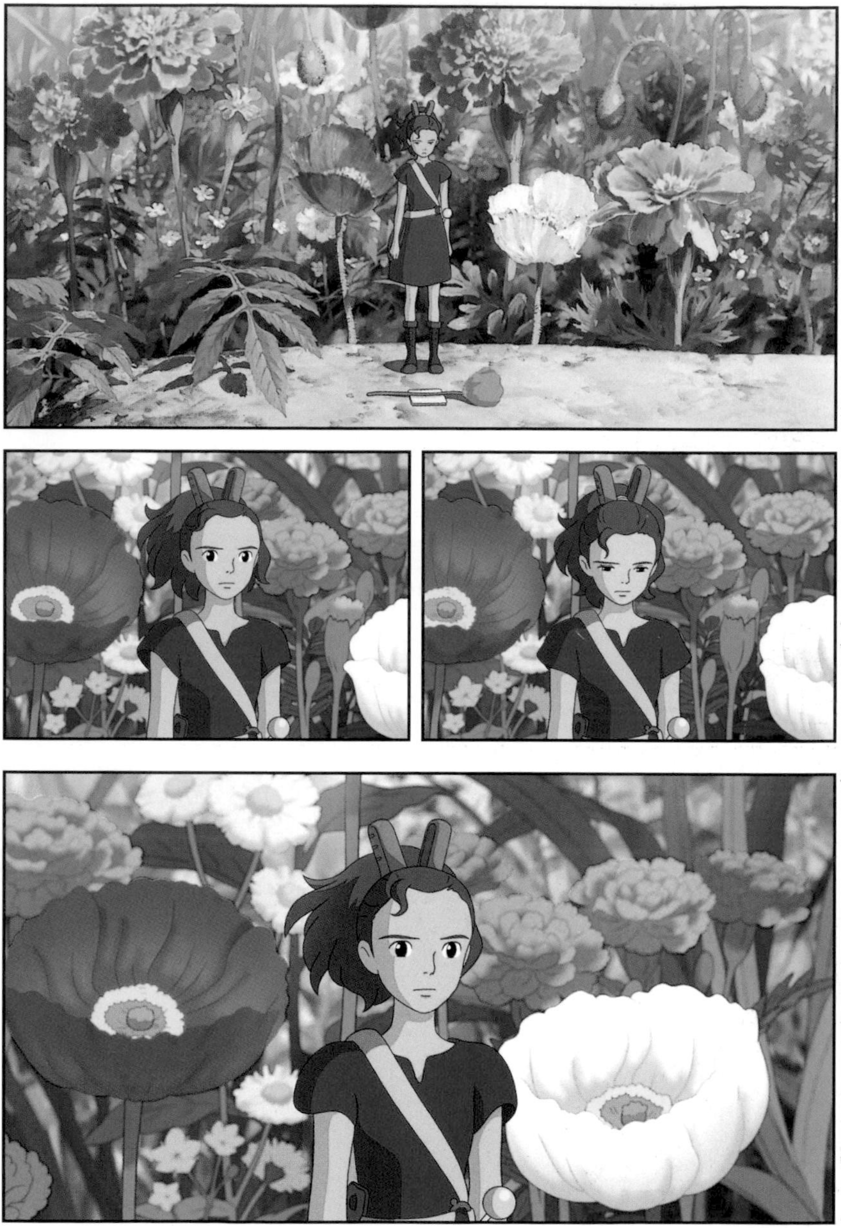

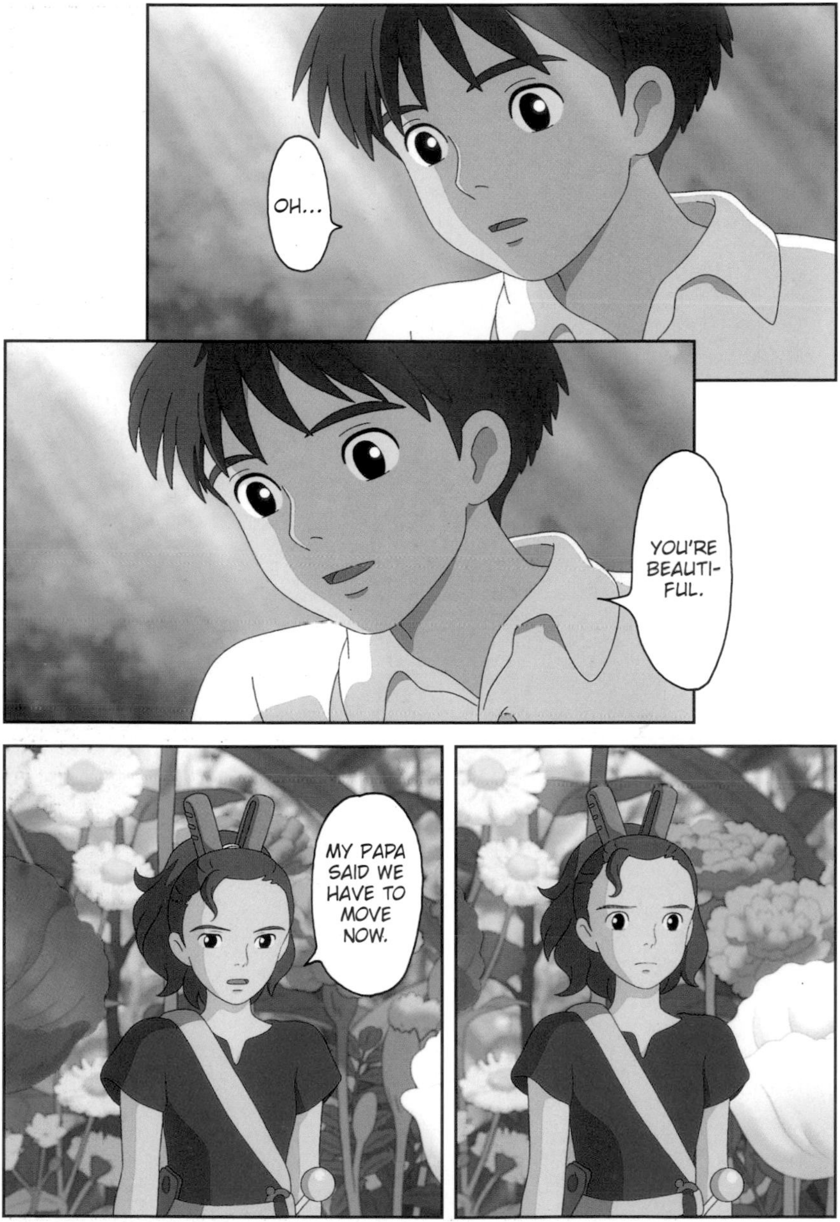
OH...
YOU'RE BEAUTI-FUL.
MY PAPA SAID WE HAVE TO MOVE NOW.

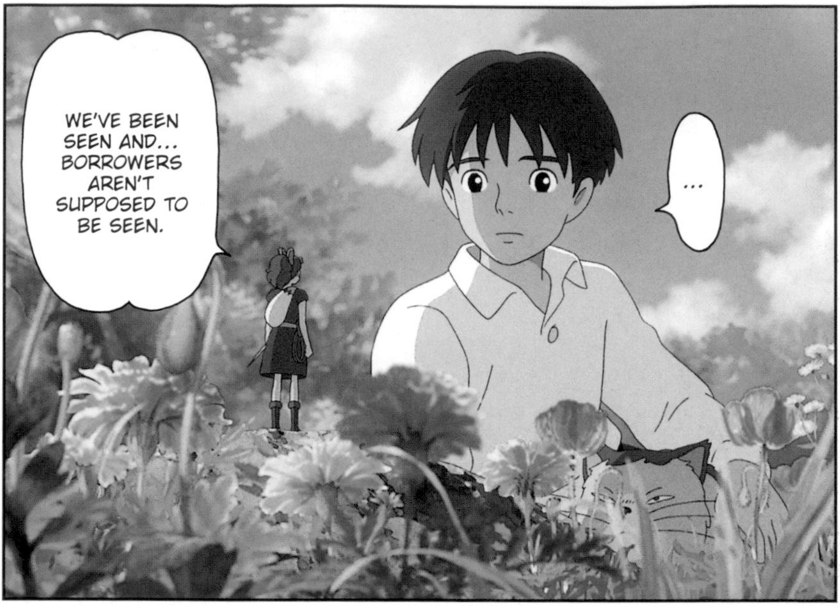
...
WE'VE BEEN SEEN AND... BORROWERS AREN'T SUPPOSED TO BE SEEN.
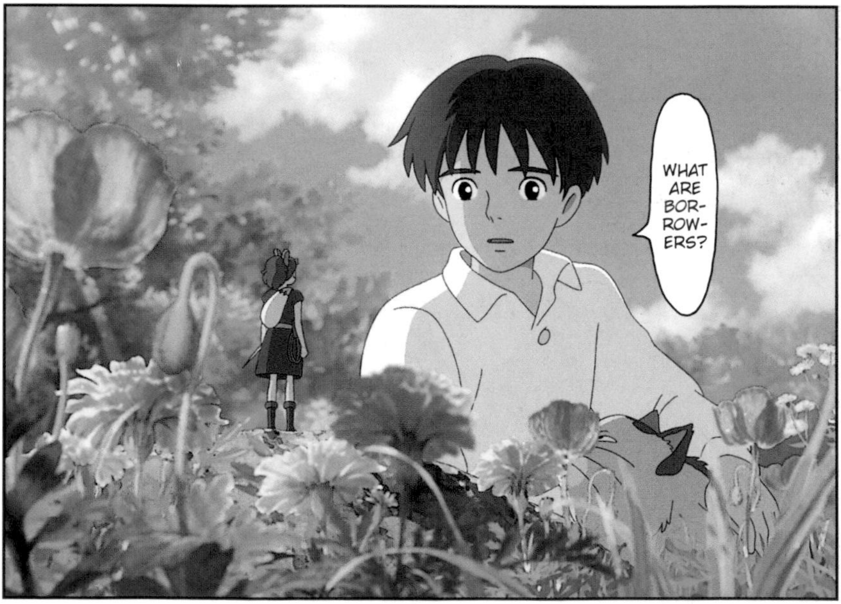
WHAT ARE BOR-ROW-ERS?

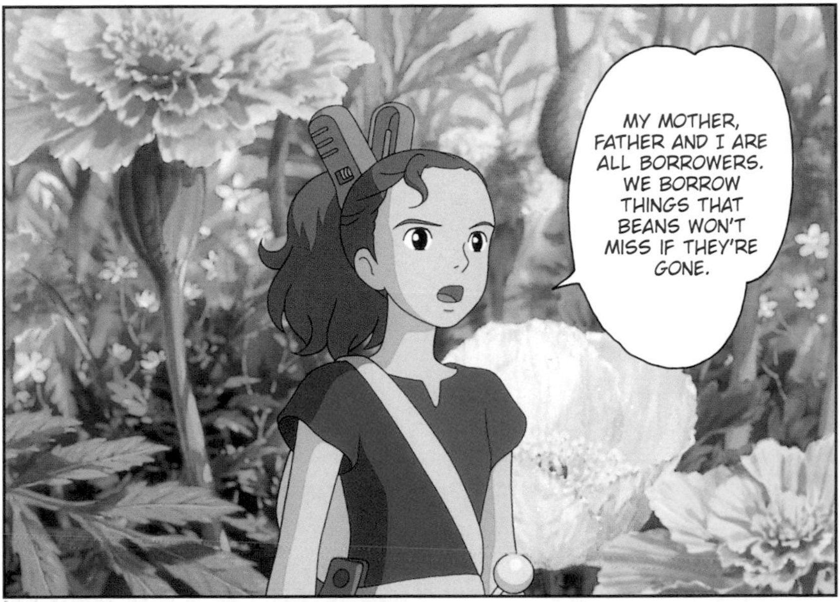
MY MOTHER, FATHER AND I ARE ALL BORROWERS. WE BORROW THINGS THAT BEANS WON'T MISS IF THEY'RE GONE.

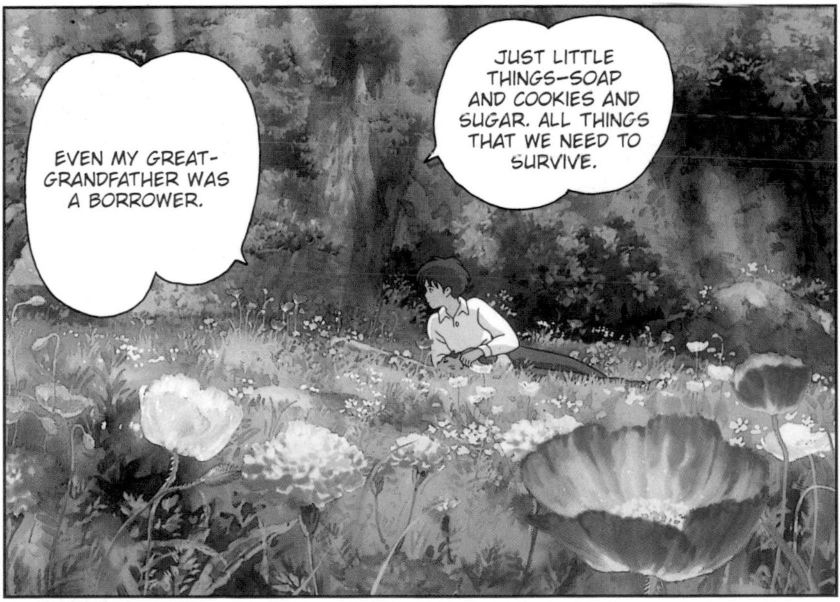
JUST LITTLE THINGS—SOAP AND COOKIES AND SUGAR. ALL THINGS THAT WE NEED TO SURVIVE.
EVEN MY GREAT-GRANDFATHER WAS A BORROWER.

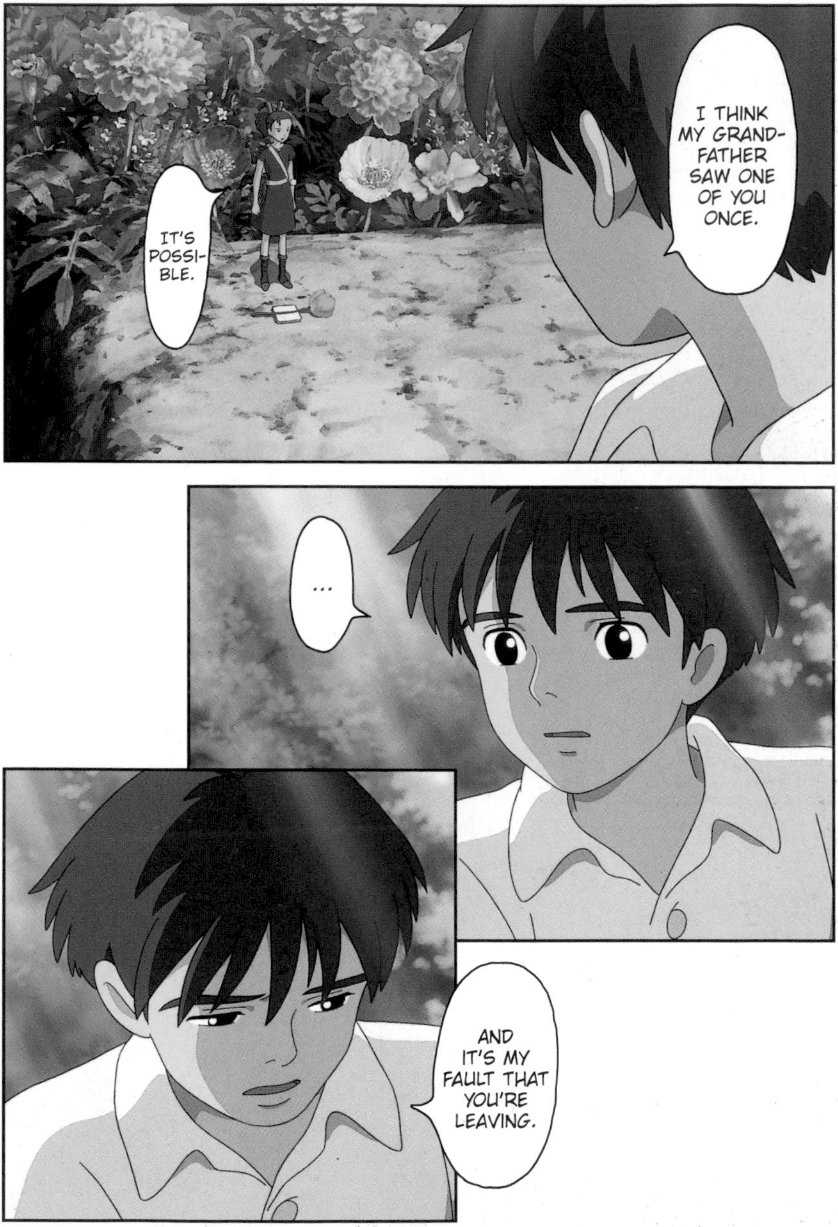
I THINK MY GRAND-FATHER SAW ONE OF YOU ONCE.
IT'S POSSI-BLE.
...
AND IT'S MY FAULT THAT YOU'RE LEAVING.

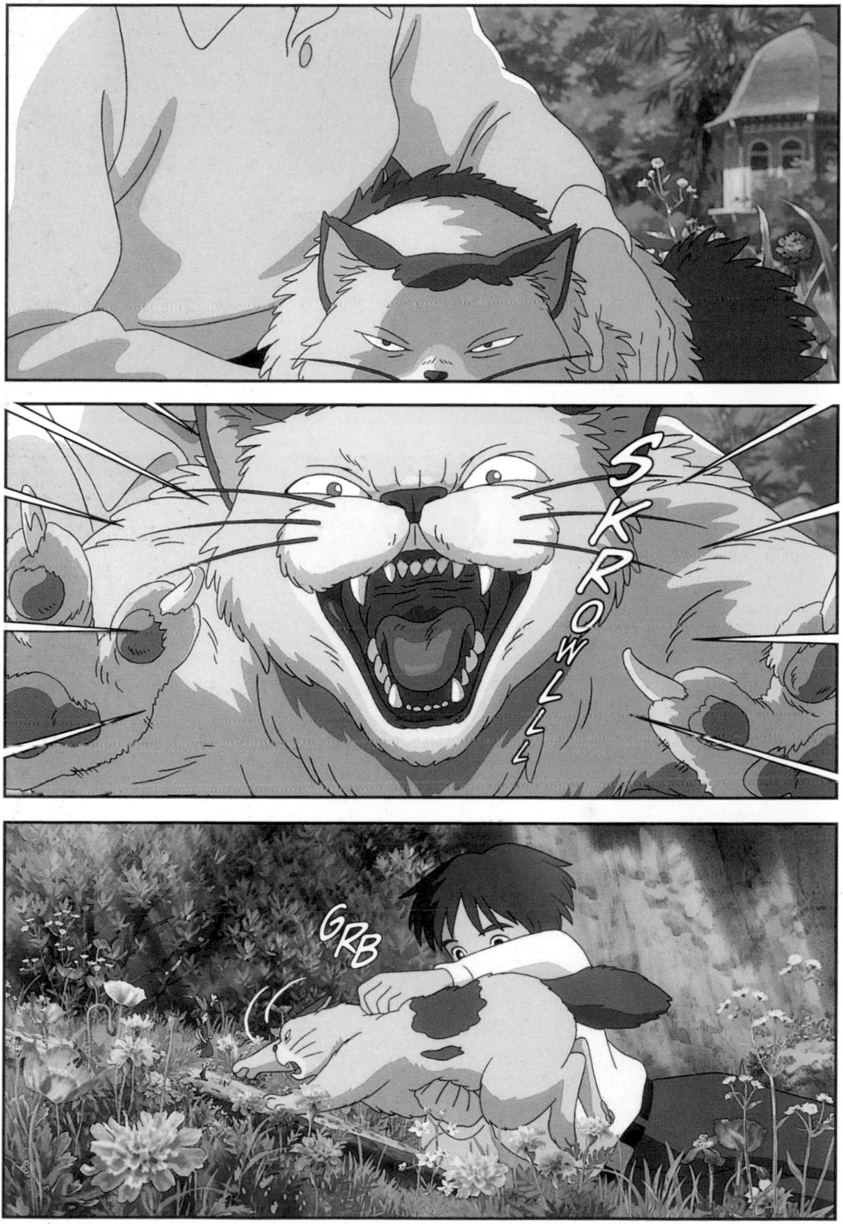
SKROWLLL
GRB

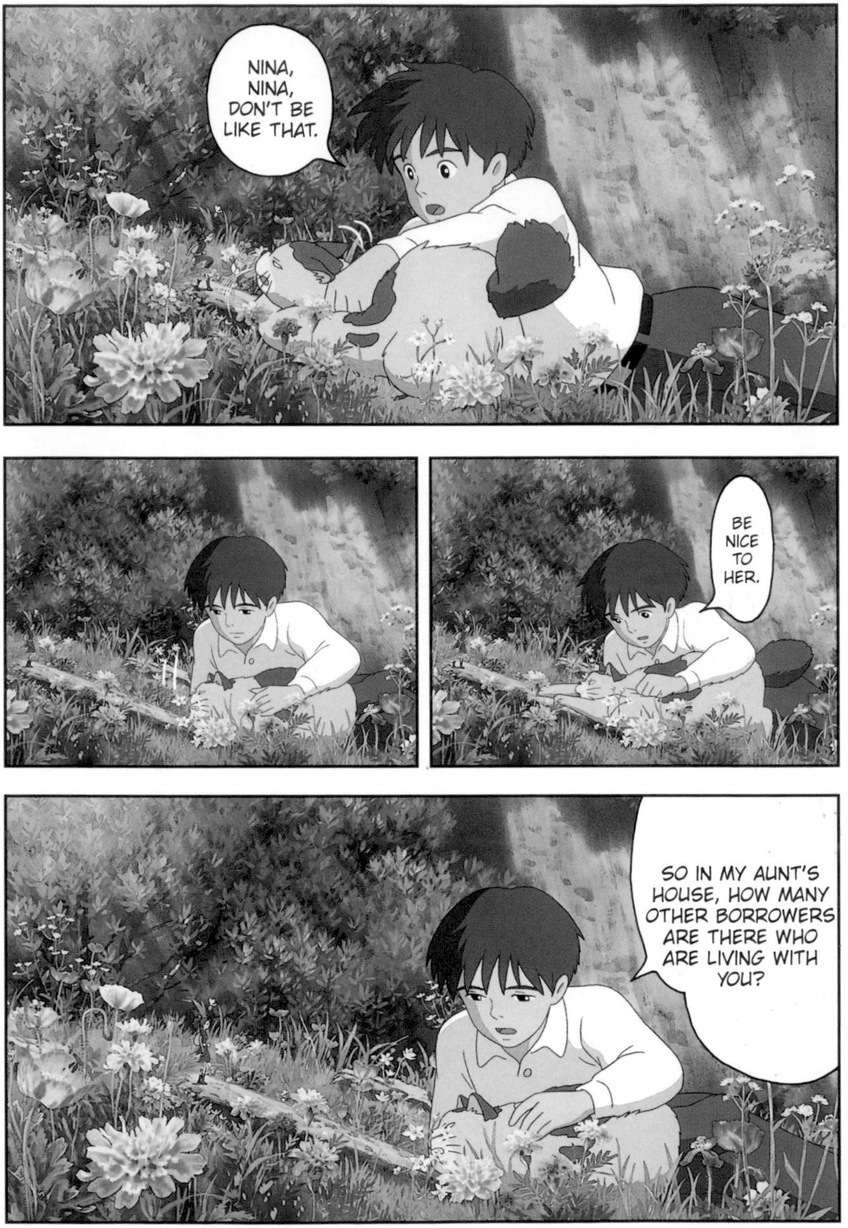
NINA, NINA, DON'T BE LIKE THAT.
BE NICE TO HER.
SO IN MY AUNT'S HOUSE, HOW MANY OTHER BORROWERS ARE THERE WHO ARE LIVING WITH YOU?

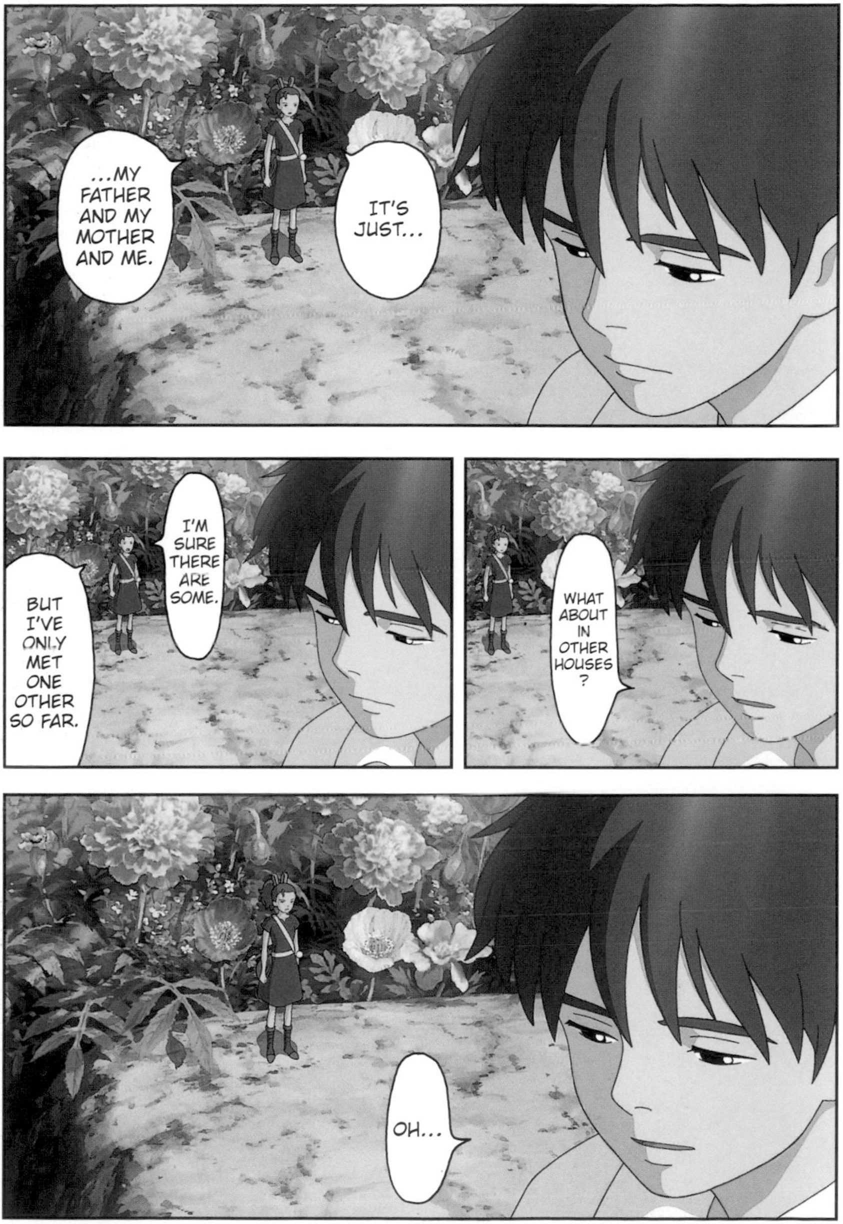
IT'S JUST...
...MY FATHER AND MY MOTHER AND ME.
WHAT ABOUT IN OTHER HOUSES?
I'M SURE THERE ARE SOME.
BUT I'VE ONLY MET ONE OTHER SO FAR.
OH...

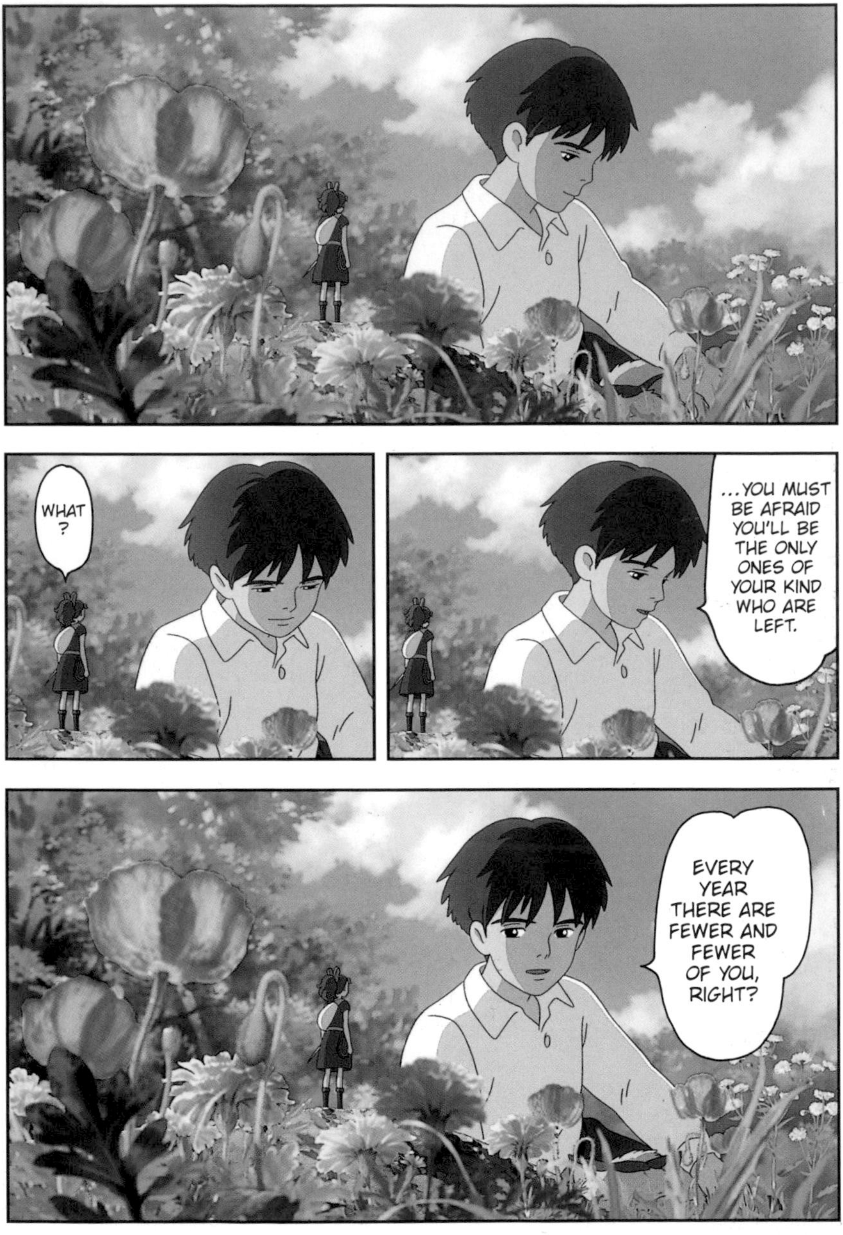
...YOU MUST BE AFRAID YOU'LL BE THE ONLY ONES OF YOUR KIND WHO ARE LEFT.
WHAT ?
EVERY YEAR THERE ARE FEWER AND FEWER OF YOU, RIGHT?

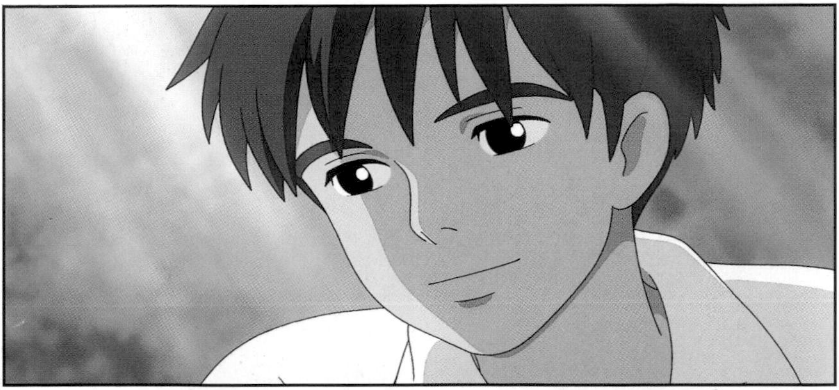
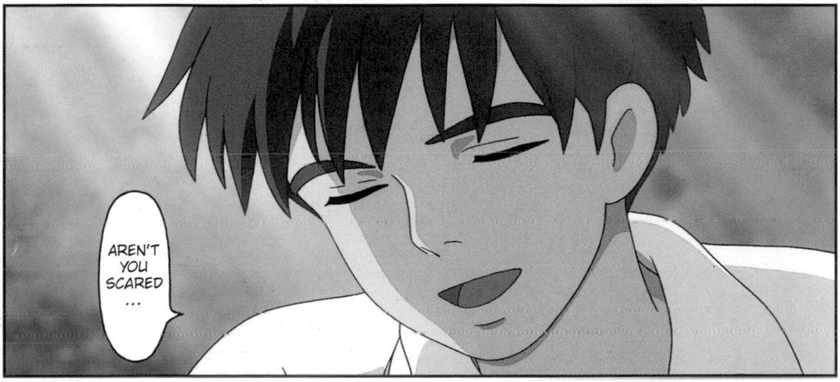
AREN'T YOU SCARED ...
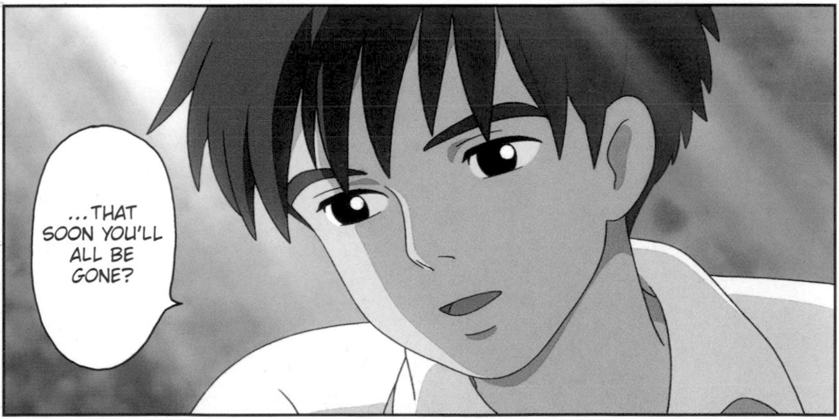
...THAT SOON YOU'LL ALL BE GONE?

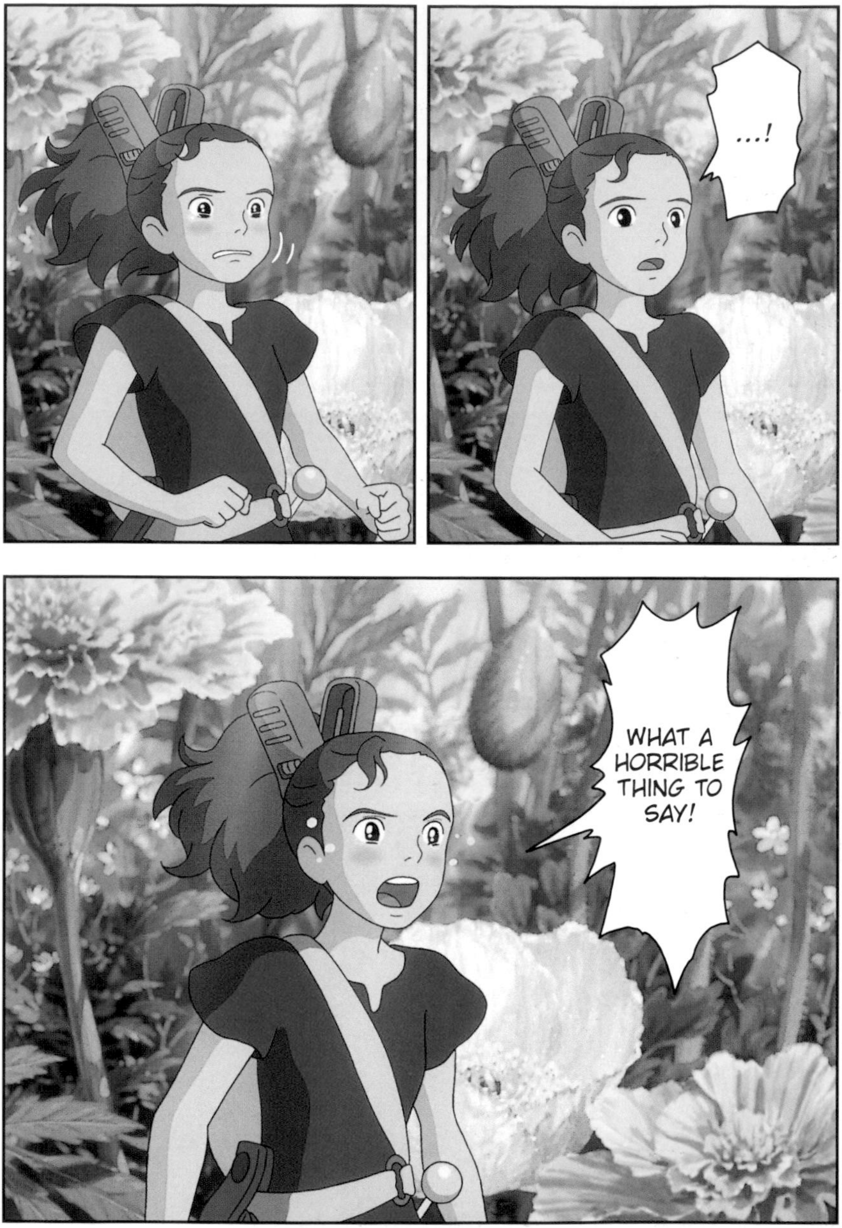
...!
WHAT A HORRIBLE THING TO SAY!

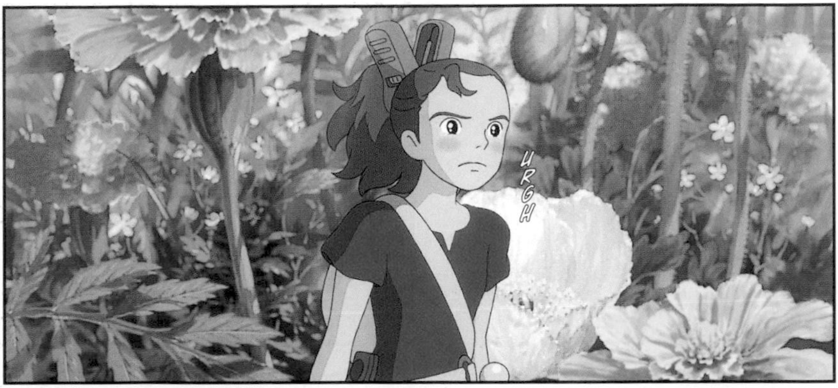
URGH

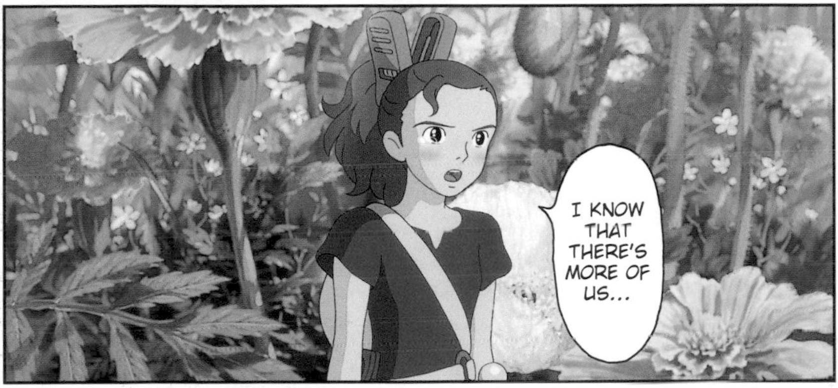
I KNOW THAT THERE'S MORE OF US...

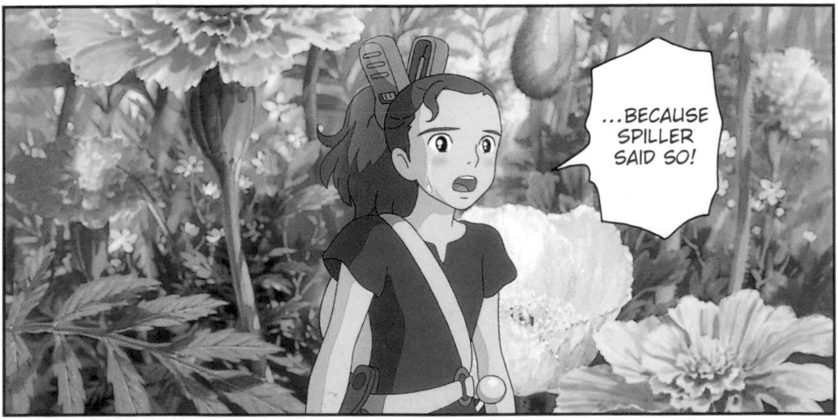
...BECAUSE SPILLER SAID SO!

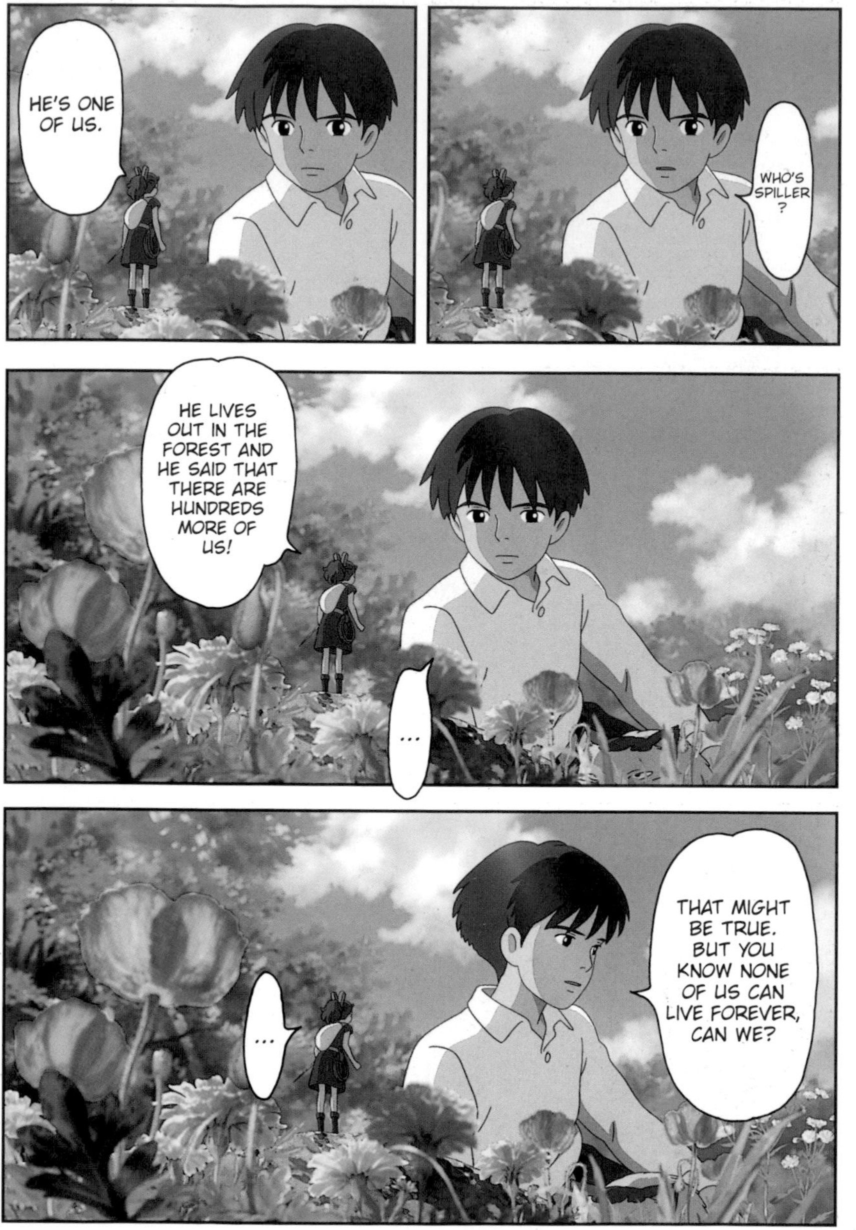
WHO'S SPILLER?
HE'S ONE OF US.
HE LIVES OUT IN THE FOREST AND HE SAID THAT THERE ARE HUNDREDS MORE OF US!
...
THAT MIGHT BE TRUE. BUT YOU KNOW NONE OF US CAN LIVE FOREVER, CAN WE?
...

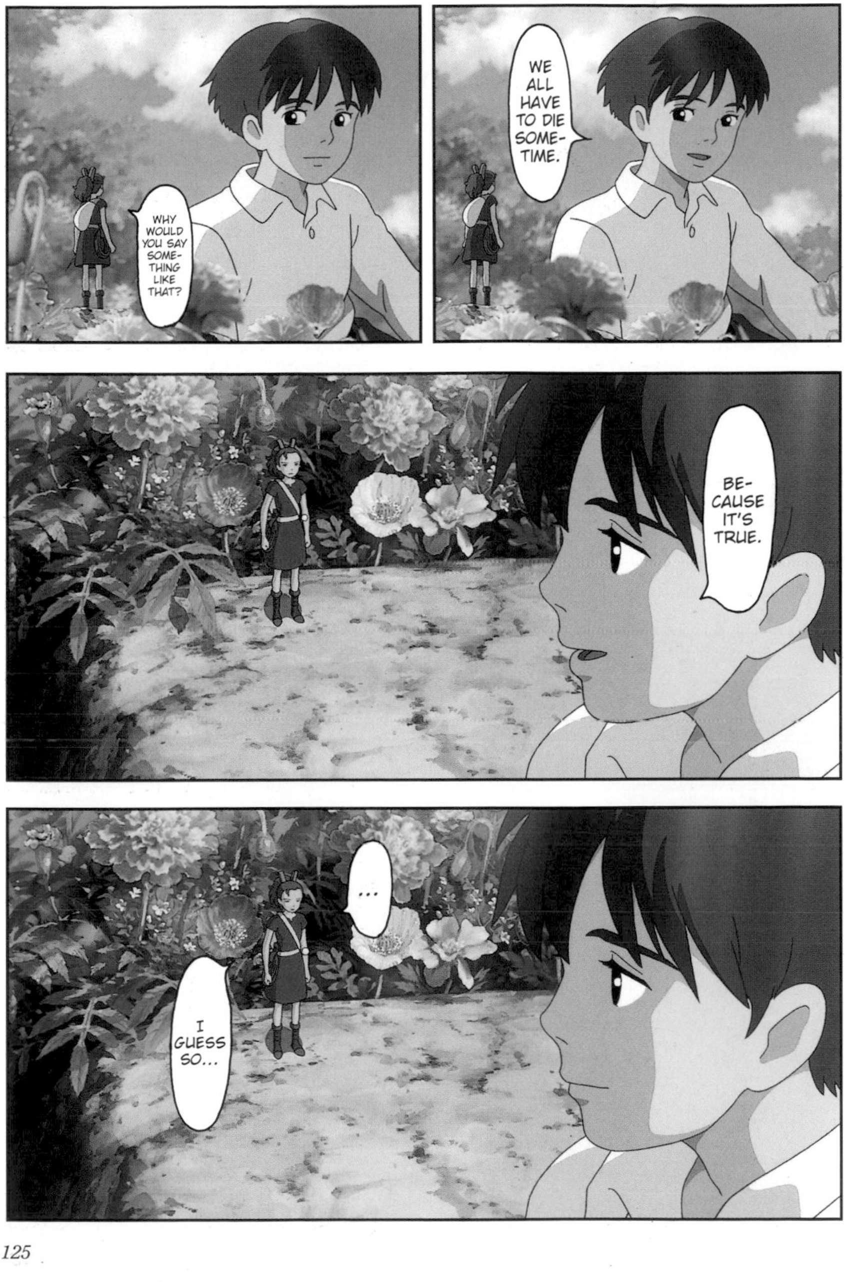
WE ALL HAVE TO DIE SOME-TIME.
WHY WOULD YOU SAY SOME-THING LIKE THAT?
BE-CAUSE IT'S TRUE.
...
I GUESS SO...

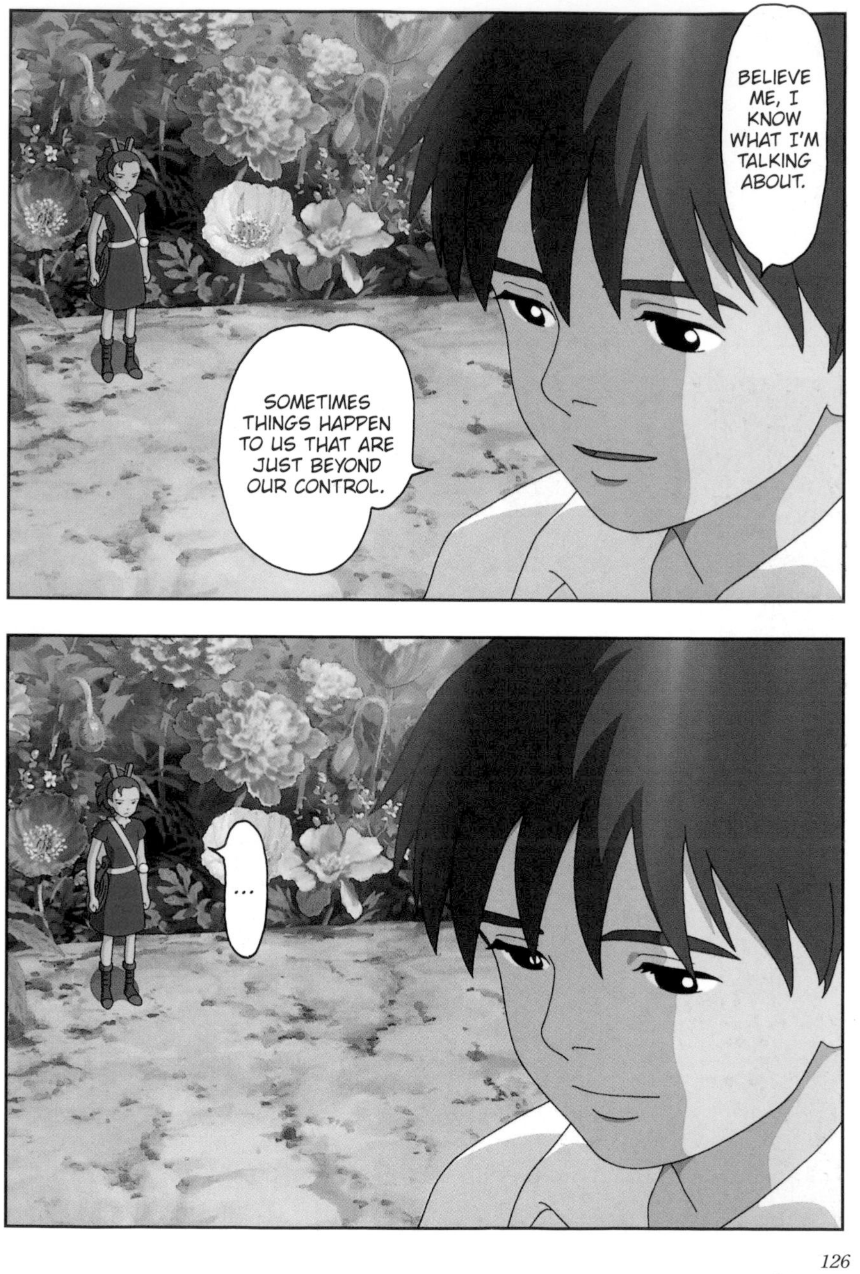
BELIEVE ME, I KNOW WHAT I'M TALKING ABOUT.
SOMETIMES THINGS HAPPEN TO US THAT ARE JUST BEYOND OUR CONTROL.
...

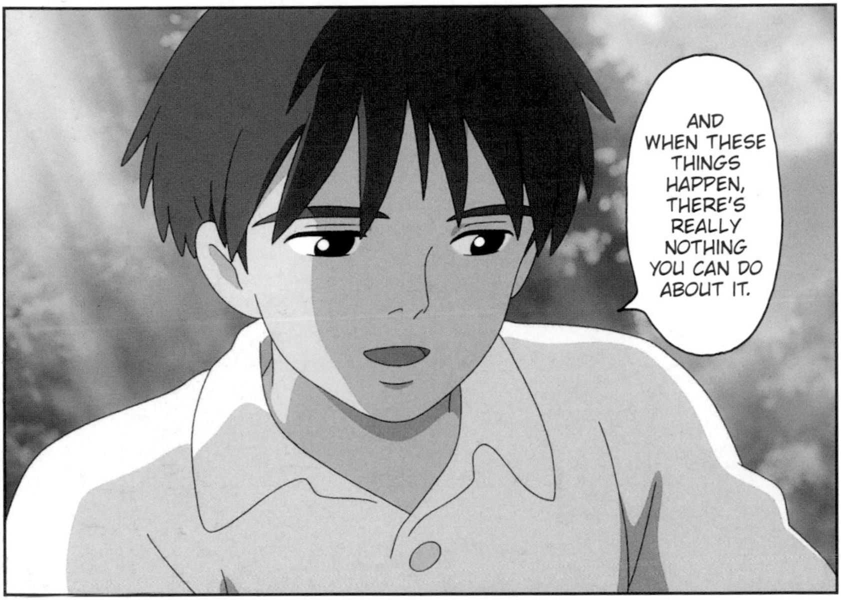
AND WHEN THESE THINGS HAPPEN, THERE'S REALLY NOTHING YOU CAN DO ABOUT IT.

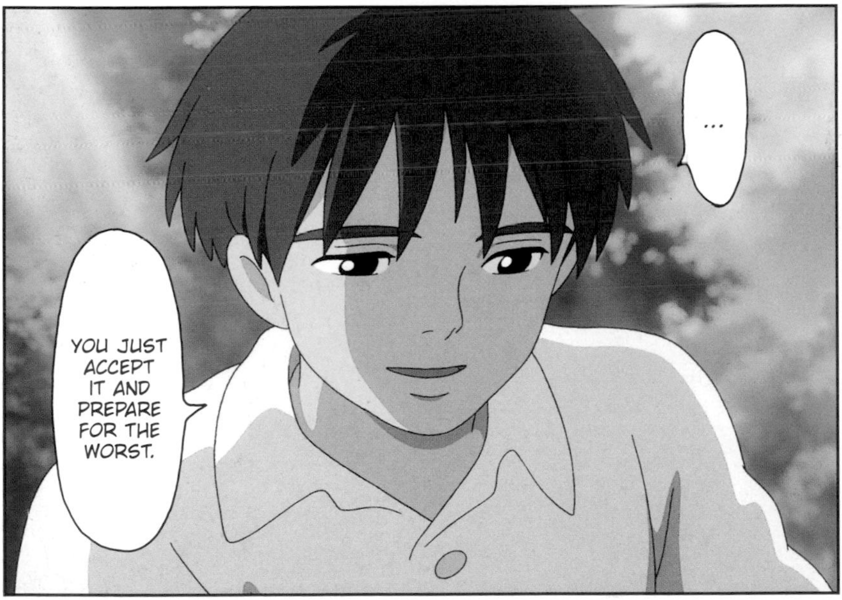
...
YOU JUST ACCEPT IT AND PREPARE FOR THE WORST.

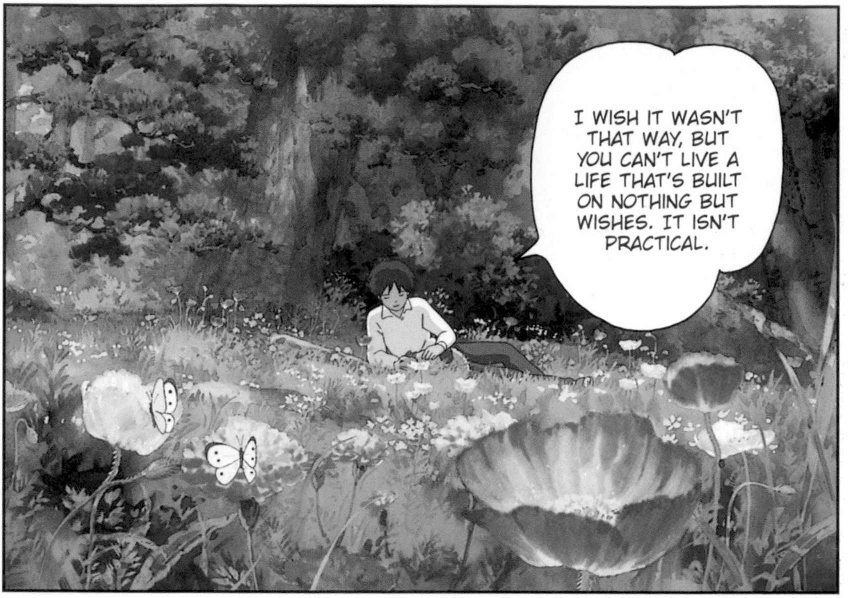
I WISH IT WASN'T THAT WAY, BUT YOU CAN'T LIVE A LIFE THAT'S BUILT ON NOTHING BUT WISHES. IT ISN'T PRACTICAL.

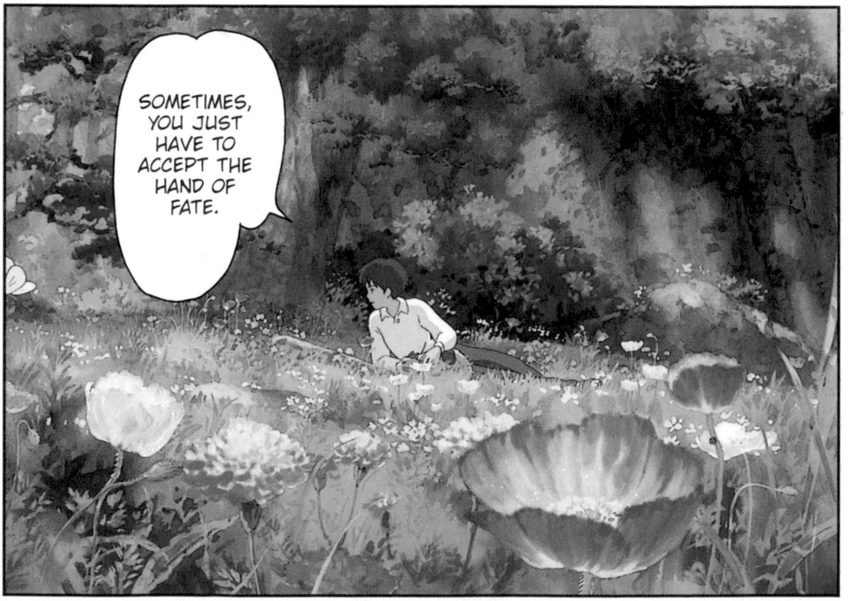
SOMETIMES, YOU JUST HAVE TO ACCEPT THE HAND OF FATE.

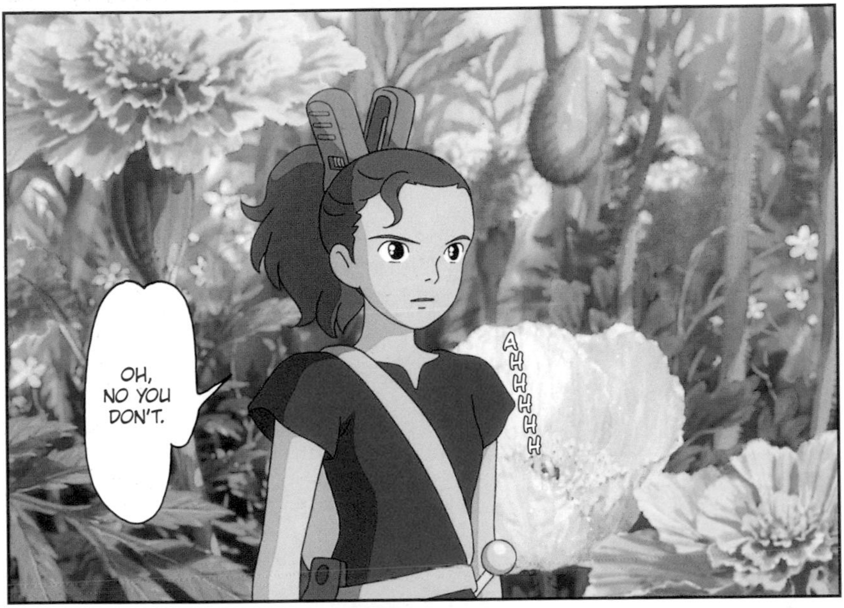
AHHHHHH
OH, NO YOU DON'T.

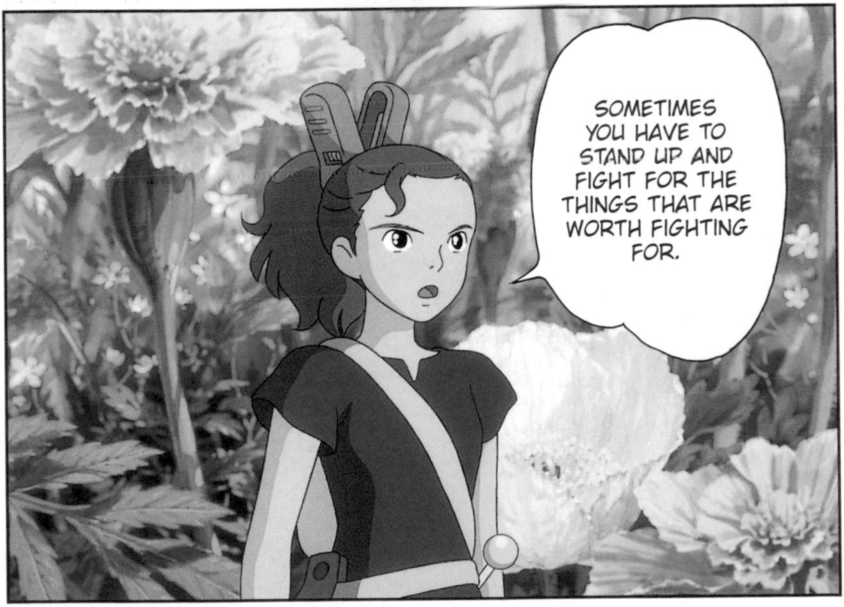
SOMETIMES YOU HAVE TO STAND UP AND FIGHT FOR THE THINGS THAT ARE WORTH FIGHTING FOR.

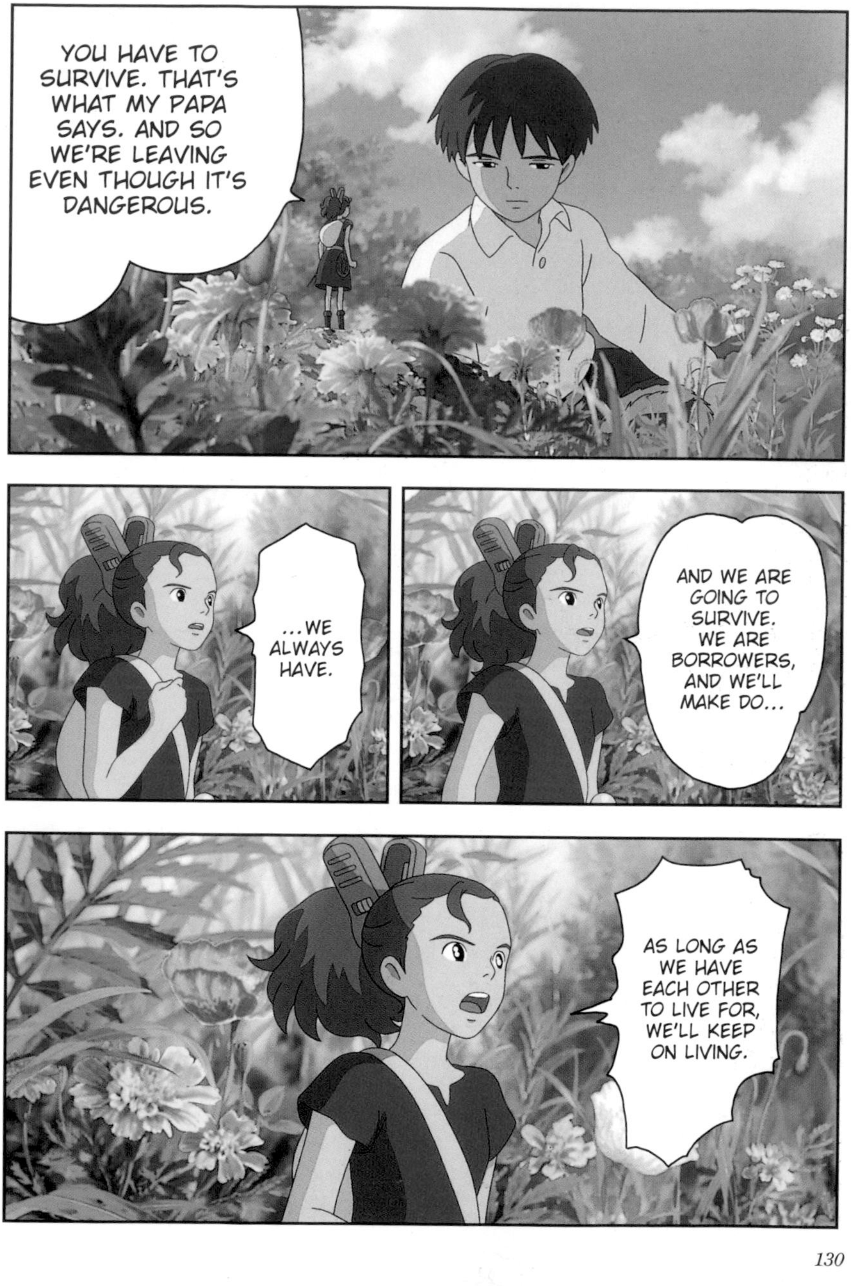
YOU HAVE TO SURVIVE. THAT'S WHAT MY PAPA SAYS. AND SO WE'RE LEAVING EVEN THOUGH IT'S DANGEROUS.
AND WE ARE GOING TO SURVIVE. WE ARE BORROWERS, AND WE'LL MAKE DO...
...WE ALWAYS HAVE.
AS LONG AS WE HAVE EACH OTHER TO LIVE FOR, WE'LL KEEP ON LIVING.

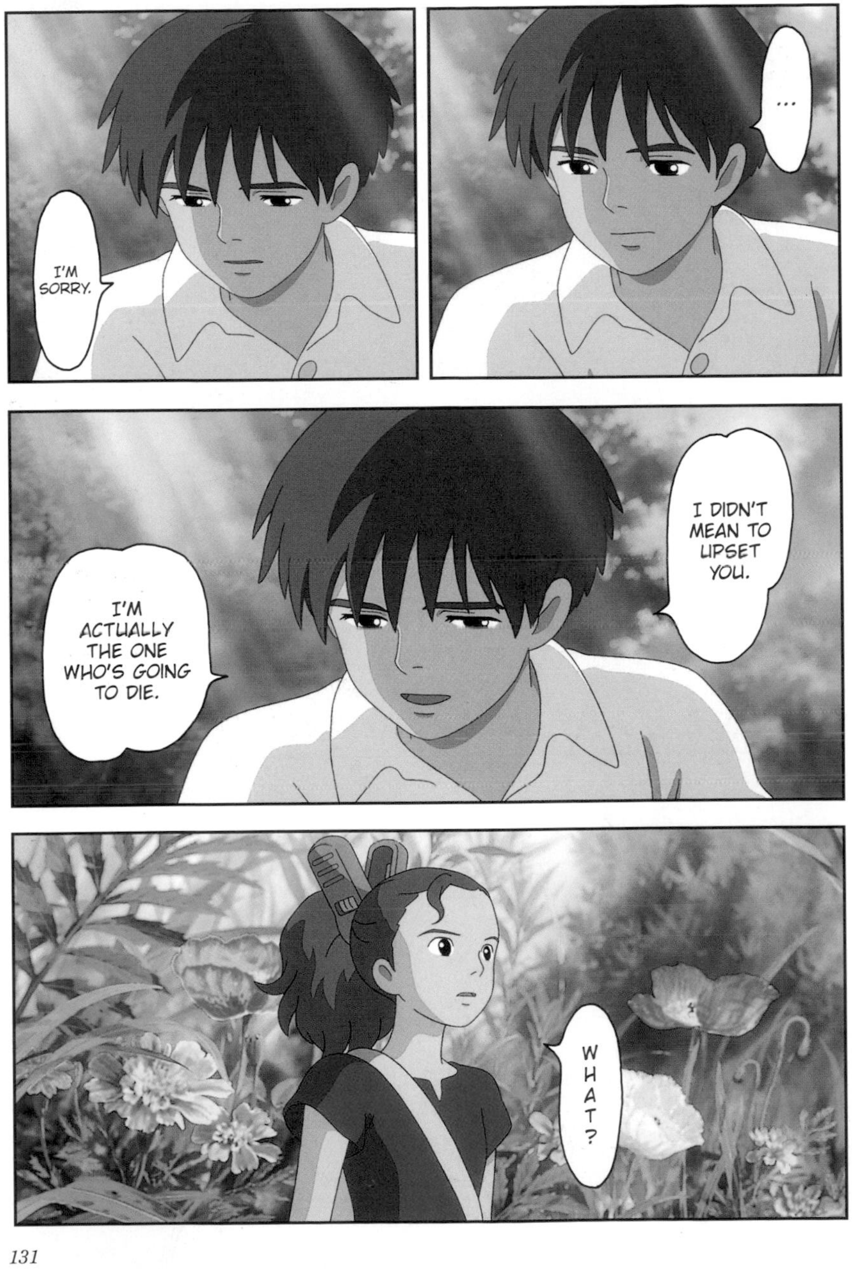
...
I'M SORRY.
I DIDN'T MEAN TO UPSET YOU.
I'M ACTUALLY THE ONE WHO'S GOING TO DIE.
WHAT?

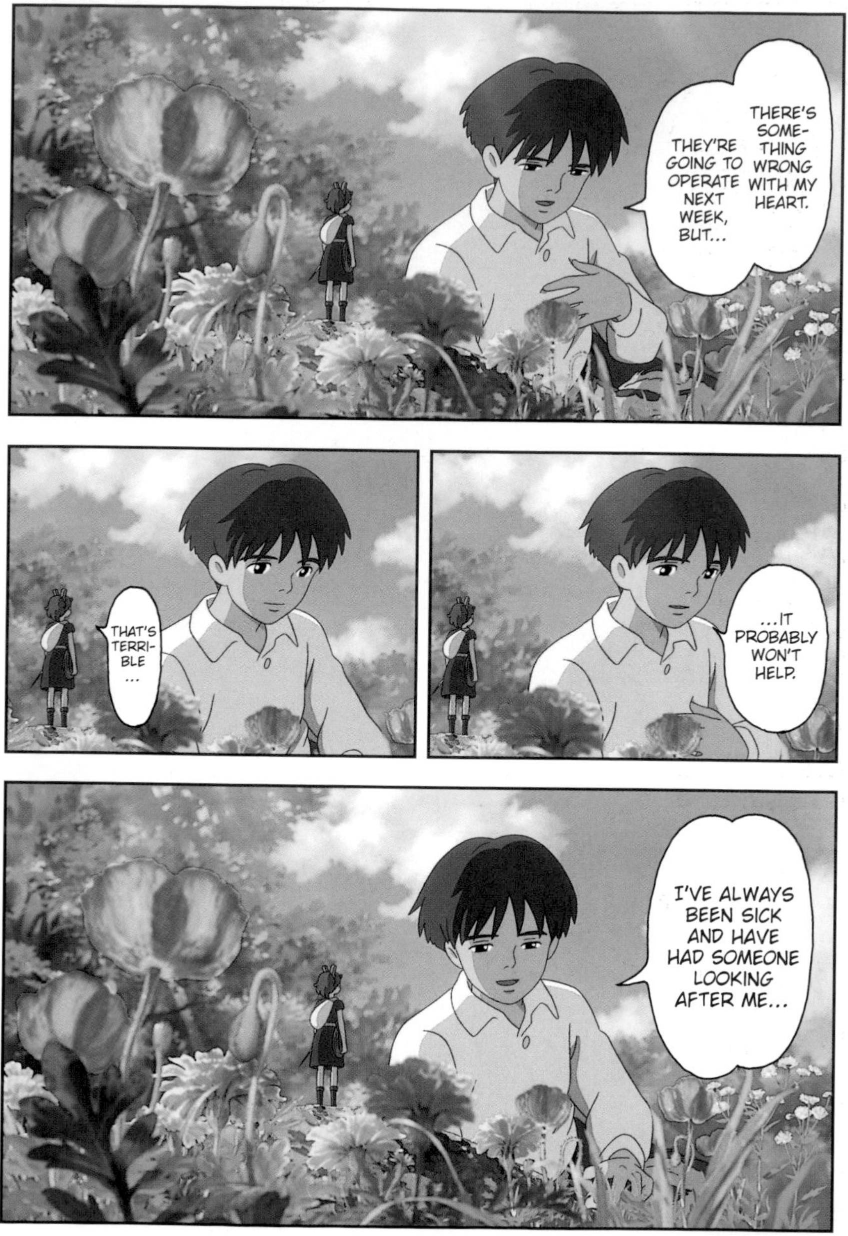
THERE'S SOME-THING WRONG WITH MY HEART.
THEY'RE GOING TO OPERATE NEXT WEEK, BUT...
...IT PROBABLY WON'T HELP.
THAT'S TERRI-BLE...
I'VE ALWAYS BEEN SICK AND HAVE HAD SOMEONE LOOKING AFTER ME...

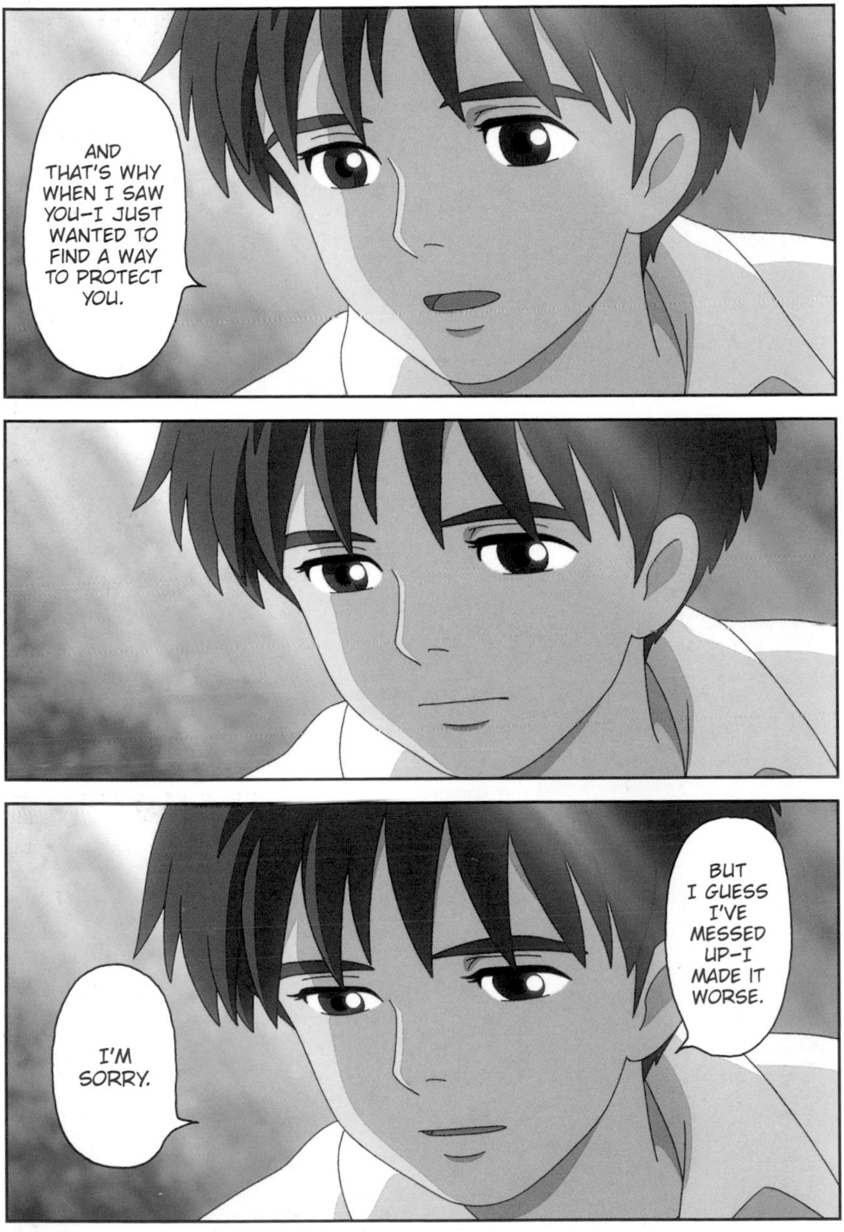
AND THAT'S WHY WHEN I SAW YOU—I JUST WANTED TO FIND A WAY TO PROTECT YOU.
BUT I GUESS I'VE MESSED UP—I MADE IT WORSE.
I'M SORRY.

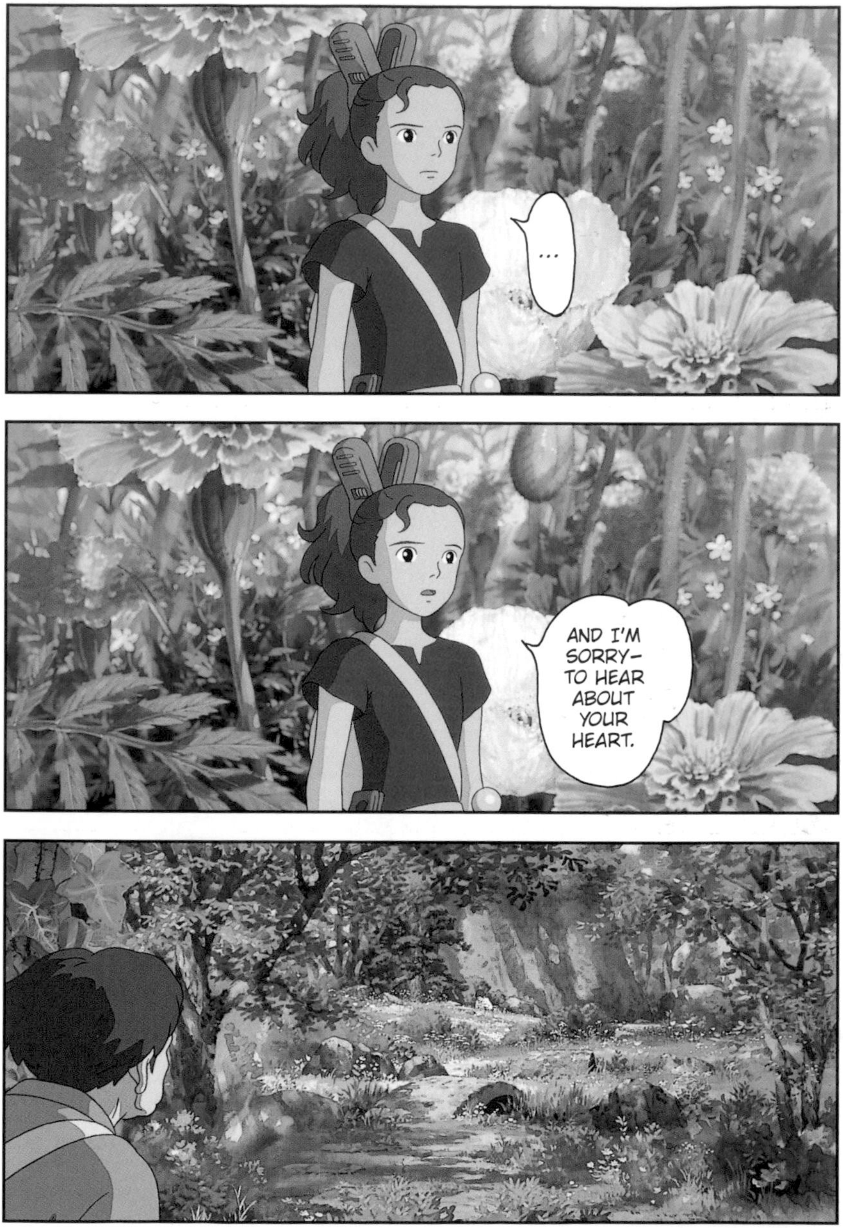
...
AND I'M SORRY— TO HEAR ABOUT YOUR HEART.

HMMM?
HMMM?

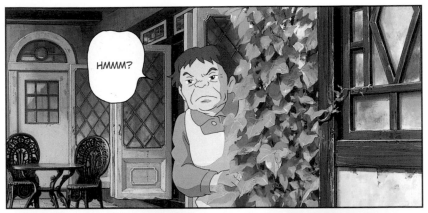

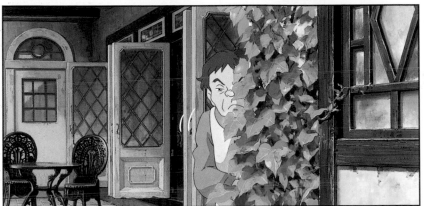

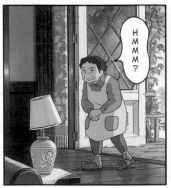

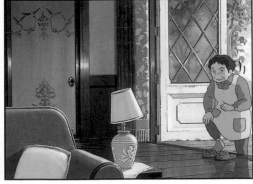

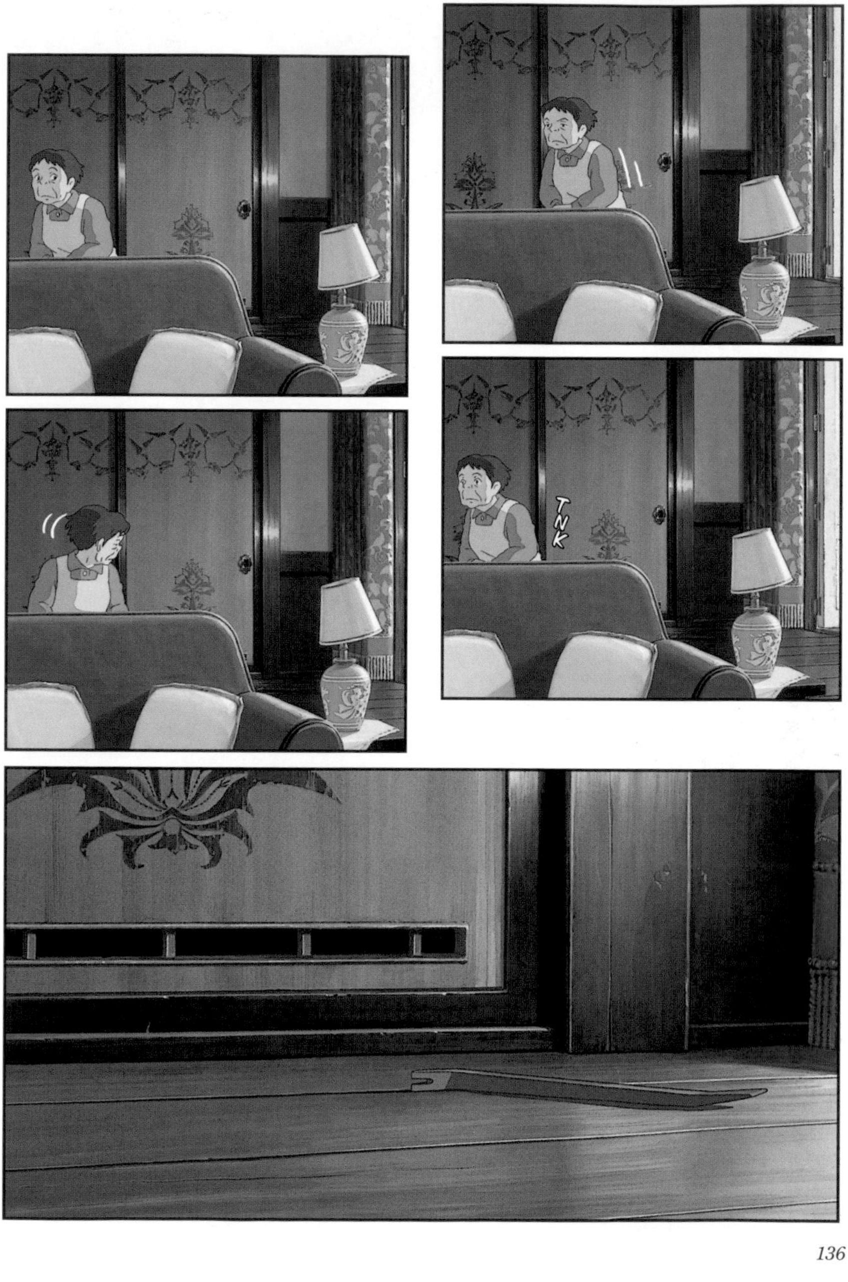
TNK

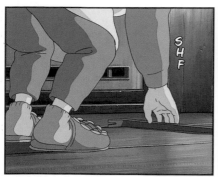

NOW WHAT ON EARTH IS THIS DOING HERE?

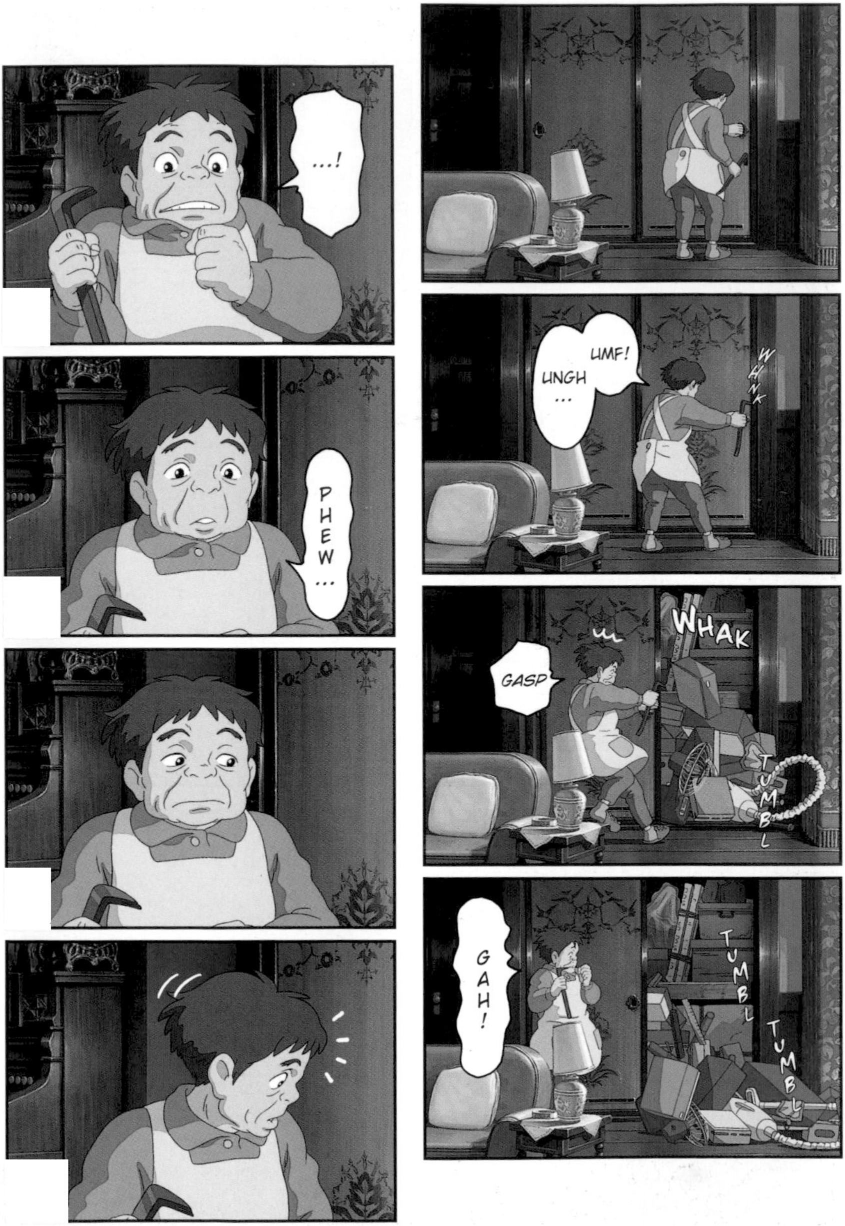

UMF!
UNGH ...
WHNK
WHAK
GASP
TUMBL
GAH!
TUMBL
TUMBL
...!
PHEW...

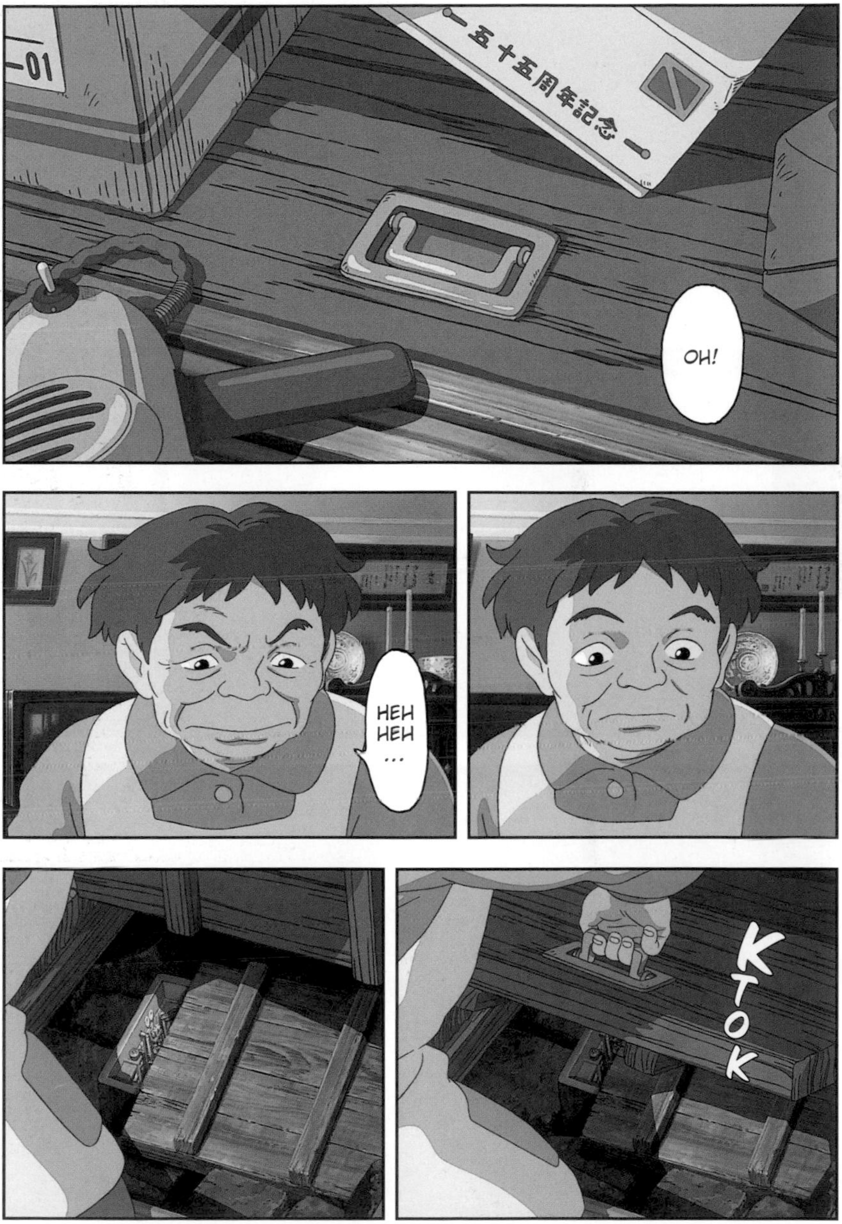
五十五周年記念
01
OH!
HEH HEH ...
KTOK

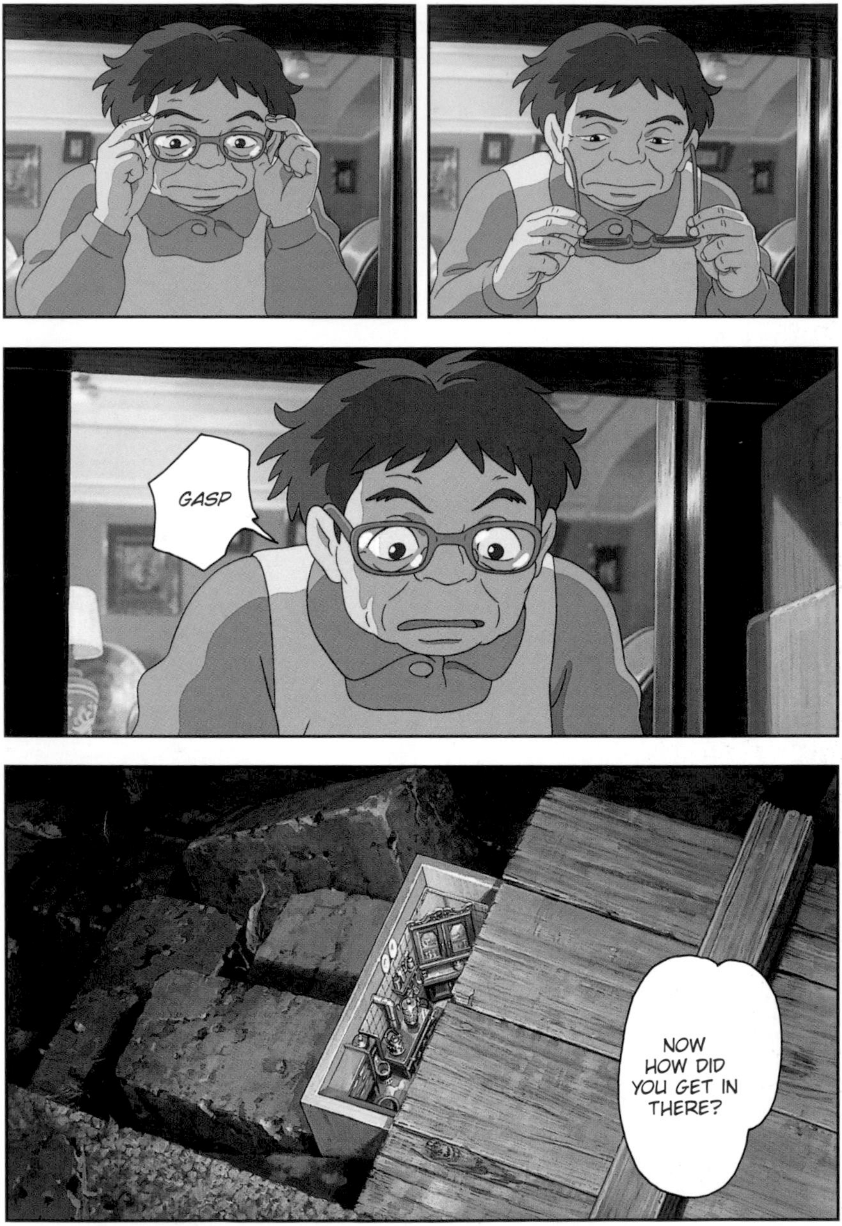
GASP
NOW HOW DID YOU GET IN THERE?

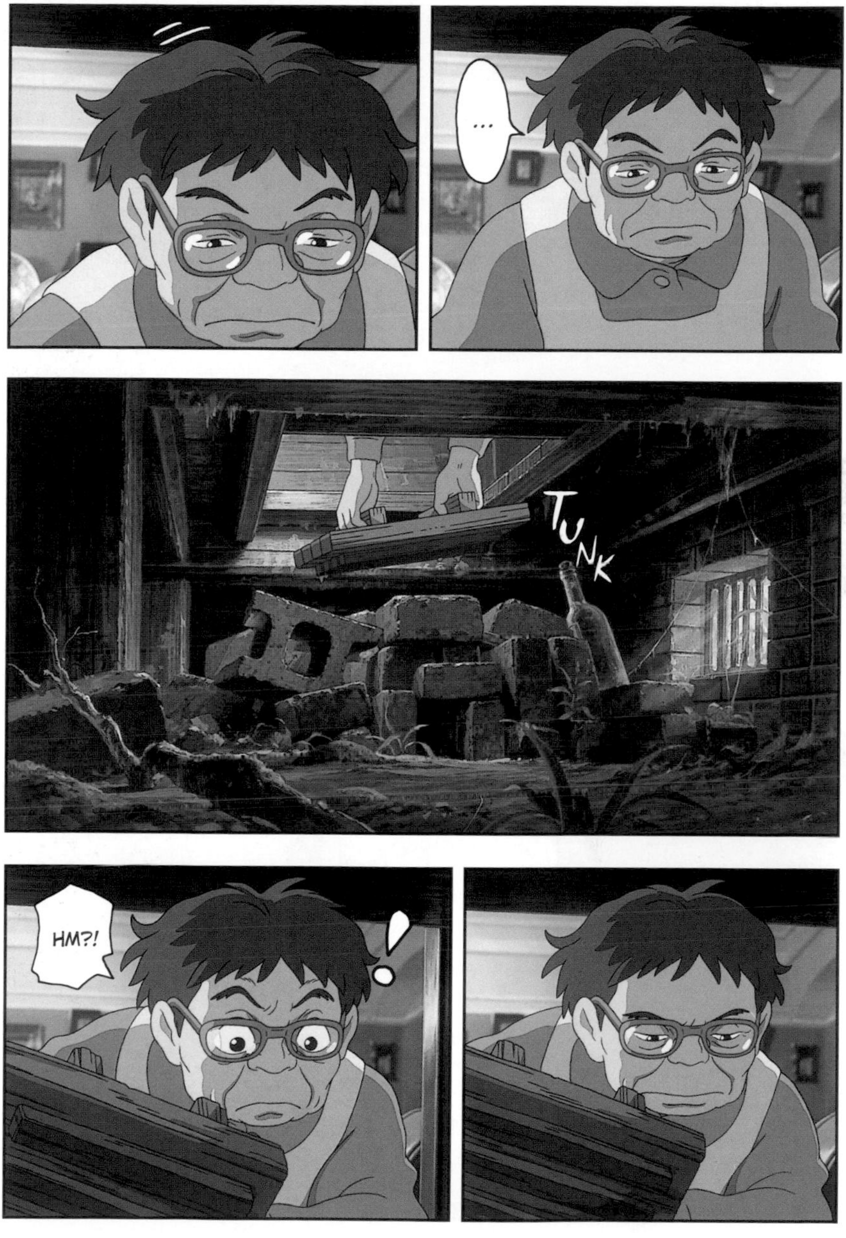
...
TUNK
HM?!
!

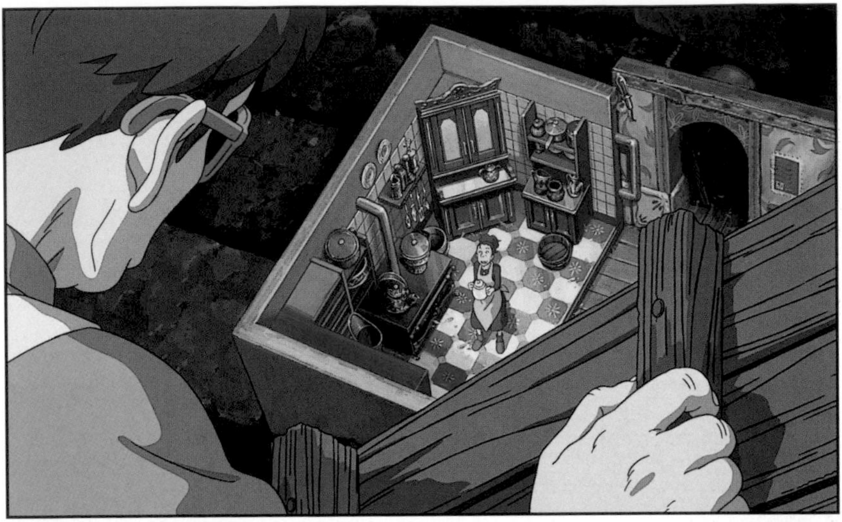

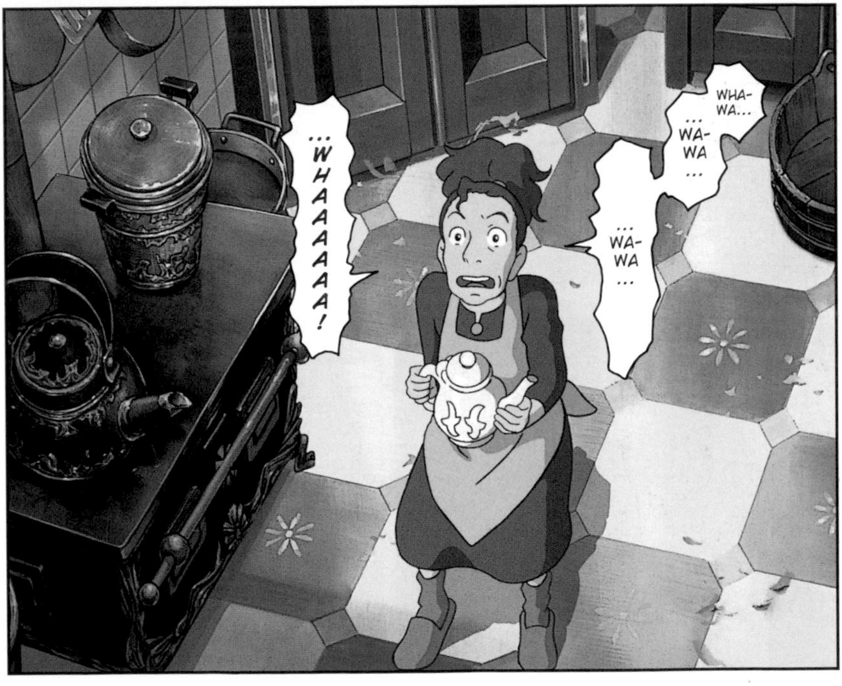
WHA-WA... ...WA-WA...
...WA-WA...
...WHAAAAAAA!

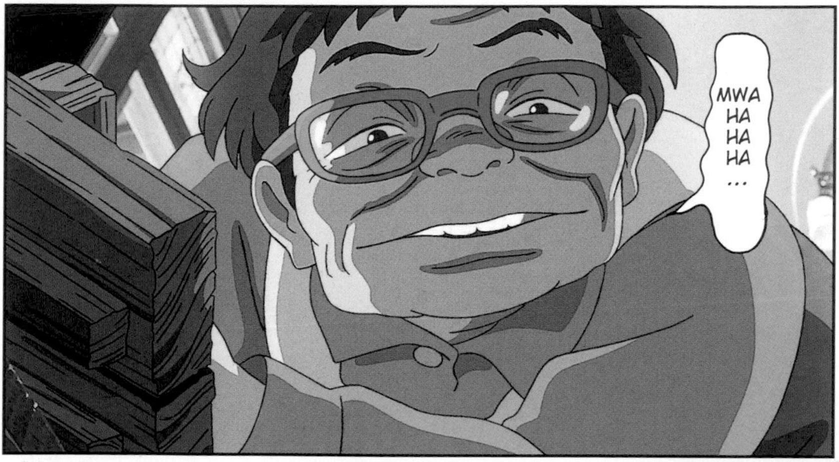
MWA HA HA HA ...

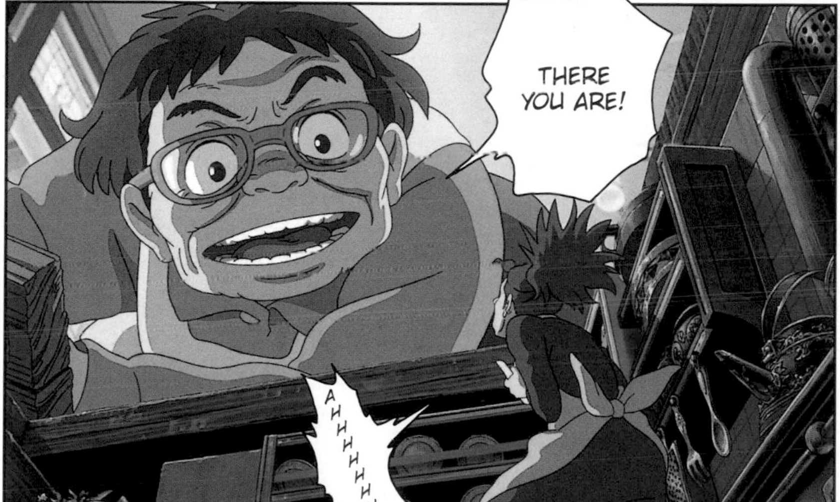
THERE YOU ARE!
AHHHHHHHHHHHH!!!

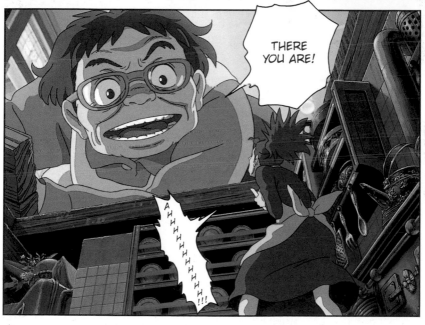

The Secret World of
Arrietty

Planning by **Hayao Miyazaki**
Based on *The Borrowers* by **Mary Norton**
Original Screenplay by **Hayao Miyazaki** and **Keiko Niwa**
Directed by **Hiromasa Yonebayashi**

Chapter 4

スタジオジブリ作品
STUDIO GHIBLI

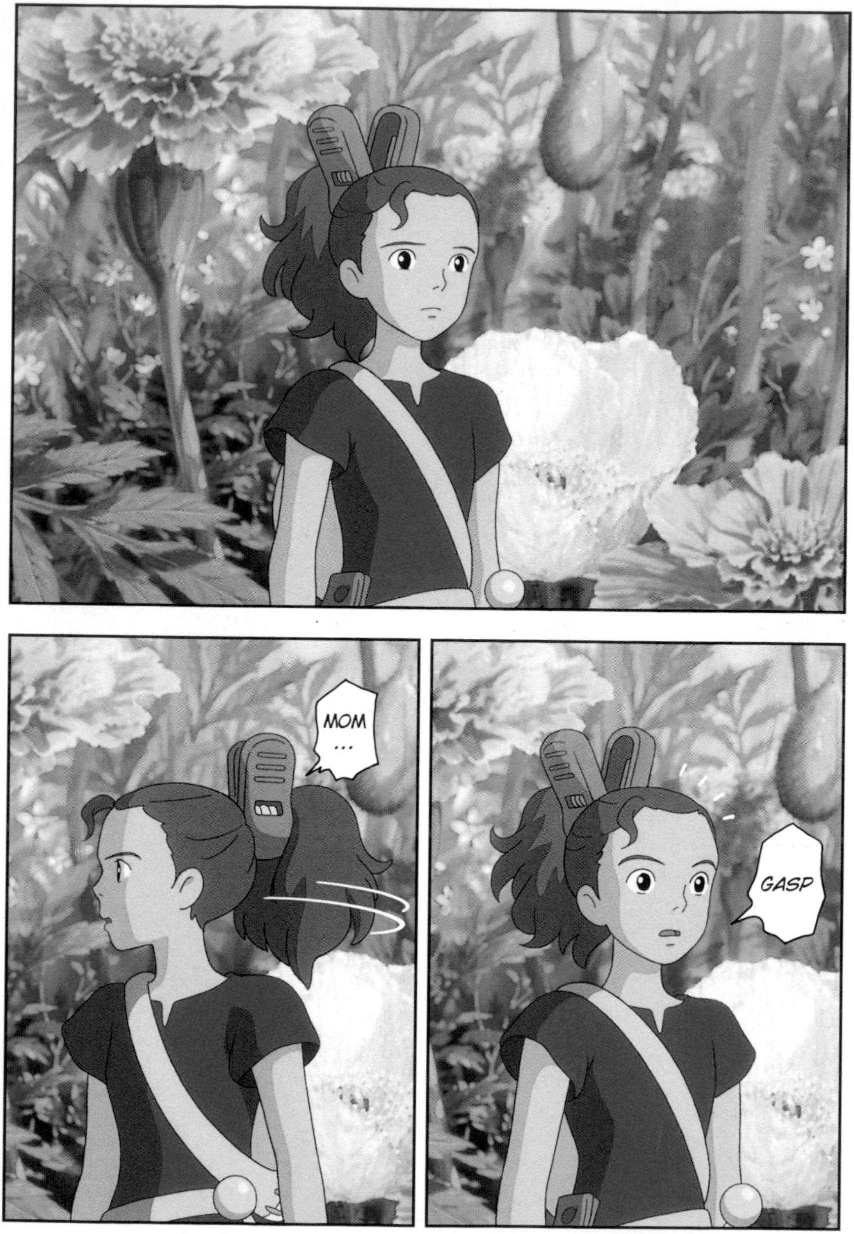
GASP
MOM ...

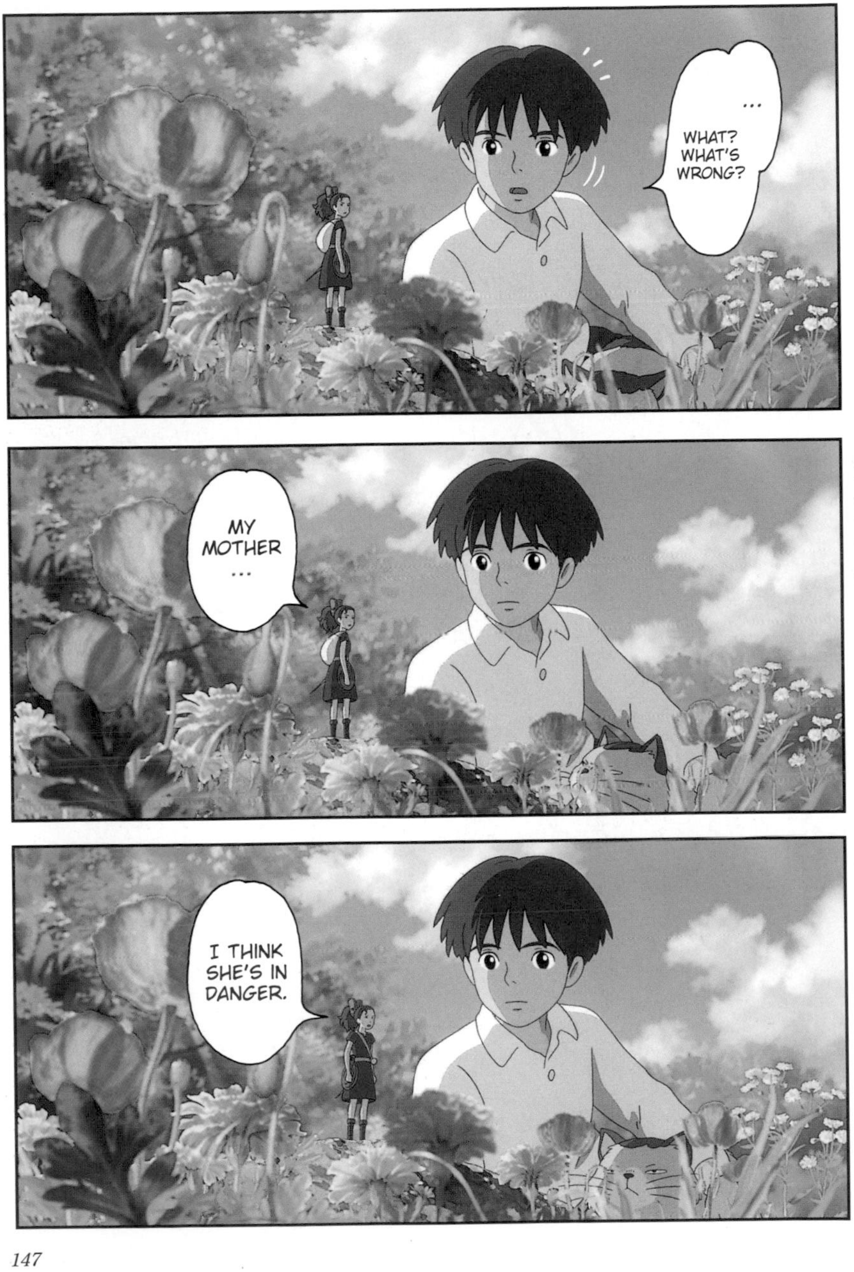
...
WHAT? WHAT'S WRONG?
MY MOTHER ...
I THINK SHE'S IN DANGER.

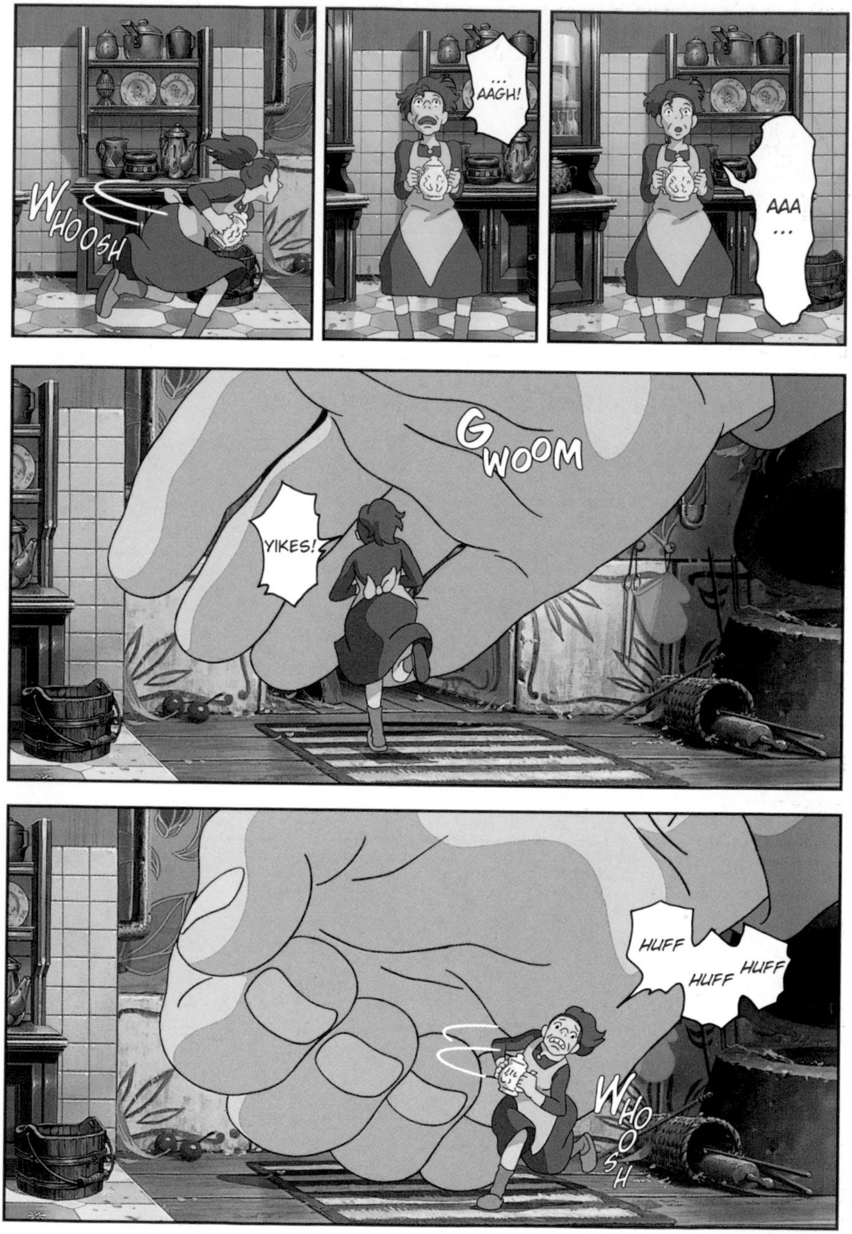
AAA ...
... AAGH!
WHOOSH
GWOOM
YIKES!
HUFF HUFF HUFF
WHOOSH

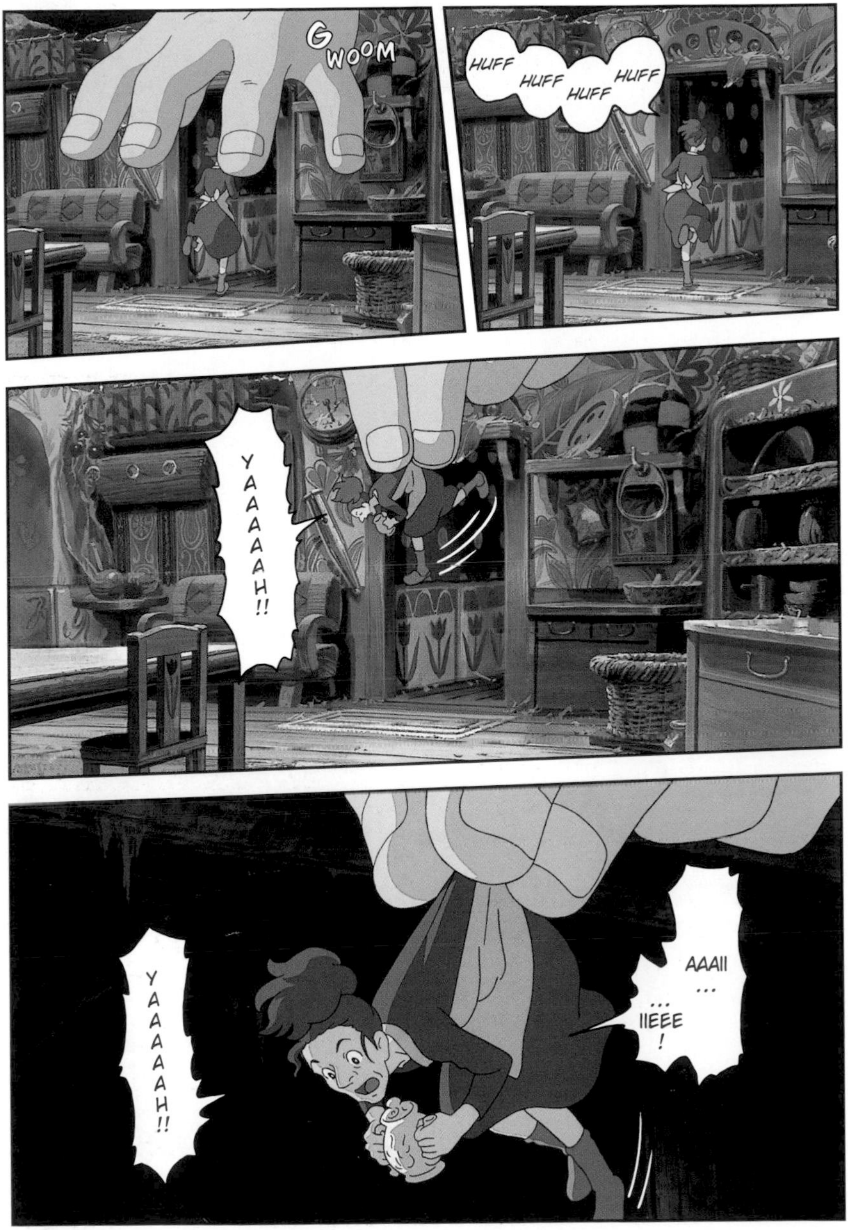
HUFF HUFF HUFF HUFF
G WOOM
YAAAAAH!!
AAAII ... ... IIEEE !
YAAAAAH!!

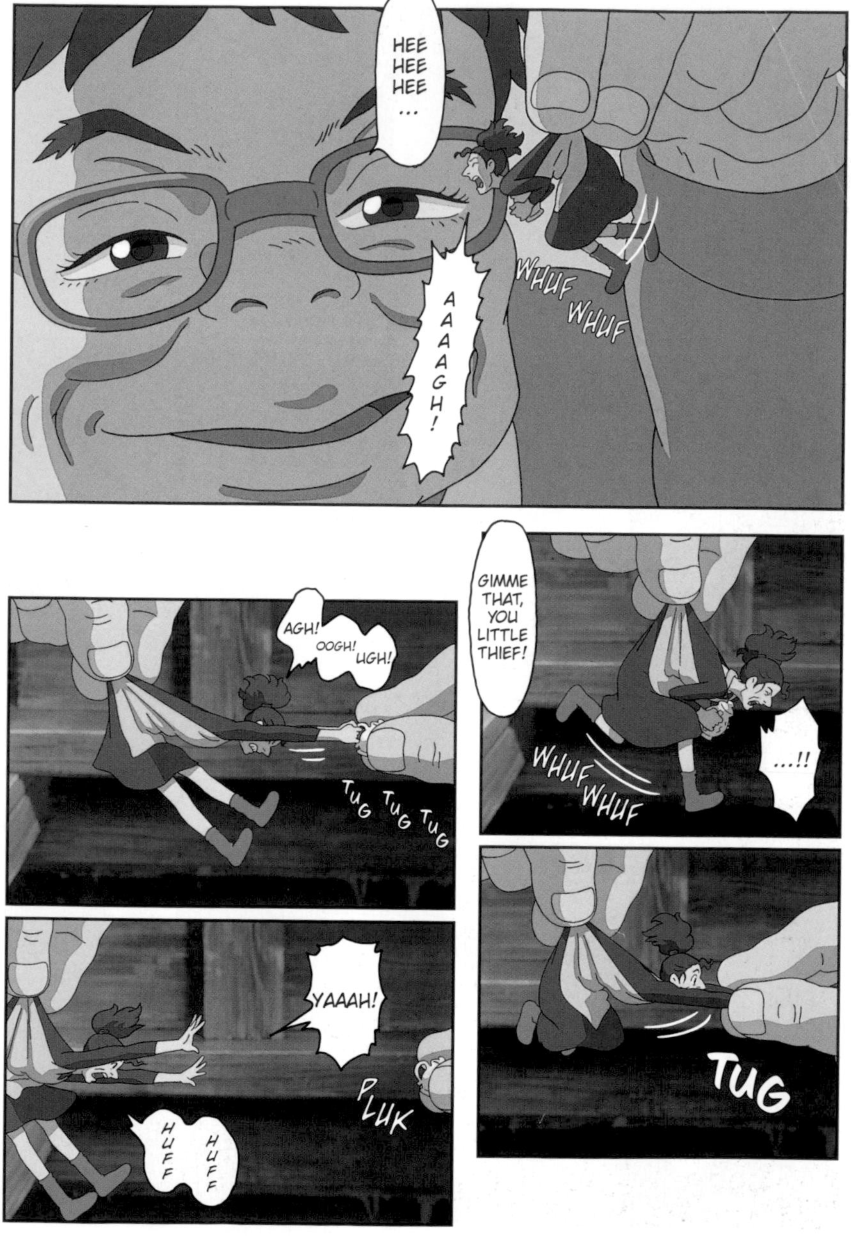
HEE HEE HEE ...
AAAAAGH!
WHUF WHUF
GIMME THAT, YOU LITTLE THIEF!
WHUF WHUF
...!!
AGH! OOGH! UGH!
TUG TUG TUG
TUG
YAAAH!
PLUK
HUFF HUFF

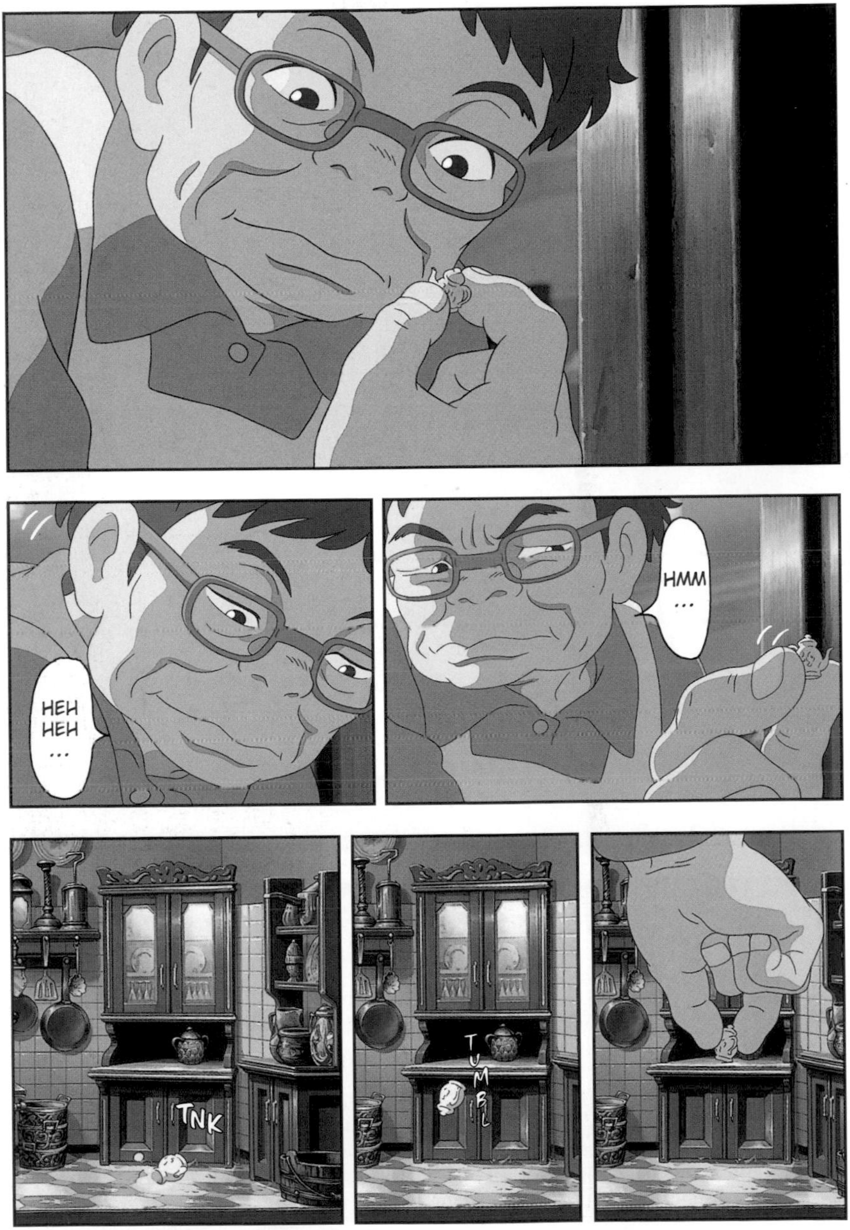
HMM ...
HEH HEH ...
TUMBL
TNK

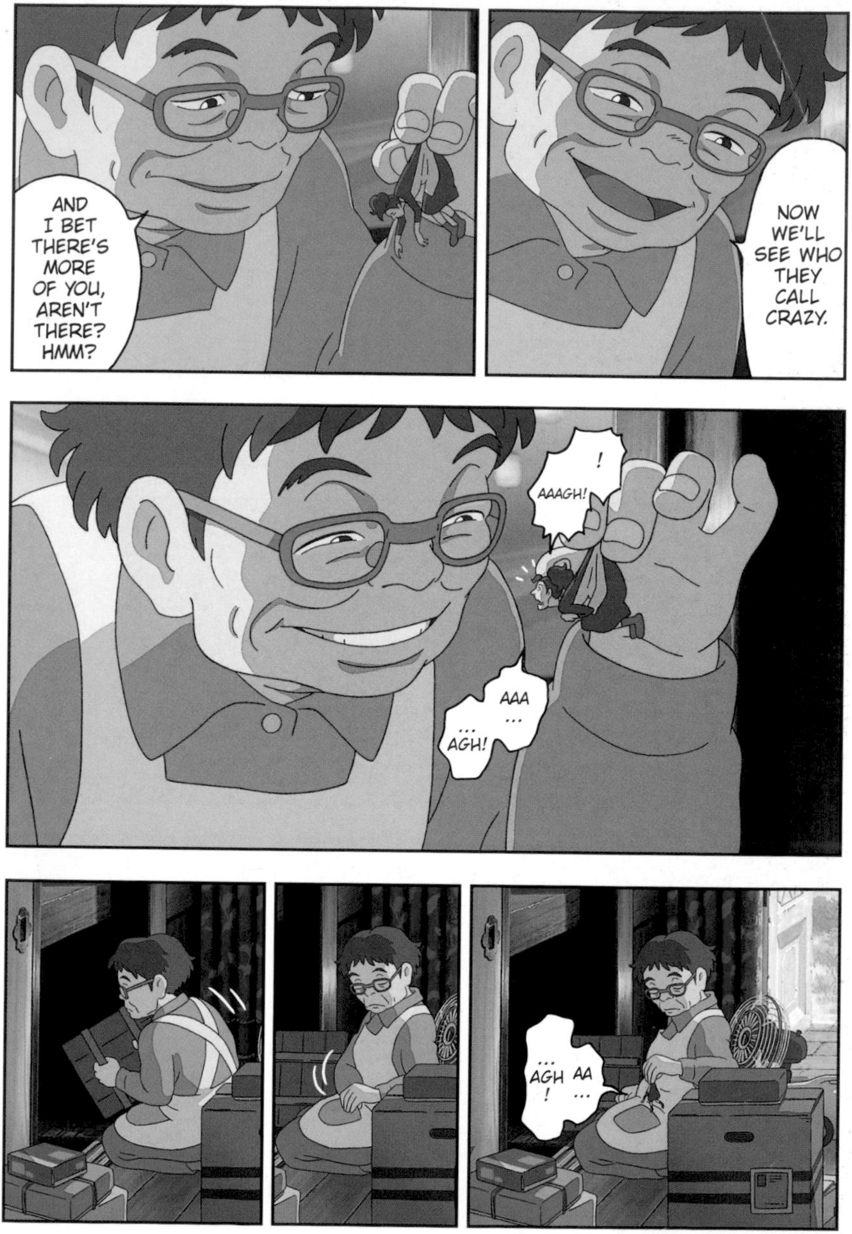
NOW WE'LL SEE WHO THEY CALL CRAZY.
AND I BET THERE'S MORE OF YOU, AREN'T THERE? HMM?
!
AAAGH!
AAA... ...AGH!
AA... ...AGH!

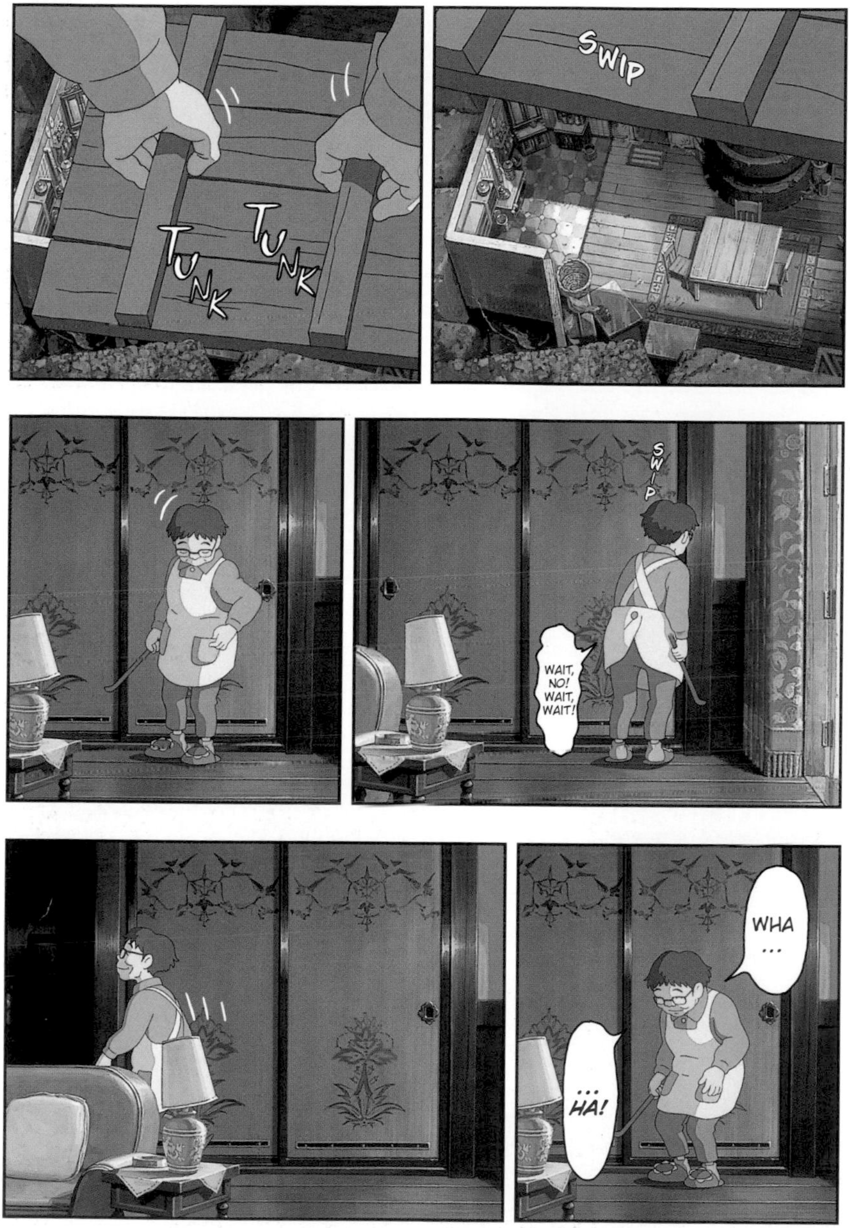
SWIP
TUNK
TUNK
SWIP
WAIT, NO! WAIT, WAIT!
WHA ...
...HA!

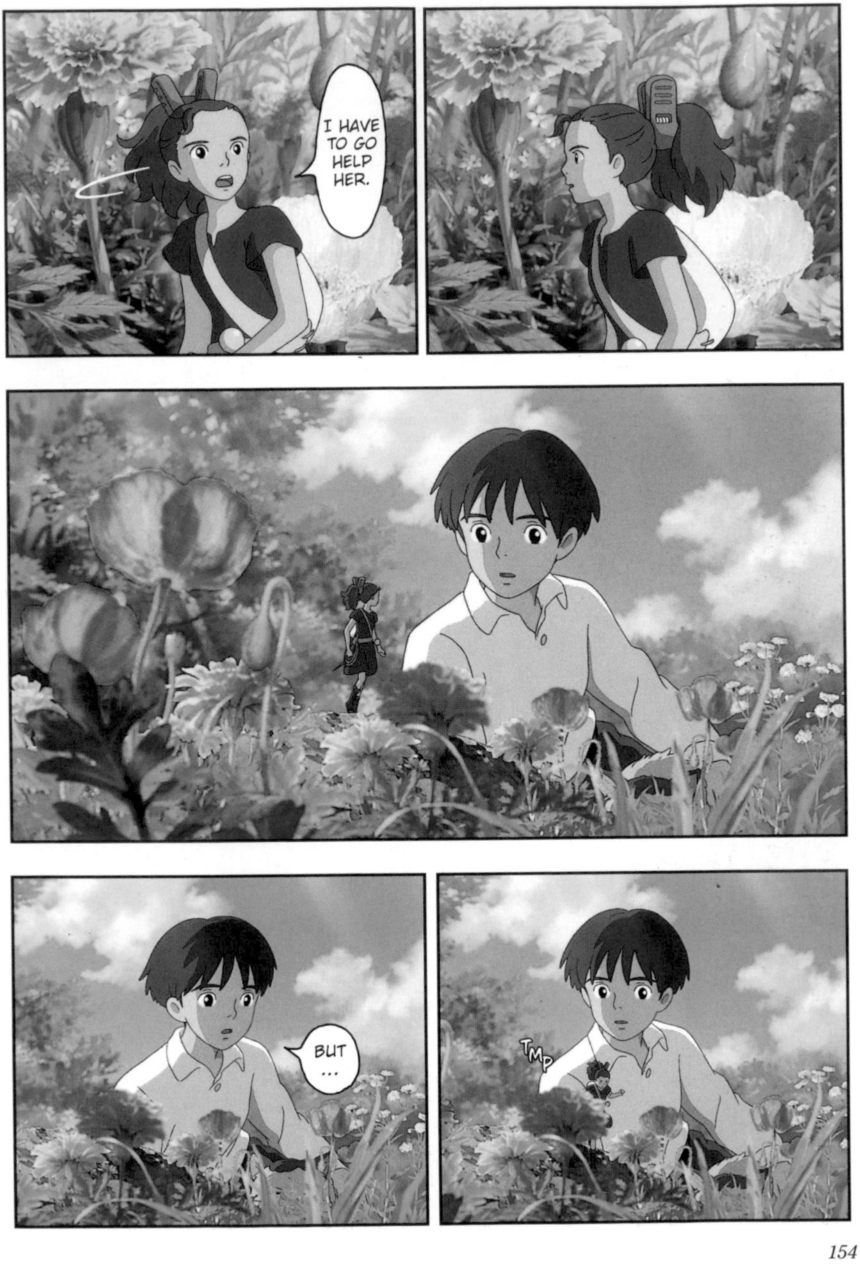
I HAVE TO GO HELP HER.
TMP
BUT ...

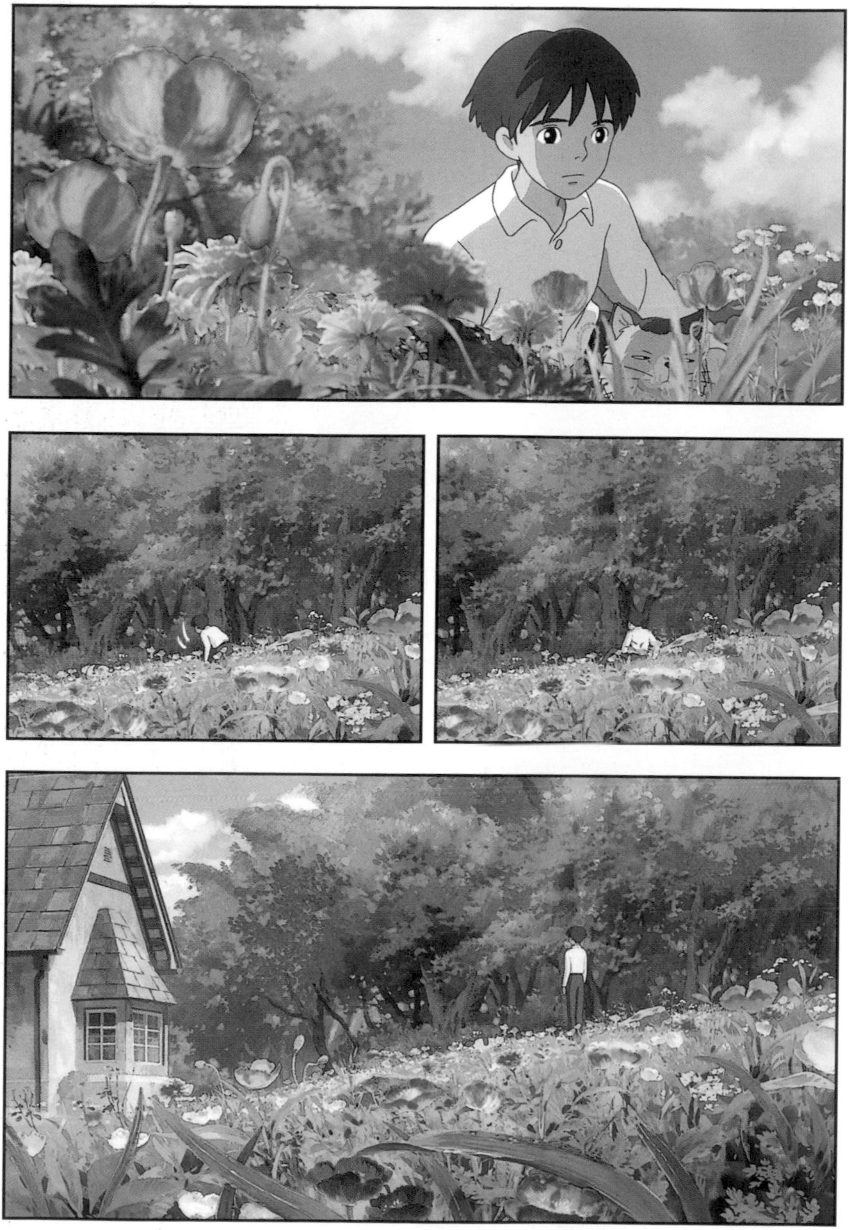

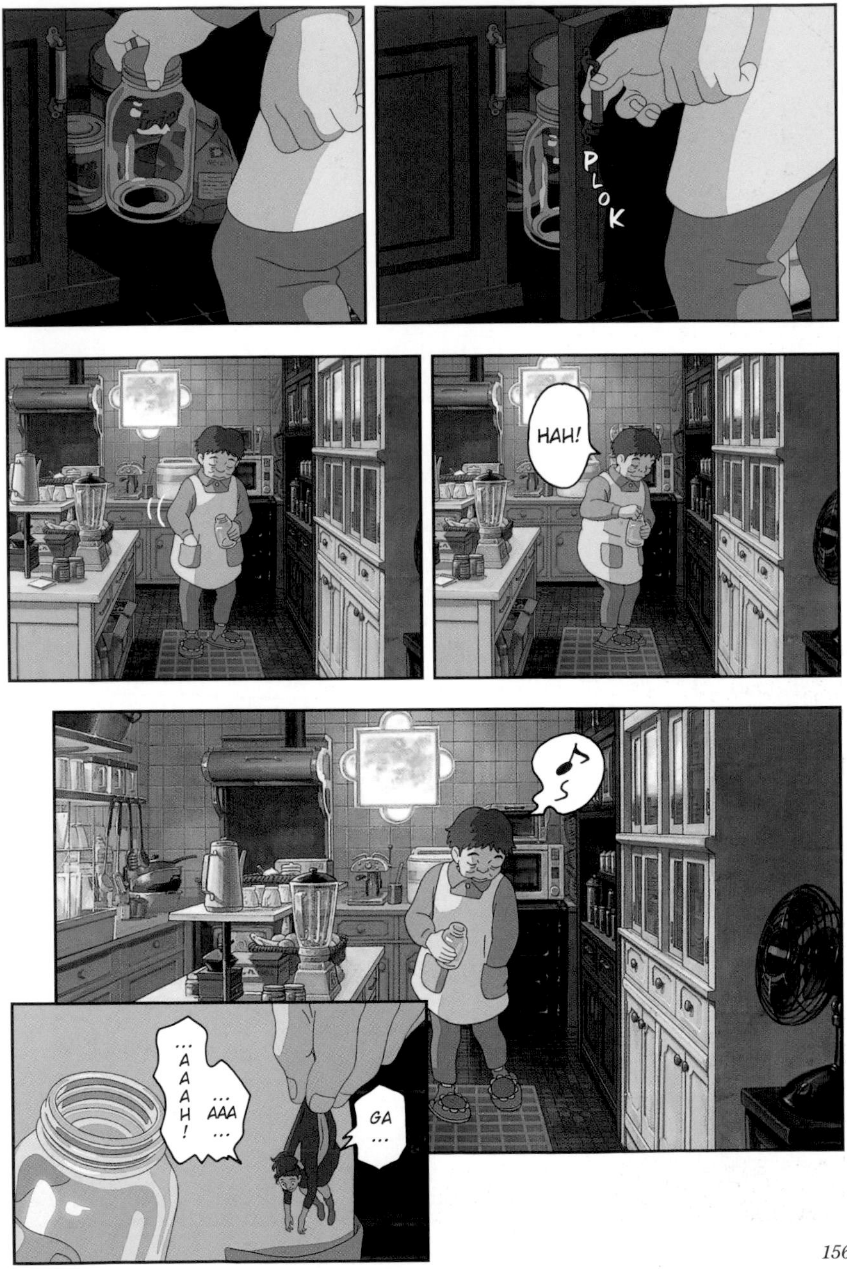
PLOK
HAH!
GA...
...AAA...
...AAAH!

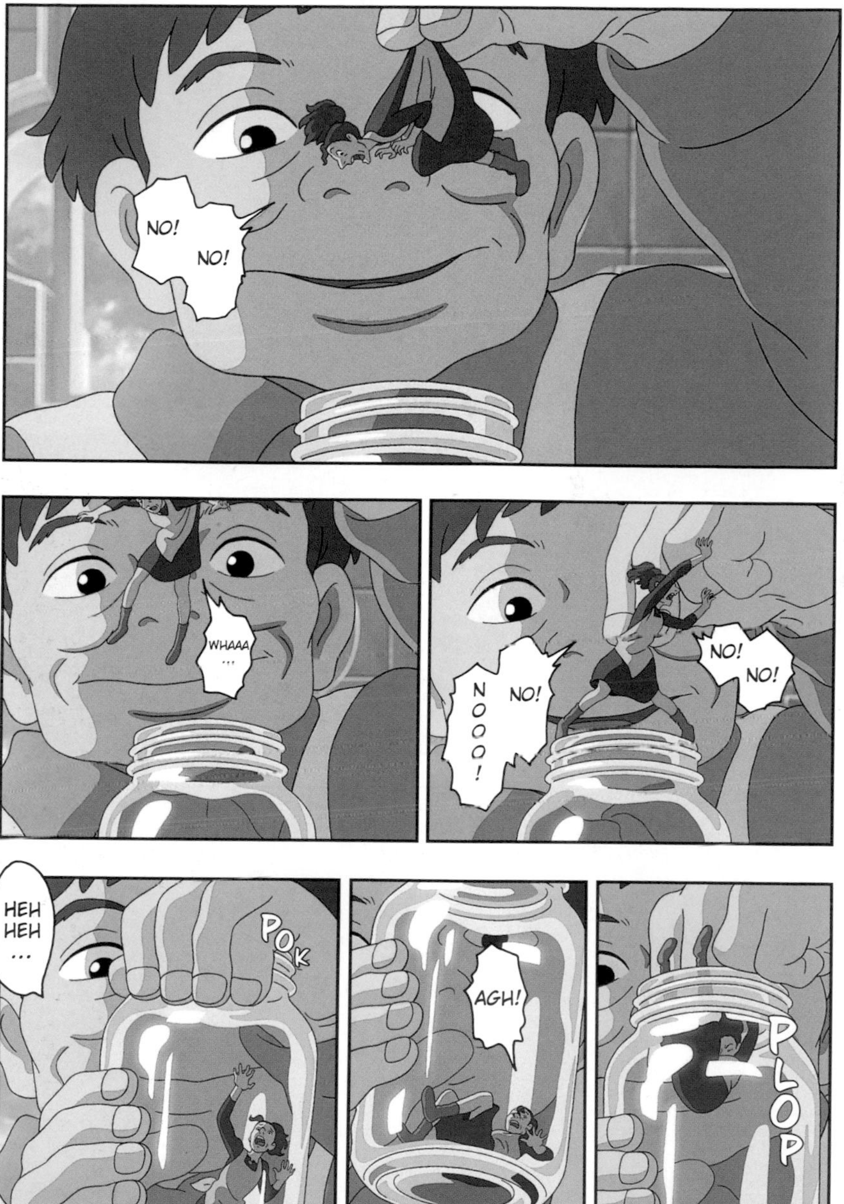
NO!
NO!
NO!
NO!
NO!
NOOOO!
WHAAA...
PLOP
AGH!
POK
HEH HEH...

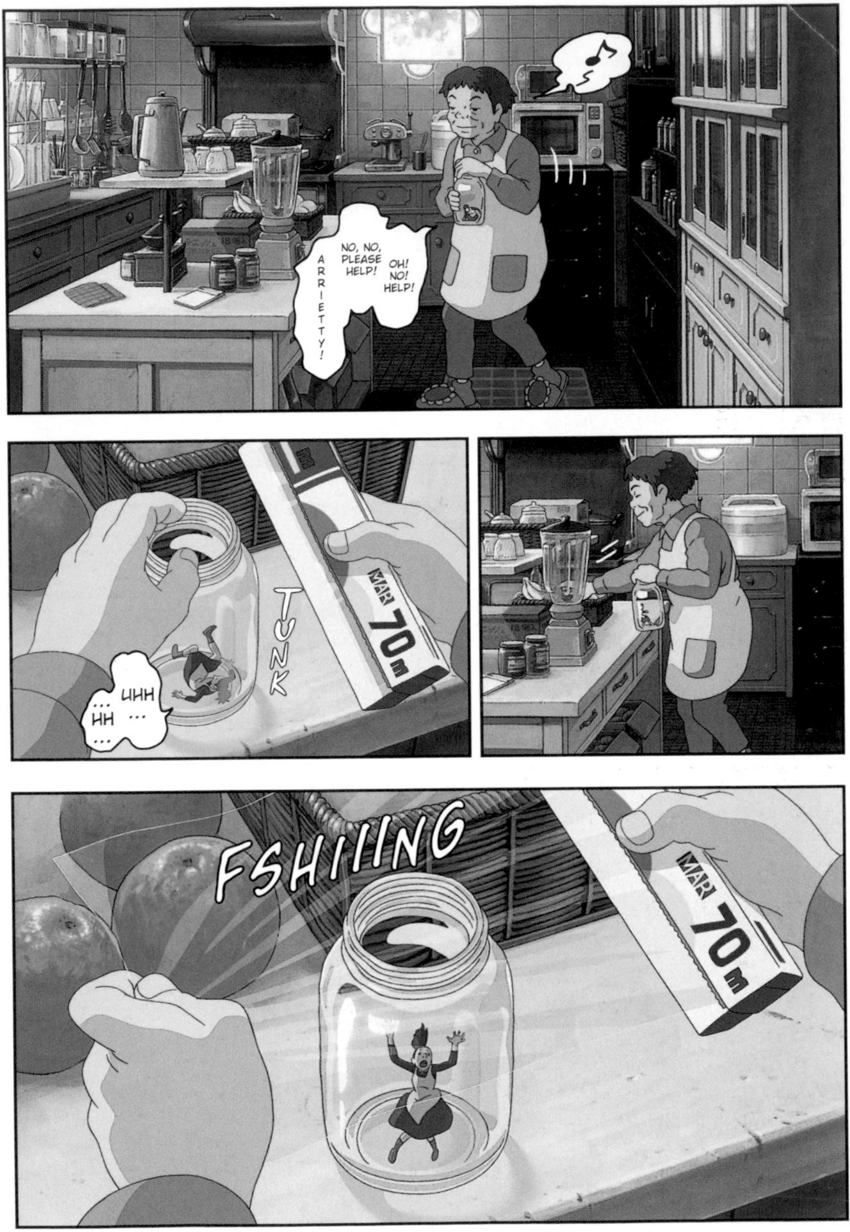
OH! NO! HELP!
NO, NO, PLEASE HELP!
ARRIETTY!
TUNK
UHH...
HH...
FSHIIING

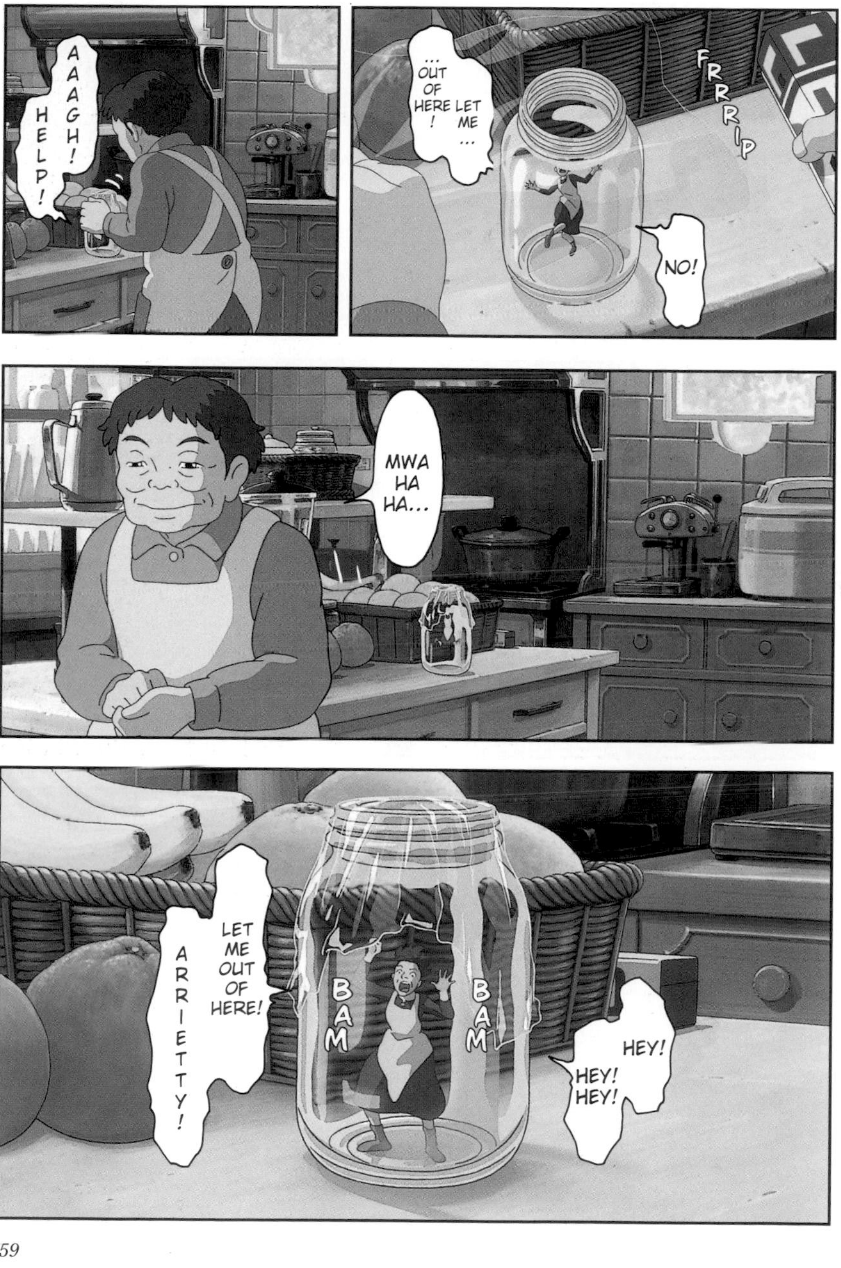
FRRRIP
...OUT OF HERE! LET ME...
NO!
AAAGH! HELP!
MWA HA HA...
HEY! HEY! HEY!
BAM
BAM
LET ME OUT OF HERE!
ARRIETTY!

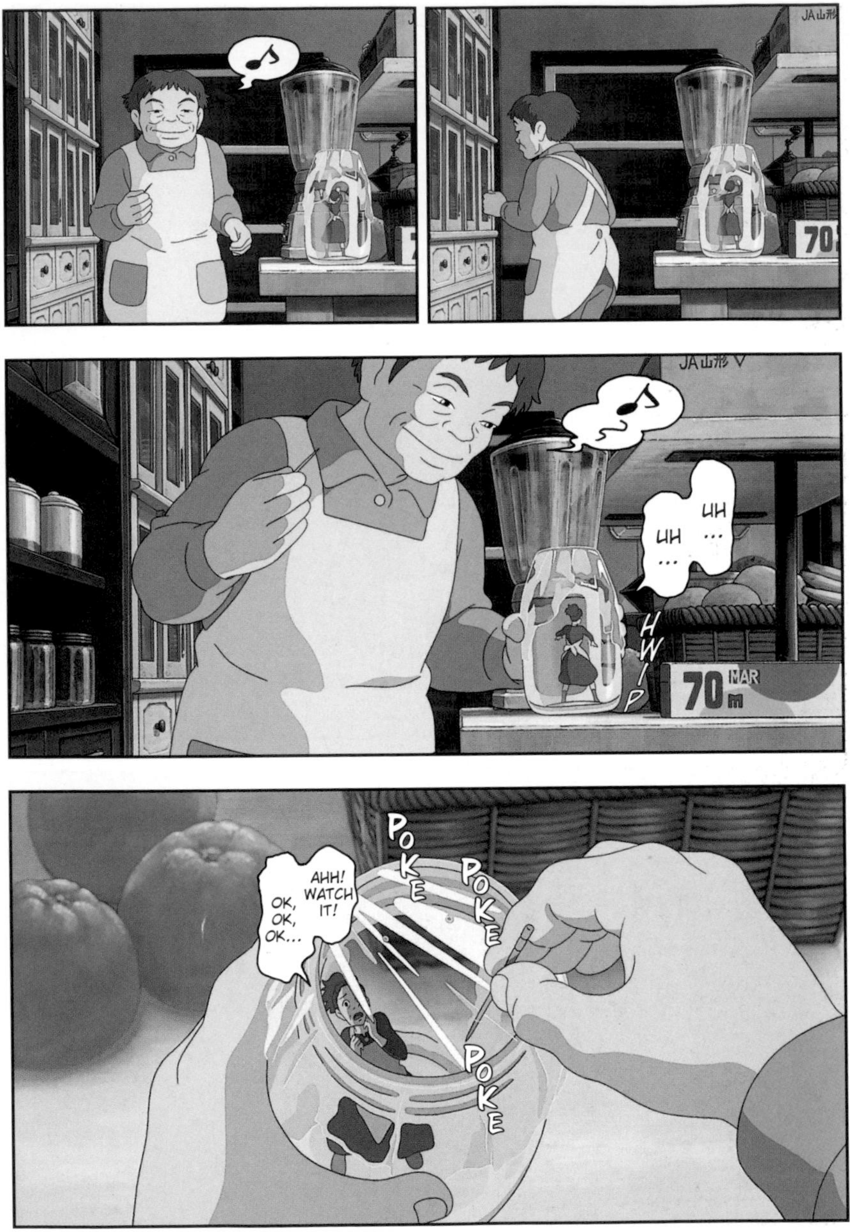
JA山形
70
♪
JA山形 ▽
♪
UH ... UH ...
HWIP
70 MAR m
POKE POKE
AHH! WATCH IT!
OK, OK, OK...
POKE

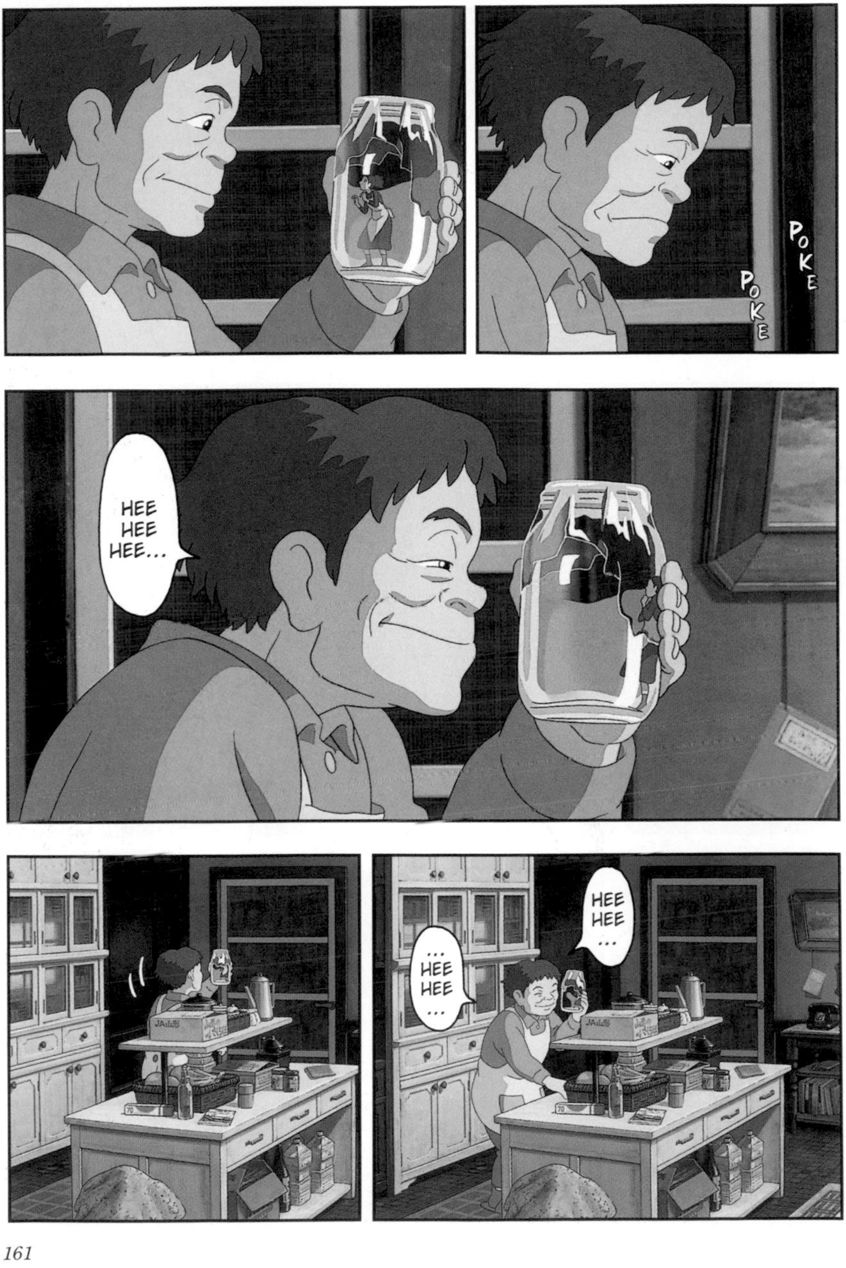
POKE
POKE
HEE HEE HEE...
HEE HEE ...
... HEE HEE ...

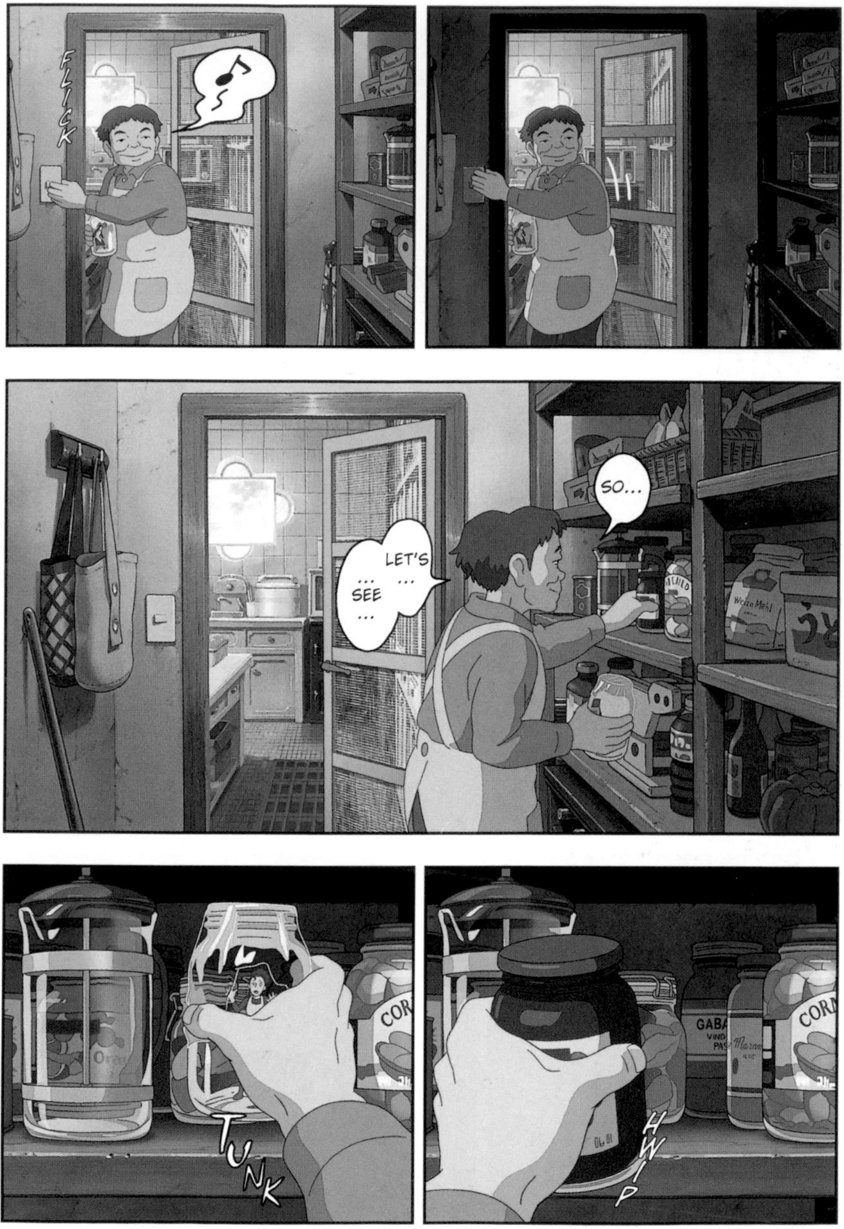
FLICK
SO...
LET'S ...
... SEE ...
HWIP
TUNK

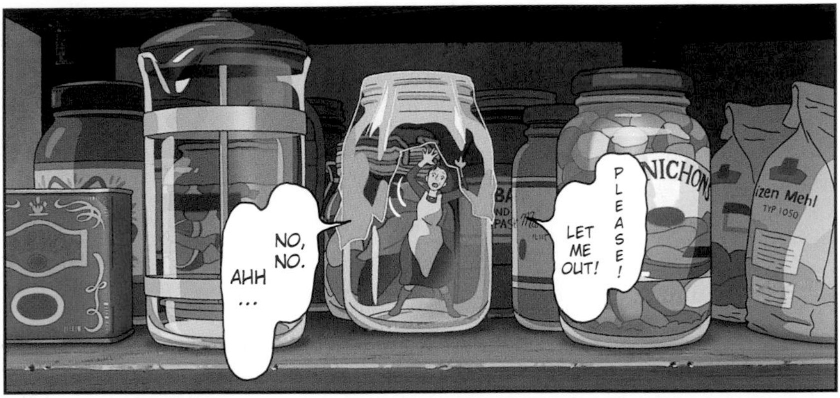
PLEASE! LET ME OUT!
NO, NO. AHH...
izen Mehl
TYP 1050
NICHONS

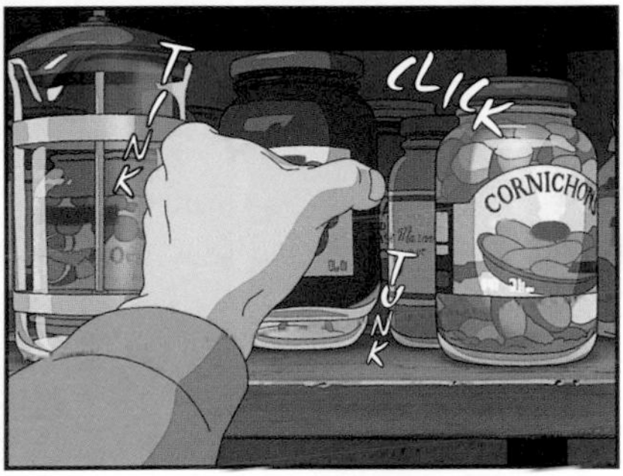
CLICK
TINK
TUNK
CORNICHONS

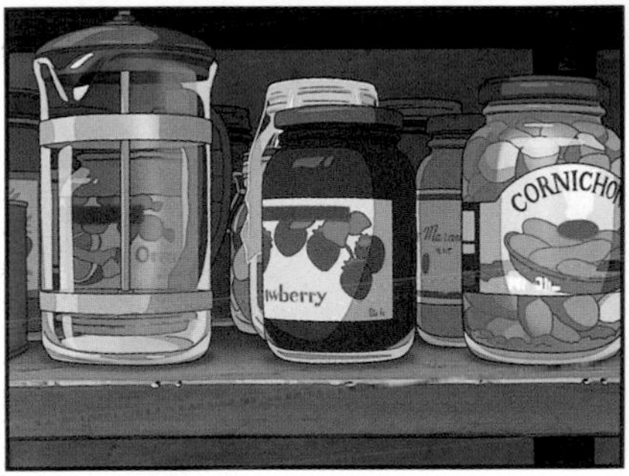
CORNICHONS
wberry

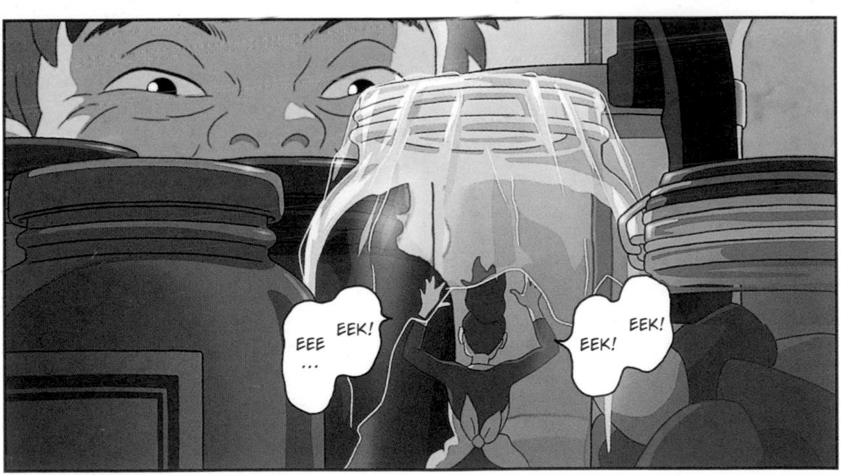
EEK! EEK!
EEK! EEE...

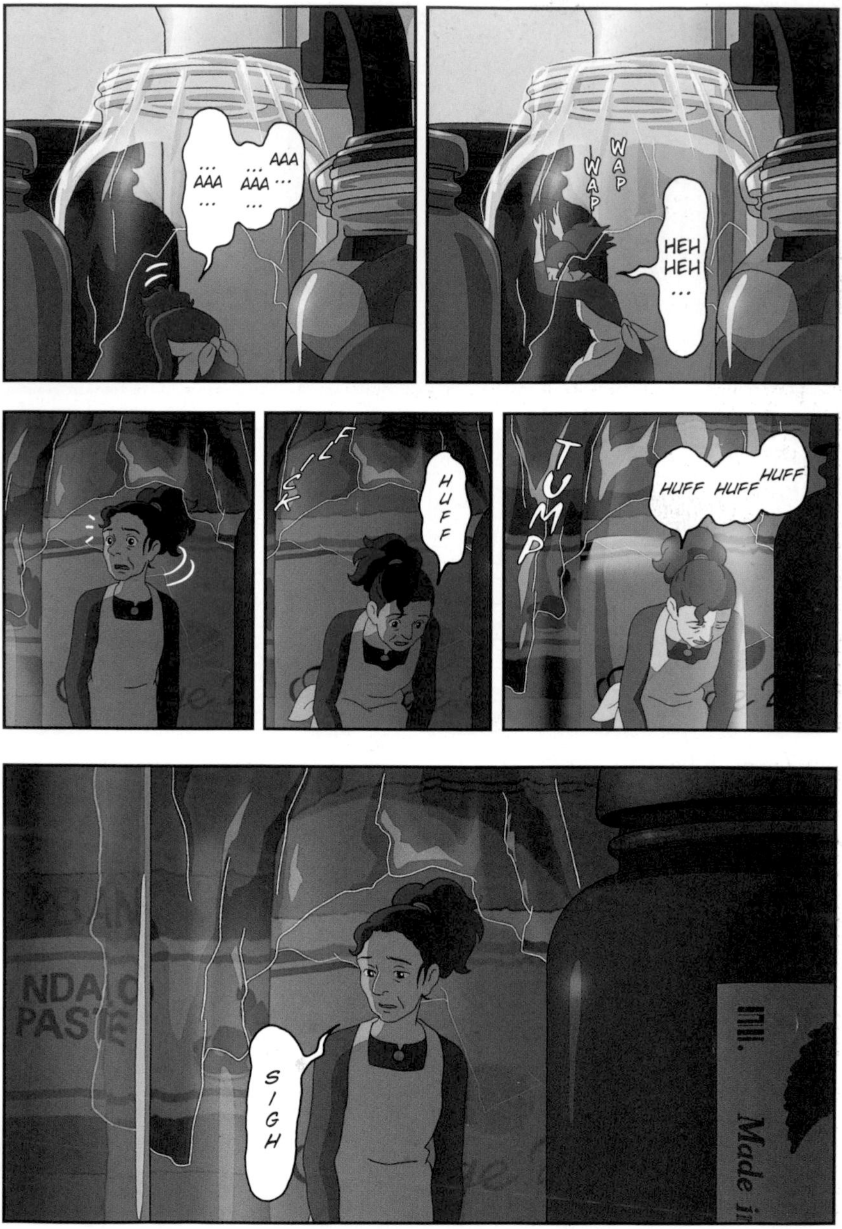
... AAA ... ... AAA ... AAA ...
WAP WAP
HEH HEH ...
FLICK
HUFF
TUMP
HUFF HUFF HUFF
NDA O PASTE
SIGH
Made i

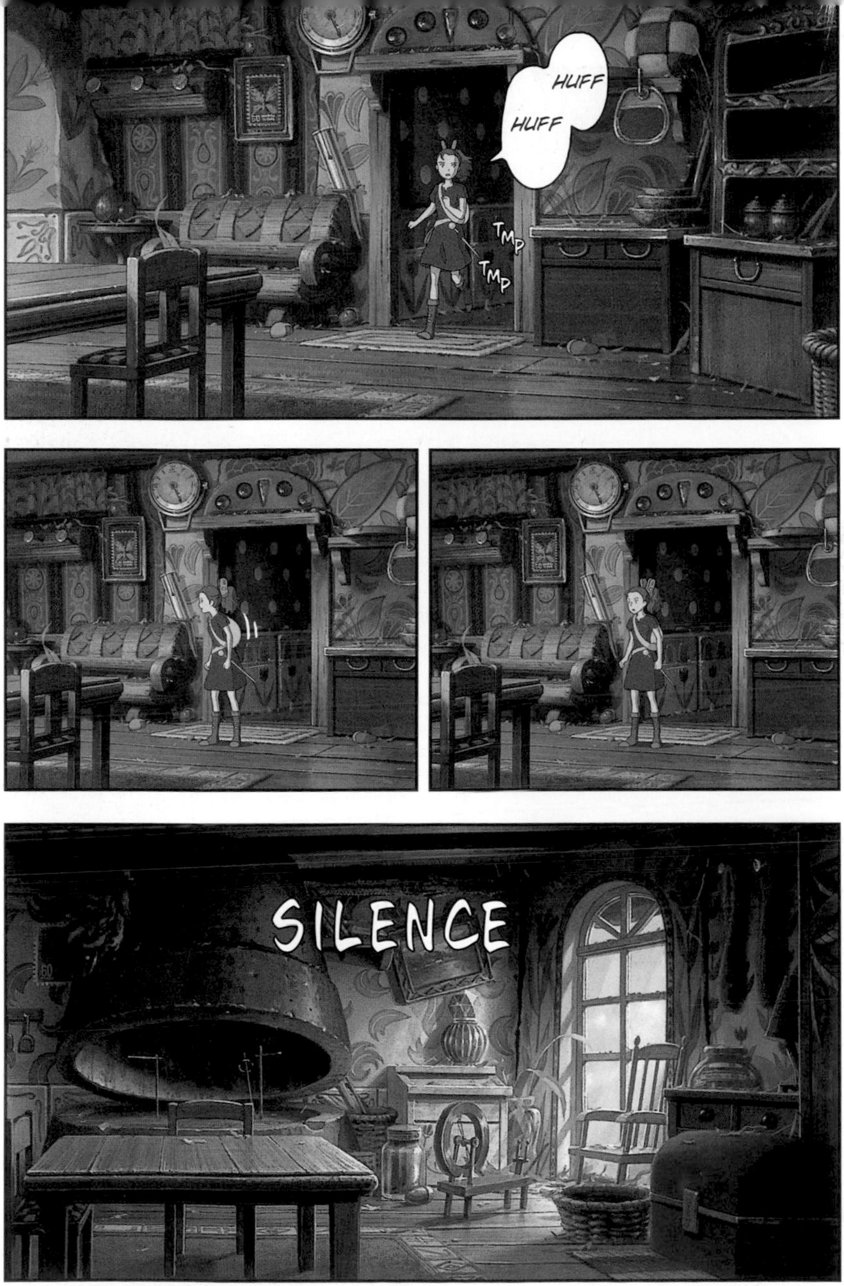
HUFF HUFF
TMP TMP
SILENCE

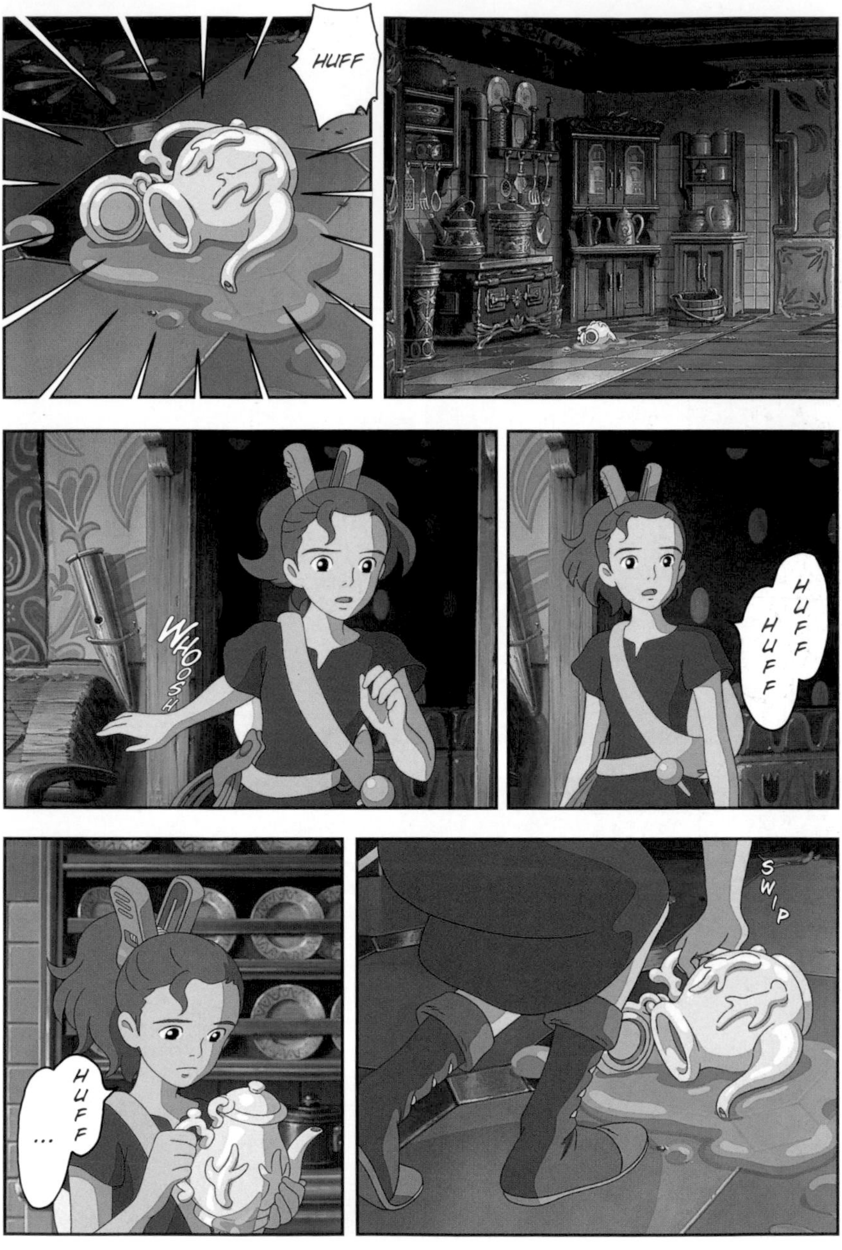
HUFF
HUFF HUFF
WHOOSH
SWIP
HUFF ...

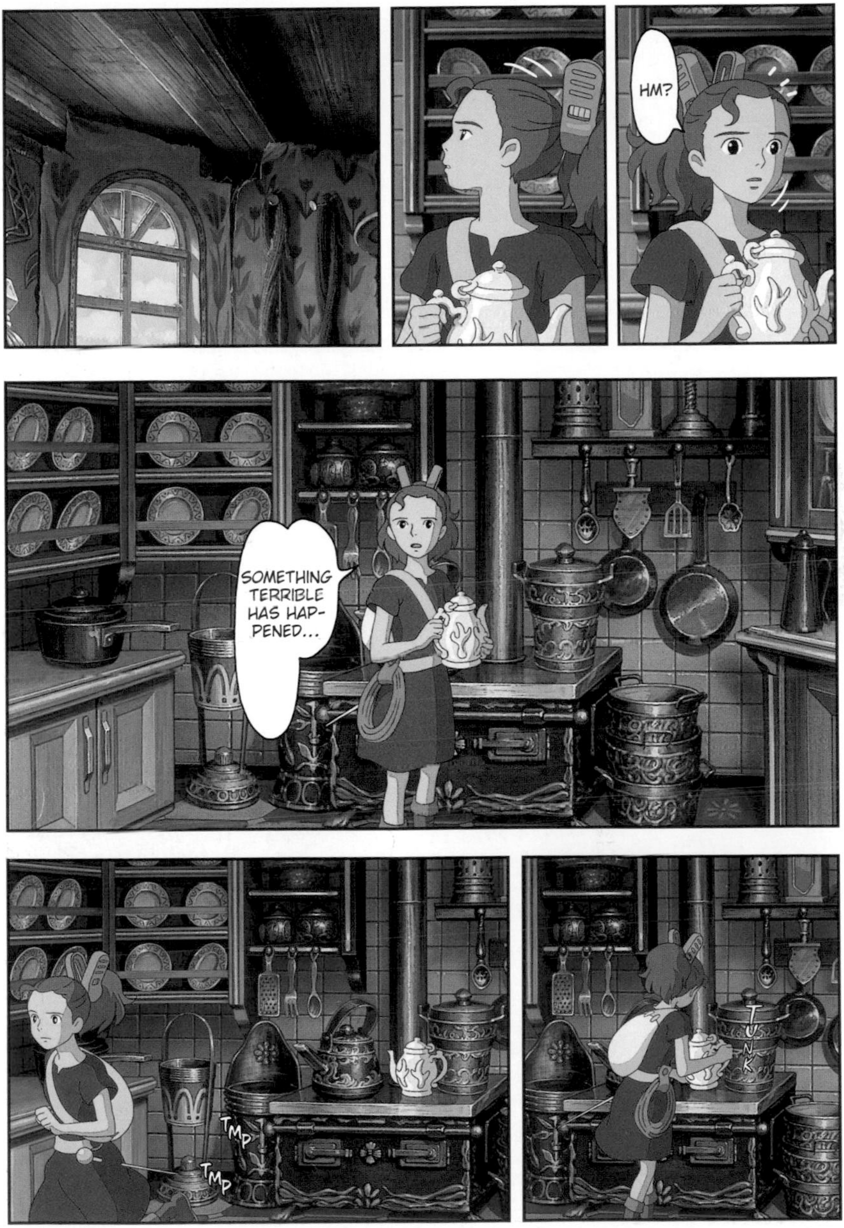
HM?
SOMETHING TERRIBLE HAS HAP-PENED...
TUNK
TMP
TMP

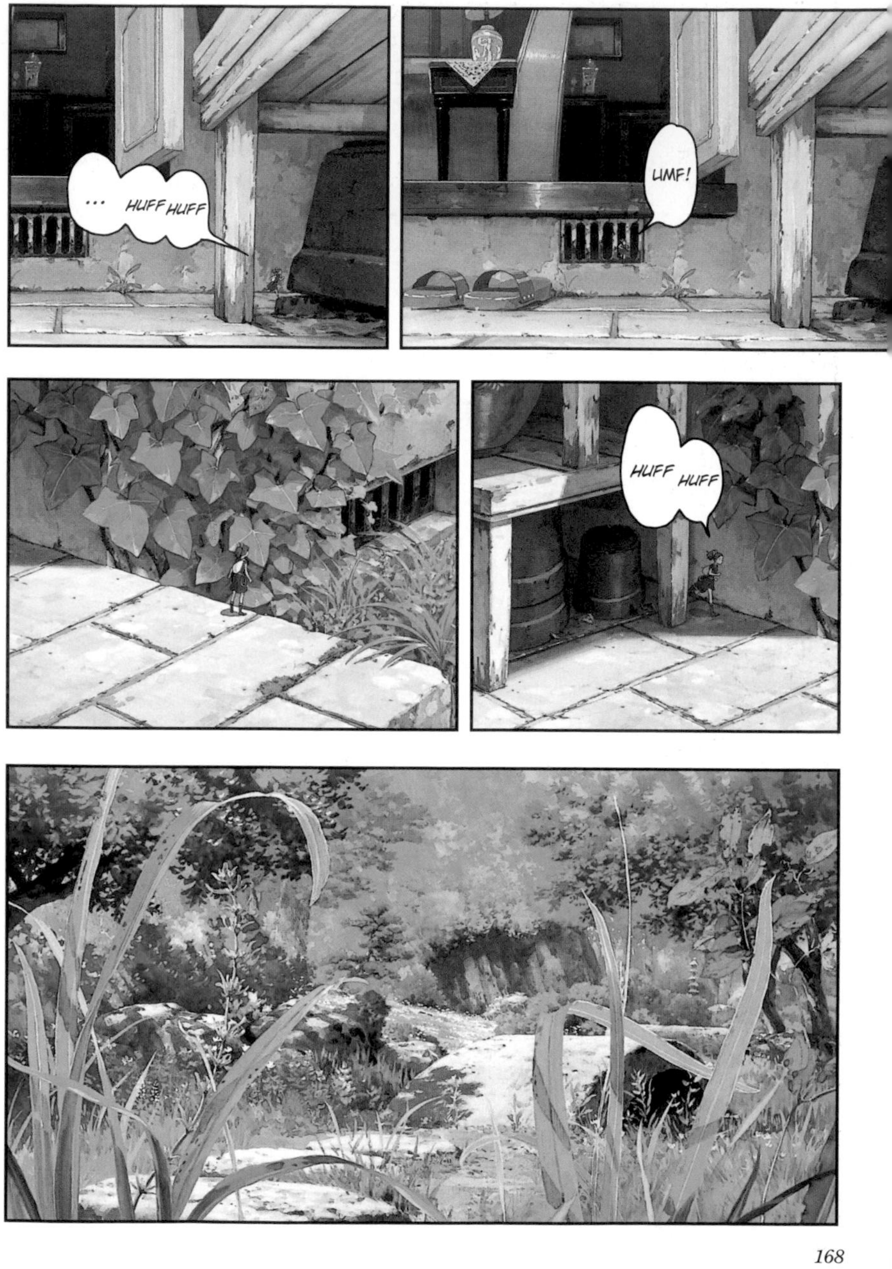
UMF!
... HUFF HUFF
HUFF HUFF

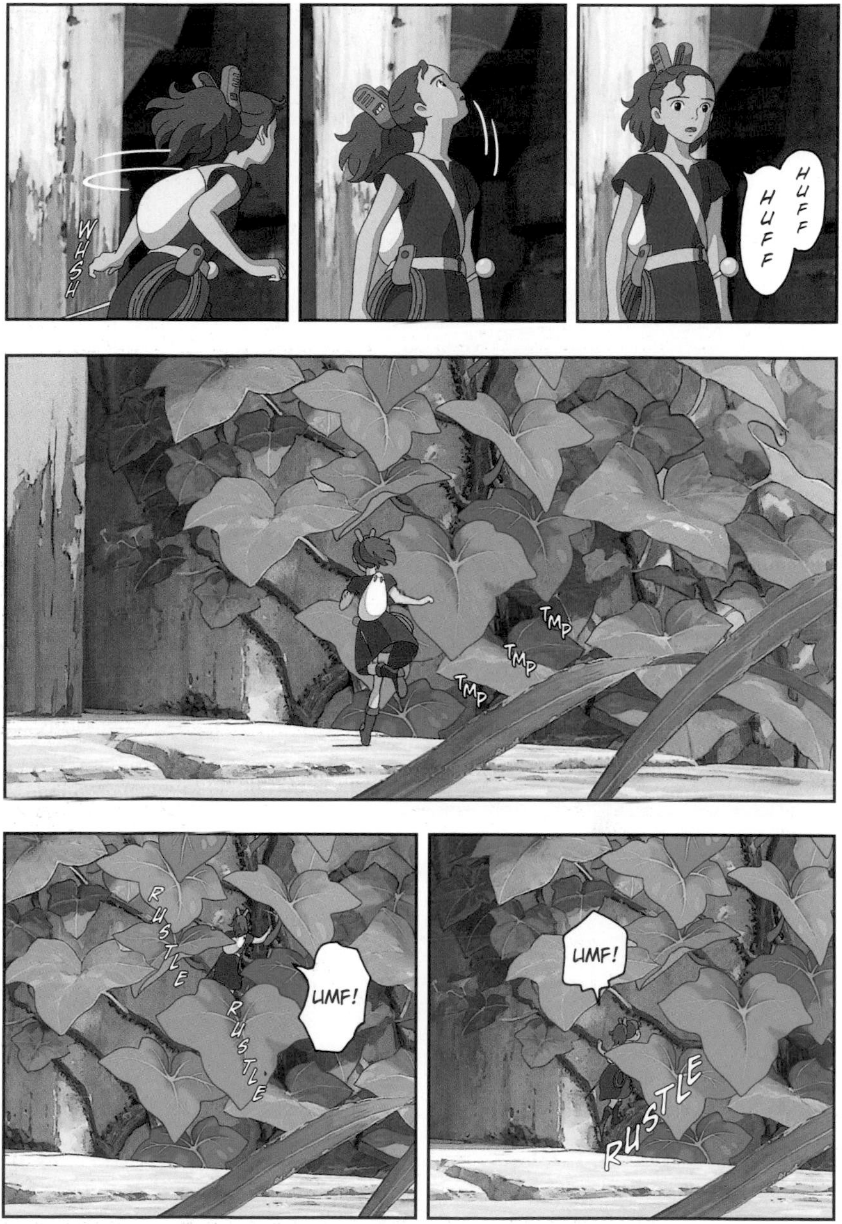
HUFF HUFF
WHSH
TMP TMP TMP
UMF!
RUSTLE
RUSTLE RUSTLE
UMF!

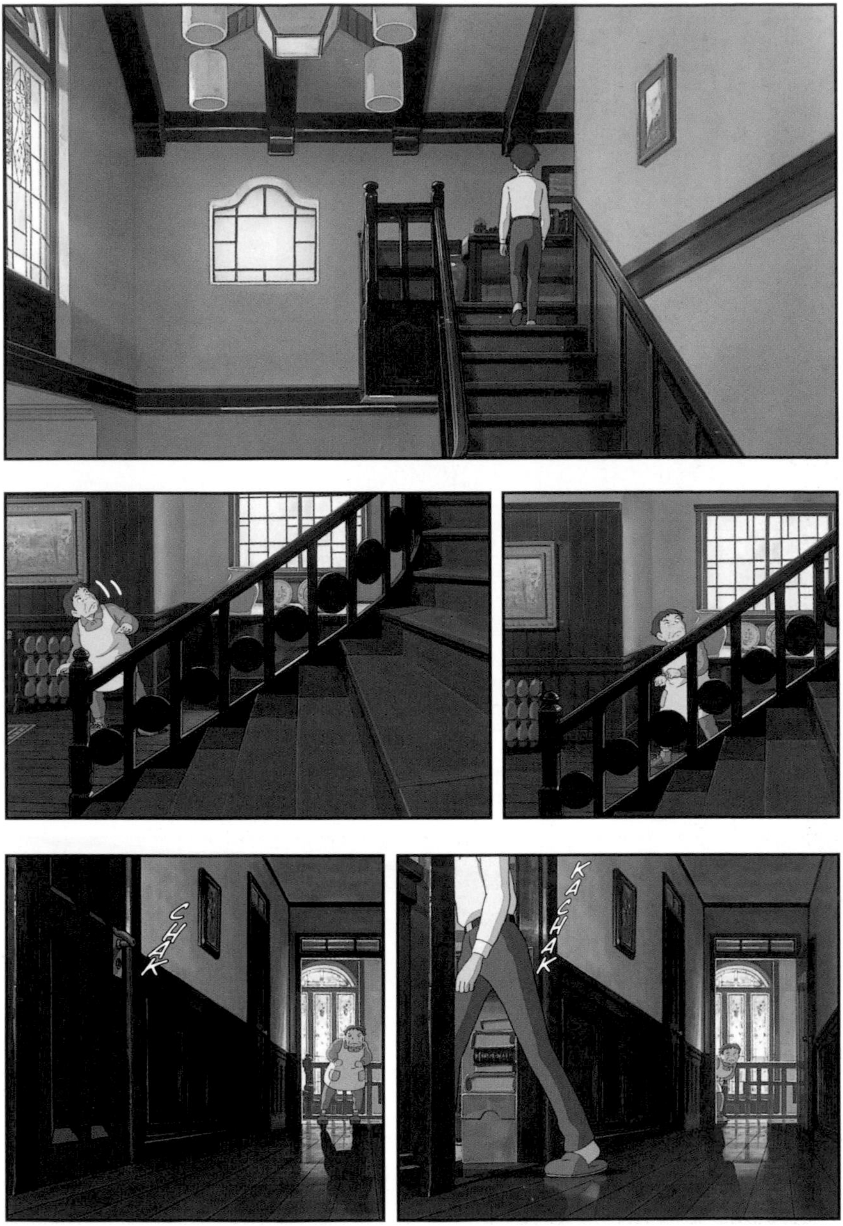
KACHAK
CHAK

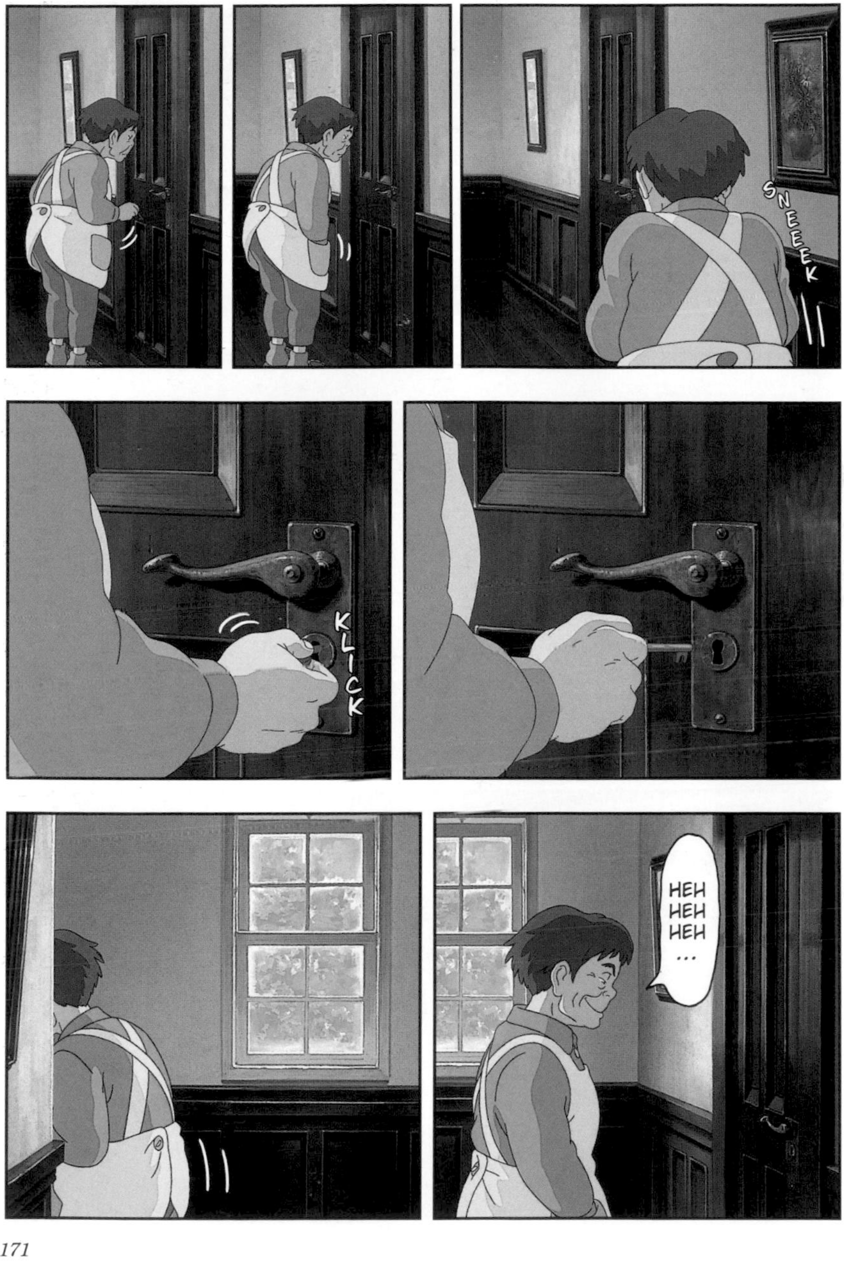
SNEEEK
KLICK
HEH HEH HEH ...

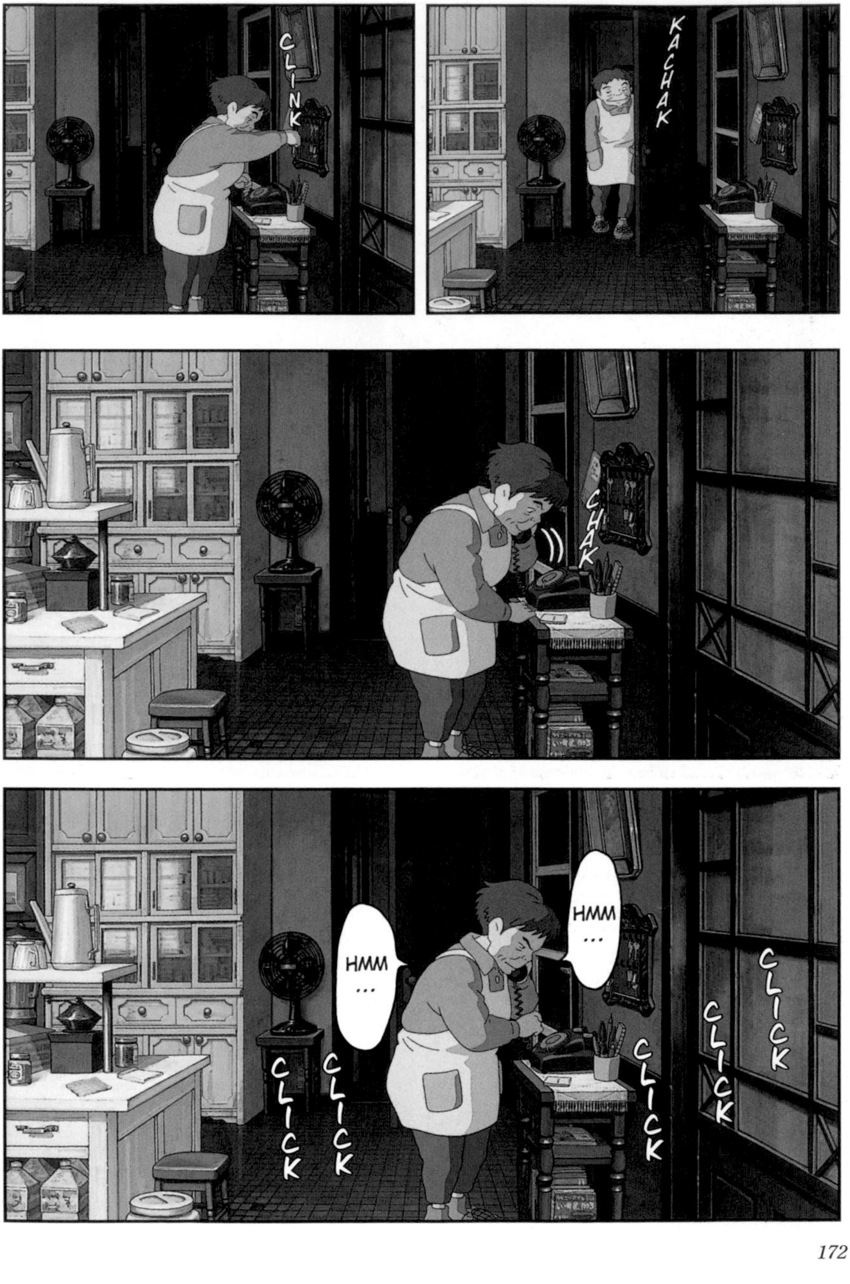
KACHAK
CLINK
CHAK
HMM...
HMM...
CLICK
CLICK
CLICK
CLICK
CLICK
CLICK

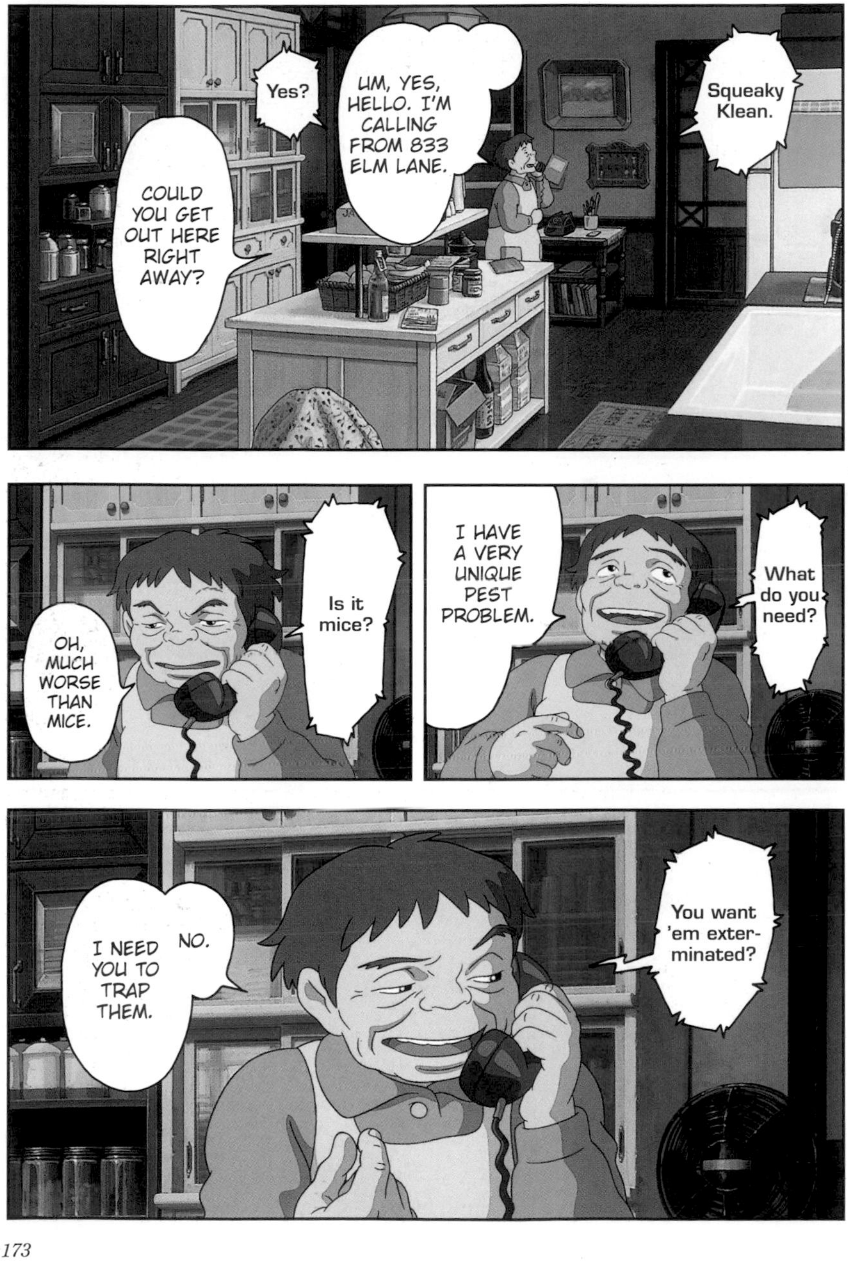
Squeaky Klean.
UM, YES, HELLO. I'M CALLING FROM 833 ELM LANE.
Yes?
COULD YOU GET OUT HERE RIGHT AWAY?
What do you need?
I HAVE A VERY UNIQUE PEST PROBLEM.
Is it mice?
OH, MUCH WORSE THAN MICE.
You want 'em exter-minated?
NO.
I NEED YOU TO TRAP THEM.

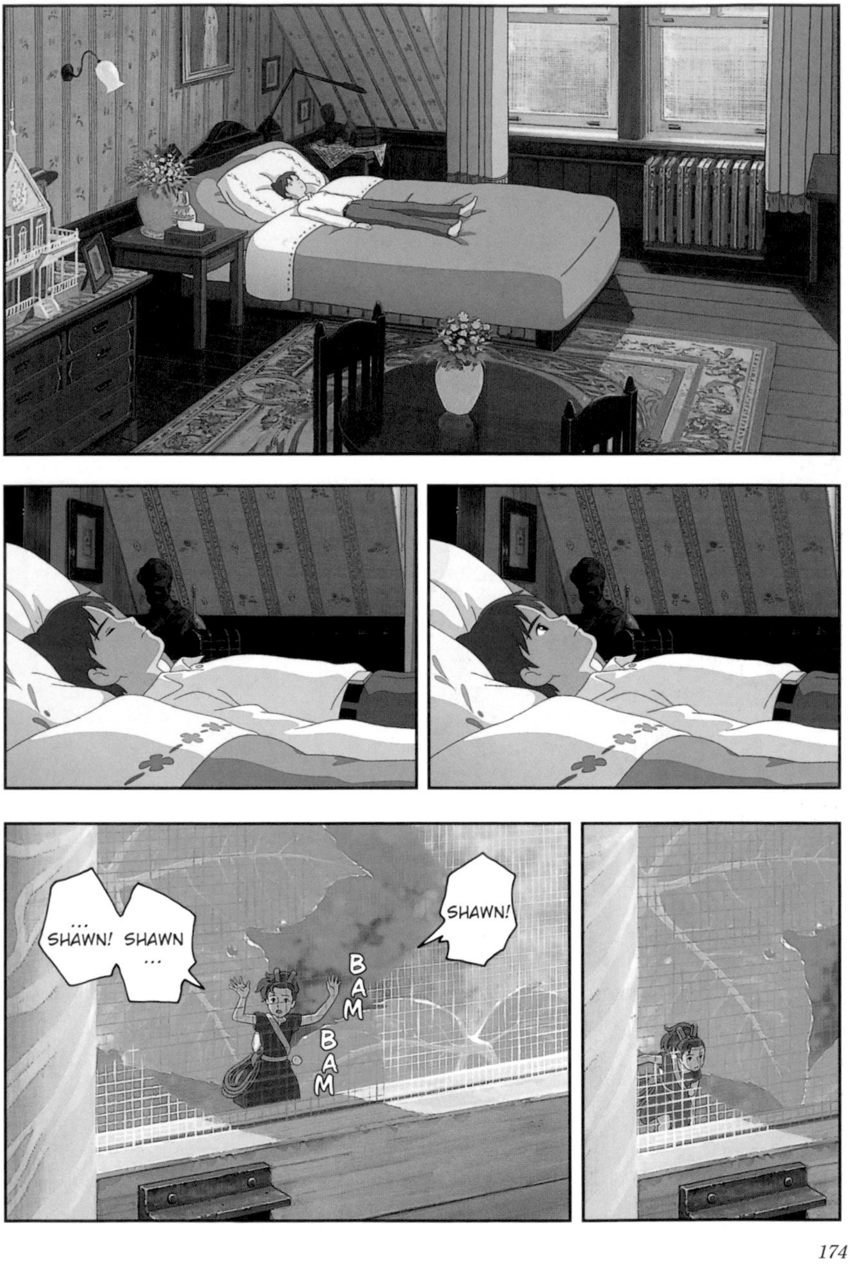
SHAWN!
BAM BAM
... SHAWN! SHAWN ...

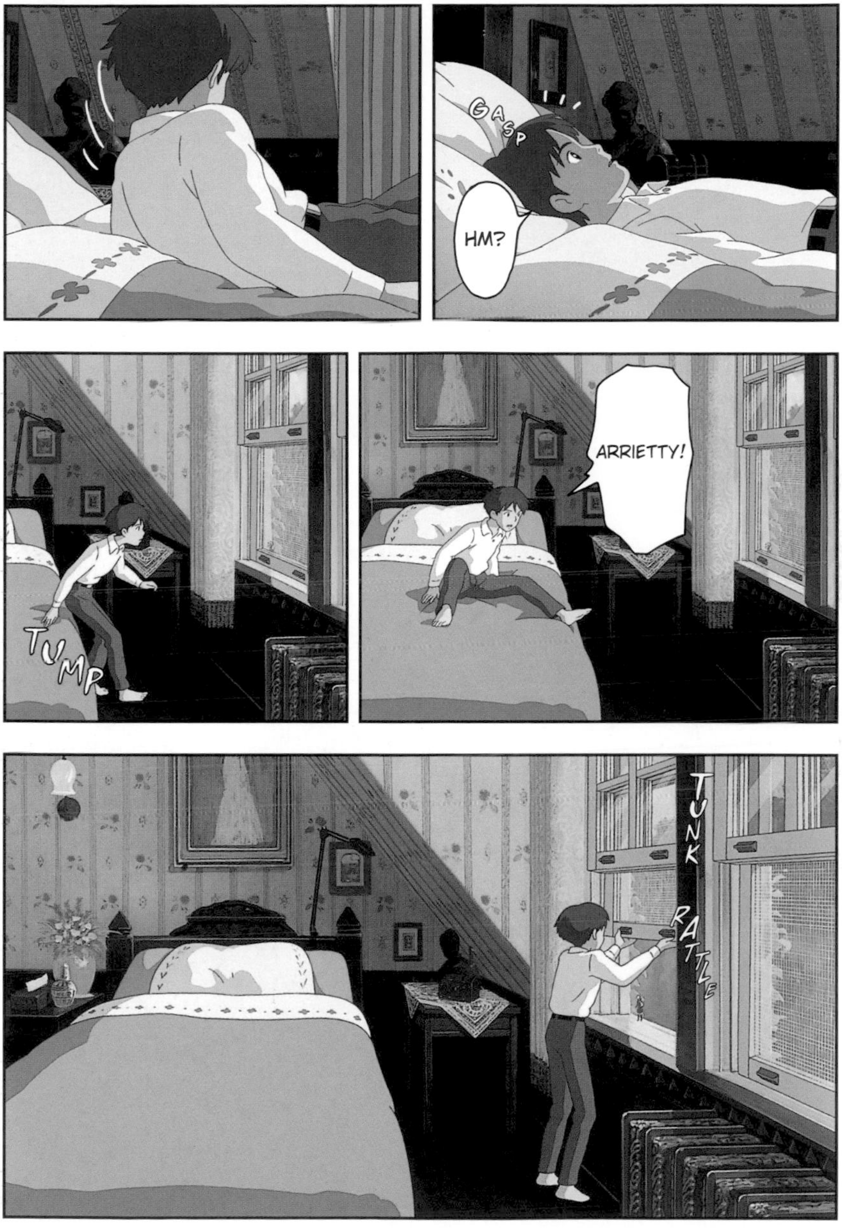
GASP
HM?
ARRIETTY!
TUMP
TUNK
RATTLE

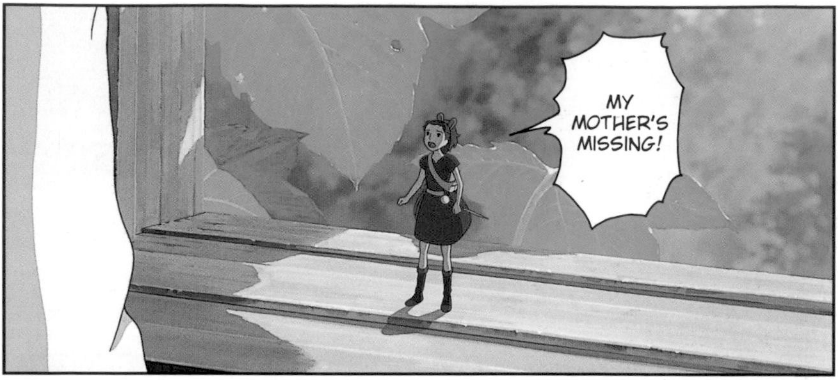
MY MOTHER'S MISSING!

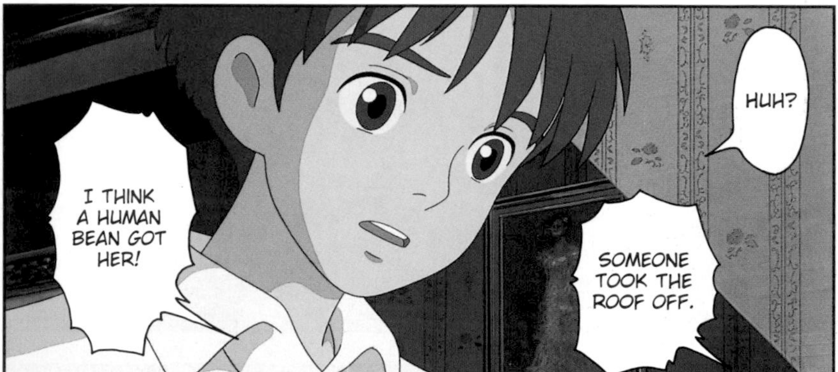
HUH?
SOMEONE TOOK THE ROOF OFF.
I THINK A HUMAN BEAN GOT HER!

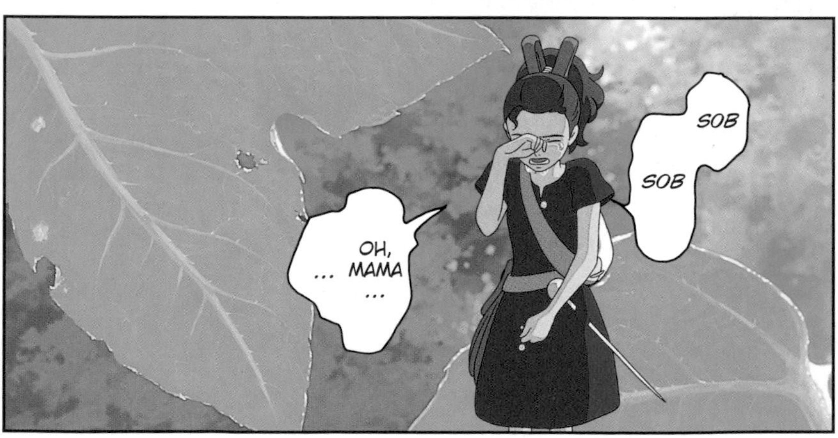
SOB
SOB
... OH, MAMA ...

SWIP

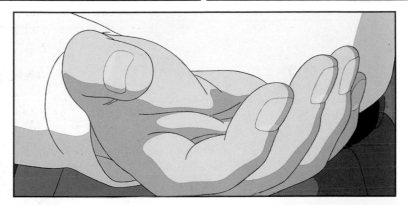

WE WILL FIND HER.

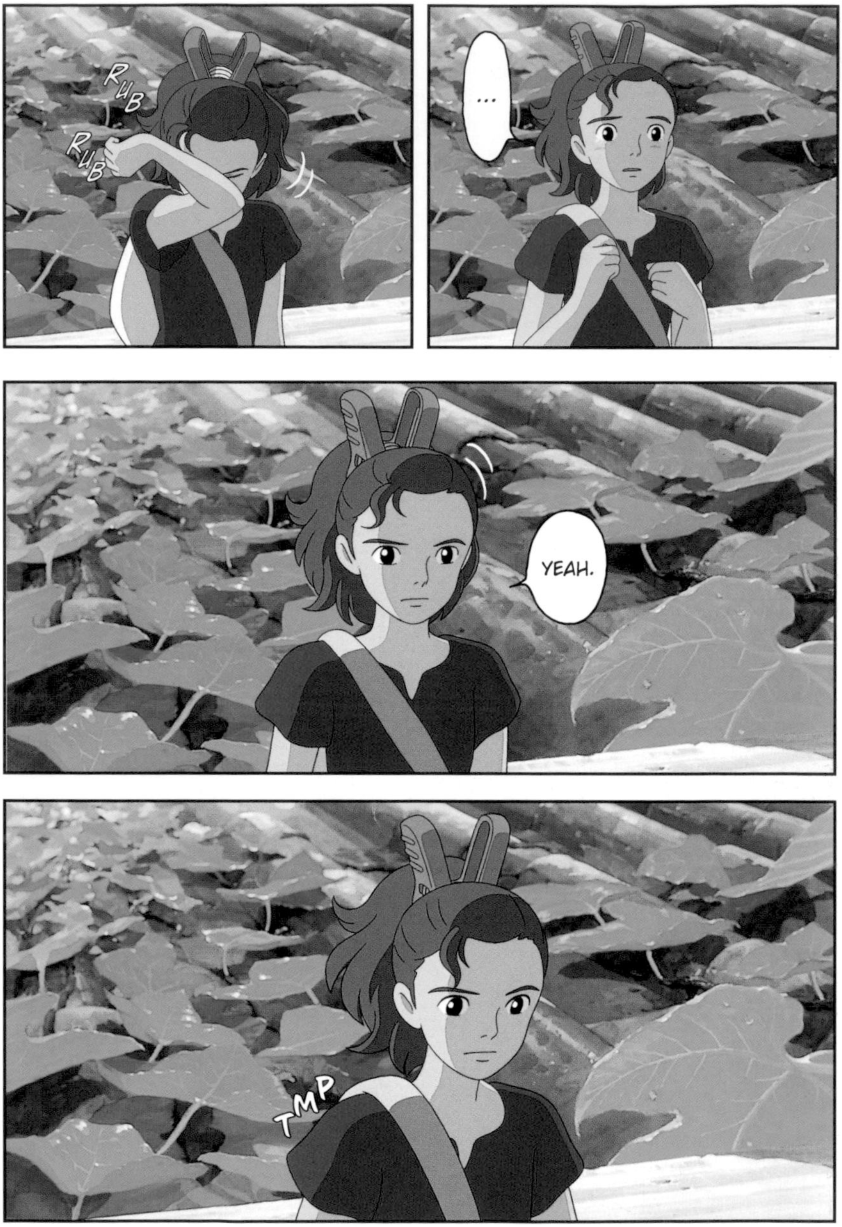
...
RUB
RUB
YEAH.
TMP

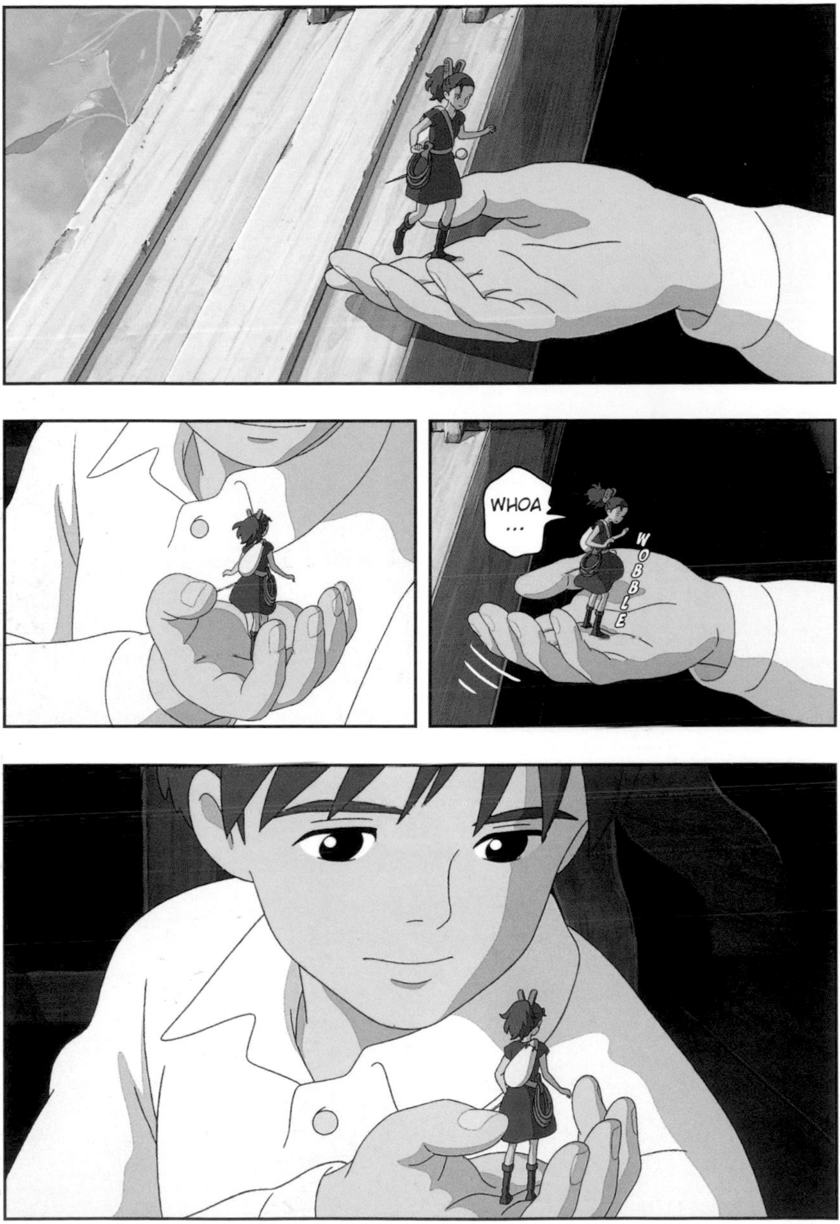
WHOA ...
WOBBLE

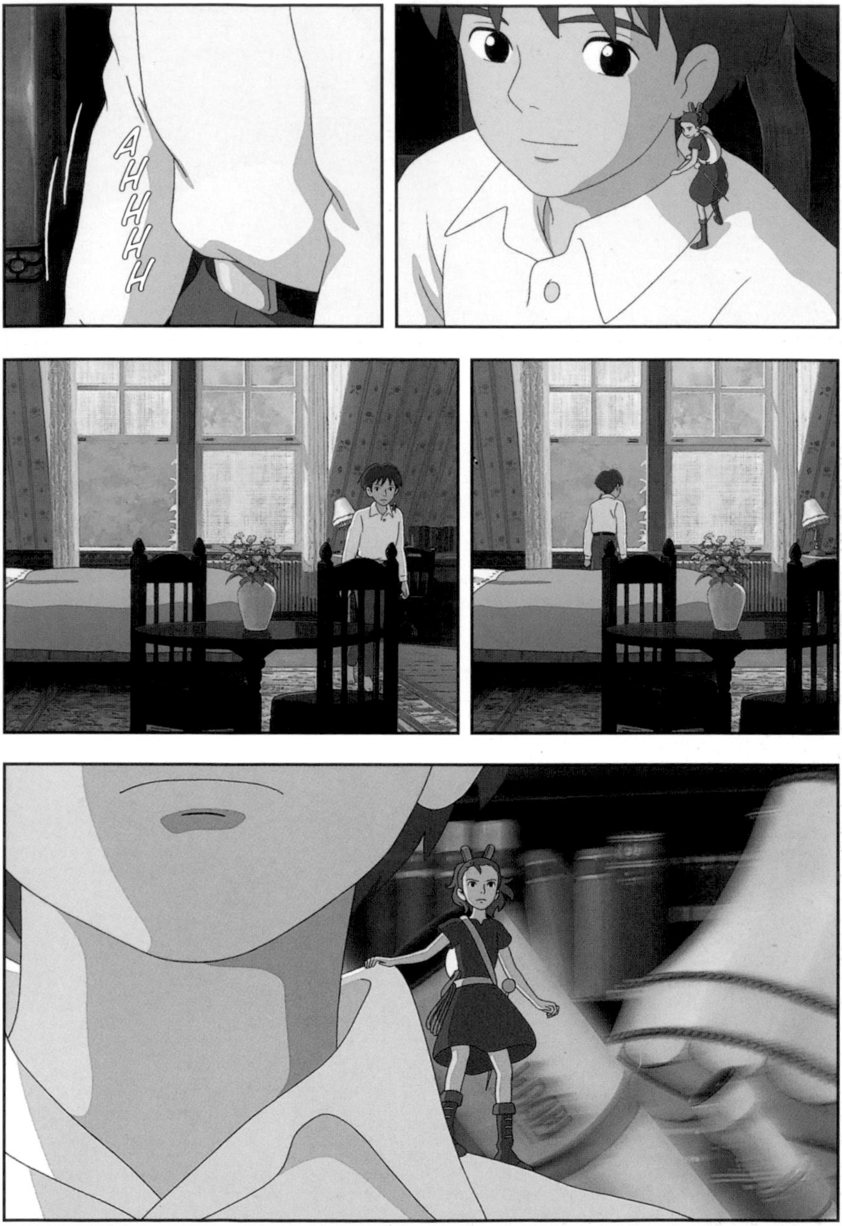
AHHHH

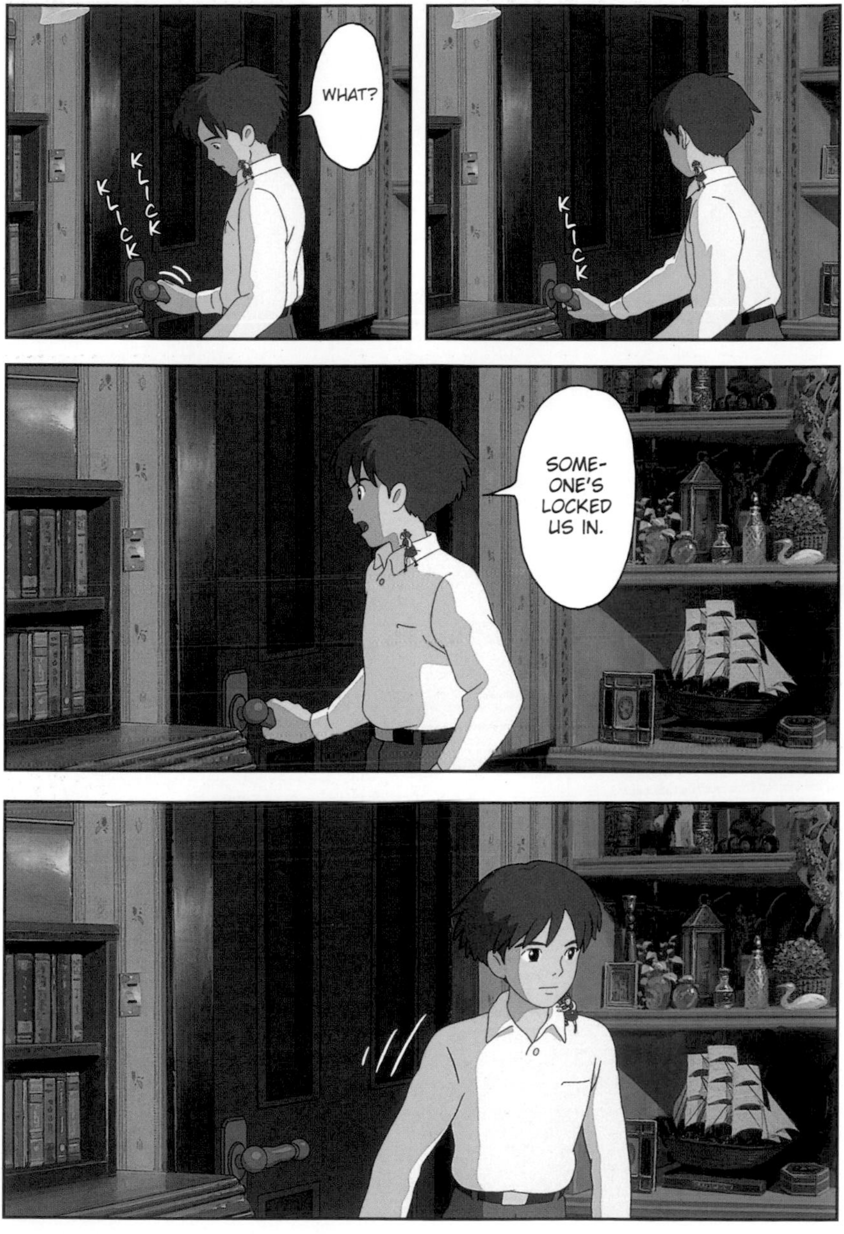
KLICK
WHAT?
KLICK
KLICK
SOME-ONE'S LOCKED US IN.

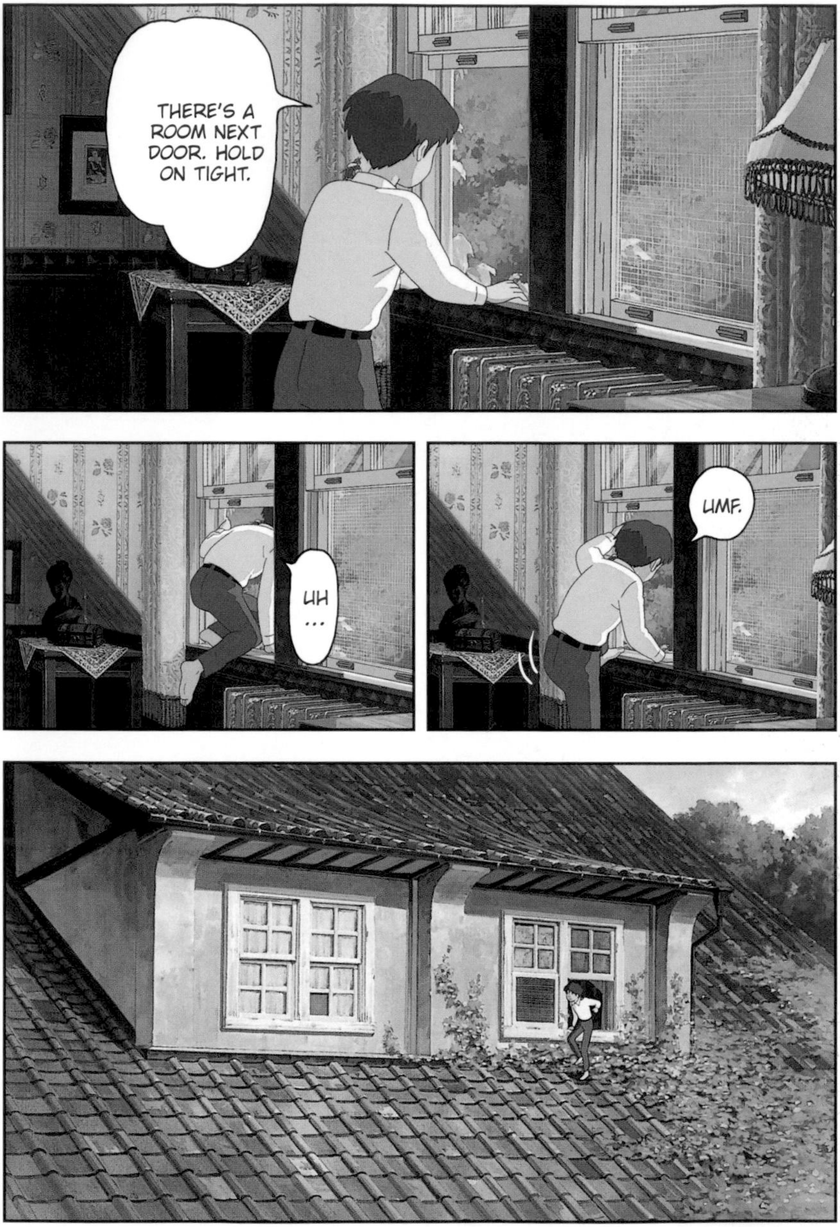
THERE'S A ROOM NEXT DOOR. HOLD ON TIGHT.
UMF.
UH ...

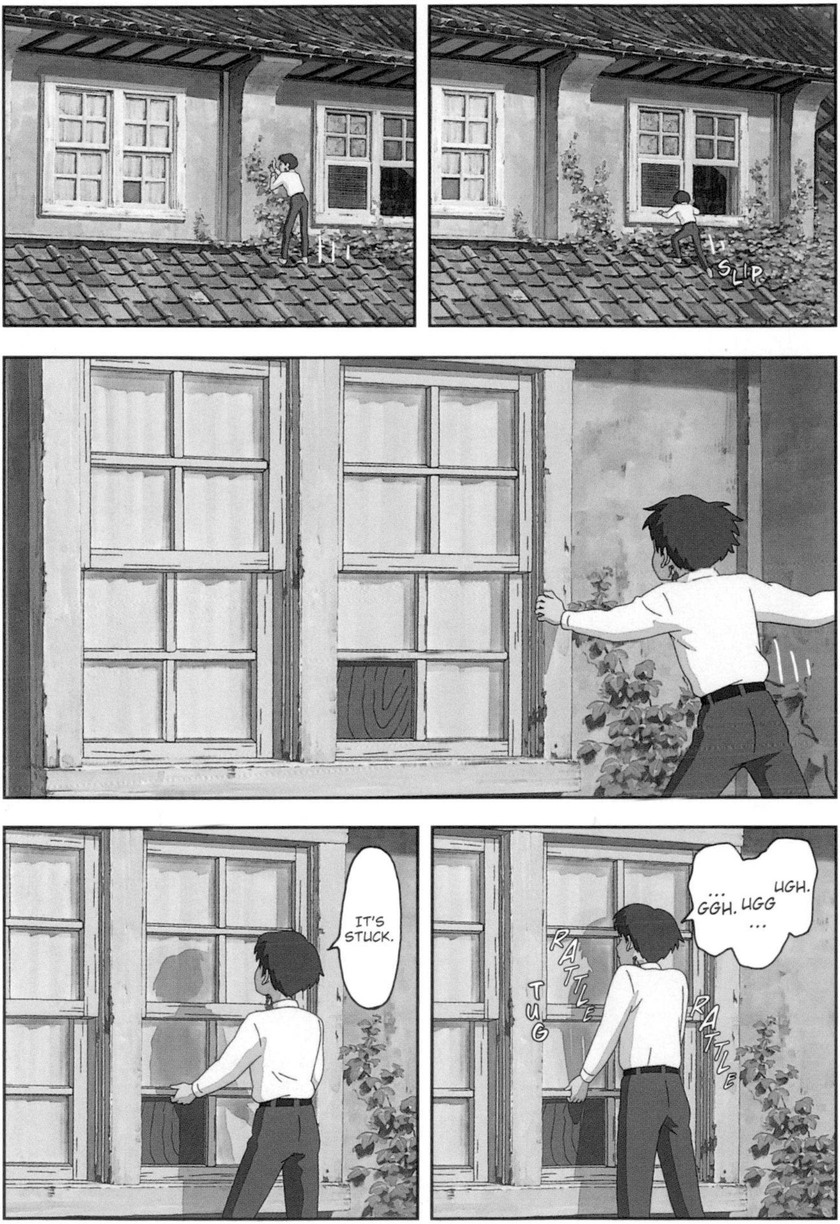
SLIP
... UGH. GGH. UGG ...
RATTLE
TUG
RATTLE
IT'S STUCK.

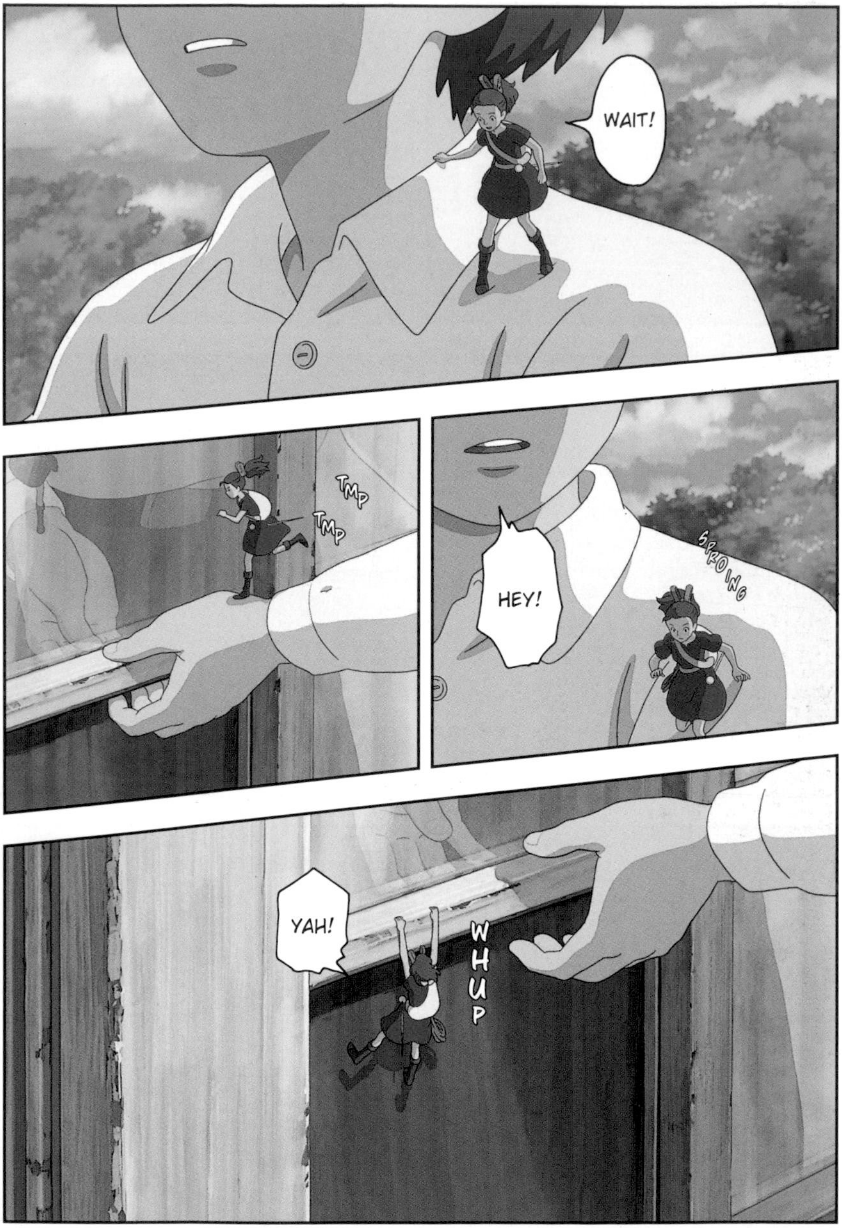
WAIT!
HEY!
SPROING
TMP
TMP
YAH!
WHUP

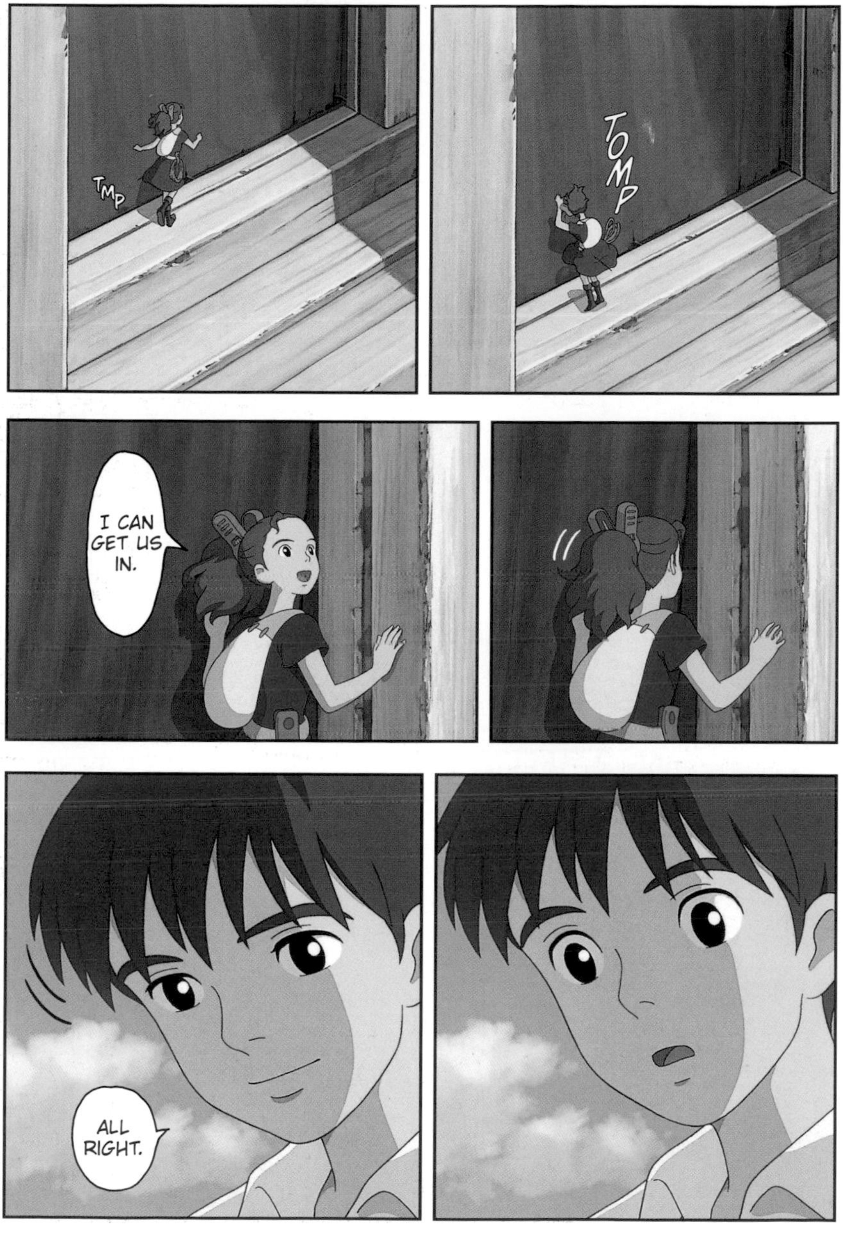
TMP
TOMP
I CAN GET US IN.
ALL RIGHT.

UGH ...
URR ... ... RRGH!
...

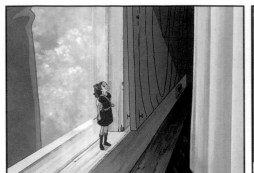

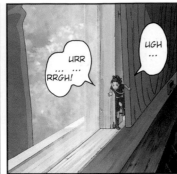

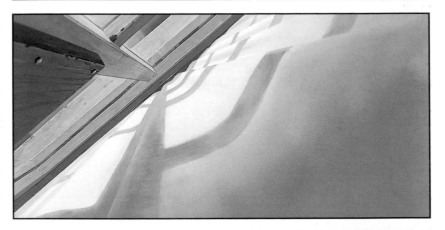

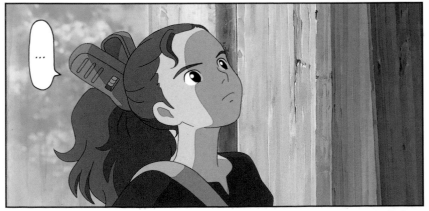

FWUP
TNK
SHTUK
UMF!
SPROING
WHOA...
HUP
SLIP
OH NO, OH NO...
SLOOMP

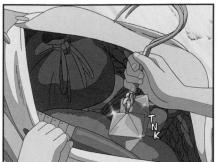

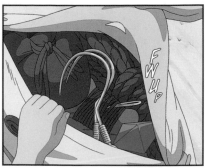

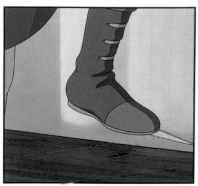

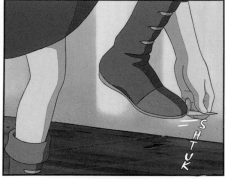

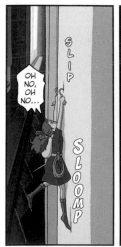

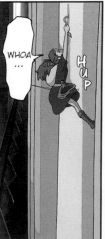

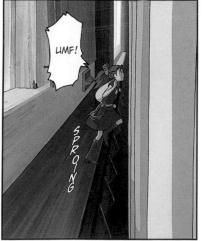

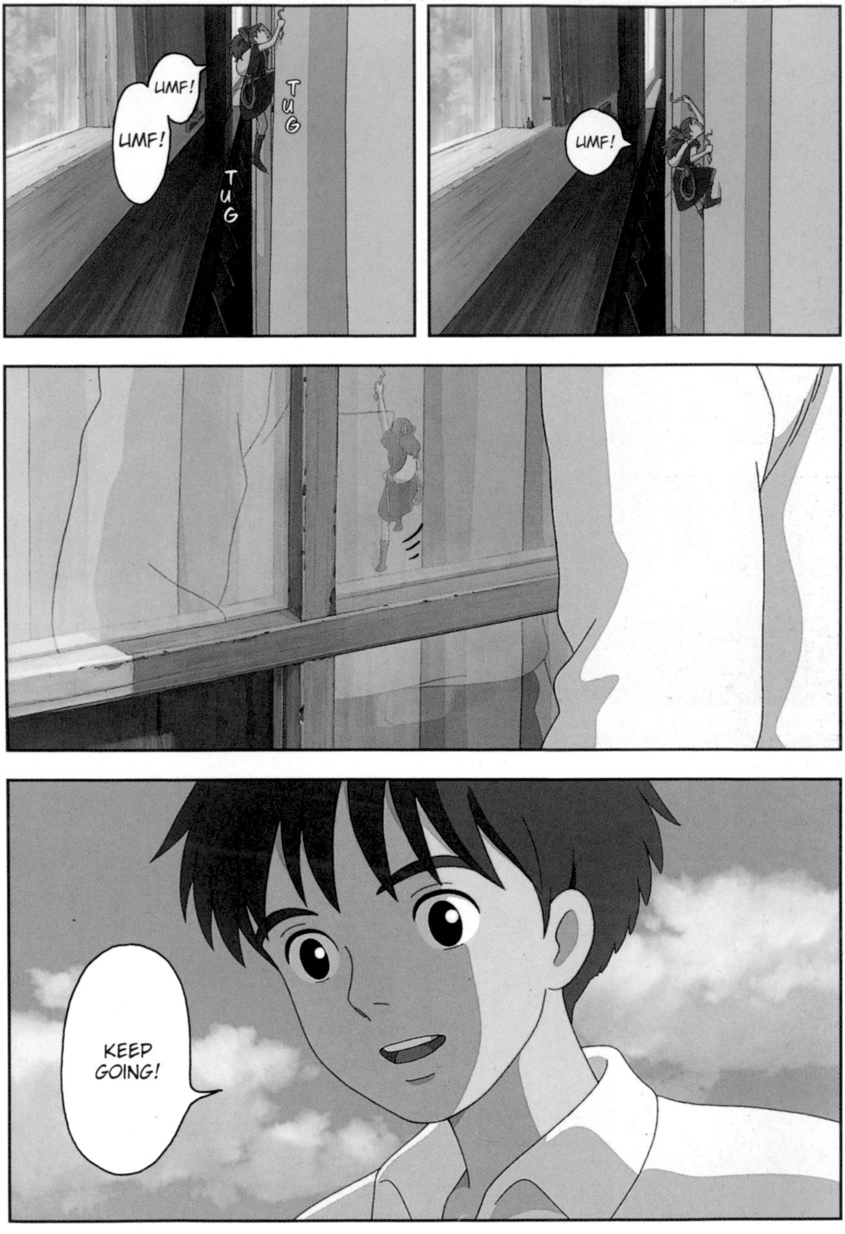
UMF!
UMF!
UMF!
TUG
TUG
KEEP GOING!

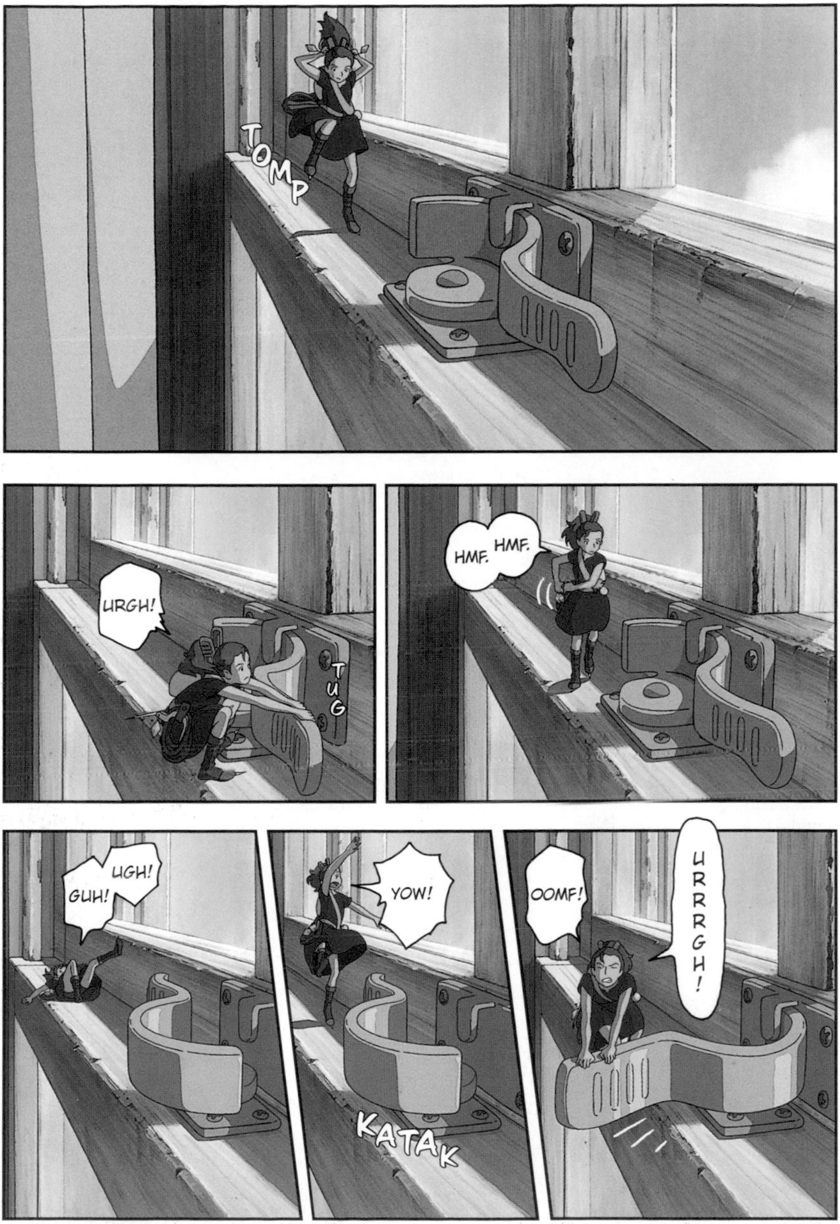
TOMP
HMF. HMF.
URGH!
TUG
URRRGH!
OOMF!
YOW!
KATAK
UGH!
GUH!

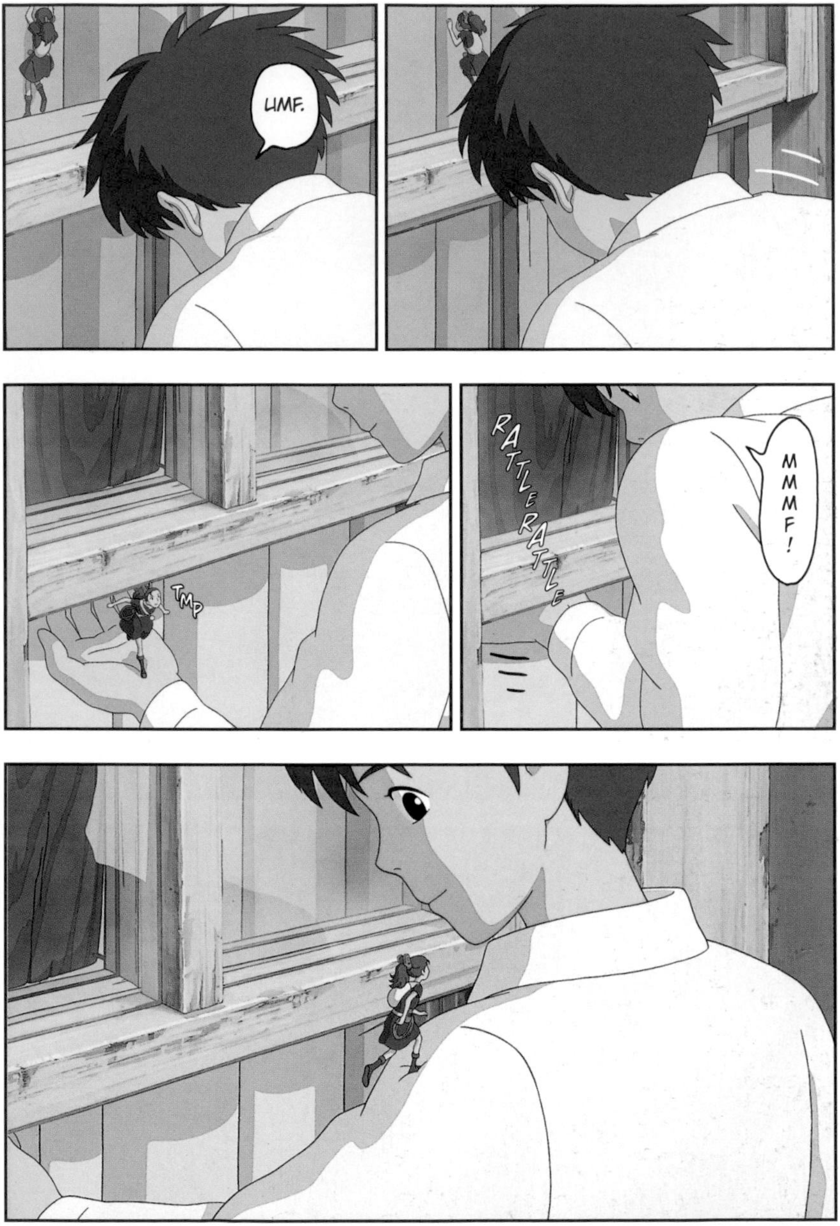
UMF.
RATTLERATTLE
MMMF!
TMP

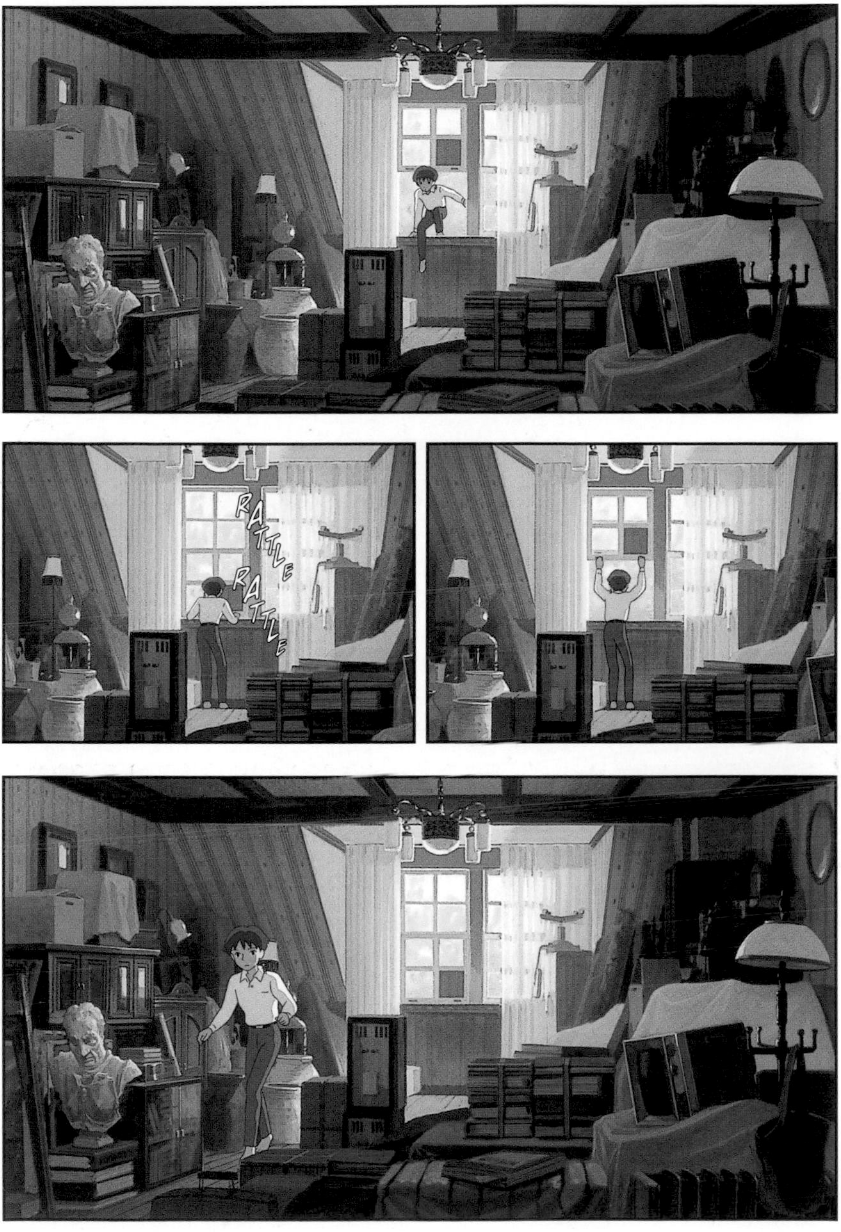
RATTLE RATTLE

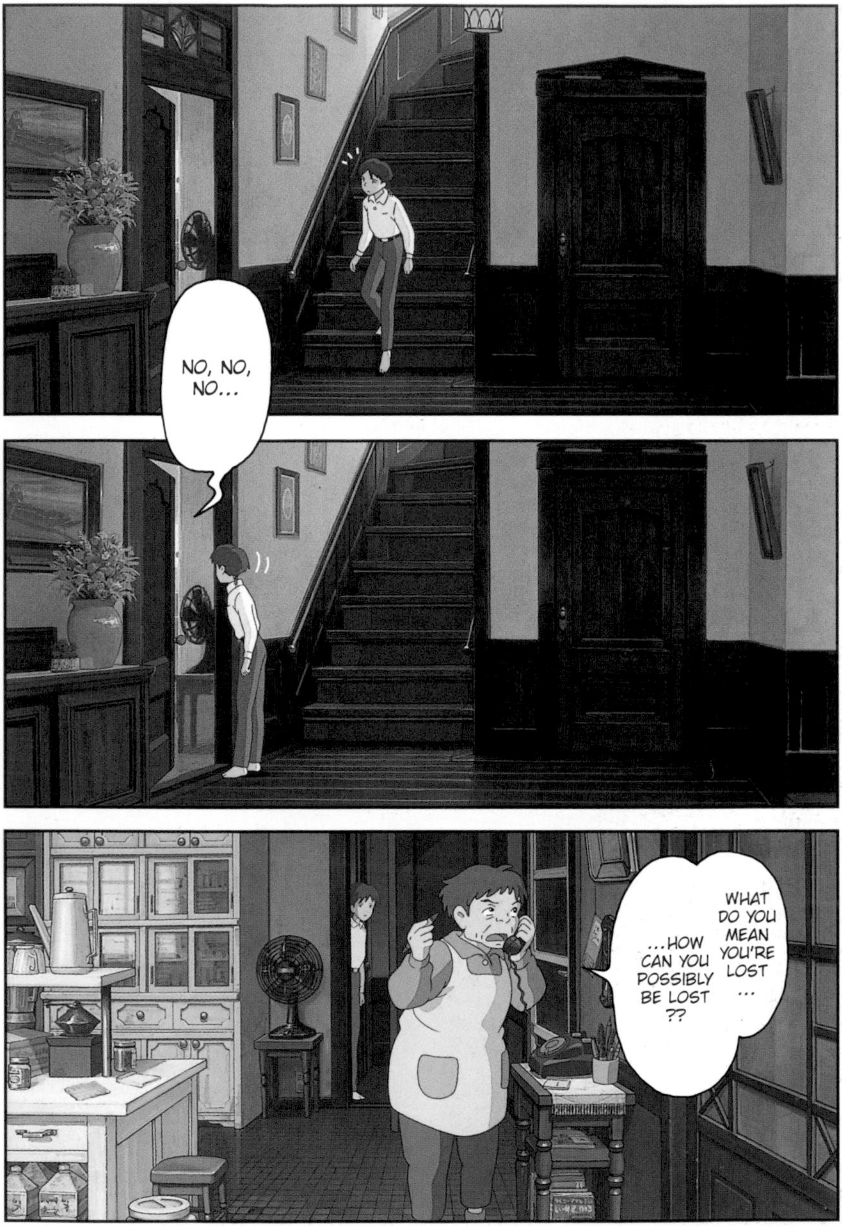
NO, NO, NO...
WHAT DO YOU MEAN YOU'RE LOST ...
...HOW CAN YOU POSSIBLY BE LOST ??

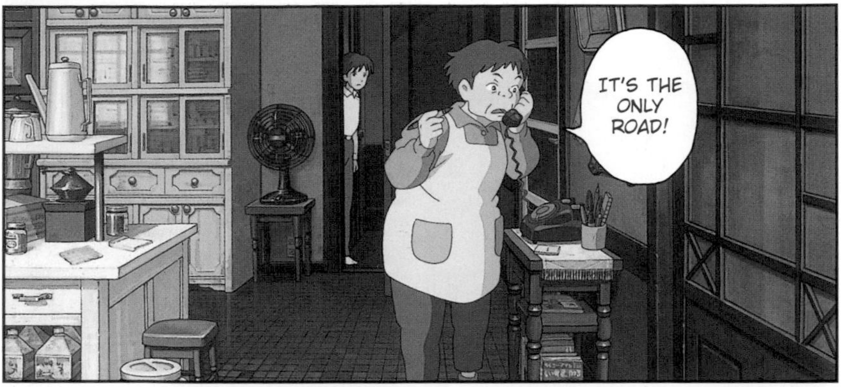
IT'S THE ONLY ROAD!

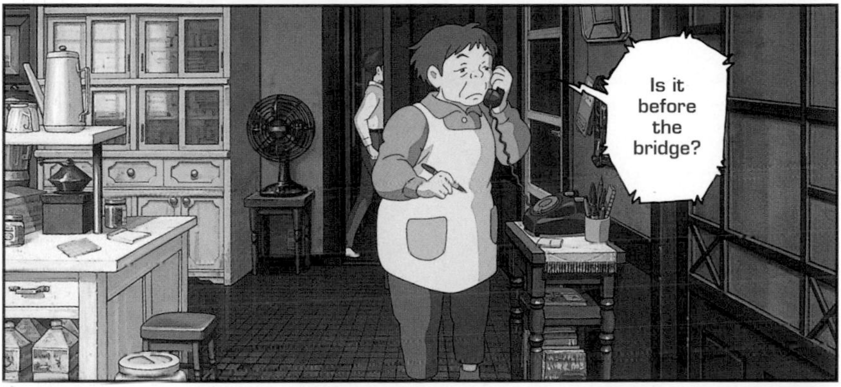
Is it before the bridge?

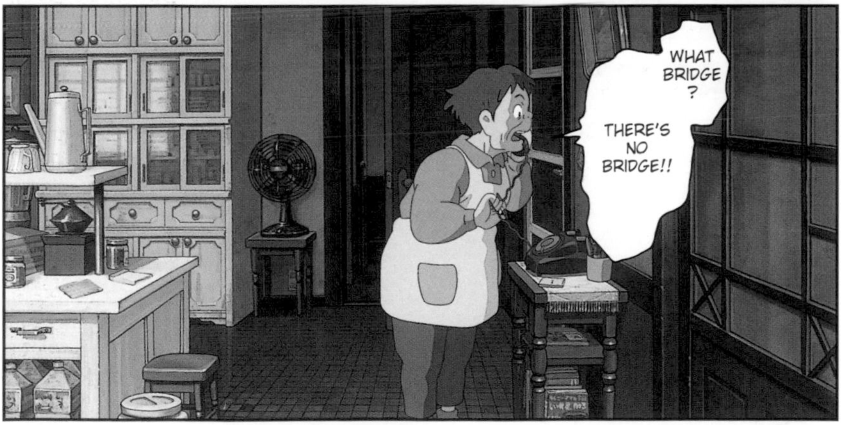
WHAT BRIDGE ?
THERE'S NO BRIDGE!!

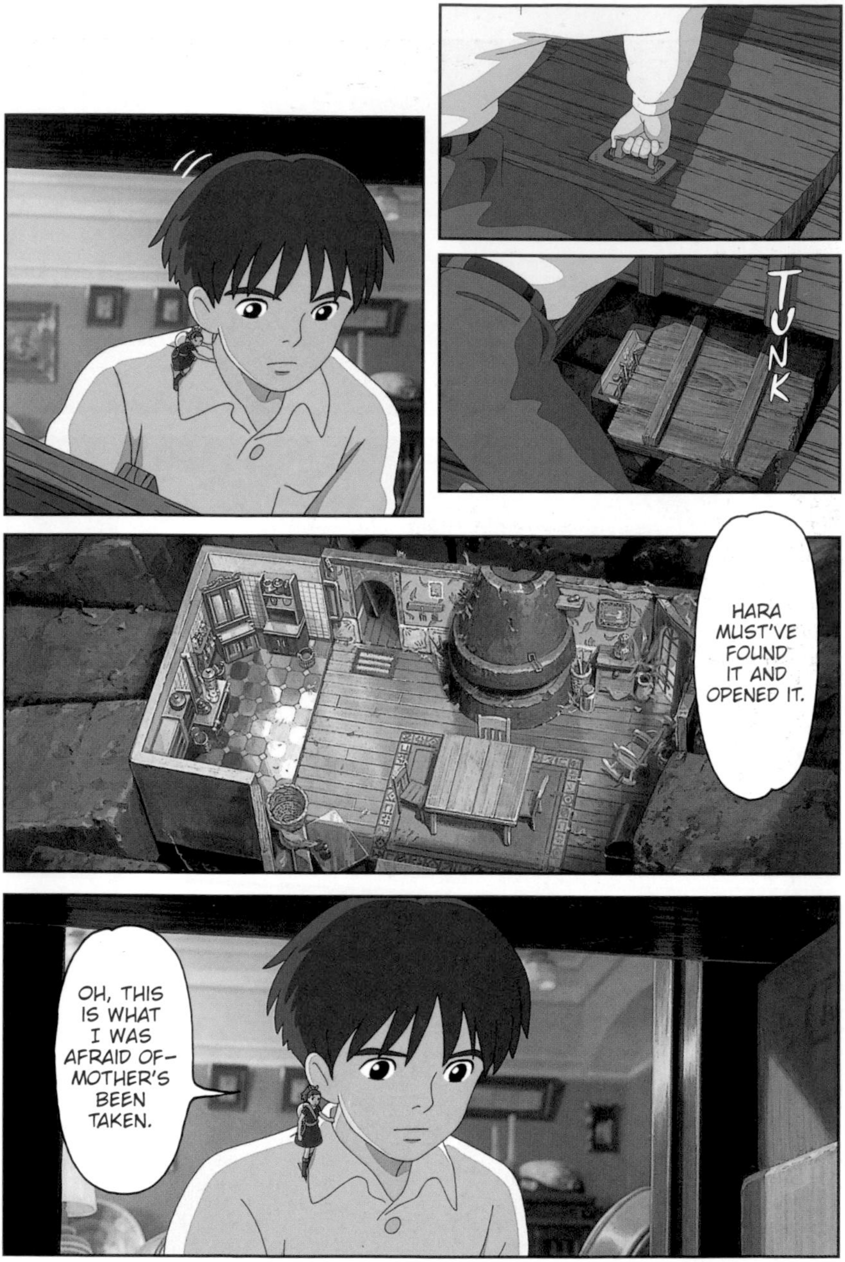
TUNK
HARA MUST'VE FOUND IT AND OPENED IT.
OH, THIS IS WHAT I WAS AFRAID OF—MOTHER'S BEEN TAKEN.

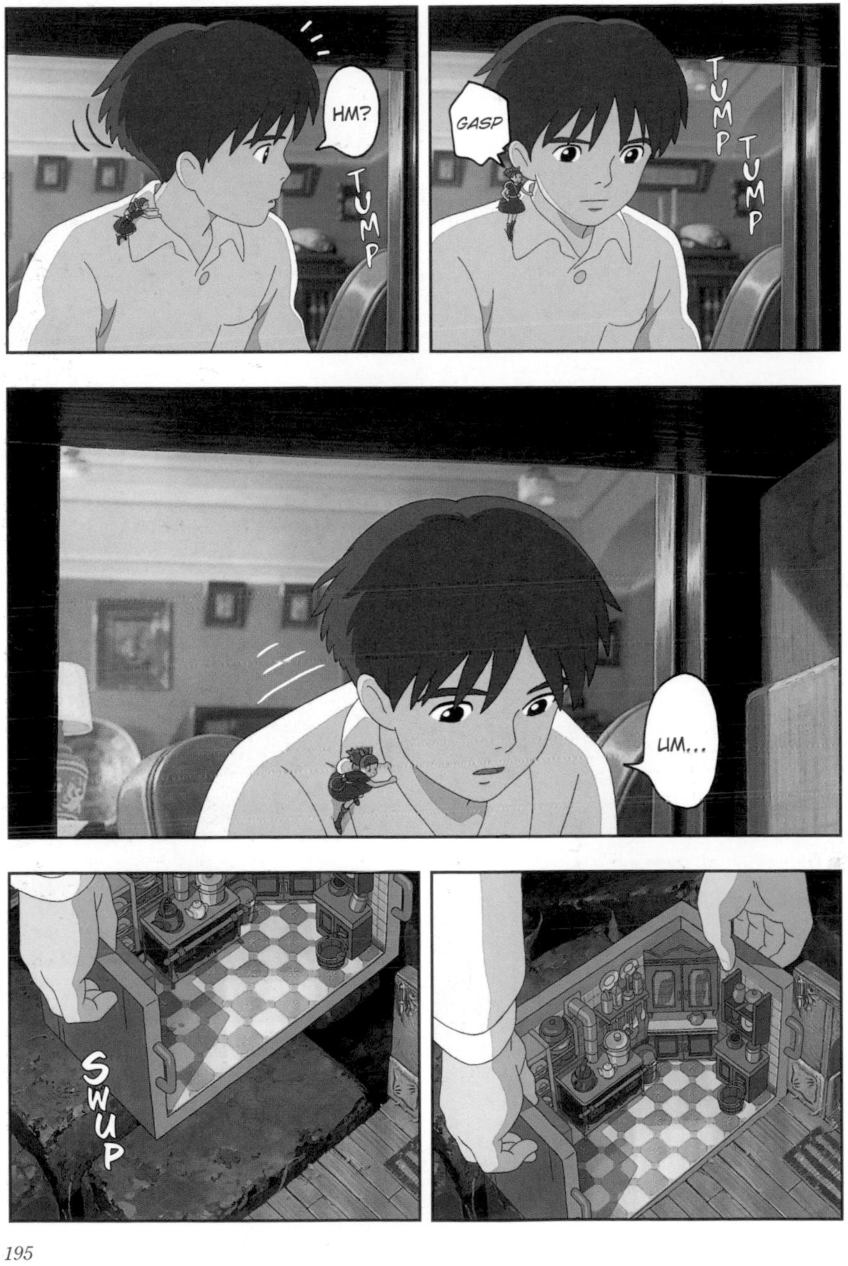
TUMP
TUMP
GASP
HM?
TUMP
UM...
SWUP

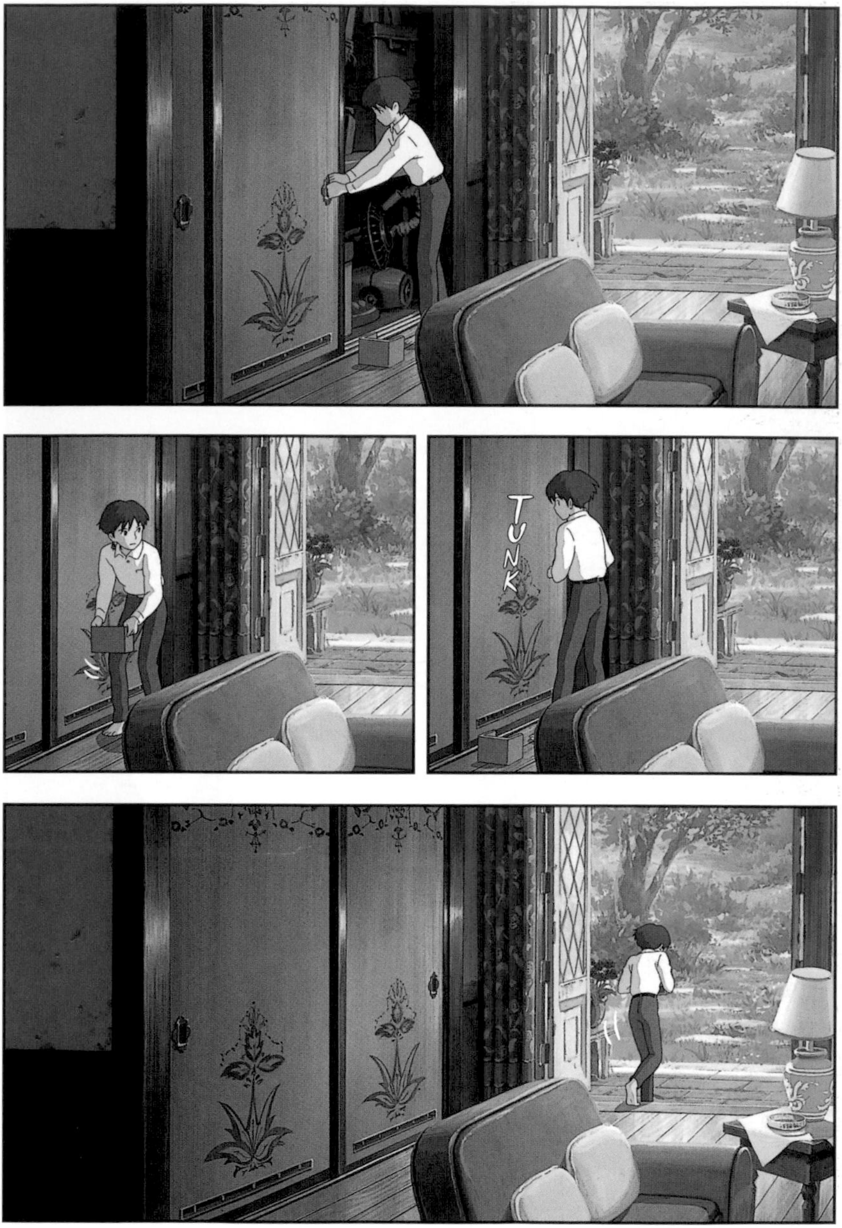
TUNK

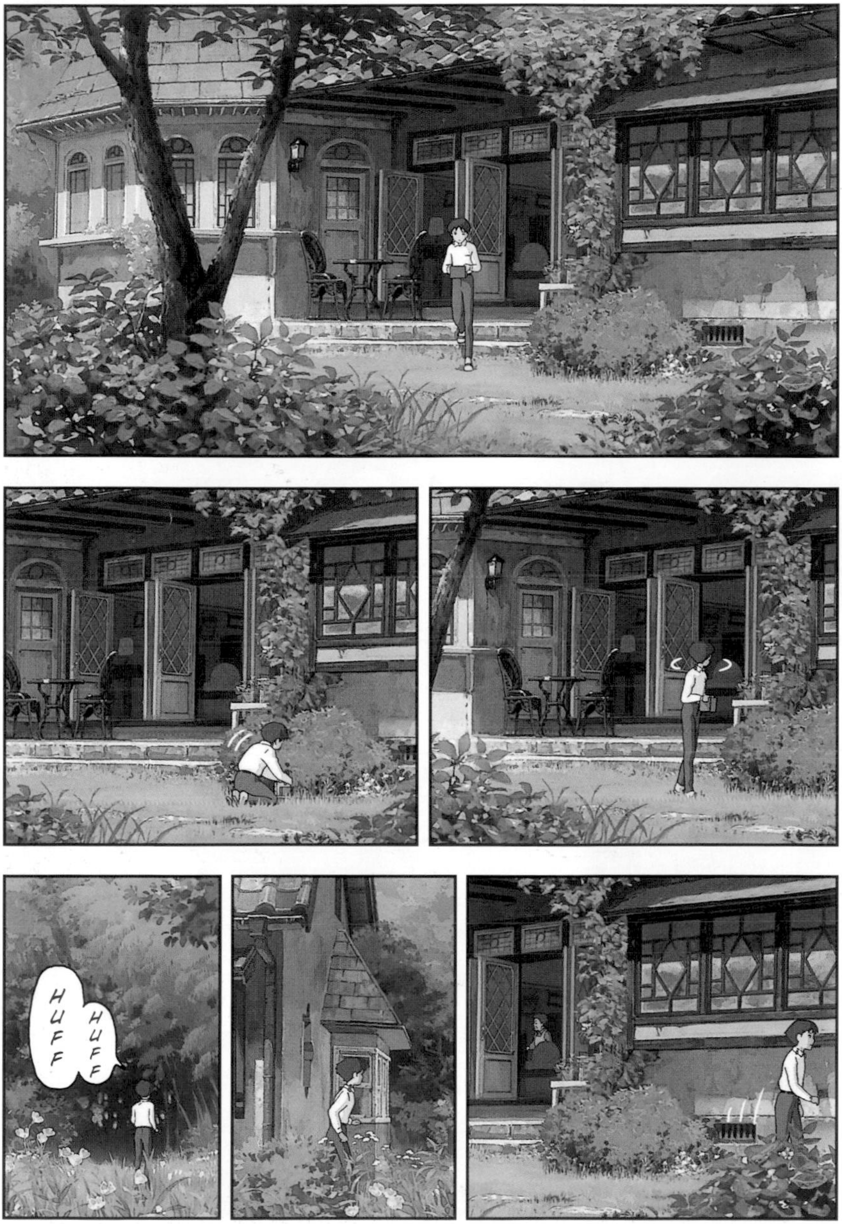
HUFF HUFF

HUFF HUFF HUFF HUFF
TMP TMP TMP
HUFF HUFF
ARE YOU OKAY?
HUFF HUFF
HUFF HUFF HUFF HUFF
NOD

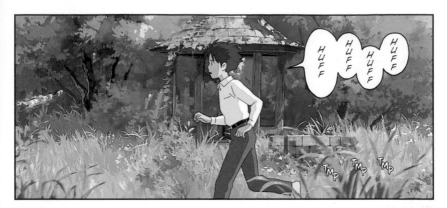

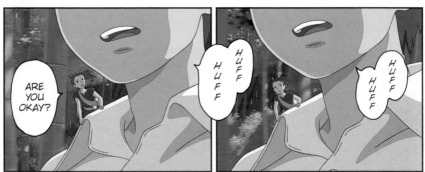

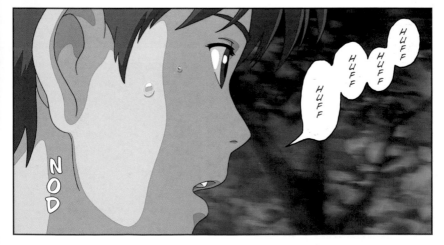

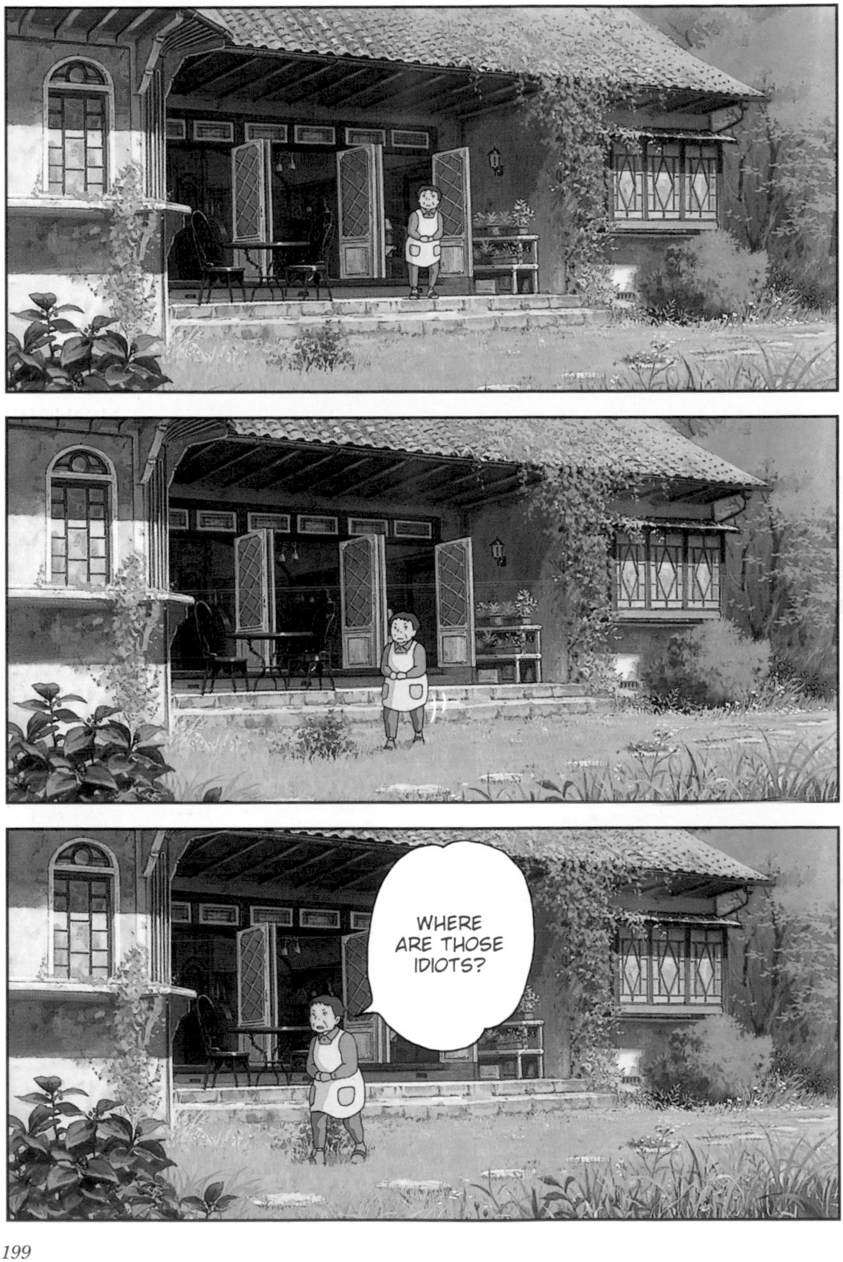
WHERE ARE THOSE IDIOTS?

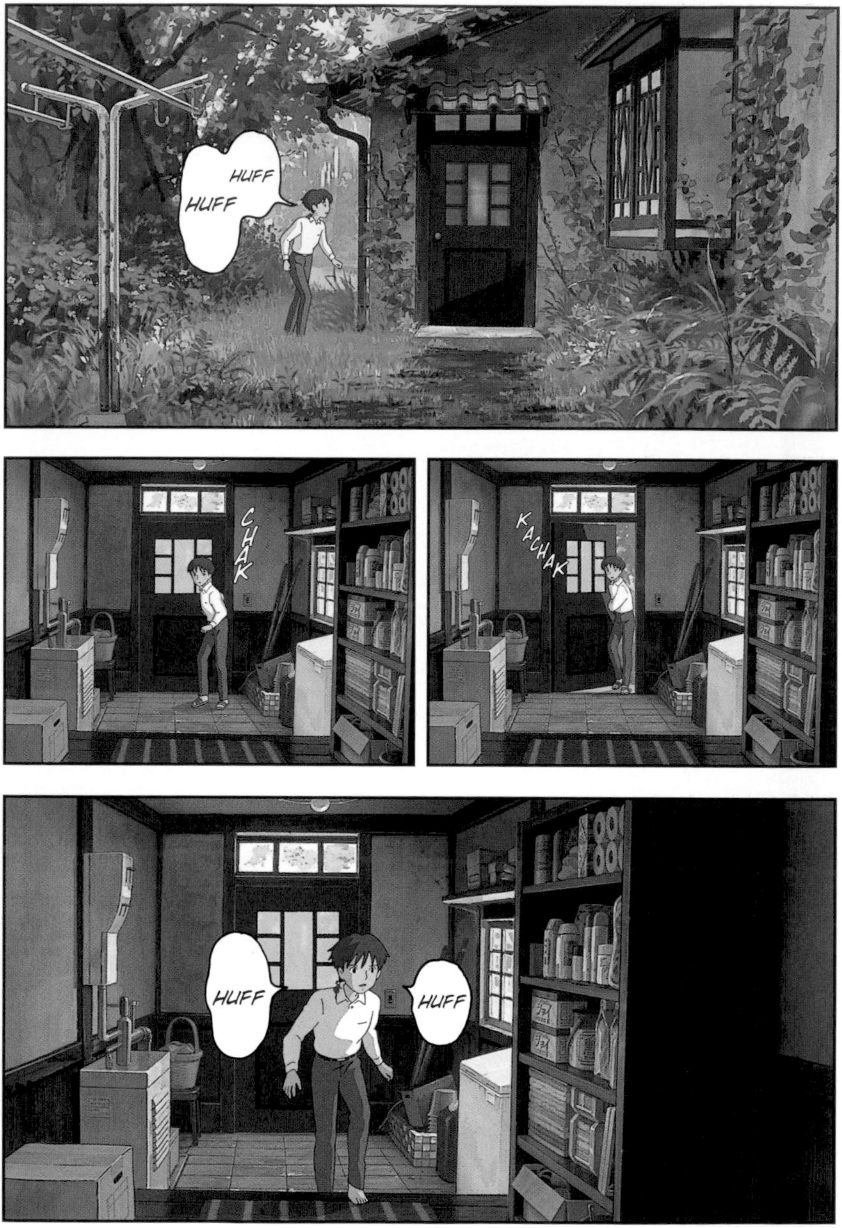
HUFF HUFF
KACHAK
CHAK
HUFF
HUFF

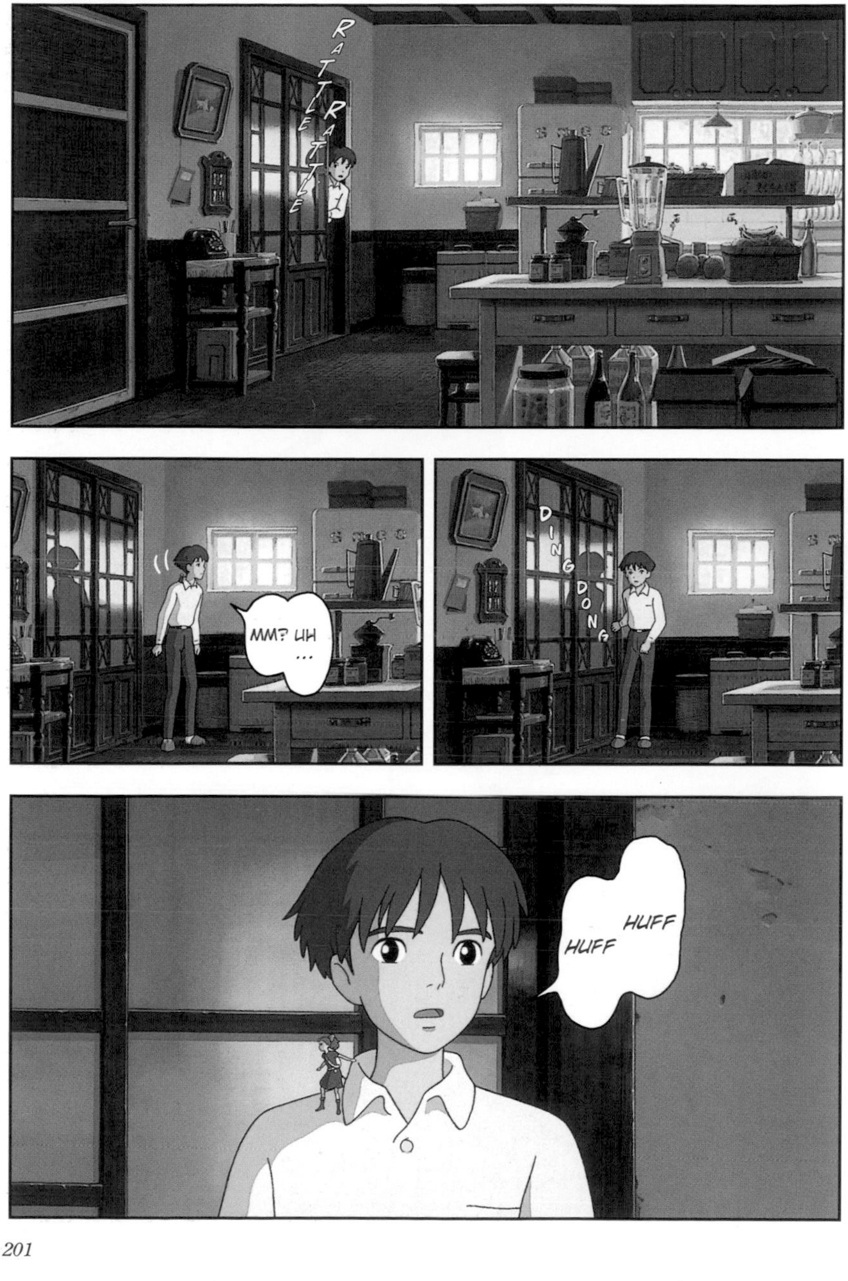
RATTLE RATTLE
DING DONG
MM? UH ...
HUFF HUFF

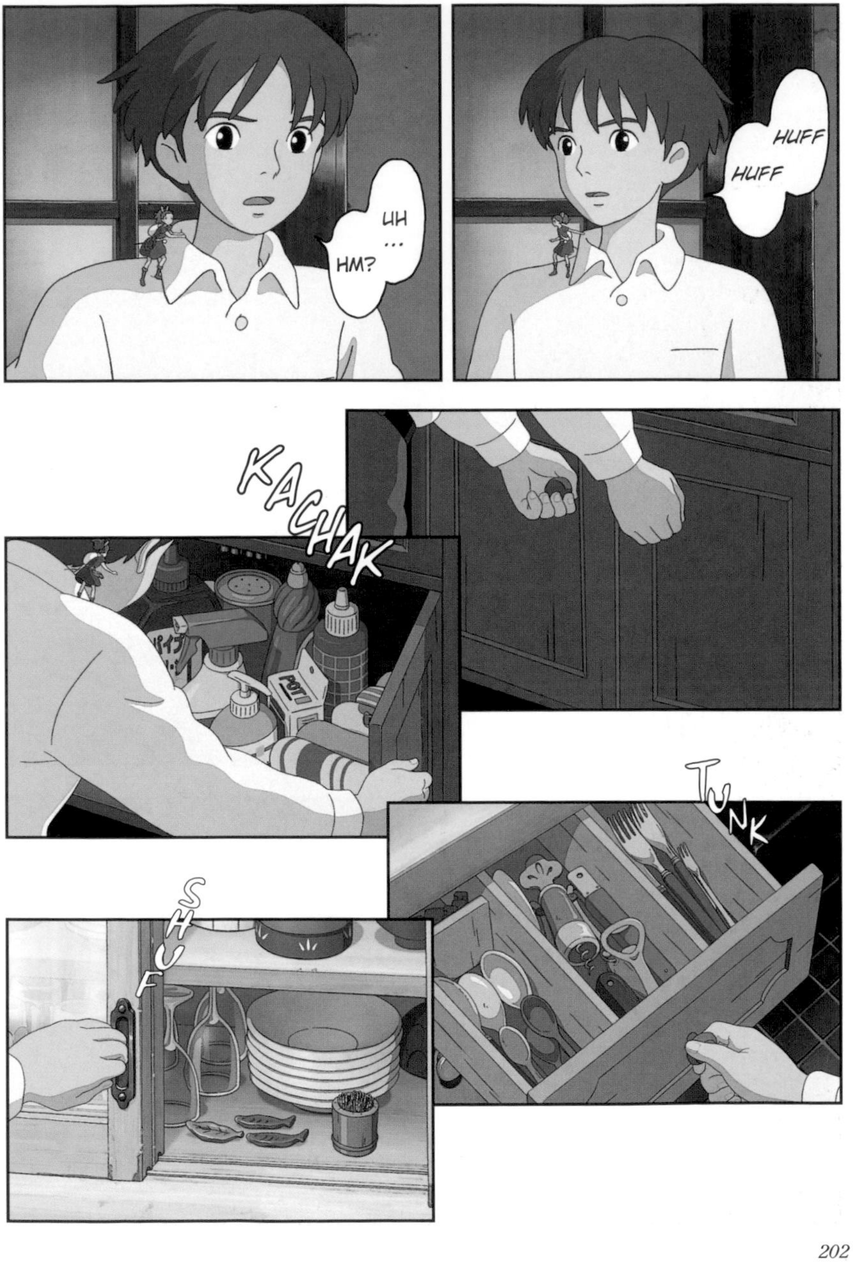
HUFF
HUFF
UH ... HM?
KACHAK
TUNK
SHUF

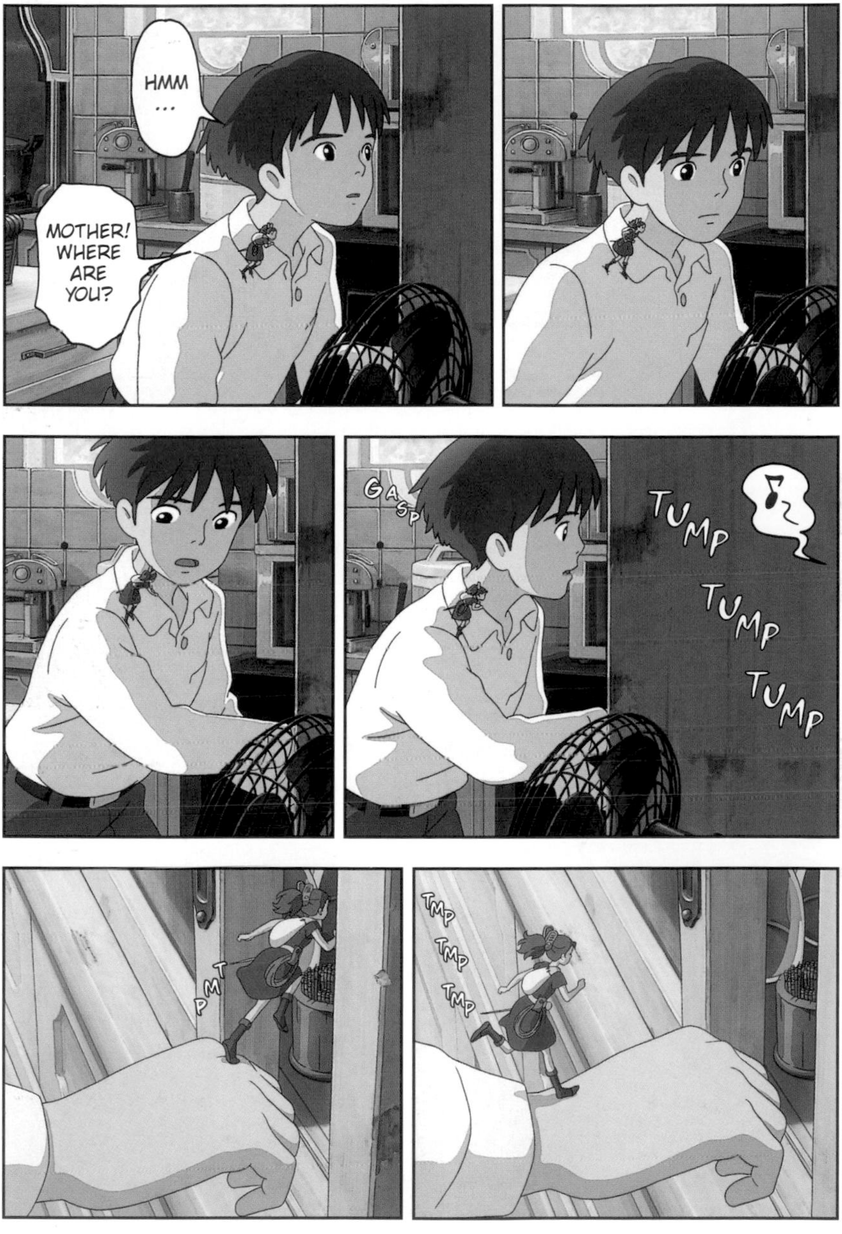
HMM ...
MOTHER! WHERE ARE YOU?
TUMP
TUMP
TUMP
TUMP
GASP
TMP
TMP
TMP
TMP

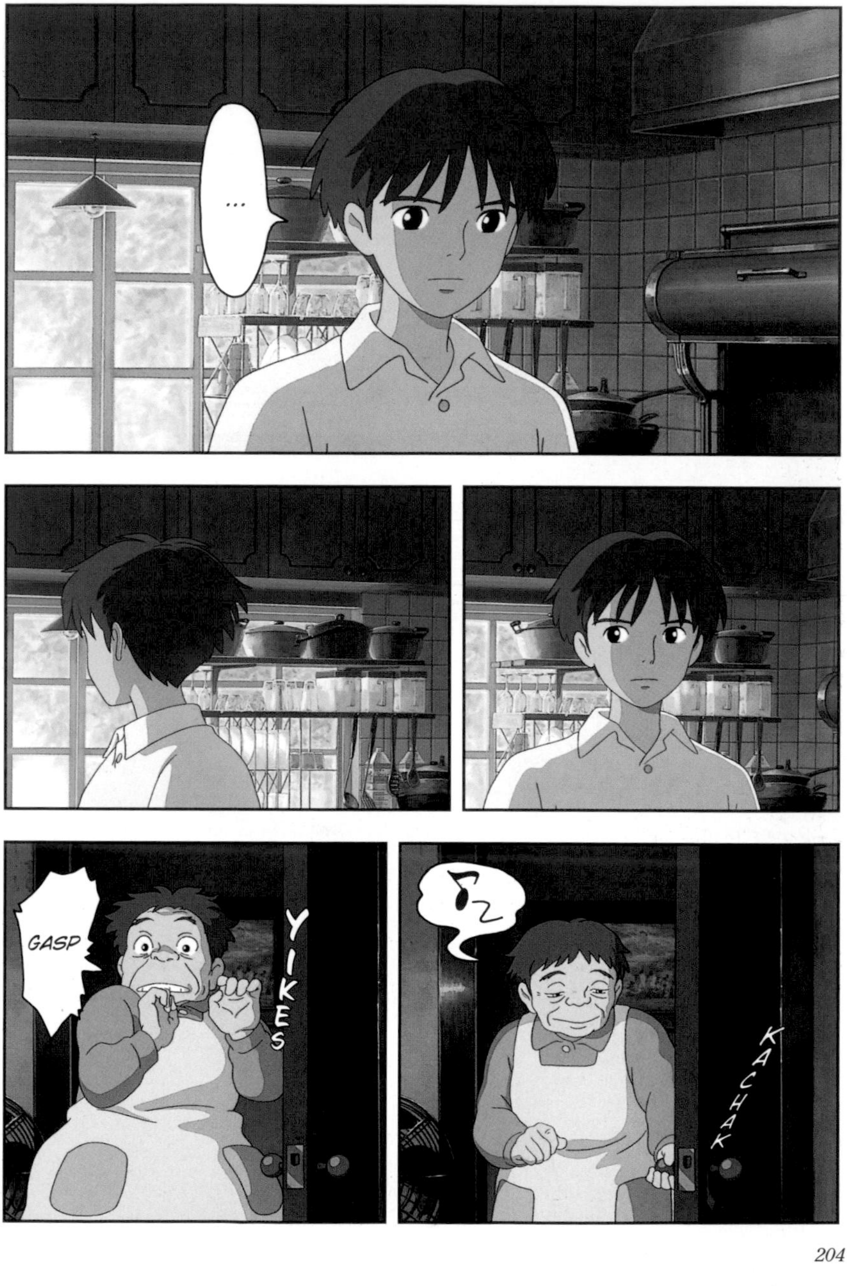
...
♪
KACHAK
GASP
YIKES

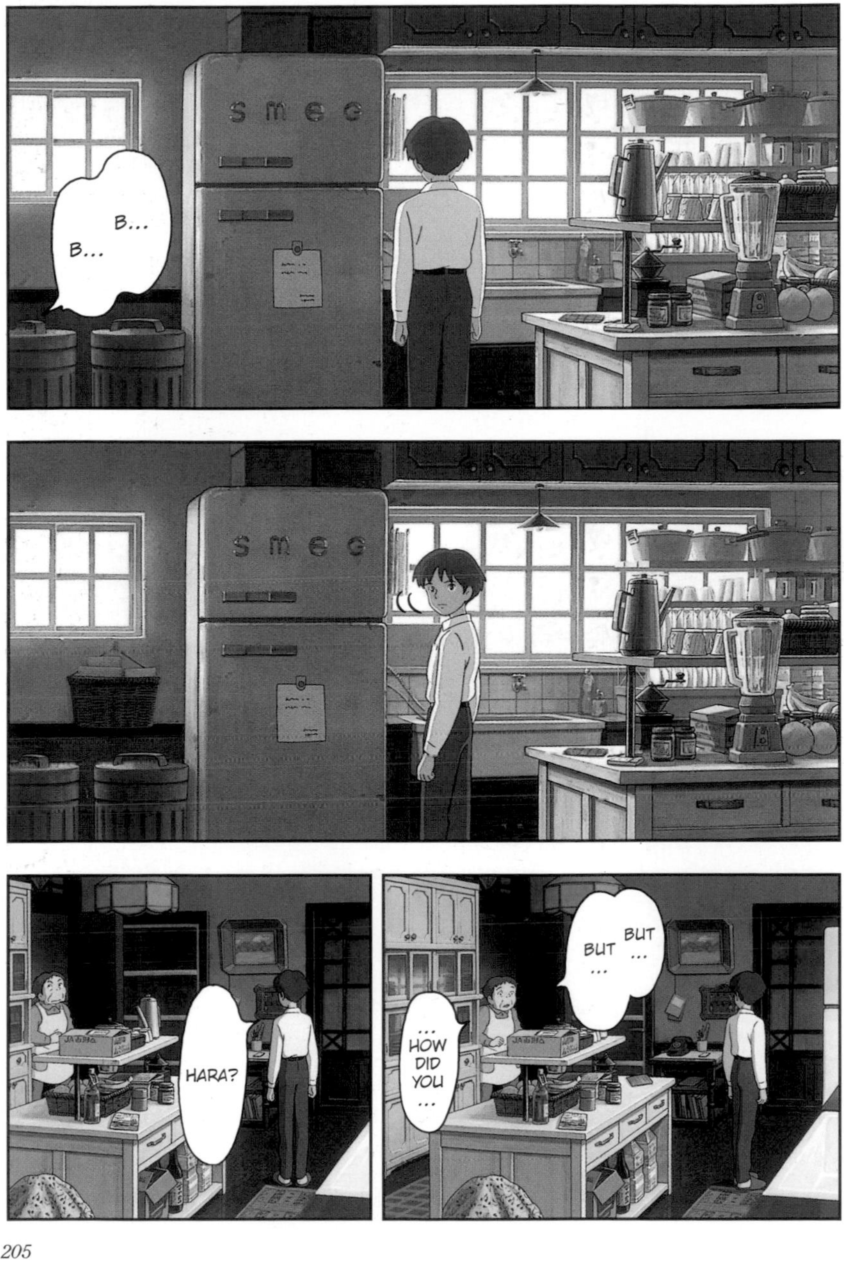
B... B...
BUT ... BUT ...
... HOW DID YOU ...
HARA?

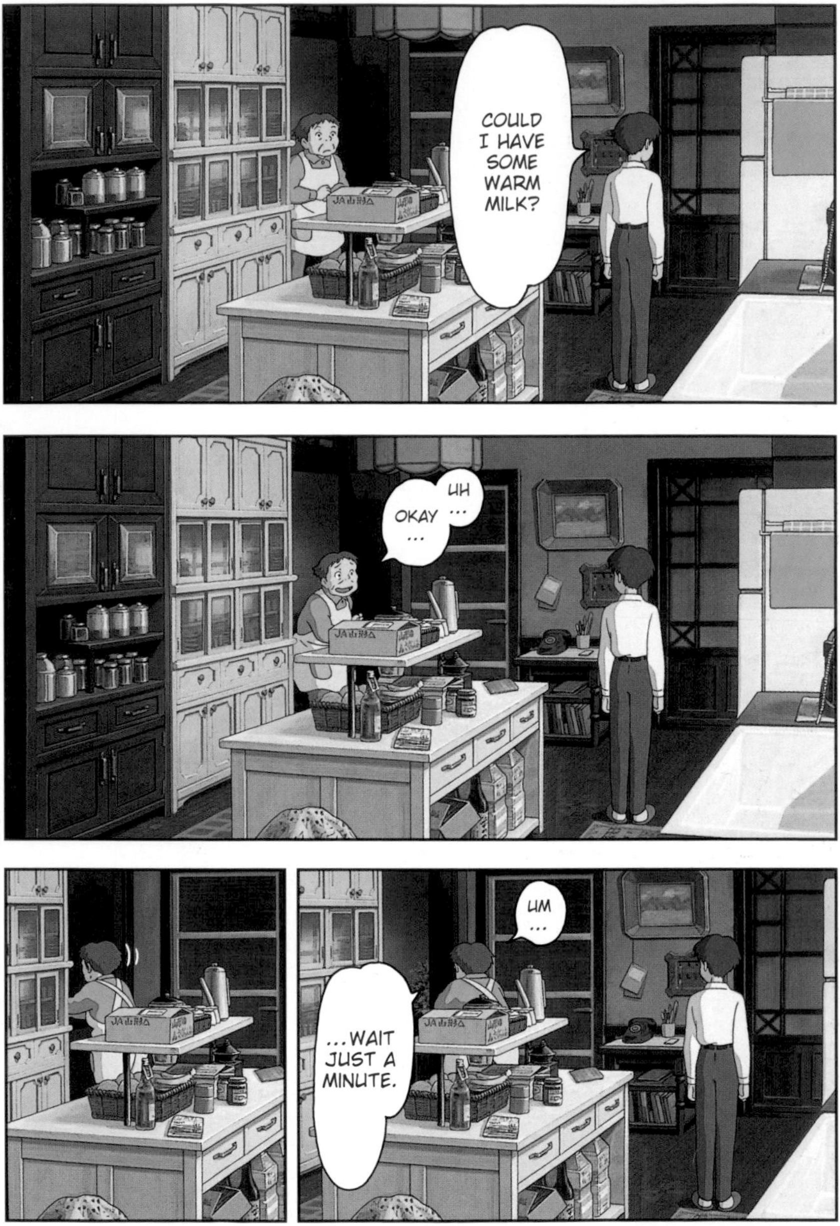
COULD I HAVE SOME WARM MILK?
UH ...
OKAY ...
UM ...
...WAIT JUST A MINUTE.

TNK
HEH HEH ...!
GLANCE

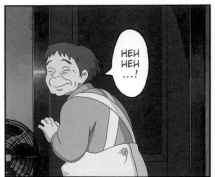

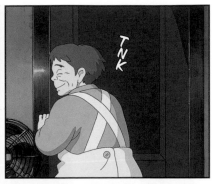

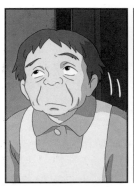

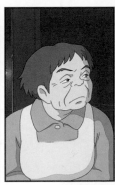

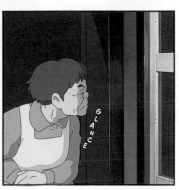

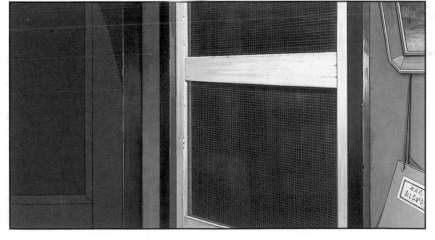

THANK YOU, HARA.
TUNK
TMP

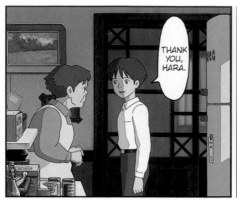

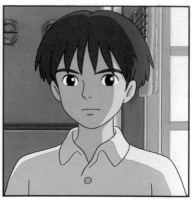

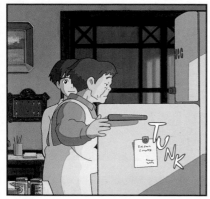

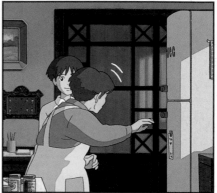

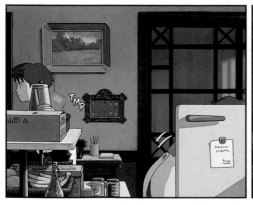

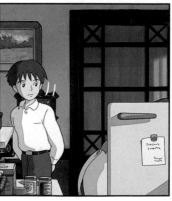

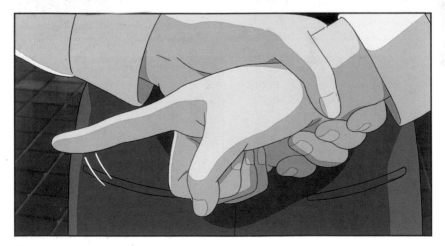

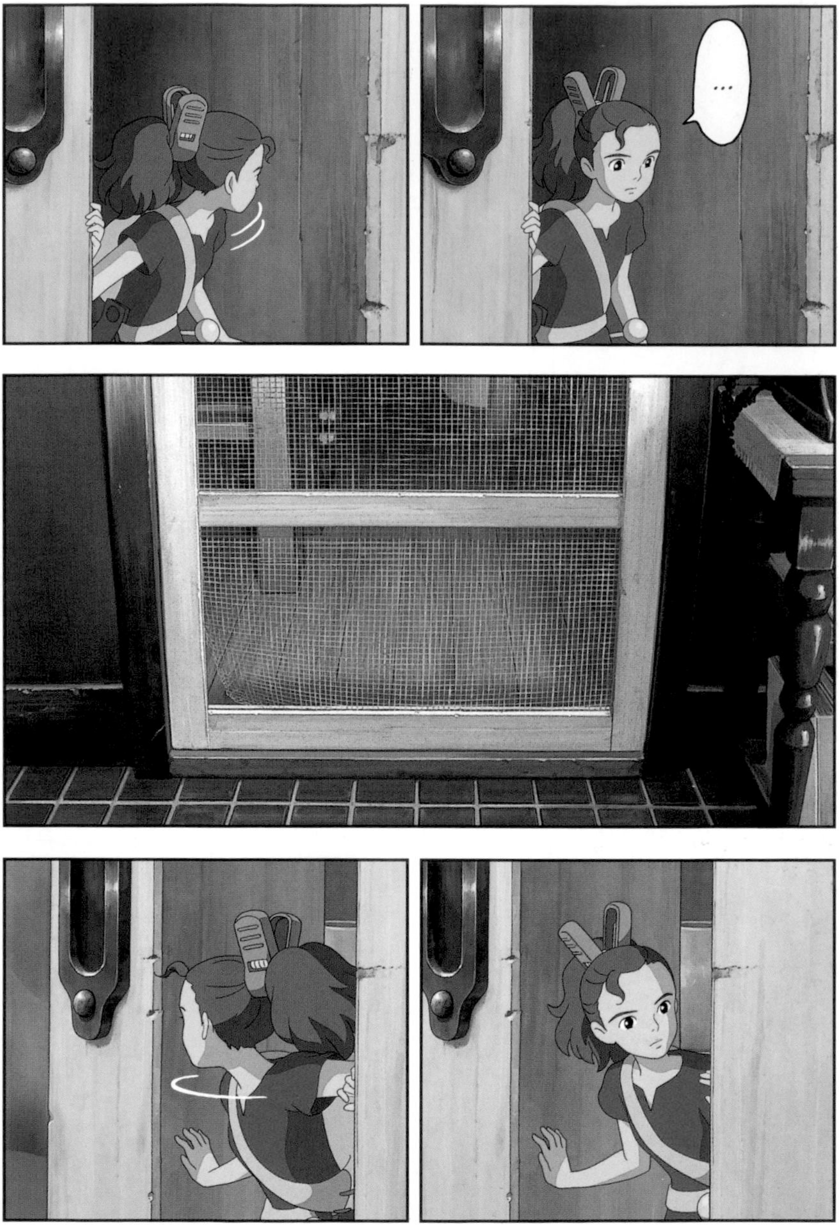
...

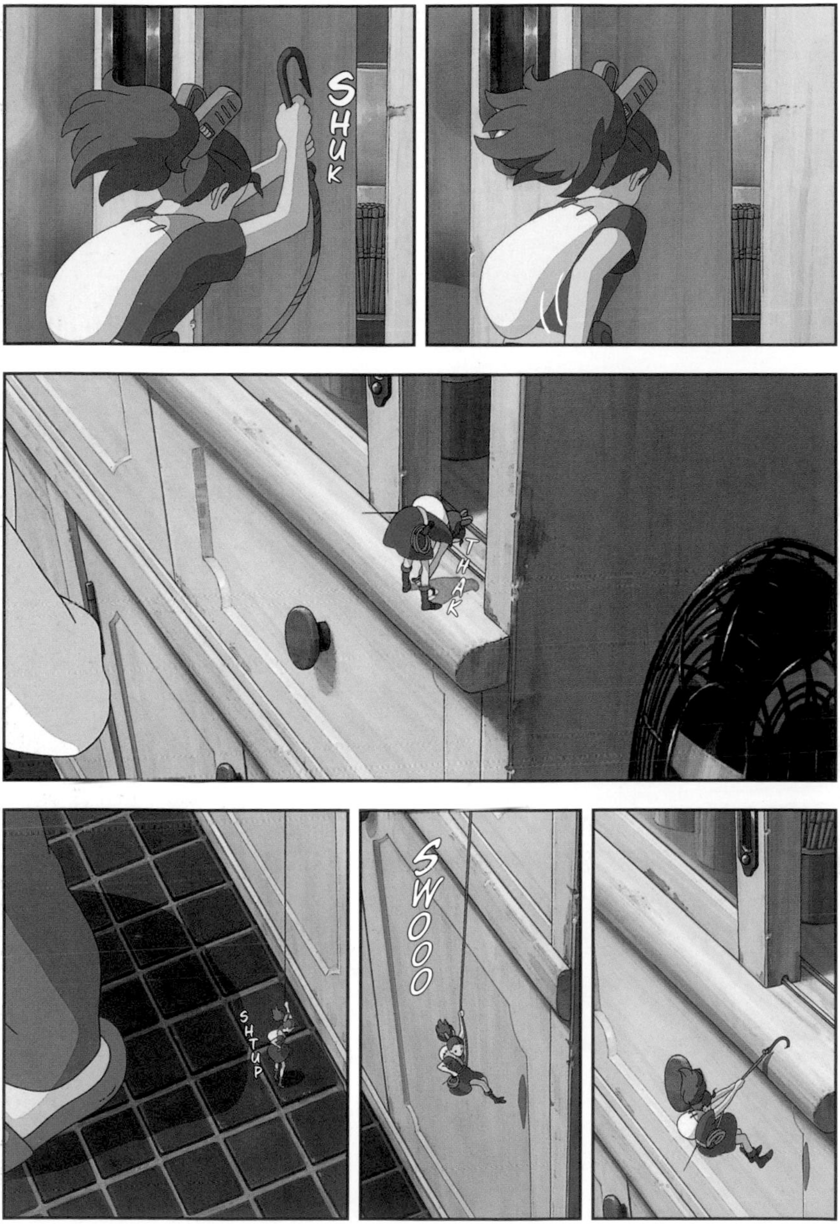
SHUK
THAK
SWOOO
SHTUP

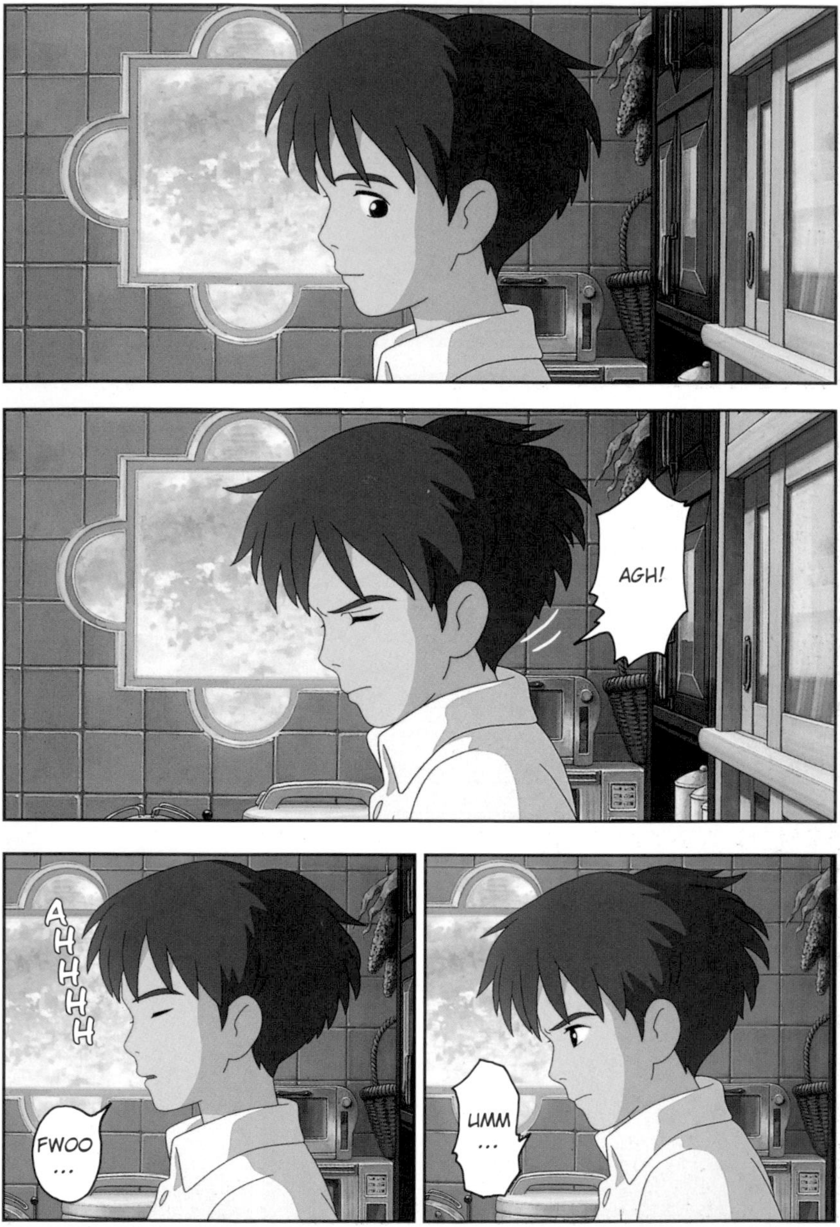
AGH!
UMM ...
AHHHH
FWOO ...

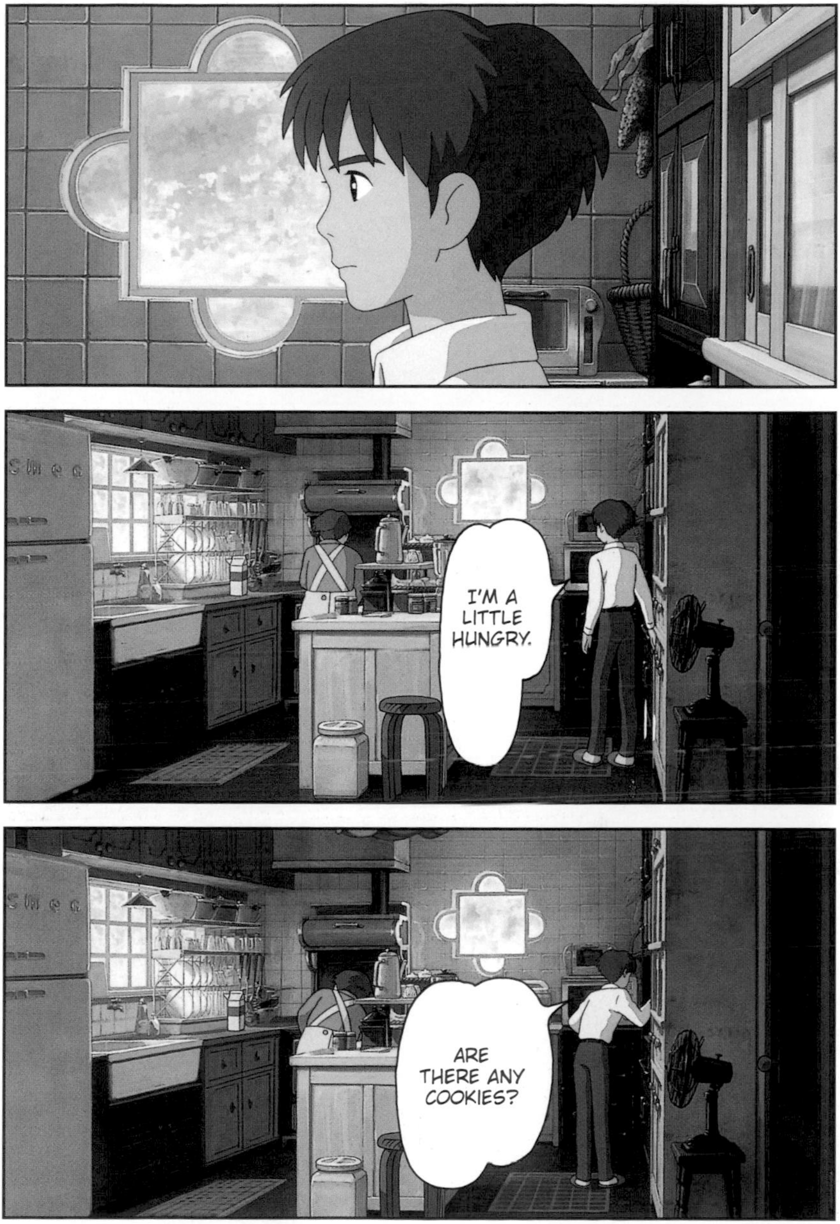
I'M A LITTLE HUNGRY.
ARE THERE ANY COOKIES?

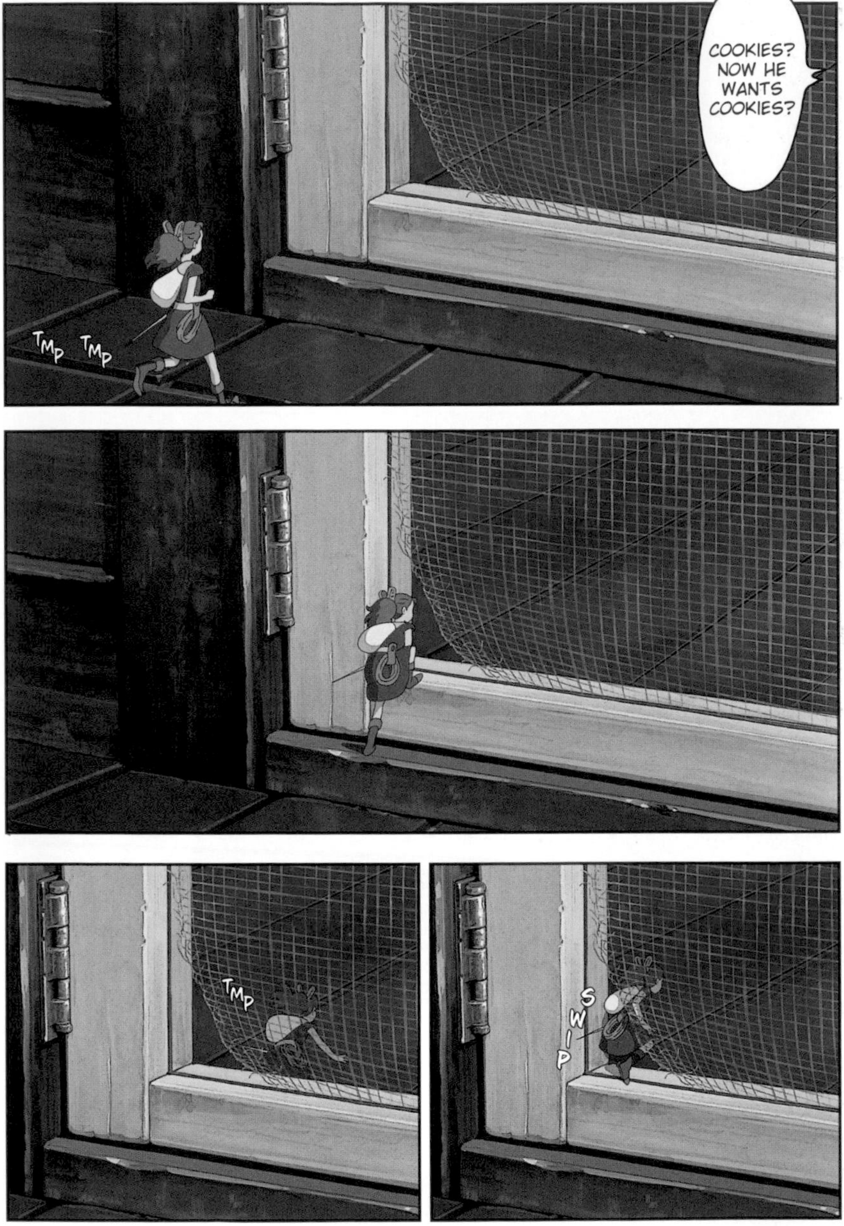
COOKIES? NOW HE WANTS COOKIES?
TMP TMP
SWIP
TMP

TMP
TMP
MOTHER!
UM...
MOTHER!

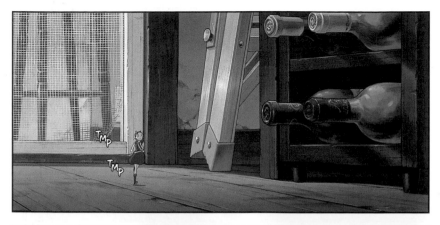

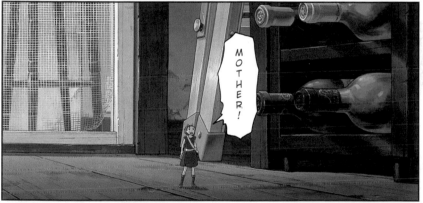

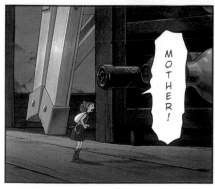

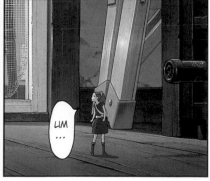

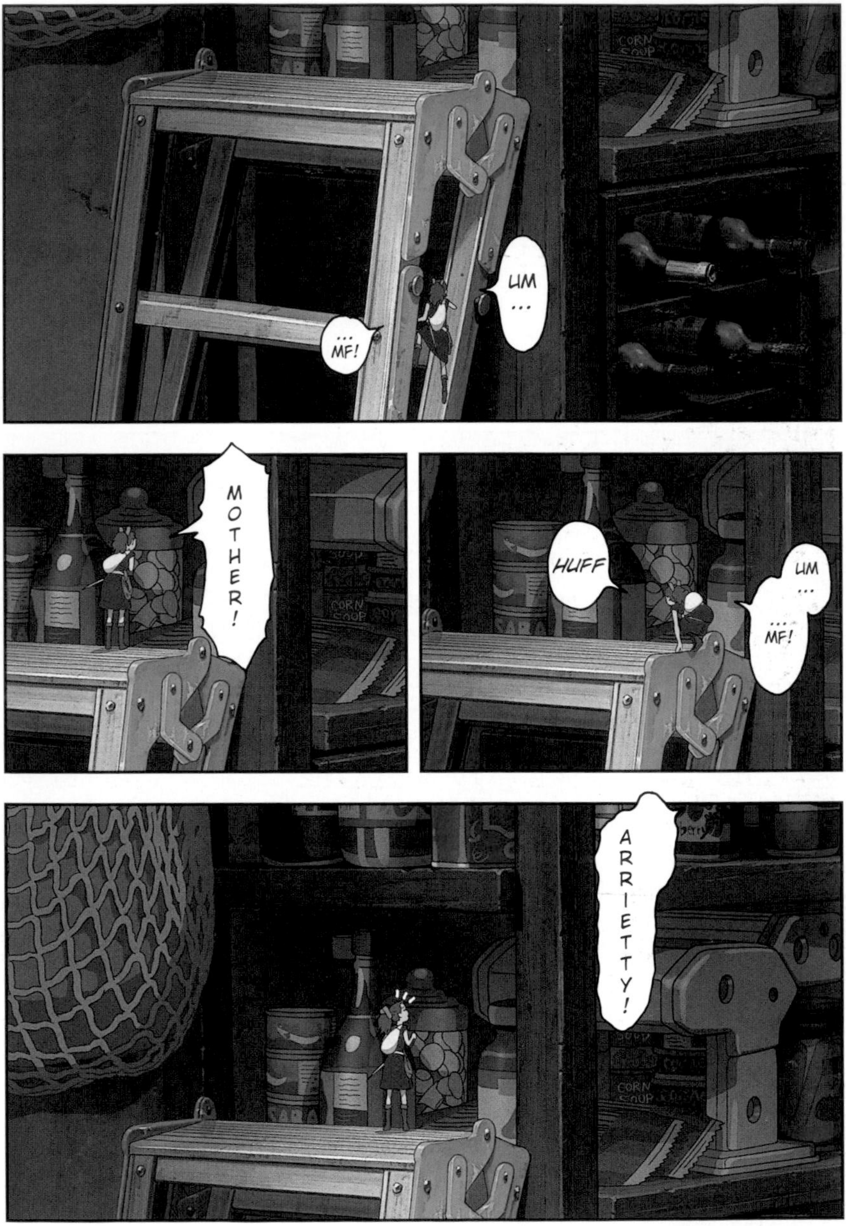
UM ...
... MF!
UM ...
... MF!
HUFF
MOTHER!
ARRIETTY!

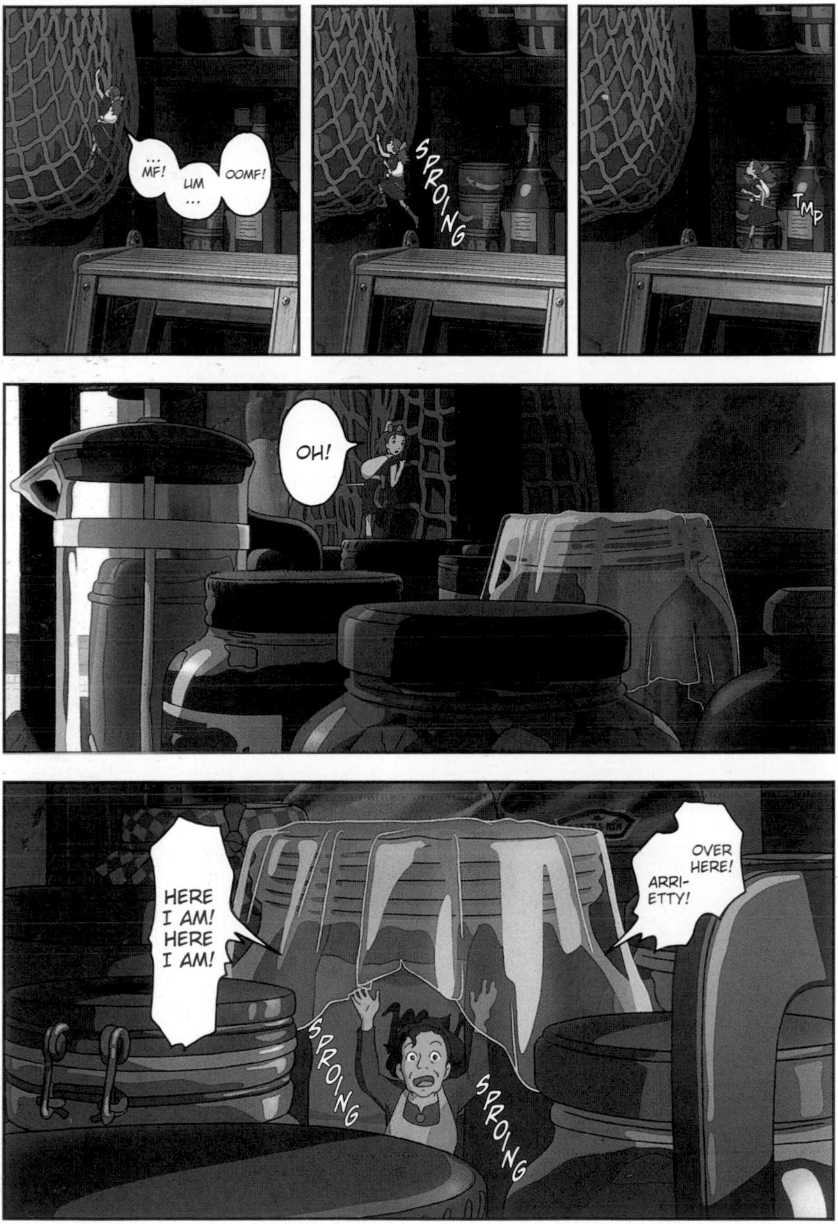
TMP
SPROING
OOMF!
... MF!
UM ...
OH!
OVER HERE! ARRI-ETTY!
HERE I AM! HERE I AM!
SPROING
SPROING

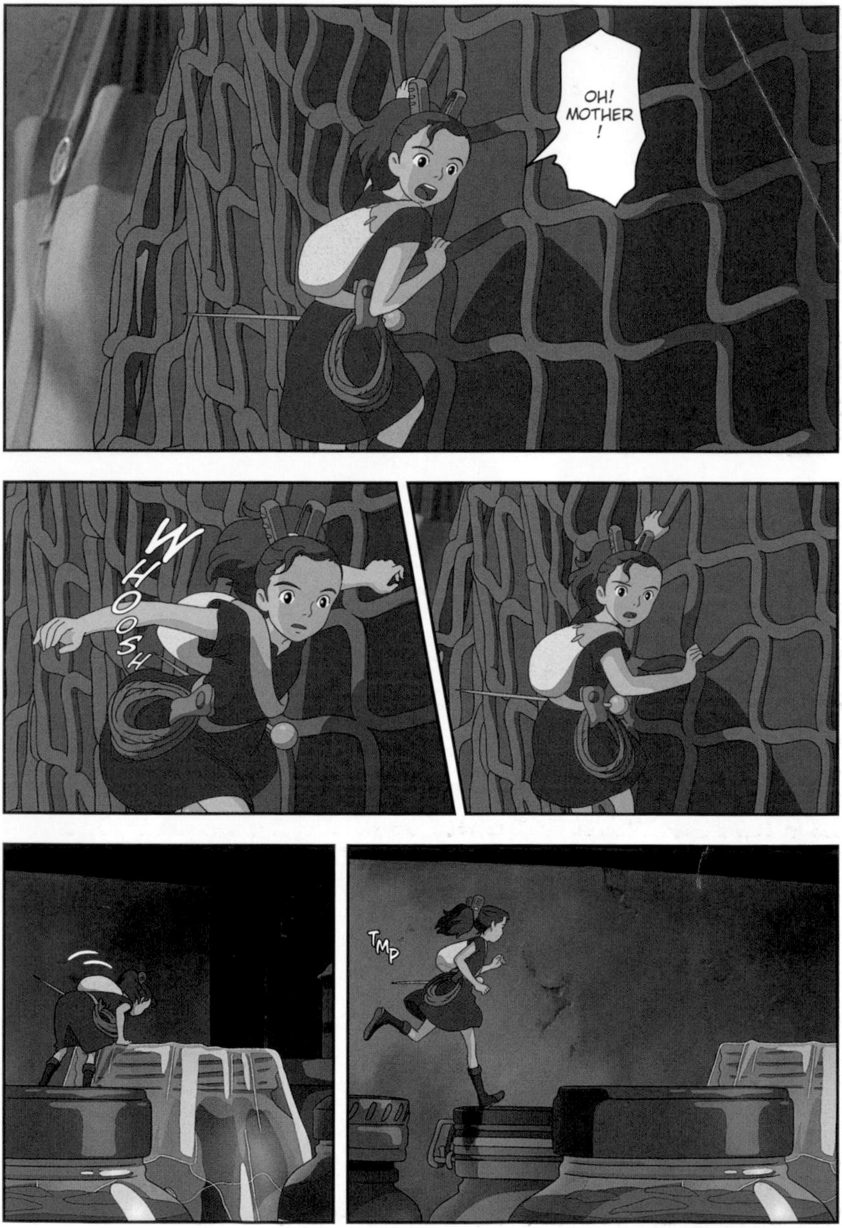
OH! MOTHER !
WHOOSH
TMP

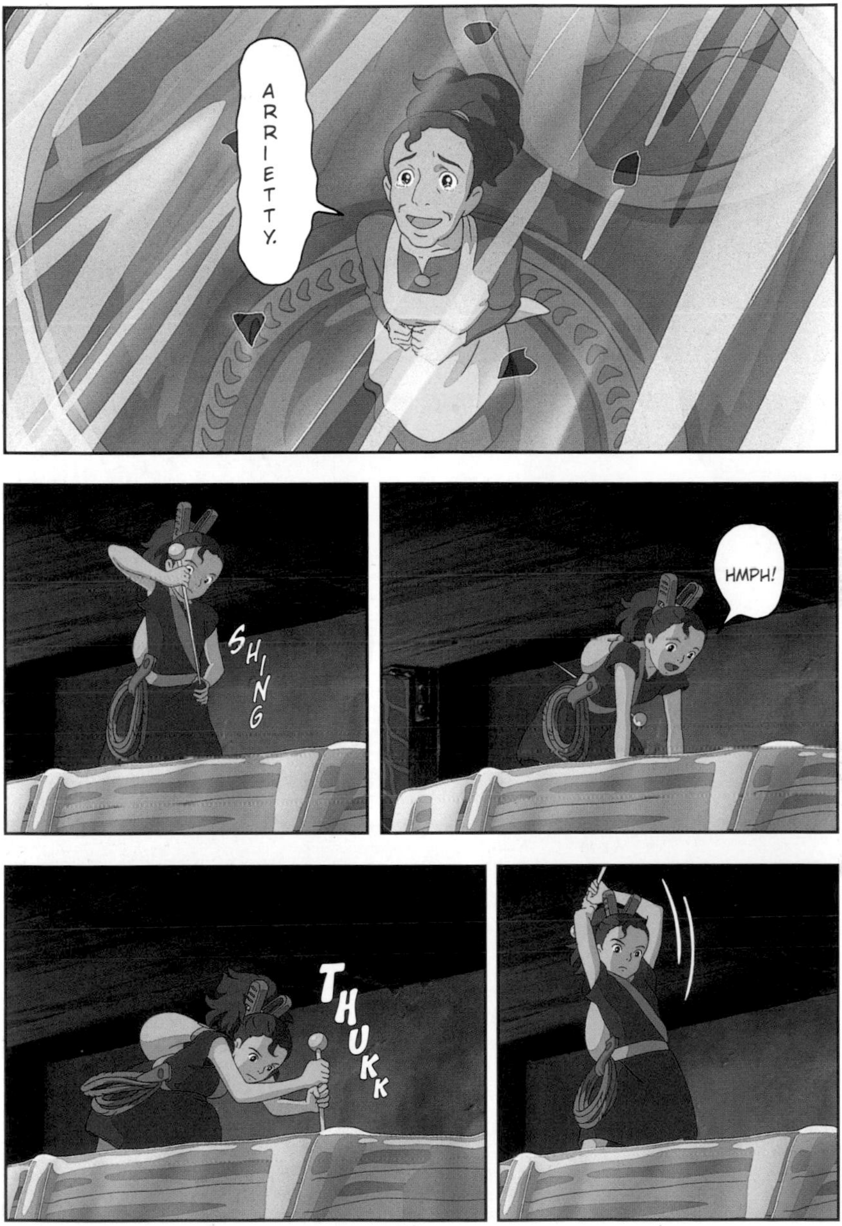
ARRIETTY.
HMPH!
SHING
THUKK

URGH
UNGH!
NNGH!
RRRIP
POKE
RRRIP
RRRIP

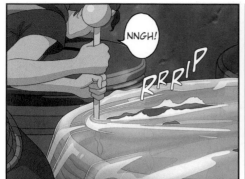

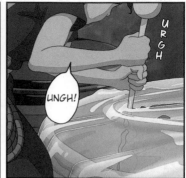

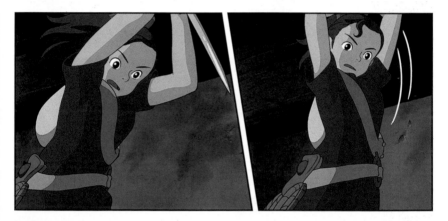

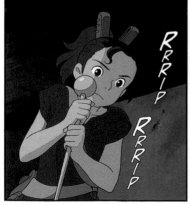

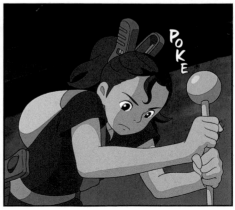

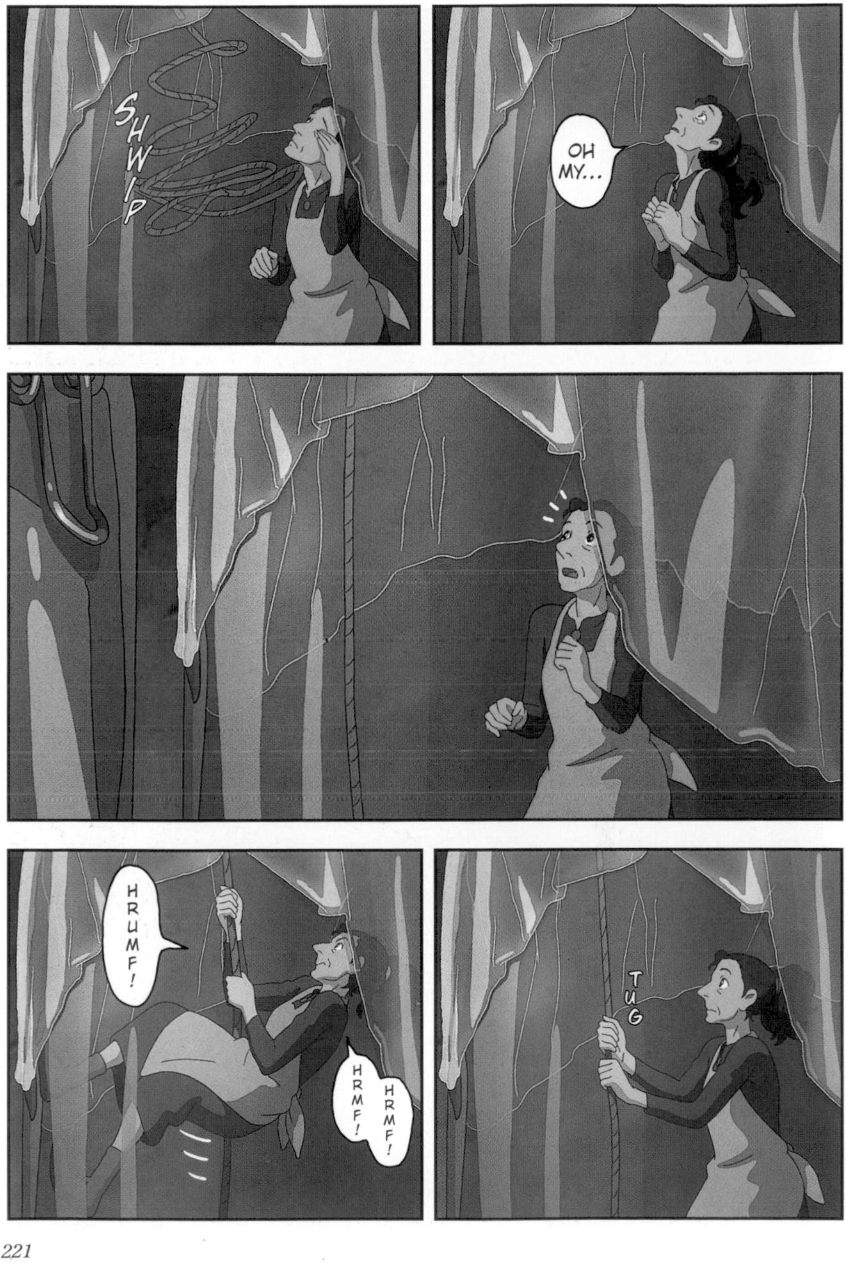
OH MY...
SHWIP
TUG
HRUMF!
HRMF! HRMF!

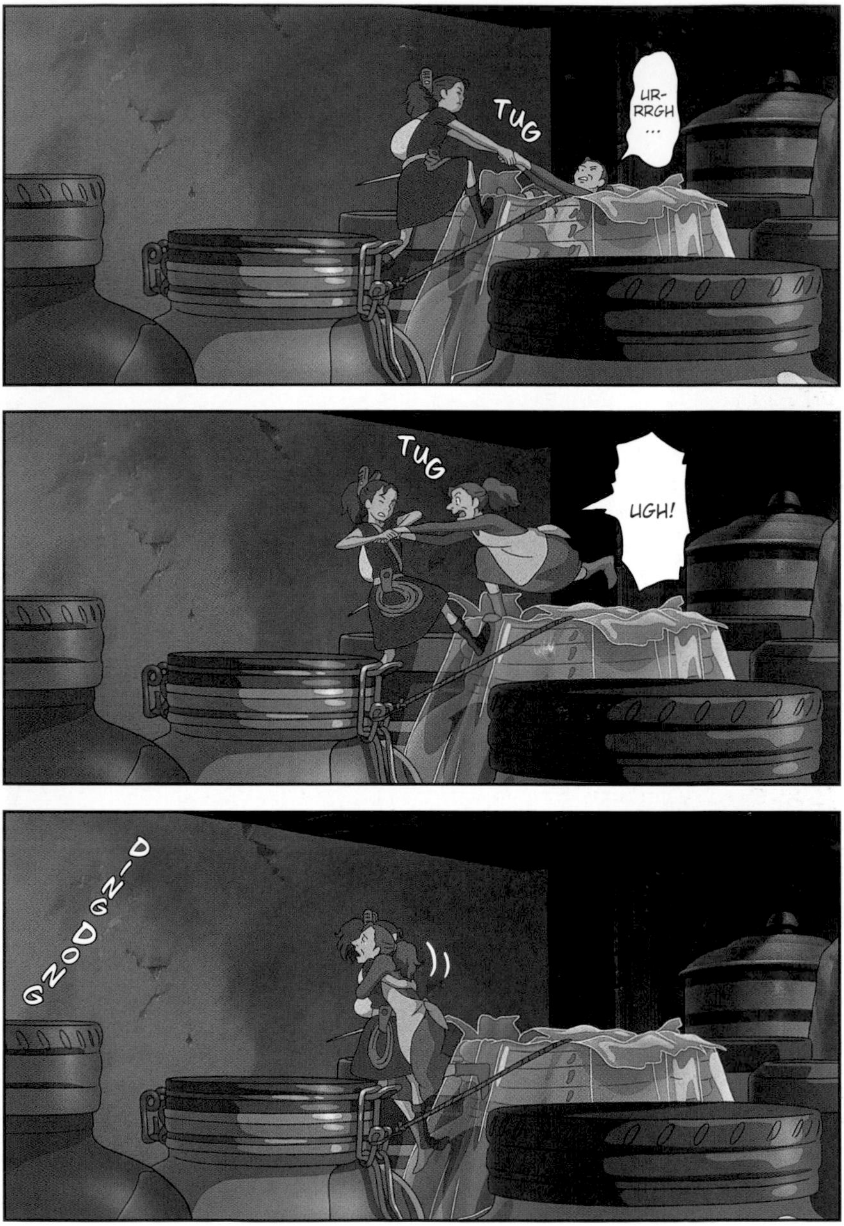
UR-
RRGH
...
TUG
UGH!
TUG
D-I-N-G
DONG

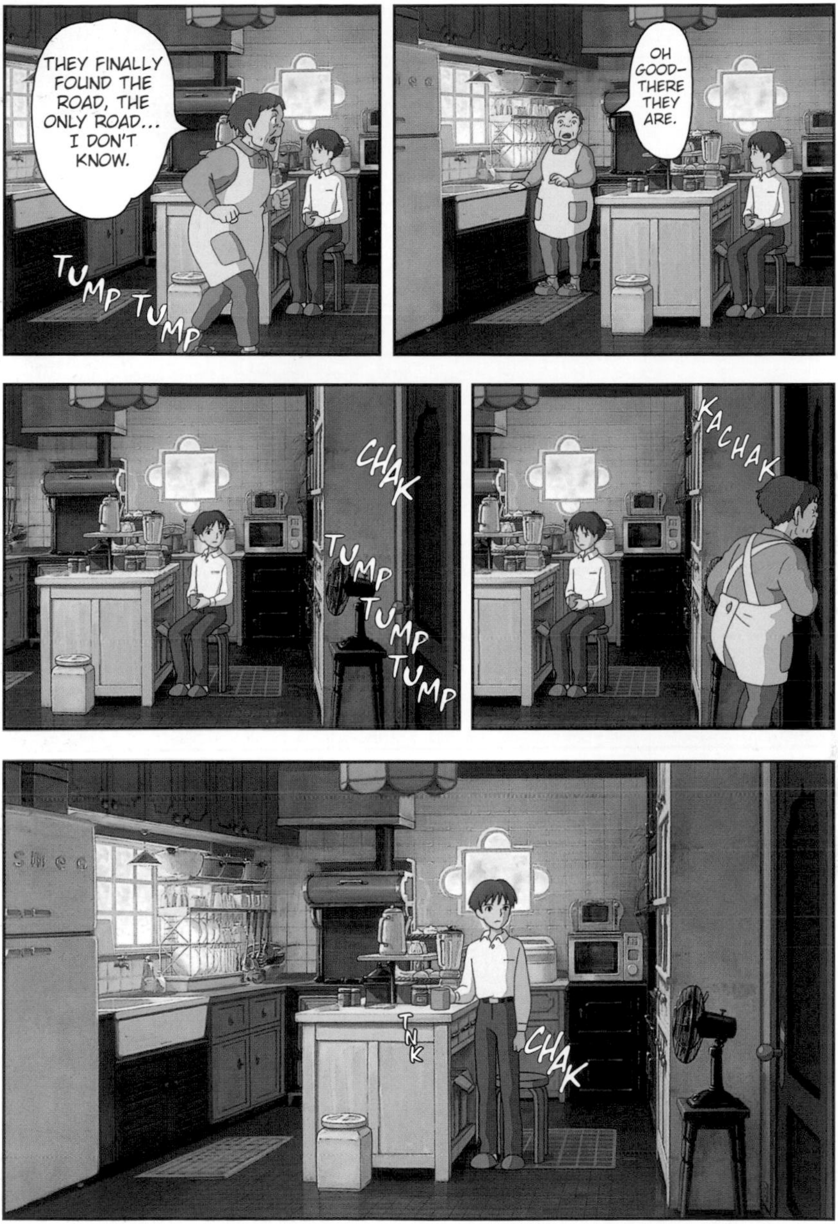
OH GOOD— THERE THEY ARE.
THEY FINALLY FOUND THE ROAD, THE ONLY ROAD... I DON'T KNOW.
TUMP TUMP TUMP
KACHAK
CHAK
TUMP TUMP TUMP TUMP
TNK
CHAK

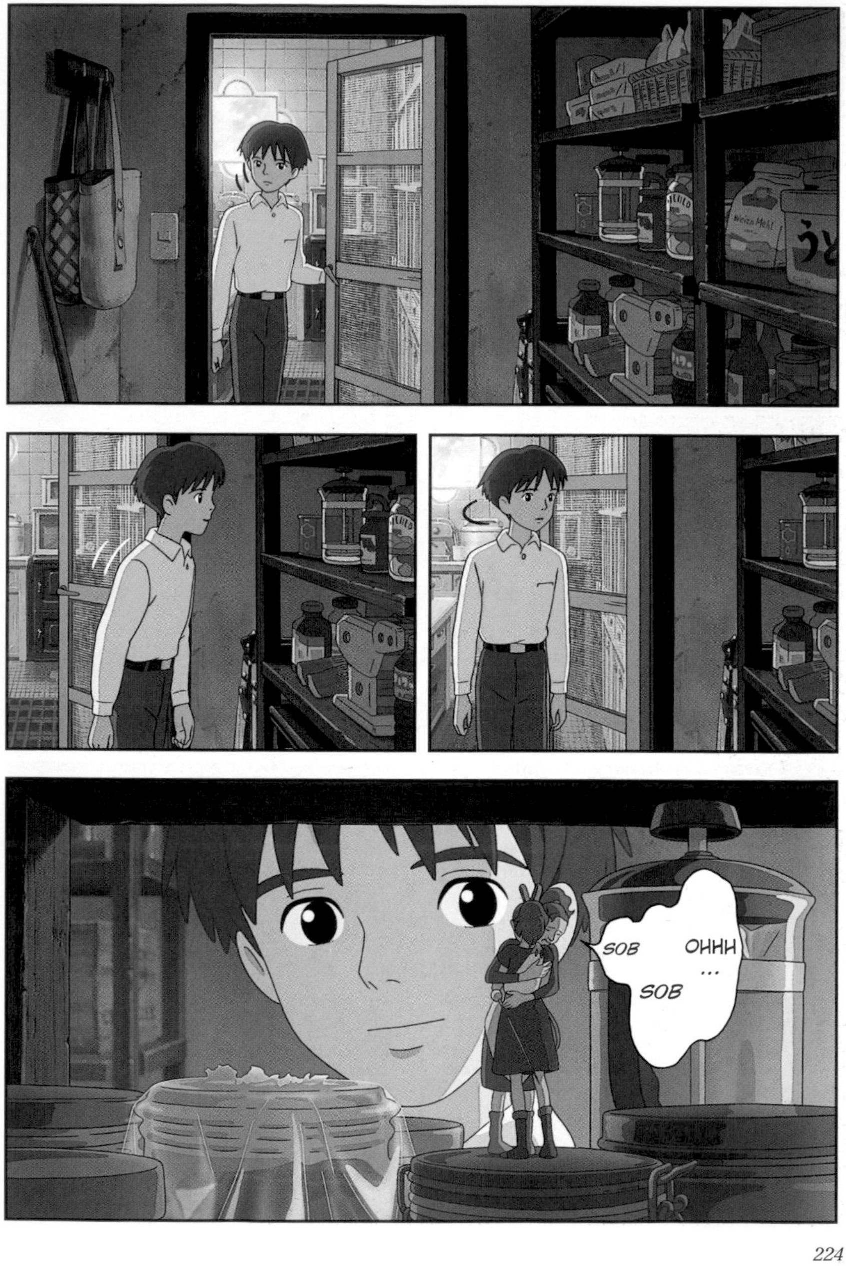
SOB
OHHH
...
SOB

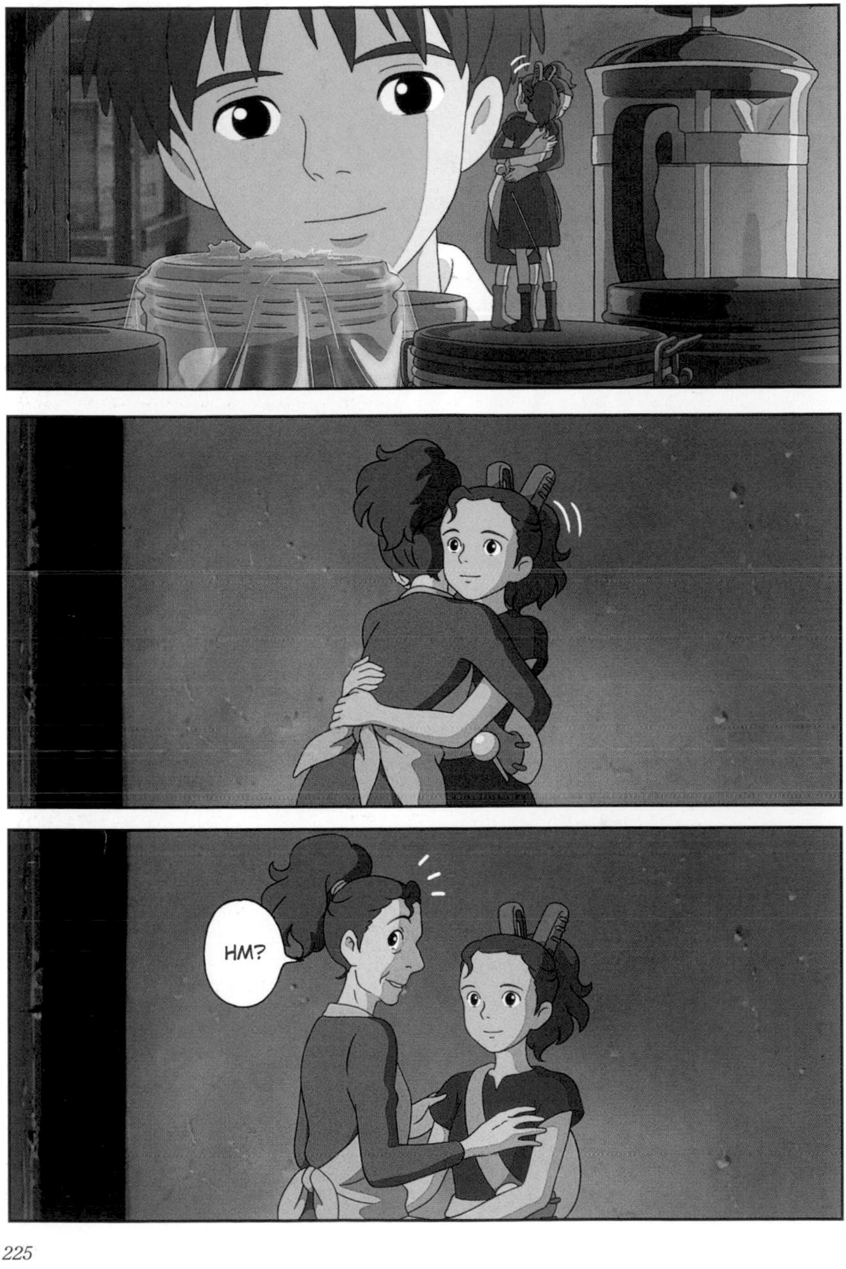
HM?

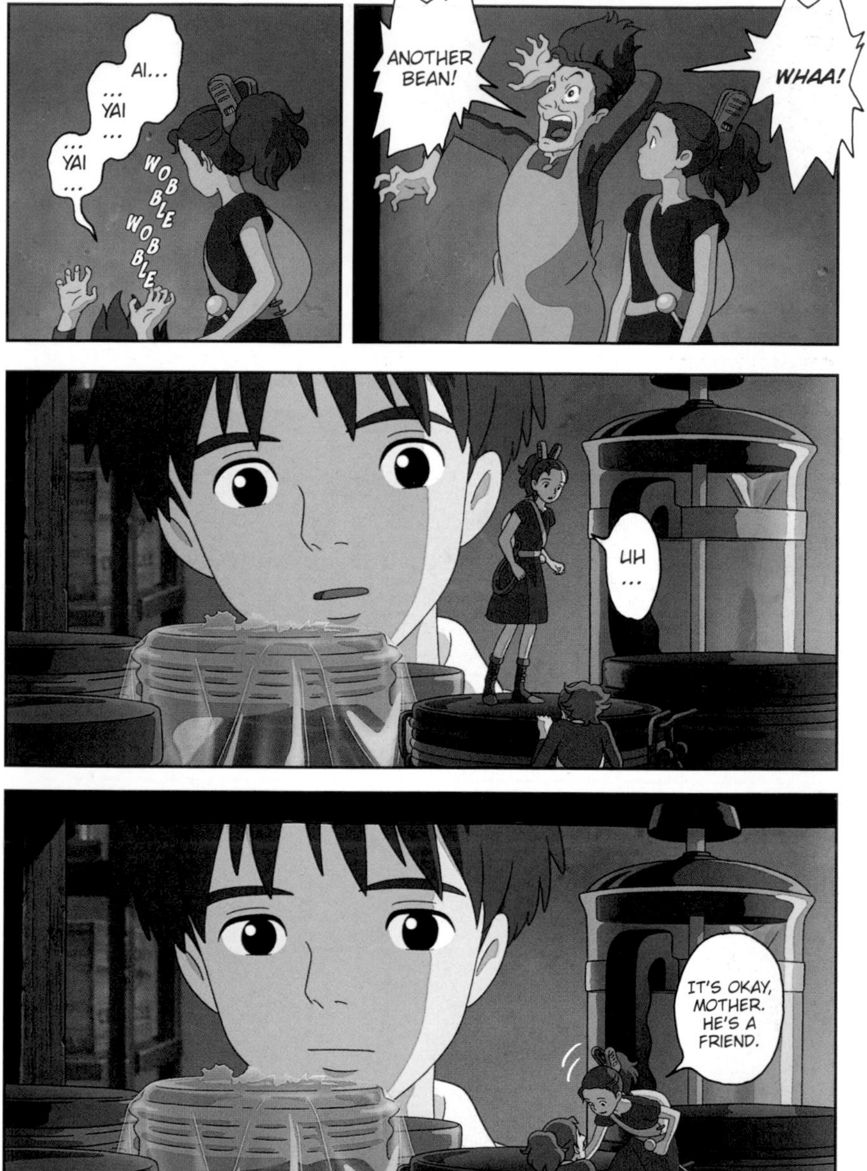

WHAA!
ANOTHER BEAN!
AI... ...YAI... ...YAI...
WOBBLE WOBBLE
UH...
IT'S OKAY, MOTHER. HE'S A FRIEND.

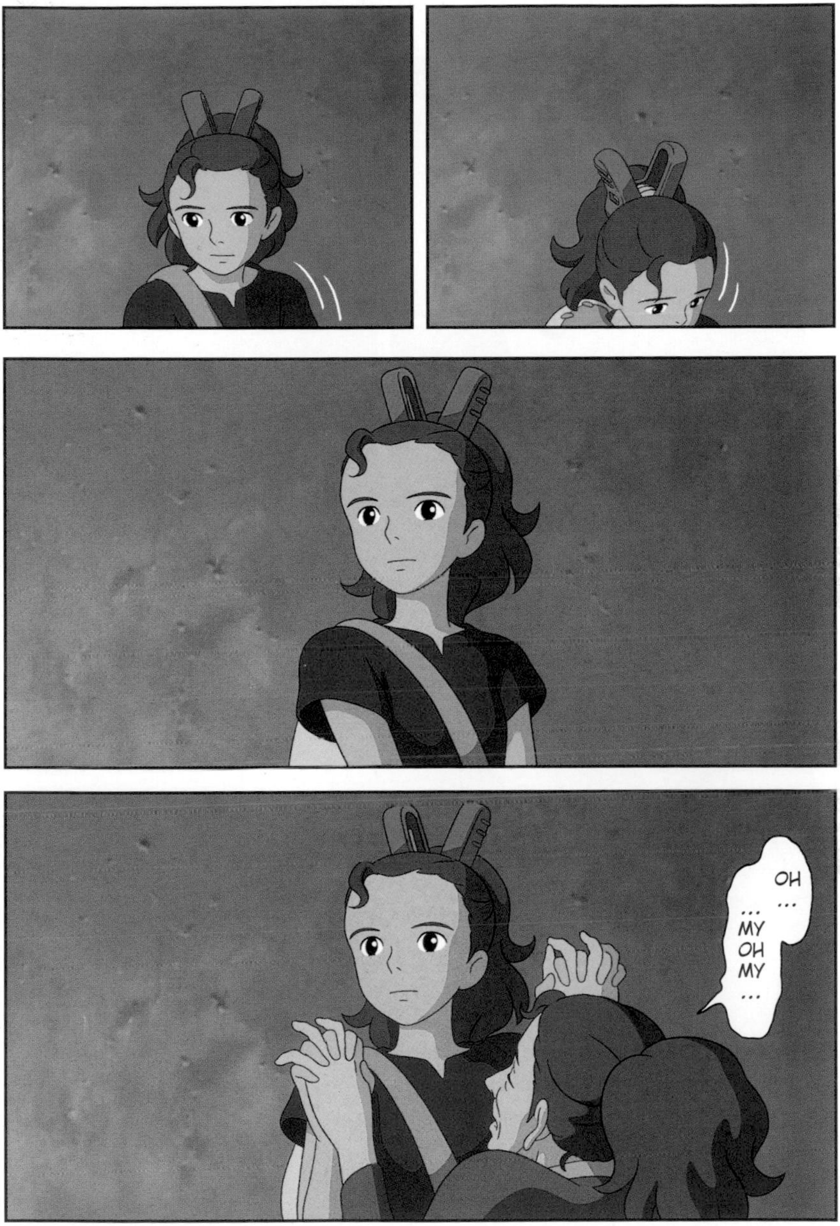
OH ... ... MY OH MY ...

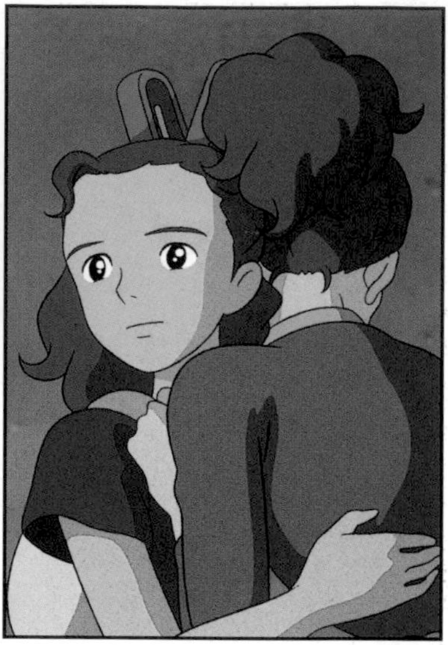

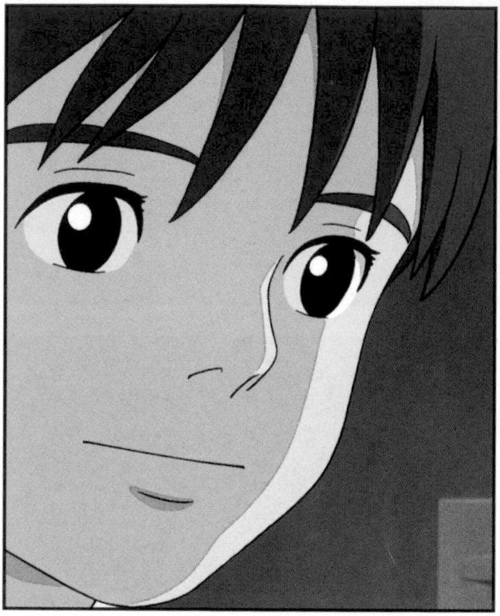

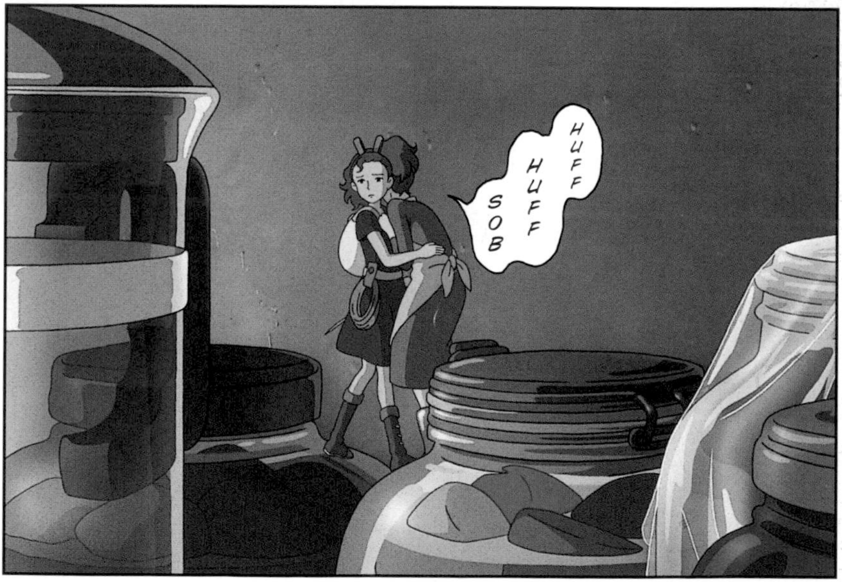
SOB
HUFF
HUFF

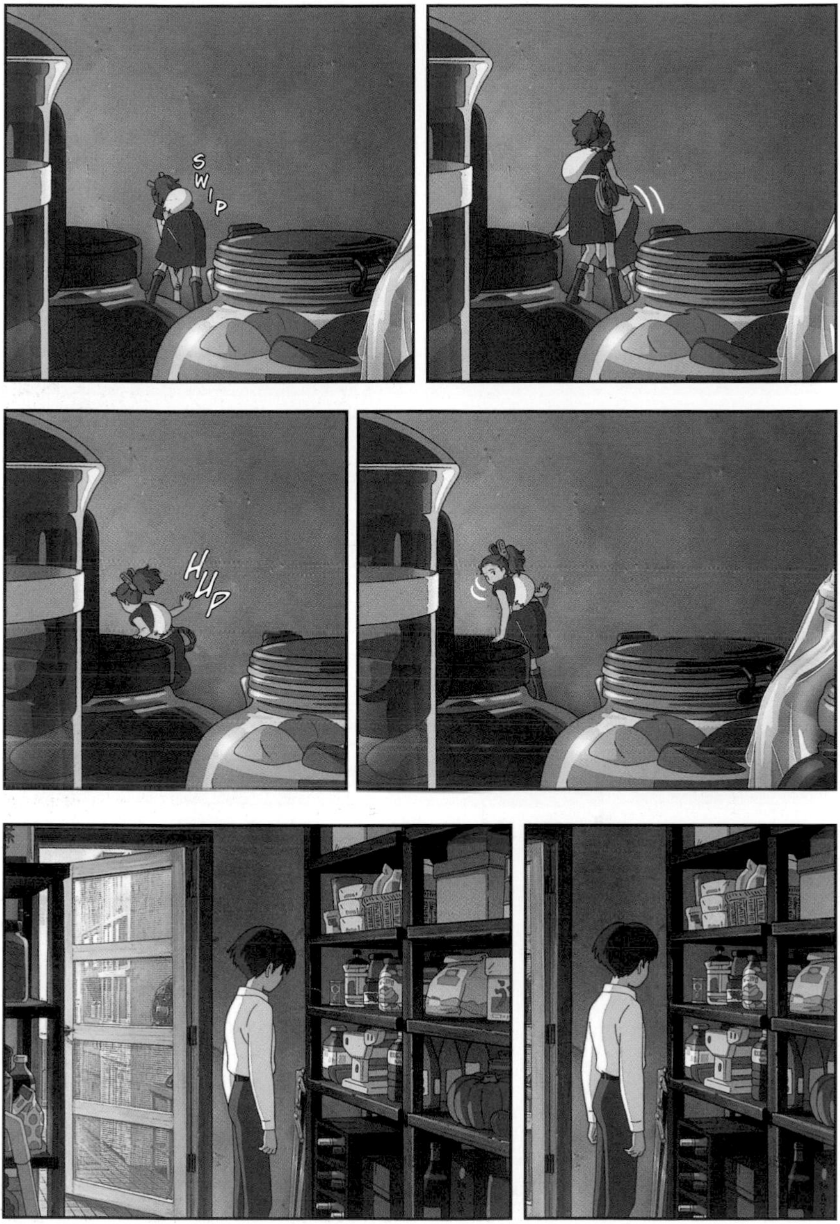
SWIP
HUP

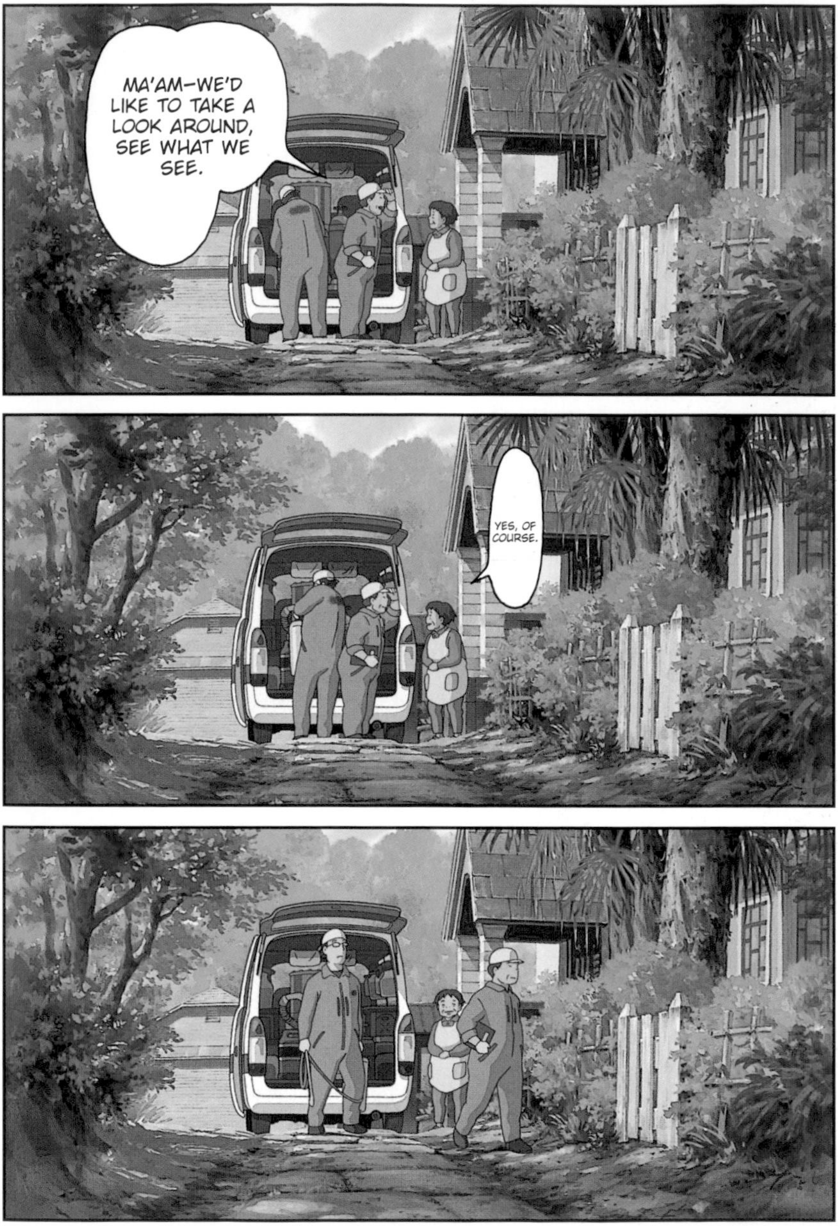
MA'AM—WE'D LIKE TO TAKE A LOOK AROUND, SEE WHAT WE SEE.
YES, OF COURSE.

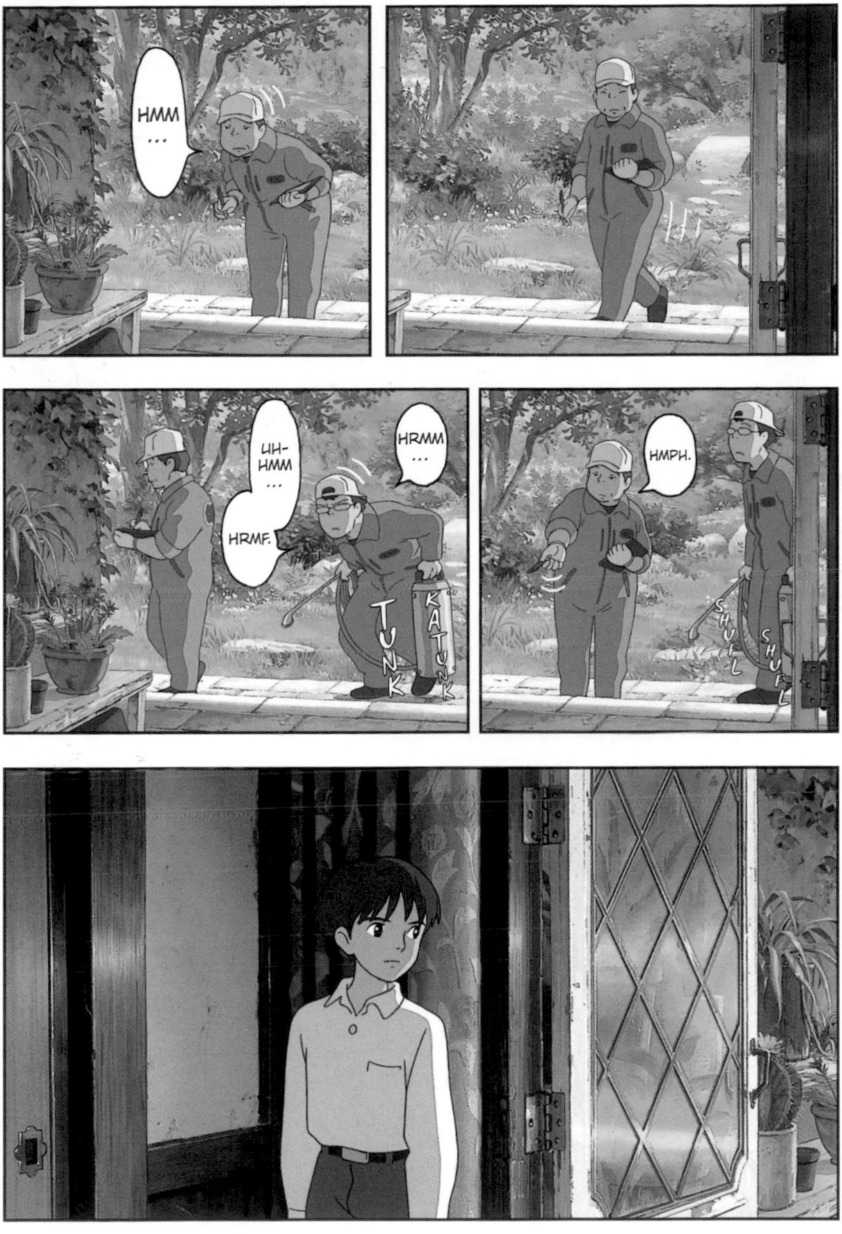
HMM ...
HMPH.
SHUFL
SHUFL
HRMM ...
UH-HMM ...
HRMF.
KATUNK
TUNK

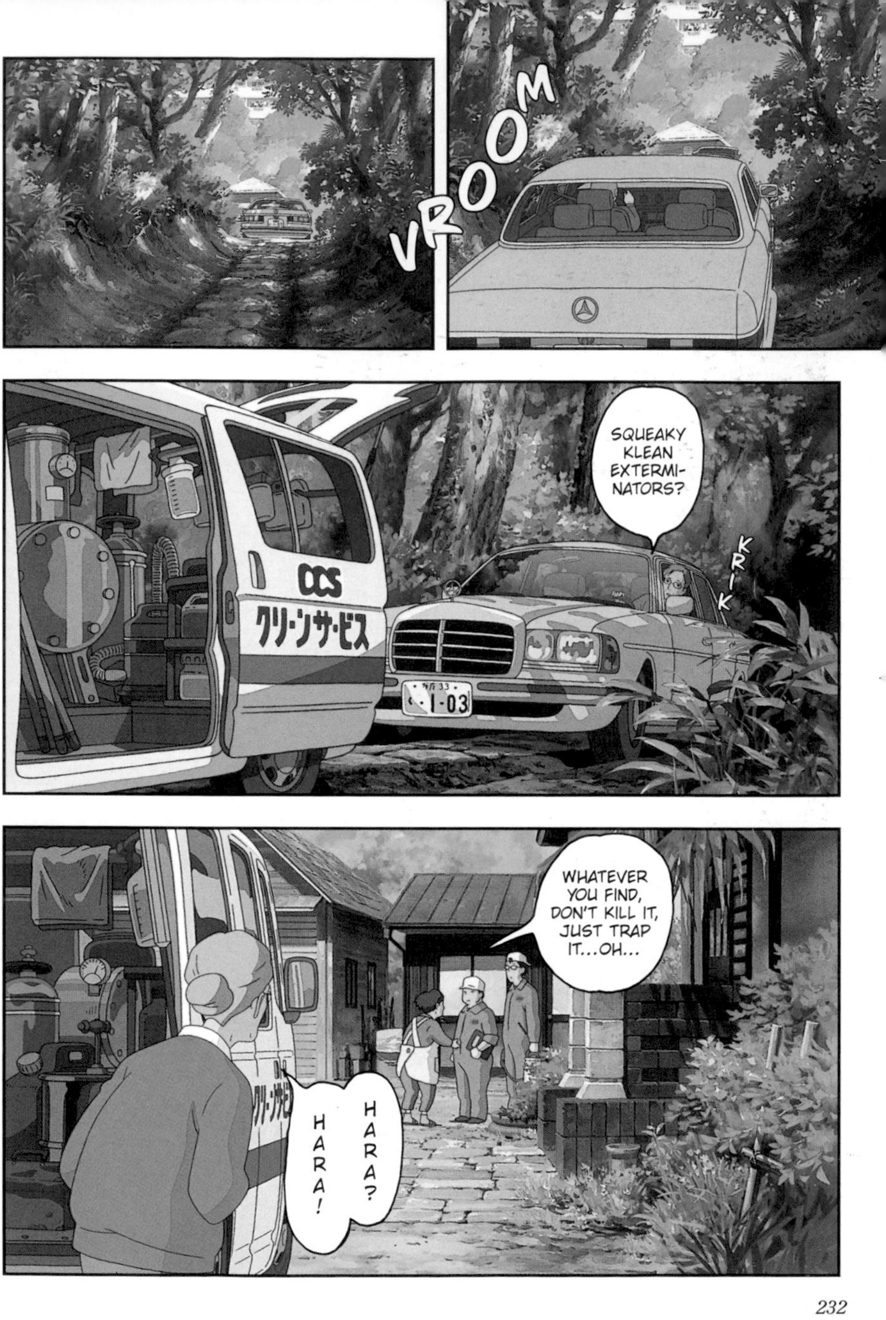
VROOM
SQUEAKY KLEAN EXTERMINATORS?
KRIK
CCS
WHATEVER YOU FIND, DON'T KILL IT, JUST TRAP IT...OH...
HARA?
HARA!

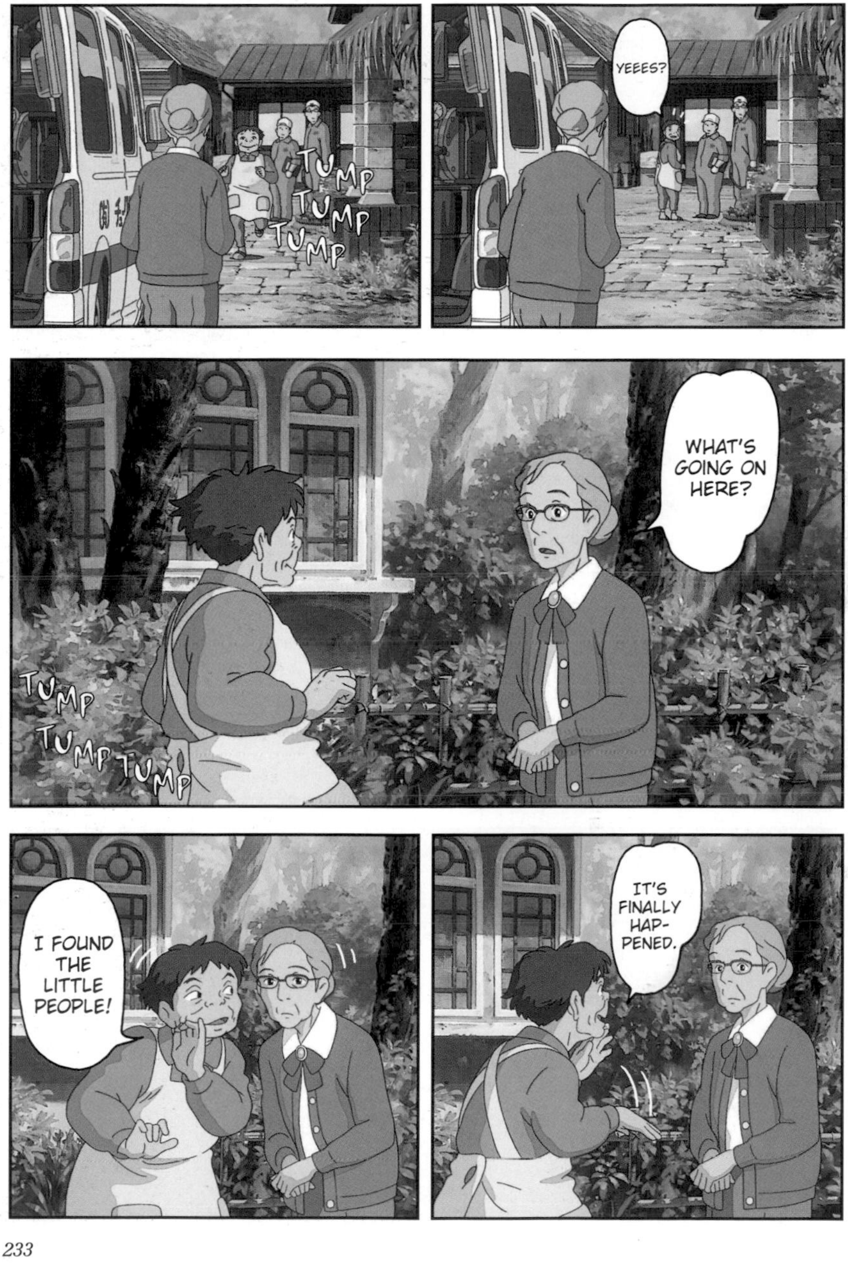
YEEES?
TUMP TUMP TUMP
WHAT'S GOING ON HERE?
TUMP TUMP TUMP TUMP
IT'S FINALLY HAP-PENED.
I FOUND THE LITTLE PEOPLE!

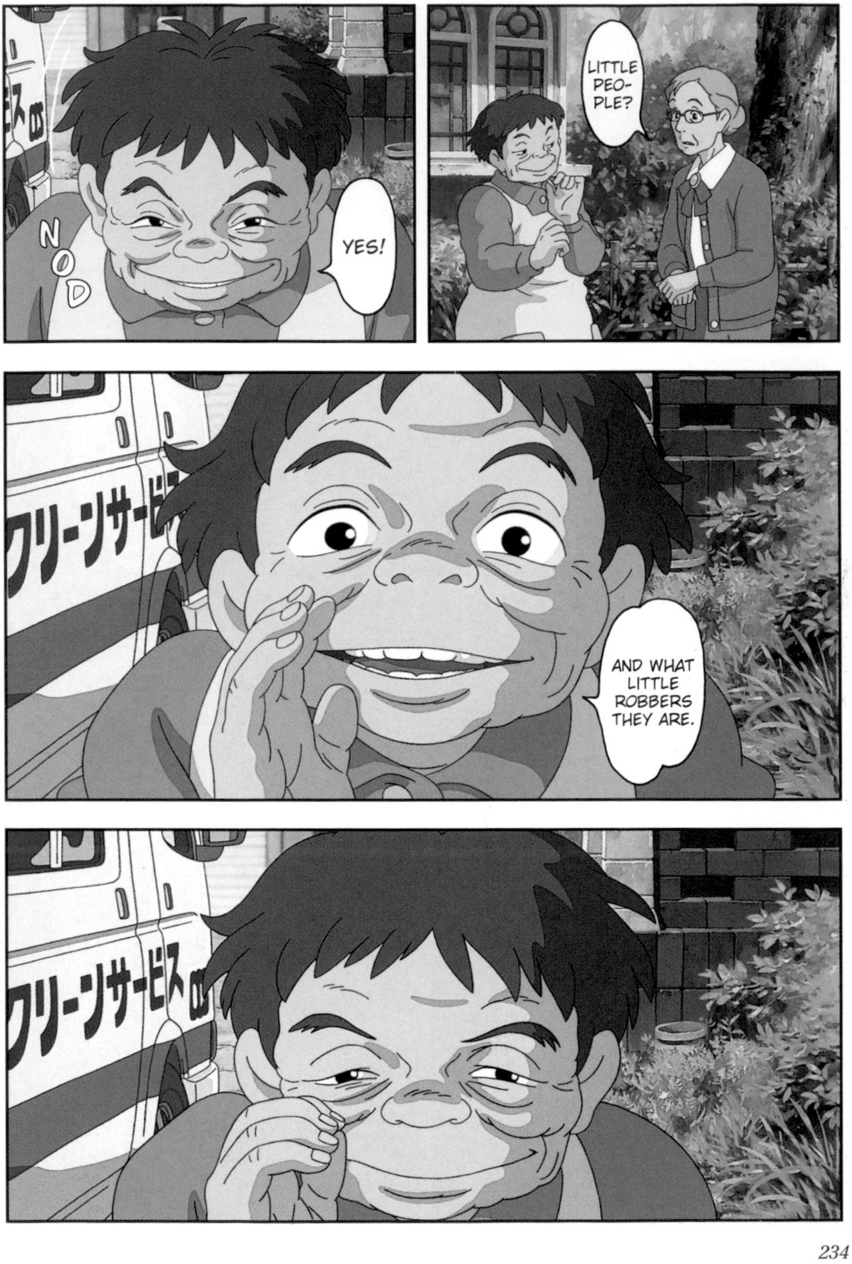
LITTLE PEO-PLE?
NOD
YES!
クリーンサービス
AND WHAT LITTLE ROBBERS THEY ARE.
クリーンサービス

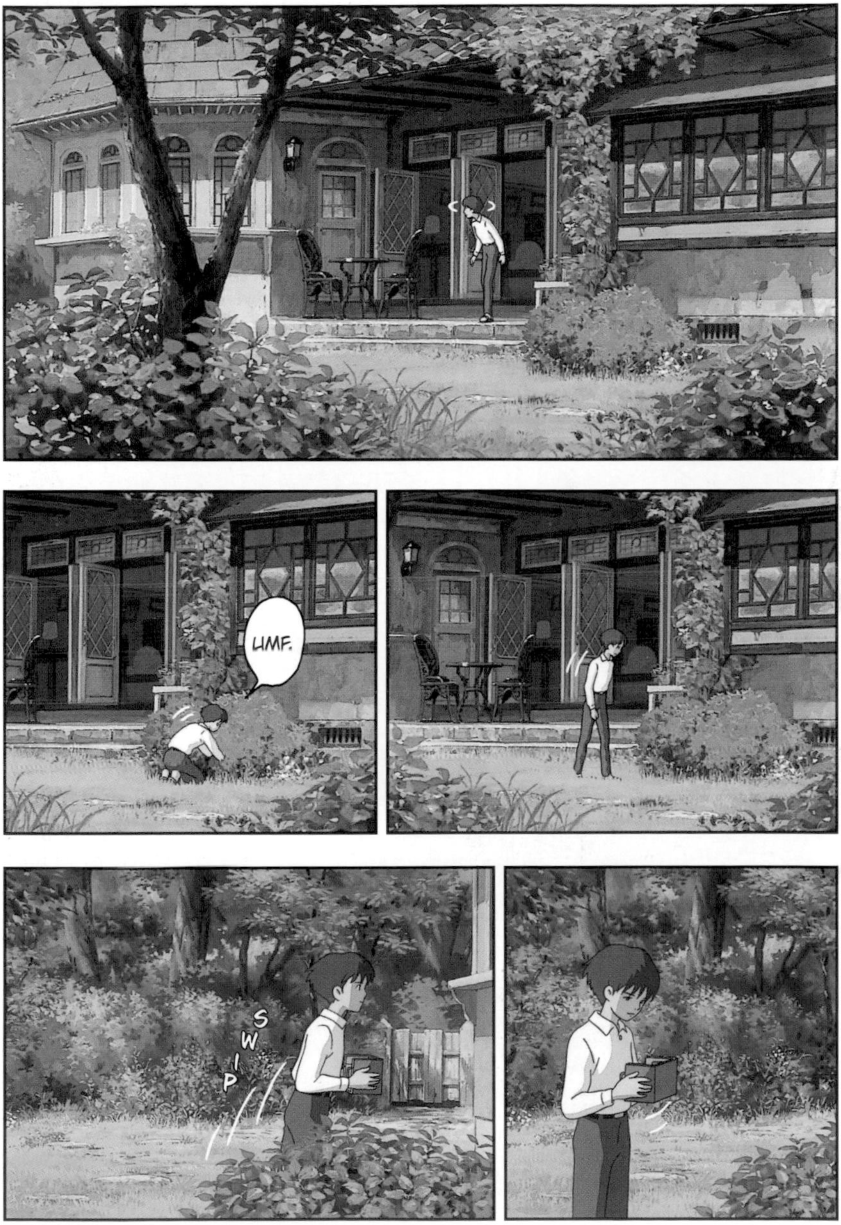
UMF.
SWIP

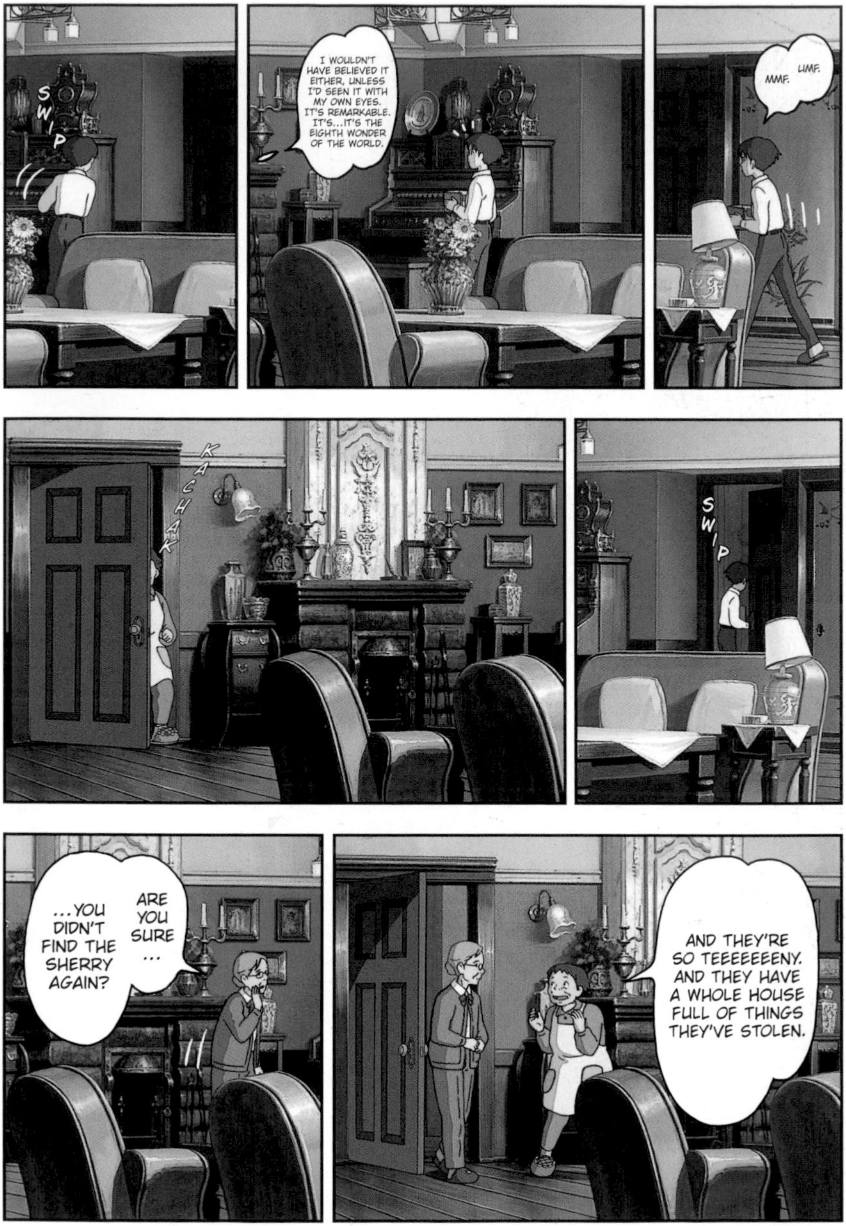
UMF.
MMF.
I WOULDN'T HAVE BELIEVED IT EITHER, UNLESS I'D SEEN IT WITH MY OWN EYES. IT'S REMARKABLE. IT'S...IT'S THE EIGHTH WONDER OF THE WORLD.
SWIP
SWIP
KACHAK
AND THEY'RE SO TEEEEEEENY. AND THEY HAVE A WHOLE HOUSE FULL OF THINGS THEY'VE STOLEN.
ARE YOU SURE ...
...YOU DIDN'T FIND THE SHERRY AGAIN?

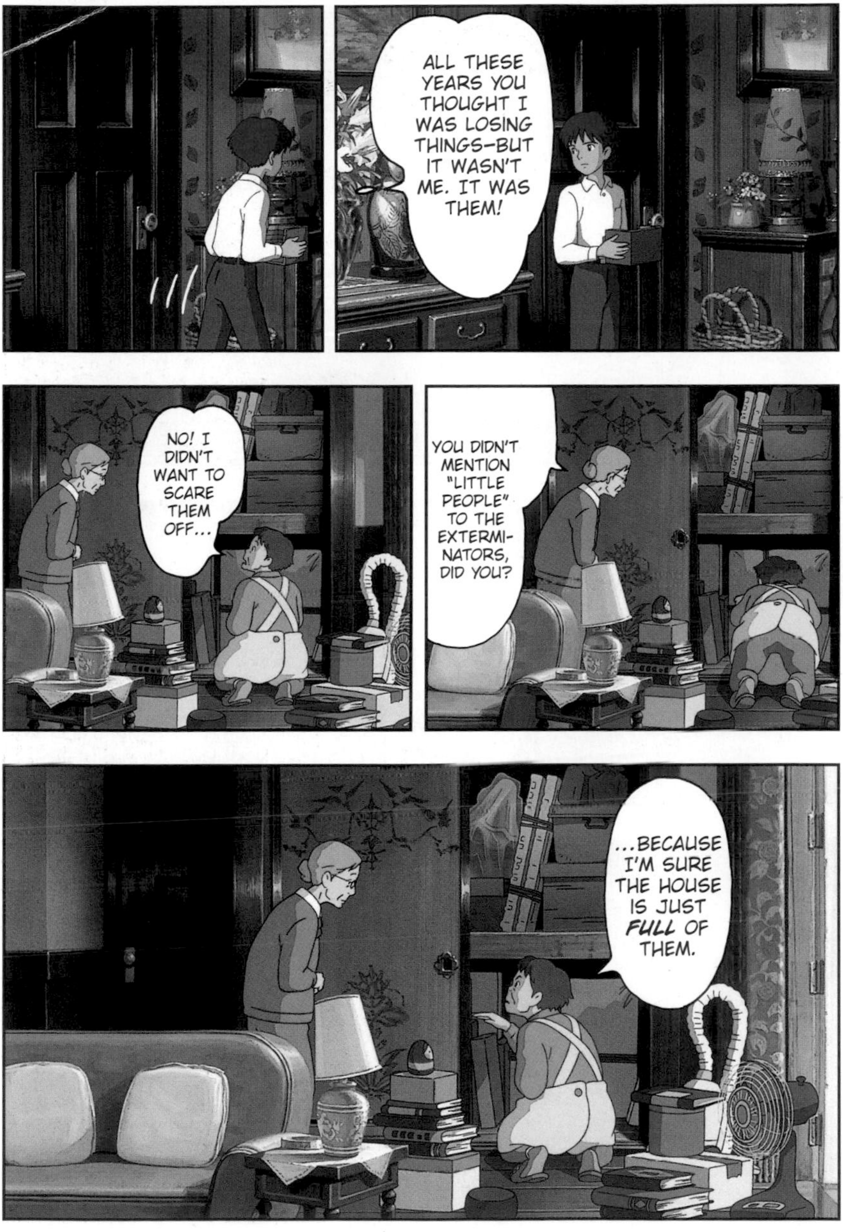
ALL THESE YEARS YOU THOUGHT I WAS LOSING THINGS—BUT IT WASN'T ME. IT WAS THEM!
YOU DIDN'T MENTION "LITTLE PEOPLE" TO THE EXTERMINATORS, DID YOU?
NO! I DIDN'T WANT TO SCARE THEM OFF...
...BECAUSE I'M SURE THE HOUSE IS JUST ***FULL*** OF THEM.

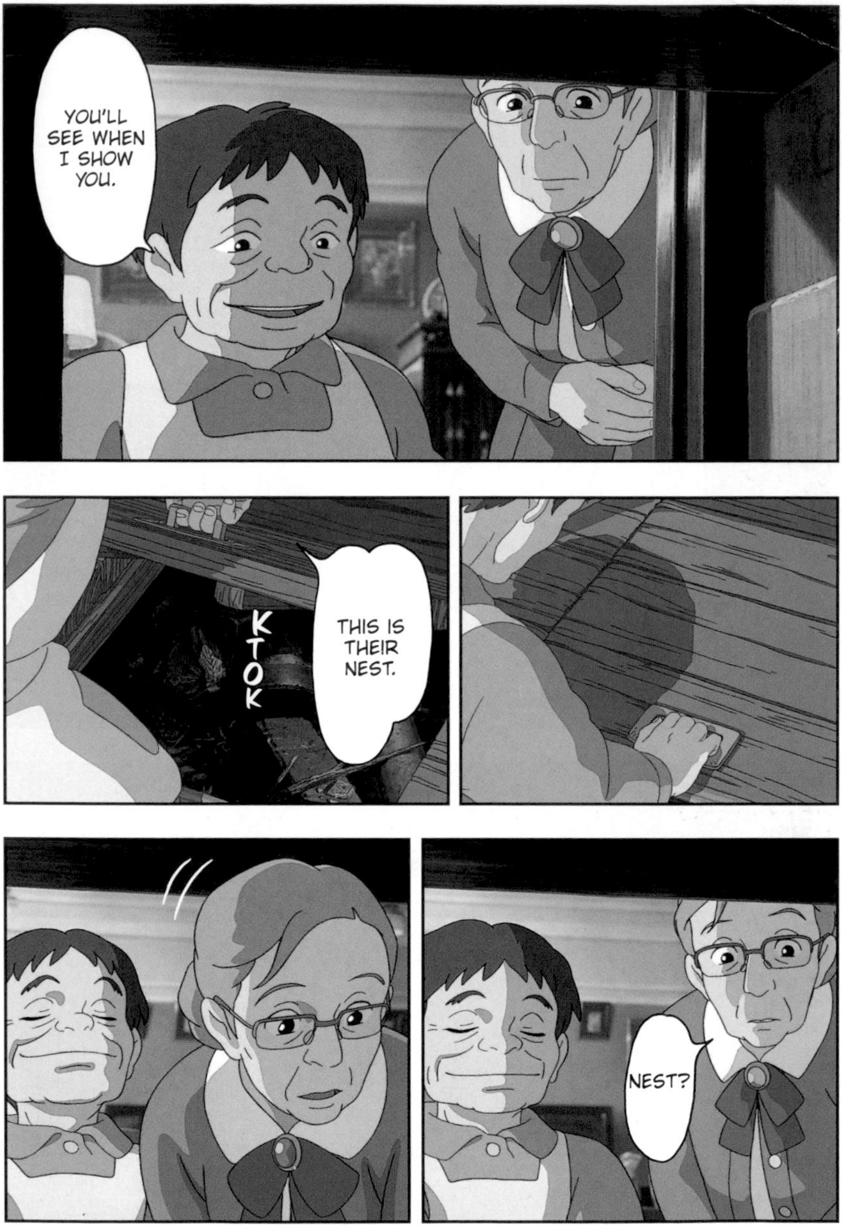
YOU'LL SEE WHEN I SHOW YOU.
THIS IS THEIR NEST.
KTOK
NEST?

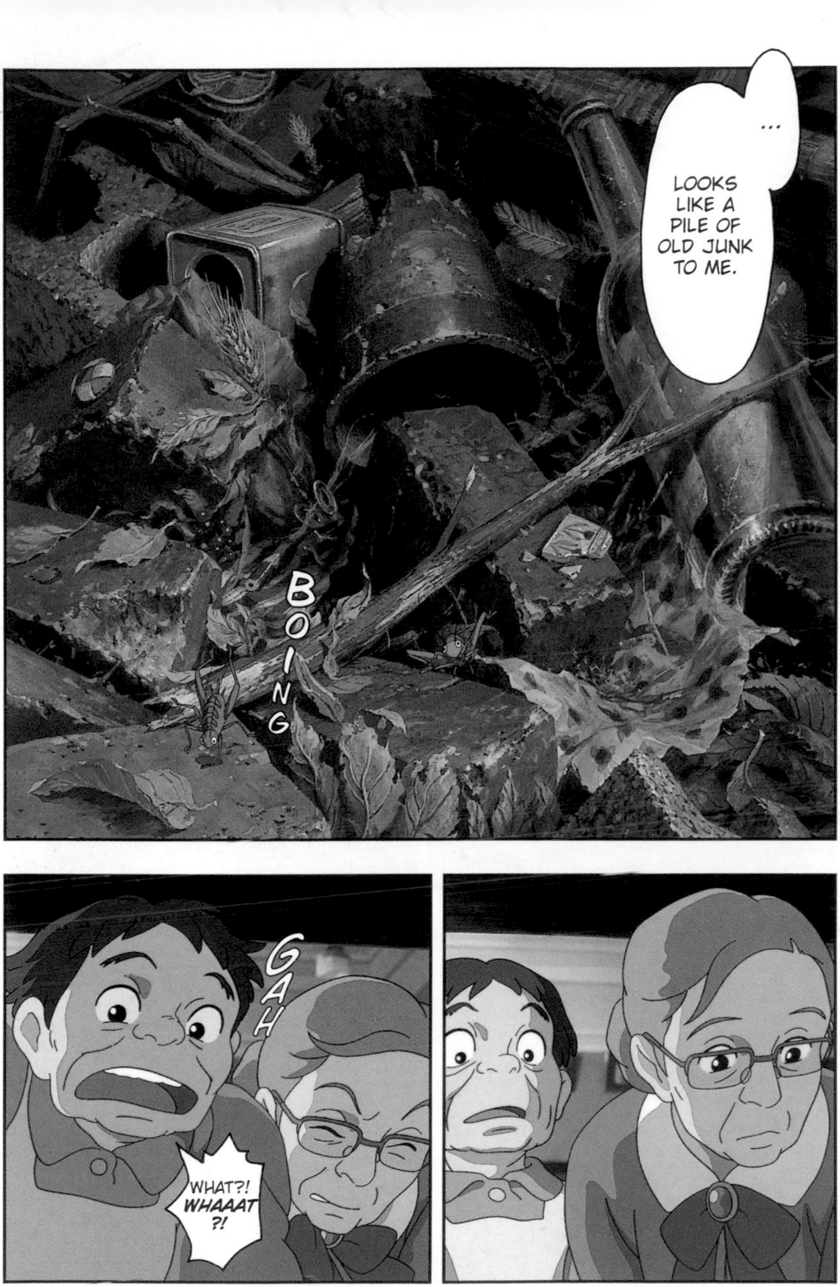
...
LOOKS LIKE A PILE OF OLD JUNK TO ME.
BOING
GAH
WHAT?! WHAAAT?!

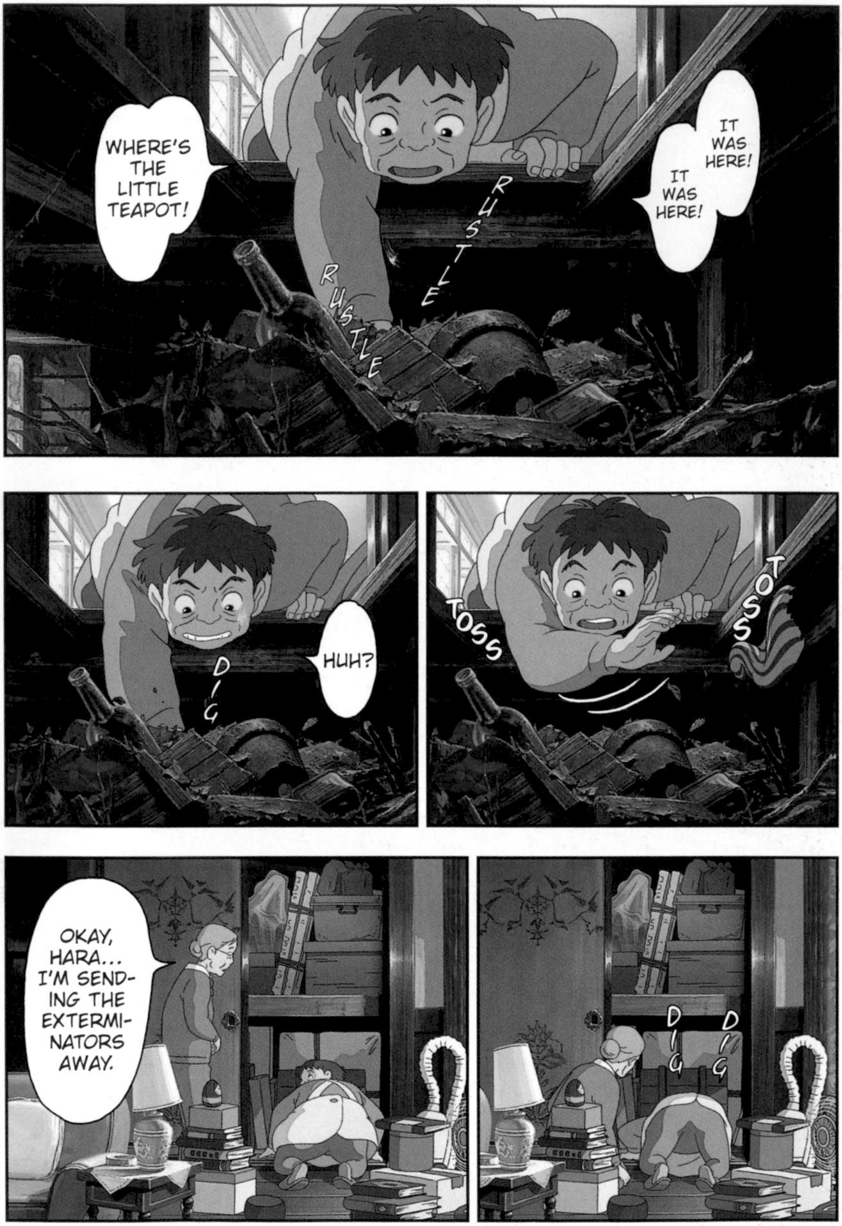
IT WAS HERE!
IT WAS HERE!
WHERE'S THE LITTLE TEAPOT!
RUSTLE
RUSTLE
TOSS
TOSS
HUH?
DIG
DIG
DIG
OKAY, HARA... I'M SENDING THE EXTERMINATORS AWAY.

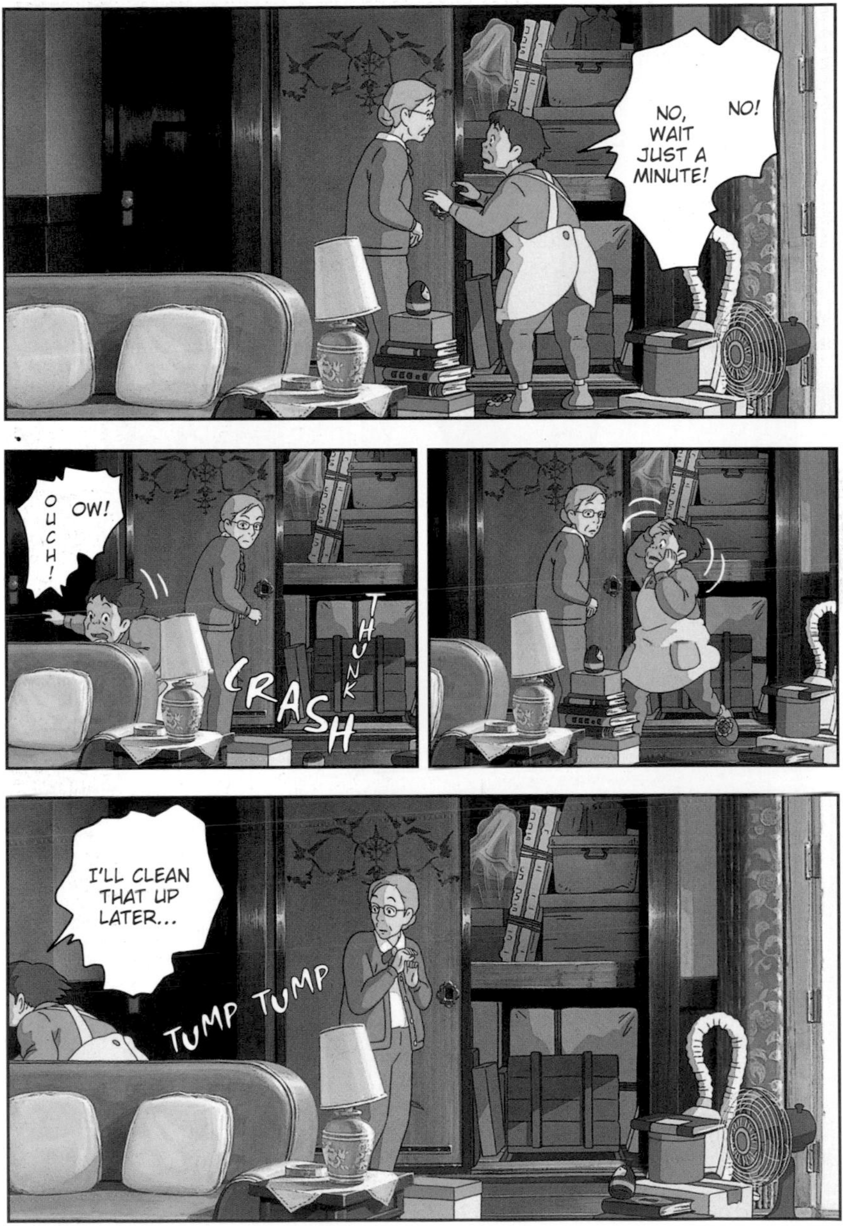
NO!
NO, WAIT JUST A MINUTE!
OUCH!
OW!
THUNK
CRASH
I'LL CLEAN THAT UP LATER...
TUMP TUMP

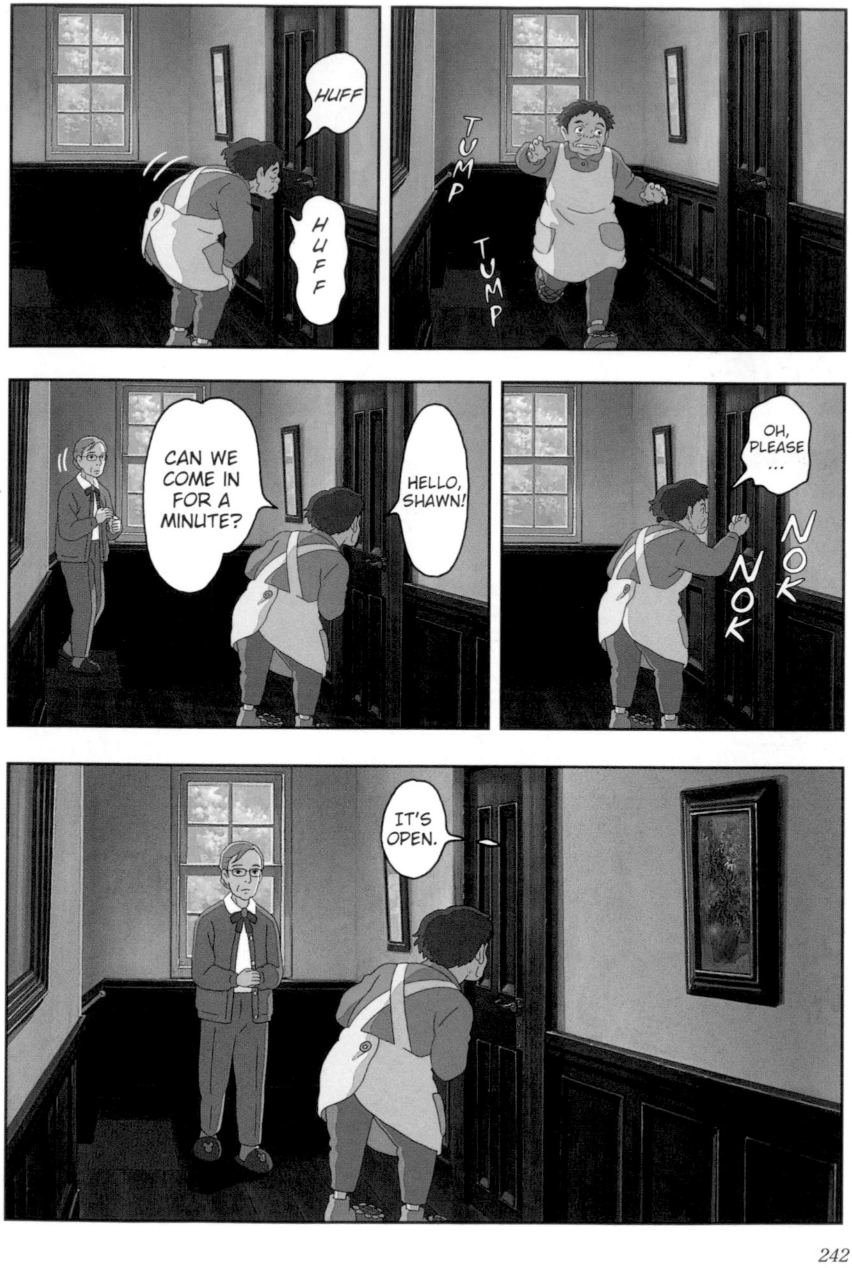
TUMP
TUMP
HUFF
HUFF
NOK
NOK
OH, PLEASE ...
HELLO, SHAWN!
CAN WE COME IN FOR A MINUTE?
IT'S OPEN.

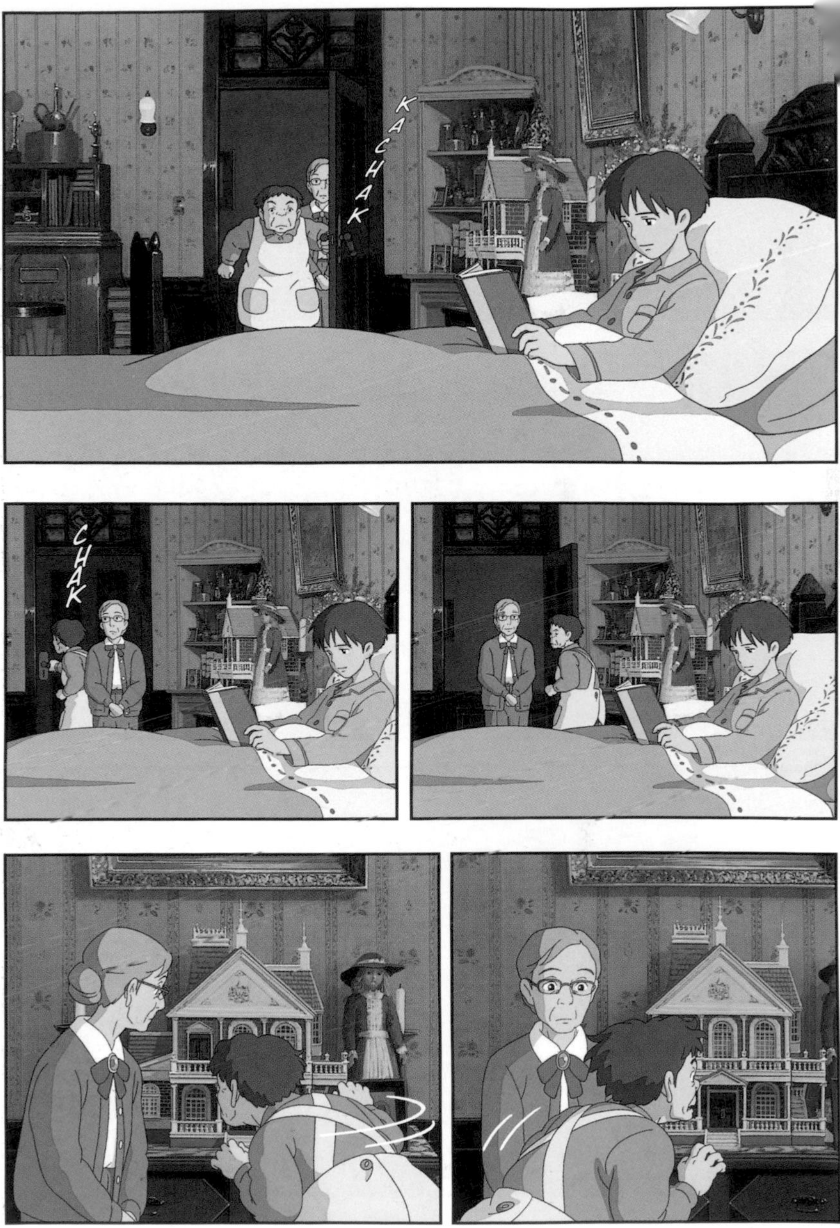
KACHAK
CHAK

YOU'LL SEE. THOSE LITTLE THIEVES STOLE THE TINY KITCHEN.

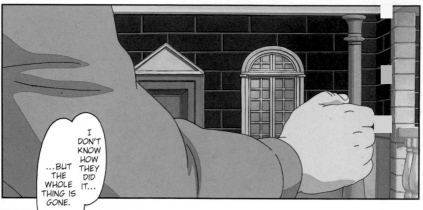

I DON'T KNOW HOW THEY DID IT...

...BUT THE WHOLE THING IS GONE.

K
T
A
K

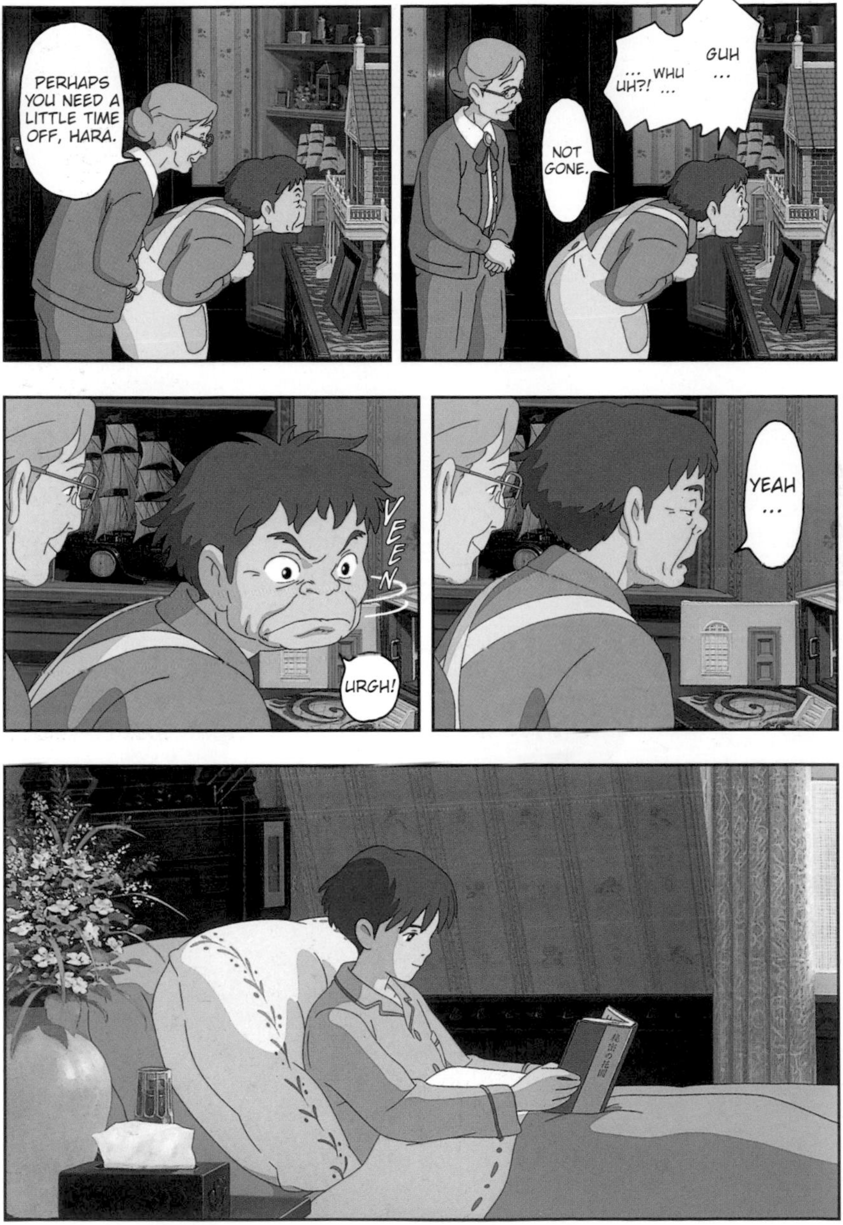
... WHU UH?! ... GUH ...
NOT GONE.
PERHAPS YOU NEED A LITTLE TIME OFF, HARA.
YEAH ...
VEEN-N
URGH!

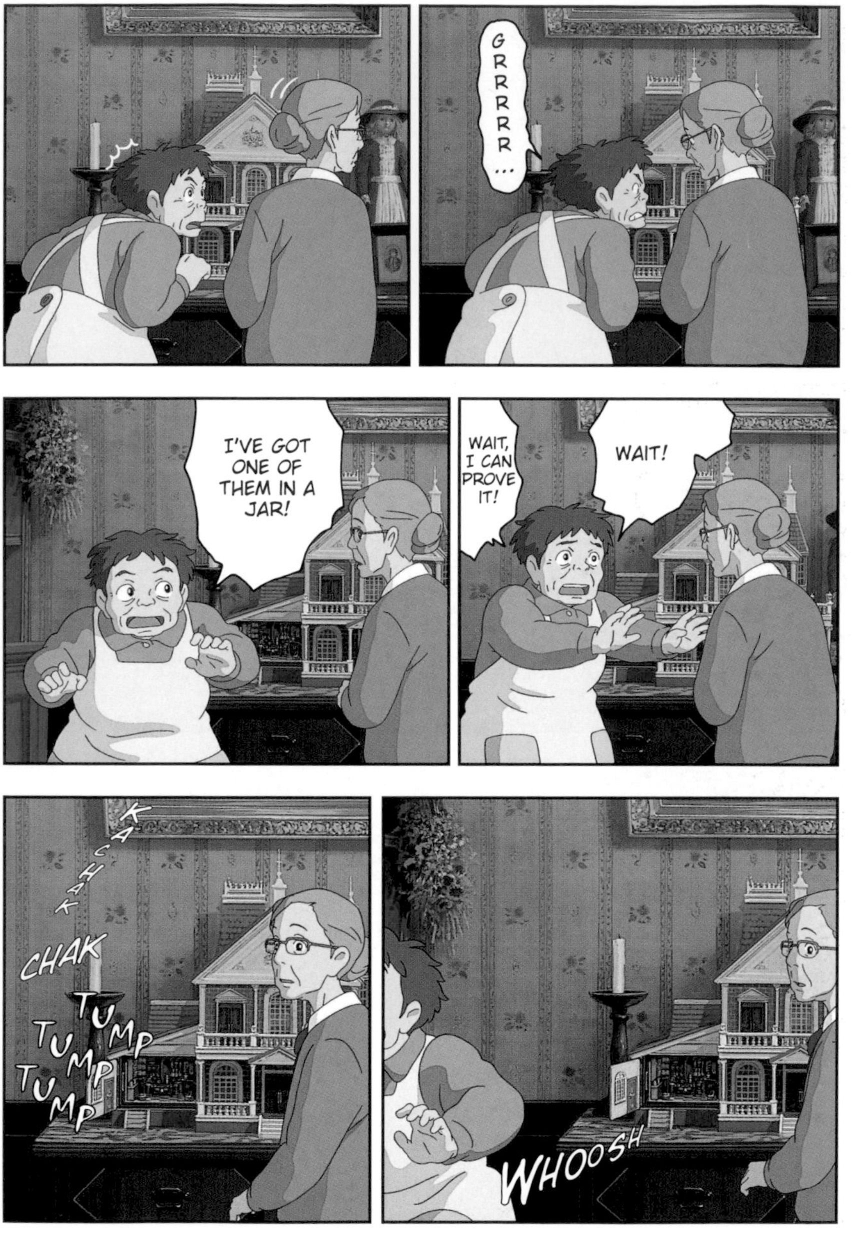
GRRRR...
WAIT!
WAIT, I CAN PROVE IT!
I'VE GOT ONE OF THEM IN A JAR!
WHOOSH
KACHAK
CHAK
TUMP TUMP TUMP

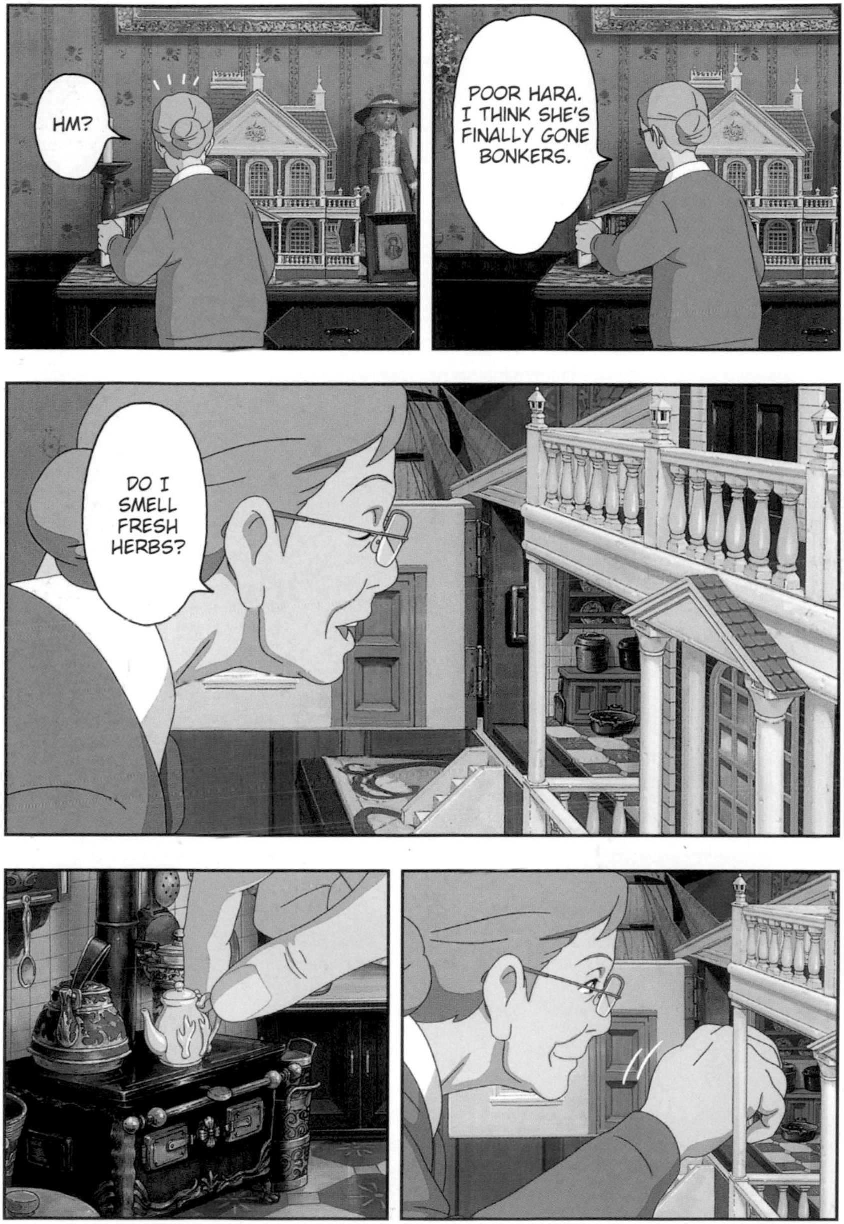
POOR HARA. I THINK SHE'S FINALLY GONE BONKERS.
HM?
DO I SMELL FRESH HERBS?

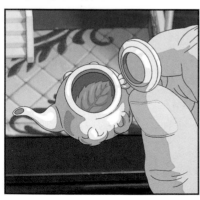

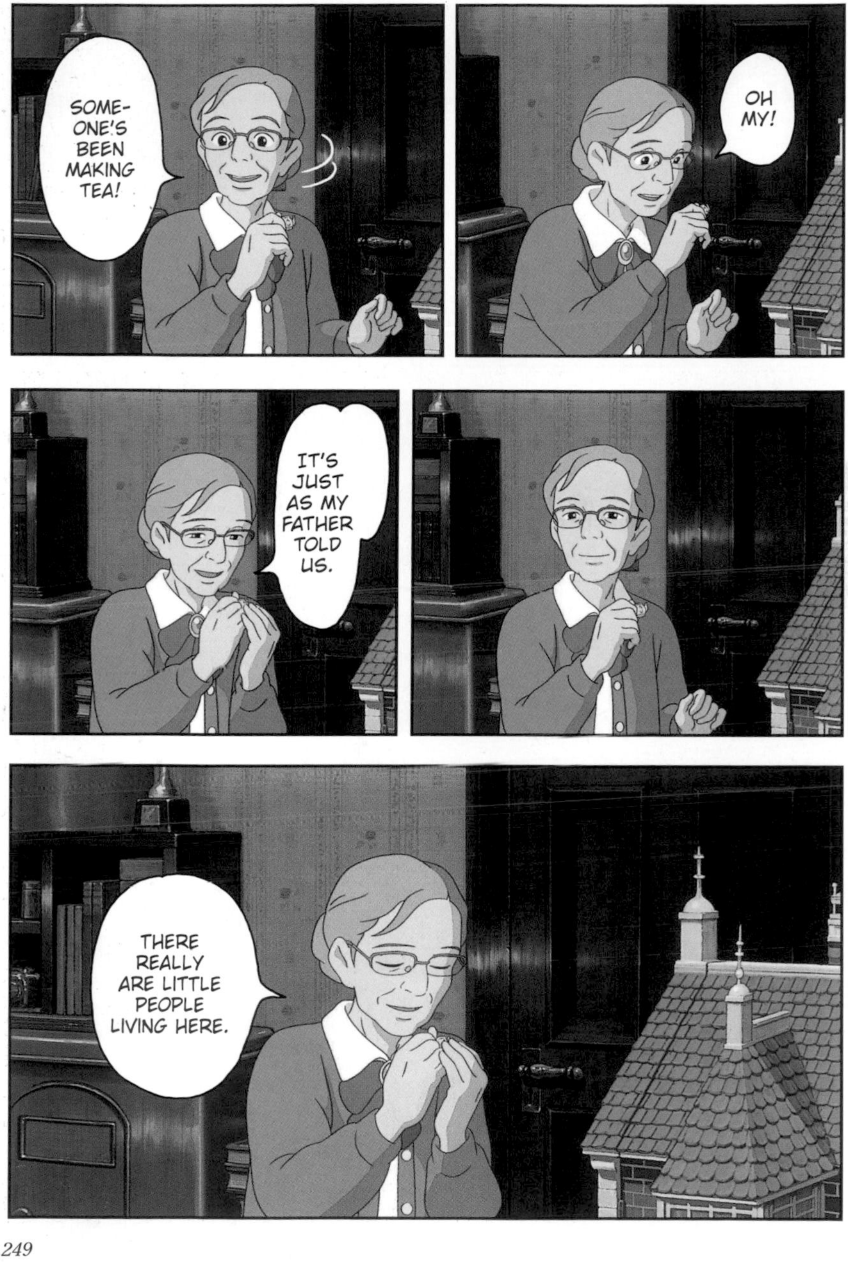
OH MY!
SOME-ONE'S BEEN MAKING TEA!
IT'S JUST AS MY FATHER TOLD US.
THERE REALLY ARE LITTLE PEOPLE LIVING HERE.

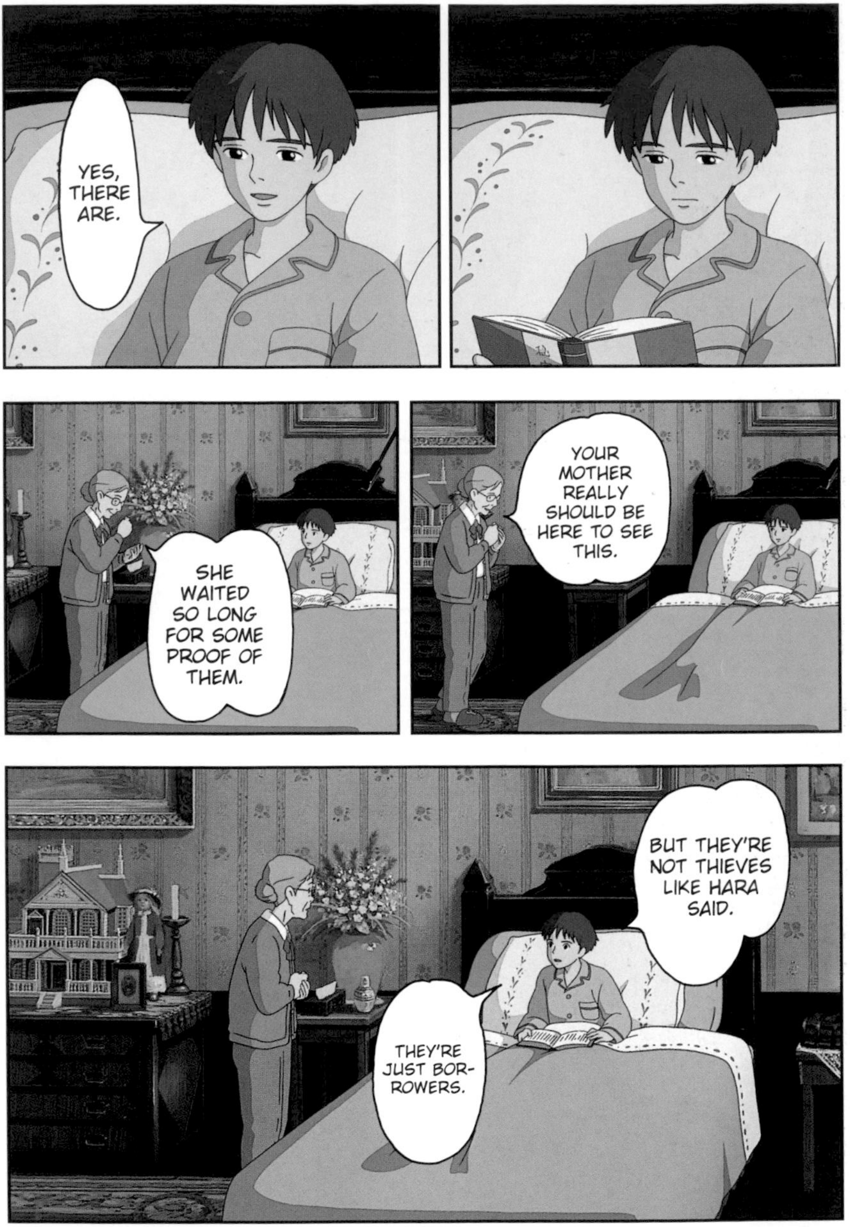
YES, THERE ARE.
YOUR MOTHER REALLY SHOULD BE HERE TO SEE THIS.
SHE WAITED SO LONG FOR SOME PROOF OF THEM.
BUT THEY'RE NOT THIEVES LIKE HARA SAID.
THEY'RE JUST BOR-ROWERS.

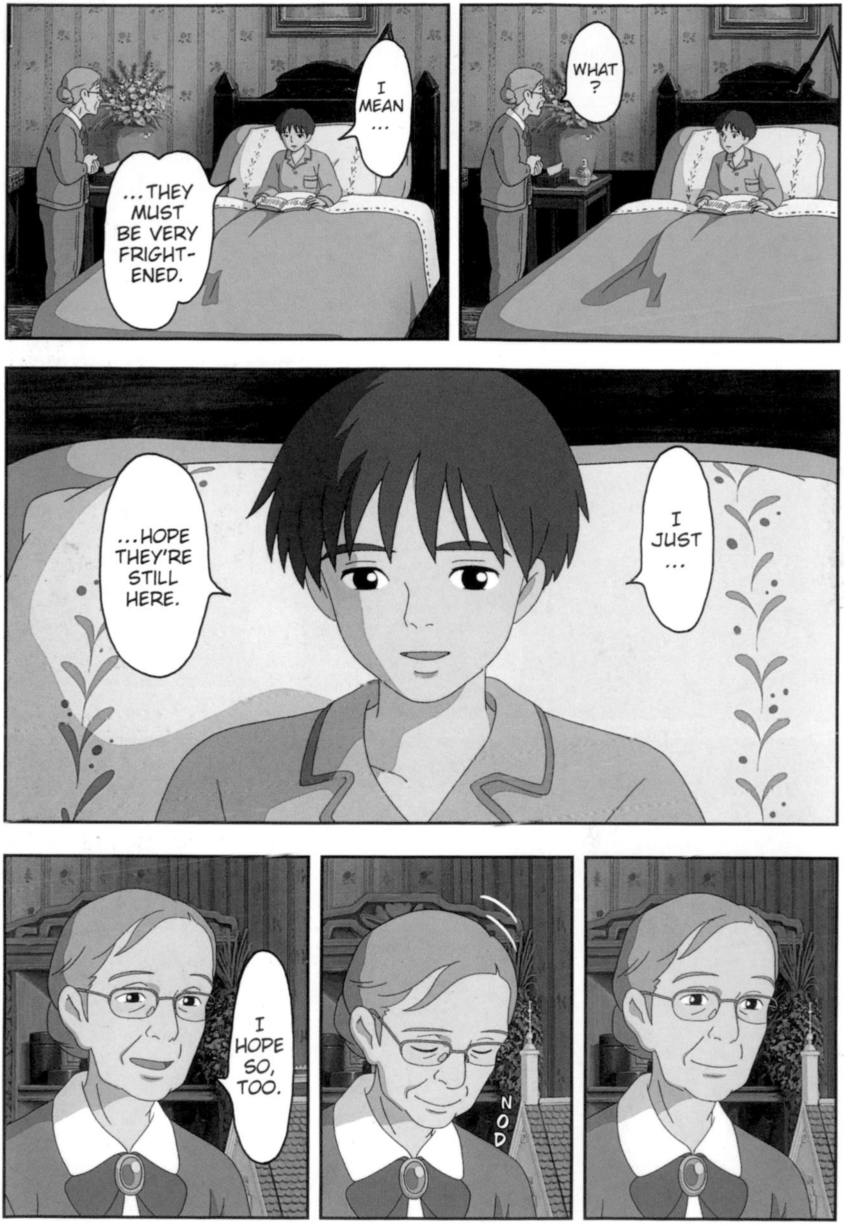
WHAT?
I MEAN...
...THEY MUST BE VERY FRIGHTENED.
I JUST...
...HOPE THEY'RE STILL HERE.
NOD
I HOPE SO, TOO.

HUFF
KACHAK
HUFF HUFF HUFF
SWIP
HU ...
GRB
... MF!
GASP

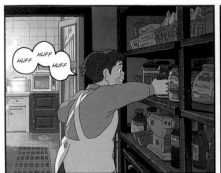

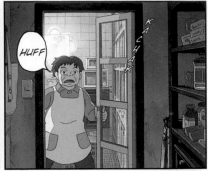

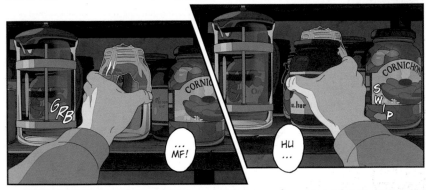

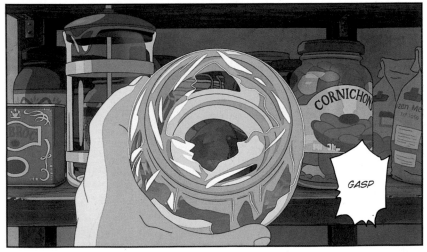

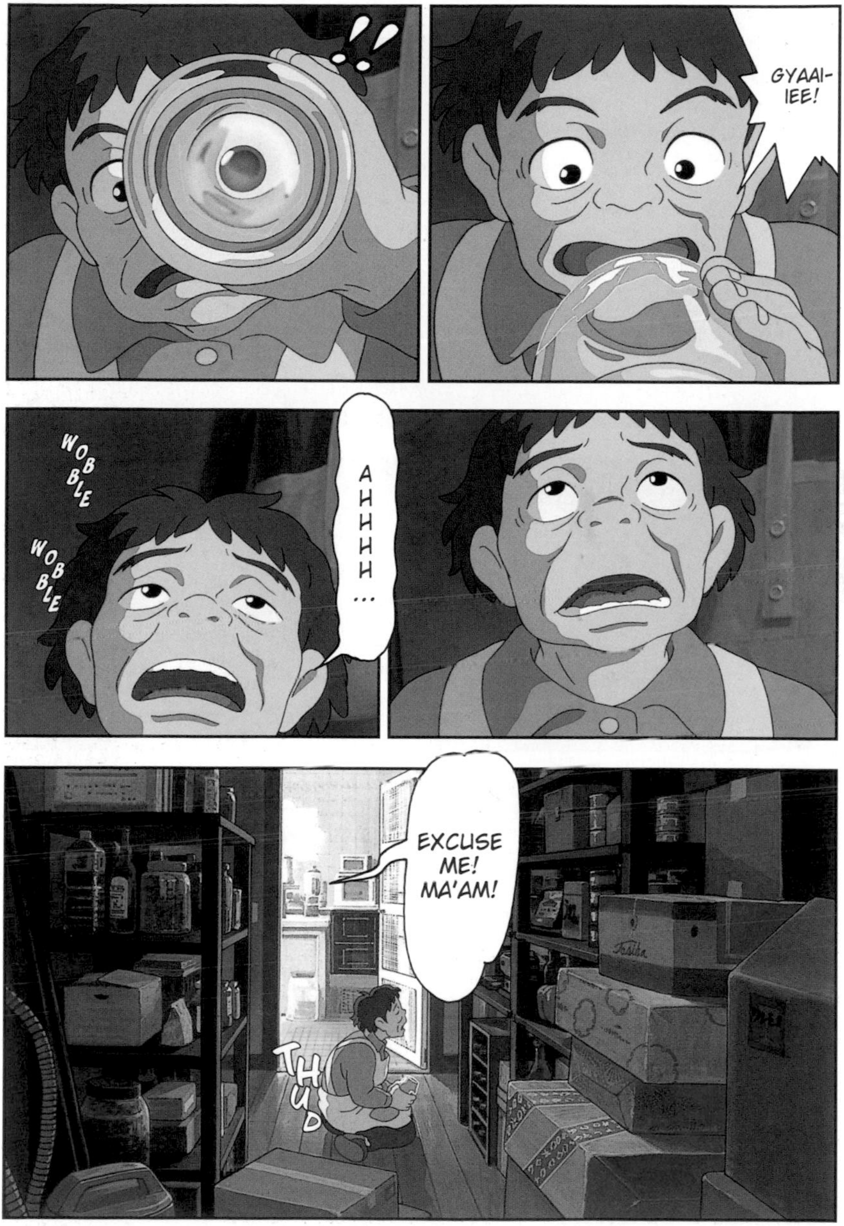
GYAAI-IEE!
!!
AHHHH...
WOBBLE
WOBBLE
EXCUSE ME! MA'AM!
THUD

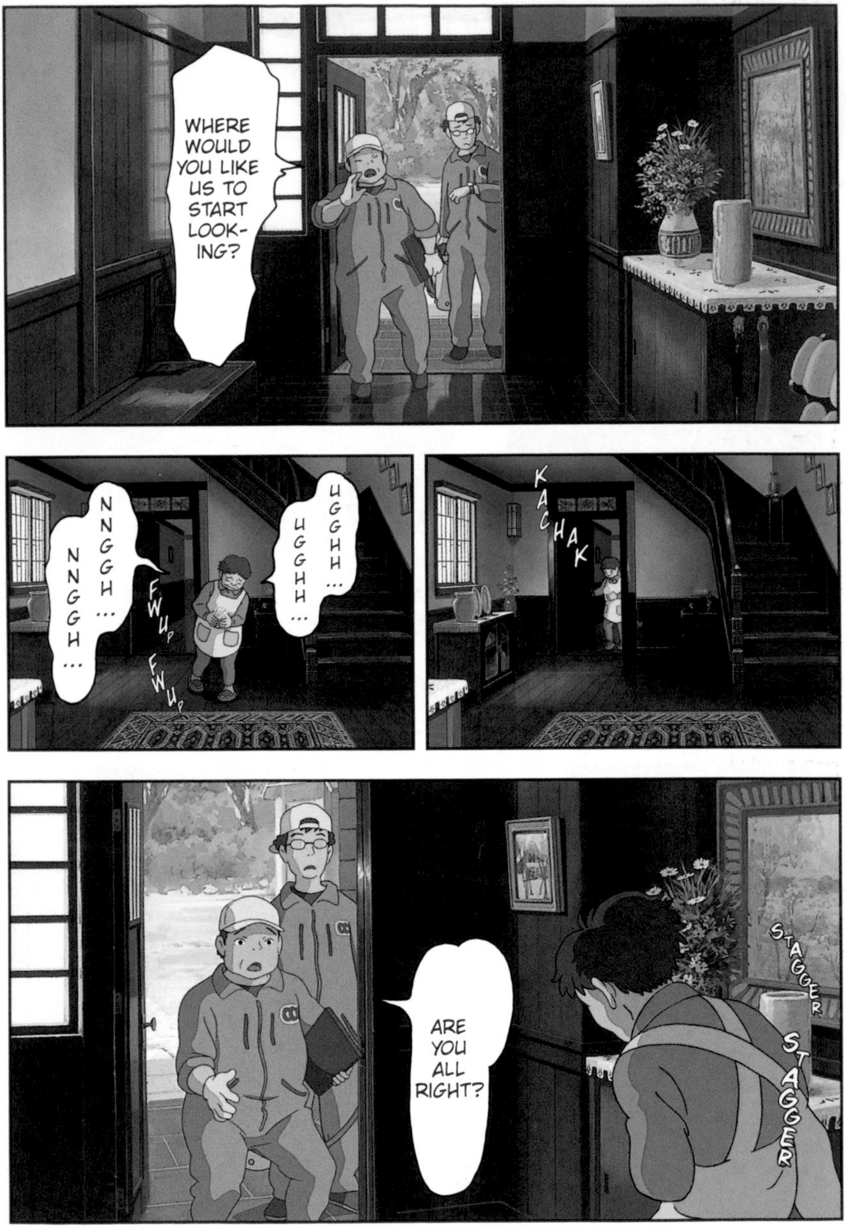
WHERE WOULD YOU LIKE US TO START LOOKING?
KACHAK
UGGHH... UGGHH...
NNGGH... NNGGH...
FWUP FWUP
STAGGER STAGGER
ARE YOU ALL RIGHT?

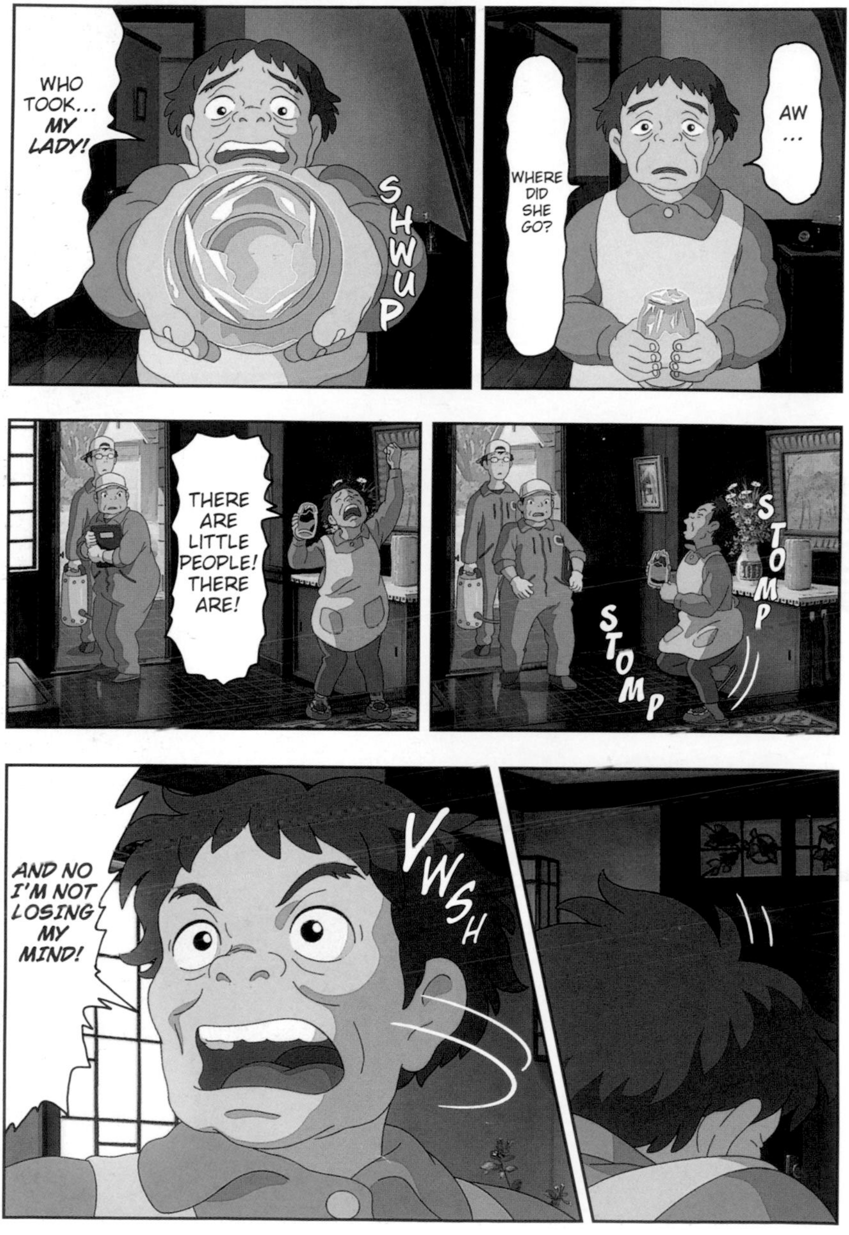
AW ...
WHERE DID SHE GO?
WHO TOOK... MY LADY!
SHWUP
STOMP
STOMP
THERE ARE LITTLE PEOPLE! THERE ARE!
VWSH
AND NO I'M NOT LOSING MY MIND!

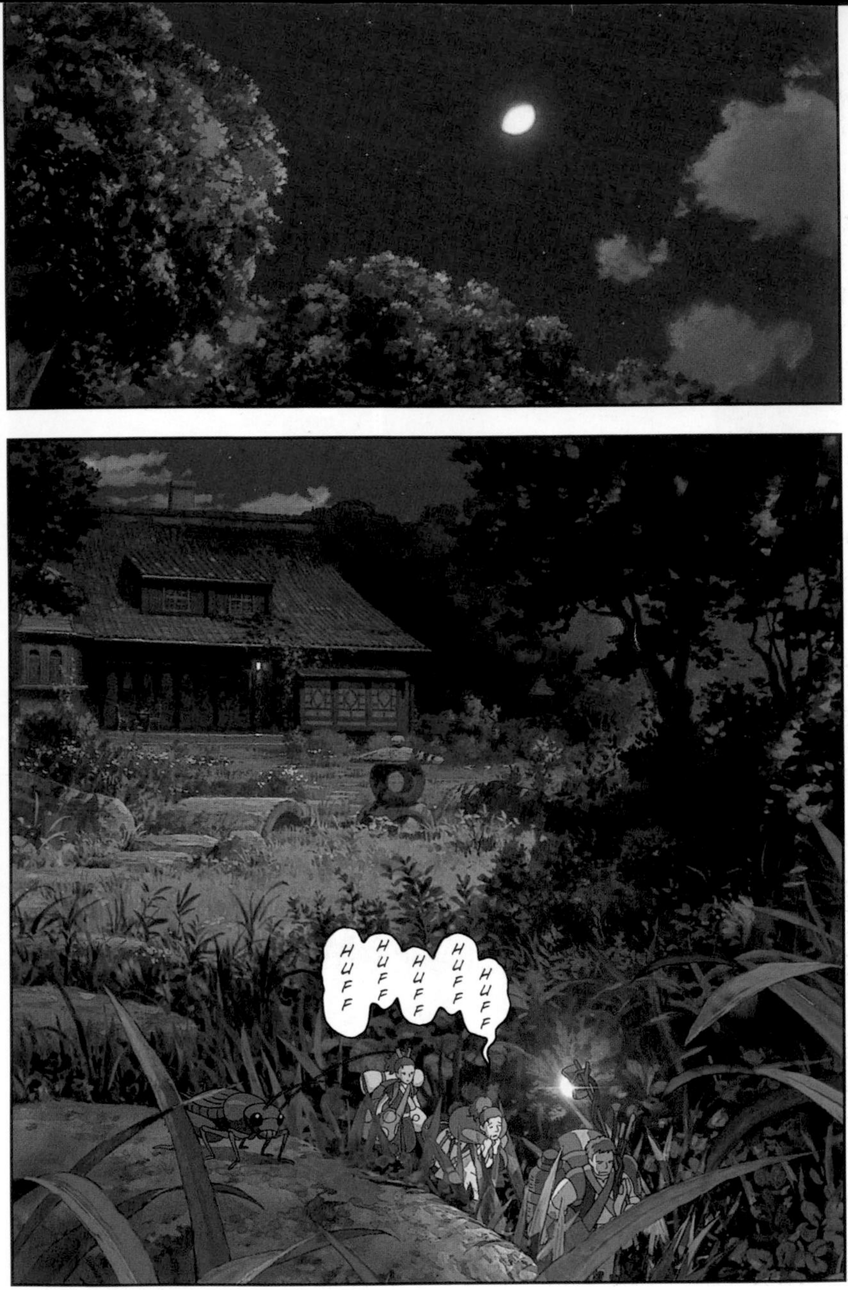
HUFF HUFF HUFF HUFF HUFF

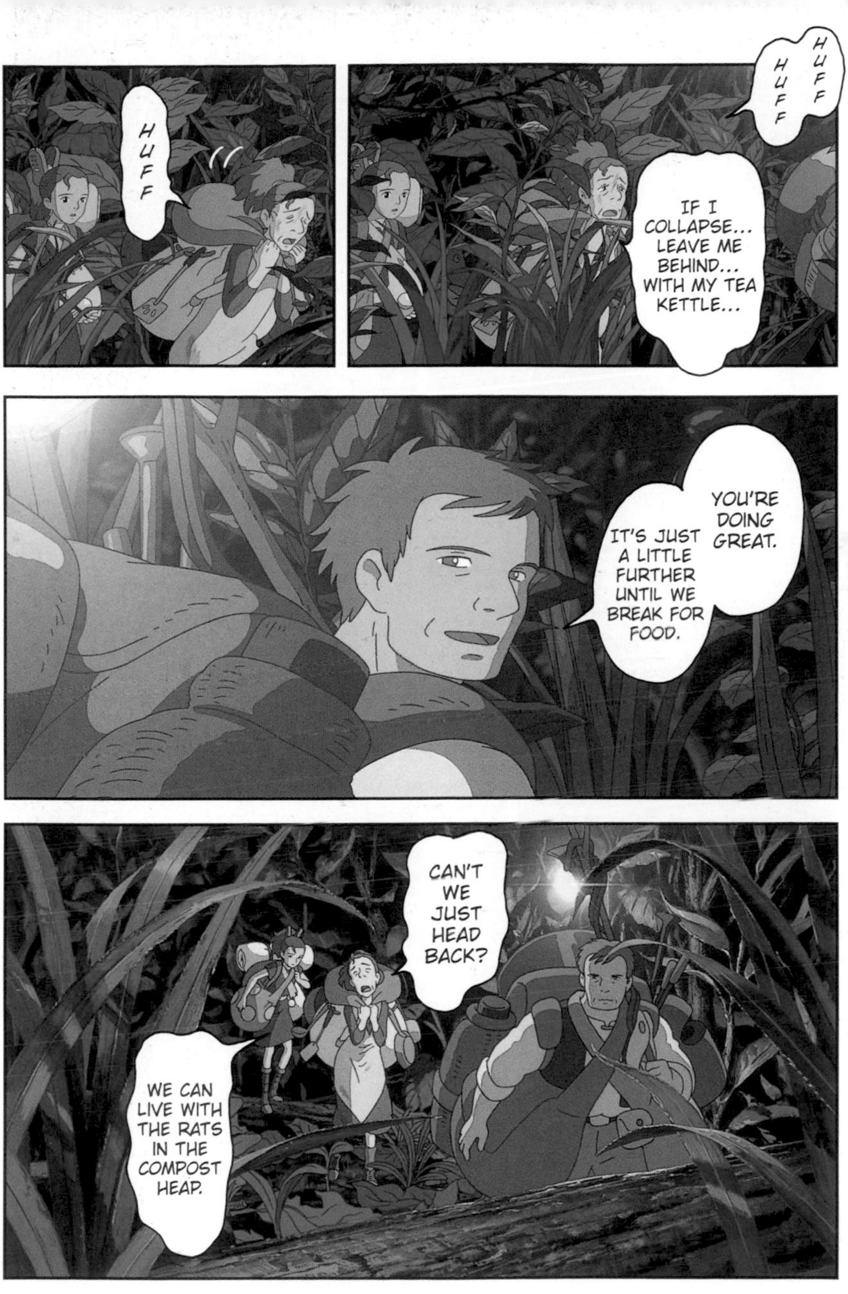
HUFF HUFF
IF I COLLAPSE... LEAVE ME BEHIND... WITH MY TEA KETTLE...
HUFF
YOU'RE DOING GREAT.
IT'S JUST A LITTLE FURTHER UNTIL WE BREAK FOR FOOD.
CAN'T WE JUST HEAD BACK?
WE CAN LIVE WITH THE RATS IN THE COMPOST HEAP.

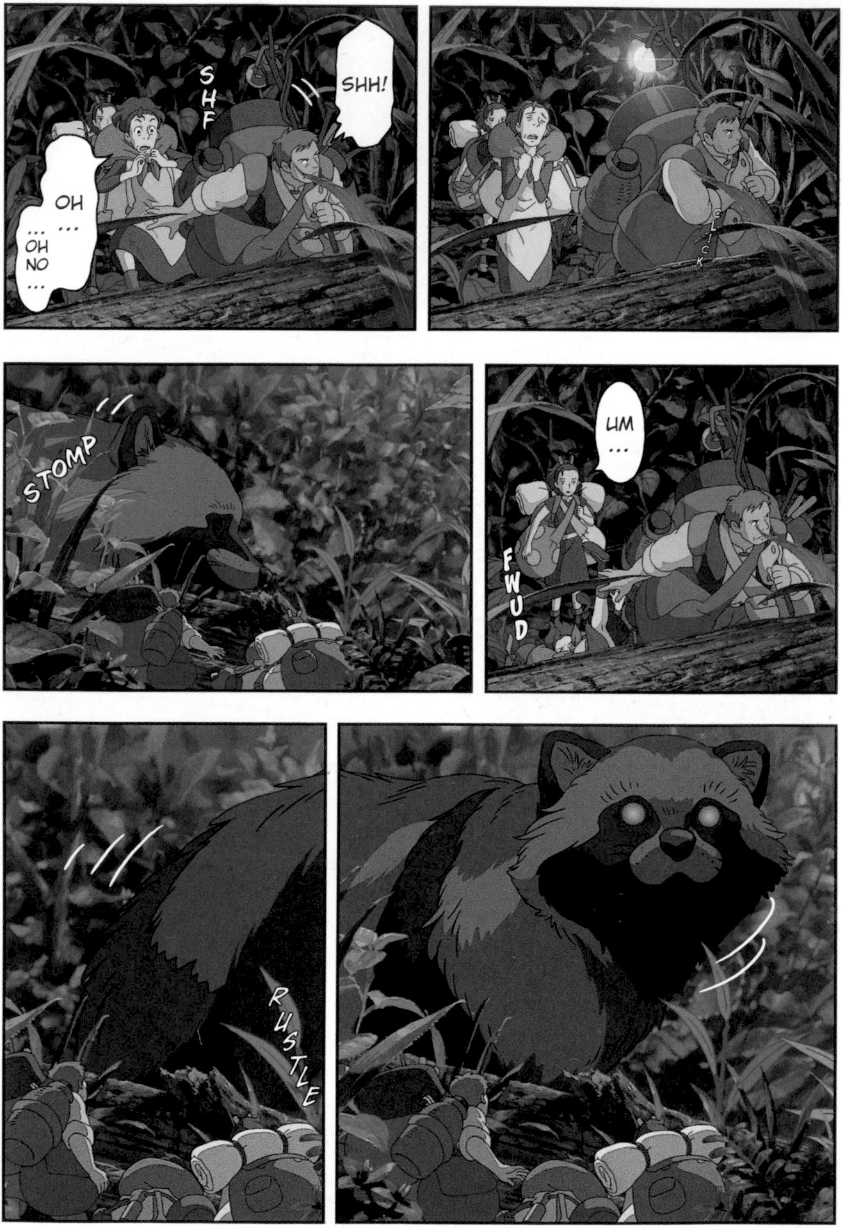
CLICK
SHH!
SHF
OH ... ... OH NO ...
UM ...
FWUD
STOMP
RUSTLE

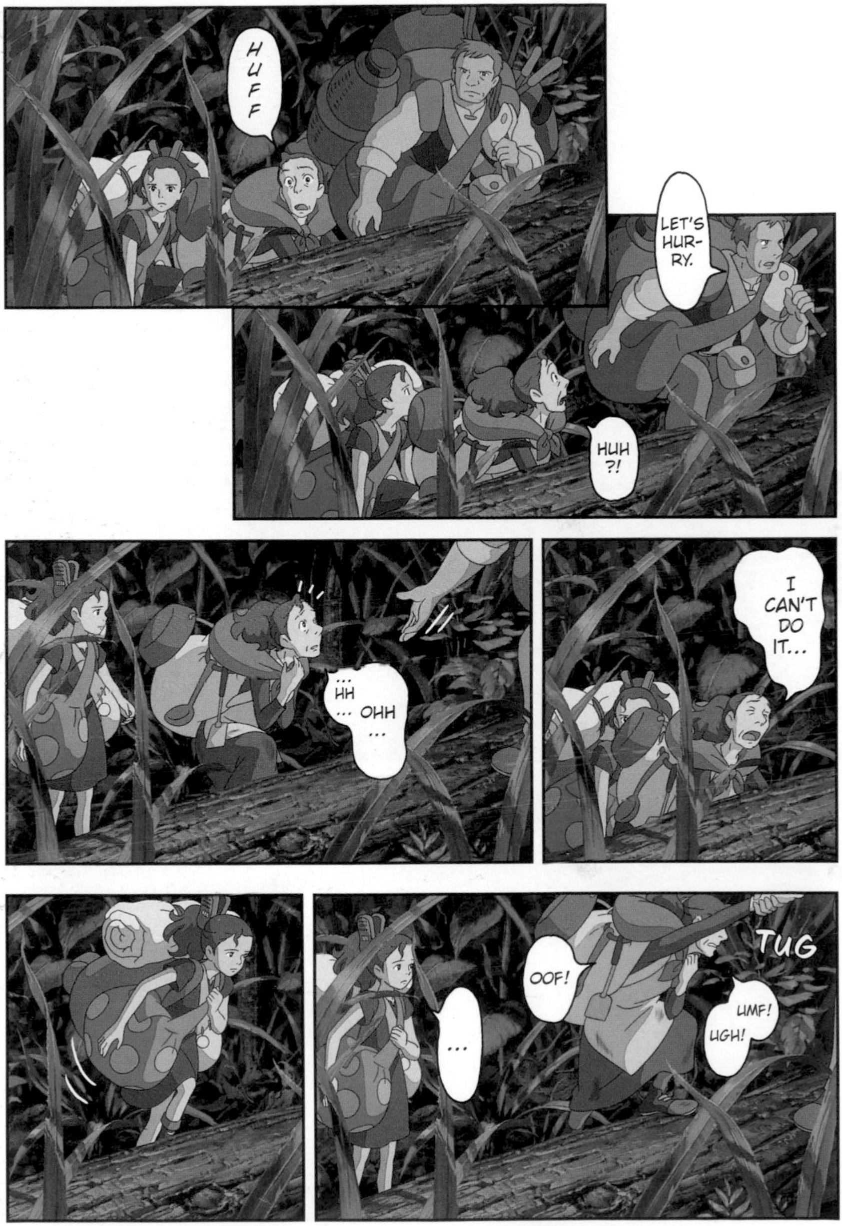
HUFF
LET'S HURRY.
HUH?!
I CAN'T DO IT...
...HH ...OHH...
TUG
UMF!
UGH!
OOF!
...

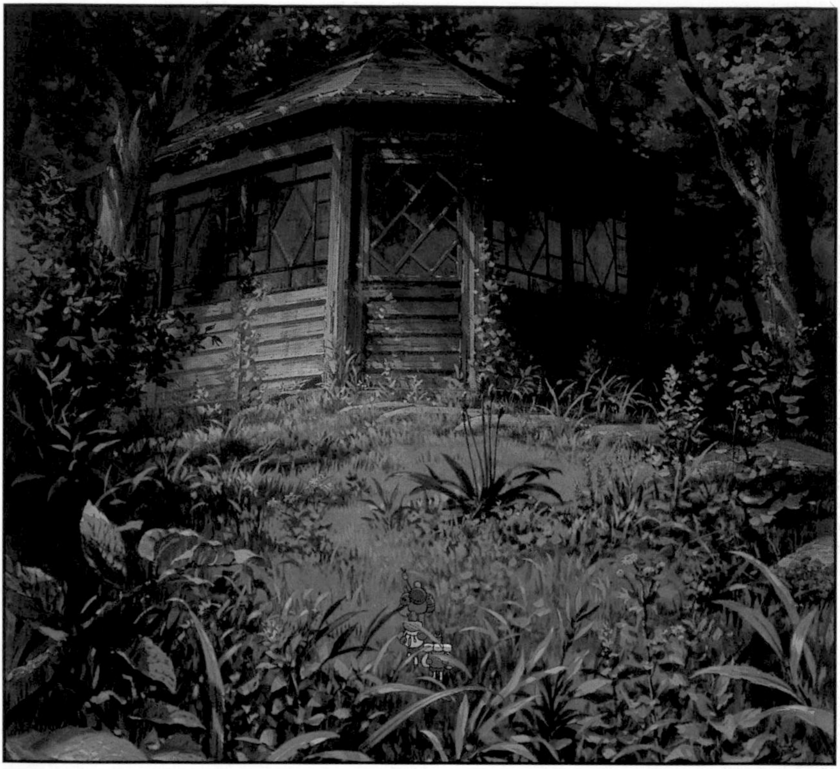

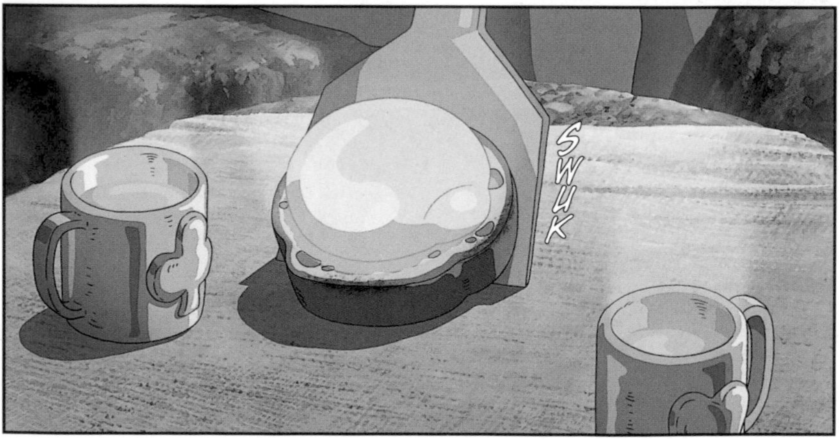
SWUK

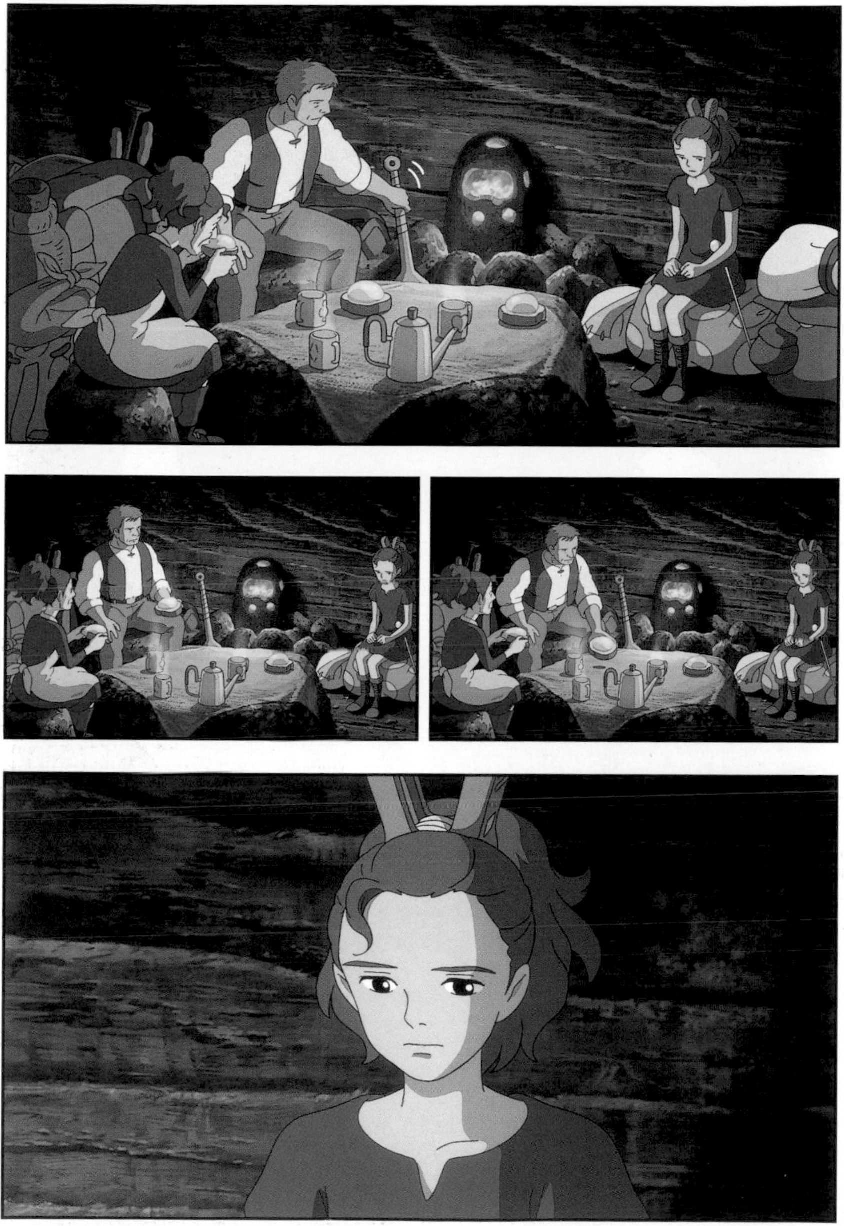

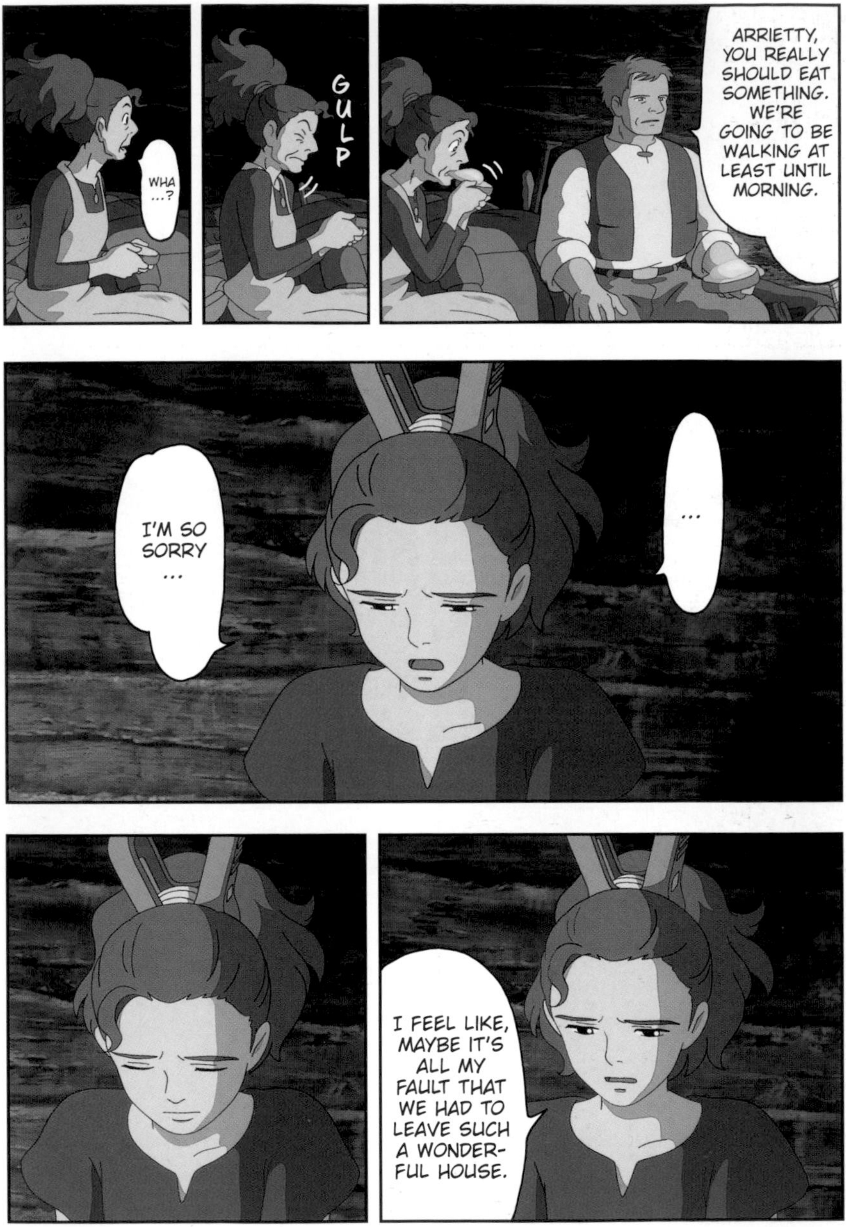
ARRIETTY, YOU REALLY SHOULD EAT SOMETHING. WE'RE GOING TO BE WALKING AT LEAST UNTIL MORNING.
GULP
WHA ...?
...
I'M SO SORRY ...
I FEEL LIKE, MAYBE IT'S ALL MY FAULT THAT WE HAD TO LEAVE SUCH A WONDERFUL HOUSE.

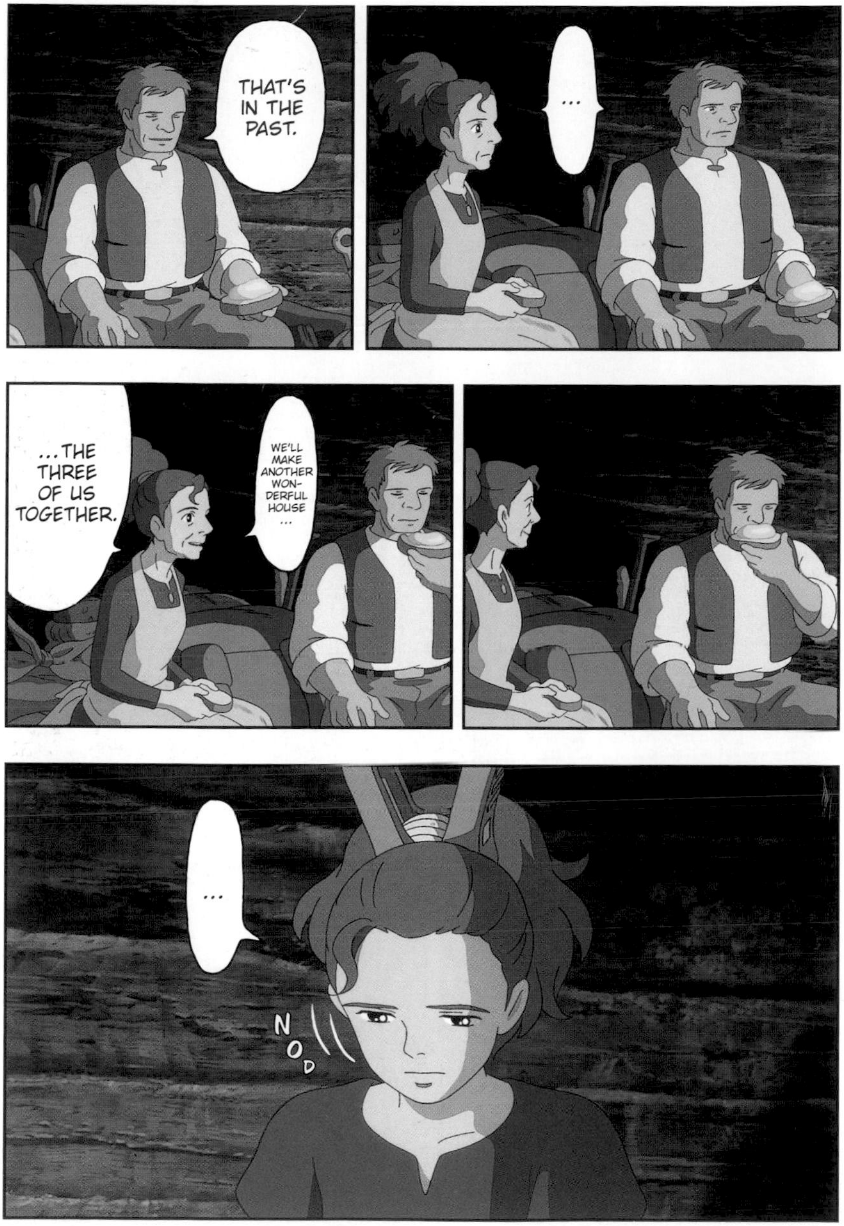
...
THAT'S IN THE PAST.
WE'LL MAKE ANOTHER WON-DERFUL HOUSE ...
...THE THREE OF US TOGETHER.
...
NOD

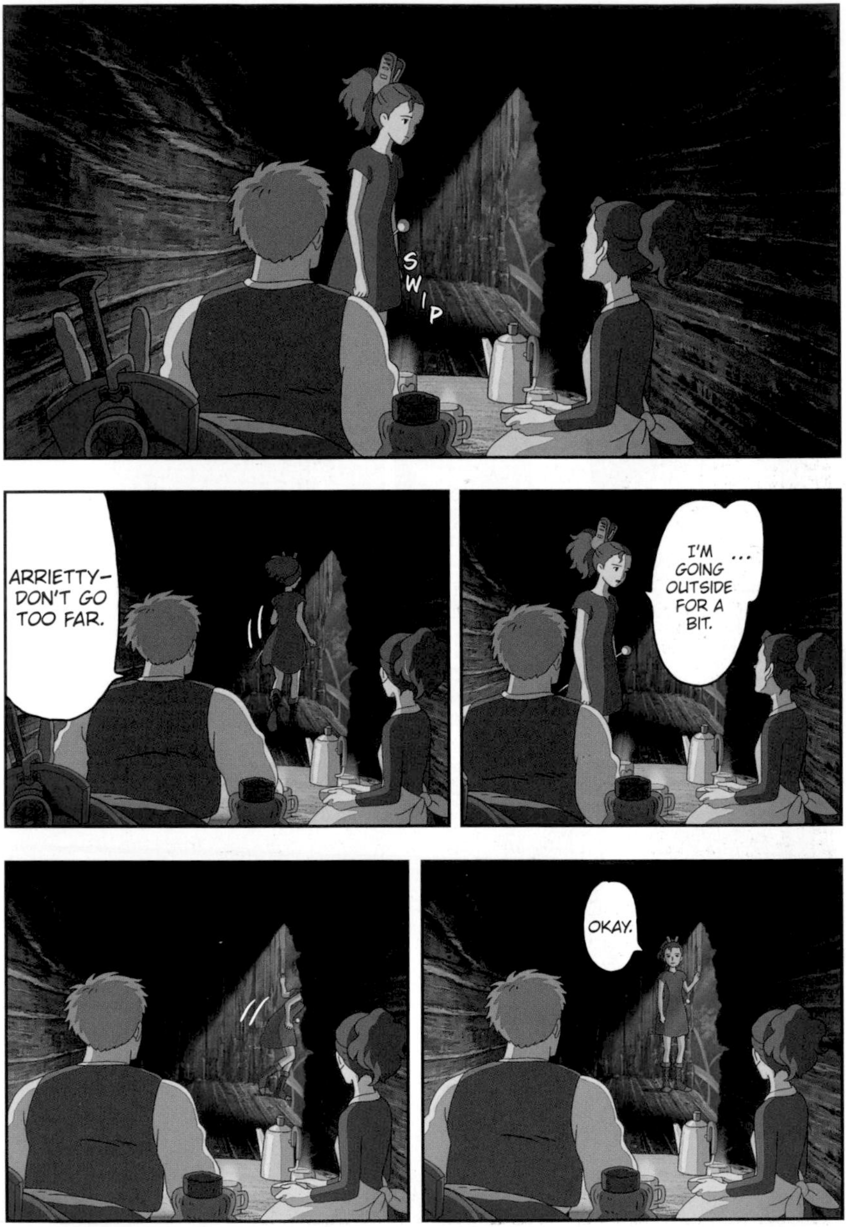
SWIP
I'M ... GOING OUTSIDE FOR A BIT.
ARRIETTY— DON'T GO TOO FAR.
OKAY.

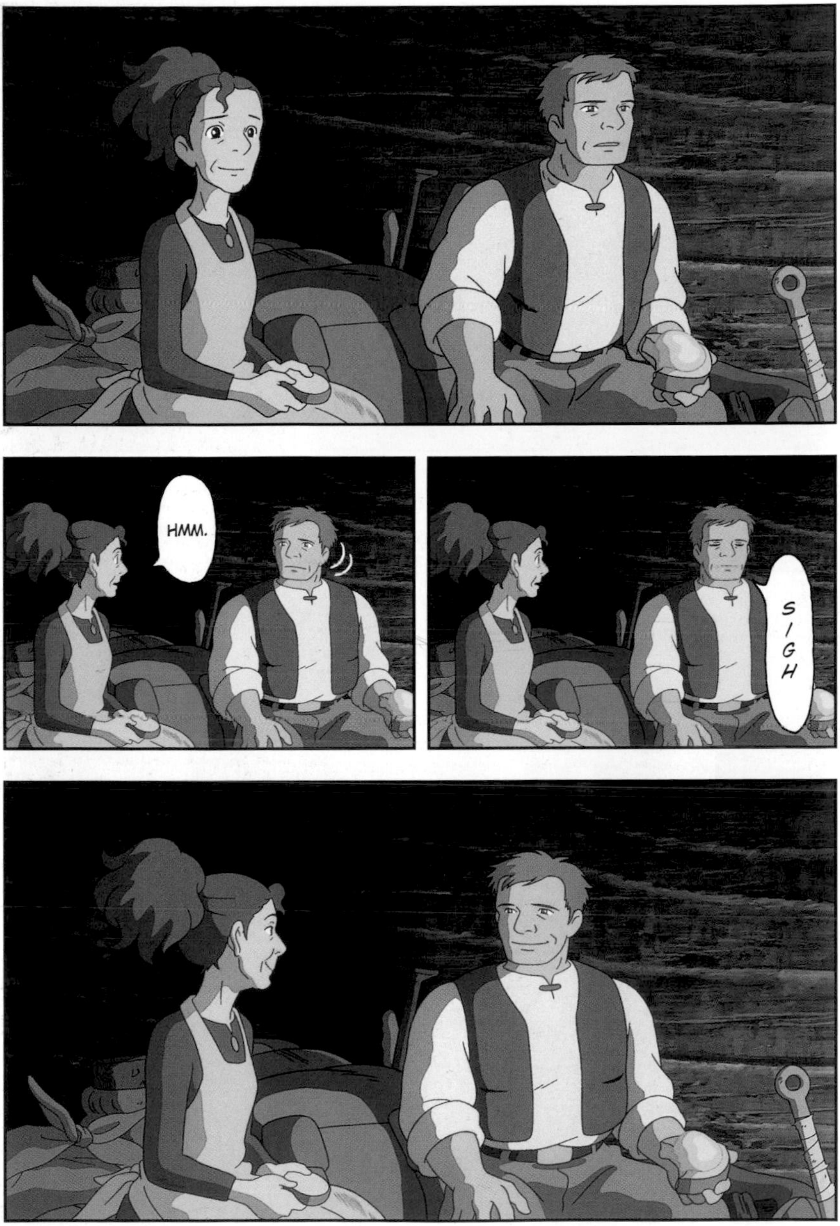
SIGH
HMM.

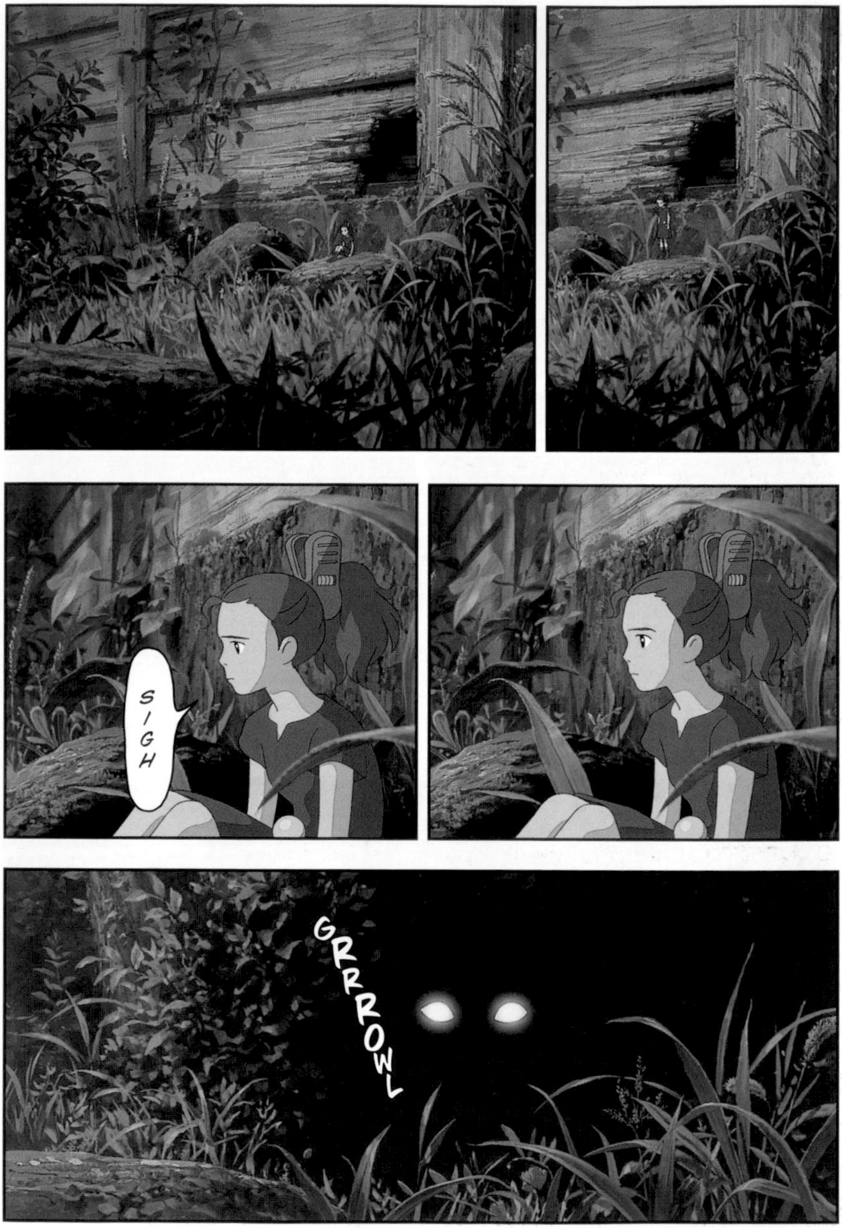
SIGH
GRRROWL

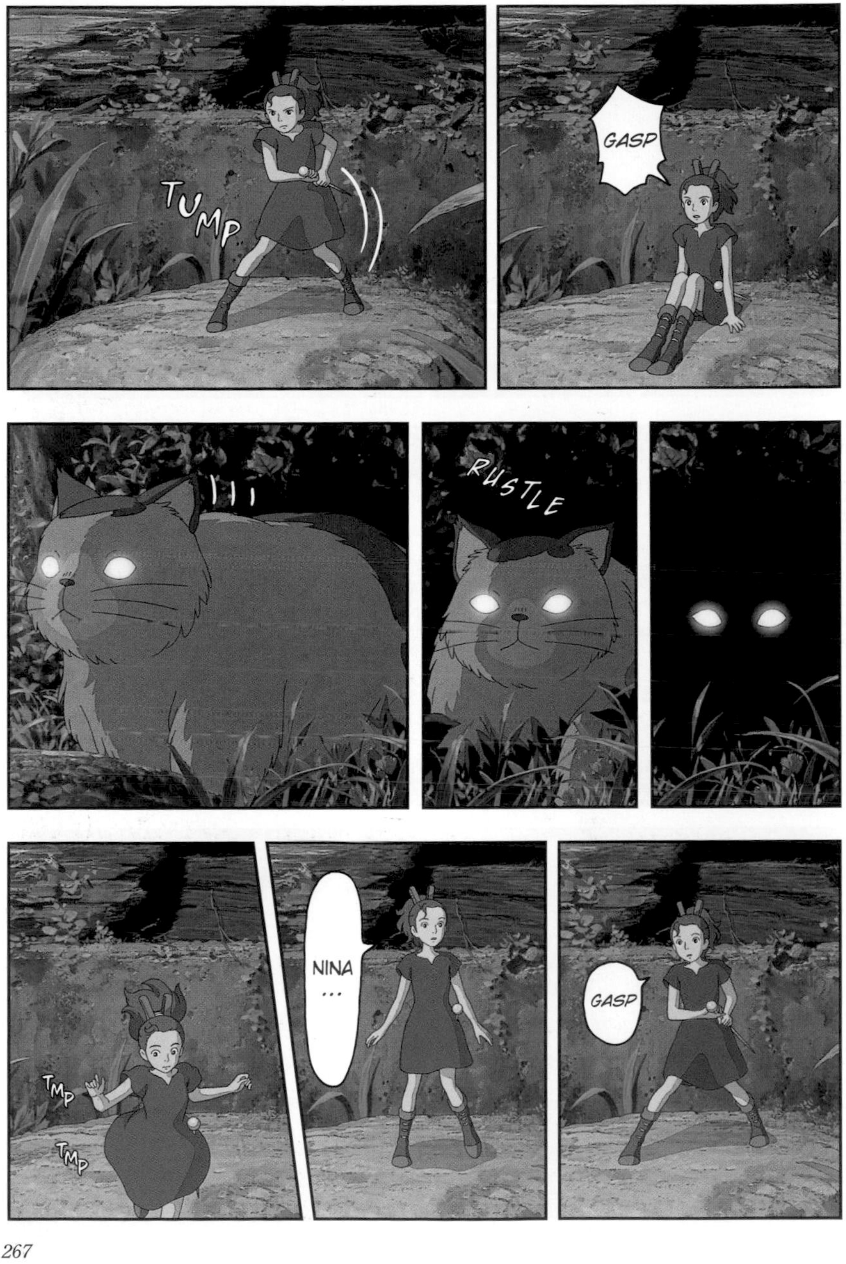
GASP
TUMP
RUSTLE
GASP
NINA ...
TMP
TMP

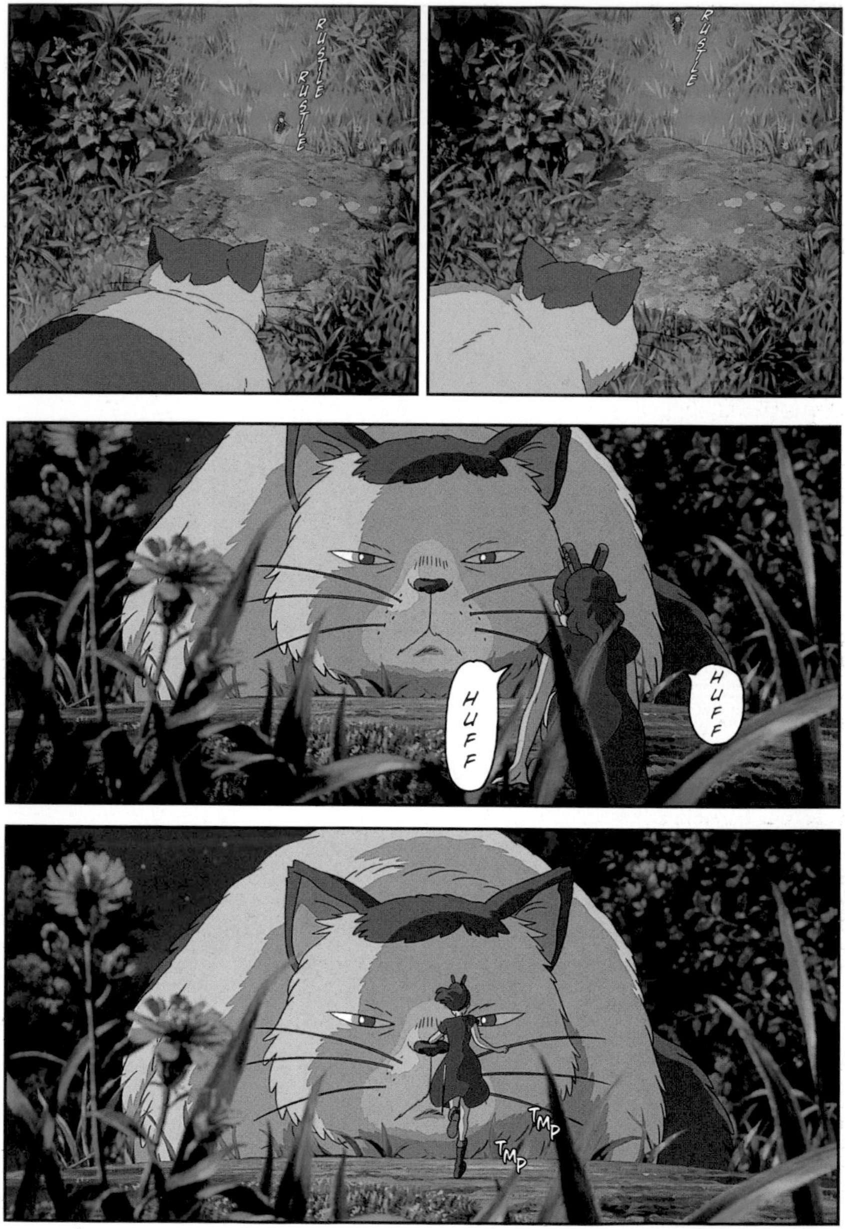
RUSTLE
RUSTLE
RUSTLE
HUFF
HUFF
TMP
TMP

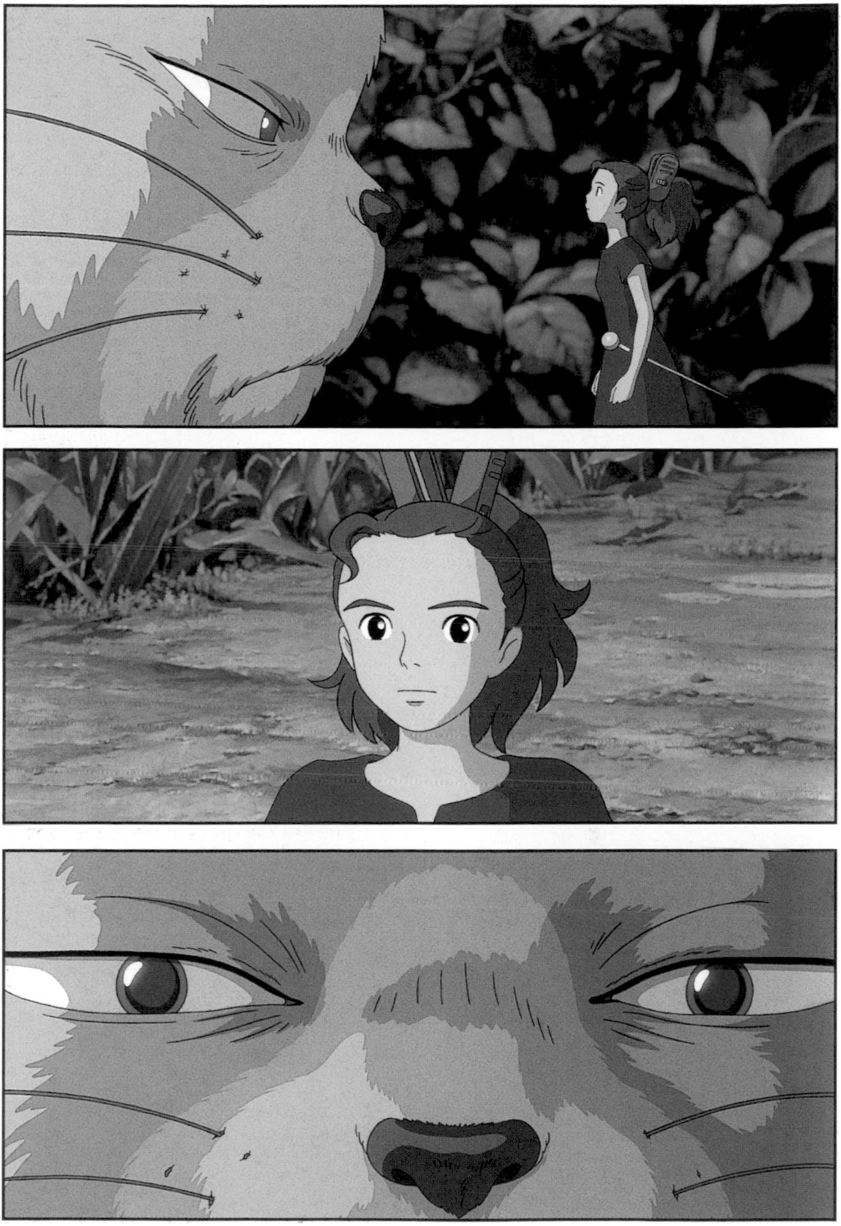

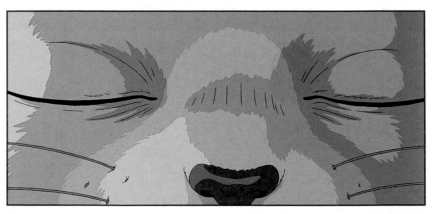

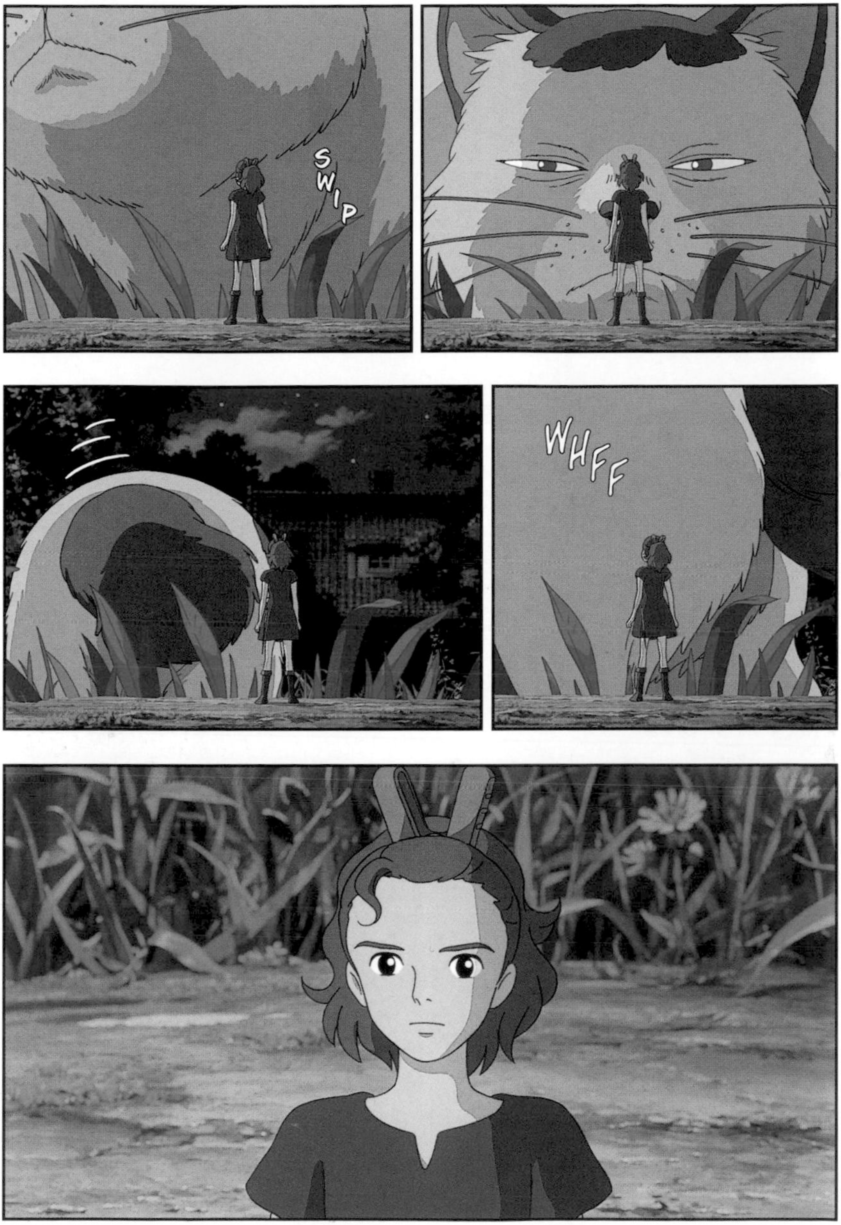
SWIP
WHFF

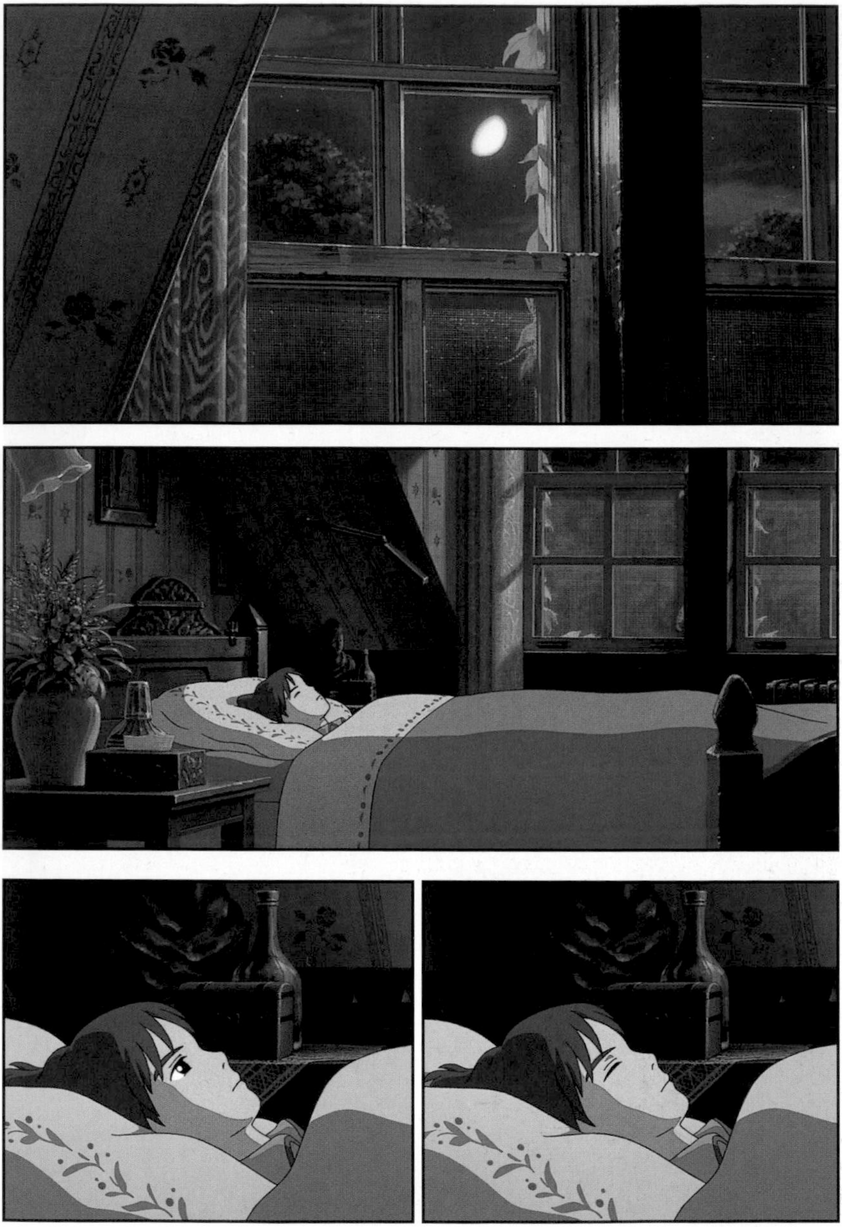

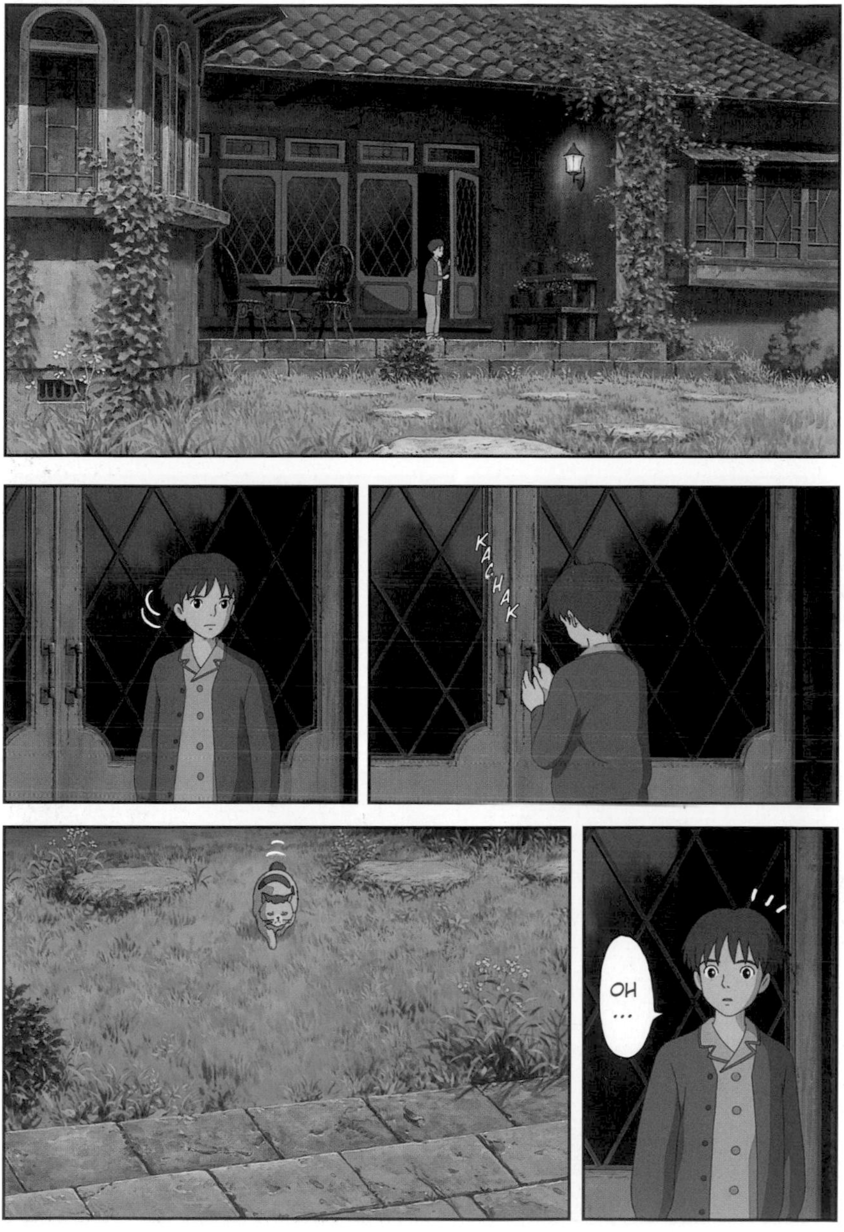
KACHAK
OH ...

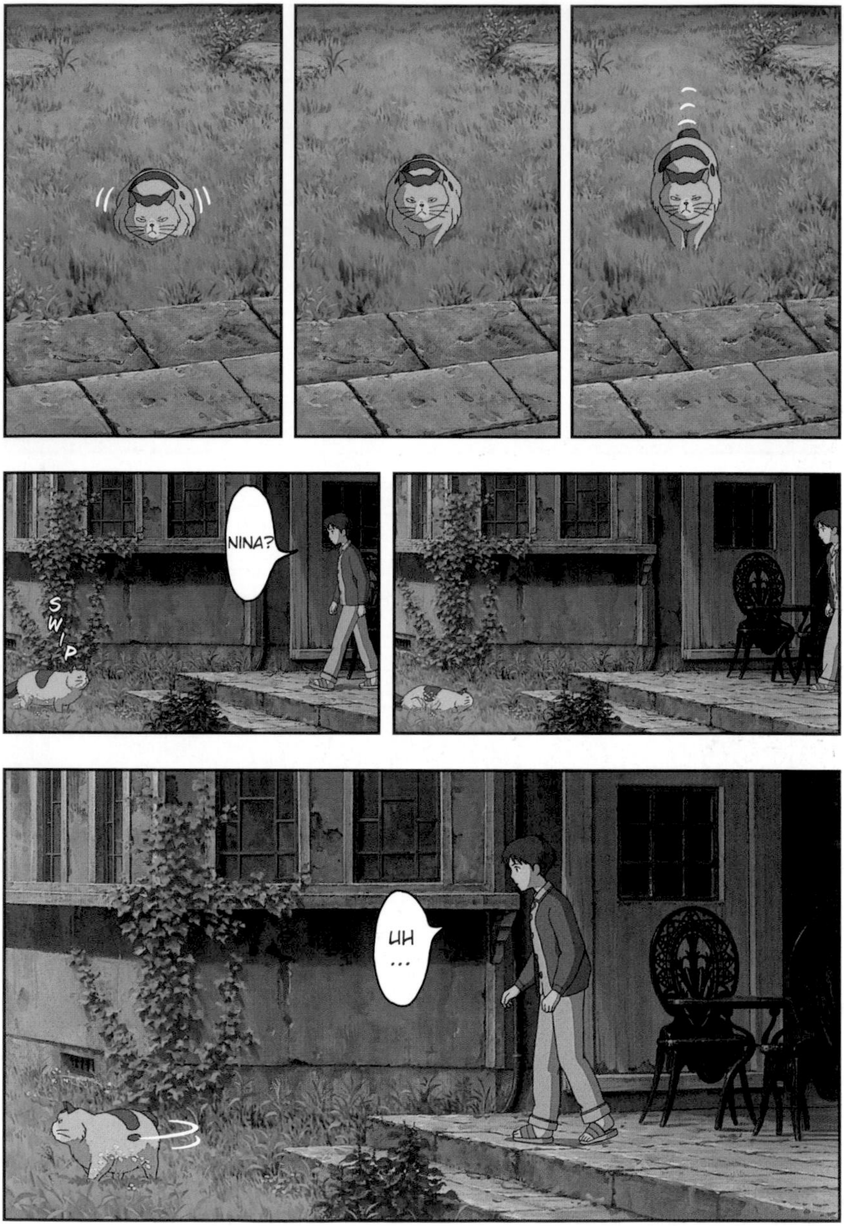
NINA?
SWIP
UH ...

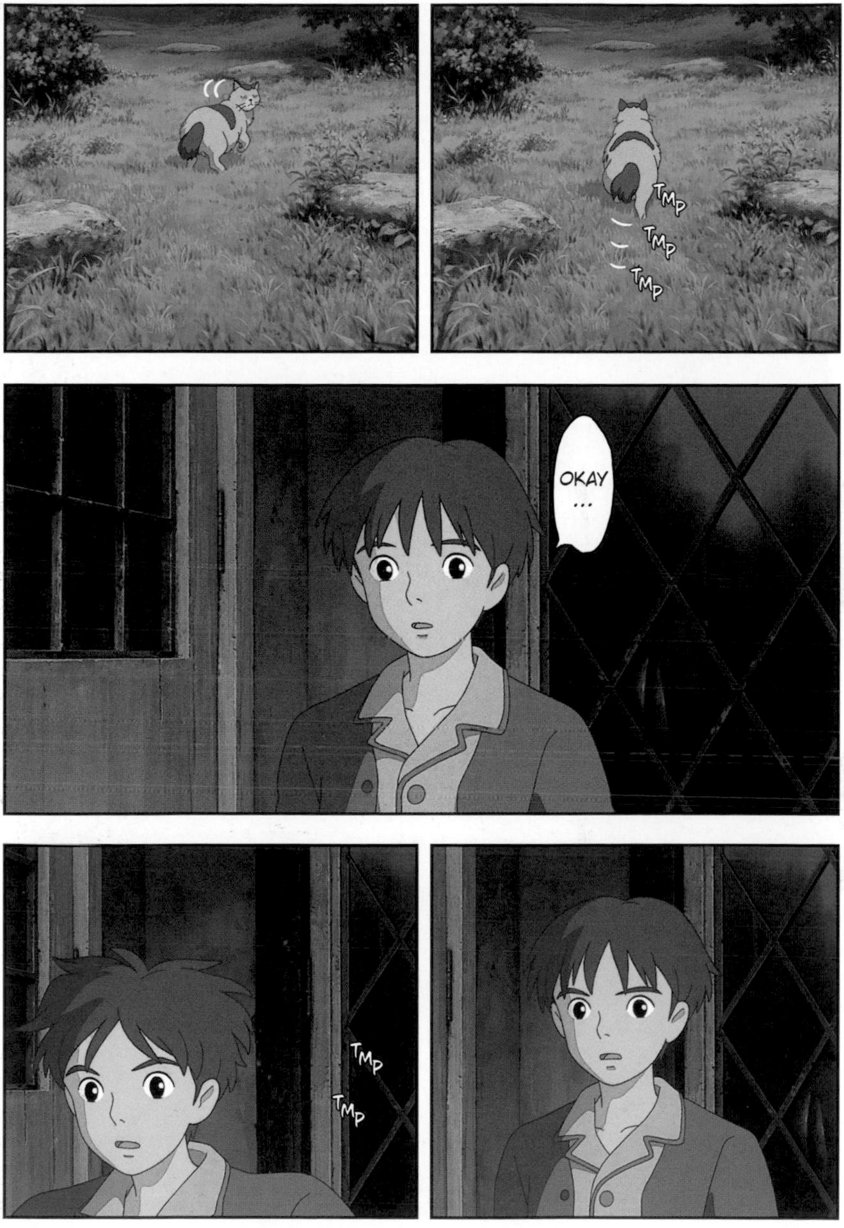
TMP
TMP
TMP
OKAY ...
TMP
TMP

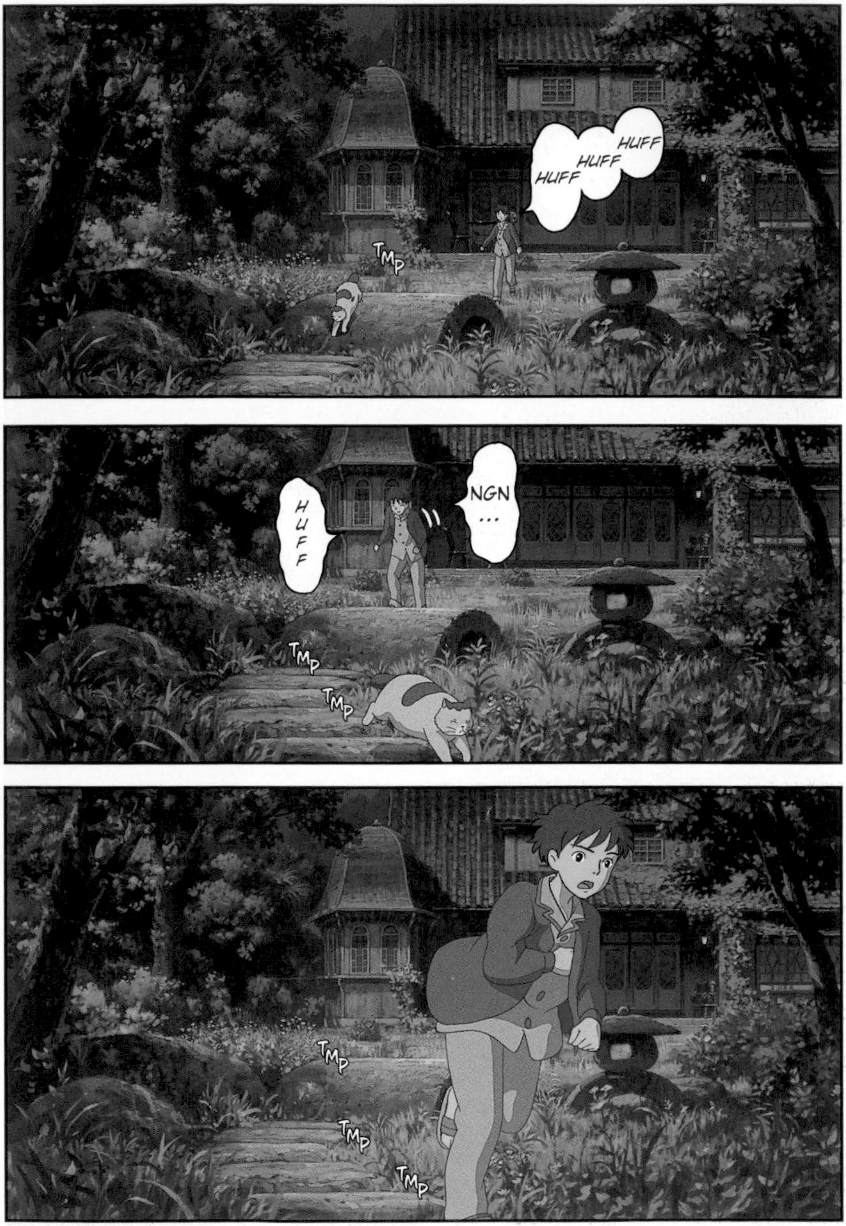
HUFF HUFF HUFF
TMP
NGN ...
HUFF
TMP
TMP
TMP
TMP
TMP

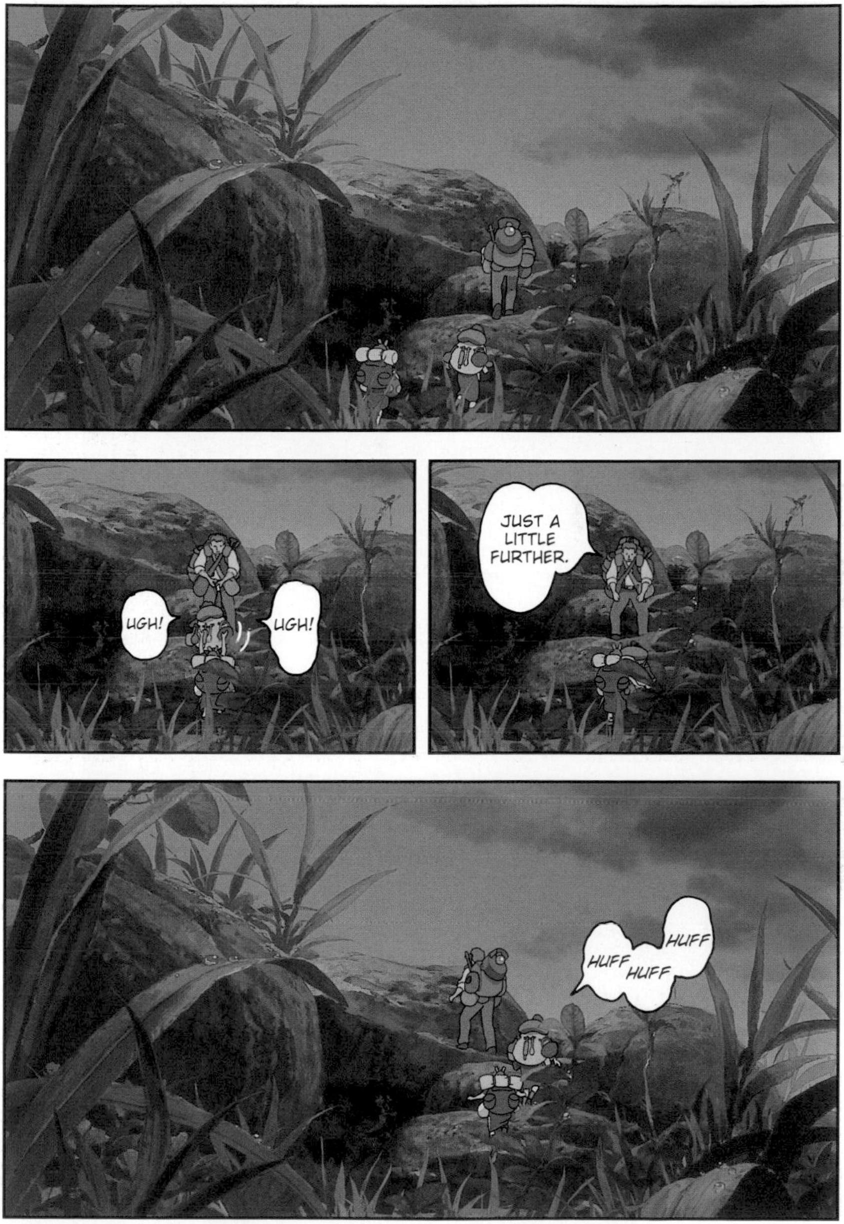
JUST A LITTLE FURTHER.
UGH!
UGH!
HUFF HUFF HUFF

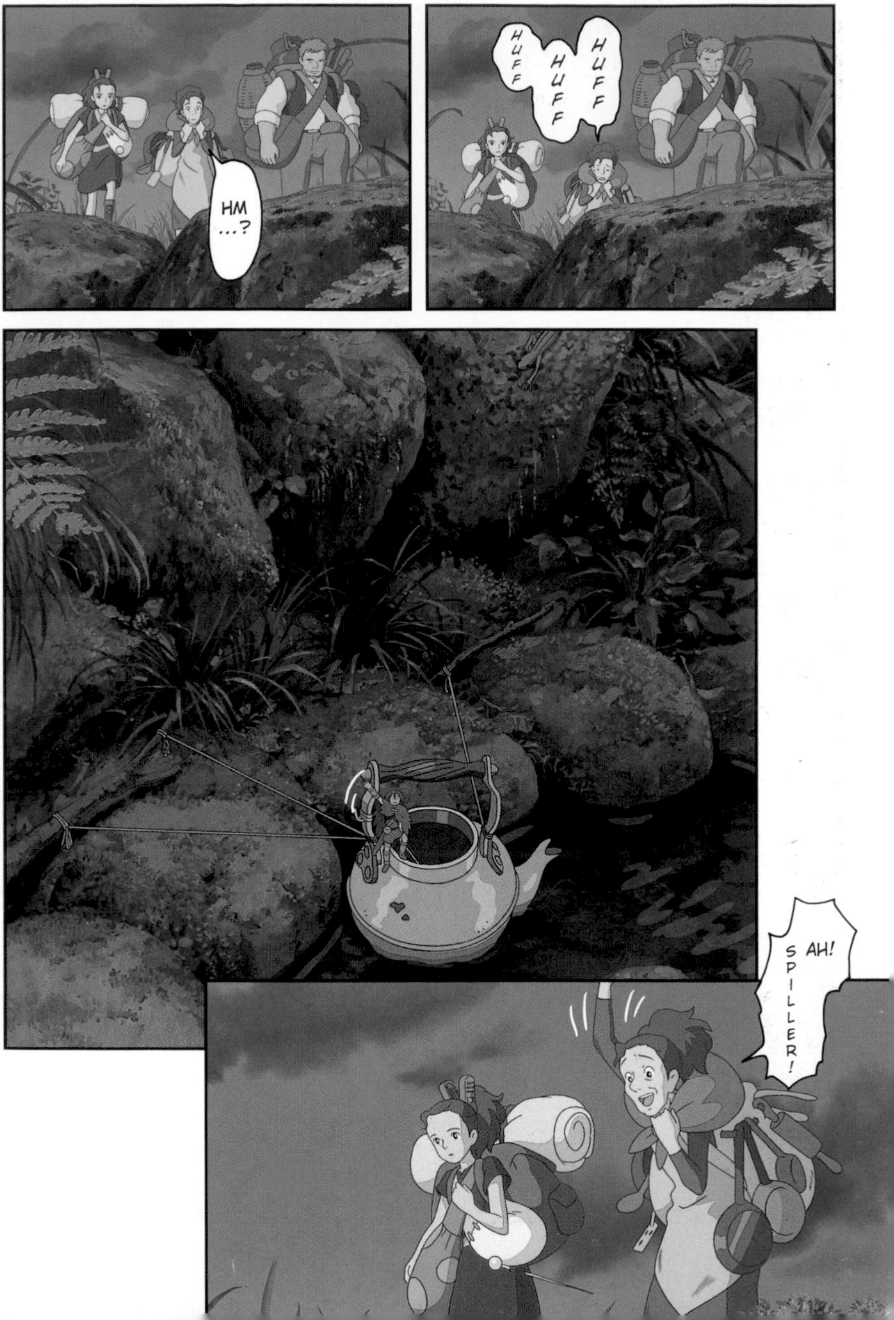
HUFF HUFF HUFF
HM ...?
AH! SPILLER!

HUFF HUFF
SHF
SHF
SHF
HUFF HUFF
SHF
SHF
HUFF HUFF HUFF
HUFF HUFF

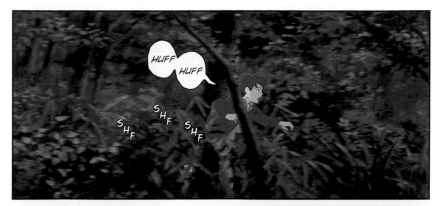

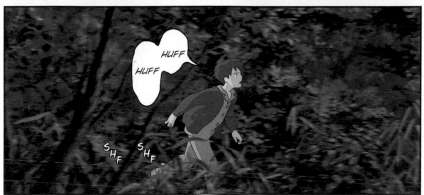

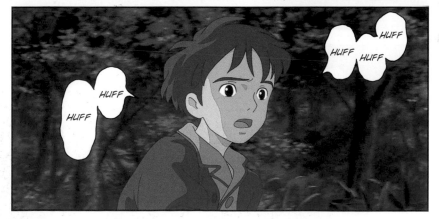

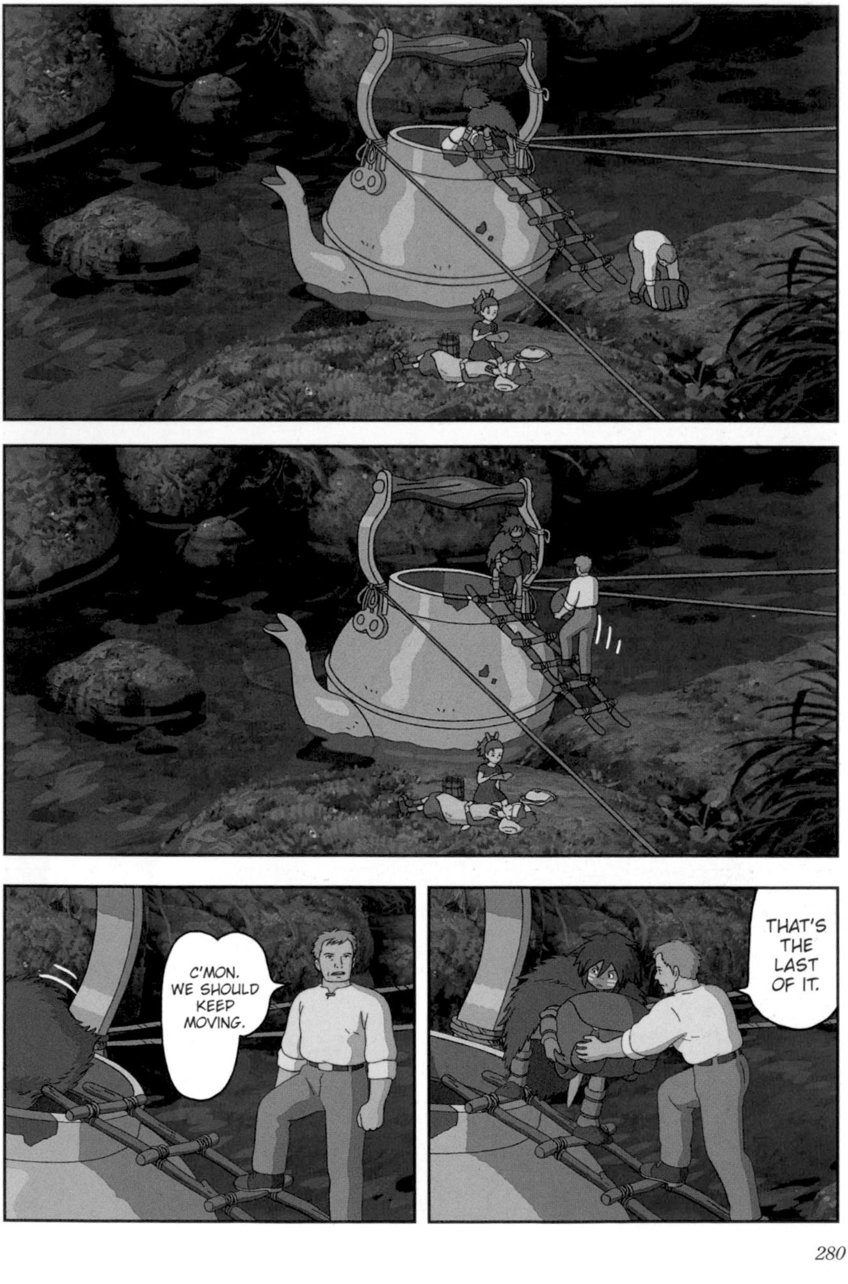
THAT'S THE LAST OF IT.
C'MON. WE SHOULD KEEP MOVING.

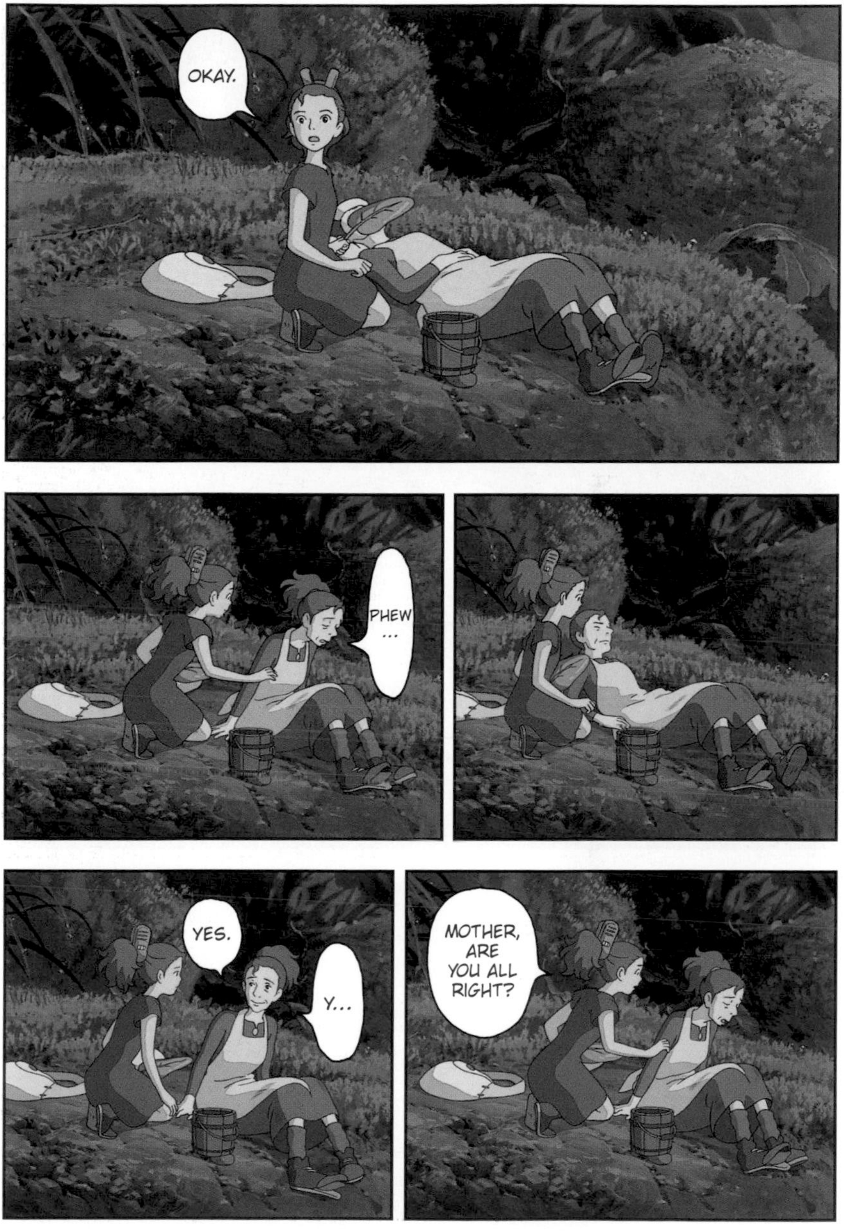
OKAY.
PHEW...
MOTHER, ARE YOU ALL RIGHT?
Y...
YES.

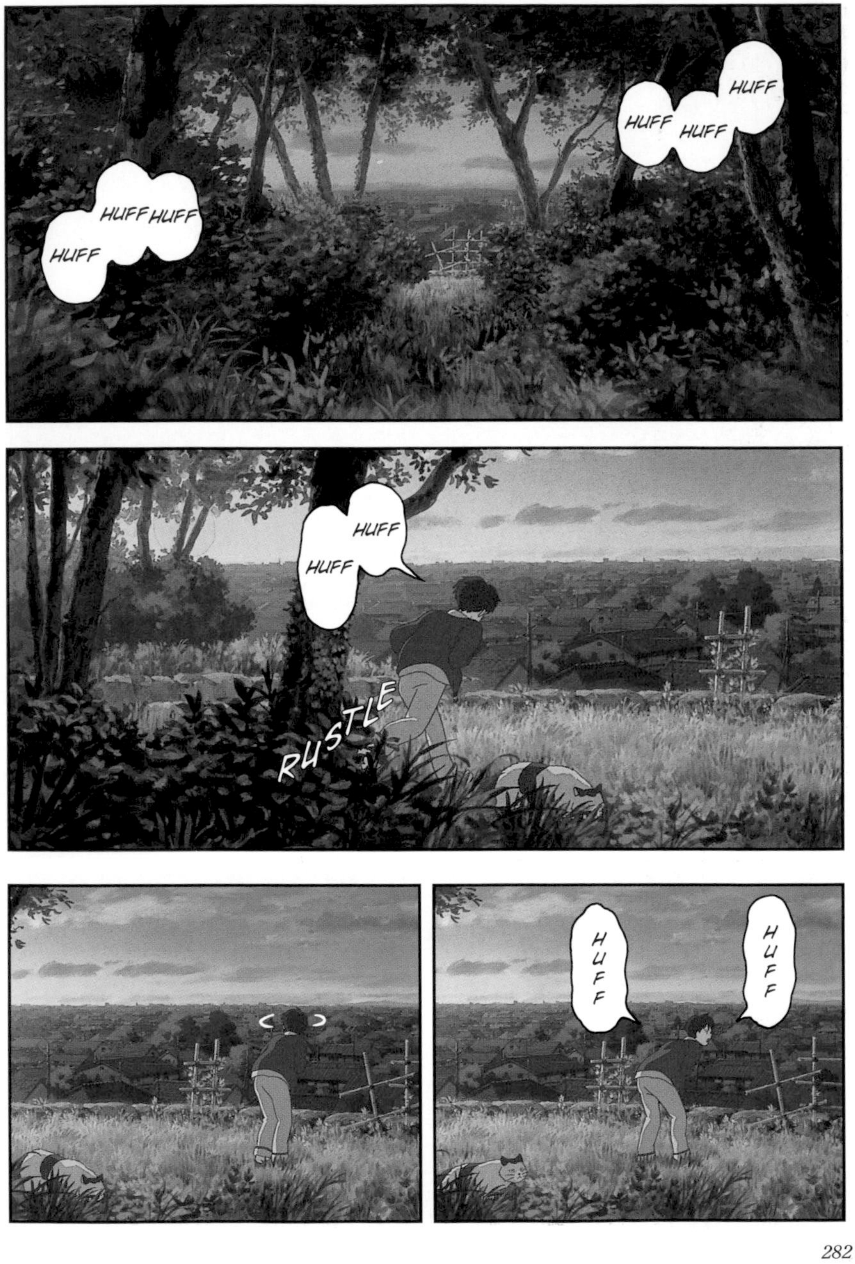
HUFF
HUFF
HUFF
HUFF HUFF
HUFF
HUFF
HUFF
RUSTLE
HUFF
HUFF

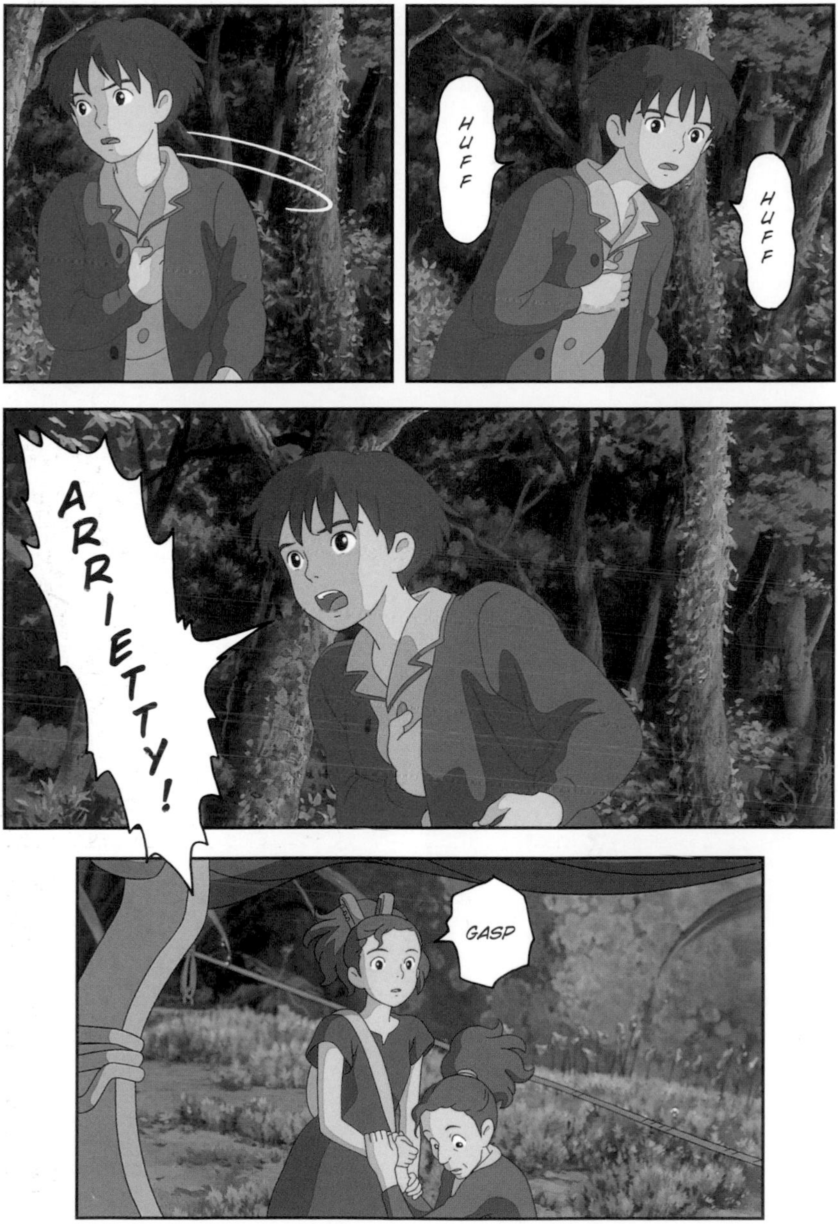
HUFF
HUFF
ARRIETTY!
GASP

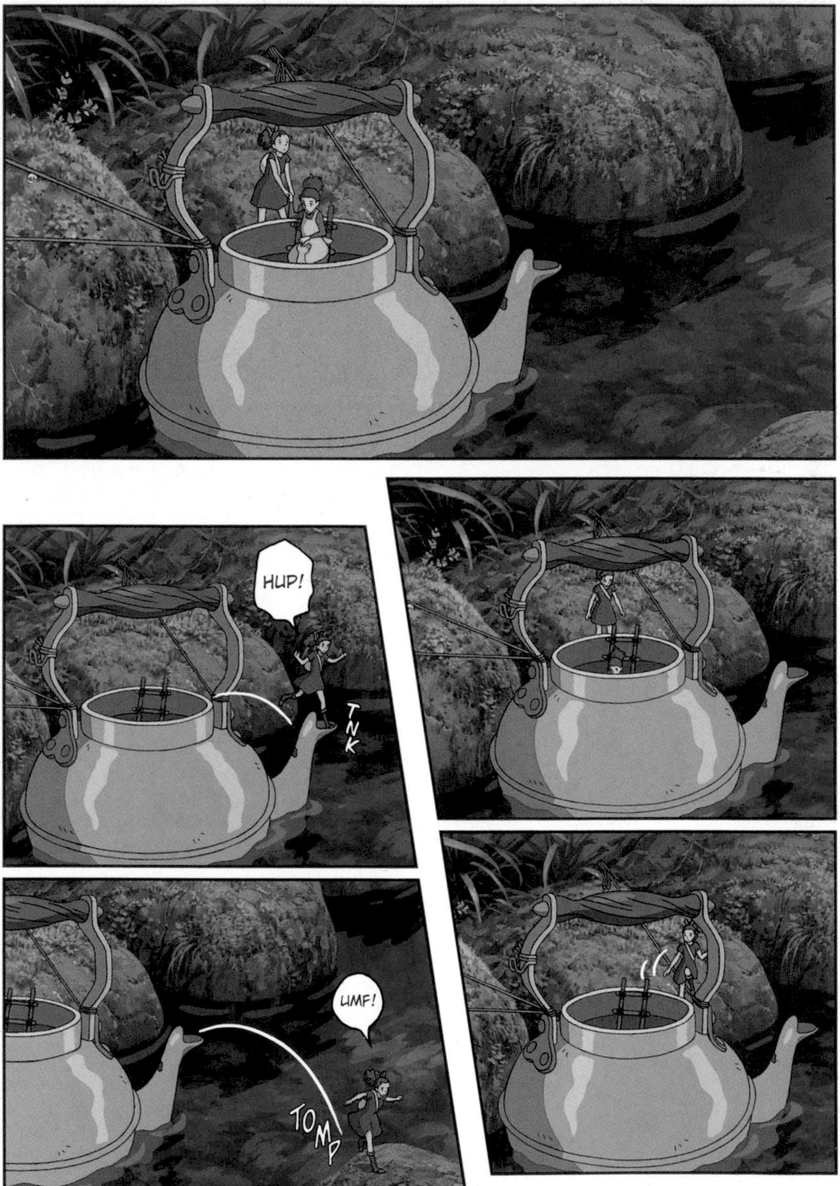
HUP!
TNK
UMF!
TOMP

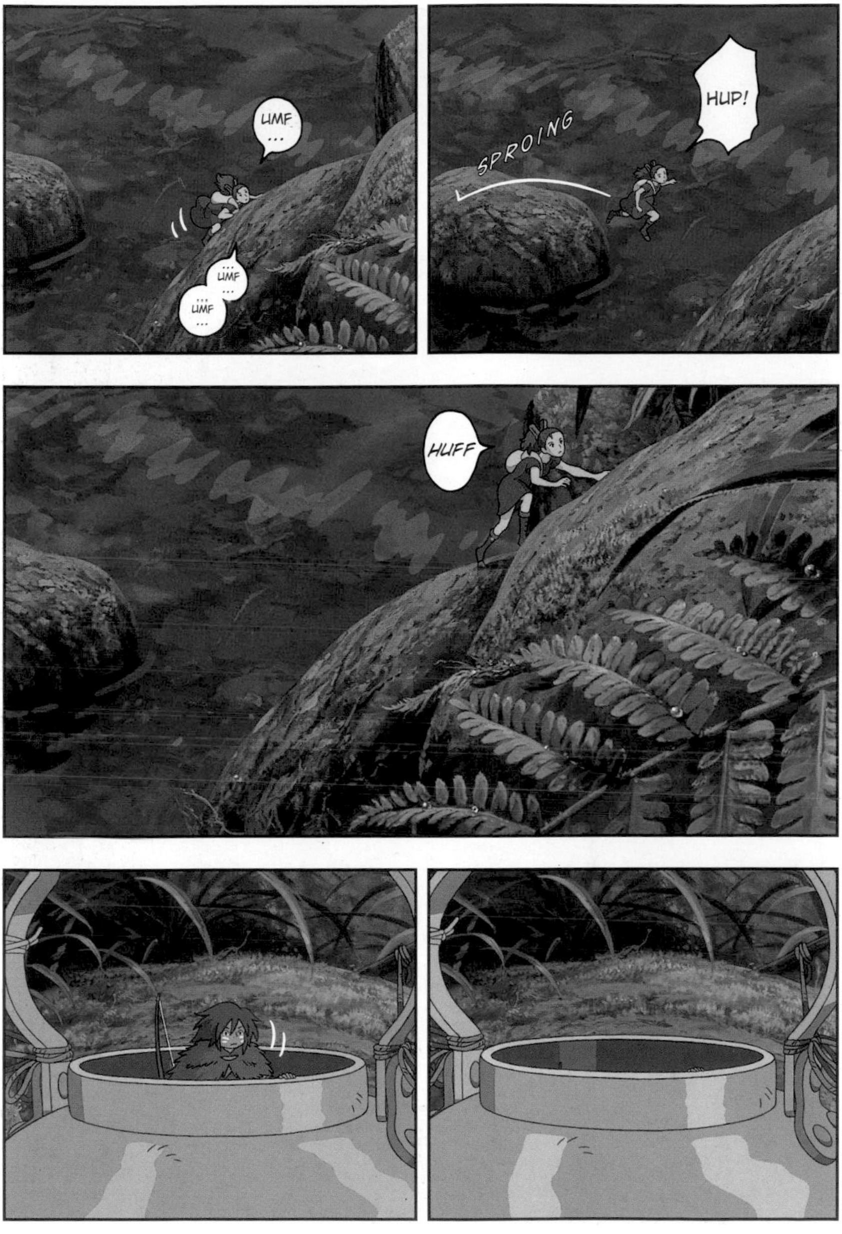
HUP!
SPROING
UMF ...
... UMF ...
... UMF ...
HUFF

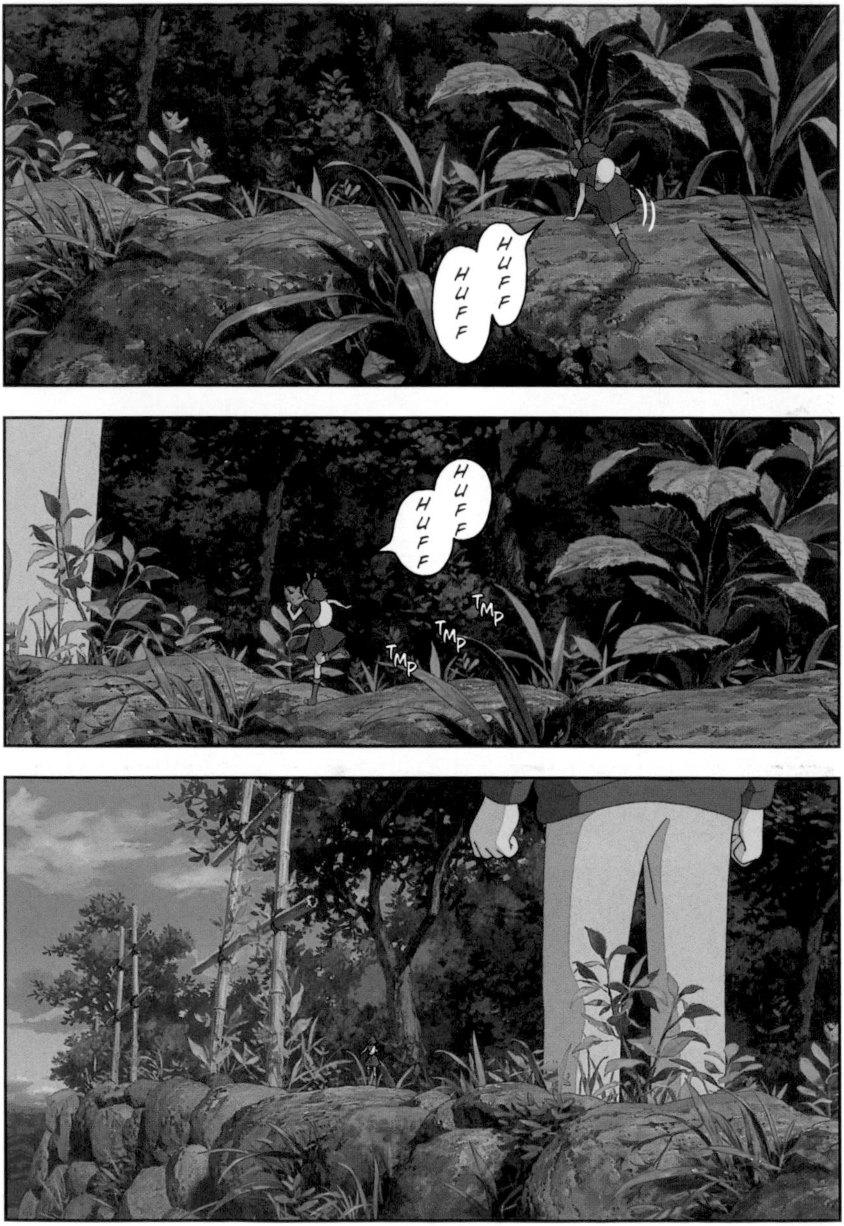
HUFF HUFF
HUFF HUFF
TMP TMP TMP

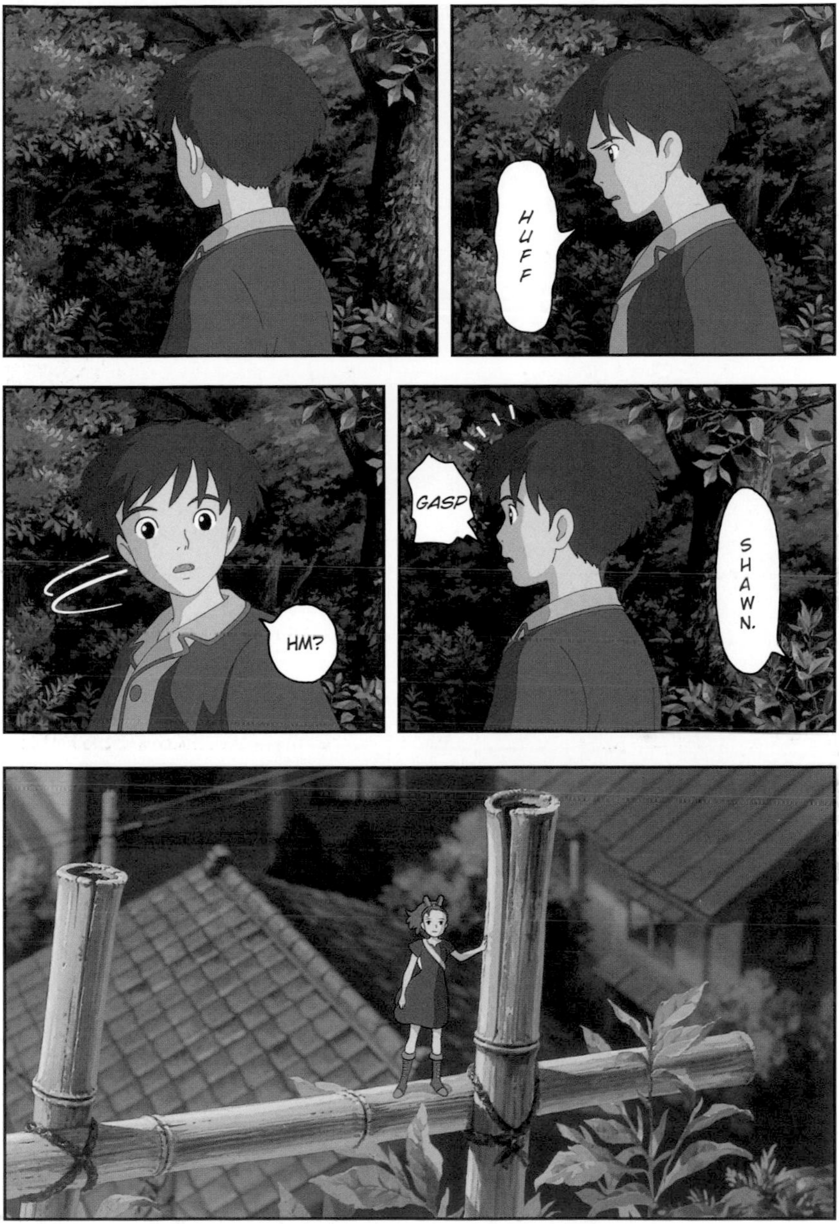
HUFF
SHAWN.
GASP
HM?

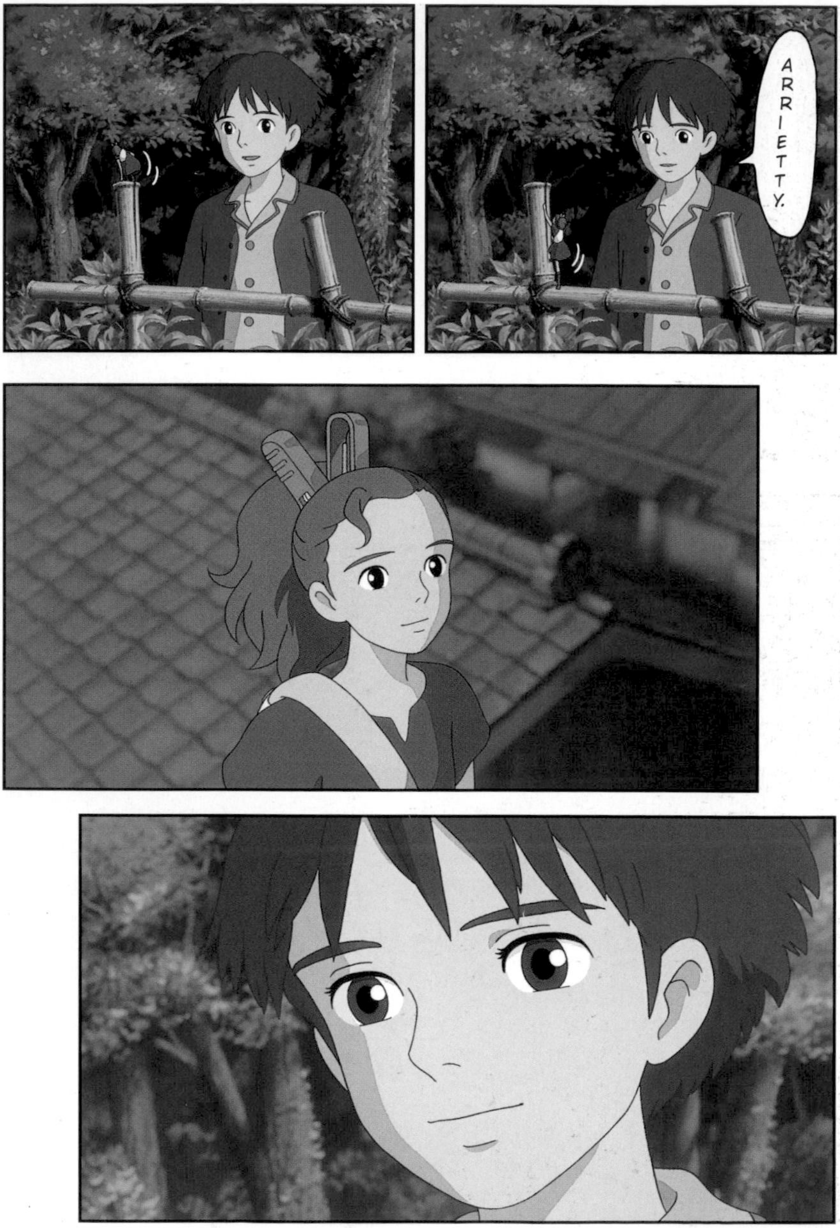
ARRIETTY.

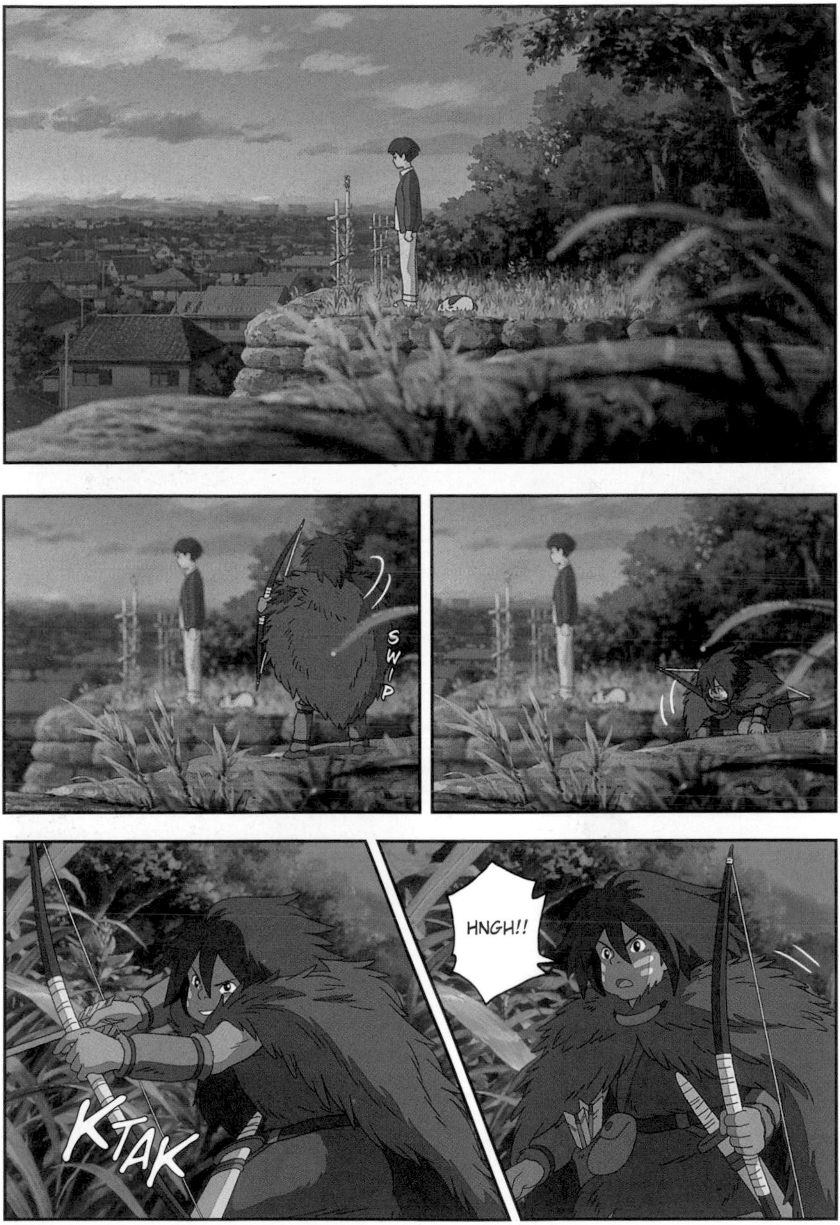
SWIP
HNGH!!
KTAK

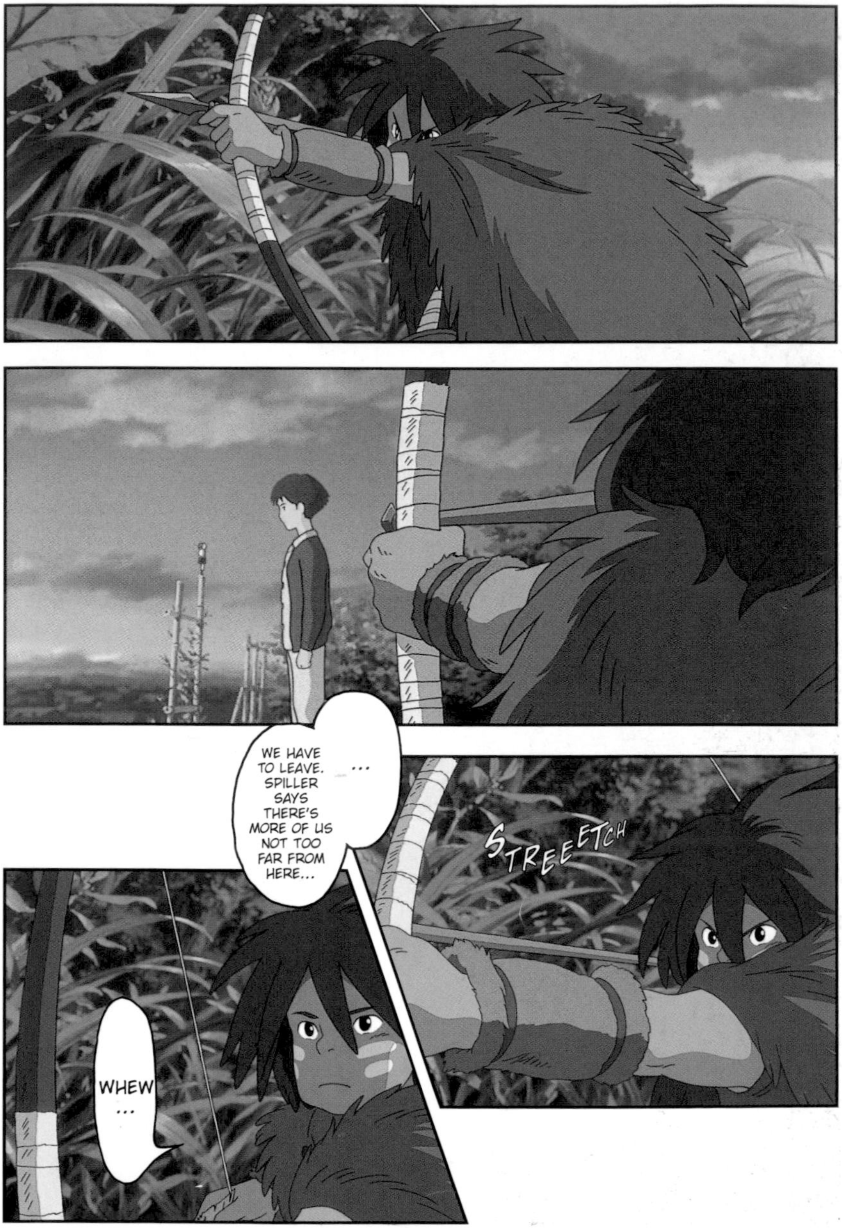
...
STREEETCH
WE HAVE TO LEAVE. SPILLER SAYS THERE'S MORE OF US NOT TOO FAR FROM HERE...
WHEW ...

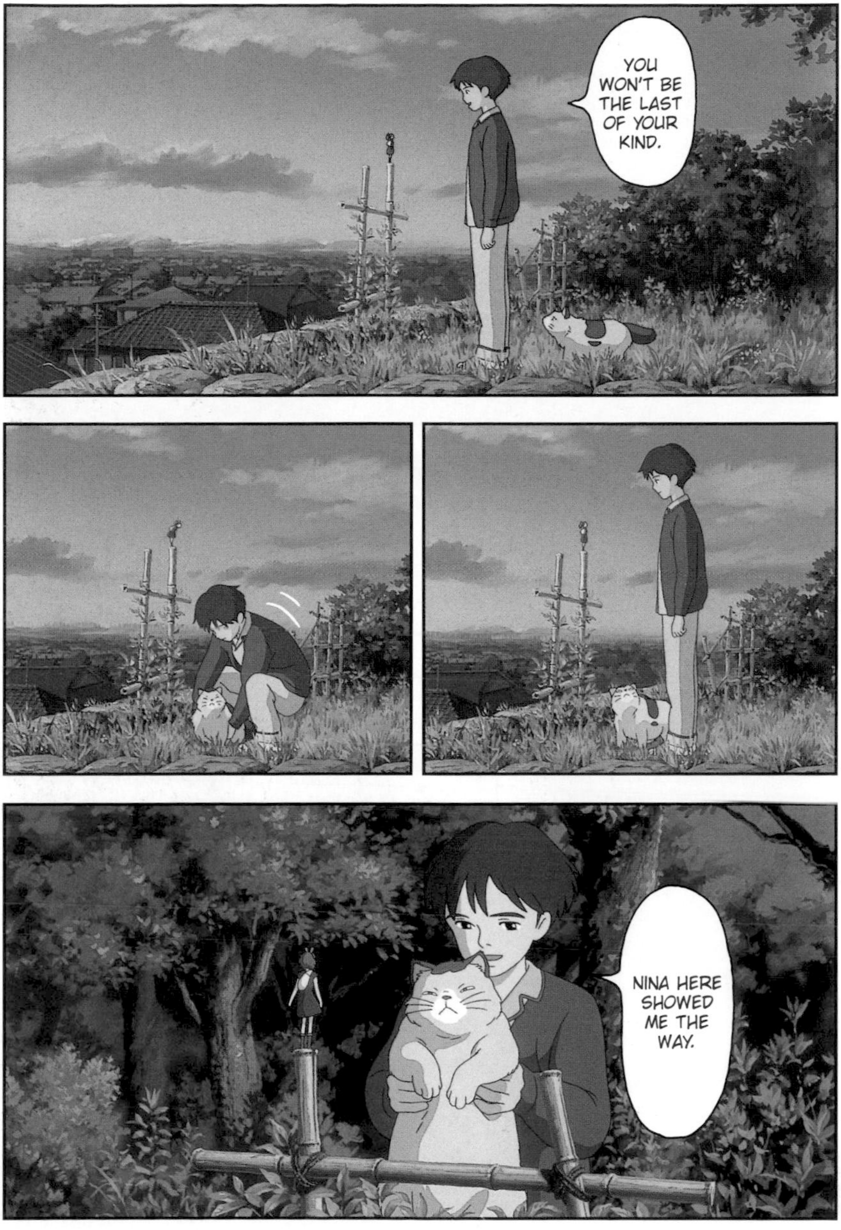
YOU WON'T BE THE LAST OF YOUR KIND.
NINA HERE SHOWED ME THE WAY.

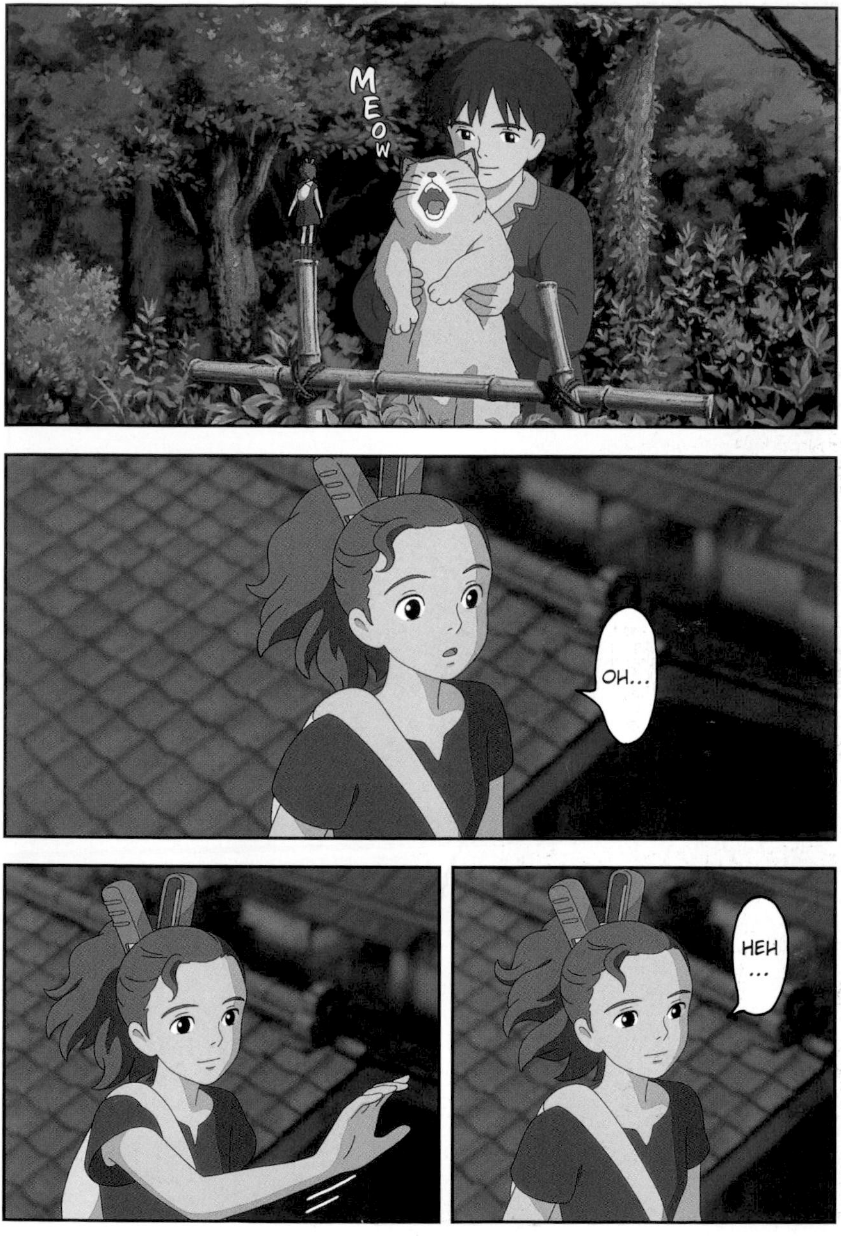
MEOW
OH...
HEH ...

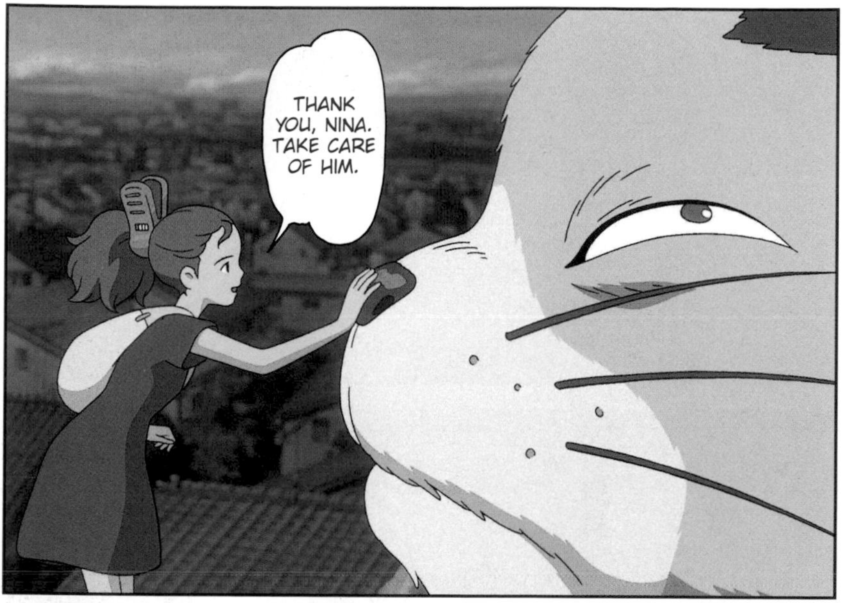
THANK YOU, NINA. TAKE CARE OF HIM.
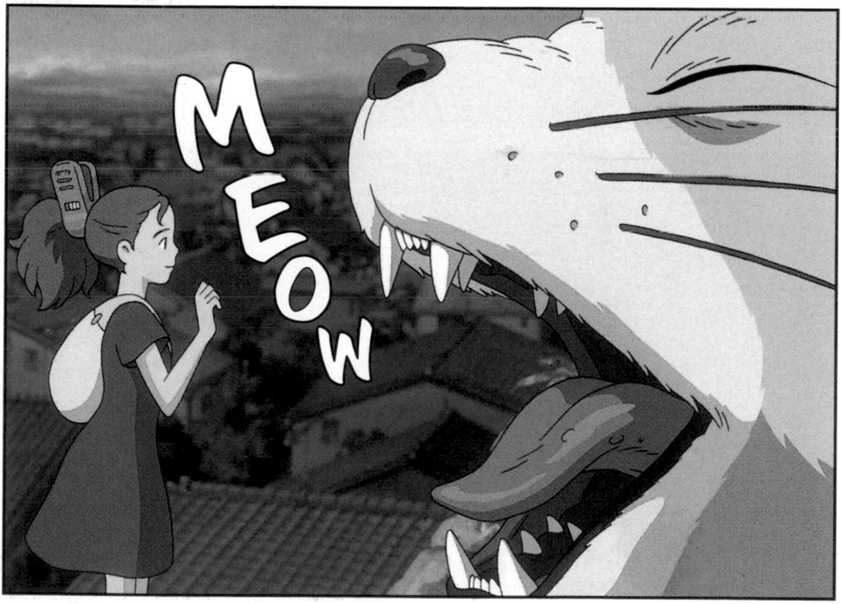
MEOW

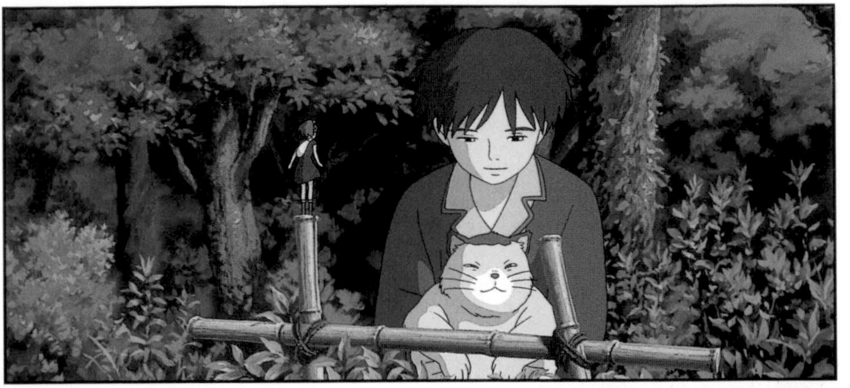
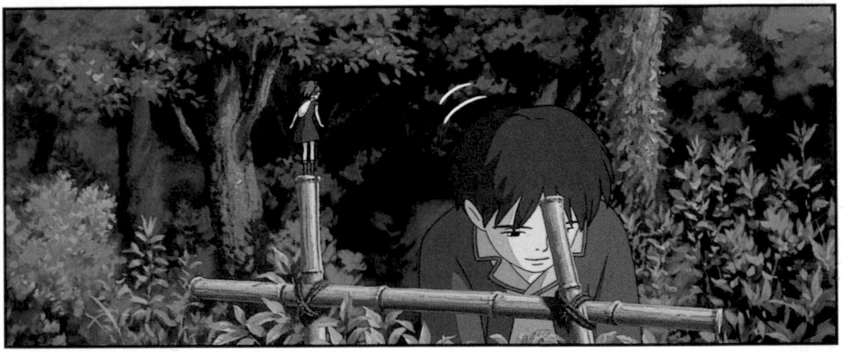
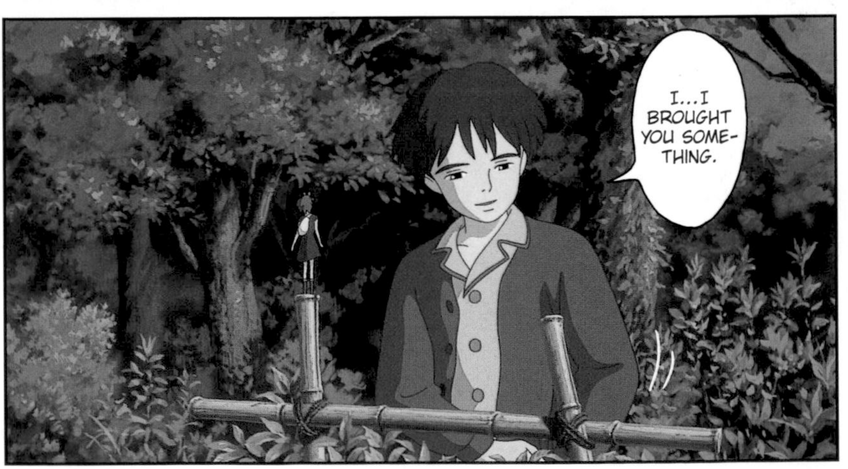
I...I BROUGHT YOU SOME-THING.

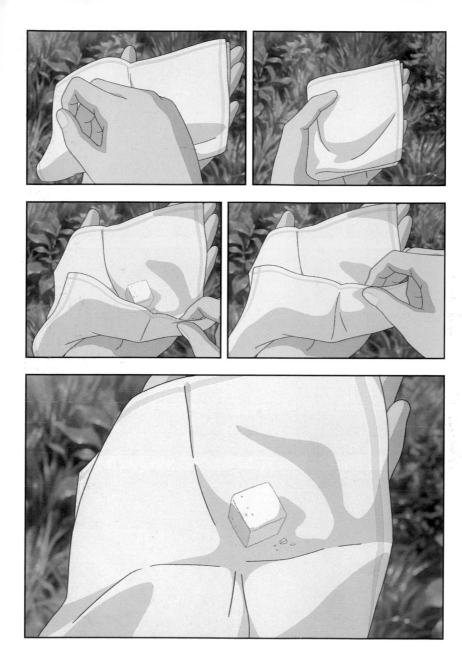

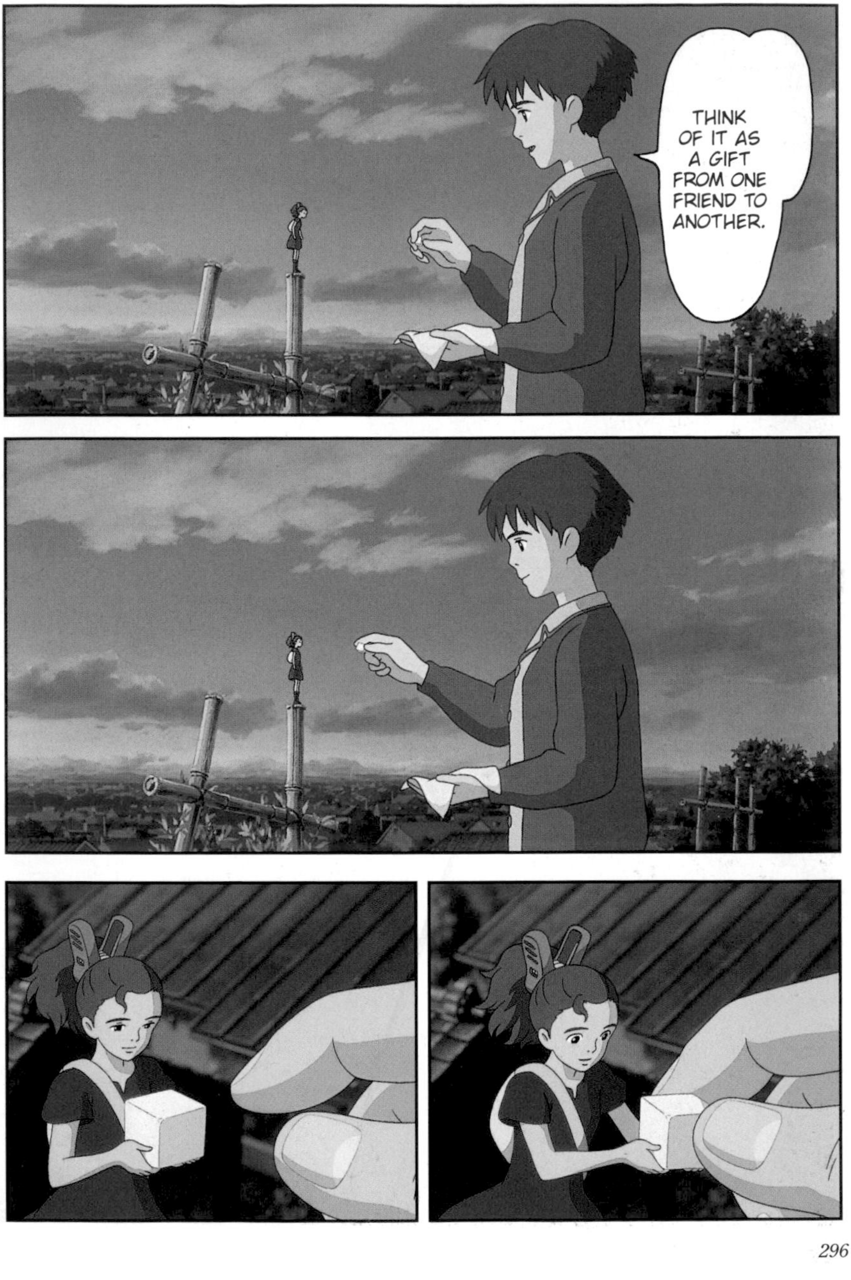
THINK OF IT AS A GIFT FROM ONE FRIEND TO ANOTHER.

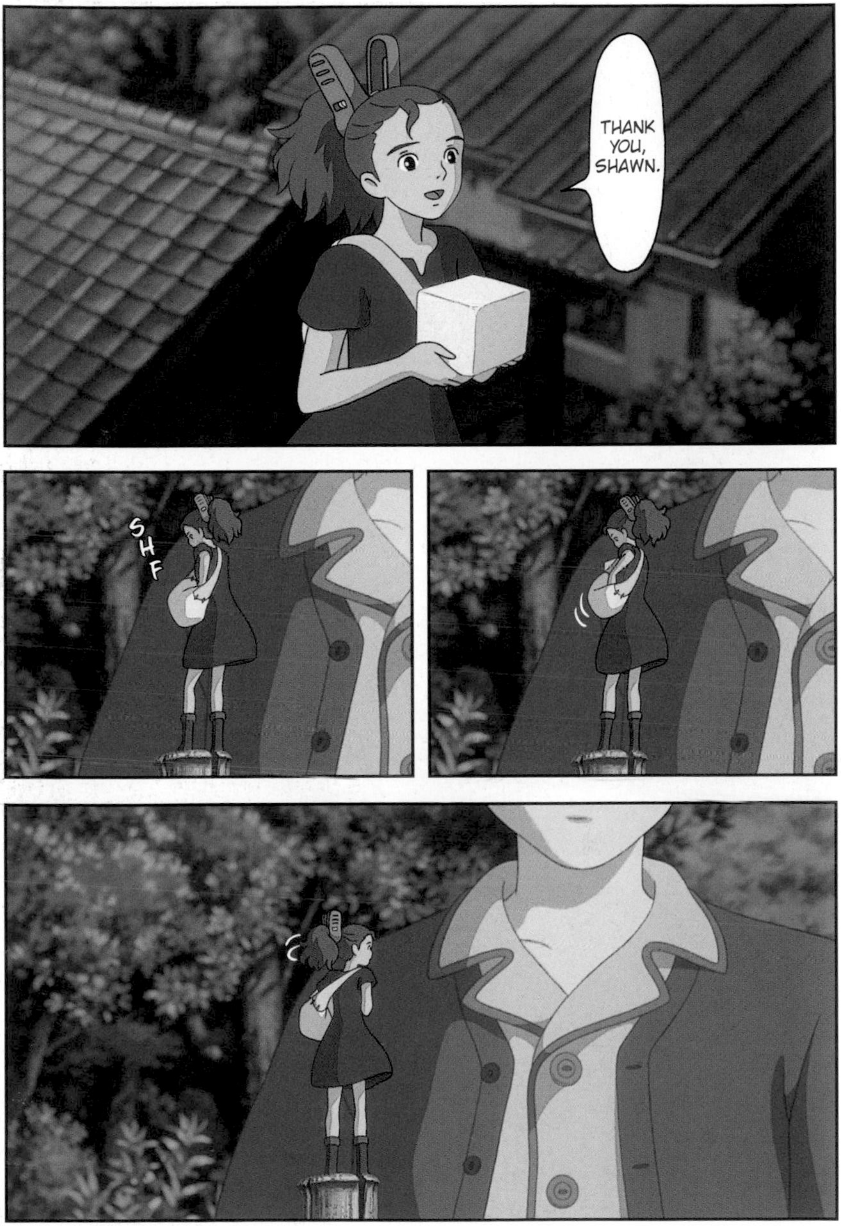
THANK YOU, SHAWN.
SHF

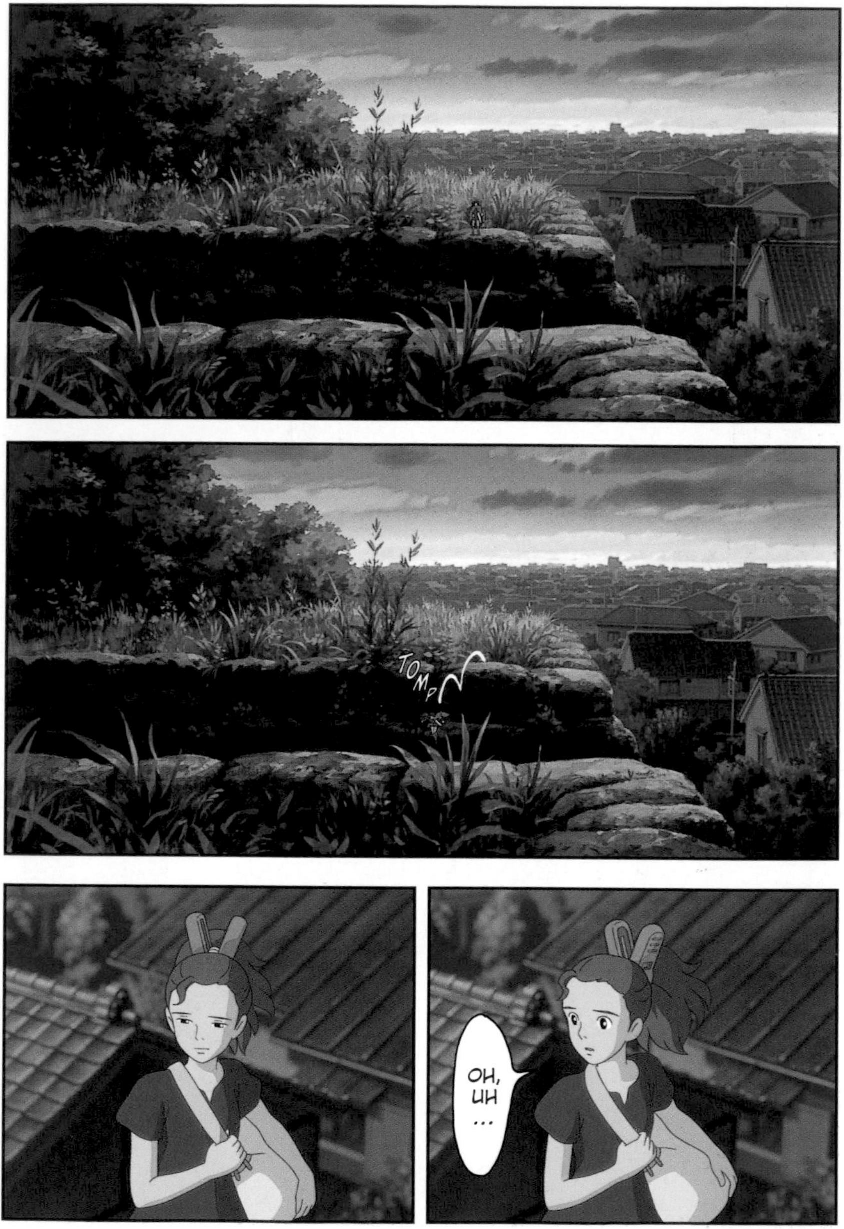
TOMP
OH, UH ...

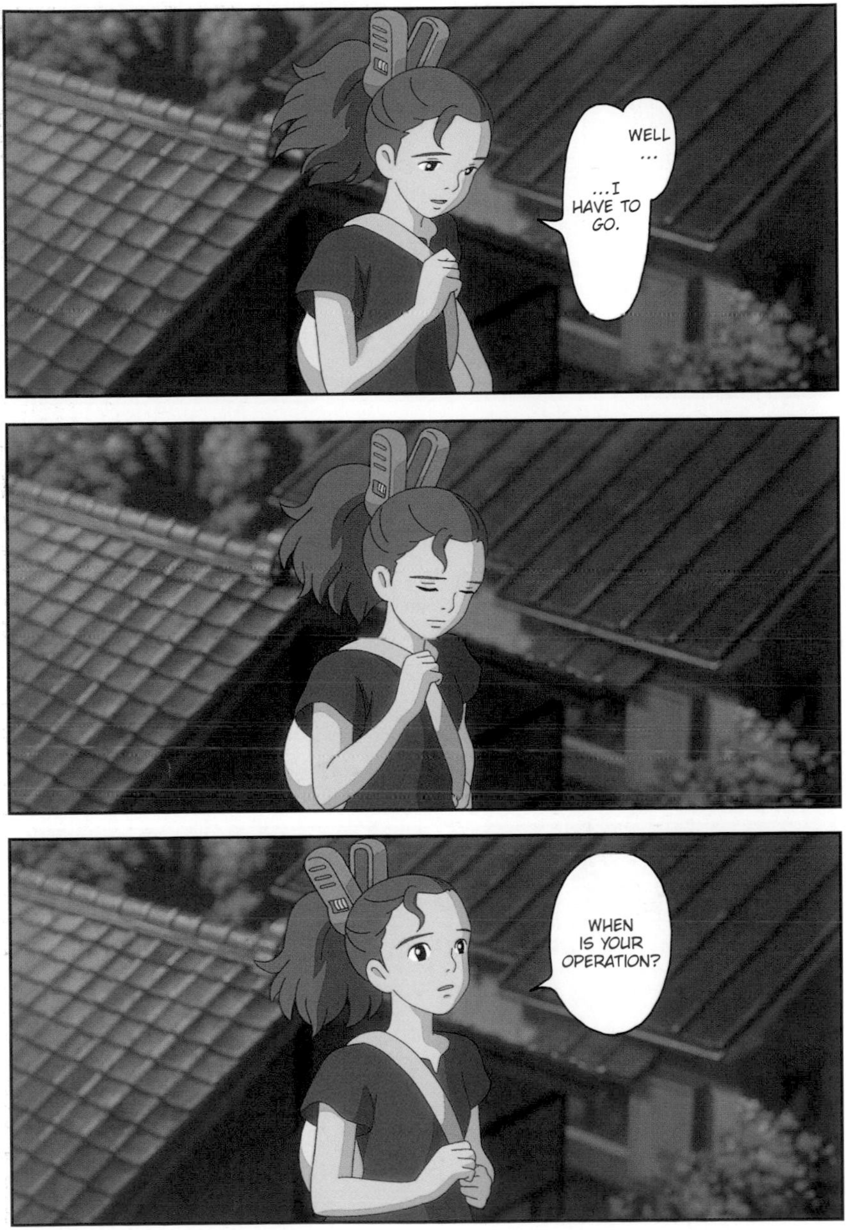
WELL ... ...I HAVE TO GO.
WHEN IS YOUR OPERATION?

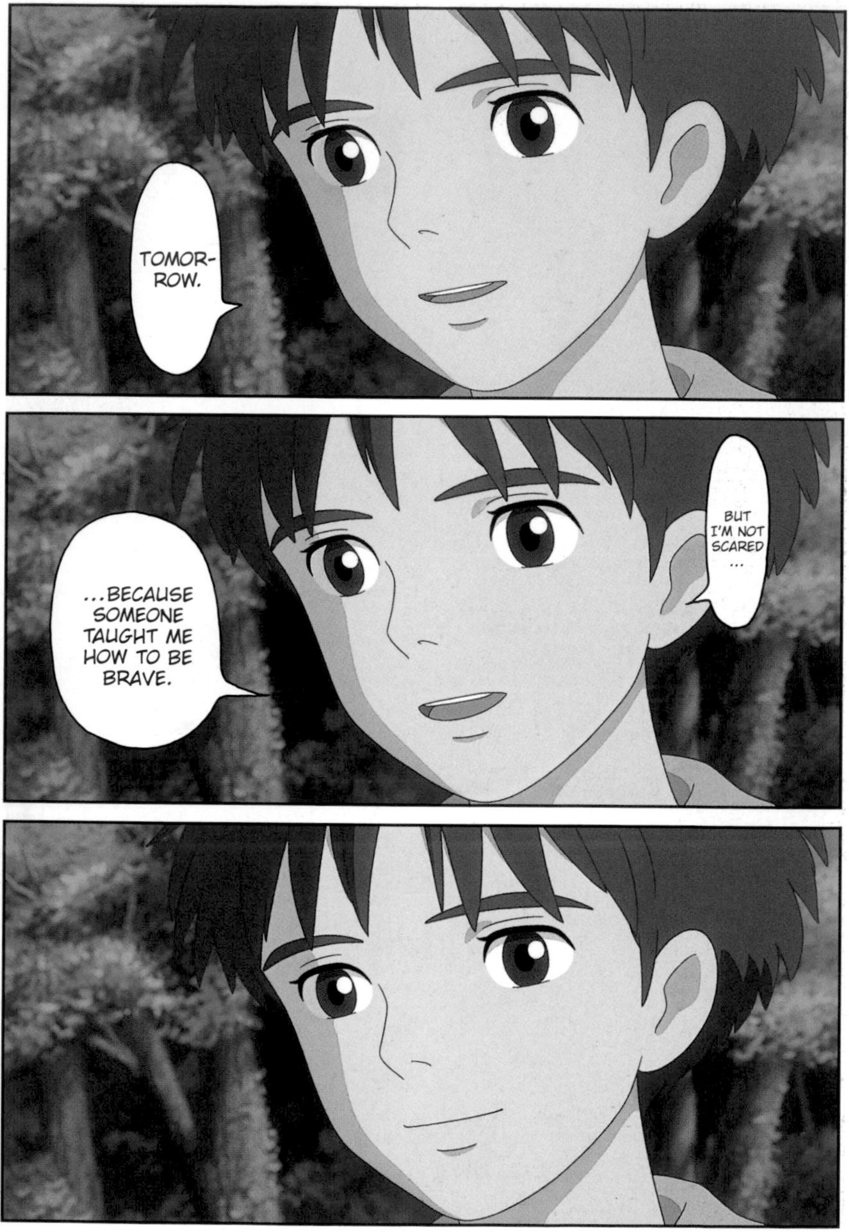
TOMOR-ROW.
BUT I'M NOT SCARED ...
...BECAUSE SOMEONE TAUGHT ME HOW TO BE BRAVE.

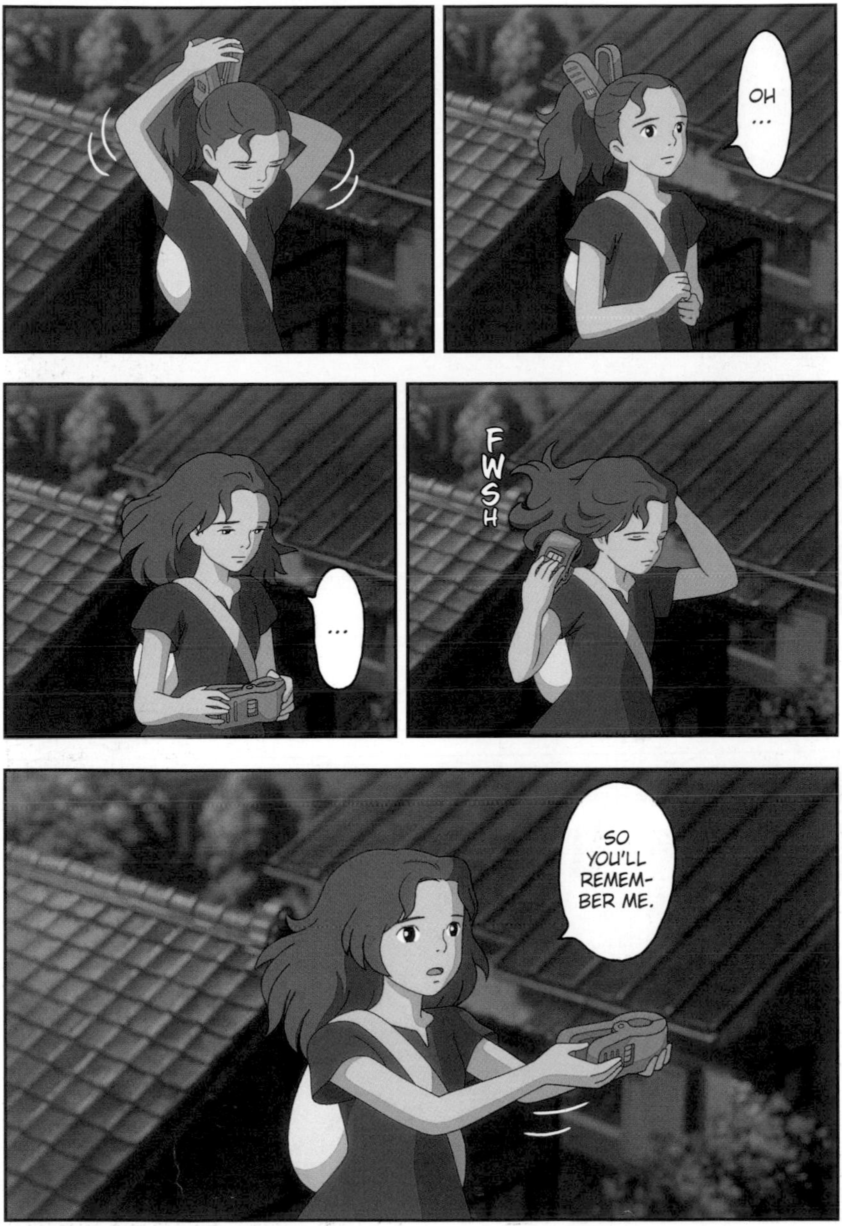
OH ...
FWSH
...
SO YOU'LL REMEMBER ME.

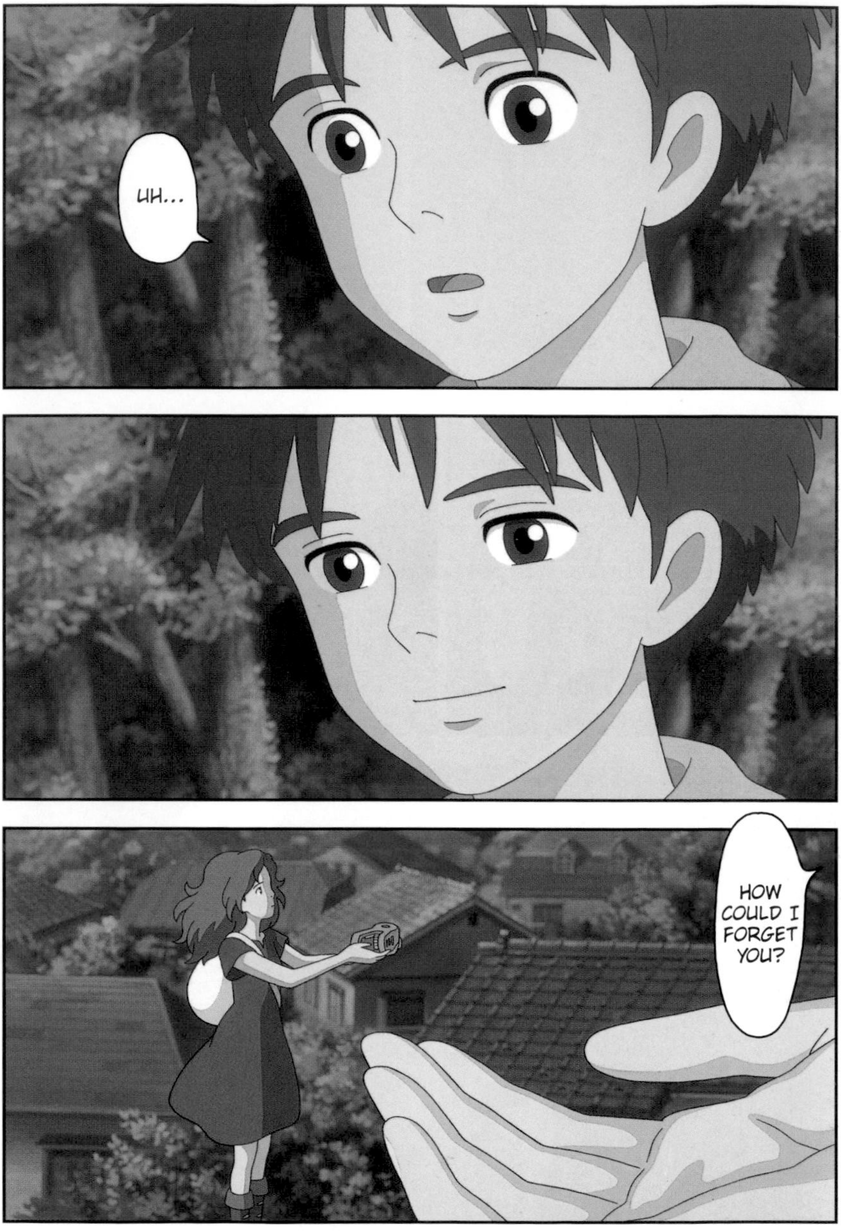
UH...
HOW COULD I FORGET YOU?

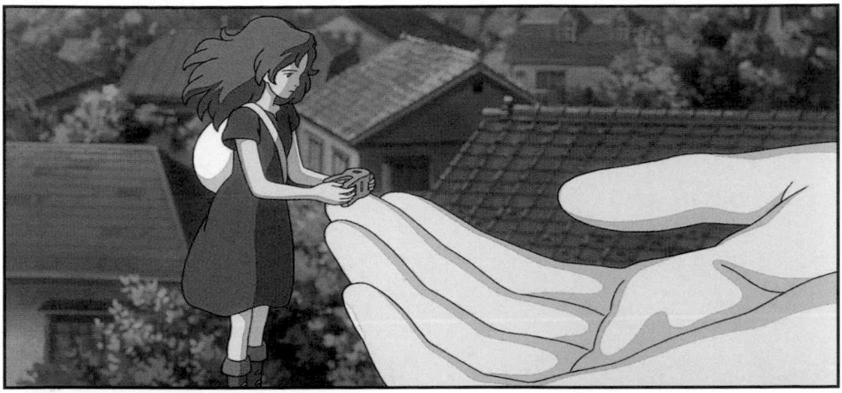

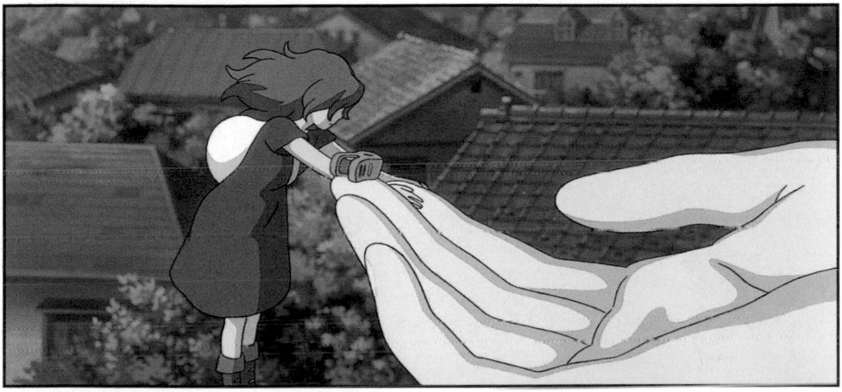

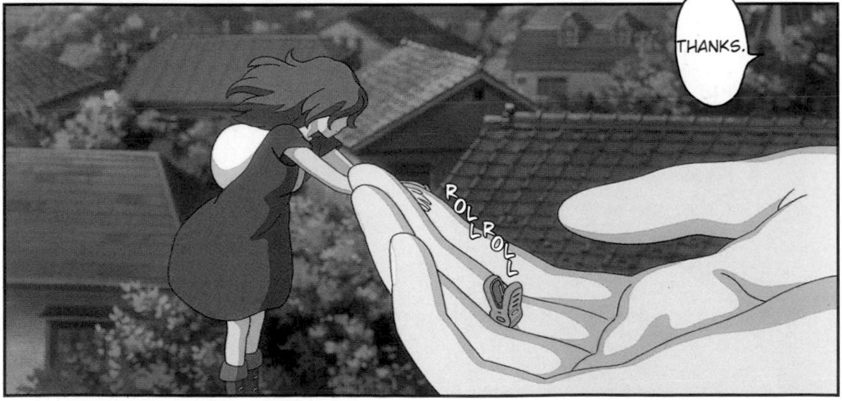
THANKS.
ROLL ROLL

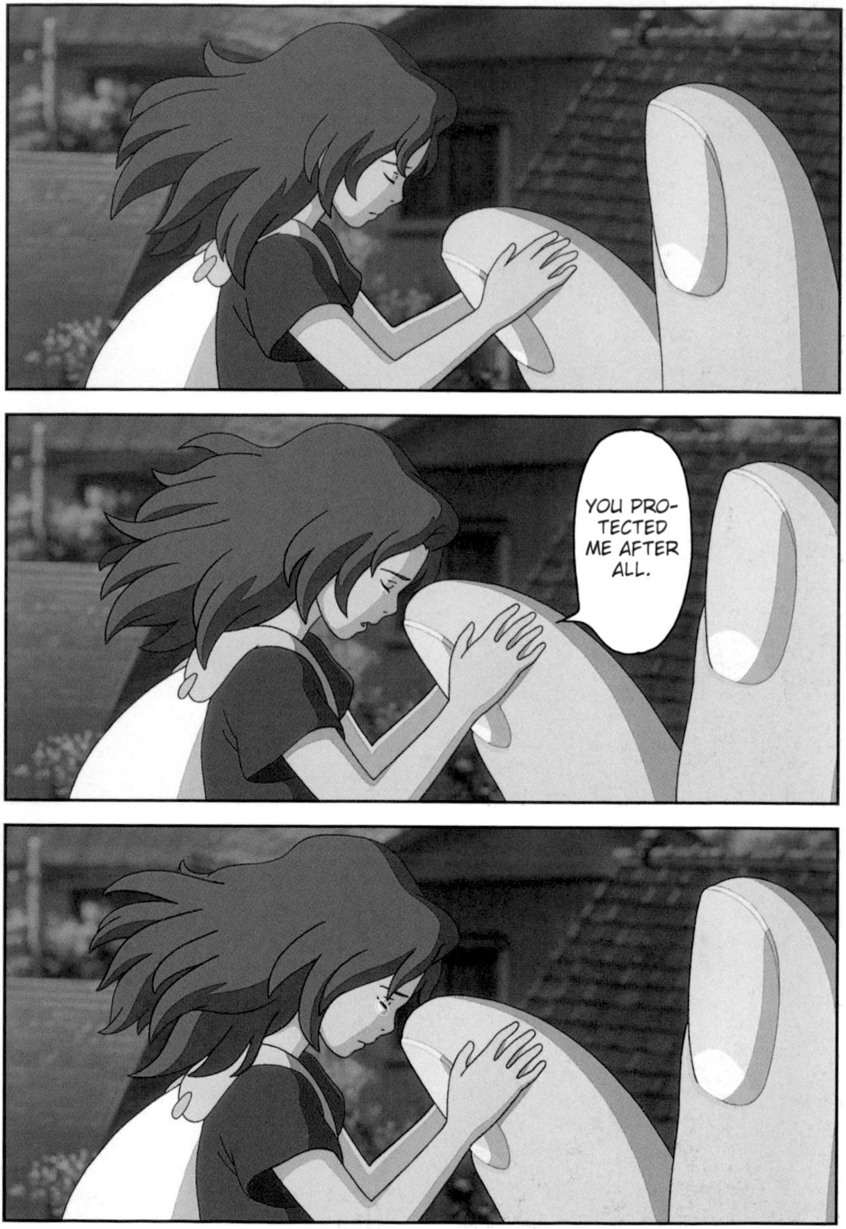
YOU PRO-
TECTED
ME AFTER
ALL.

ARRIETTY...

I HOPE YOU... HAVE A HAPPY LIFE.

PLIP

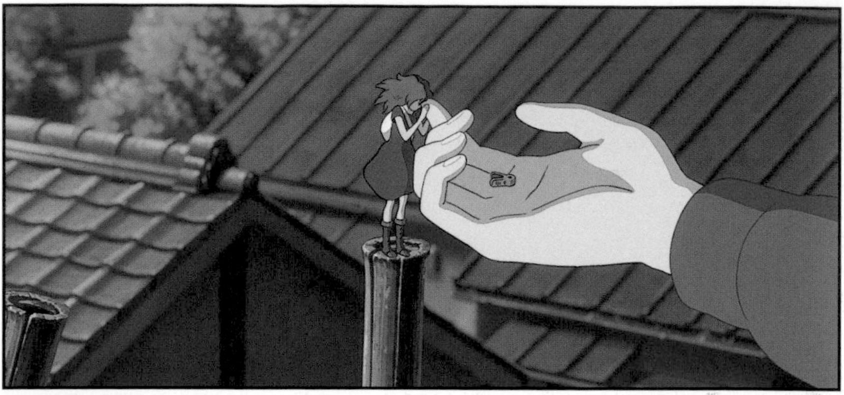

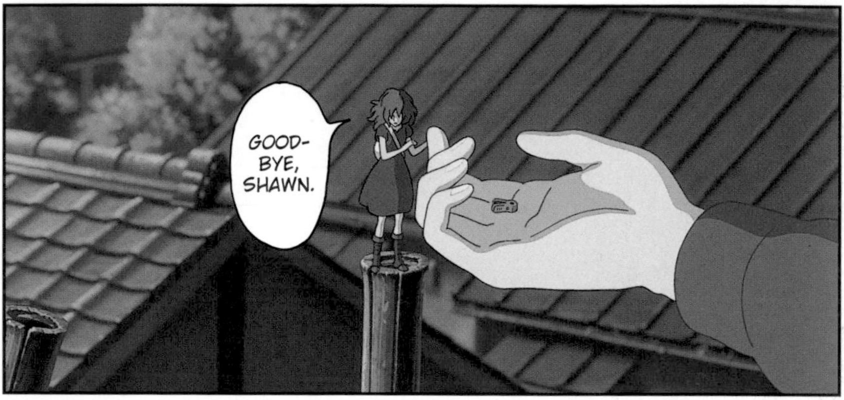
GOOD-BYE, SHAWN.

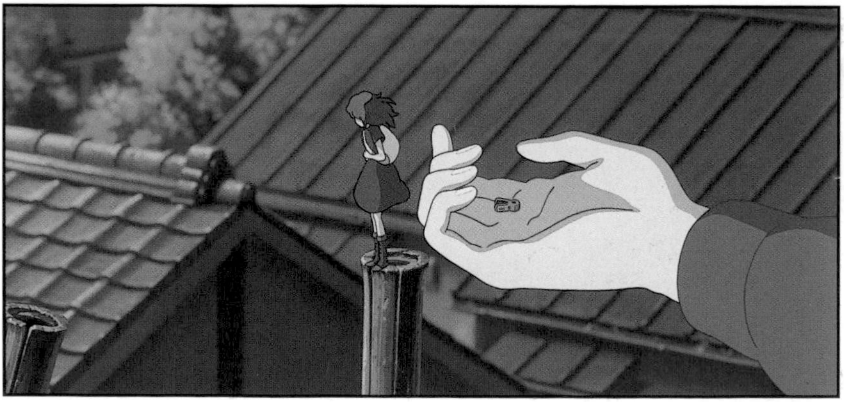

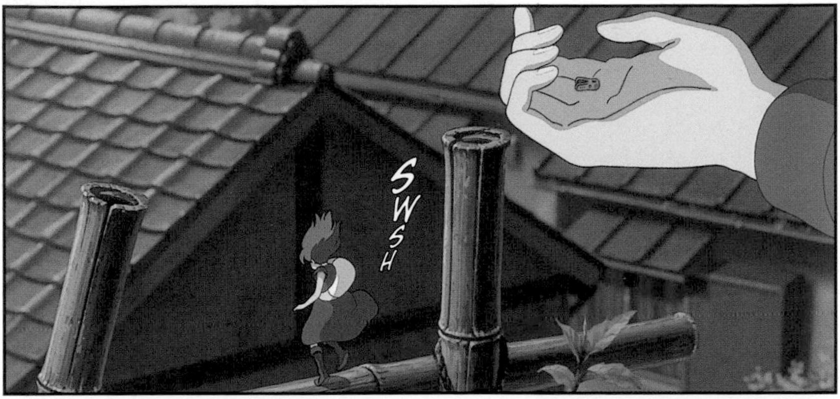
SWSH
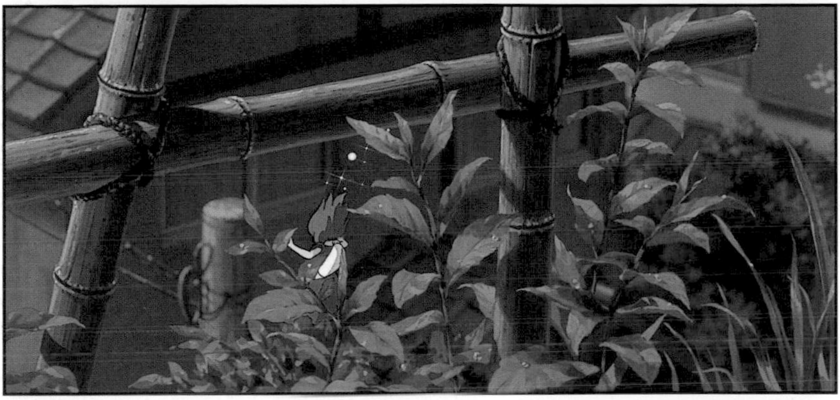
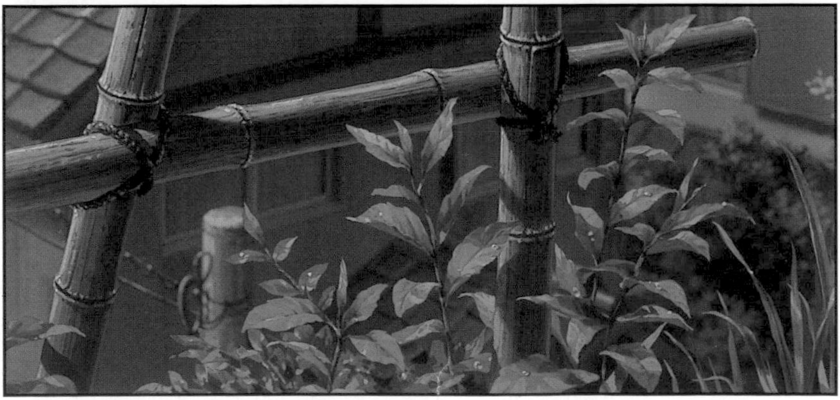

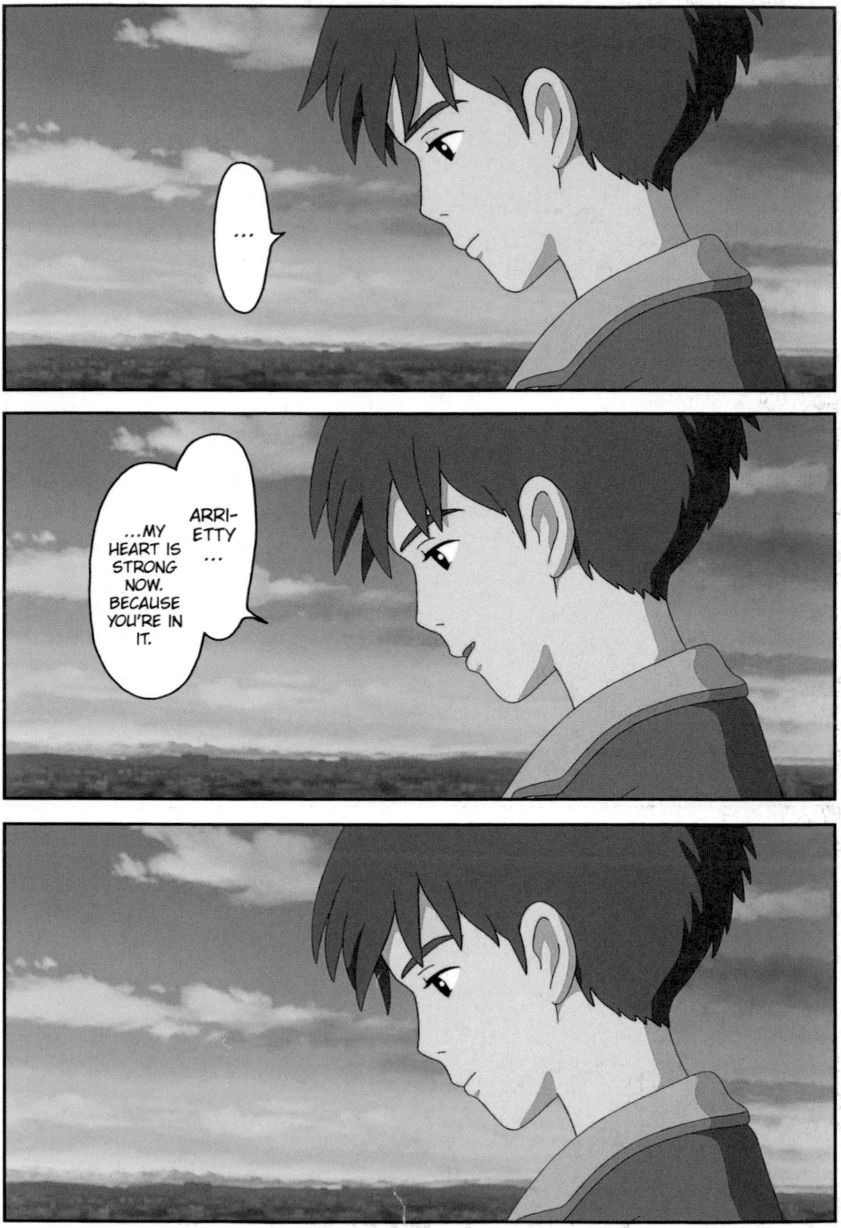
...
ARRI-ETTY... ...MY HEART IS STRONG NOW. BECAUSE YOU'RE IN IT.

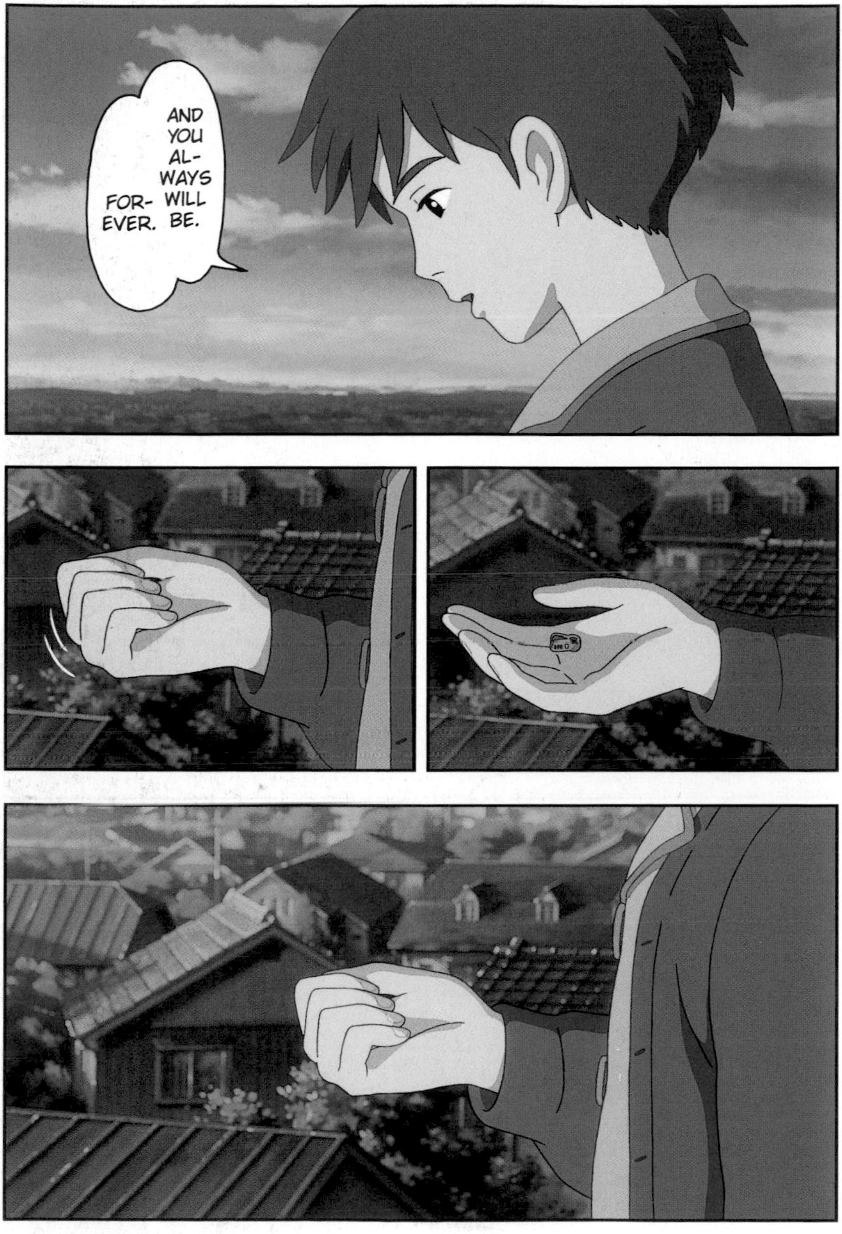
AND YOU AL- WAYS WILL BE. FOR- EVER.

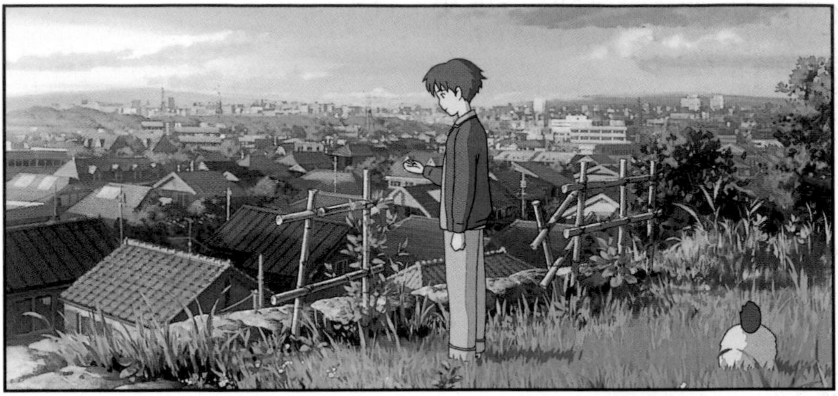

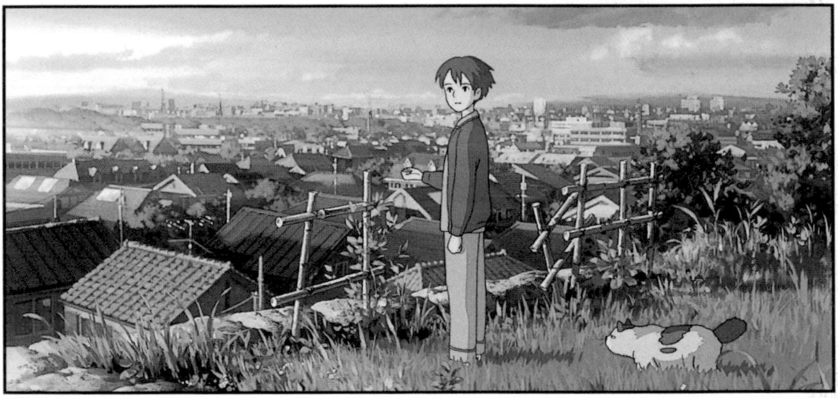

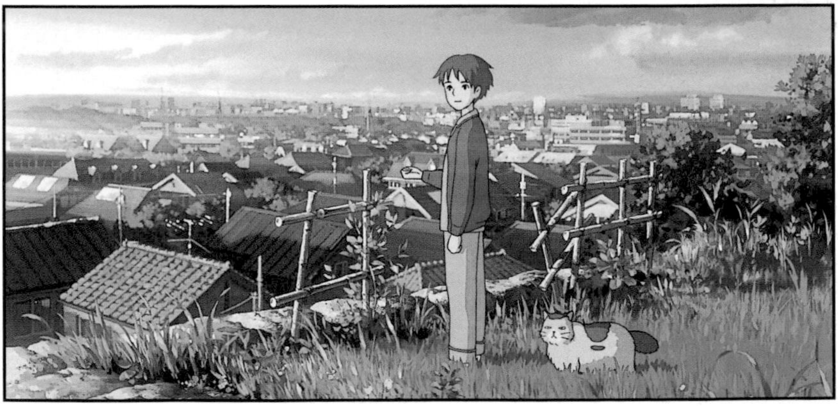

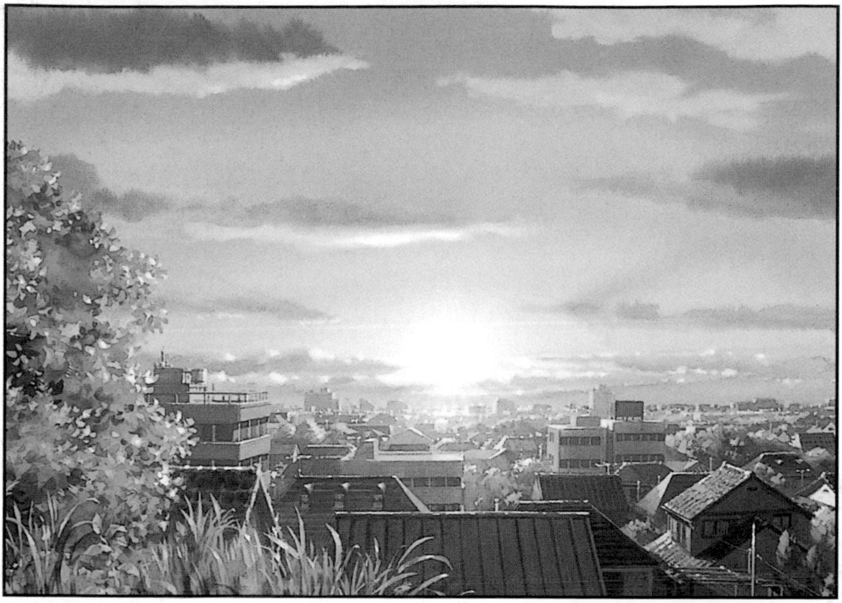
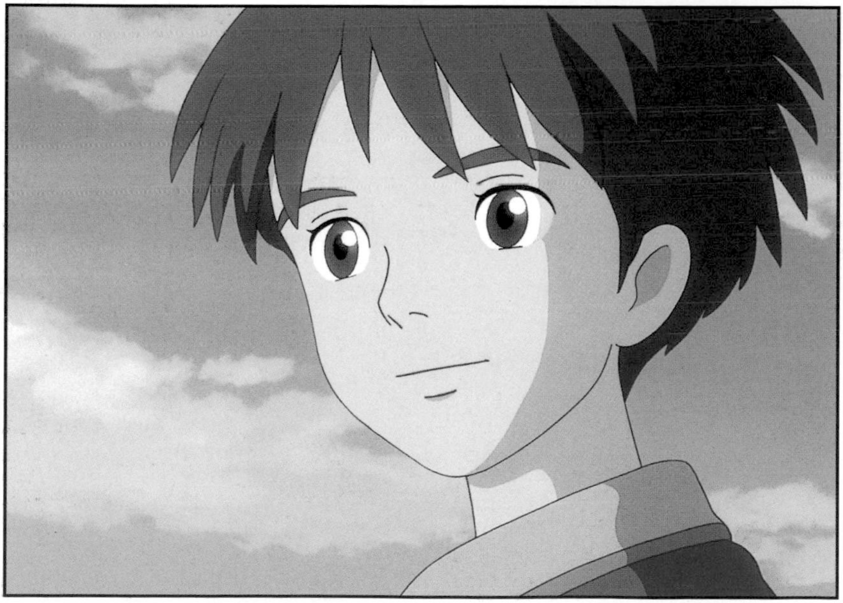

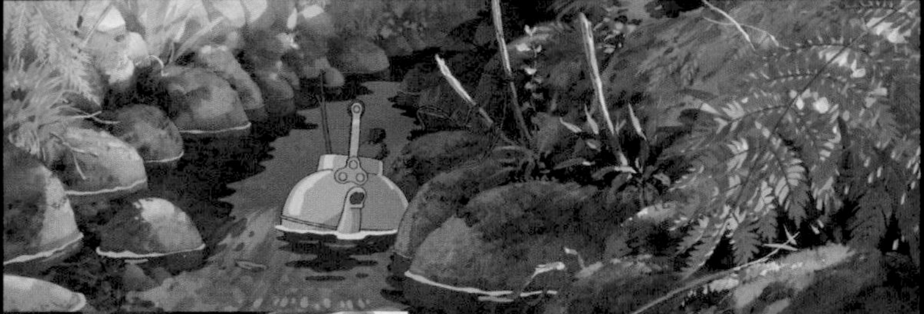

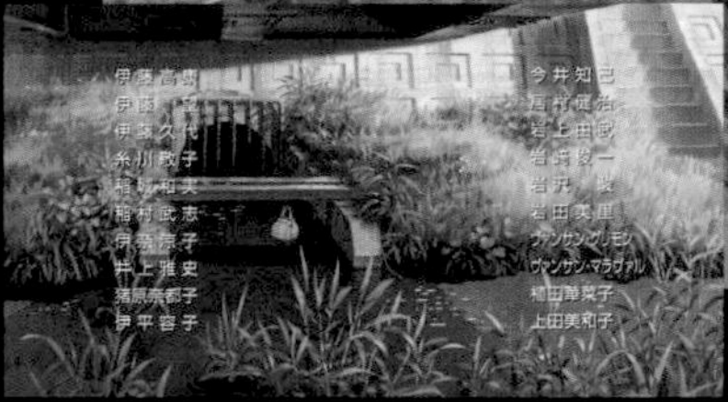

伊藤高志
伊藤久代
糸川敦子
稲村武志
井上雅史
猪原奈都子
伊平容子
今井知己
岩上田敦
岩崎俊一
岩田美里
ヴァンサン・マラヴァル
上田美和子

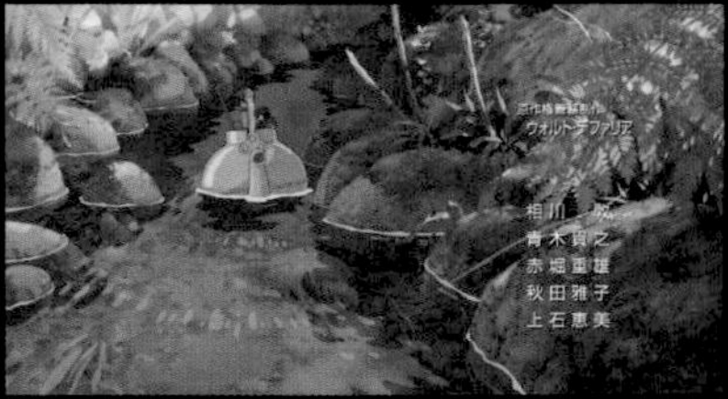

ウォルト・ディズニー・ジャパン
相川
青木貴之
赤堀重雄
秋田雅子
上石恵美

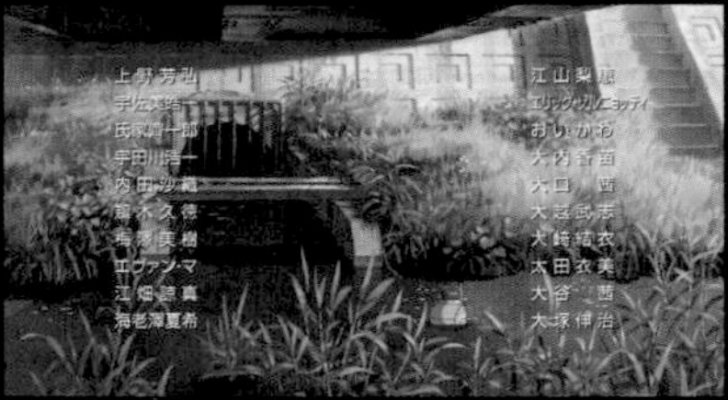

上野芳弘
氏家伸一郎
宇田川浩一
エヴァン・マ
海老澤夏希
江山梨恵
おいかわ
大内香苗
大口茜
大坂武志
大崎結衣
太田衣美
大谷茜
大塚伸治

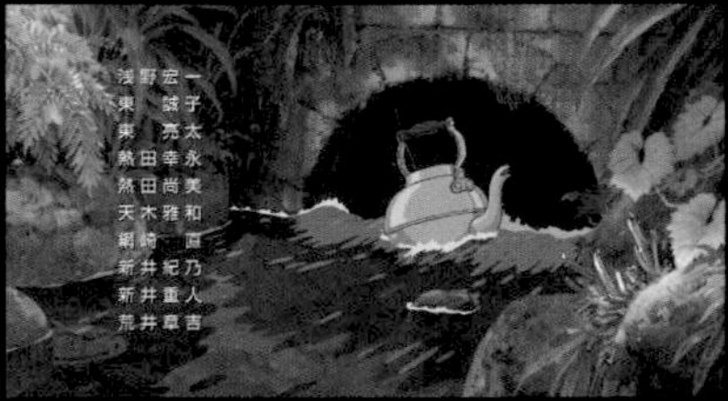

浅野宏一
東誠子
東亮太
熱田幸永
熱田尚美
天木雅和
網崎茜
新井紀乃
新井重人
荒井章吉

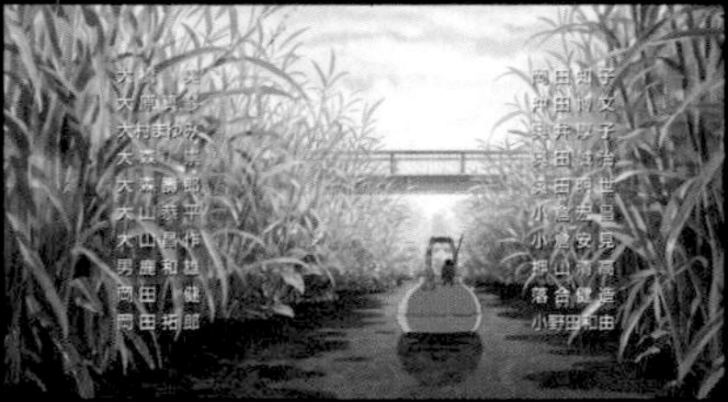

大村まゆみ
大森寿郎
大山泰平
大山昌作
男鹿和雄
岡田健
岡田拓郎
小倉安見
落合健造
小野田和由

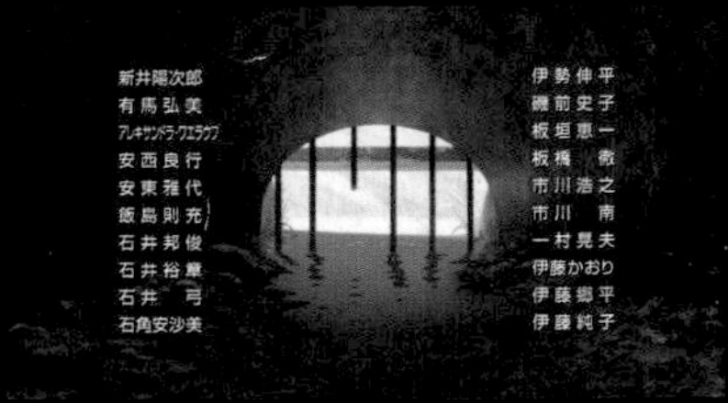

新井陽次郎
有馬弘美
アレキサンドラ・ワエラウフ
安西良行
安東雅代
飯島則充
石井邦俊
石井裕章
石井弓
石角安沙美
伊勢伸平
磯前史子
板垣恵一
板橋徹
市川浩之
市川南
一村晃夫
伊藤かおり
伊藤郷平
伊藤純子

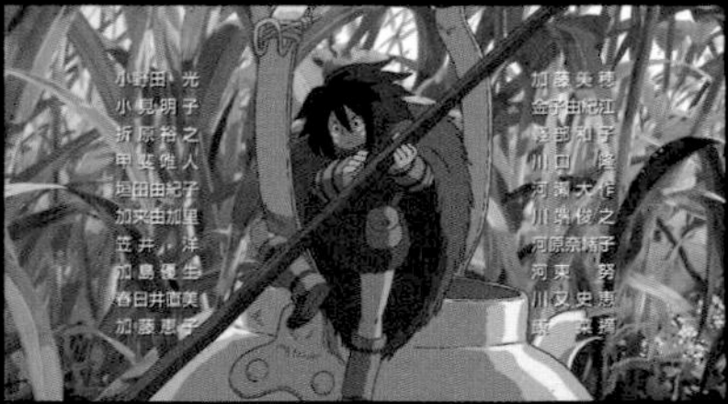

小見明子
折原裕之
加来由加里
笠井洋
加島優生
春日井直美
加藤恵子
加藤美穂
金子由紀江
川口隆
河瀬大作
河原奈緒子
河東努
川又史恵

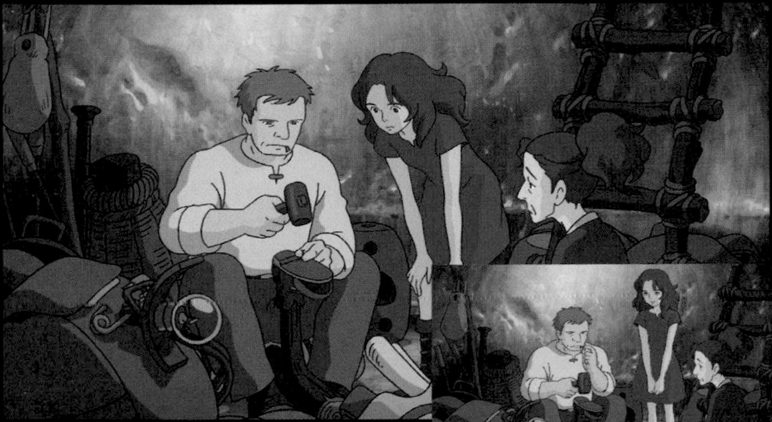

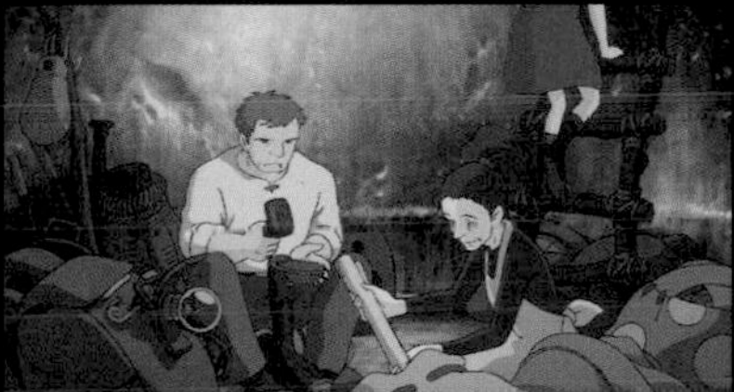

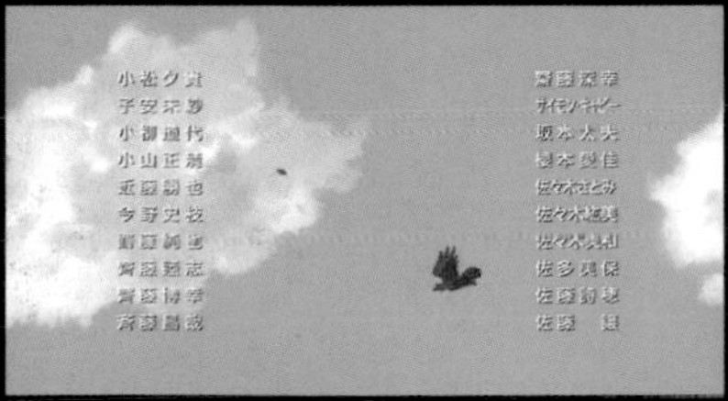
今野史枝
佐々木さとみ
佐多真保

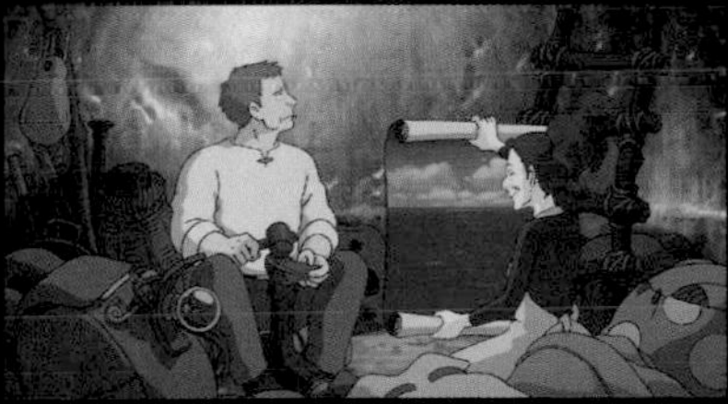

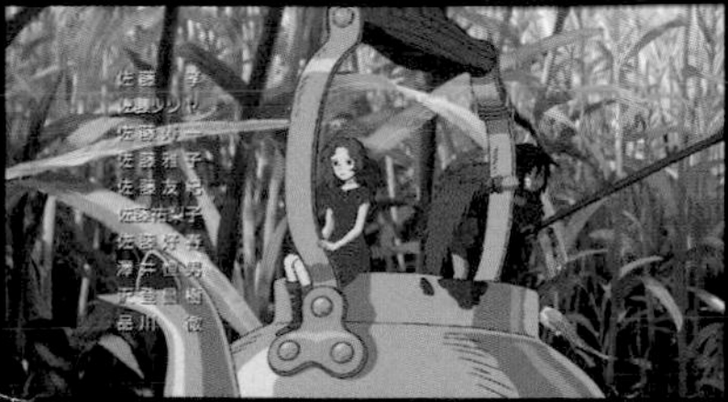
佐藤雅子
佐藤好春
品川 徹

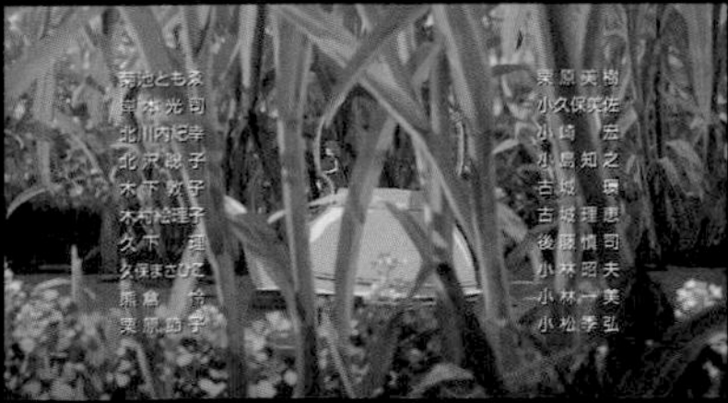
岸本光司
北川内紀幸
木村絵理子
久保まさひこ
小島知之
古城 環
古城理恵
後藤慎司
小林昭夫
小林一美

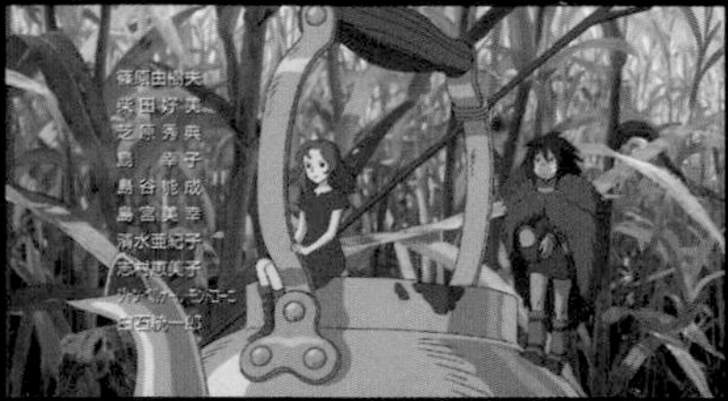
柴田好美
芝原秀典
島 幸子
島谷能成
清水亜紀子

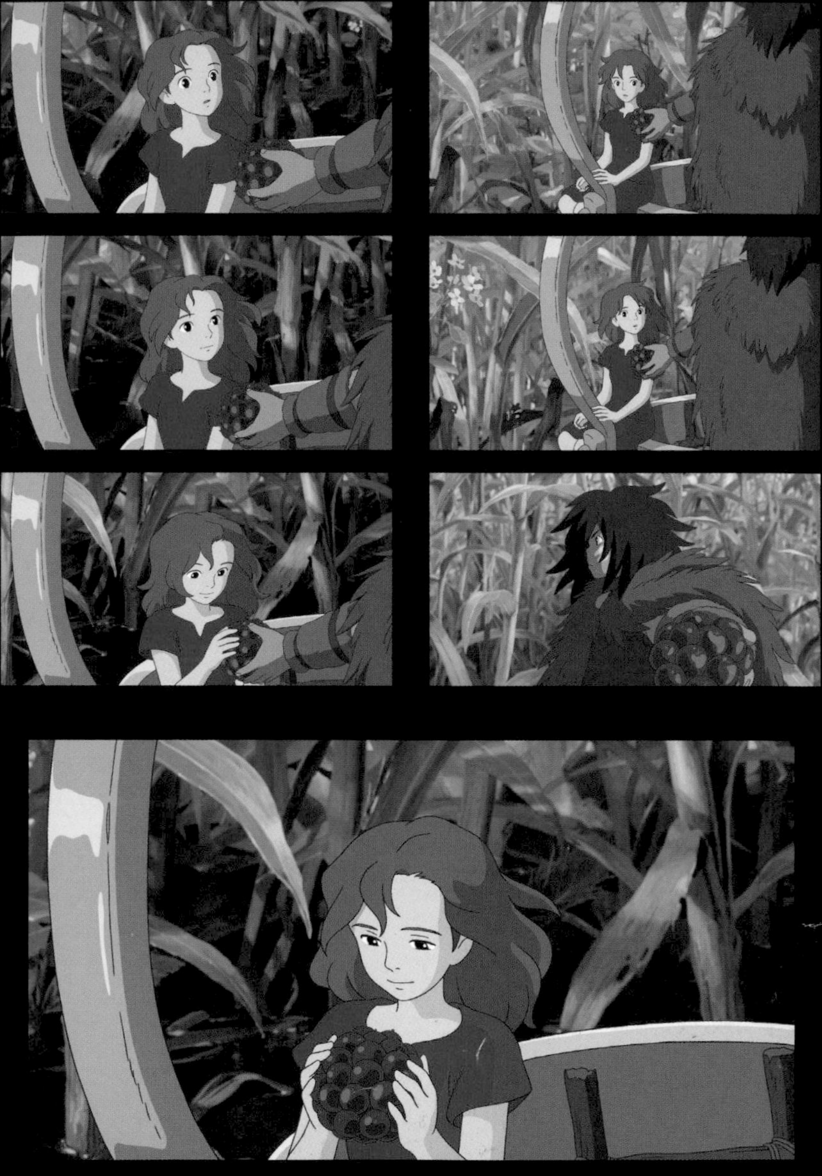

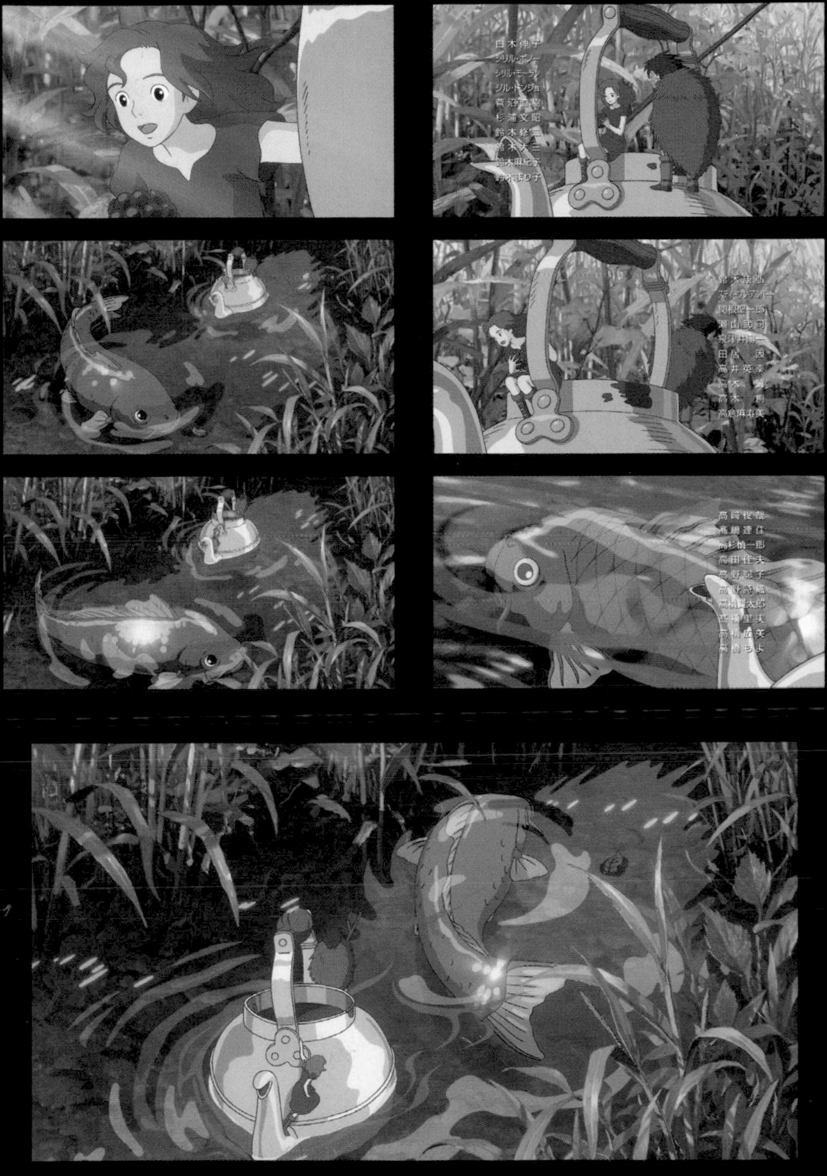
白木伸子
シリル・ボノー
シリル・モーラン
杉浦文昭
鈴木麻紀子
鈴木まり子
スティーブン・アルパート
田居 因
高井英幸
高木 剛
高田佳夫
高橋広美
高橋ちよ

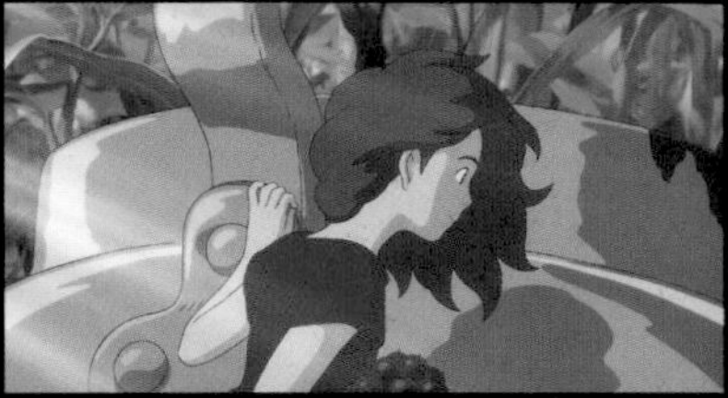
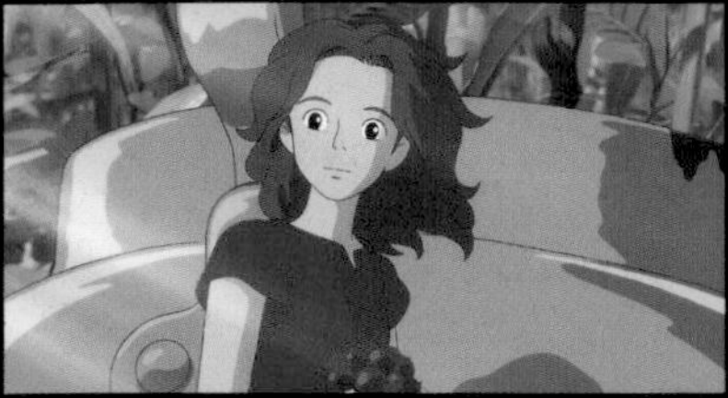
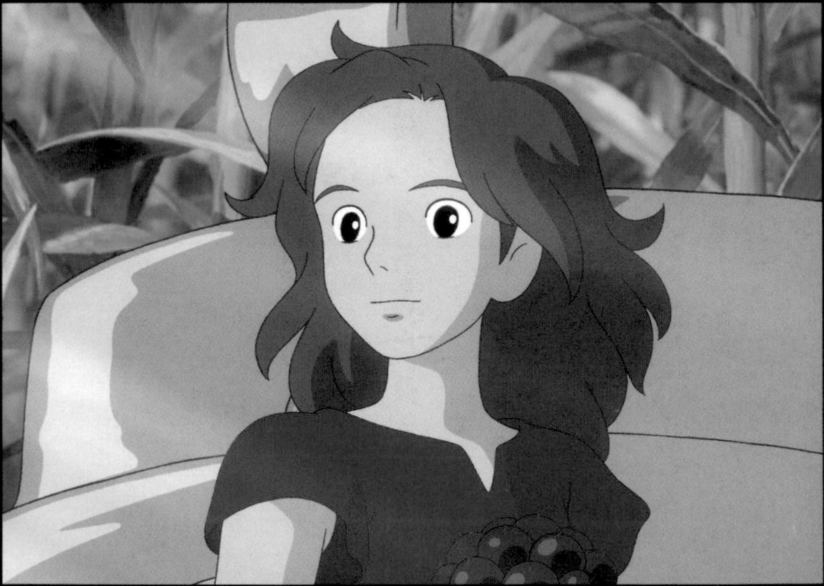
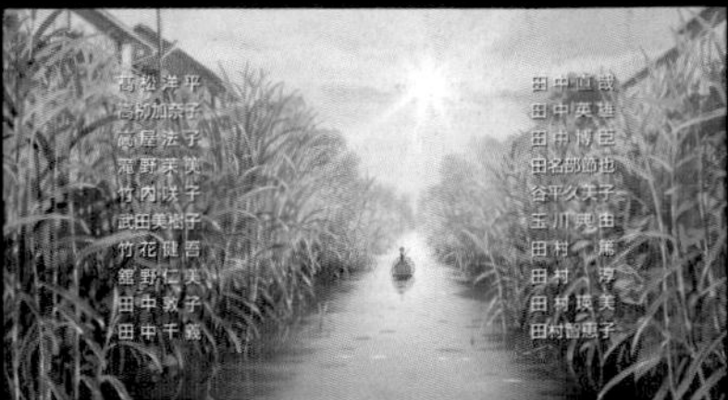
高松洋平
高柳加奈子
高屋法子
竹内咲子
武田美樹子
竹花健吾
舘野仁美
田中敦子
田中千義
田中直哉
田中英雄
田名部節也
谷平久美子
玉川明由
田村 淳
田村瑛美
田村智恵子
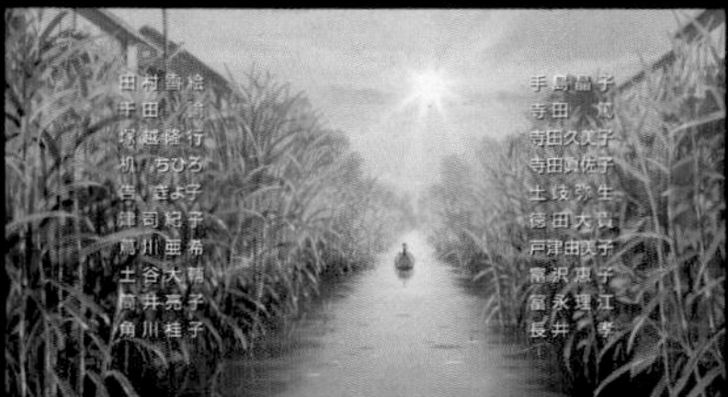
田村雪絵
塚越隆行
机 ちひろ
津司紀子
鶴川亜希
土谷大輔
筒井亮子
角川桂子
手島晶子
寺田久美子
寺田真佐子
土岐弥生
徳田大貴
富沢恵子
富永理江
長井 孝

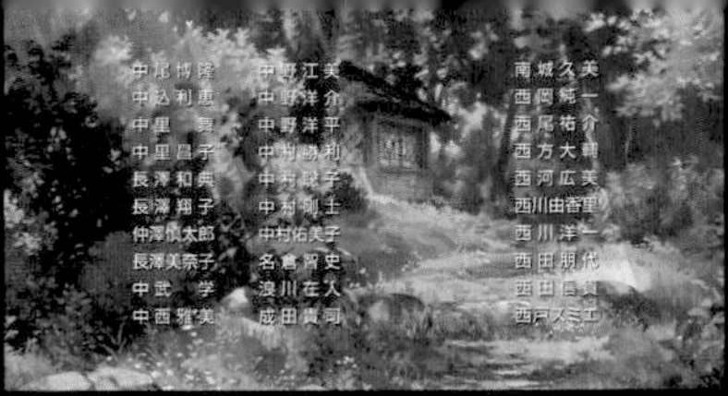

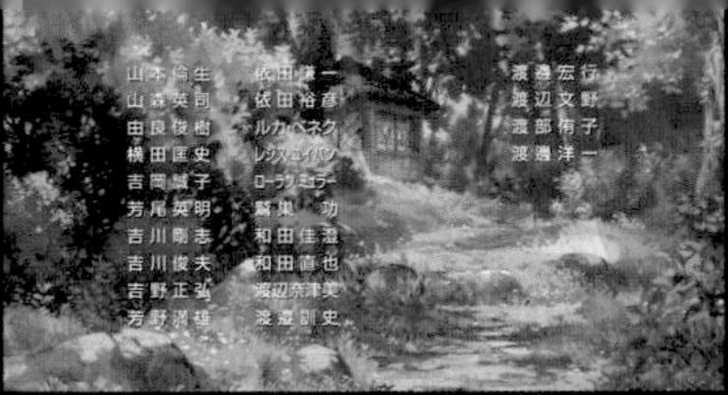

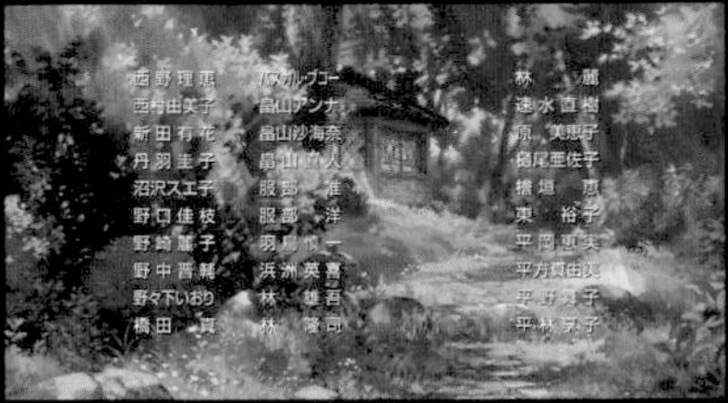

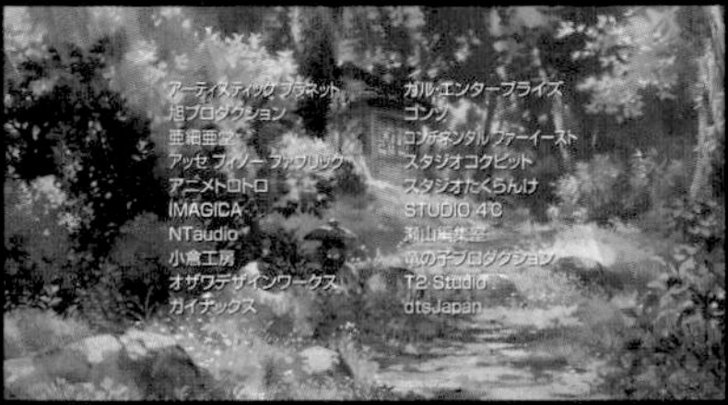
アーティスティック プラネット
旭プロダクション
亜細亜堂
アニメトロトロ
IMAGICA
NTaudio
小倉工房
オザワデザインワークス
ガイナックス
カル・エンタープライズ
コンツ
コンチネンタル ファーイースト
スタジオコクピット
スタジオたくらんけ
STUDIO 4℃
竜の子プロダクション
T2 Studio
dtsJapan

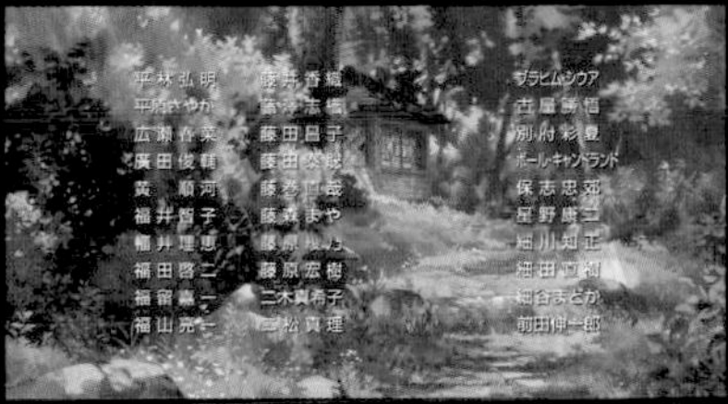

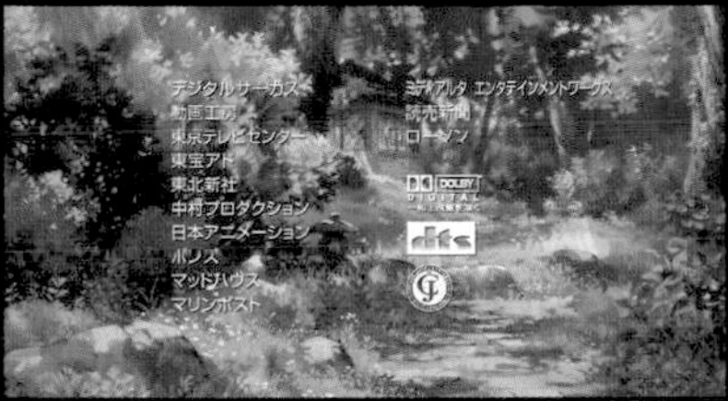
デジタルサーカス
動画工房
東京テレビセンター
東宝アド
東北新社
中村プロダクション
日本アニメーション
ボンズ
マッドハウス
マリンポスト
読売新聞
ローソン

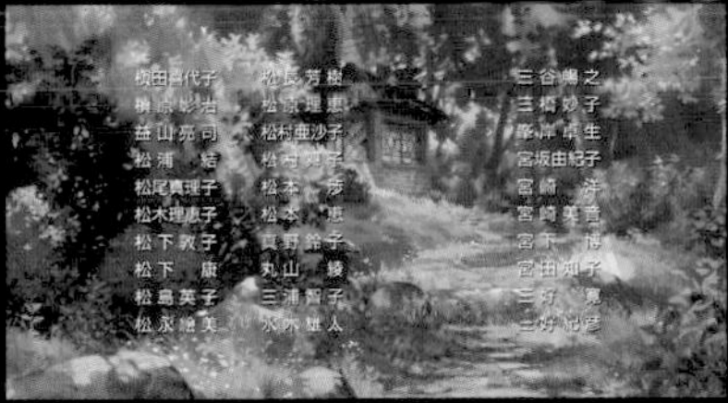

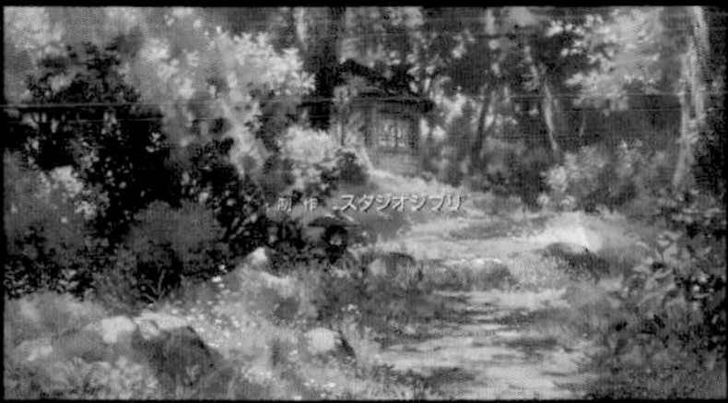
制作 スタジオジブリ

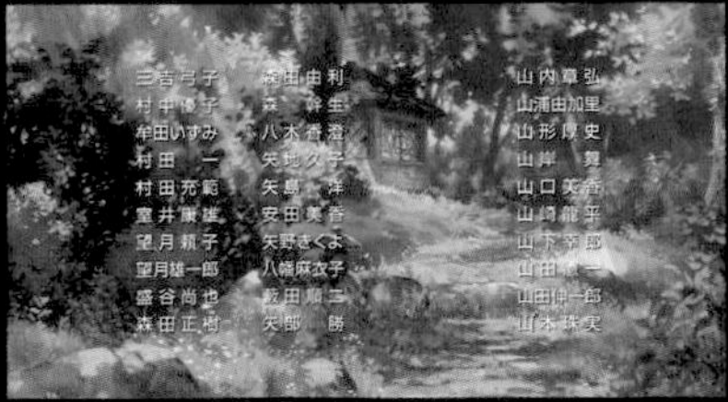

THE END

This book should be read in its original Japanese right-to-left format.
Please turn it around to begin!

The Secret World of
Arrietty

2

Volume 2 of 2

Planning by Hayao Miyazaki
Based on *The Borrowers* by Mary Norton
Directed by Hiromasa Yonebayashi
Original Screenplay by Hayao Miyazaki and Keiko Niwa
Translated from the Original Japanese by Rieko Izutsu-Vajirasarn and Jim Hubbert
English Language Screenplay by Karey Kirkpatrick

Film Comic Adaptation/HC Language Solutions, Inc.
Lettering/Erika Terriquez
Design/Yukiko Whitley
Editor/Josh Bettinger
Senior Editorial Director/Masumi Washington

Printed in Singapore

Published by
VIZ Media, LLC
295 Bay St. San Francisco, CA 94133

First printing, January 2012

PARENTAL ADVISORY
ARRIETTY is rated A and is
suitable for readers of all ages.
ratings.viz.com